ENCYCLOPEDIA OF
AMERICAN
SUBMARINES

ENCYCLOPEDIA OF
AMERICAN
SUBMARINES

Wilbur Cross

and

George W. Feise, Jr.

with

James W. Blanchard, Captain, USN (Retired)

TECHNICAL CONSULTANT

Joseph T. Talbert, Jr.
Captain, USN (Retired)

FOREWORD BY

Albert H. Konetzni
Vice Admiral, USN
Deputy Commander in Chief
U.S. Atlantic Fleet
and Former Commander, Submarine Force
U.S. Pacific Fleet

☑®

Facts On File, Inc.

ENCYCLOPEDIA OF AMERICAN SUBMARINES

Facts On File, Inc.
132 West 31st Street
New York NY 10001

Library of Congress Cataloging-in-Publication Data

Cross, Wilbur, and Feise, George W.
The encyclopedia of American submarines / Wilbur Cross, and George W. Feise, Jr.
p. cm.
Includes bibliographical references and index.
ISBN 0-8160-4460-0 (hardcover : alk. paper)
1. Submarines (Ships)—United States—Encyclopedias. I. Title.
V858 .C76 2002
359.9'3'097303—dc21   2001054473

Facts On File books are available at special discounts when purchased in bulk quantities for businesses, associations, institutions, or sales promotions. Please call our Special Sales Department in New York at (212) 967–8800 or (800) 322–8755.

You can find Facts On File on the World Wide Web at
http://www.factsonfile.com

Text design by Erika K. Arroyo
Cover design by Cathy Rincon

Printed in the United States of America

VB FOF 10 9 8 7 6 5 4 3 2 1

This book is printed on acid-free paper.

IN MEMORIAM

This volume is dedicated to the late James W. ("Doc") Blanchard, Jr., Captain, United States Navy (Retired), who was the catalyst and consultant in the planning, starting, and initial research, seeing the encyclopedia well on its way, until his untimely death in the fall of 2000.

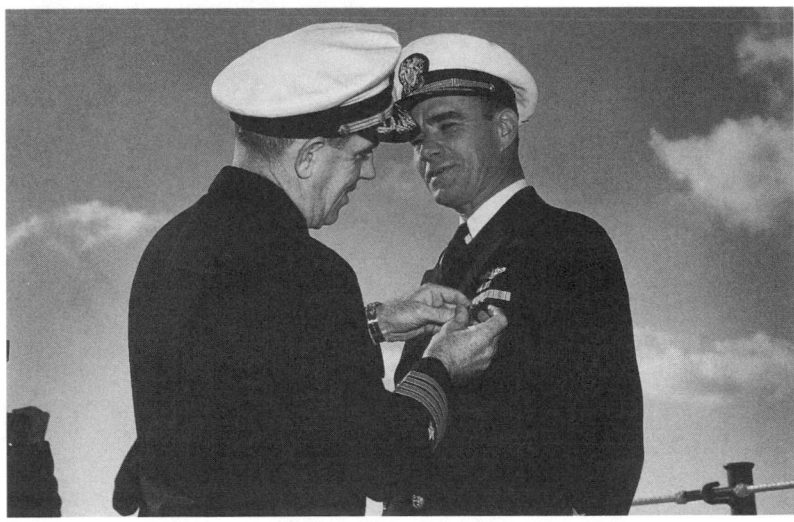

Presentation of the Navy Cross to Rear Admiral James W. Blanchard, Senior, father of the officer to whom this book is dedicated, in 1945 when he commanded *Albacore*, the first American submarine to sink a Japanese aircraft carrier, *Tahio* (31,000 tons). Within weeks after Blanchard was transferred from *Albacore* the submarine disappeared on her 10th patrol and was never heard from again. *(Mrs. James W. Blanchard, Jr.)*

CONTENTS

MAPS

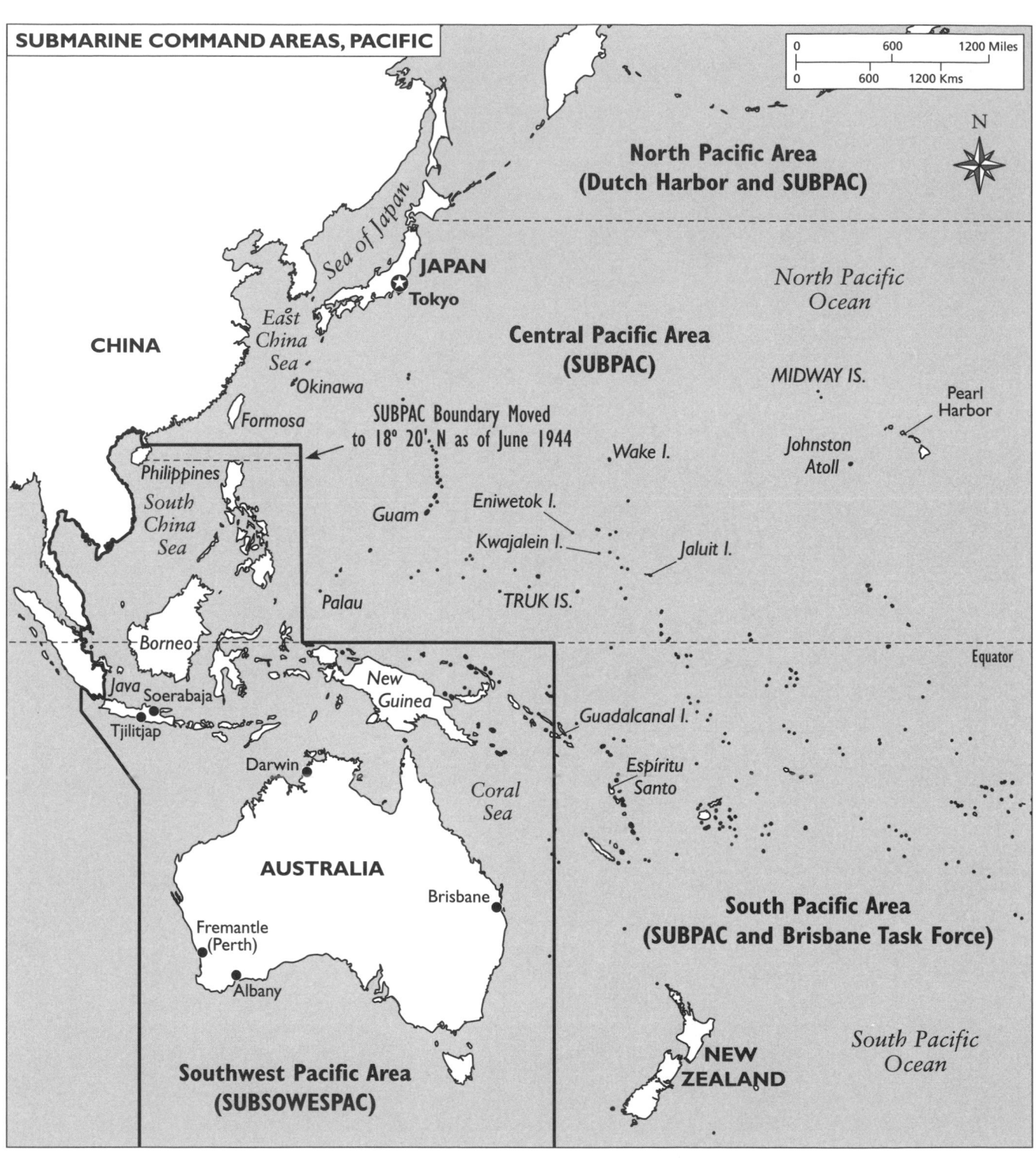

SUBMARINE COMMAND AREAS, PACIFIC

North Pacific Area
(Dutch Harbor and SUBPAC)

North Pacific Ocean

JAPAN
Tokyo

Sea of Japan

East China Sea

CHINA

Okinawa

Formosa

Central Pacific Area
(SUBPAC)

MIDWAY IS.

Pearl Harbor

SUBPAC Boundary Moved
to 18° 20' N as of June 1944

Wake I.

Johnston Atoll

Philippines

South China Sea

Guam

Eniwetok I.

Kwajalein I.

Jaluit I.

Palau

TRUK IS.

Borneo

Equator

Java
Soerabaja
Tjilitjap

New Guinea

Guadalcanal I.

Darwin

Coral Sea

Espíritu Santo

AUSTRALIA

Brisbane

South Pacific Area
(SUBPAC and Brisbane Task Force)

Fremantle
(Perth)

Albany

NEW ZEALAND

South Pacific Ocean

**Southwest Pacific Area
(SUBSOWESPAC)**

0   600   1200 Miles
0   600   1200 Kms

N

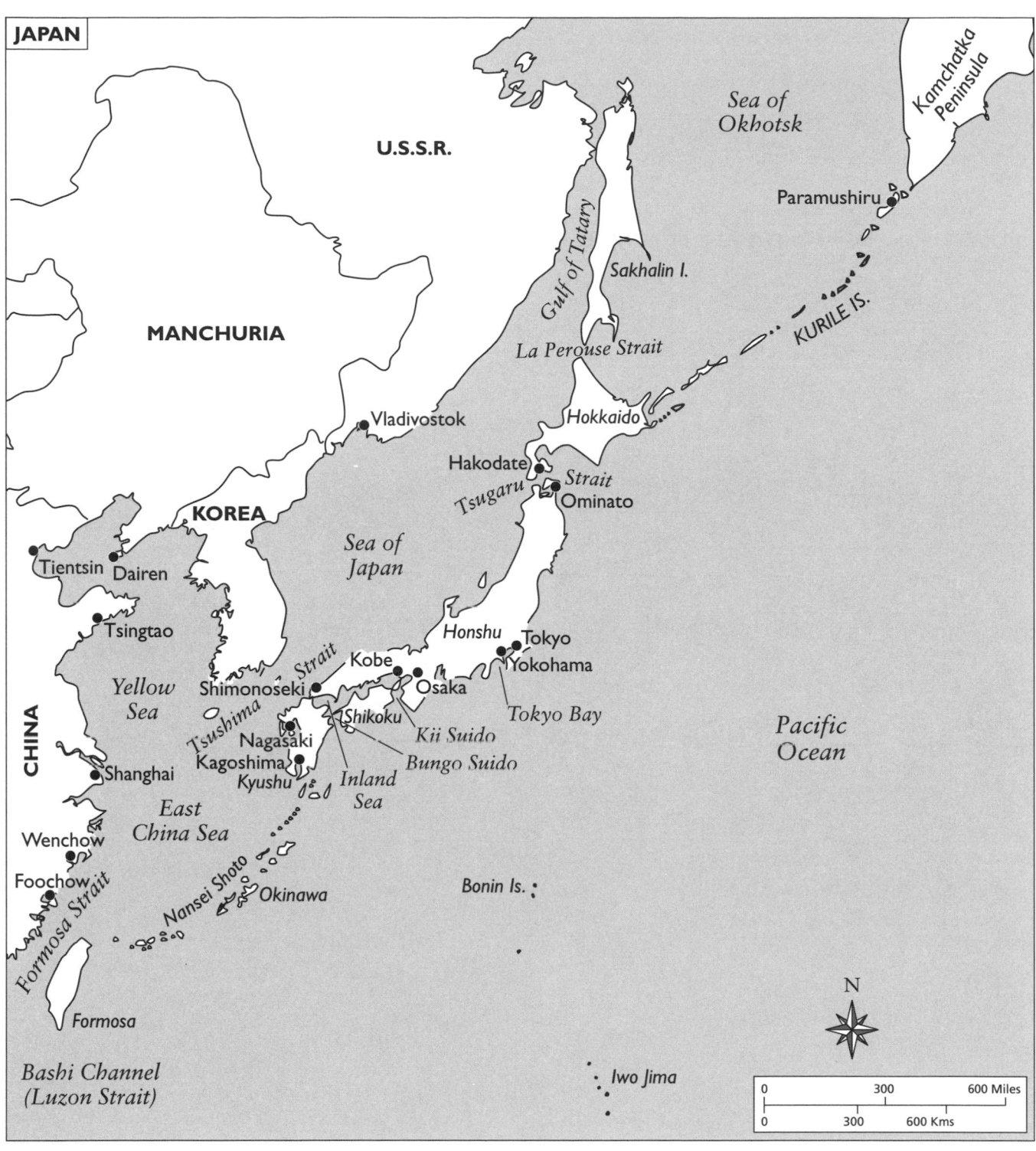

JAPAN

U.S.S.R.

MANCHURIA

Sea of
Okhotsk

Kamchatka
Peninsula

Paramushiru

Sakhalin I.

Gulf of Tatary

La Perouse Strait

KURILE IS.

KOREA

Vladivostok

Hokkaido

Hakodate

Tsugaru
Strait
Ominato

Tientsin
Dairen

Sea of
Japan

Tsingtao

Honshu
Tokyo
Yokohama

Yellow
Sea

Kobe
Shimonoseki
Strait

CHINA

Tsushima

Osaka

Shikoku

Tokyo Bay

Kii Suido

Nagasaki
Kagoshima

Bungo Suido

Pacific
Ocean

Shanghai

Kyushu

Inland
Sea

East
China Sea

Wenchow

Nansei Shoto

Okinawa

Foochow

Formosa Strait

Bonin Is.

Formosa

N

Bashi Channel
(Luzon Strait)

Iwo Jima

| 0 | 300 | 600 Miles |
| 0 | 300 | 600 Kms |

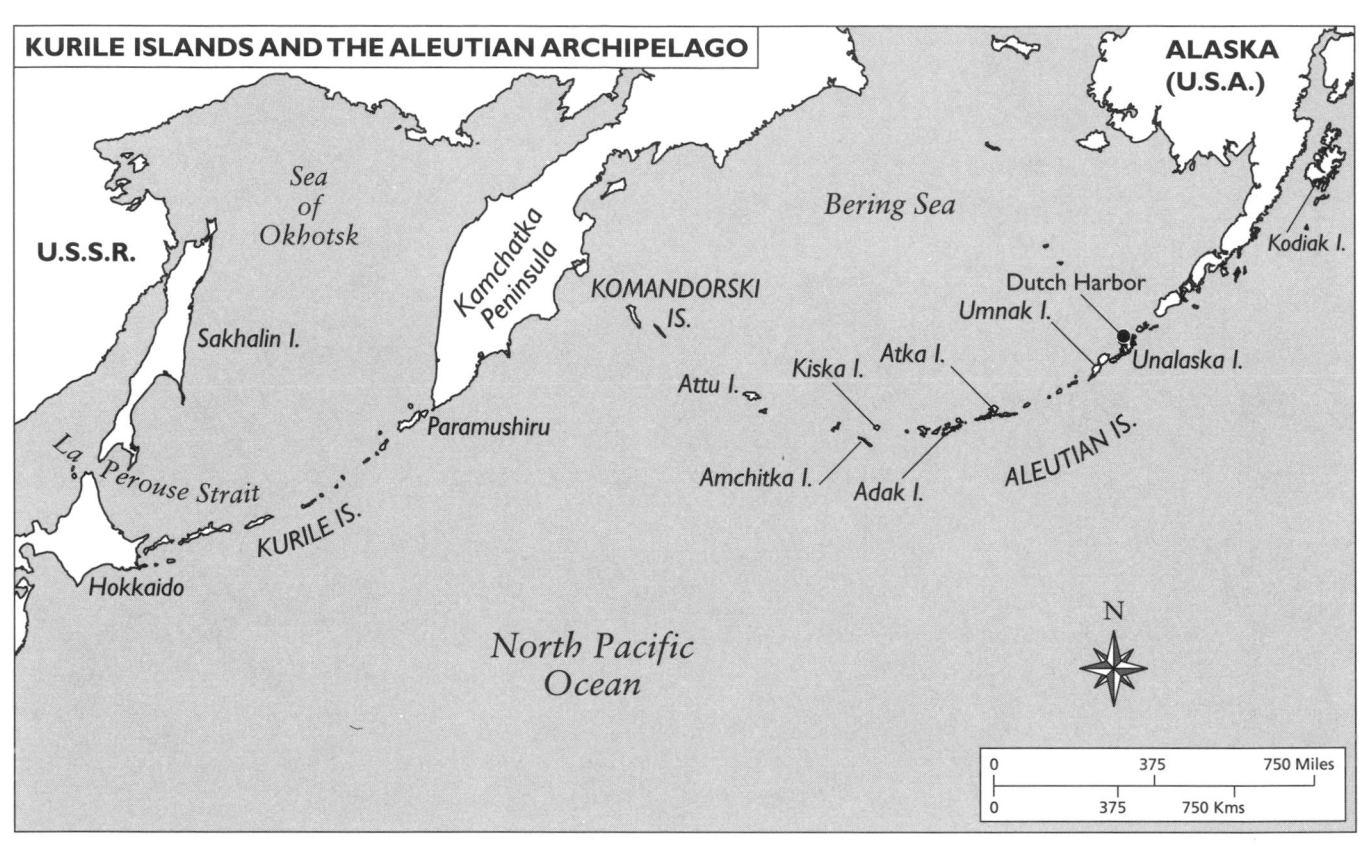

KURILE ISLANDS AND THE ALEUTIAN ARCHIPELAGO

ALASKA (U.S.A.)

U.S.S.R.

Sea of Okhotsk

Kamchatka Peninsula

Bering Sea

KOMANDORSKI IS.

Sakhalin I.

Kodiak I.

Dutch Harbor

Umnak I.

Atka I.

Unalaska I.

Kiska I.

Attu I.

Paramushiru

Amchitka I.

Adak I.

ALEUTIAN IS.

La Perouse Strait

KURILE IS.

Hokkaido

North Pacific Ocean

N

0   375   750 Miles

0   375   750 Kms

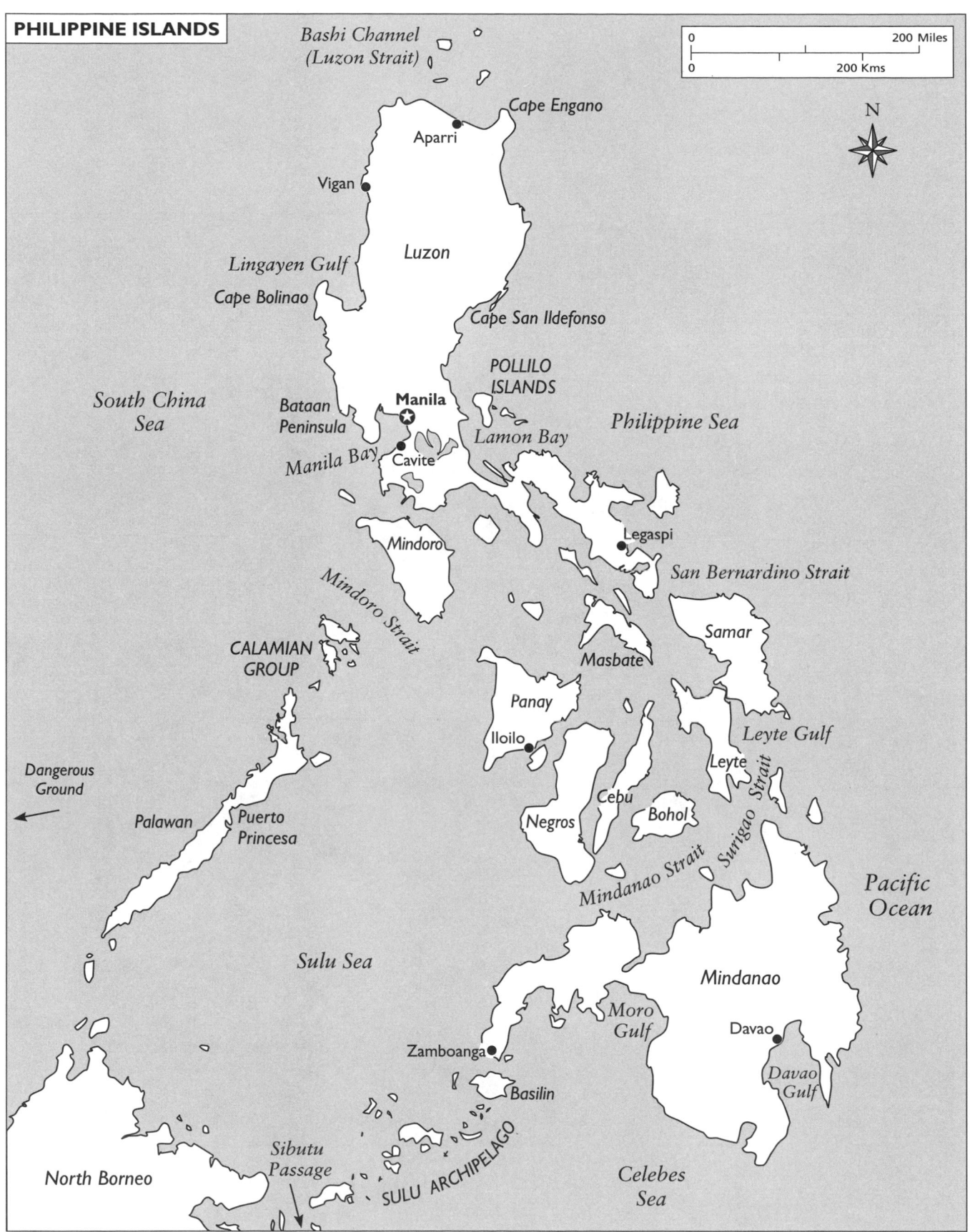

PHILIPPINE ISLANDS

Bashi Channel
(Luzon Strait)

Cape Engano

Aparri

Vigan

Luzon

Lingayen Gulf

Cape Bolinao

Cape San Ildefonso

POLLILO
ISLANDS

South China
Sea

Bataan
Peninsula

Manila

Manila Bay

Cavite

Lamon Bay

Philippine Sea

Mindoro

Legaspi

San Bernardino Strait

Mindoro Strait

CALAMIAN
GROUP

Masbate

Samar

Dangerous
Ground

Palawan

Puerto
Princesa

Panay

Iloilo

Cebu

Negros

Bohol

Leyte Gulf

Leyte

Surigao Strait

Mindanao Strait

Pacific
Ocean

Sulu Sea

Mindanao

Moro
Gulf

Davao

Zamboanga

Basilin

Davao
Gulf

Sibutu
Passage

SULU ARCHIPELAGO

Celebes
Sea

North Borneo

N

0   200 Miles

0   200 Kms

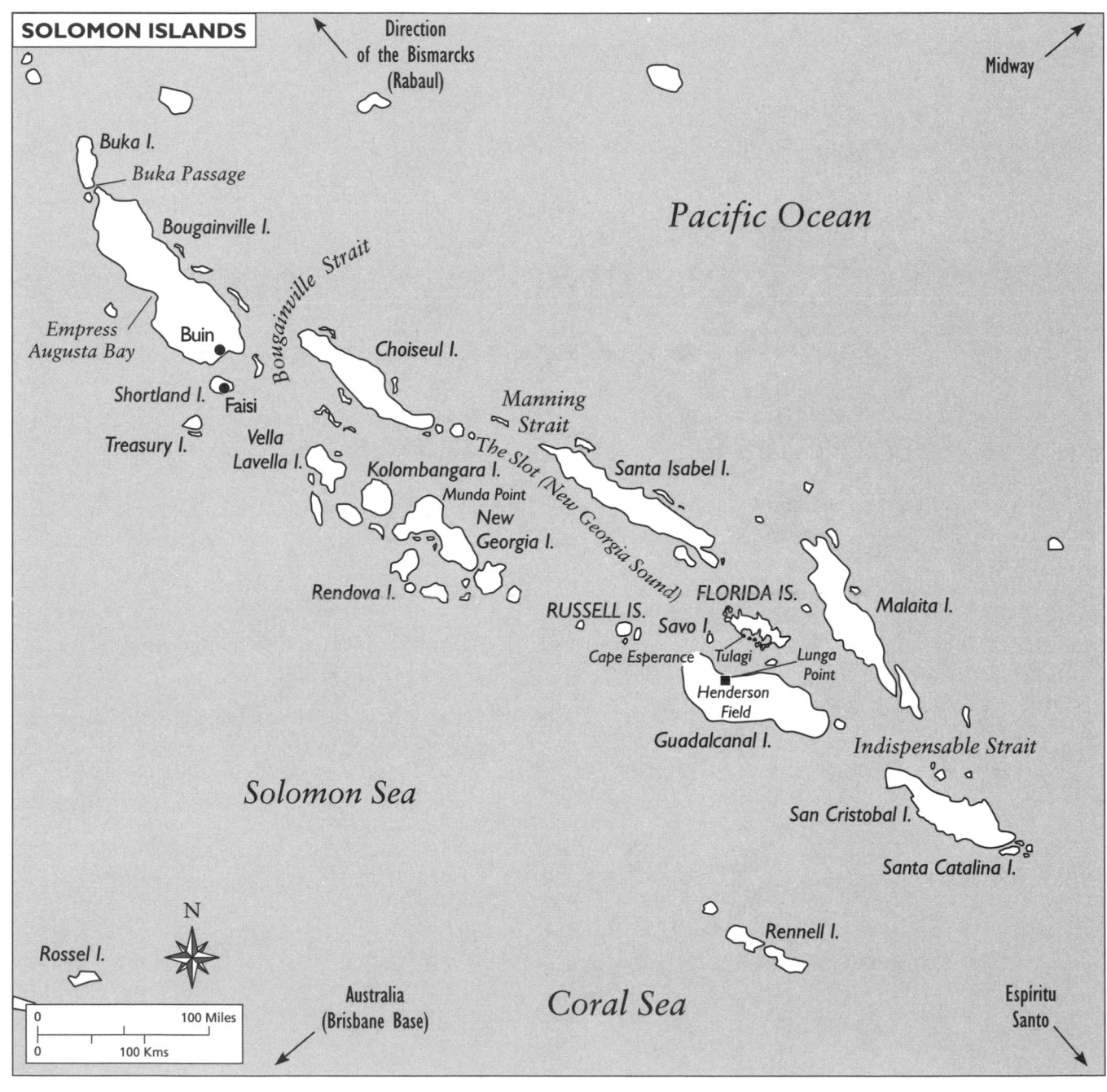

SOLOMON ISLANDS

Direction
of the Bismarcks
(Rabaul)

Midway

Pacific Ocean

Buka I.

Buka Passage

Bougainville I.

Bougainville Strait

Empress
Augusta Bay

Buin

Choiseul I.

Manning
Strait

Shortland I.

Faisi

Treasury I.

Vella
Lavella I.

The Slot (New Georgia Sound)

Santa Isabel I.

Kolombangara I.

Munda Point

New
Georgia I.

Rendova I.

RUSSELL IS.

Savo I.

FLORIDA IS.

Malaita I.

Cape Esperance

Tulagi

Lunga
Point

Henderson
Field

Guadalcanal I.

Indispensable Strait

San Cristobal I.

Santa Catalina I.

Solomon Sea

N

Rossel I.

Rennell I.

Espiritu
Santo

Australia
(Brisbane Base)

Coral Sea

0   100 Miles

0   100 Kms

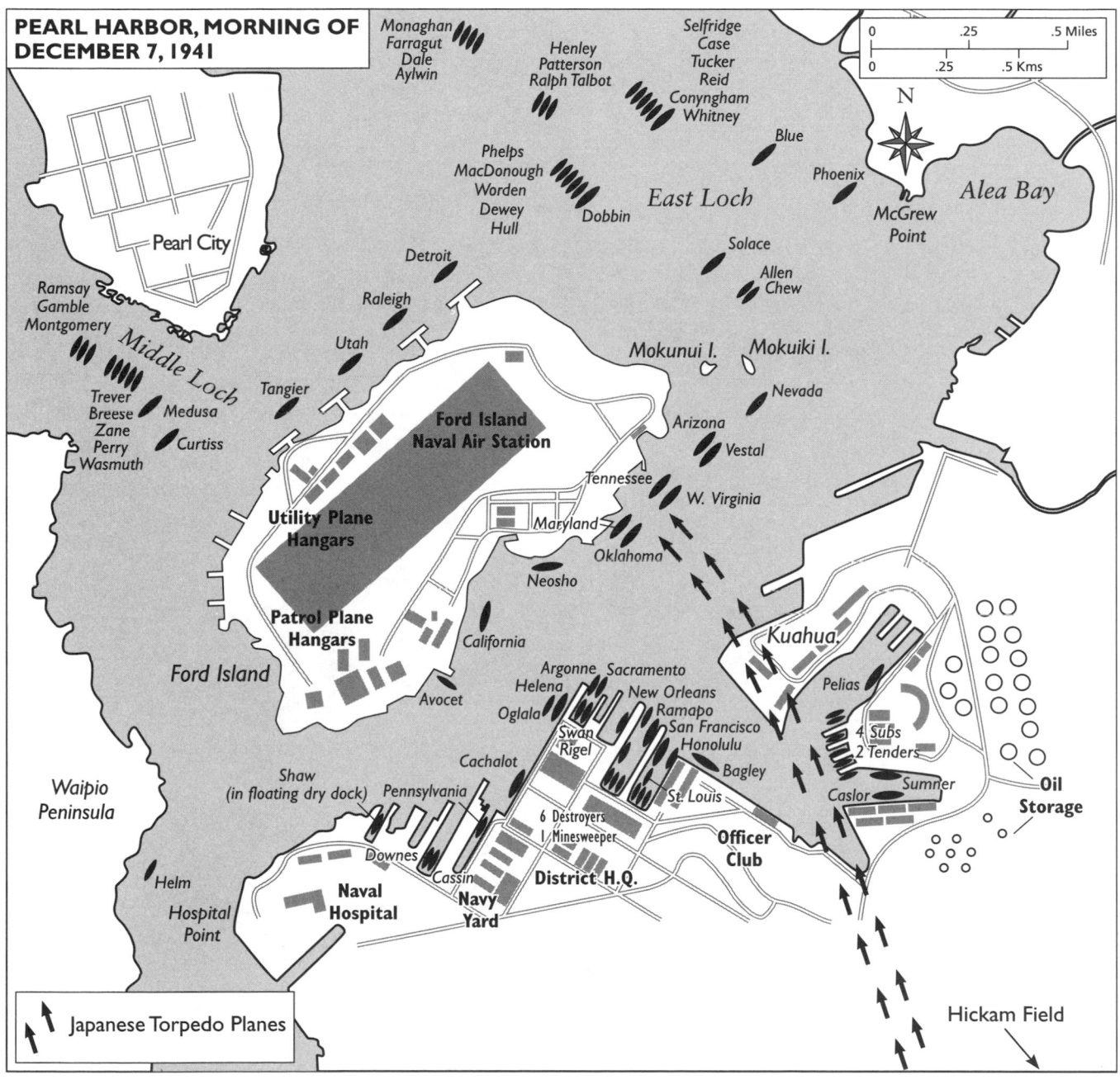

PEARL HARBOR, MORNING OF DECEMBER 7, 1941

Monaghan
Farragut
Dale
Aylwin

Henley
Patterson
Ralph Talbot

Selfridge
Case
Tucker
Reid
Conyngham
Whitney

Blue

Phoenix

Alea Bay

McGrew
Point

Phelps
MacDonough
Worden
Dewey
Hull

Dobbin

East Loch

Solace

Allen
Chew

Pearl City

Detroit

Raleigh

Utah

Tangier

Mokunui I.

Mokuiki I.

Nevada

**Ford Island
Naval Air Station**

Arizona

Vestal

Ramsay
Gamble
Montgomery

Middle Loch

Trever
Breese
Zane
Perry
Wasmuth

Medusa

Curtiss

Tennessee

W. Virginia

**Utility Plane
Hangars**

Maryland

Oklahoma

Neosho

**Patrol Plane
Hangars**

Ford Island

California

Avocet

Kuahua

Pelias

Argonne
Helena
Oglala

Sacramento

New Orleans
Ramapo
San Francisco
Honolulu

4 Subs
2 Tenders

*Waipio
Peninsula*

Shaw
(in floating dry dock)

Cachalot

Swan
Rigel

Bagley

St. Louis

Sumner

Caslor

**Oil
Storage**

Pennsylvania

Downes

Helm

Cassin

**Naval
Hospital**

*Hospital
Point*

**Navy
Yard**

6 Destroyers
1 Minesweeper

District H.Q.

**Officer
Club**

0		.25	.5 Miles
0	.25	.5 Kms	

N

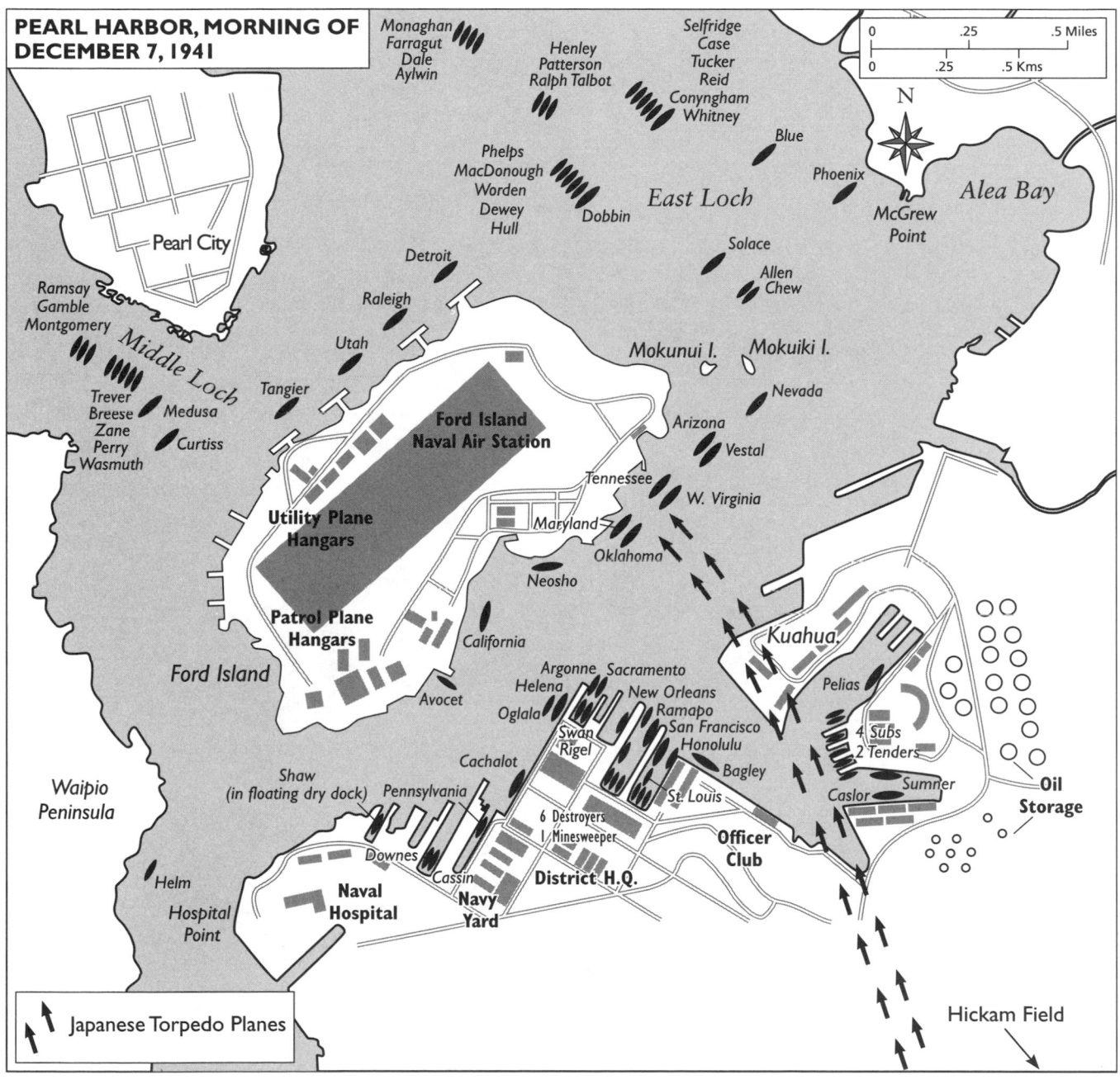 Japanese Torpedo Planes

Hickam Field

xv

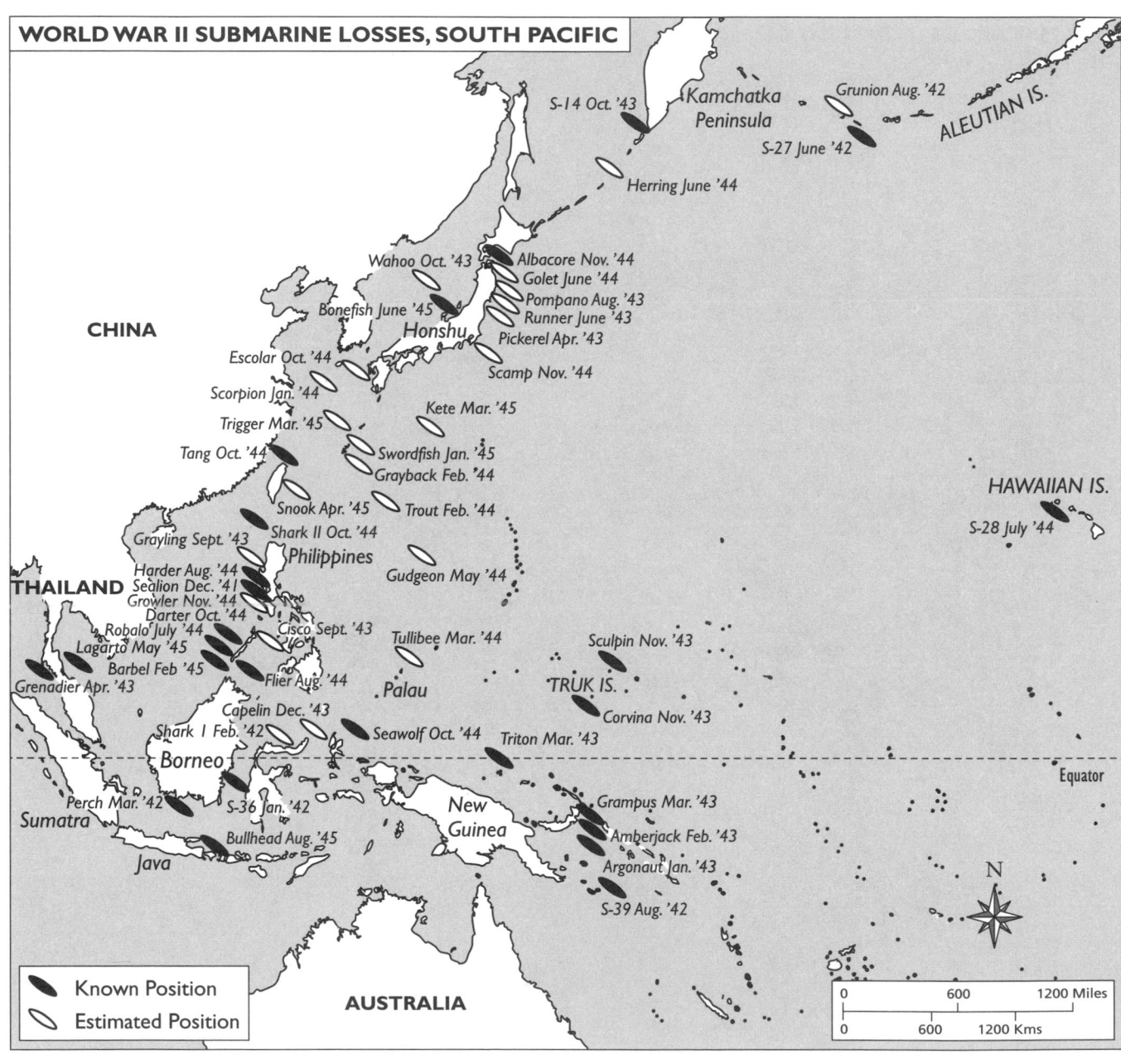

WORLD WAR II SUBMARINE LOSSES, SOUTH PACIFIC

Grunion Aug. '42

S-14 Oct. '43

Kamchatka Peninsula

ALEUTIAN IS.

S-27 June '42

Herring June '44

Wahoo Oct. '43   Albacore Nov. '44
Golet June '44
Bonefish June '45   Pompano Aug. '43
Runner June '43

CHINA

Honshu   Pickerel Apr. '43

Escolar Oct. '44   Scamp Nov. '44

Scorpion Jan. '44   Kete Mar. '45

Trigger Mar. '45

HAWAIIAN IS.

Tang Oct. '44   Swordfish Jan. '45
Grayback Feb. '44   S-28 July '44

Snook Apr. '45   Trout Feb. '44

Grayling Sept. '43   Shark II Oct. '44

Harder Aug. '44   Philippines   Gudgeon May '44
Sealion Dec. '41
Growler Nov. '44
Darter Oct. '44   Cisco Sept. '43
Robalo July '44   Tullibee Mar. '44   Sculpin Nov. '43
Lagarto May '45
Barbel Feb. '45   Flier Aug. '44   Palau   TRUK IS.
Grenadier Apr. '43   Capelin Dec. '43   Corvina Nov. '43
THAILAND

Shark I Feb. '42   Seawolf Oct. '44   Triton Mar. '43

Borneo   Equator

Perch Mar. '42   Grampus Mar. '43
Sumatra   S-36 Jan. '42   New
Guinea   Amberjack Feb. '43
Bullhead Aug. '45   N
Java   Argonaut Jan. '43

S-39 Aug. '42

▬ Known Position
◖ Estimated Position

AUSTRALIA

0   600   1200 Miles
0   600   1200 Kms

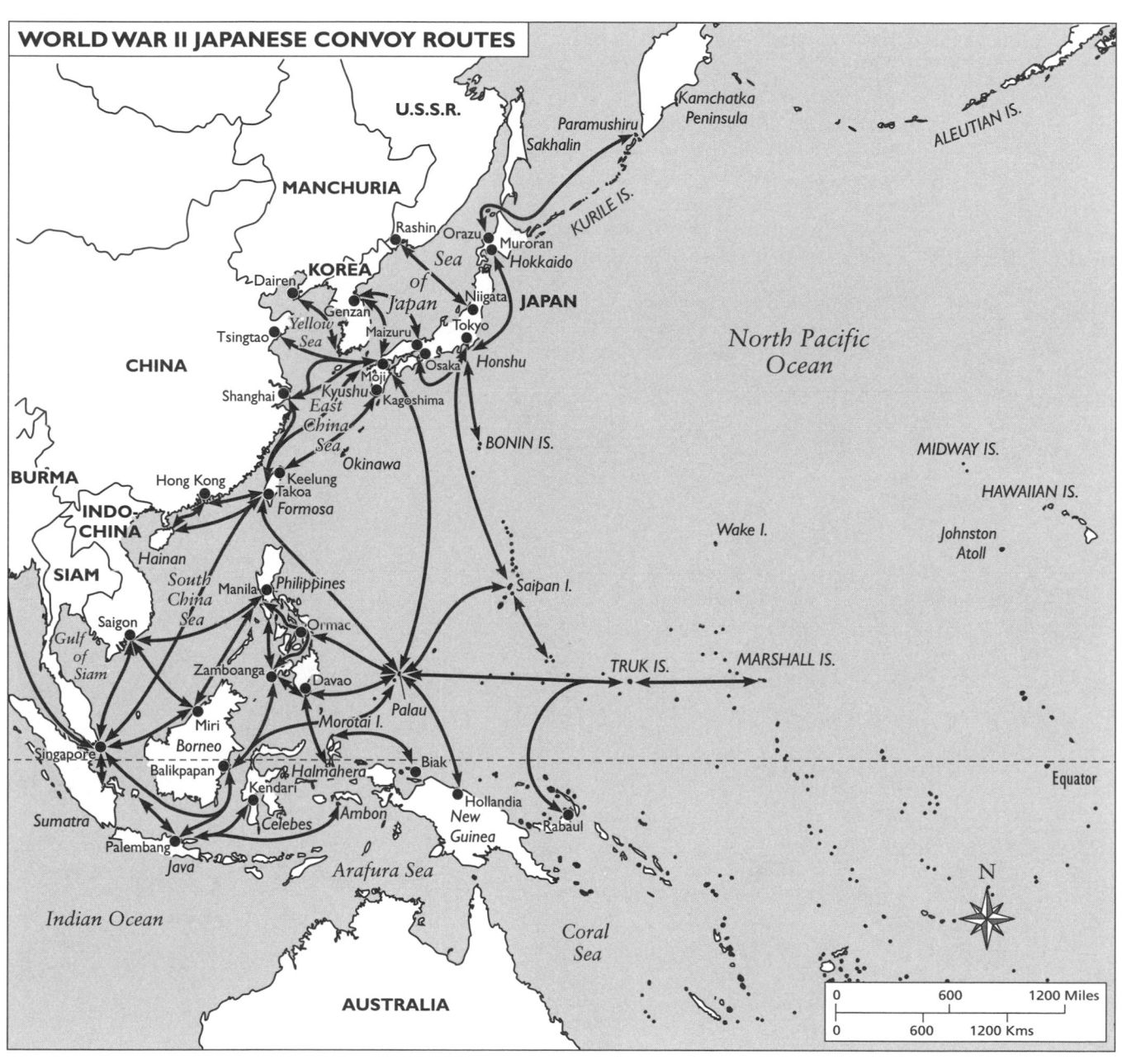

WORLD WAR II JAPANESE CONVOY ROUTES

U.S.S.R.

MANCHURIA

Kamchatka
Peninsula

Paramushiru

Sakhalin

ALEUTIAN IS.

KURILE IS.

Rashin Orazu Muroran
KOREA   Hokkaido

Dairen Genzan Niigata JAPAN

Yellow   Maizuru Tokyo

Sea Sea
of
Japan

Tsingtao

CHINA Moji Osaka Honshu

Shanghai Kyushu Kagoshima

East North Pacific
China   Ocean
Sea

Okinawa

BONIN IS.

BURMA Hong Kong Keelung MIDWAY IS.

INDO- Takoa
CHINA   Formosa HAWAIIAN IS.

SIAM Hainan Wake I. Johnston
        Atoll

South Manila Philippines Saipan I.
Saigon China
        Sea Ormac

Gulf   TRUK IS. MARSHALL IS.
of Zamboanga
Siam   Davao

        Palau

Miri Morotai I.
Singapore Borneo
        Biak Equator
Balikpapan
Kendari Halmahera Hollandia
Sumatra   Ambon New
        Celebes Guinea Rabaul
Palembang
Java Arafura Sea

Indian Ocean N

        Coral
        Sea

AUSTRALIA

| 0 | 600 | 1200 Miles |

| 0 | 600 | 1200 Kms |

xvii

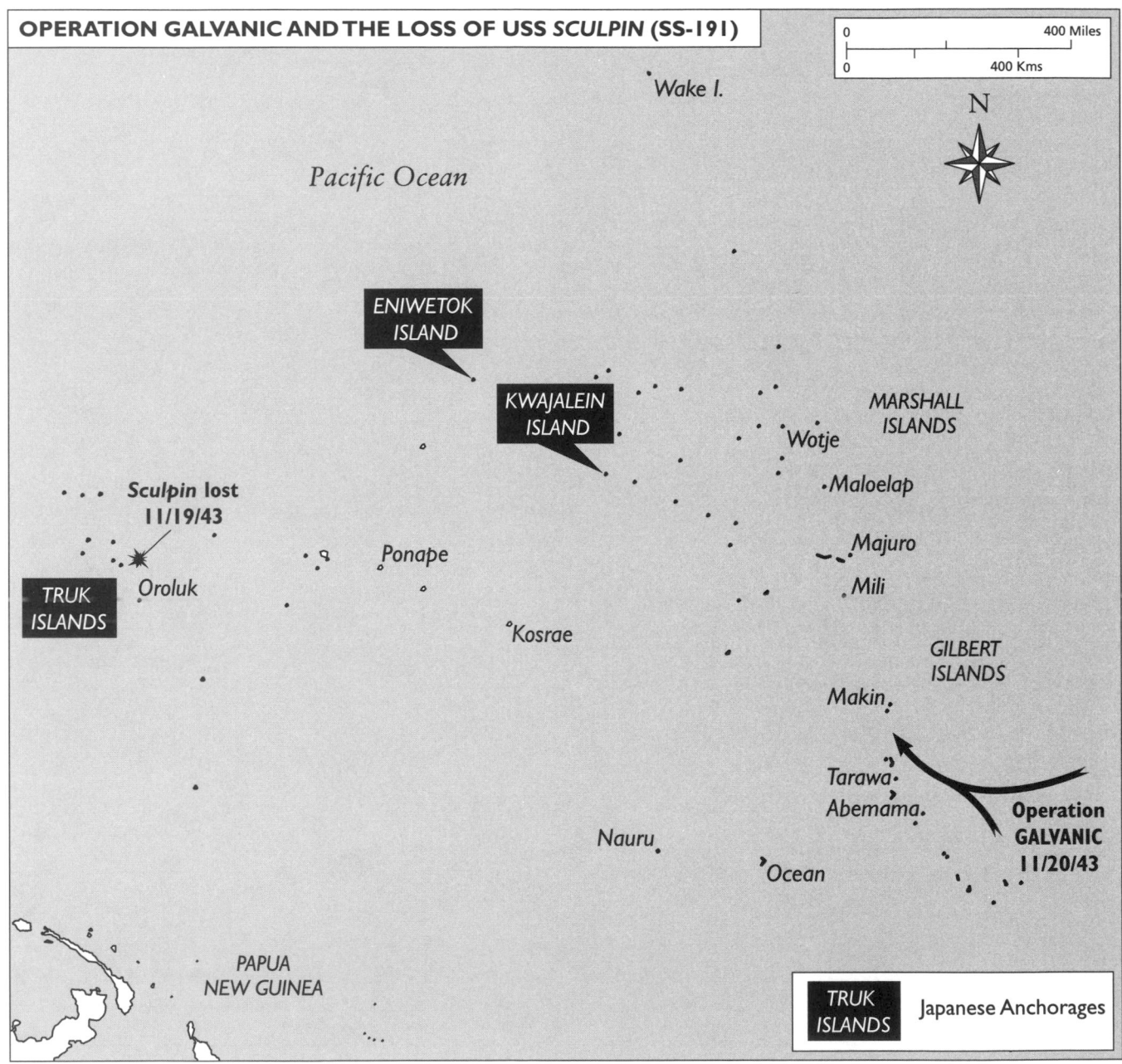

OPERATION GALVANIC AND THE LOSS OF USS *SCULPIN* (SS-191)

FOREWORD

Innovation, vision, honor, courage, professionalism, and pride are only a few of the characteristics of the United States Submarine Force. Each class of submarine—from the Confederate navy's *Hunley* or our latest operational attack submarine, USS *Connecticut*—has been at the vanguard of naval design and construction. Our nation has been blessed to have these "engineering works of art" in her defense arsenal.

Having recently celebrated a centennial of submarines, the United States Submarine Force is again on the cusp of the future. The construction of the Virginia-class fast-attack submarine brings to bear the latest in technology, allowing operational commanders unprecedented advantages in the undersea battle space. The ingenious redesign of our Trident ballistic missile submarines into cruise missile launching arsenal ships will provide our leaders a stealthy and conventional deterrent to would-be aggressors. But technology alone has never been the defining element behind the success of the American submarine force.

While technological capabilities and advances are important in warfare, the true mettle of the American submarine force has been our people. As George Orwell once said, "We sleep safe in our beds because rough men stand ready in the night to visit violence on those who would do us harm." These "rough men," these submariners, have come from all parts of America, from different backgrounds and varied experiences. Even so, they have displayed common traits; among them, great flexibility, common sense, team spirit, and a strong love of freedom. These men include visionaries like John Holland and Admiral Hyman G. Rickover and gallant leaders like Admiral Gene Fluckey and Captain Doc Blanchard. Submariners past and present accepted and continue to accept the challenges and sacrifices necessary to maintain our freedom. They set the standards for war-fighting during both world wars and the long cold war. They will play a major role in the war on terrorism!

Al Konetzni, Jr., Vice Admiral, U.S. Navy, Deputy Commander in Chief, U.S. Atlantic Fleet. *(Vice Admiral Albert H. Konetzni, Jr.)*

It has been my honor to serve side by side with these "rough men," watching history in the making for nearly 40 years. This compendium of history and technology will serve you well as a ready reference to the past with an ever-watchful eye on the future.

Best Regards and Welcome Aboard,
Albert H. Konetzni, Jr.
Vice Admiral, United States Navy

PREFACE

When we undertook the challenging assignment of authoring an entire encyclopedia of American submarines, we realized that there was absolutely no way we could adequately integrate information on all of the submarines that have been placed in service down through the generations, particularly after the United States Navy activated its building and commissioning program in 1900. So our emphasis has been more on past history than on current events in the story of American submarines, for it is obvious that the stories of submarines currently in service can be told only in a very limited way, for security reasons, while accounts of navy submarines put into service during the past two decades or so will be told independently and collectively in the near and distant future in the nation's press, books, and service publications. And so it seemed reasonable to infer that these accounts would be more valuable in a later edition of the current encyclopedia.

We have placed considerable emphasis on the more dramatic and readable accounts, such as the stirring narratives of World War II missions, the tragedies of peacetime sinkings, and the reports of the heroic sacrifices of submariners on "Eternal Patrols." But we have also focused on those people and events and circumstances vital to the overall history of American submarines, going back more than 200 years. And we have covered many individual submarines in brief in collective reports about the different classes of boats over the years. We ask those readers to bear with us if we have omitted references and accounts of particular interest and concern to them, and welcome suggestions for inclusion in any future edition of this encyclopedia that may be contemplated.

In the selection of illustrations, our goal has been to provide readers with an exciting, active overview of the subject, rather than a categoric display of the type that might be found in such works as naval classifications of ships. Our hope is that this volume will be a fitting tribute to the achievements of submariners present and the memories of submariners past.

ACKNOWLEDGMENTS

It goes without saying that the authors are indebted to dozens of sources in the United States Navy, as well as to individuals and organizations outside of the government but with interests in, and extensive knowledge about, submarines. Among those in the first category are the submarine force commanders of the Atlantic and Pacific Fleets; the naval submarine bases at New London, Connecticut, Pearl Harbor, Hawaii, Norfolk, Virginia, and King's Bay, Georgia; the Naval Submarine School, the Naval Undersea Warfare Center; the Portsmouth, Boston, and Mare Island Shipyards; the Naval Historical Center, the United States Naval Institute, the United States Naval Academy, the Submarine Force Library, and the many submarine museums spread across the United States, in particular the ones at the Groton/New London Submarine Base and the Naval Academy.

In the second category, we are especially grateful for the detailed data and most of the illustrations for this book, which were supplied by SubPride, whose curator, Don Scott, has been compiling a vast submarine collection going back more than 40 years, and which is known to thousands of submariners as a source of pictures and data about boats in which they have a personal interest. During the last two years of preparation for this volume, we relied heavily on some of the private collections of undersea data, in particular the St. Mary's Submarine Museum in St. Mary's, Georgia, as well as on dozens of Internet websites, both public and private. These include, among many others, the United States Navy official website; Submarine Warfare Division home page; Navy Online; The Submarine Center; New Attack Submarine home page; Subnet; DANFS Online; SubPride; Ron Martini's Submarine World Network; United States Submarine Veterans; Cyber Sub Base, Houston, Texas; Navets USA; Deep Domain; Green Board; Kackman's Submarine page; Gordy's Sub Groupie page; Yahoo USN Submarines; Greg's home page; and the many websites maintained by navy submarine bases and operational offices. Our thanks also to submarine shipbuilders, but most importantly to the Electric Boat Company, now a division of General Dynamics, founded in 1900, and the oldest submarine builder in existence.

Since submariners have long been known for their intense pride in the service, and their allegiance in terms of alumni associations and fraternal societies, we turned to many of these organizations for facts, personal accounts, and illustrations, not to mention a considerable amount of inspiration. Among these groups are the United States Submarine Veterans, Inc. (USSVI); the Naval Submarine League; Submarine Old Comrades Association; Submarine Wives Club; Cyberspace Association of U.S. Submariners; Submarine Veterans of World War II; Submarine Veterans, Inc.; and many of the more than 100 individual sub alumni associations.

Finally, we owe our warmest thanks to the family and many friends of the late James ("Doc") Blanchard, Captain, United States Navy (Retired), who was a major catalyst for the start of this project, and to whom this book is fondly dedicated.

INTRODUCTION*

ONE HUNDRED YEARS OF THE AMERICAN SUBMARINE FORCE

At the beginning of the centennial recognition of the submarine force in the U.S. Navy, the U.S. Naval Historical Center published an article to commemorate the event. The following is a condensation of that text.

The past 100 years have witnessed the evolution of a force that mastered submersible warfare, introduced nuclear propulsion to create the true submarine, and for decades patrolled the deep-ocean front line. The navy's involvement with the submarine dates from 1888 when the Bureau of Construction and Repair sponsored a design competition that inspired John Holland to build the experimental *Plunger*. As the new century dawned, a few American naval leaders called the submarine a real threat to international surface forces, leading the navy to acquire its first submarine in 1900 when it bought Holland's 64-ton sub for $160,000, and commissioned it *Holland*, with a gasoline engine for surface runs and electric motors for submerged operations.

Because of the volatility of gasoline, American designs began to adopt the diesel engine in 1909 with the Electric Boat Company's F class (SS-20–23). Combining diesel propulsion with the submersible designs of Holland and Lake, U.S. boats took on a familiar configuration through American entry into World War I. Submarines of the E, H, K, L, M, N, O, and R classes ranged in displacement from 287 to 610 tons, with the fastest boats displaying a top surface speed of barely 14 knots on diesel power.

During World War I the U.S. Navy separated these submersibles into two groups according to mission. Boats of the N and O classes, as well as some of the E type, patrolled American coasts and harbors following a defensive strategy. Other submarines drew assignments that sent them to hostile European waters after 1917. Some K-, L-, O-, and E-class boats conducted offensive, open-sea operations from the Azores and Bantry Bay in Ireland. They sup-

ported the Allied effort to maintain open sea lanes along the European coast and in the approaches to the British Isles. The Navy Department's plans reflected the prevailing thinking, which saw the submersible as a type of torpedo boat to function with the battle fleet. Thus the first submarine designs produced the faster 16-knot, S-class submarine in 1916. At the same time, Electric Boat was commissioned to design three boats of the 20-knot T, or AA class, whose characteristics brought the navy one step closer to the "fleet submarine," which could keep pace with the battle fleet. But there were flaws in the early designs, and the navy was constantly faced with the question of *identity:* how should the navy use submarines and what would be their primary strategic roles? Another question was how to provide them with the necessary aggressive tactics and capabilities and yet avoid the stigma of the German U-boats of World War I, which had been damned by many nations for the torpedoing of neutral commercial vessels and the killing of innocent civilians.

American commanders realized that war in all its brutality, not peacetime politics, would determine future challenges faced by the submarine force. Thus, the boats built in the 1930s reflected assertive, offensive strategic thinking as the country came to terms with the Great Depression and the engineers resolved the submarine technological and propulsion dilemmas. The new Salmon-Sargo designs were intended for long-range independent patrols, with requisite food, fuel, and weapons capacity. The fleet exercises during the late 1930s were actually based on the strategy that submarines should be free to attack warships, convoy escort ships, and even certain convoys identified as critical to enemy supplies. By 1940, the submarine force had answered its fundamental strategic questions and had the vessels to carry out the conse-

---

* Adapted from "One Hundred Years of the American Submarine Force," by Dr. Gary E. Weir, courtesy of the U.S. Naval Historical Center.

quent roles and missions. It came as no surprise when Admiral Thomas Hart proclaimed unrestricted submarine warfare against Japan the day after the Pearl Harbor attack in December 1941. The submarine force knew what to do.

Employing the extremely reliable boats of the Gato, Balao, and Tench classes, the submarine force scored the most victories of any force in any theater of the war. Despite a hesitant beginning, the submarine force destroyed 1,314 enemy ships for 55 percent of all enemy ships lost. The price was substantial; out of 16,000 submariners, the force lost 375 officers and 3,131 enlisted men in 52 submarines, but the accomplishments were superb. While the Japanese advanced quickly after Pearl Harbor and the navy struggled to recover from its initial defeat, the submarine force brought the war to the enemy while operating from American and Australian bases. American submarines had extraordinary success against both Japanese merchantmen and warships. Refining their methods of attack made American submariners the worst enemy of any ship flying the Japanese flag. One such method was to split command: while the executive officer manned the periscope and made observations, the commander was left free to evaluate the entire combat situation, making possible swift, informed, and effective approach and attack decisions. As a result, one submarine, Wahoo, sank almost 32,000 tons of enemy shipping on a single patrol. Later in the war, Wahoo's executive officer, Richard O'Kane, now in command of Tang, received the Congressional Medal of Honor and became the submarine force's leading ace of the war, credited with destroying 31 ships for 227,800 tons.

Apart from their attack records, American submarines played both humane and special operations roles in their campaign against Japan. In many of the hardest fought battles of the war, submarine crews rescued unlucky fighter and bomber pilots who ended up in the sea. Fleet submarines also delivered troops tasked with special missions against Japanese Pacific strongholds, such as reconnaissance and the transportation of marine raiders and coast-watchers to strategic combat areas. In the final months of the war, American submarines had difficulty finding targets because the Japanese had virtually no ships left to sink. Undaunted, submarine commanders pursued the enemy right into his own harbors and hiding places.

Undersea warfare experienced a remarkable evolution after World War II, and the submarine force led the way. Building on the advanced designs created by the Germans during World War II, the navy foresaw boats of the future going deeper, staying down longer, and cruising much faster. Indeed, in reports submitted in 1950, naval and civilian advisers warned that U-boat technology exploited by the Soviets might present the greatest postwar naval threat to the United States. No warship of the time, it was predicted, could effectively detect and track a submarine like the German Type 21, which could sustain a 17-knot submerged speed for at least 30 minutes. Thus, shortly after the war, with this potential threat in mind, the U.S. Navy began experimenting with high-speed, sophisticated silencing techniques, sensitive sonic detection, and deeper diving potential. The result: the greater underwater propulsive power, or GUPPY, conversions that changed the configuration of wartime submersibles to enhance submerged speed and hydrodynamic efficiency. The Tang class, the first truly new postwar construction, represented an initial step on a new road toward greater speed and endurance below the surface. It also provided the basic hull form used for the first true nuclear submarine, the Nautilus, which went to sea propelled by a pressurized-water nuclear reactor plant in January 1955, setting a totally new standard. Its submerged endurance was limited only by the crews' periodic needs. Rather than a surface ship capable of submerging when the need arose, this submarine's natural environment lay below the surface. Seawolf and the Skate-class hunter-killer submarines quickly followed Nautilus, and together they demonstrated the new extent of submarine effectiveness.

The advent of nuclear submarines provided the final piece to a number of promising technical puzzles. Research into the quest for greater submerged speed and endurance provided insights into the ideal hull form for high-speed submarines. With the experimental Albacore, submarines attained an extraordinary submerged speed. In the fast-attack submarine Skipjack, the endurance of nuclear propulsion and the high speed of the Albacore teardrop hull were wed to form the new paradigm. Every American submarine since 1958 has followed this same basic formula. The attack submarines proved very effective during the cold war in addressing the Soviet submarine threat in the Atlantic and Pacific through surveillance and deterrence. The Nautilus-Albacore combination also served to extend the reach of the submarine force. While the navy experimented with launching missiles like the Regulus from surfaced submarines during the late 1950s, the mobility, stealth, and endurance of nuclear submarines based on the Skipjack model proved the ideal platform for submerged launching of ballistic missiles. From the Polaris in 1960, to subsequent generations of missiles suitable for submerged launching, the navy's fleet ballistic missile submarines (SSBN) have provided the ultimate nuclear deterrent. As opposed to easily targeted land-based missiles, SSBNs are in constant motion. Hiding deep in the ocean, with virtually unlimited endurance, SSBNs are capable of reaching almost any target. With the current Ohio-class SSBNs, the submarine force employs the most effective and survivable component of current American strategic nuclear defense.

Since the 1970s, the submarine force has also provided the navy with a stealthy way of applying tactical firepower against land and sea targets. Designed at first for torpedo tube launch, the Tomahawk cruise missile has enhanced the effectiveness of the attack submarine fleet. Now capable of firing these missiles from a vertical launch system in the bow, the latest flight of the submarine force's front-line, Los Angeles-class SSNs has proven very useful in the challenging environment of modern war at sea. During Desert Storm, submarine-launched Tomahawks proved their extraordinary effectiveness during the first combat use of the submarine force's new capability. With their stealth, endurance, diverse weapons array, and ability to detect threats while communicating with the fleet at great range, American submarines conduct both independent tactical and strategic patrols as well as operations in support of carrier battle groups. The effort to integrate the submarine more thoroughly with air and surface forces suggests that naval warfare of the future will require a flexible mix of assets designed for a future filled with constantly changing defense demands.

ENTRIES A–Z

A

acoustic warfare

Action that involves the use of underwater acoustic energy to determine, exploit, reduce, or prevent hostile use of the underwater acoustic spectrum—and actions that retain friendly use of the underwater acoustic spectrum. There are three divisions within acoustic warfare:

1. **Acoustic Warfare Support Measures** Acoustic warfare involving actions to search for, intercept, locate, record, and analyze radiated acoustic energy in water for exploitation of the radiations. The use of acoustic warfare support measures involves no intentional underwater acoustic emission and is generally not detectable by the enemy.
2. **Acoustic Warfare Countermeasures** Actions taken to prevent or reduce an enemy's effective use of the underwater acoustic spectrum. Acoustic warfare countermeasures involve international underwater acoustic emissions for deception and jamming.
3. **Acoustic Warfare Counter-countermeasures** Actions taken to ensure friendly, effective use of the underwater acoustic spectrum despite the enemy's use of underwater acoustic warfare. Acoustic warfare counter-countermeasures involve anti-acoustic warfare support measures and anti-acoustic warfare countermeasures, and may not involve underwater acoustic emissions.

Adder (SS-3)

One of the earliest U.S. Navy submarines, she was built by the Crescent Shipyard, Elizabethport, New Jersey, and launched July 22, 1901. She was known as a "submarine torpedo boat," and carried a complement of one officer and six enlisted men. After initial experimental duty at the Naval Torpedo Station at Newport, *Adder* was towed to the Norfolk Navy Yard by tug in December 1903, and assigned to the Reserve Torpedo Flotilla. In July 1909, she was loaded on board a collier and transported to the Philippine Islands, where she was assigned to duty with the First Submarine Division, Asiatic Torpedo Fleet. Over almost a decade, the submarine torpedo boat operated from Cavite, principally in training and experimental work. During World War I, she carried out patrols off the entrance to Manila Bay and around the island of Corregidor. She was decommissioned in December 1919, and ended duty as a target in January 1922.

Advanced Seal Delivery System (ASDS)

A minisubmarine, generally 65 feet in length, operated by a two-man crew and used to transport a Navy Sea-Air-Land (SEAL) squad or special operations forces from other services. This vessel assists in the conduct of long-range clandestine operations in support of special operations missions. It can be launched either from a host submarine or from the well decks of amphibious ships. The battery-powered submersible is specifically designed to carry SEALs, or other occupants, close to their area of operations, thus decreasing exposure to cold water and reducing physical and mental fatigue.

Albacore (AGSS-569)

Almost 10 years after World War II, *Albacore* was declared missing and presumably sunk, and a more modern vessel of the same name was launched in August 1953, at the

1

The USS *Adder/A-2* (SS-3), Submarine Torpedo Boat #3, patrolled Manila Bay and Corregidor during World War I.
(United States Navy)

Portsmouth (New Hampshire) Navy Yard as an experimental submarine to test changes in hull form to increase speed and agility underwater. During the following years, she underwent continual changes in design and controls, each time with extensive testing to help shape the submarine of the future, and was finally deactivated in December 1972. *Albacore's* service as an experimental submersible for more than two decades steadily increased the navy's knowledge in the design of faster, quieter, more maneuverable, and safer submarines.

Albacore (SS-218)

A Gato-class boat, launched in February 1942. She was ordered to Pearl Harbor in August and began war patrols in the Pacific. She made several attacks on Japanese shipping, inflicting some degree of damage, but had her first important kill after being stationed in New Guinea, when she sank the light cruiser *Tenryu* at the end of December. In February 1943, she sank a destroyer and a frigate off the north coast of New Guinea. On patrols during 1943, she suffered many attacks and considerable damage by Japanese ships and aircraft, without inflicting much damage in return. But on June 18, after American forces began landing on Saipan, she attacked the 31,000-ton carrier *Taiho*, the newest and largest carrier in the Japanese fleet, and sent her down, along with 1,650 officers and men. *Albacore* damaged another large carrier in July, and in August was credited with sinking two vessels, a cargo ship and a submarine chaser, before returning to Pearl Harbor for servicing. In October, she headed west again and stopped at Midway for refueling. On the 28th she departed and was never heard from again.

Albuquerque (SSN-706)

A nuclear-powered fast-attack submarine of the Los Angeles class, built by Electric Boat Company and launched in March 1982, *Albuquerque* has a displacement of 6,900 tons (submerged), cruises at 25 knots on the surface and more than 30 knots submerged, and is armed with Mark 48 advanced capability torpedoes, Tomahawk land-attack cruise missiles, and mines. She carries a complement of 14 officers and 120 enlisted men. Since commissioning, *Albuquerque* has completed many deployments in both the Atlantic Ocean and Mediterranean Sea, including combat missions in Operations Allied Force/Noble Anvil in 1999 against the former Republic of Yugoslavia. She has been awarded three Meritorious Unit Commendations.

All Hands

A magazine published by the U.S. Navy and available on subscription to anyone who is interested. Produced by the Naval Media Center, the publication focuses from time to time on subjects dealing with submarines, but with an emphasis on the officers and men who make up the submarine force and their contributions to the strength and operation of undersea operations. As the *All Hands* mission states, the publication "supports the Chief of Naval Information's mission of keeping the Navy/Marine Corps team up-to-date on issues that affect their careers and their lives."

Alligator

The first submarine purchased by the U.S. Navy was built in Philadelphia in 1862. Intended to mine Confederate harbors, she sank while under tow in April 1863, with no casualties. The *Alligator,* though ungainly and all but unmanageable, was ahead of its time in one respect: it contained two crude air purifiers, a chemical-based system for producing oxygen and bellows to force stale air through lime. Unlike other early submarines, which utilized a screw propeller cranked by hand, *Alligator* used a system of 16 oars that functioned like a duck's web feet, closing when in the forward position and opening up when moved backward.

Alvin

A deep-sea submersible operated by the Woods Hole (Massachusetts) Oceanographic Institution, *Alvin* is among the most famous submersibles and played an important role in the exploration of the sunken British liner *Titanic*. *Alvin* also took part in the search for, and recovery of, a nuclear weapon lost off the coast of Spain in 1966. *Alvin* itself sank in 1968 in more than 5,000 feet of water while preparing for a dive near Cape Cod, Massachusetts. Lifting lines on the craft's tender broke, and *Alvin* sank with its hatch open. *Alvin* was recovered in 1969 with the help of Reynolds Aluminum's submersible *Aluminaut,* which had participated with *Alvin* in the search for the lost nuclear weapon off Spain.

Amberjack (SS-219)

Launched at the Electric Boat Company in March 1942, this submarine of the Gato class had a spotty career in the Pacific. In September of that year she achieved her first success by sinking a Japanese cargo and troop vessel, followed two weeks later by the demise of a cargo vessel. She reported some further small successes, which could not be confirmed because, on February 14, 1943, while stalking transport routes near Rabaul, and after making the last

The USS *Albuquerque* (SSN-706) is a Los Angeles–class submarine that displaces 6,900 tons and carries a crew of 127 U.S. Navy personnel. She was launched March 13, 1982, sponsored by Mrs. Pete B. Domenici, with Commander Richard H. Hartman in command. *(United States Navy)*

radio transmission ever received from her, she was presumed lost.

Amberjack (SS-522)

The second submarine of the same name, and of the Tench class, she was built by the Boston Naval Shipyard and launched in December 1944, and later converted to a GUPPY II boat. She conducted training missions in the North Atlantic, and was later assigned to the East Coast and the West Indies, where she operated for 11 years. *Amberjack* was later based in Charleston, South Carolina, and in several European ports. She was decommissioned at Key West, Florida, in October 1973, and then shortly afterward transferred to the Brazilian navy, where she was commissioned as *Cerea* (S-12).

American Submariner magazine

This periodical, a bimonthly, is the official publication of United States Submarine Veterans, Inc. (USSVI), and is available on subscription to members of that organization.

The magazine contains reports on submarine bases and organizations, submarine-related news and events, current and past submarine history, profiles of individuals in the news, boat reunions, obituaries, listings of USSVI members, officers and committees, book reviews, and advertising for submarine-related products. Submariners use the magazine and its website and e-mail address to search for former shipmates or to obtain personalized information.

AN/BPS-16

A Litton Sperry search and navigation radar, with touch-screen controls, embedded trainer scenarios, on- and off-line fault monitoring, and a hydraulic raise and rotate mechanism for the antenna.

AN/BQR-15

A thin-line, submarine-towed array passive sonar system, it can be streamed, retrieved, or adjusted by use of a hydraulic drive winch, while the submarine is submerged.

Annapolis (SSN-760)

Built by the Electric Boat Division of General Dynamics, this submarine of the Los Angeles class was launched in May 1991 and commissioned in April 1992.

See LOS ANGELES.

antisubmarine warfare (ASW)

Antisubmarine warfare—more recently termed undersea warfare (USW)—is a designated U.S. Navy warfare mission area, the objective of which is to deny an adversary the effective use of its submarines. ASW involves the proper deployment and employment of a wide range of sensors that may include visual sensors, magnetic sensors, passive and active electronic sensors, and passive and active acoustic sensors (sonar) in order to detect, locate, track, and, if necessary, destroy, the adversary's submarine(s). While ASW is a primary mission of U.S. submarines, the conduct of a full-scale ASW effort may also include ASW-capable surface ships and aircraft.

Apogon (SS-308)

This submarine of the Balao class was launched in March 1943, and was ordered a few months later to Pearl Harbor, getting underway for her first war patrol in early November. During the course of the war, she survived eight patrols in the Pacific, sank more than 7,000 tons of Japanese shipping and survived one ramming by an enemy ship in a convoy, which sheared off part of her periscope and demolished her radar masts. She ended her short career with the dubious distinction of being prepared as a target for atomic bomb testing at Bikini Atoll, where she was sunk on July 25, 1946. *Apogon* received six battle stars for World War II service.

Archerfish (SS-311)

A submarine of the Balao class, built by the Portsmouth Naval Shipyard and launched in May 1943. Sent to the Pacific theater, she completed four war patrols without inflicting much damage against Japanese shipping. But on her fifth patrol, during the evening of November 28, 1944, while on patrol in enemy waters, she sighted a large Japanese aircraft carrier, screened by four escorts, leaving Tokyo Bay. After a dogged surface pursuit of this elusive, high-speed target, *Archerfish* finally obtained a favorable firing position ahead of her quarry and unleashed six torpedoes. Shortly thereafter, the first torpedo exploded and a glowing ball of fire was seen climbing up the ship's side. The crew of the *Archerfish* subsequently heard an additional series of tremendous explosions as the vessel disintegrated. Not until after the war was it learned that the *Archerfish* had sunk the Shinano, a 59,000-ton Japanese aircraft carrier, probably the largest warship ever sunk by a submarine. Her sixth and seventh patrols were relatively uneventful, but on August 15, when word of the Japanese capitulation was received, she was at Hokkaido and became one of 12 submarines that entered Tokyo Bay at the end of the month to tie up at the Yokosuka Navy Yard. During her peacetime years, she was assigned to research operations, especially "Sea Scan," a scientific study of marine weather conditions and ocean depths, before being decommissioned in October 1968. *Archerfish* received seven battle stars and one Presidential Unit Citation for her World War II service.

Argonaut V-4, later SS-166

A submarine and, later, a class. Built by the Portsmouth Naval Shipyard, she was launched in November 1927 as the first of the second generation of V-boats, primarily designed to be a minelayer, and the first and only such experimental boat ever built. At the time of her construction, *Argonaut* was the largest submarine ever built in the United States, with a complement of eight officers and 80 enlisted men. On a trial dive she set a record of 318 feet. After peacetime operations off the West Coast and Hawaii, where she became the squadron flagship, she was on patrol duty near Midway Island when the Japanese attacked Pearl Harbor. She had the distinction of making the first wartime submarine approach on enemy naval forces in World War II, but since she had been sighted by a Japanese ship, she decided not to do battle with the two destroyers she detected and wisely withdrew. Later she was assigned

Apogon (SS-308), a member of the large Balao class, was typical of these World War II submarines, carrying a complement of six officers and 60 enlisted men, displaces 2,400 tons submerged, and armed with six 21-inch torpedo tubes forward and four aft and a five-inch deck gun (not pictured). *(United States Navy)*

to transport and land marine commandos in the Gilbert Islands campaign. On January 10, 1943, *Argonaut*, then on patrol in the South Pacific in hazardous waters between New Britain and Bougainville attacked one of three destroyers escorting five Japanese freighters. In the counterattack, she was subjected to a furious depth charge attack. By chance, a U.S. Army Air Force aircraft patrolling in the area witnessed one of the destroyers hit by a torpedo. The plane also observed the submarine's bow suddenly break the water at an unusual angle. She slipped back below the surface and was never heard from again.

One hundred and five officers and men went down with the submarine. *Argonaut* won two battle stars posthumously for her World War II service.

Argonaut (SS-475)

The second to bear this name, this submarine of the Tench class was built by the Portsmouth Naval Shipyard and launched in October 1944. She began her first war patrol in the Pacific in June, but encountered very few enemy vessels because of the waning Japanese fleet presence in her assigned patrol areas, sinking only one small vessel with surface fire before the war's end. In 1952, she was converted to a Fleet Snorkel at the Philadelphia Naval Shipyard. During the following peacetime years, she served in a number of areas, including the Mediterranean, Caribbean, North Atlantic, and the southern coastal region. Decommissioned in December 1968, she was sold to Canada, where she resumed service in the Royal Canadian Navy under the name *Rainbow II*. *Argonaut* won one battle star for her World War II service.

ASDIC

In 1917, during WORLD WAR I, when the menace of the German submarine fleet had reached a critical stage, the British and French established the Allied Submarine Detection Investigation Committee (ASDIC). The committee concluded that there were three methods of detecting submerged submarines: echo-sounding, monitoring their noise, and measuring their magnetic displacement. The same three methods, although far more sophisticated, are still employed in antisubmarine warfare. ASDIC is known by the American term *sonar* and is similar to commercial echo sounders.

Because sound travels at a known, steady speed through water, the depth of an object (or the seabed) can be calculated from the time it takes the sound pulse to travel from the ship's transmitter back to the receiver. If the submarine is moving, a bearing can be obtained by measuring the change of pulse, or what is known as the Doppler effect. Submarines also can be detected by measuring the changes they cause in the earth's magnetic field because they are made of a large mass of metal. This is known as magnetic anomaly detection (MAD) and has been used commercially for many years to find deposits of minerals and oil from MAD-equipped aircraft.

Asheville (SSN-758)

A submarine of the Los Angeles class, and the fourth navy vessel to bear the name of the North Carolina mountain city, she was built by Newport News Shipbuilding and

Being the first and only such experimental ship ever built, USS *Argonaut/V-4* (SS-166) was designed primarily as a minelayer and had two minelaying tubes aft. *(United States Navy)*

Drydock Company and launched in October 1989. As a fast-attack nuclear submarine, she has participated in what the navy refers to as "many diverse and difficult operations while deployed, none of which can be commented upon." She and her class displace 6,900 tons submerged, carry a complement of 12 officers and 115 enlisted men, and are equipped with vertical launch cruise missiles, the Submarine Advanced Combat Control System, and a state-of-the-art direction finding capability. In addition to these tactical advances, retractable bow planes and a hardened sail provide the capability to surface through an ice cover, allowing *Asheville* to operate freely in any of the world's oceans.

Aspro (SS-309)

A submarine of the Balao class, she was built by Portsmouth Naval Shipyard and launched in April 1943. Assigned to the Pacific theater, she was ordered to the waters around Taiwan where she encountered two Japanese convoys in succession in mid-December. During the second, she attacked several freighters and tankers, claiming to have sunk three vessels and damaged three others, none of which were ever substantiated. Her first confirmed victory came on February 15, 1944, during her second war patrol when she attacked and sank a large Japanese submarine, and later damaged a freighter. On her third patrol, she attacked a freighter convoy, sinking one ship and later one of the escorts. On her fourth patrol, in late July, she sank one medium-sized ship, damaged a second, and left a third grounded and consumed by fire. In August, she attacked two more freighters and watched them listing and apparently sinking before having to leave the scene. On her fifth patrol, in the South China Sea, she again claimed three more victims—a tanker and two freighters. On her sixth patrol, in early January 1945, she was assigned lifeguard duties west of Taiwan to support carrier strikes. While on station, she attacked and sank a large, damaged tanker, but was given even more credit for rescuing four downed American aviators.

Her seventh, and final, patrol began in late June, where she was assigned lifeguard duties right in the heart of Japan's homeland waters in support of planes flying from Iwo Jima for strikes on military targets in Japan, during which time she sank an enemy tug with her final torpedo spread of the war. Her most notable achievement was a daring rescue of a downed American pilot within five miles of the Japanese coast and under repeated air attacks. *Aspro's* career ended with peacetime duties along the West Coast, with a short break in the western Pacific. She was decommissioned in October 1962, and later sunk as a target by another navy submarine, the *Pomodon* (SS-486).

Aspro (SSN-648)

The second *Aspro,* of the Sturgeon class, was built by Ingalls Shipbuilding Company and launched in November 1967. From the start, she received navy commendations for superior performance as a fast-attack nuclear submarine, serving along the West Coast and in the mid-Pacific, western Pacific, and Indian Ocean. From October to December 1982, she conducted an extended deployment to the Arctic Ocean, where she remained under the polar ice canopy for 43 days and conducted the first winter rendezvous at the North Pole with the submarine *Tautog* (SSN-639). After having distinguished herself with yet another navy commendation, she was decommissioned in March 1995.

Atlanta (SSN-712)

Built by the Electric Boat Division of General Dynamics, this submarine of the Los Angeles class was launched in August 1980, commissioned in March 1982, and deactivated in 1999. She had a displacement of 6,900 tons (submerged), was armed with four 21-inch torpedo tubes amidships, aft of the bow, and carried a complement of 12 officers and 115 enlisted men.

See LOS ANGELES.

Atlantic, Battle of the (1915–1917)

During World War I, the main surface fleets of Britain and Germany were used cautiously, acting primarily as blockading forces. They met in battle only on a few occasions. The British surface fleet had quickly established domination of the seas, and German merchant ships were forced to seek refuge in neutral ports. This eventually led to severe shortages in supplies and raw materials in Germany. As a result, the German navy turned to the submarine to increase economic pressure on Britain, which depended for its survival on supplies brought by sea. It waged a three-year war—with some interruptions—against merchant ships in the Atlantic Ocean and elsewhere. The U-boat blockade of Britain began on February 18, 1915, when it was announced that Allied shipping of all kinds that entered the "war zone" would be torpedoed without warning. Among the victims of this first campaign were an American tanker and a number of American citizens who were passengers on two British liners, the *Lusitania,* sunk May 7, 1915, and the *Arabic.* These incidents outraged American opinion, although it was nearly two years before the United States entered the war.

Following the destruction of the second passenger ship on August 19, 1915, the Germans were compelled to announce, on September 1, an end to unrestricted submarine warfare. The German government said that in the future, no liners would be attacked without warning and the safety of noncombatants would be assured as long as no resistance was offered. The destruction of Allied merchant vessels, which were unaffected by this policy change, continued to rise. A million tons of shipping were lost in 1915–16. Following the sinking of the *Sussex,* a Channel steamer, in the spring of 1916, U.S. president Woodrow Wilson secured a promise from Germany that it would not attack any more merchantmen without warning and would do its "utmost to confine the operations of war for the rest of its duration to the fighting forces of the belligerents." However, pressure from the German navy to reintroduce unrestricted submarine warfare grew during 1916 as it became clear that Germany could not hope to win the war by the efforts of its army alone, so it resumed full U-boat attacks on February 1, 1917, on the assumption that Britain would be starved out within six months, well before any American intervention could become effective. With 127 U-boats in service, Allied shipping losses did begin to rise at an alarming rate: 259 ships were destroyed in February, 325 in March, and 423 in April, when losses reached a peak. This was well in excess of the rate of replacement, and Britain was in danger of being cut off. The Royal Navy introduced countermeasures, but the use of improved mines, hydrophones, and depth charges was not sufficient to provide the protection required.

The Royal Navy had long opposed the introduction of the convoy system, but this system proved to be the only way of winning the battle against the U-boat in the Atlantic. Following the intervention of Britain's Prime Minister David Lloyd George, convoys were introduced on May 10, 1917. Shipping losses gradually diminished during the remainder of the year as the system was extended, eventually to cover neutral as well as Allied ships. By the last quarter of 1917, the destruction of Allied shipping tonnage was running at a little more than half that of six months earlier. Allied losses continued to fall in the following year. By May 1918, the Allies were building more shipping than was being destroyed by U-boats. The first Battle of the Atlantic had been won and the threat to Britain's supply lifeline was virtually over.

Atlantic, Battle of the (1939–1945)

The battle for control of the Atlantic was a key determinant of the outcome in both world wars and offered Germany perhaps the best prospect of defeating her opponents. As in World War I, Britain's survival depended on the preservation of the North American supply route, while the defeat of Germany would entail transporting large numbers of U.S. troops across the Atlantic. Neither the British nor the German navies were fully prepared for the longest battle of the war when fighting began in 1939. A U-boat construction program was well under way and

98 submarines had been built (compared with Britain's 70). However, this was not a sufficient number of boats for the task of disrupting the Atlantic supply routes. Nonetheless, under the energetic direction of Admiral Karl Dönitz, Germany was well advanced in training crews and developing the wolf pack tactics that were to prove so effective, at first.

The Royal Navy was better prepared to combat the U-boat threat in 1939 than it had been during World War I. Its extensive experience of the convoy system was soon put to full use, and it was confident that it had the technology to locate and destroy enemy submarines. However, at least initially, the British Admiralty overlooked the importance of air power in defeating the U-boat. Unconstrained submarine warfare on the part of Germany quickly became the pattern in World War II as the U-boat war intensified. Losses of Allied shipping mounted as more U-boats entered service; auxiliary cruisers and long-range aircraft also played an important role in the German offensive in the Atlantic. With the German occupation of France and Norway in 1940, U-boats could be based much closer to the North Atlantic shipping lanes, their main intended area of operations. Other weaknesses in the British position quickly became evident. In the early stages of the war Britain had insufficient convoy escort vessels, and air protection was virtually nonexistent. The British were also ill-equipped to respond effectively to German wolf pack tactics. Allied shipping losses rapidly mounted, and a three-year struggle for control of the Atlantic ensued. British efforts were underpinned by growing American support and direct involvement in convoy escort duties from May 1941 onward. Convoy escort techniques improved with experience, and more escort vessels, increasingly equipped with radar, appeared. Moreover, the British had access to information from enemy signals traffic. Air protection gradually increased, although a shortage of long-range aircraft meant that there was a greater vulnerability to U-boat attack in the mid-Atlantic.

These developments laid the foundation for the decisive struggle in the winter of 1942–43, when the balance gradually tipped in the Allies' favor. By mid-1943 U-boat losses had reached unsustainable levels and the Germans were forced to abandon the fight in the Atlantic. There is no single explanation for this gradual reversal of fortunes. The Allies' greater provision of long-range air cover and the introduction of the escort aircraft carrier, which provided immediate air support for each protected convoy, were key factors in shifting the balance of power. Other major contributory factors were a substantial increase in the number of escort vessels and improvements in the methods of detecting and attacking enemy submarines. The Germans also lost their Atlantic U-boat bases when the Allies invaded France in 1944. U-boats continued to operate against Allied shipping for the duration of the war, but they were never again able to mount a serious challenge. The introduction of new U-boats with longer range and higher speed might have changed the balance of advantage, but the war ended before many were built. The Battle of the Atlantic produced some 50,000 Allied and 32,000 German casualties. The Germans had sunk 2,575 Allied and neutral ships for the loss of 781 U-boats.

attack submarines

The term *attack submarine* was used initially (that is, prior to and during World War II) to designate any boat properly designed and equipped to attack surface vessels during war at sea. Not until the end of World War II did the term extend to underwater attacks against other submarines. During the 1950s, the navy developed a major type of fast-attack nuclear submarine, described as "a fish-shaped cylinder 360 feet long—the length of a football field with end zones included, and roughly 33 feet in diameter." A new class of attack submarine was initiated in 1962 with the authorization of the *Sturgeon* (SSN-637); 37 other boats in this class followed and were designed to be deep-diving and quiet. With the advent of nuclear power, submarines achieved a new dimension in warfare: the ability to attack other submarines as well as surface ships. This was made possible by their ability to stalk enemy undersea craft for long enough periods of time to get a bearing on them and by their increased capability to use sonar more effectively than surface ships. In addition, they could operate close to enemy fleets and bases in ways not possible for surface ships and lie in ambush, undetected, awaiting a propitious time to strike. Modern attack submarines of the Los Angeles class brought the attack submarine to maturity by arming them not only with torpedoes but also with rocket-launched nuclear depth bombs for antisubmarine warfare and underwater-launched missiles capable of destroying surface ships almost 100 miles away. According to the chief of naval operations, "fast attack submarines exemplify a truly multi-mission platform—from open ocean anti-submarine warfare to surveillance and intelligence gathering in the prevention of regional crises. They are agile assets for Battle Group and Joint Task Force commanders. They can transit at high speeds, undetected, independent of sea state, and arrive on station ready for action . . . lethal against enemy submarines, surface ships, and critical shore targets."

Atule (SS-403)

A submarine of the Balao class, built by the Portsmouth Naval Shipyard and launched in March 1944. Assigned to the Pacific, *Atule* headed for the Marianas as a member of a wolf pack, with two other submarines, *Jallao* and *Pintado*. The pack made its first score when *Jallao* sent a Japanese light cruiser to the bottom, and its second when *Atule* tracked and sank a 16,975-ton transport ship in late October. A few days later, *Pintado* got her share of the pack's success by sinking a destroyer. After a game of hide-and-seek with Japanese planes equipped with radar and magnetic detection devices, the pack moved toward Formosa, where on November 20 *Atule* sank a minesweeper, and four days later a small transport and a patrol boat. She returned from her first patrol with a credit of 27,000 tons of enemy shipping destroyed. On her second patrol in the Yellow Sea, in January 1945, *Atule* bagged a 6,888-ton freighter and undertook the dangerous assignment of sighting and destroying mines in waters where American ships were sailing. She saw further action, which was cut short with the capitulation of the Japanese in August. Her following peacetime career found her assisting with Operation Nanook, to help establish advanced weather stations in the Arctic; participating in Fleet and NATO training exercises in the Atlantic, the Caribbean, and the Mediterranean; joining a goodwill operation to promote cooperation between naval forces of the United States and participating South American countries; and helping with fleet training exercises. *Atule* was converted to a GUPPY IA at Portsmouth Naval Shipyard in 1951. She was decommissioned in April 1970, and later sold to Peru and renamed *Pacocha*. *Atule* earned four battle stars for World War II service.

Augusta (SSN-710)

A submarine of the Los Angeles class, *Augusta* was built by the Electric Boat Division of General Dynamics and launched in January 1984. She had a displacement of 6,900 tons, was armed with four 21-inch torpedo tubes amidships, aft of the bow, and was designed for a complement of 12 officers and 115 enlisted men.

See LOS ANGELES.

B

Balao (SS-285)

Submarine whose name also designates a class; built by the Portsmouth Naval Shipyard and launched in February 1943. The *Balao*'s war operations spanned a period from July 25, 1943, until August 27, 1945, during which she completed 10 war patrols. She is credited with having sunk six Japanese ships totaling 32,108 tons, in addition to sinking by gunfire 1,100 tons of miscellaneous enemy small craft, for which she was credited with nine battle stars. After World War II, she was assigned to the Atlantic Fleet where she was based at Key West, Florida, and engaged in various exercises, fleet maneuvers, and submarine warfare training. She was decommissioned in July 1963.

ballistics

In the field of submarine weaponry, the science of ballistics has always been of primary concern—even before 1900 and with the very first navy submarines and their emphasis on torpedoes and the most effective means of moving them from sub to target. In scientific terminology, "*Ballistics* is the science or art that deals with the motion, behavior, appearance, or modification of missiles or other vehicles acted upon by propellants, whether explosives, mechanics, wind, gravity, temperature, or any other modifying substance, condition, or force." A submarine ballistic missile, as it has become known today, is any projectile that does not rely upon aerodynamic surfaces to produce lift and consequently follows a ballistic trajectory when thrust is terminated. A ballistic trajectory is the path that is traced after the propulsive force is terminated and the body is acted upon only by gravity and aerodynamic drag.

Bang (SS-385)

A submarine of the Balao class, built by the Portsmouth Naval Shipyard and launched in August 1943; she conducted World War II operations from March 1944 until May 1945, during which time she completed six war patrols. She is officially credited with sinking eight Japanese merchant ships totaling 20,177 tons while operating in the South China and Philippine Seas. *Bang* arrived at Portsmouth Navy Yard June 22, 1945, and after repairs proceeded to New London where she went into reserve on February 12, 1947. She was converted to a GUPPY IIA-type submarine and brought back into active service in 1952 and conducted training off the East Coast and in the Caribbean, and later east of Iceland, off Scotland, and in the Mediterranean, where she was when the Beirut crisis broke out in the summer of 1958. She was diverted to patrol between Iceland and the coast of Europe to alert if ship movements were observed coming around from Russia to interfere at Beirut. *Bang* was decommissioned in October 1972. She was loaned to Spain in 1973, and later was sold to Spain in November 1974.

Barb (SS-220)

A submarine of the Gato class, *Barb* was built by the Electric Boat Company and launched in April 1942. Her World War II operations spanned the period from mid-October 1942, until early August 1945, during which time she completed 12 war patrols. During her first mission, she carried out reconnaissance duties relating to the invasion of North Africa. Operating out of Roseneath, Scotland, until July 1943, she conducted her next four patrols against the Axis blockade runners in European waters.

Following an overhaul in New London, Connecticut, she departed for Pearl Harbor and a series of patrols that compiled one of the outstanding submarine records of the war. During the seven war patrols she conducted between March 1944 and August 1945, she sank 17 enemy vessels, totaling 96,628 tons, including a Japanese escort carrier.

Her 11th patrol, under the command of Eugene Fluckey, along the east coast of China, was highlighted by one of the outstanding submarine attacks of World War II. As his official citation for this victory reads (in part), "Commander Fluckey, in an exceptional feat of brilliant deduction and bold tracking on 23 January [1945], located a concentration of more than 30 enemy ships in the lower reaches of Nakuan Chiang (Mamkwan Harbor). Fully aware that a safe retirement would necessitate an hour's run at full speed through the uncharted, mined, and rock-obstructed waters, he bravely ordered 'Battle station-torpedoes!' In a daring penetration of the heavy enemy screen, and riding in five fathoms of water, he launched the *Barb's* last forward torpedoes at 3,000-yard range. Quickly bringing the ship's stern tubes to bear, he turned loose four more torpedoes into the enemy, obtaining eight direct hits on six of the main target ships to explode a large ammunition ship and cause inestimable damage by the resultant flying shells and other pyrotechnics."

On the way home, *Barb* also sank a large Japanese freighter and then concluded her wartime service on her 12th patrol by setting a different kind of record. For the first time in submarine history, she successfully employed rockets against Japanese ports and emplacements, resulting in widespread destruction of enemy targets. In her postwar operations, *Barb* served with the Atlantic fleet and in 1954 underwent conversion to a GUPPY IB submarine. She received the Presidential Unit Citation, Navy Unit Commendation, and eight battle stars for her World War II service, and Commander Fluckey was decorated with the Congressional Medal of Honor.

Barb (SSN-596)

Built by the Ingalls Shipbuilding Company and launched in February 1962, this submarine of the Permit class displaced 3,500 tons submerged, could attain an undersea speed of 28 knots, and carried a complement of nine officers and 76 enlisted men. After extensive service, she was decommissioned in December 1989.

Barbel (SS-316)

A submarine built by the Electric Boat Company and launched in November 1943; she was ordered to the Pacific theater, and on her fourth war patrol, in January 1945, sailed from Fremantle, Australia, on a mission to Lombok Strait, Java Sea, and Karmata. She later joined a wolf pack of other submarines, including the *Perch* and *Gabil*, to cover the western approaches to Balabac and the southern entrance to Palawan Passage. On February 3, 1945, *Barbel* sent a message to her sister submarines reporting numerous aircraft contacts daily. She had been attacked by aircraft three times with depth charges, and would transmit a message "tomorrow night" giving information. This was the last contact with her, and although the other submarines searched and sent repeated messages, they were unsuccessful in determining her fate. After the war, Japanese records indicated that on February 4, 1945, a plane attacked a submarine in a position southwest of the Philippines from which had come *Barbel's* last report, scoring one hit near the bridge with one of two bombs dropped. It appears almost certain that this attack sank *Barbel*. During her brief war career, however, she sank six ships for 15,263 tons and damaged two ships for 14,000 tons during her three completed patrols. Her first

USS *Balao's* (SS-285) war operations span a period from July 25, 1943, until August 27, 1945. During this period she completed 10 war patrols. She is credited with having sunk six Japanese ships totaling 32,108 tons, in addition to sinking by gunfire 1,100 tons of miscellaneous enemy small craft. *(United States Navy)*

was made in the Nansei Shoto chain. She sank three medium freighters and a tanker. In the same area on her second patrol, *Barbel* sank a freighter and two escort vessels. She also damaged another freighter and a tanker. During her third patrol, conducted in the South China Sea, *Barbel* probably sank two medium freighters. *Barbel* received three battle stars for her World War II service.

Barbel (SS-580)

Built by the Portsmouth Naval Shipyard and launched in July 1958, *Barbel* was the first of a new class of diesel-electric attack submarines, with a submerged displacement of 2,639 tons and designed for a crew of eight officers and 69 enlisted men. She was armed with six 21-inch torpedo tubes forward and had a submerged speed of more than 18 knots. She was one of the first submarines, along with *Skipjack,* to incorporate the experimental Albacore hull form, with rounded bow and stern that were almost similar to each other. Other innovations were push-button ballast control and an improved arrangement of control spaces. Her test depth was 700 feet. *Barbel* served long and well with the fleet, and was decommissioned in December 1989.

Barbero (SS-317)

A submarine of the Balao class, she was built by the Electric Boat Company and launched in December 1943. Her war operations spanned the period from August 1944 until January 1945, during which time she completed two war patrols. She is officially credited with sinking three Japanese merchant ships totaling 9,126 tons while patrolling in the Java and South China Seas. On December 27, 1944, en route to Fremantle, Australia, *Barbero*, while at periscope depth, received an aerial bomb close aboard aft. This near-miss damaged the port reduction gear and put her out of action for the remainder of the war. In September 1945 she was ordered to Mare Island Navy Yard where she underwent pre-inactivation overhaul and was placed in commission in reserve in April 1946. Following conversion to a cargo submarine (reclassified SSA-317) in March 1948, she was recommissioned and assigned to the Pacific Fleet. Between October 1948 and March 1950 she took part in an experimental program to evaluate her capabilities as a cargo carrier. Experimentation was discontinued in early 1950 and she went out of commission in June 1955. She entered Mare Island Naval Shipyard for her second conversion. Her designation was changed to SSG-317 (guided missile submarine) in October 1955. She operated off the coast of California until April 1956 when she transited the Panama Canal and joined the Atlantic Fleet, subsequently returning to the Pacific until decommissioning in June 1964. She received two battle stars for her World War II service.

USS *Barbel* (SS-580) was the first of the Barbel-class diesel-powered submarines having the teardrop hull design that greatly enhances submerged maneuverability and speed. *(United States Navy)*

Barracuda (B-1)

Launched in July 1924, *Barracuda* was the second submarine to bear this name and was designed for a complement of six officers and 50 enlisted men. She was armed with four 21-inch torpedo tubes forward, and two aft, and had a surface cruising speed of more than 18 knots. Her design called for a larger conning tower and a covered bridge to protect the personnel on duty there—which became standard in American submarines thereafter. She was assigned to the New England coast, and later saw service in the Caribbean, the West Coast, the Canal Zone, and Hawaii. *Barracuda* had many other unique features, which were largely experimental. These included extra buoyancy tanks forward, which gave her a bulbous look in the bow, a complicated forward torpedo room hatch to expedite loading, escape hatches, a third periscope, and a double hull. But she proved to have poor operational performance and, after an experiment to transform her into an undersea cargo vessel, was decommissioned just before World War II.

Barracuda (SS-21)

The first submarine of this name was built by Union Iron Works, of San Francisco, in August 1909. Launched three years later, she joined the First Submarine Group, Pacific Torpedo Flotilla, in operations between San Diego and San Pedro, the flotilla base. She continued to play an important part in developing tactics and coordinating the use of undersea craft with the fleet during an extended training period in the Hawaiian Islands, from August 1914 through November 1915. In 1917, she became the flagship of SubDiv1, Submarine Force, Pacific Fleet. Returning to operations out of San Pedro, she participated in surface and submerged exercises, torpedo proving practice, experiments in balancing at various depths, and trained prospective crews of new submarines. In September 1919, she was placed in reserve commission at San Pedro to be used in elemental school work until decommissioned in March 1922.

Barracuda (SST-3)

The third submarine of this name was built by Electric Boat Company and launched in March 1951. She joined Submarine Development Group 2 with her home port at

Because of her partial double hull, USS *Barracuda B-1* (SS-163) featured a complex tank arrangement and a noncircular cross section. The bulbous profile at the bow bore a startling resemblance to a shark with an anchor gripped between its jaws. *(United States Navy)*

New London, Connecticut. She cruised along the Atlantic coast of the United States and Canada, in the Caribbean, and made a voyage to Greenock and Rothesay, Scotland, in June 1955. During intervals between and after these cruises, she has operated along the eastern seaboard carrying out training and experimental exercises. In August 1959 her classification was changed from SSK to SST, becoming SST-3.

Bass [ex-V-2] (B-2) (SS-164)

Bass [ex-V-2] (SS-164) experienced a fire that started in the after battery in August 1942, taking the lives of 25 of her crew. Although *Bass* survived the fire, she was subsequently converted to a cargo submarine and ultimately used as a target, being sunk on March 14, 1945. *Bass* is now a favorite diving spot, being located off the coast of Rhode Island in 155 feet of water.

bathyscaphe

A navigable diving vessel developed by the Swiss educator and scientist Auguste Piccard, designed to reach great depths in the ocean. The first bathyscaphe, the *FNRS 2*, built in Belgium between 1946 and 1948, was damaged during 1948 trials in the Cape Verde Islands. Substantially rebuilt and greatly improved, the vessel carried out a series of descents under excellent conditions, including one of 13,000 feet, into the Atlantic off Dakar, Senegal, in February 1954. A second, improved bathyscaphe, the *Trieste,* was launched in August 1953, and dived to 10,300 feet in the same year. In 1958 the *Trieste* was acquired by the United States Navy, taken to California, and equipped with a new cabin designed to enable it to reach the seabed of the great oceanic trenches. Several successive descents were made into the Pacific by Jacques Piccard, and on January 23, 1960, Piccard, accompanied by Lieutenant Don Walsh of the U.S. Navy, dived to a record 35,810 feet in the Pacific's Mariana Trench. The bathyscaphe consists of two main components: a steel cabin, heavier than water and resistant to sea pressure, to accommodate the observers; and a light container called a float, filled with gasoline, which, being lighter than water, provides the necessary lifting power. The cabin and float are closely linked. On the surface, one or more ballast tanks filled with air provide enough lift to keep the bathyscaphe afloat. When the ballast tank valves are opened, air escapes and is replaced by water, making the whole device heavy enough to start its descent. The gasoline is in direct contact with the sea water and so is compressed at a rate almost exactly in proportion to the prevailing depth. Thus, the bathyscaphe gradually loses buoyancy as it descends, and the speed of its descent tends to increase rapidly.

USS *Bass* B-2 (SS-164) in the 1930s; *Bass* was launched December 27, 1924, and sunk as a target on March 14, 1945. In August 1942, *Bass* experienced a fire on board that started in the after battery and spread rapidly to the after room. While fighting the fire, which was eventually brought under control and finally extinguished, 25 members of the crew perished. *(United States Navy)*

bathysphere

A spherical steel vessel for use in undersea observation, provided with portholes and suspended by a cable from a boat. Built by the American zoologist William Beebe and the American engineer Otis Barton, the bathysphere made its first dives in 1930, when, on June 11, it reached a depth of 1,300 feet; and in 1934, Beebe and Barton reached a deeper depth of about 3,000 feet. Although the bathysphere proved to be a great step forward in undersea exploration, it had critical faults, one of which was the difficulty of operation, which made for potential risks. A break in the suspension cable, for example, caused by surface waves and strain, would have meant certain death for the observers. Because of these disadvantages, the bathysphere was supplanted by the safer, more maneuverable mesoscaphe and bathyscaphe.

Battle Group

A standing naval task group consisting of a carrier or battleships, surface combatants, and submarines, which are assigned to operate in mutual support with the task of destroying hostile submarine, surface, and air forces within the group's assigned area of responsibility. Related missions are striking at targets along hostile shorelines or projecting fire power inland.

Baya (SS-318)

A submarine of the Balao class, built by the Electric Boat Company and launched in May 1944, the *Baya* was dispatched to Pearl Harbor three months later and, from then until the end of July 1945, completed five war patrols in the South China Sea, Gulf of Siam, Java Sea, and the Philippine Sea. She was credited with sinking four Japanese vessels totaling 8,855 tons and an 8,407-ton passenger-cargo ship in conjunction with a sister submarine, *Hawkbill*. Although placed on the inactive list after World War II, for which she received four battle stars, she was recommissioned in February 1948 and converted to an electronics experimental submarine by the Mare Island Naval Shipyard and the Naval Electronics Laboratory (NEL). *Baya* conducted experiments for NEL; participated in local operations near San Diego; and served with the Joint American-Canadian Task Force that gathered scientific data off the west coast of Canada during November and December 1948. During 1949, she was turned over to NEL at San Diego, California, to be a sonar test ship, at which time all torpedo-loading and handling gear in the forward torpedo room was removed to provide space for experimental electronic equipment. In August 1949, *Baya* was reclassified as AGSS-318, the designation for an "Auxiliary Submarine."

During the period July through September 1949, *Baya* made a cruise to the Arctic to gather valuable scientific data in the Bering and Chukchi Seas. Between July and October 1955, she was deployed to Pearl Harbor for further experimental research. During 1958 and 1959, she was completely reworked to test the LORAD equipment, an experimental long-range sonar. The forward torpedo tubes were removed and replaced by a blunt bow with a mushroom anchor in the bottom of the hull. A 23-foot section was added between the former forward torpedo room and the forward battery compartment, with quarters for 12 scientists. These modifications increased her overall length to 330 feet, her surface displacement to 2,220 tons, and her submerged displacement to approximately 2,600 tons. During 1962 and 1963, further alterations were made, followed, in 1964, by the installation of the BRASS-11 sonar equipment and a second set of LORAD hydrophone "wings." During 1967, all remaining fire-control and weapons equipment was removed, leaving the ship completely demilitarized. *Baya* continued to serve NEL in this capacity until she was decommissioned in October 1972.

Becuna (SS-319)

A submarine of the Balao class, built by the Electric Boat Company and launched in May 1944, she was sent to join the Pacific Fleet in July 1944 and undertook war operations extending from August 1944 to late July 1945. During this period she completed five war patrols in the Philippines, South China Sea, and Java Sea, and was credited with having sunk two Japanese tankers totaling some 4,000 tons. She continued missions in peacetime in the Pacific until April 1949 when she was ordered to Submarine Force, Atlantic Fleet, as a unit of Submarine Squadron 8. There she conducted refresher training exercises until, in November 1950, she returned to Electric Boat Company for a complete modernization overhaul, being refitted as a GUPPY IA-type submarine. Thereafter, she operated with the Atlantic Fleet, making two cruises with the Sixth Fleet in the Mediterranean and one to Scotland, with a majority of her time spent as a training boat at New London prior to decommissioning in November 1969.

Benjamin Franklin (SSBN-640)

The prototype for this class of nuclear fleet ballistic missile submarines—and the other boats that followed—was launched in the mid-1960s, displaced 7,320 tons on the surface and 8,251 tons submerged, and was designed for a complement of 14 officers and 126 enlisted men, each in two crews. These submarines, equipped with 16 missile tubes and four torpedo tubes, differed from the earlier Lafayette class because of their quieter machinery and other minor differences. They were built to carry the Polaris submarine-launched ballistic missile (SLBM), and were subsequently modified to carry the Poseidon C-3 missile. In the early 1990s, they were converted to special operations submarines. The conversions consisted of deactivating the missile tubes and creating the capability to carry two drydeck shelters, side by side over the former missile tube area (aft of the sail), each containing one swimmer delivery vehicle, a decompression chamber, and an access section allowing for submerged entry. More than 65 special operations troops could be transported in the new configuration. These submarines were designed originally for a 20-year service life, but in the early 1980s the navy determined that they could operate successfully for 30 years. While these boats train with, and are most likely to operate with, Navy SEAL teams, exercises with Marine Recon units have shown that many types of special operations teams can be accommodated.

The other submarines in this class include

Simon Bolivar (SSBN-641)

Kamehameha (SSBN-642)

George Bancroft (SSBN-643)

Lewis & Clark (SSBN-644)

James K. Polk (SSBN-645)

George C. Marshall (SSBN-654)

Henry L. Stimson (SSBN-655)

George Washington Carver (SSBN-656)

Francis Scott Key (SSBN-657)

Mariano G. Vallejo (SSBN-658)

Will Rogers (SSBN-659)

Bergall (SS-320)

A submarine of the Balao class, built by the Electric Boat Company and launched in February 1944, she was assigned to the Pacific Fleet five months later and ordered to Fremantle, Australia, for missions against the Japanese fleet. She made five war patrols between early September 1944 and mid-June 1945 in the South China Sea, Java Sea, Lombok Strait, and north of the Malay Barrier. During these patrols, she sank two merchantmen and a coastal minesweeper totaling 14,884 tons and one 740-ton frigate. While patrolling off the Malay coast, in June 1945, she was damaged aft by a mine explosion and forced to retire to Subic Bay, Luzon, for emergency repairs. This ended her wartime career; she was then assigned to peacetime duties with the Pacific Fleet and later to the Atlantic Fleet, making two Mediterranean cruises before being decommissioned and sold to Turkey. *Bergall* was converted to a Fleet Snorkel submarine by Philadelphia Naval Shipyard in 1952.

Besugo (SS-321)

A submarine of the Balao class, built by the Electric Boat Company and launched in February 1944, she was assigned to the Pacific Fleet in July of that year and made five war patrols between late September 1944 and late July 1945, operating in Bungo and Makassar Straits, Java Sea, and South China Sea. During these patrols she attacked and sank the German submarine *U-183*, on April 23, 1945; and later, one 10,020-ton tanker; one LSV, one frigate, and a minesweeper totaling 2,260 tons. After an overhaul in San Diego at the end of the war, she returned to the Central Pacific, operating out of Guam until being transferred to Pearl Harbor for the next eight years, during which time she made two Far Eastern tours. In August 1954 *Besugo* shifted her base of operations to San Diego and operated along the West Coast until decommissioning in March 1958. However, she was recommissioned during the 1960s and loaned temporarily to Italy before being stricken from the Navy list in 1975. *Besugo* received four battle stars for her World War II service and one for Korea.

Billfish (SSN-676)

This submarine of the Sturgeon class was built by the Electric Boat Division of General Dynamics and launched in May 1970. She had a displacement of 4,762 tons (submerged), was armed with four 21-inch torpedo tubes amidships, aft of the bow, and carried a complement of 12 officers and 95 enlisted men. She was commissioned in March 1971, and deactivated in January 1999, after some 28 years of service on a multitude of missions around the world.

Bismarck Sea, Battle of the (March 2–5, 1943)

Sea and air battle between Japanese and Allied forces in the Pacific during WORLD WAR II. The Allies attacked a Japanese troop convoy of 16 ships (eight transports and eight destroyers) that had left Rabaul, New Britain, bound for northeast New Guinea with essential troop reinforcements (some 7,000 men) for the occupying forces. On March 2, 1943, as the convoy crossed the Bismarck Sea, it came under attack from American B-17 Flying Fortress bombers, and one transport was sunk. The escorting destroyers rescued some 850 survivors who were delivered to New Guinea. These were the only troops carried by the convoy to reach their intended destination. Over the next two days, this attack was followed by sorties by B-25s and other American aircraft as well as by Australian Bristol Beauforts and Beaufighters. Helped by new low-level bombing techniques, the Allied aircraft sank seven Japanese transport ships and four accompanying destroyers, and some 3,000 Japanese died. Allied losses amounted to no more than five aircraft. The surviving ships, with some 3,000 troops on board, were forced to return to Rabaul. This successful operation confirmed Allied air superiority over the Bismarck Sea and proved that the Japanese on New Guinea could now be supplied only by submarine.

Blackfin (SS-322)

A submarine of the Balao class, built by the Electric Boat Company and launched in March 1944, she completed five war patrols in her operating areas, which included the South China and Yellow Seas. She sank the Japanese destroyer *Shigure* in January 1945, and a cargo ship for a total of 4,325 tons. The termination of hostilities occurred while *Blackfin* was on her fifth war patrol. After occupying a lifeguard station and destroying 61 floating mines, she retired to Guam in September 1945, shortly thereafter proceeding to San Diego where she joined Submarine Squadron 1. Through July 1948, *Blackfin* continued on active duty in the Pacific, mainly off the Hawaiian and Mariana Islands. In June and July 1946, she participated in Operation Iceberg, which took her across the Arctic Circle. In late 1950, she began conversion to a GUPPY IA submarine at Mare Island Naval Shipyard and was then assigned to Submarine Force, Pacific Fleet, based at San Diego for four years and thereafter at Pearl Harbor. During that time she completed two tours in the Far East, conducted training operations, and made several simulated war patrols until her final decommissioning in September 1972. *Blackfin* received three battle stars for her World War II service.

Blackfish (SS-221)

This submarine of the Gato class was launched at the Electric Boat Company in April 1942, and was assigned to Submarine Squadron 50 in Europe. She completed five war patrols in waters extending from Dakar, West Africa, to the north of Ireland, and was credited with sinking a German patrol boat of the north coast of Spain in February 1943. She returned to the United States and after refitting was deployed to the Pacific where she completed seven war patrols in areas that included the Solomon Islands, New Guinea, South China Sea, and the Yellow Sea. She sank one Japanese cargo vessel, effectively bombarded Japanese shore installations, and was awarded eight battle stars for her World War II service. *Blackfish* operated on peacetime missions thereafter on the East Coast and was decommissioned in May 1954.

Blenny (SS-324)

A submarine of the Balao class, she was built by the Electric Boat Company and launched in April 1944. Between mid-November 1944 and mid-August 1945, she conducted four war patrols in the Java and South China Seas, sinking eight Japanese vessels totaling 18,262 tons, and, in addition, destroying more than 62 Japanese small craft by gunfire. With the cessation of hostilities, the boat was assigned to San Diego during the remainder of 1946. Between 1946 and 1951, she made one cruise to China; participated in a midshipman cruise to Canada; made two winter cruises in Alaskan waters; and participated in fleet maneuvers off Hawaii and local operations near San Diego. In 1951, she underwent conversion to a GUPPY IA submarine at San Francisco Naval Shipyard and spent the remainder of the year operating in the San Diego area, followed by service in the Far East, during which time she conducted a 35-day reconnaissance patrol in support of Korean operations. The boat spent 1953 conducting local operations along the West Coast, moved to the Atlantic Fleet the following year, and was assigned to operations with a submarine development group engaged in evaluating new equipment, before being decommissioned in November 1969. She received four battle stars for her World War II service.

Blower (SS-325)

A submarine of the Balao class, built by the Electric Boat Company and launched in April 1944, she was assigned to Pearl Harbor in December 1944, and left on her first war patrol in January 1945. She completed three war patrols before the termination of hostilities, all in the Java and South China Seas. All three patrols proved unprofitable, and she arrived at Fremantle, Australia, from her last patrol in July 1945. *Blower* departed the southwest Pacific in September 1945, and, after engaging in training exercises around the Mariana and Caroline Islands for several months, proceeded to San Diego in January 1946. From 1946 through 1949, she was attached to Submarine Force, Pacific Fleet. She operated mainly along the West Coast, but also had missions in Japan, the Marianas, and Alaska, patrolling along the contour of the arctic ice pack in the Chukchi Sea, carrying out radar tracking and sonar exercises. Returning to San Diego, the ship continued scheduled operations until early 1950 when she departed for the East Coast to join Submarine Force, Atlantic Fleet. She was decommissioned in November 1950, and transferred to Turkey under the Mutual Defense Assistance Program. She was lost in April 1953 while serving in the Turkish navy as *Dumlupinar*, after being rammed by the Swedish freighter *Naboland*.

Blueback (SS-326)

A submarine of the Balao class, and the first of two boats to bear the *Blueback* name, she was built by the Electric Boat Company and launched in May 1944. She was ordered to join the Pacific Fleet, and during the period from mid-December 1944 through July 1945, she completed three war patrols in the South China and Java Seas. She was credited with sinking a 300-ton submarine chaser, as well as eight smaller vessels by war's end, after which she was deployed to Guam. She conducted training exercises, and later made tours to the West Coast, Truk, Subic Bay, Tsingtao, Shanghai, and the Mediterranean. In May 1948, she cruised to Turkey, where she was decommissioned and transferred to the Turkish navy.

Blueback (SS-581)

A diesel-electric submarine of the Barbel class, built by Ingalls Shipbuilding Company and launched in May 1959, she was among the last class of diesel submarines built by the U.S. Navy. This class of submarine was the first to have the "teardrop" hull design, which greatly enhances submerged maneuverability and speed. After commissioning, she became a unit of the Submarine Force, U.S. Pacific Fleet, homeported in San Diego. In March 1961, she embarked on her first deployment to the western Pacific (WesPac) for duty with the U.S. Seventh Fleet. Completing the deployment in September 1961, *Blueback* set a new record by transiting the 5,340 miles from Yokosuka, Japan, to San Diego, California, totally submerged. *Blueback*'s second WesPac deployment began in April 1963, in time to participate in the Coral Sea Festival, which also included a visit to Australia. The years

1967–68 marked the boat's third and fourth western Pacific deployments. In 1970–71 *Blueback* conducted two WesPac deployments and was awarded the Meritorious Unit Commendation and two consecutive Battle Efficiency "E" awards. In 1973 *Blueback* departed for her seventh WesPac deployment, following which she was presented with the Fire Control Excellence Award for the fourth time. In 1977, she steamed over 13,000 miles, twice transiting the Panama Canal, while conducting joint antisubmarine exercises with the navies of Colombia, Ecuador, Peru, and Chile. In 1978, she represented the submarine force at the Rose Festival in Portland, Oregon, for the first time, and began her eighth WesPac, following which she was awarded another Battle Efficiency "E." In 1980 *Blueback* marked her ninth WesPac deployment and was awarded Submarine Group Five Top Gunner Award and Supply "E." In 1981 *Blueback* returned to Portland to participate in the Rose Festival and later that year was awarded the Fleet Communications "C" in recognition of superior communications performance. In January 1982, she departed on her 10th and last WesPac deployment, conducting operations with surface units of the U.S., Korean, and Japanese navies. In 1984 and 1985, *Blueback* won three more awards for efficiency and in 1988 embarked on one of the most aggressive and rewarding years in her history, not only winning honors but also receiving the coveted Golden Anchor Award from CinCPacFleet for 100 percent retention in all categories. Despite her age, *Blueback* continued to demonstrate her exceptional worth by supporting a high-priority special project for the chief of naval operations until early September 1990, after which she was decommissioned. Since May 1994, *Blueback* has been serving as a Memorial Ship at the Oregon Museum of Science and Industry, in Portland.

Bluefish (SS-222)

A submarine of the Gato class, she was built by the Electric Boat Company and launched in February 1943. She was ordered to Brisbane, Australia, in August 1943, and completed nine war patrols between September of that year and the end of July 1945. Her operating area extended from the Netherlands East Indies to the waters south of Honshu. *Bluefish* sank 12 Japanese ships totaling 50,839 tons, including the destroyer *Sanae;* a Japanese submarine; and a submarine chaser. In addition, she assisted the submarine *Puffer* (SS-268) in sinking a large tanker. With the cessation of hostilities *Bluefish* returned to the United States, where she underwent repairs and was recommissioned for service with the Atlantic Fleet. After operations along the East Coast of the United States, she was placed out of commission in November 1953. *Bluefish* received 10 battle stars for her World War II service.

Bluefish (SSN-675)

This submarine of the Sturgeon class was built by the Electric Boat Division of General Dynamics and launched January 1970. With displacement (submerged) of 4,762 tons, she was armed with four 21-inch torpedo tubes amidships, aft of the bow, and carried a complement of 12 officers and 95 enlisted men. After some 25 years of service on worldwide missions, she was decommissioned and struck from the Navy list in June 1996.

Bluegill (SS-242)

A submarine of the Gato class, built by the Electric Boat Company and launched in August 1943. She was attached to the Pacific Fleet and completed six war patrols during the period from the end of that year until June 1945, in an area extending from New Guinea to Formosa and through the South China and Java Seas. She sank 10 Japanese vessels totaling 46,212 tons, including the light cruiser *Yubari* and a submarine chaser. During January 1945 *Bluegill* made reconnaissance in support of American reoccupation of the Philippines. On May 28 she conducted a reconnaissance and bombardment of Pratas Island. Twelve men were landed and discovered that the island had recently been evacuated by the Japanese naval garrison. In a fitting ceremony on May 29 her crew raised the American flag on Pratas Island and proclaimed it to be "Bluegill Island." After her last war patrol, she was stationed at Pearl Harbor and continued to serve with the Pacific Fleet until March 1946, when she was placed out of commission and in reserve at Mare Island Naval Shipyard. Later she underwent conversion to a "killer" submarine and was reclassified SSK-242 and recommissioned in May 1953. Later that year she was deployed to the western Pacific where she participated in training exercises and operations with various United Nations forces. She returned to San Diego the following year and took part in intensive antisubmarine exercises with other fleet units in the area. In July 1955 her home port was changed to Pearl Harbor from where she conducted cruises in the Far East and local operations in the vicinity of the Hawaiian Islands before being decommissioned in June 1969. She was subsequently sunk in Hawaiian waters to be used as a salvage trainer. She was awarded four battle stars for World War II service.

Boarfish (SS-327)

A submarine of the Balao class, built by the Electric Boat Company and launched in May 1944. She was assigned to the Pacific Fleet in December of that year and made four war patrols in the South China Sea, Java Sea, and Gulf of Siam by the end of World War II. She was credited with sinking one freighter of 6,968 tons and com-

An interesting photo of the USS *Bonefish* (SS-582) conning tower. *(United States Navy)*

A view of USS *Bonefish* (SS-582) showing her Barbel-class teardrop hull design. *(United States Navy)*

bined with units of the 14th Air Force to sink another 6,890 tons. After the war, she operated out of Guam on training exercises and then returned to San Diego, arriving early in February 1946. She remained on the West Coast until October 1946 when she began a cruise to Midway Island, Marcus Island, Okinawa, Tsingtao (China), and Guam, which lasted until November. Except for a voyage to Pearl Harbor in February 1947 and one to Alaska and Canada during July–November 1947, *Boarfish* remained in the San Diego area until November 1947. She then went to Mare Island Naval Shipyard for overhaul preparatory to transfer to Turkey, where she was turned over to the Turkish navy in May 1948.

Boise (SSN-764)

Built by Newport News Shipbuilding and Drydock Company, this submarine of the Los Angeles class was launched in March 1991, and commissioned in November 1992. With a displacement of 6,900 tons, she carries a complement of 12 officers and 115 enlisted men, and is armed with four 21-inch torpedo tubes amidships, aft of the bow, and 12 vertical launch tubes (VLT) forward.

See LOS ANGELES.

Bonefish (SS-223)

A submarine of the Gato class, built by the Electric Boat Company and launched in March 1943, she was the first to carry her name. She was deployed to Pearl Harbor to join the Pacific Fleet and had a very active record of war patrols until May 1945 when, in company with the submarines *Tunny* (SS-282) and *Skate* (SS-305), she departed Guam on the 28th to conduct her eighth war patrol. This coordinated attack group, which was one of three groups then penetrating the Japan Sea, was ordered to transit Tsushima Strait on June 5, 1945, and to conduct offensive patrol in the Sea of Japan off the west-central coast of Honshu. She then made rendezvous with *Tunny* on June 16, 1945, reporting that she had sunk one large transport and one medium freighter. Two days later, she requested permission to conduct a submerged daylight patrol in Toyama Wan, in the mid-part of western Honshu, and having received it, departed for Suzu Misaki. She was never seen or heard from again. In the operation order governing this patrol group provisions had been made for submarines, in case of necessity, to proceed to Russian waters to claim a 24-hour haven, or to submit to internment in extreme need, or for them to make their exit from the Japan Sea prior to or after June 24. When all of these possibilities had been examined, and she had not been seen or heard from by July 30, 1945,

USS *Bonita* V-31 (SS-165) was launched June 9, 1925 and is shown above doing test submergence on June 12, 1926. *(United States Navy)*

Bonefish was reported as presumed lost. Japanese records of antisubmarine attacks mention an attack made on June 18, 1945, in Toyama Wan. A great many depth charges were dropped, and wood chips and oil were observed. This undoubtedly was the attack that sank *Bonefish*.

The record shows that *Bonefish* sank 31 enemy vessels, for a total tonnage of 61,345. She began her career as an active member of the submarine force with a patrol in the South China Sea in September and October 1943. She sank three freighters, two transports, a tanker, and a schooner, and damaged a fourth freighter. On her second war patrol, conducted in the Celebes Sea and near Borneo, she sank two freighters and an escort vessel, and damaged a minelayer. Again in the South China Sea on her third patrol, she sank a very large tanker, a medium freighter, and a schooner, and damaged a second large tanker. This boat went to the Celebes and Sulu Seas for her fourth patrol and sank two freighters, a transport, and a tanker, and damaged a subchaser. Postwar information also reveals that on May 14, 1944, while firing at the large tanker that she sank, *Bonefish* also sank a Japanese destroyer.

This boat's fifth patrol was in the same area as her fourth, and she sank two small freighters, a large tanker, and five miscellaneous small craft, while she damaged a second tanker. *Bonefish* covered a South China Sea area in her sixth patrol, and sank two large tankers and a freighter during September and October 1944. She also damaged two medium freighters. Then, after a thorough overhaul and the installation of much new equipment in San Francisco, *Bonefish* made her seventh patrol in the East China Sea. She had only one attack opportunity and did no damage. However, she took two Japanese prisoners from a downed enemy plane, and performed reconnaissance work at the southern end of Korea. *Bonefish* was awarded the Navy Unit Commendation for the period of her first and third through sixth patrols.

Bonefish (SS-582)

The third, and last, of the Barbel class of modern diesel-electric attack submarines, built by New York Shipbuilding Corporation and launched in November 1958. *Bonefish* had an Albacore hull form, a submerged displacement of 2,639 tongs, and a submerged speed of more than 18 knots. She was designed for a crew of eight officers and 69 enlisted men. She was armed with six 21-inch torpedo tubes and her test depth was 700 feet. After commissioning, and for most of her active career, she was assigned to the Submarine Force, U.S. Pacific Fleet, first being homeported in San Diego and then Pearl Harbor. She served with distinction throughout her career, having conducted numerous training operations and deployments to the Western Pacific. Her homeport was ultimately shifted to Charleston, South Carolina, and in April 1988, 160 miles off of the coast of Florida, while engaged in an exercise with the guided missile frigate USS *Carr* (FFG-52) she suffered a major casualty. While operating submerged, water leaked directly onto cables and bussing in a battery cableway, causing arcing between cables, which caused an explosion and fire within minutes. Temperatures in the battery spaces reached 1,200 degrees; heat so intense that it melted the soles of the shoes on crewmembers located in the spaces above. *Bonefish* surfaced immediately, and the order to abandon ship was given. During the course of fighting the fire, three crewmembers were lost. Eighty-nine crewmembers were safely rescued by whaleboat and helicopter crews from the USS *Carr*, and helicopter crews from the USS *John F. Kennedy* (CV 67). *Bonefish* was towed into Charleston, where it was determined the damage was too extensive to repair, resulting in her deactivation and decommissioning on September 28, 1988.

Bonita (C-4) (SS-15)

One of the early navy submarines built by the Fore River Shipbuilding Company, and launched in June 1909, she was assigned first to the Atlantic Torpedo Fleet, and later to the Atlantic Submarine Flotilla. She plied East Coast waters until May 1913, when she cleared Norfolk, Virginia, for Guantanamo Bay, Cuba. Her tactical exercises and development operations continued here and from Cristobal, Panama Canal Zone, where she reported in December 1913. During August 1917, sailing with two other submarines, she explored the suitability of Panamanian ports as advance submarine bases. She was berthed at Coco Solo, Panama Canal Zone, from mid-November 1918 until mid-August 1919, and was decommissioned in April 1920.

Bonita (SS-165)

This submarine of the Barracuda class was built by the Mare Island Shipyard and launched in June 1925. She was commissioned in May 1926, her first skipper being Charles A. Lockwood, then a lieutenant commander and later to become known as one of the top submarine officers in the Pacific. Bonita served largely as a training ship during World War II and was decommissioned and struck from the Navy list in March 1945.

Bonita (SS-552)

The third submarine of this name was built at the Mare Island Naval Shipyard, Vallejo, California, and launched as

SS-K3 in June 1951. She joined SubRon7 at Pearl Harbor May 15, 1952 and operated on experimental and normal submarine duties, making a cruise to Alaskan waters in August–September 1956. She was decommissioned in November 1958, then a year later, after modifications, recommissioned, and her hull number changed to SS-552.

Boston (SSN-703)

This submarine of the Los Angeles class was built by the Electric Boat Division of General Dynamics and launched in April 1980. With a displacement of 6,900 tons (submerged) and armed with four 21-inch torpedo tubes amidships, aft of the bow, she carried a complement of 12 officers and 115 enlisted men. She was deactivated in March 1999.

See LOS ANGELES.

Bowfin (SS-287)

A submarine of the Balao class, built by the Portsmouth Naval Shipyard and launched in May 1943. She was ordered to Brisbane, Australia, in August 1943. Between that month and early July 1945 she completed nine war patrols, operating from the Netherlands East Indies to the Sea of Japan and the waters south of Hokkaido. *Bowfin* sank 15 merchantmen and one frigate for a total of 68,032 tons. She also shared credit with the submarine *Aspro* for sinking a 4,500-ton merchantman. At the end of the war, she sailed to the East Coast of the United States and operated with the Atlantic Fleet until placed out of commission and in reserve at New London, Connecticut, in February 1947. She was recommissioned at New London in July 1951, and was deployed to the Pacific, where she operated from San Diego on local missions and naval reserve training exercises for 10 years. She was decommissioned in December 1971, and now serves as a museum boat at Bowfin Park in Pearl Harbor. *Bowfin* received the Presidential Unit Citation for her second war patrol, the Navy Unit Commendation for her sixth war patrol, and eight battle stars during World War II.

Bream (SS-243)

A submarine of the Gato class, she was built by the Electric Boat Company and launched in October 1943. She was assigned to the Pacific Fleet and conducted war operations from early June through mid-June 1945. During this period she completed six war patrols operating in the Java, Celebes, Sulu, and South China Seas and the Gulf of Siam. She sank two Japanese vessels totaling 6,934 tons, and shared with two other submarines the destruction of a 6,806-ton passenger-cargo vessel. In October 1944, while patrolling off western Luzon, *Bream* made a daring surface attack on a Japanese formation, damaging the heavy cruiser *Aoba.*

After the war, she was inactivated in San Francisco and was placed out of commission and in reserve in January 1946. She was recommissioned in June 1951 and reported to SubRon3, Pacific Fleet. From June 1951 to August 1952 *Bream* engaged in training and services to the Fleet Sonar School, San Diego. She was later converted to a killer submarine and reclassified SSK-243 on February 18, 1953. Following recommissioning in June 1953, *Bream* participated in all phases of peacetime submarine operations in the Pacific Ocean. She conducted an Alaskan training cruise in September 1954, returning to San Diego to carry out operations off California until she was assigned to Pearl Harbor in May 1955. Her next departure was in March 1956, for a cruise in the Western Pacific, which terminated at San Francisco in early 1957. In November 1969 she was sunk as a target off the coast of southern California by the *Sculpin* (SSN-590). *Bream* was awarded four battle stars for her World War II service.

Brill (SS-330)

A submarine of the Balao class, she was built by the Electric Boat Company and launched in June 1944. Deployed in the Pacific in January 1945, she conducted three war patrols in the South China Sea and the Gulf of Siam. *Brill* made few contacts worthy of torpedo fire during her patrols and consequently had to settle with the damaging of an unidentified ship of approximately 1,000 tons as her only score. After the war, she continued operations briefly in the central Pacific and Philippines before making cruises in Alaska and along the West Coast. These were followed by training operations out of Pearl Harbor, overhaul at the San Francisco Naval Shipyard, and decommissioning in May 1948, after which she was turned over to Turkey. She received one battle star for her World War II service.

Buffalo (SSN-715)

This submarine of the Los Angeles class was built by the Newport News Shipbuilding and Drydock Company and launched in May 1982. With a displacement of 6,900 tons, she was designed for a complement of 12 officers and 115 enlisted men.

See LOS ANGELES.

Bugara (SS-331)

A submarine of the Balao class, built by the Electric Boat Company and launched in July 1944, she was sent to the Pacific where she completed three war patrols, from late February to the end of hostilities, in the Flores, Java, and South China Seas and the Gulf of Siam. While the first two patrols proved uneventful, her third war patrol might be classified as one of the most colorful ever made during the war. This patrol in the Gulf of Siam was highlighted by a series of excellently conducted gun attacks, which disposed of 57 small ships totaling 5,284 tons. All except two of these vessels were boarded and their native crews put safely ashore with their personal belongings. One of the many interesting incidents of this patrol was an encounter with a Japanese ship manned by a Chinese crew being attacked by Malay pirates. *Bugara* rescued the Chinese, sank the Japanese ship, and then disposed of the pirates. After her last war patrol, she sailed to Subic Bay, Philippine Islands, and joined the other units of her squadron. For the remainder of 1945 she operated out of Subic Bay. In January 1946 she returned to San Diego via Pearl Harbor. After a rehabilitation period on the West Coast she returned to Pearl Harbor in May 1946. She was overhauled at Pearl Harbor Naval Shipyard in 1946 and during the fall of that year made a training cruise in the Bering Sea and then returned to Pearl Harbor. She later conducted operations off the West Coast, the mid-Pacific, Yokosuka (Japan), Guam, Melbourne, Buckner Bay, and Tsingtao. She returned to Pearl Harbor August 24, 1948. After an overhaul in January 1950, she conducted operations out of Pearl Harbor until early December 1954. In 1951 she was converted to a Fleet snorkel submarine at Pearl Harbor Naval Shipyard. Twice during this period she served in the Far East supporting the Korean operations. She was decommissioned in October 1969, but, several years later, while under tow near Cape Flattery, Washington, swamped and sank accidentally. *Bugara* received three battle stars for her World War II service.

Bullhead (SS-332)

A submarine of the Balao class, she was launched in July 1944, and ordered to the Pacific, where she embarked on her first war patrol, to the South China Sea. Although she made no enemy contacts, she bombarded Japanese shore positions and rescued three airmen from a downed B-29, following its air strike on the China Coast. During her second patrol, in May and June 1945, *Bullhead* sank two freighters, a schooner, and a subchaser. She started on her third war patrol, this time in the Java Sea, in late June 1945, from which she did not return. After the war, it was assumed that she had been depth-charged by a Japanese plane during the first week in August and was sunk with all hands. *Bullhead* received two battle stars for World War II service.

Bumper (SS-333)

A submarine of the Balao class, she was built by the Electric Boat Company and launched in August 1944. While on duty in the Pacific between mid-April and war's end, she completed two war patrols in the Java and South China Seas and the Gulf of Siam. During this time she sank a tanker, destroyed another small tanker at anchor, and sank four miscellaneous small craft by gunfire. She arrived at Fremantle, Australia, from her last war patrol and departed for Subic Bay, Philippine Islands, where she served as a unit of Submarines, Philippine Sea Frontier, until February 1946, when she returned to California for repairs. Repairs completed, she reported for duty with Submarine Squadron 5 at Pearl Harbor and operated in the vicinity of the Hawaiian Islands until December 1946, when she went on a simulated war patrol covering Truk, the Caroline Islands; Subic Bay, the Philippine Islands; Yokosuka, Japan; and Midway. She also spent six weeks with Northern Training Group, Western Pacific, at Tsingtao, China, and in the Yellow Sea. She later participated in a second simulated war patrol in the western Pacific, in the fall of 1949, before being assigned to operations along the Atlantic seaboard until November 1950, when she was decommissioned and sold to Turkey. She received one battle star for her World War II service.

buoyancy

Unlike other navy vessels, the submarine is designed to operate chiefly below water, while at the same time having capabilities to function when necessary on the surface. To be able to undertake this dual role, the submarine must possess unusual features of both construction and design. The basic feature is the possession of ballast tanks and the means to increase or decrease ballast. Using these, the crew can adjust the buoyancy of the boat in quick order to make it operate effectively on the surface or at any assigned depth.

In submarines a measure of a boat's ability to float may be classed as positive, negative, or neutral. Positive buoyancy results when a submarine weighs less than an equal volume of water and floats on the surface. Negative buoyancy occurs when the boat floods its ballast tanks and submerges to a specified depth. Neutral buoyancy can be said to occur when it rests below the surface, neither rising nor sinking. Submarines submerge and surface through buoyancy control. Admitting water to tanks between the submarine's outer hull and inner "pressure" hull results in negative buoyancy, which allows the submarine to submerge. Pumping compressed air into the tanks expels water and produces positive buoyancy, which lets the submarine rise to the surface. Neutral buoyancy occurs when just enough water is present in the tanks to let the submarine maintain a certain depth. Problems with buoyancy control may sink a submarine, as has happened most notably and frequently in cases of accident or damage inflicted by enemy attack. A fourth category of buoy-

(United States Navy)

ancy—associated only with submarines—can be referred to as "artificial buoyancy." This might occur, for example, when a sub is sinking (negative buoyancy) but has enough power to be propelled to the surface by increasing propeller speed and pointing the bow planes upward.

Burke, Arleigh Albert (1901–1996)

American naval officer, born in Boulder, Colorado, on October 19, 1901. Burke graduated from the U.S. Naval Academy and was commissioned in 1923 and embarked upon a career that would lead him to become a famous destroyer squadron commander in WORLD WAR II, as well as the youngest chief of naval operations (during the 1950s). Because he was a specialist in ordnance, he was stationed in shore and sea billets dealing with this work well into World War II, although he requested combat duty. In March 1943 he was given command of successive destroyer divisions that engaged the Japanese while escorting cruiser forces in the SOLOMON ISLANDS. In October 1943 he commanded Destroyer Squadron 23, known as the "Little Beavers," displaying exceptional battle tactics and bravery in sinking various Japanese vessels during actions in the South Pacific.

He then became chief of staff to Admiral Marc Mitscher, participating in actions such as the battles of the Philippine Sea, LEYTE GULF, IWO JIMA, and OKINAWA. Following the war he headed the controversial section of the Navy Department, Op 23, that campaigned to ensure for the navy a role in America's nuclear arsenal. Further commands followed, including that of a cruiser division during the KOREAN WAR (1950–53) and service as a United Nations delegate at the Panmunjom peace talks. Raised over the 87 officers above him by President Eisenhower, Admiral Burke became chief of naval operations in 1955. He held the post successfully for an unprecedented six years, running the navy during many critical phases of the cold war, before retiring in 1961.

Burrfish (SS-312)

A submarine of the Balao class whose keel was laid by the Portsmouth Naval Shipyard and launched in June 1943. Her wartime operations extended from early February 1944 to mid-May 1945, during which period she com-

pleted six war patrols, sinking one 5,894-ton Japanese tanker. Her operating area extended from the western Caroline Islands to Formosa and the waters south of Japan. *Burrfish* also participated with the submarine *Ronquil* in the destruction of a patrol vessel. During her third war patrol the ship accomplished several special missions, conducting reconnaissance of the beaches of Palau and Yap where landings were planned. After the war she saw service, following modifications and conversion, as a radar-picket submarine. She was assigned to Submarine Squadron 6 at Norfolk, and later, between February 1950 and June 1956, she completed three tours with the Sixth Fleet in the Mediterranean; participated in several major type and intertype exercises; and operated along the eastern seaboard as a radar-picket ship. She was later loaned to the Canadian navy (RCN) and commissioned HMCS *Grilse II* until being returned to the United States and struck from the Navy list in July 1969. *Burrfish* received five battle stars for her World War II service.

Bushnell, David (1742–1824)

American inventor, educated at Yale, who created the first operational submarine in 1776. A year earlier he had established that dynamite would explode underwater, but it was as the inventor of the *Turtle* during the American War of Independence (1775–83) that he made his main contribution to the development of naval warfare. A small, hand-powered submarine, the *Turtle* floated upright in the water and could be partially submerged when two internal water tanks were filled. Power was provided by a hand-cranked propeller. She was armed with a detachable explosive charge that could be attached to the hull of an enemy warship secretly. The first-ever submarine attack against an enemy surface vessel took place on September 6–7, 1776, when Admiral Richard Howe's flagship, the HMS *Eagle,* which was blockading the Hudson River, was selected as *Turtle*'s intended victim. However, the attack failed because *Turtle*'s explosive charge could not be attached to *Eagle*'s copper-clad hull. Bushnell experimented with two other submarine prototypes but neither was a success. Although he abandoned his career as a naval architect at the end of the war, his contribution to the early history of the submarine was firmly established.

C

C-2 (SS-13)

A small submarine, later named *Stingray,* of only 275 tons (submerged), built by the Fore River Shipbuilding Company of Quincy, Massachusetts, in 1908 and launched in April 1909. With a crew of 14 enlisted men and one officer, she was originally christened *Stingray* and assigned to the Atlantic Torpedo Fleet and later to the Atlantic Submarine Flotilla. She had a top speed of nine knots submerged and 11 on the surface, and cruised in East Coast waters until May 1913, when she was reassigned for six months of operations from Guantanamo Bay, Cuba. In December, she based at Cristobal in the Panama Canal Zone and began an operating schedule of torpedo practice, exploration of anchorages, and harbor defense duty at ports of the Panama Canal Zone. During the latter part of World War I, *C-2* patrolled off the Florida coast. She was decommissioned in December 1919.

C-4 (Trident I)

The U.S. Navy's Trident I (C-4) submarine-launched ballistic missile (SLBM) is the successor to the Poseidon (C-3) SLBM, with twice the yield and twice the accuracy. (The original design criteria for the Trident was primarily to obtain an increase in range over the Poseidon while remaining compatible with existing Poseidon submarines.) Development began in 1972 and initial operational capability (IOC) was achieved in October 1979. No longer in production, but still in service, some 570 missiles had been produced by the end of the century.

C-5 [ex-*Snapper*] (SS-16)

An early submarine built by the Fore River Shipbuilding Company and launched in June 1909. The submarine fitted out at the Boston Navy Yard, then began three years of training and tests along the East Coast and in Chesapeake Bay. She ran experiments with radio, submarine signaling apparatus, different types of batteries, and other equipment, all of which later became standard in submarines of the "Silent Service." She joined in fleet maneuvers, helping to develop submarine tactics in submerged attacks on combatant ships, and engaged in operations with airplanes in the infancy of naval aviation. A highlight of the period was a review of the fleet by President William Howard Taft in November 1911. *C-5* operated in Panamanian waters, conducting exercises and patrolling on harbor defense, as well as studying the suitability of various ports of Panama for submarine bases. She was decommissioned at Coco Solo, Panama Canal Zone, in December 1919.

Cabezon (SS-334)

A submarine of the Balao class, built by the Electric Boat Company and launched in August 1944. She departed New London in February 1945 for Key West, Florida, where she underwent three weeks of training and provided services for the Fleet Sound School. She then sailed to Pearl Harbor for duty with the Pacific Fleet, conducting war patrols from late May until the end of the war. On her first patrol, in the Sea of Okhotsk, she sank a 2,631-ton Japanese cargo vessel. She refitted at Midway until early

August, then departed for Saipan to serve as target ship for surface force training exercises. From September 1945 until January 1946 she engaged in local operations and training in Philippine waters, based at Subic Bay, before being deployed to San Diego and later to Pearl Harbor. She participated in local operations and training cruises for submariners of the Naval Reserve there and on the West Coast, with intervening cruises to the South Pacific, the North Pacific, and across the Arctic Circle. She also made two cruises to the Far East in 1950 and 1952, the second of which included a reconnaissance patrol in the vicinity of La Perouse Strait, between Hokkaido, Japan, and Sakhalin, U.S.S.R. She sailed for Mare Island in April 1953, and was placed out of commission in October. *Cabezon* received one battle star for service in World War II.

Cabrilla (SS-288)

A submarine of the Balao class built by the Portsmouth Naval Shipyard and launched in December 1942. She arrived at Pearl Harbor in late August 1943, and two weeks later departed on the first of eight war patrols. After a daring exploit in which four Filipino guerrillas were taken off Negros Island, *Cabrilla* completed her patrol at Fremantle, Australia, her base for the next five patrols. During her second patrol, she laid mines in the Gulf of Siam, and sank her first Japanese merchantman, then returned to Fremantle to prepare for her third patrol, a reconnaissance of Sunda Strait. Her fourth and fifth patrols, off Makassar and in the Celebes and Sulu Seas, found her again striking with telling results against Japanese merchant shipping. Most successful of her patrols was the sixth, in the South China Sea and off Luzon from mid-September to late October 1944. During this period, she sank a total of 24,557 tons of shipping, including a 10,059-ton tanker. *Cabrilla* made her seventh war patrol in vicious weather in the Kuriles of northern Japan, and her last patrol found her on lifeguard duty for aviators downed at sea while carrying out attacks on Japan. Her tally in seven war patrols was seven ships for a total of 39,707 tons. Homeward-bound after two arduous years, she cleared Fremantle, Australia, at the end of August 1945 for the States. Following overhaul at Philadelphia, she sailed for the Canal Zone for exercises in February and March 1946, then returned to Philadelphia and was placed out of commission in August 1946. *Cabrilla* received six battle stars for World War II service.

Cachalot (SS-33) (K-2)

The first of two submarines of this name, and originally designated a K boat, *Cachalot* was constructed by the Fore River Shipbuilding Company and launched in October 1913. She had a complement of two officers and 26 enlisted men. After trials and exercises in New England waters throughout the spring and summer of 1914, she became a unit of SubDiv4 of the Atlantic Torpedo Flotilla at Newport, Rhode Island, in October 1914. For almost three years, she cruised the East Coast of the United States, from New England to Florida, conducting experiments to develop the techniques of submarine warfare. As World War I raged in Europe, guarding the vital shipping lanes across the Atlantic Ocean became imperative, since German U-boats interfered heavily with Allied shipping bound for Europe during that conflict. *Cachalot* and three other K boats were the first American submarines to operate in European waters during the First World War. Leaving the naval submarine base at New London/Groton, Connecticut, on October 12, 1917, the four submarines, accompanied by the submarine tender USS *Bushnell,* set course for their new base at Ponta Delgada in the Azores. For over a year, these boats searched for the German submarines and surface raiders reputed to be operating in the Azores area. However, no contacts with the enemy were ever made. *Cachalot* continued these war patrols until October 1918, when she transited to Philadelphia, and commenced operating off the East Coast of the United States. From 1919 to 1923, she cruised along the Atlantic coast of the United States, from New England to Florida, conducting experimental exercises. The development of submarines was greatly accelerated through the technology learned from these experiments. New listening devices, storage batteries, and torpedoes were tested; and their later adoption contributed greatly toward enhancing American submarine superiority and strength on the high seas. She was decommissioned in March 1923.

Cachalot (SS-170) (ex-V-8)

A submarine built by Portsmouth Naval Shipyard and launched in October 1933, she was a boat of 1,650 tons (submerged) and carried a complement of three officers and 39 enlisted men. Although she had a surface speed of 17 knots, her submerged limit was only eight knots. She was initially assigned to San Diego, where in October 1934 she joined the Submarine Force, U.S. Fleet. Operating until 1937 principally on the West Coast, she engaged in fleet problems, torpedo practice, antisubmarine, tactical, and sound training exercises. She cruised to Hawaiian waters and the Canal Zone to participate in large-scale fleet exercises. In June 1937, she was ordered to duty in experimental torpedo firing for the Newport Torpedo Station and sound training for the New London Submarine School, until late October 1937. A year later she sailed for participation in a fleet problem, torpedo practice, and sound training in the Caribbean, and in June 1939 reported at Pearl Harbor for duty with the Submarine Scouting Force. War came to *Cachalot* as she lay in Pearl Harbor Navy Yard. In the Japanese attack of December 7,

1941, one of her men was wounded, but the submarine suffered no damage. Yard work on her was completed at a furious pace, and on January 12, 1942, she sailed on her first war patrol. After fueling at Midway, she conducted a reconnaissance of Wake, Eniwetok, Ponape, Truk, Namonuito, and Hall Islands, returning with vitally needed intelligence of Japanese bases. Her second war patrol, for which she cleared from Midway in early June, was conducted off the Japanese home islands, where she damaged an enemy tanker. Returning to Pearl Harbor, she cleared for her final war patrol September 23, in the frigid waters of the Bering Sea in support of Aleutians operations. Overage for strenuous war patrols, *Cachalot* still had a role to play as training ship for the Submarine School at New London. She served there until late June 1945, when she sailed to Philadelphia and was decommissioned three months later. *Cachalot* received three battle stars for World War II service.

Caiman (SS-323)

A submarine of the Balao class, built by Electric Boat Company and launched in March 1944. She sailed from Pearl Harbor on her first war patrol in November 1944, operating in the South China Sea, where she combined offensive patrol with lifeguard duty to rescue aviators downed in air strikes on enemy-held territory. Aggressive American submarine and naval air attacks had already greatly reduced the Japanese merchant fleet; hence, *Caiman* made no contacts on this patrol, from which she returned to Fremantle, Australia, in January to refit. Her second patrol in this area also yielded no contacts, but on her third, which began at Subic Bay in the Philippines in April, she sank two small schooners. Their use illustrated graphically the almost complete loss of merchant ships, which the Japanese had suffered largely at the hands of the U.S. Navy. Returning to Fremantle in June from her patrol area off southern Indochina and western Borneo, she refitted for her fourth war patrol, during which she performed three dangerous special missions, landing and later evacuating agents from the coast of Java. On this patrol, which took place from July 22 to the end of hostilities, she sank another Japanese schooner. She returned to Subic Bay, then sailed for the West Coast. She operated out of San Diego, Guam, and Pearl Harbor in 1946. In 1947 she made an arctic familiarization cruise out of Seattle. Thereafter, based in Seattle, she served as a reserve training ship until April 1951 when she began a GUPPY IA conversion at Mare Island Naval Shipyard. Then based at Pearl Harbor and San Diego, *Caiman* alternated local operations and fleet exercises with tours of duty in the Far East at 18-month intervals. She was decommissioned in June 1972. *Caiman* received two battle stars for service in World War II.

Cape Esperance, Battle of (October 11, 1942)

An engagement between American and Japanese naval units to the northwest of Cape Esperance on Guadalcanal in the Pacific during World War II. It was part of the continuing struggle for control of the Solomon Islands during the first two years of the war. An American strike force consisting of the heavy cruisers *San Francisco* and *Salt Lake City*, the light cruisers *Boise* and *Helena*, and five destroyers commanded by Rear Admiral Norman Scott was sent to intercept and destroy enemy ships in the channel between the eastern and western Solomons. Shortly before midnight, the *Helena's* radar identified a Japanese squadron some 14 nautical miles away. Consisting of two heavy cruisers and two destroyers, it was under orders to bombard Guadalcanal airfield. Some minutes before he was notified of the radar information, Rear Admiral Scott had ordered his squadron to reverse course as a result of information received from his spotter planes about Japanese movements. By this time the two naval forces were only four miles apart. Although the American commander was unsure of the location of some of his destroyers for a while, he went ahead with the attack. The Japanese were taken completely by surprise when the *Helena* and a destroyer opened fire. The cruisers were damaged and a destroyer was sunk. One U.S. cruiser and a destroyer were also crippled in the final phase of the action, but the engagement was a modest success for the Americans, who had successfully attacked the Japanese at sea for the first time and prevented the bombardment of Guadalcanal. Exaggerated American claims of Japanese losses were made at the time, but in fact the Japanese lost no more than a cruiser and a destroyer.

Capelin (SS-289)

A submarine of the Balao class, built by Portsmouth Naval Shipyard and launched in January 1943. Assigned to the Pacific Fleet, her first war patrol, in November 1943, west of New Guinea, resulted in the sinking of a 3,127-ton Japanese freighter, but the actions also revealed in a defective conning tower hatch, radar tube, and bow planes. These flaws were corrected and the boat then departed for her second patrol in late November. Her area was in the Molucca and Celebes Seas, and she was to pay particular attention to Kaoe Bay, Morotai Strait, Davao Gulf, and trade routes in the vicinity of Siaeo, Sangi, Talaud, and Sarangani islands. She was to leave her area at dark on December 6; however, nothing was ever positively heard from *Capelin* after she departed and attempts by other naval craft in the area to reach her by radio elicited no response. Japanese records later revealed that an American submarine was attacked off Kaoe Bay, Halmahera. However, the Japanese stated that this attack was broken off, and the evidence of contact was rather thin. The only positive statement that can be made is that *Capelin* was lost in the Celebes Sea, or in Molucca Passage or the Molucca Sea, probably in December 1943. Enemy minefields are now known to have been placed in various positions along the north coast of Celebes in *Capelin's* patrol area, and she may have been lost because of a mine explosion. *Capelin* received one battle star for World War II service.

Capitaine (SS-336)

A submarine of the Balao class, built by Electric Boat Company and launched in October 1944. After initial training the boat was ordered to Pearl Harbor and left on her first war patrol in March 1945. Although the patrol was of 62 days' duration and ended at Fremantle, Western Australia, on July 13, 1945, *Capitaine* had sighted no major targets and had sunk only one small patrol boat. With the war ending, she was ordered to the Philippines to conduct training exercises before her return to San Diego in March 1946. She was engaged in simulated war patrols during 1947 and 1948, and training cruises along the West Coast. During the 1950s, she also made cruises to the central and far Pacific. She then operated locally off the coast of southern California until departing for Puget Sound to provide submarine services for ASW units in that area, as well as for the Naval Ordnance Test Station and the Scripps Institute of Oceanography. These services continued through the 1960s, and she was decommissioned in March 1966 and sold to Italy.

Carbonero (SS-337)

A submarine of the Balao class, built by the Electric Boat Company and launched in October 1944. She was a typical World War II–type diesel submarine that was later modernized and equipped with a streamlined sail and a fleet snorkel. During the remaining months of World War II, *Carbonero* participated in two successful war patrols. No major Japanese shipping was sighted in either the Gulf of Siam or the Formosan waters patrolled, but a number of smaller craft were destroyed by gunfire. When the war ended she was ordered to Seattle, Washington, for training and in the following months participated in a variety of operations including two trips to the Orient. In April 1947, *Carbonero* was ordered into the Submarine Guided Missile Program. Late in 1951 she was converted to a Fleet Snorkel submarine with a streamlined sail, allowing her to operate her diesel engines and to receive fresh air for prolonged periods while underwater. In May 1957, she was transferred to Pearl Harbor where she later became the flagship of SubDiv12. She participated in the 1962 nuclear tests in the central Pacific off Christmas Island and Johnston Island, entitled Operation Dominic. *Carbonero* was decommissioned on December 1, 1970. On April 27,

1975, she was taken to sea for the last time and used as a test target for a Mark 48 torpedo fired by the USS *Pogy*. She now rests in Hawaiian waters where she spent the last 13 years of her commissioned life.

Carp (F-1) (SS-20)

An early submarine built by Union Iron Works of San Francisco and launched in March 1912. She was assigned to the First Submarine Group, Pacific Torpedo Flotilla, and operated in the San Francisco area on trials and tests through January 1913, when she joined the flotilla for training at sea, between San Diego and San Pedro and then in San Diego Harbor. Between July 1914 and November 1915, the flotilla was based at Honolulu for development operations in the Hawaiian Islands. There *Carp* served with the Patrol Force, Pacific, making surface and submerged runs to continue her part in the development of submarine tactics. Her base during this time was San Pedro. On December 17, 1917, while maneuvering in exercises at sea, *Carp* and a sister submarine, *F-3*, collided, the former sinking in 10 seconds, her port side torn for-

Carp/F-1 (SS-20), built by Union Iron Works and commissioned in 1912, with the crew topside to show how narrow these boats were and how cramped it was below decks. *(United States Navy)*

ward of the engine room. Nineteen of her men were lost, while the others were rescued by the submarines with whom she was operating.

Carp (SS-338)

The second submarine to bear this name was of the Balao class, built by the Electric Boat Company and launched in November 1944. Assigned to the Pacific Fleet, she left on her first and only war patrol, from early June to early August 1945, cruising off the coast of Honshu, destroying small craft and patrolling for the carriers of the Third Fleet engaged in air strikes on the mainland. Undergoing refit at Midway when hostilities ended, she was ordered to San Diego as flagship for SubDiv71; Carp operated along the West Coast with occasional training cruises to Pearl Harbor. Between February and June 1947 she made a simulated war patrol to the Far East, and in 1948 and 1949 undertook two exploratory cruises to extreme northern waters, adding to the knowledge of an increasingly important strategic area for submarine operations. She was converted at the San Francisco Naval Shipyard to a Fleet Snorkel submarine in February 1952, which added to her submerged speed and endurance, Carp supported United Nations forces in the Korean War during a cruise from late September 1952 to April 1953 in the Far East. Arriving at Pearl Harbor, her new home port, on March 15, 1954, Carp remained on active duty with the fleet from that port through July 1959. During this time she continued to make cruises to the Far East, one of which included a goodwill visit to Australia and participation in a Southeast Asia Treaty Organization exercise, and also a cruise to Alaskan waters. On August 1, 1959, Carp departed Pearl Harbor for her new assignment with the Atlantic Fleet. Arriving at Norfolk, Virginia, on August 28, 1959, the submarine conducted training exercises off the East Coast and in the Caribbean through 1963. Carp was decommissioned in March 1968 and placed in reserve until December 1971 when she was struck from the Navy list. Carp received a battle star for her service in World War II.

Casimir Pulaski (SSBN-633)

This submarine of the Lafayette class was built by the Electric Boat Division of General Dynamics and launched in February 1964. With a displacement of 8,251 tons and armed with 16 missile tubes and four 21-inch torpedo tubes forward, she was designed for a complement of 14 officers and 126 enlisted men (each in two crews). After almost three decades of service, conducting vital missions in many parts of the globe, Casimir Pulaski was decommissioned and struck from the Navy list in December 1994.

See LAFAYETTE.

Catfish (SS-339)

A submarine of the Balao class, constructed by Electric Boat Company and launched in November 1944. Ordered to the Pacific, she departed from Guam on August 8, 1945, on a special mission to locate a minefield off Kyushu. When the cease-fire order was given August 15, Catfish was ordered to the Yellow Sea for surface patrol and lifeguard duty. She returned to Guam in September, and thence to the West Coast. Based at San Diego, Catfish operated locally on the West Coast and made two cruises to the Far East during which she conducted simulated war patrols and provided services to the Seventh Fleet. In August 1948 Catfish departed for an overhaul and conversion to a GUPPY II. This conversion streamlined the hull superstructure and included a new sail to replace the open conning tower fairwater and periscope/radar shears, installation of a snorkel system, four high-capacity batteries, and other enhancements. These modifications allowed Catfish to run submerged ("snorkel depth") on diesels rather than batteries. In 1950 Catfish embarked on a training cruise to the Far East. While at Guam, the Korean conflict broke out, and Catfish remained in the Far East, where she made one patrol in the Sea of Japan in support of U.N. forces in Korea. Throughout the 1950s and 1960s, she made training cruises and tours in Alaska and the Far East. She also participated in joint antisubmarine warfare exercises with Canadian forces, and conducted training cruises for Naval Reservists. Catfish was decommissioned in 1971, but had an untimely end. Sold to Argentina and renamed Santa-Fe, in 1982 during the Falklands War, she was hit by British forces. Deemed too costly to repair as a war prize, she was sunk in waters off South Georgia. Catfish was awarded one battle star for World War II service.

Cavalla (SS-244)

The first boat of this name was built by the Electric Boat Company and launched in November 1943 as a member of the Balao class. In May 1944, she departed on an unusual mission on her maiden patrol of distinguished service that would earn her a Presidential Unit Citation. En route to her station in the eastern Philippines, she made contact with a large Japanese task force, June 17, 1944. Cavalla tracked the force for several hours, then relayed invaluable information that contributed heavily to the overwhelming United States victory scored in the battle of the Philippine Sea, the famous "Marianas Turkey Shoot," on June 19–20, 1944. With this great service completed, Cavalla continued her pursuit. On June 19, she caught the carrier Shokaku landing planes and quickly fired a spread of six torpedoes for three hits, enough to send the carrier to the bottom. After a severe depth charging by three destroyers, Cavalla escaped to continue her mission. Her second patrol took her to the Philippine Sea as a member of a wolf pack operating in support of the invasion of Peleliu, September 15, 1944. On November 25, 1944, during her third patrol, *Cavalla* encountered two Japanese destroyers and made a daring surface attack, which sank the first one with a great explosion. The companion destroyer began depth charging while the elusive *Cavalla* evaded on the surface. Later in the same patrol, January 5, 1945, she made a night surface attack on an enemy convoy and sank two converted net tenders.

Cavalla cruised the South China and Java Seas on her fourth and fifth war patrols. Targets were few and far between, but she came to the aid of an ally on May 21, 1945. A month out on her fifth patrol, the submarine sighted HMS *Terrapin*, damaged by enemy depth charges and unable to submerge or make full speed. *Cavalla* stood by the wounded submarine and escorted her on the surface to Fremantle. She received the cease-fire order of August 15 while lifeguarding off Japan on her sixth war patrol. A few minutes later, she was bombed by a Japanese plane that apparently had not yet received the same information. She joined the fleet units entering Tokyo Bay at the end of August, remained for the signing of the surrender, and then departed for New London, Connecticut. Temporarily out of commission, she was reactivated and assigned to SubRon8 and engaged in various fleet exercises in the Caribbean and off Nova Scotia. Then, in September 1952, she entered the Electric Boat Company yard for conversion to a hunter-killer submarine (SSK), after which she participated in fleet exercises, testing her new capabilities. She also cruised to European waters several times to take part in North Atlantic Treaty Organization exercises. She remained active with the fleet through 1963; she was decommissioned in 1969. She has since become a memorial at Galveston, Texas. In addition to the Presidential Unit Citation, *Cavalla* received four battle stars for service in World War II, during which she sank four enemy ships, including an aircraft carrier, for a total of 34,180 tons.

Cavalla (SSN-684)

This submarine of the Sturgeon class was launched in February 1972, at the Electric Boat Division of General Dynamics. She had a displacement of 4,762 tons (submerged), was armed with four 21-inch torpedo tubes amidships, aft of the bow, and carried a complement of 12 officers and 95 enlisted men. After many strategic missions over a period of a quarter of a century, *Cavalla* was decommissioned and struck from the Navy list in March 1998.

See STURGEON.

celestial navigation

Also known as *nautical astronomy*, this is the art of finding position by observing the sun, moon, stars, and planets. Since the apparent positions of celestial bodies change with time and with changes in an observer's position on the nearly spherical Earth, the location of a ship or other craft may be determined by careful observations of celestial bodies. At any instant of time every celestial body is directly above or in the zenith of some point on the Earth's surface. This point lies on a line connecting the body and the center of the Earth, and is called the geographical position of the body. A line from the center of the Earth through the geographical position of an observer would extend to a point on the celestial sphere. This point is called the zenith of the observer. From that point, it can be determined by instrumentation, exactly where a vessel at sea is geographically located.

To put this theory into practice, a navigator measures with a sextant the altitudes of two or more celestial bodies. He carefully notes the exact time at which he made his observations. He obtains the time from radio signals or from accurate clocks called chronometers. These are set to Greenwich mean time, or GMT, for this is the time the navigator must know as he turns next to the *Nautical Almanac*, a book of astronomical tables from which may be found, for every second of every day, the positions on the celestial sphere of the sun, the stars, the moon, and the planets used in navigation. Knowing the altitudes of the bodies he observed and their geographical positions, the navigator has the information necessary to construct the circles of equal altitude that define his position. The navigator does not plot on his chart the full circles since, from dead reckoning or other means, he knows his approximate latitude and longitude. All he needs, then, are segments of the circles so short that, without loss of accuracy, they may be drawn as straight lines, which, like the lines obtained from bearings in piloting, are called lines of position. In modern submarines, the periscope have built-in sextants.

Cero (SS-225)

A submarine of the Gato class, built by the Electric Boat Company and launched in April 1943. She was assigned to the Pacific and in late September of that year sailed from Pearl Harbor on her first war patrol, which was conducted in the East China and Yellow Seas. At dawn on October 12, she made her first attack on a convoy of three freighters escorted by two destroyers. After heavily damaging one of the merchantmen, *Cero* was forced to plunge deep to survive the depth charging that followed. During the same patrol, she damaged two other freighters, and a small patrol boat, which she engaged on the surface. In December, she made her second war patrol, an unproductive one, along the Truk-New Ireland route, then put in to Milne Bay, New Guinea, for three weeks. Returning to the Truk-New Ireland shipping lanes in February 1944, she attacked a freighter (later sunk by one of her sister submarines) and inflicted damage on another merchantman.

She put in to Brisbane, Australia, and sailed on her fourth war patrol in early April, to be conducted off the Palau Islands. In late May, she attacked two freighters and a tanker, sinking one cargo ship and damaging the tanker. On her next patrol, in early August, she sent a Japanese tanker to the bottom. Fifteen days later she arrived at Brisbane, and on September 19 cleared Darwin, Australia, for the Mindanao and Sulu Seas. She called en route at Mios Woendi, where she took on board 17 tons of supplies for Philippine guerrillas, along with 16 soldiers headed for behind-the-lines operations in Luzon. Although not permitted by her orders to attack escorted merchantmen while on this mission, *Cero* encountered two small craft on October 27, and in the resulting gun action, damaged both and forced them ashore. On November 3, north of Manila, she made contact with the guerrillas, landed the soldiers and supplies, and took four evacuees on board. Later taken under attack by a Japanese submarine, *Cero* was able by alert bridge action to evade a torpedo aimed at her. Mission completed, she returned to Pearl Harbor on November 24, then sailed to the West Coast for overhaul.

Cero departed Pearl Harbor once more on March 31, 1945, on her seventh and most productive war patrol. Cruising off Honshu and Hokkaido, she not only provided lifeguard services for air strikes on Japan, but also sank two Japanese picket boats and damaged another, and sent three freighters and a large trawler to the bottom. Later refitted at Guam, she was ordered to do life-guard and picket duty off Honshu for her eighth war patrol. On July 15, she rescued three survivors of a downed bomber, and later that day bombarded the Japanese lighthouse and radio station at Shiriya Saki, Honshu. On July 18, while sailing for the Kurile Islands, *Cero* came under enemy air attack, and was damaged so severely by a bomb landing close aboard that she was forced to leave her patrol area for Pearl Harbor. During her battle career she sank five vessels for a total of 18,159 tons. After the war, *Cero* was placed in reserve, but then activated for training cruises in the Caribbean and aided in the work of the Fleet Sonar School. She was decommissioned in December 1953. *Cero* received seven battle stars for World War II service.

Charlotte (SSN-76)

This submarine of the Los Angeles class was built by the Newport News Shipping and Drydock Company and launched in October 1992. After commissioning, two years later, she embarked on the first of many strategic missions. With a displacement of 6,900 tons (submerged), *Charlotte* was armed with four 21-inch torpedo tubes amidships, aft of the bow, and 12 vertical launch tubes (VLT) forward, and was designed for a complement of 12 officers and 115 enlisted men.

See LOS ANGELES.

Charr (SS-328)

A submarine of the Balao class, built by the Electric Boat Company and launched in May 1944. Assigned to the Pacific, she left Pearl Harbor on December 30, 1944, to patrol the northeast coast of French Indochina. The patrol was highlighted by the unusual rescue of a naval aviator, a crew member of a PBY patrol plane that had been forced down, just off the coast. *Charr* lay at anchor four miles off the coast in broad daylight, an easy target for Japanese planes, while two men went ashore in a rubber boat. The aviator was brought aboard and three successive attempts were made, without success, to pick up the remaining nine members of the plane's crew, but contact with them could not be reestablished. *Charr* completed her 64-day patrol by escorting the badly damaged Dutch submarine *Zwaaruisch* through the Java Sea and Lombok Straits, arriving at Fremantle, Western Australia, on the third day of March, where she was refitted for her second war patrol. The second patrol began in late March 1945 and resulted in the sinking of a 5,200-ton cruiser and a four-day chase, with two other American submarines, which ended up with a joint record of two sinkings: a cruiser and one of its escorts. *Charr's* third patrol located no targets, since it was at the end of the war and Japanese shipping had been almost totally destroyed. After the war, following repairs, *Charr* spent the rest of the 1940s and 1950s in operations along the West Coast, with occasional cruises out into the Pacific. She was converted to a Fleet Snorkel submarine at Mare Island Naval Shipyard in 1951. In 1961, she conducted exercises with the Seventh Fleet in the western Pacific, and during the 1960s was variously deployed for service along the West Coast and lengthy cruises in the Pacific. In 1965, she participated in "Exercise Sea Horse," in support of the Vietnam conflict, at one time rescuing a downed navy pilot. In 1967, she left San Diego for the South China Sea to participate in "Exercise Sea Dog." She was decommissioned in June 1969. *Charr* received one battle star for her service during World War II.

Cheyenne (SSN-773)

This submarine of the Los Angeles class was built by the Newport News Shipbuilding and Drydock Company and launched in April 1995. She has a displacement of 6,900 tons (submerged), is armed with four 21-inch torpedo tubes amidships, aft of the bow, and 12 vertical launch tubes (VLT) forward, and carries a crew of 12 officers and 115 enlisted men. This boat, the fourth to carry the name, was the last of her class, and benefits from capabilities that are improved over her sister ships in such matters as fire control systems, VLTs, nuclear propulsion plant, and sonar system.

See LOS ANGELES.

Chivo (SS-341)

This submarine of the Ballao class was built by the Electric Boat Company (later to be the Electric Boat Division of General Dynamics) and launched in January 1945. She had a displacement of 2,391 tons (submerged), was armed with a five-inch deck gun, six 21-inch torpedo tubes forward and four aft, and carried a crew of six officers and 60 enlisted men.

Chivo was not commissioned until April 1945, and was ordered to the Pacific area too late to carry out any battle missions. However, she conducted training and strategic exercise during the postwar period for a quarter of a century before being decommissioned and struck from the Navy list and sold to Argentina in July 1971.

Chopper (SS-342)

A submarine of the Balao class, built by the Electric Boat Company and launched in February 1945. She was midway between Panama and the Philippine Islands when the war in the Pacific ended. However, she continued to the Philippine Islands via Guam, where she spent approximately three months in training before heading for San Diego for permanent duty. In July 1947, *Chopper* departed for a simulated war patrol to China, covering more than 18,000 miles and earning the boat the Battle Efficiency Pennant as one of the outstanding submarines in the Pacific Fleet. In September 1950, after service on the West Coast and in the Caribbean, *Chopper* returned to the Electric Boat Company to be converted from a fleet-type submarine to a modern GUPPY IA type. In January 1952, she joined the Sixth Fleet operating in the Mediterranean Sea. Her mission was to participate in exercises with U.S. Navy and NATO units. She visited Gibraltar; Augusta, Palermo and Naples, Italy; Malta; Marseilles and Cannes, France; Suda Bay, Crete; Messina and Taranto, Italy; Bone and Oran, Algeria. From then until August 1955, she operated locally out of Key West, Florida, including trips to Guantanamo Bay, Cuba, as well as the ports of Santiago de Cuba, Cuba; Port au Prince, Haiti; Kingston and Montego Bay, Jamaica. The Cuban Missile Crisis of 1962 found *Chopper* and her sister SubRon12 submarines on blockade barrier patrol on the Cuba sea approaches to interdict and repulse any Soviet flag vessels carrying Soviet missiles to Cuba. She revisited Guantanamo Bay several more times, but almost faced tragedy when, on what was to be her last trip to Guantanamo Bay, she suffered a control problem, causing her to exceed her rated test depth before the crew was able to recover control of the ship and resurface. Upon reentry to Guantanamo Bay, the badly damaged boat was extensively surveyed by marine engineers, and was given approval for a surface transit back to Key West under escort. After further inspection and repair, *Chopper* was removed from active service. She served as a salvage and rescue training hulk until July 21, 1976, when she was rigged as a tethered underwater target. Flooding sounds were heard, and the boat was lost as she sank in 2,400 fathoms off the Florida coast.

Admiral Christie *(United States Navy)*

Christie, Ralph W. (1893–1987)

After graduating from the Naval Academy in 1915, Christie joined the budding submarine service, had his first command in the *C-1*, and during the World War I period became a specialist in torpedo weaponry, where there were many problems. By World War II, he had reached top command levels, operating out of Brisbane, Australia, where he focused a great deal of attention on the problems of submarine skippers whose torpedoes misfired, were erratic, or in some instances threatened to circle back to the point from which they had been fired. He was elevated to the rank of vice admiral and was closely involved in many of the major submarine battles of the Pacific during the war. After the war, he wound up with two years in command of the Bremerton Navy Yard and retired in August 1949.

chronometer

A timekeeping device of great accuracy, particularly when used for, and fundamental to, determining longitude at sea. Although practical chronometers were in use at sea as early as the 18th century, it was not until recent times that they were developed to the 100th fractions of a second needed for the highly critical maneuvers of submarines. The modern chronometer resembles a large, meticulously refined watch, suspended in gimbals (a set of two rings connected by bearings) so poised as to remain horizontal whatever the inclination of the ship. It is important to understand that chronometers may not be accurate with respect to true time, but they have a continually monitored drift rate and, as such, the face time can be corrected to true time. Additionally, since the advent of the first SSBNs, nuclear submarines are equipped with electronic chronometers, which are much more accurate, in addition to regular windup mechanical chronometers.

Chubb (SS-329)

A submarine of the Balao class, built by the Electric Boat Company and launched in June 1944. Deployed to the Pacific, she set out on her first war patrol in mid-February, where, in the Tonkin Gulf and the Java and South China Seas, she found her skill and determination tried in four hairbreadth escapes from destruction. On March 3, she was attacked by an enemy submarine whose torpedoes she evaded. On March 29, she began a long surface chase after an escort group, which she carried through the next day, even though forced six times to go deep by enemy aircraft. On their last pass, they dropped bombs, a clear indication that *Chubb*'s chase had to be broken off. The next day she was off Yulikan Bay, and while American and Japanese planes fought in the skies above, *Chubb* rescued three downed pilots as they and she were strafed. With two Japanese patrol craft looming out of the harbor, *Chubb* raced away. Then, on April 12, she was bombed by an enemy patrol plane as she started to dive. Bomb damage caused a temporary loss of power, and with depth control lost, she broached. Fortunately, the enemy bomber had apparently dropped its entire load on the first run. *Chubb* put in to Fremantle for a month of repair and then sailed for the Java Sea and her second war patrol. During this patrol, she attacked two freighters, and sank a minesweeper, which had come out hunting for her. The damage already done to Japanese shipping made targets few by this time, and *Chubb* put in to Subic Bay from June 21 to July 15 to refit. Her third war patrol found her again in the Java Sea, sinking a few small craft, although attacked by the remnant of Japanese air strength. Returning to Fremantle at war's end, she sailed on to Subic Bay for training through the rest of 1945, then returned to the West Coast. During the years 1946

to 1948, she served on the West Coast, in Alaska, and in the Far East. In late May 1948, she was transferred briefly to Turkey, but then returned to the United States and was decommissioned. *Chubb* received three battle stars for World War II service.

Chuuk Islands, Battle of (1942)

Formerly referred to as Truk, these are a cluster of 14 much-eroded high volcanic islands in Micronesia, in the western Pacific Ocean. They were annexed by Japan in 1914 and strongly fortified, but were heavily attacked, bypassed, and blockaded by the Allies during the war. American submarines played a role, not so much in battle as in reconnoitering the islands preparatory to the attacks by surface ships and planes. The sunken hulls of Japanese ships remain in the surrounding waters, along with ruined weapons and fortifications on land. Chuuk, together with the other islands in what are now the Federated States of Micronesia, was part of the U.S.-administered United Nations Trust Territory of the Pacific Islands from 1947 to 1986.

Cincinnati (SSN-693)

Built by Newport News Shipbuilding and Drydock Company, this submarine of the Los Angeles class was launched in February 1977, and commissioned in June 1978. She had a displacement of 6,900 tons submerged, was armed with four 21-inch torpedo tubes amidships, aft of the bow, and had a complement of 12 officers and 115 enlisted men. During her relatively short life of 17 years, she conducted training and strategic exercise in many waters of the world, and was decommissioned and struck from the Navy list in July 1995.

See LOS ANGELES.

Cisco (SS-290)

A submarine of the Balao class, built by Portsmouth Naval Shipyard and launched in December 1942. Venturing out for her first war patrol, she left Port Darwin, Australia, in mid-September 1943, having returned once for a repair to her hydraulic system. Her assigned area was a large rectangular one in the South China Sea between Luzon and the coast of French Indochina. In order to reach it, she was to pass through the Arafura Sea area, the Banda Sea, Manipa Strait, Molucca Passage, the Celebes Sea, Sibutu Passage, the Sulu Sea, and Mindoro Strait. On September 28, *Cisco* should have been due west of Mindanao in the center of the Sulu Sea. On that day a Japanese antisubmarine attack was made, slightly north and east of *Cisco*'s expected position. In reporting the attack the Japanese report later stated, "Found a sub tailing oil. Bombing. Ships cooperated with us." The attack would seem to have been made by planes in cooperation with ships. No submarine that returned from patrol reported having been attacked at this time and position. The navy report was brief: "Nothing has been seen of or heard from *Cisco* since her departure from Darwin, and on 4 and 5, November 1943, Headquarters Task Force Seventy-One was unable to make radio contact with her. At the time of her loss it was considered very unlikely that a recurrence of trouble with her main hydraulic system could explain her sinking, and the only other possible clue was the fact that a Japanese plane was reported over Darwin at twenty thousand feet on the morning of her second departure. The attack listed above is thought to probably explain this loss. No enemy mine fields are known to have been in her area, or enroute to it."

Clamagore (SS-343)

A submarine of the Balao class, built by Electric Boat Company and launched in February 1945. World War II came to an end while *Clamagore* was on a training cruise off Panama. In January 1946, she became flagship of Submarine Squadron Four based in Key West, Florida, a title she held until August 1959. She was converted at Electric Boat to a high-speed GUPPY II submarine in the summer of 1948. During the 1950s, she made trips to Guantanamo Bay and Havana, Cuba, and to other ports in the Caribbean and along the East Coast, and participated in Operation UNITAS II, a joint antisubmarine warfare training exercise with eight South American countries—Argentina, Brazil, Chile, Colombia, Ecuador, Peru, Venezuela, and Uruguay—during which she steamed around the southern tip of the South American continent. In 1963, she was converted to a Guppy III submarine. During this conversion, the ship was cut in half and a 15-foot, 55-ton section was added. The latest and most sophisticated electronics and fire control system were also installed. In early April 1965, she joined in a NATO operation south of Iceland with British, Dutch, American, and French submarines and aircraft. She undertook a variety of operations in the first half of the 1970s, mainly in the Caribbean, Mediterranean, the Norwegian Sea, and the East Coast. *Clamagore* was decommissioned in June 1975, and now serves as a museum ship at Patriot's Point, Charleston, South Carolina.

classes of submarines

Almost from the beginning of U.S. Navy development of submarines in 1900, boats have been designed, built, and commissioned in distinct classes. The earliest example is the Holland class. As undersea technology advanced and new and better designs were perfected, submarines received class designations, meaning in effect that a series of submarines would be built alike until such time as a better role model was perfected. In some instances, new classes represented models that were improved over previous ones. Thus, the earlier classes designated by the letters K, L, N, O, and R during the World War I period were succeeded by the S boats, which were highly successful for their day during the 1920s and 1930s. The S boats were later discontinued in favor of the Gato and Balao classes that were so successful during World War II. In other instances, class designations were used in the same time period but applied to boats designed for different tactical and operational purposes, such as submarines designed primarily for attacking enemy vessels at short range and those bearing guided missiles for long-range deterrent objectives.

Following are descriptions of seven major classes of submarines built between 1934 and 1946 that formed the basis of the fleet during their years in service. Their names are the Shark, Salmon, Sargo, Tambor, Gato, Balao, and Tench. Of the 439 boats ordered during this 12-year period, 248 were completed and proved very instrumental in the United States's winning World War II. Their numbers are SS-174 through SS-522, and they were built by six different shipbuilding companies: Electric Boat, Portsmouth, Mare Island, Manitowoc, Cramp, and Boston. They ranged in length from 298 feet, 1 inch to 311 feet, 9 inches and in breadth from 25 feet, 1 inch to 27 feet, 3 inches. Most important, they represented the most powerful submarine force the world had ever known.

SHARK CLASS

Specifications

Overall length x maximum breadth: 298 ft. 1 in. x 25 ft. 1 in.
Displacement: 1,316 tons surfaced; 1,968 tons submerged
Operating depth: 250 ft.
Watertight compartments: 7, plus conning tower
Pressure hull plating: approx. 5/8 in. mild steel
Torpedo tubes: 4 bow; 2 stern (2 bow deck tubes added to SS 175 in 1942)
Torpedo load, maximum: 16; 18 with deck tubes
Deck guns: 1 3-in./50-cal.
Maximum speed: 18 knots surfaced; 8 knots submerged
Cruising range: 11,000 miles surfaced at 10 knots
Submerged endurance: 36 hours at minimum speed
Fuel capacity: 85,946–86,675 gallons
Patrol endurance: 75 days
Propulsion: Diesel-electric reduction gear with 4 main generator engines; 2 auxiliary generators; 4 main motors with 4,300 shaft horsepower; 2 120-cell main storage batteries

Construction

Number of boats: 2 boats ordered in 1934
Builders: Electric Boat

SALMON CLASS

Specifications

Overall length x maximum breadth: 308 ft. x 26 ft. 2 in.
Displacement: 1,449 tons surfaced; 2,198 tons submerged
Operating depth: 250 ft.
Watertight compartments: 7, plus conning tower
Pressure hull plating: approx. 11/16 in. mild steel
Torpedo tubes: 4 bow; 4 stern
Torpedo load, maximum: 20 internal; 4 external (later removed)
Deck guns: 1 3-in./50-cal.
Maximum speed: 17 knots surfaced; 8.75 knots submerged
Cruising range: 11,000 miles surfaced at 10 knots
Submerged endurance: 48 hours at 2 knots
Fuel capacity: 96,025 gallons
Patrol endurance: 75 days
Propulsion: Composite with 2 main propulsion engines, 2 main generator engines, 2 auxiliary generator engines; 4 main motors with 2,660 shaft horsepower; 2 126-cell main storage batteries

Construction

Number of boats: 6 boats ordered in 1936
Builders: Electric Boat (SS-182–184); Portsmouth (SS-185, 186); Mare Island (SS-187)

SARGO CLASS

Specifications

Overall length x maximum breadth: 310 ft. 6 in. x 27 ft. 1 in.
Displacement: 1,460 tons surfaced; 2,350 tons submerged
Operating depth: 250 ft.
Watertight compartments: 7, plus conning tower
Pressure hull plating: approx. 11/16 in. mild steel
Torpedo tubes: 4 bow; 4 stern
Torpedo load, maximum: 20 internal; 4 external (later removed)
Deck guns: 1 3-in./50-cal.
Maximum speed: 20 knots surfaced; 8.75 knots submerged
Cruising range: 11,000 miles surfaced at 10 knots
Submerged endurance: 48 hours at 2 knots
Fuel capacity: 109,000 gallons
Patrol endurance: 75 days
Propulsion: Composite with 2 main propulsion engines; 2 main generator engines; 2 auxiliary generator engines; 4 main motors with 2,740 shaft horsepower; 2 126-cell main storage batteries

Construction

Number of boats: 6 boats ordered in 1937
Builders: Electric Boat (SS-188–190); Portsmouth (SS-191, 192); Mare Island (SS-193)

TAMBOR CLASS

Specifications

Overall length x maximum breadth: 307 ft. 3 in. x 27 ft. 3 in.
Displacement: 1,475 tons surfaced; 2,370 tons submerged
Operating depth: 250 ft.
Watertight compartments: 7, plus conning tower
Pressure hull plating: approx. 11/16 in. mild steel
Torpedo tubes: 6 bow; 4 stern
Torpedo load, maximum: 24
Deck guns: 1 3-in./50-cal.
Maximum speed: 20 knots surfaced; 8.75 knots submerged
Cruising range: 11,000 miles surfaced at 10 knots
Submerged endurance: 48 hours at 2 knots
Fuel capacity: 93,993–96,365 gallons
Patrol endurance: 75 days
Propulsion: Diesel-electric reduction gear with 4 main generator engines; 2 auxiliary generators; 4 main motors with 2,740 shaft horsepower; 2 126-cell main storage batteries

Construction

Number of boats: 12 boats ordered in 1939–1940
Builders: Electric Boat (SS-198–200; 206–208), Portsmouth (SS-201, 202, 209, 210), Mare Island (SS-203, 211)

GATO CLASS

Specifications

Overall length x maximum breadth: 311 ft. 9 in. x 27 ft. 3 in.
Displacement: 2,025–2,060 tons surfaced; 2,424 tons submerged
Operating depth: 300 ft.
Watertight compartments: 8, plus conning tower
Pressure hull plating: approx. 11/16 in. mild steel
Torpedo tubes: 6 bow; 4 stern; max. load = 24
Deck guns: 1 3-in./50-cal.
Maximum speed: 20.25 knots surfaced; 8.75 knots submerged
Cruising range: 11,000 miles surfaced at 10 knots
Submerged endurance: 48 hours at 2 knots
Fuel capacity: 94,400 gallons
Patrol endurance: 75 days
Propulsion: Diesel-electric reduction gear with 4 main generator engines; 1 auxiliary generator; 4 main motors with 5,400 shaft horsepower; 2 126-cell main storage batteries

Construction

Number of boats: 77 boats ordered between 1941 and 1943
Builders: Portsmouth (SS-275–280, 228–235); Manitowoc (SS-265–274, 361–364); Electric Boat (SS-212–227, 240–264); Mare Island (SS-236–239; 281–284)

BALAO CLASS

Specifications

Overall length x maximum breadth: 311 ft. 9 in. x 27 ft. 3 in.
Displacement: 2,010–2,075 tons surfaced; 2,415 tons submerged
Operating depth: 400 ft.

Watertight compartments: 8, plus conning tower
Pressure hull plating: approx. 7/8 in. high tensile steel
Torpedo tubes: 6 bow; 4 stern; max. load = 24
Deck guns: 1 4-in./50-cal. or 1 5-in./25-cal.
Maximum speed: 20.25 knots surfaced; 8.75 knots submerged
Cruising range: 11,000 miles surfaced at 10 knots
Submerged endurance: 48 hours at 2 knots
Fuel capacity: 116,000 gallons
Patrol endurance: 75 days
Propulsion: Diesel-electric reduction gear with 4 main generator engines; 1 auxiliary generator; 4 main motors with 2,740 shaft horsepower; 2 126-cell main storage batteries

Construction

Number of boats: 256 boats ordered between 1942 and 1945; 119 completed
Builders: Portsmouth (SS-285–291, 308–312, 381–410); Manitowoc (SS-361–369); Electric Boat (SS-313–352, 370–378); Mare Island (SS-304–307; 411–416); Cramp (SS-292–295; 297–303)

TENCH CLASS

Specifications

Overall length x maximum breadth: 311 ft. 8 in. x 27 ft. 3 in.
Displacement: 1,980–2,000 tons surfaced; 2,415 tons submerged
Operating depth: 400 ft.
Watertight compartments: 8, plus conning tower
Pressure hull plating: approx. 7/8 in. high tensile steel
Torpedo tubes: 6 bow; 4 stern; max. load = 28
Deck guns: 1 or 2 5-in./25-cal.
Maximum speed: 20.25 knots surfaced; 8.75 knots submerged
Cruising range: 11,000 miles surfaced at 10 knots
Submerged endurance: 48 hours at 2 knots
Fuel capacity: 118,510 gallons
Patrol endurance: 75 days
Propulsion: Diesel-electric direct with 4 main generator engines; 1 auxiliary generator; 2 main motors with 5,400 shaft horsepower; 2 126-cell main storage batteries

Construction

Number of boats: 80 boats ordered between 1943 and 1946; 26 completed
Builders: Portsmouth (SS-417–424, 475–489); Cramp & Sons (SS-425); Electric Boat (SS-435); Boston (SS-522)

Coast Guard

The United States Coast Guard is a separate military service under the Department of Transportation, and is responsible for the enforcement of laws in those coastal waters and high seas subject to the jurisdiction of the United States. However, at the direction of the president, the Coast Guard can become a part of the navy (as it was during both world wars) or it can operate in a specific war zone, to assist navy surface vessels, submarines, and aircraft. In this respect, it has been essential in cooperating with the navy, especially in rescue operations. The Coast Guard operates its fleet under the direction of two primary district commands: Atlantic Command and Pacific Command, which can be coordinated with navy commands and geographically extended in times of conflict or emergencies. During its long history, the Coast Guard has been instrumental in going to the aid of stricken submarines, rescuing survivors, and conducting searches.

The Coast Guard uses the term "vessels" for all watercraft operated by the service. Within that classification, the term "cutter" is used for ships that have a permanently assigned crew, with living quarters and facilities to support such a crew for an extended period of time. Like the submarine service, all Coast Guard vessels are referred to as "boats," regardless of size, class, or capabilities. The Coast Guard insignia, a narrow blue and white stripe next to a wider orange stripe, with the Coast Guard shield superimposed on the latter, is carried on the bows of all vessels.

Cobbler (SS-344)

A submarine of the Balao class, built by the Electric Boat Company and launched in April 1945. She came into service too late for any overseas war operations and began her career in the Caribbean, moving later to more northerly reaches of the East Coast. *Cobbler* was converted to a GUPPY II submarine in 1949 at Electric Boat Company. Her operations in the Caribbean and off the East Coast continued until early January 1958, when she departed Norfolk for a tour of duty in the Mediterranean. Upon her return she continued in familiar waters, and was assigned to the Atlantic Fleet's Antisubmarine Development Force. She was decommissioned in November 1973, and sold to Turkey to serve as *Canakkale* (S-341).

Cobia (SS-245)

A submarine of the Gato class, built by the Electric Boat Company and launched in November 1943. Ordered to join the Pacific Fleet, she put out to sea on her first war patrol in June 1944, bound for the Bonin Islands. In July, she sank three Japanese freighters, and later three small ships in running gun battles. One of them rammed *Cobia*, causing minor damage, but she continued her mission, sinking a converted yacht of 500 tons, one of whose survivors she rescued as her first prisoner of war. After refitting, in September 1944, *Cobia* sailed into the Luzon Straits for her second war patrol, a mission punctuated again and again by attacks by Japanese aircraft. On October 22, she rescued two survivors of a Japanese ship previously sunk by one of *Cobia*'s sisters. She put into Fremantle to refit, and cleared on her third war patrol in late November. Sailing into the South China Sea, she sank a minelayer off the southeast coast of Malaya in mid-January. Next day she rescued two Japanese from a raft on which they had been adrift 40 days. In mid-February 1945, she sailed to the Java Sea for her fourth war patrol. On February 26 she engaged two sea trucks, one of which resisted with machine-gun fire, which killed one of *Cobia*'s crew and damaged her radar equipment. After sinking both sea trucks, she interrupted her patrol for repairs at Fremantle, then returned to the Java Sea, where on April 8 she rescued seven men, the surviving crew of a downed army bomber. In early May, she put out for the Gulf of Siam and her fifth war patrol, and attacked a cargo ship, but was driven deep by depth charges hurled by a minesweeper. Her luck improved when she contacted a tanker convoy, and sank both a tanker and the landing craft *Hakusa*. She refitted once more at Fremantle, then sailed for her sixth and final war patrol. After landing intelligence teams along the coast of Java in late July, she sailed to act as lifeguard during air strikes on Formosa until the end of hostilities, returning to Saipan in late August. After a period in reserve at New London, she was reactivated and served on the East Coast as a training boat during the 1950s and 1960s. In 1959, *Cobia* was assigned as a Naval Reserve dockside trainer in Milwaukee, Wisconsin, a role she performed until July 1970 when she was struck from the Navy list. She was then transferred to the Manitowoc Submarine Memorial Association and towed to Manitowoc, Wisconsin, where she serves as a museum ship. *Cobia* received four battle stars for her services during World War II, during which she sank six Japanese vessels for a total of 16,835 tons.

Cochino (SS-345)

A submarine of the Balao class, built by the Electric Boat Company and launched in April 1945. She was readied for service too late to have a World War II career, like most of the Balao-class boats, and was converted to a GUPPY II submarine at the Electric Boat Company in 1949. That year, *Cochino* made history in an unexpected and undesirable way. In late August 1949, she was on a mission due west of Ireland in company with another submarine, *Tusk*, when they were caught in a storm that made cruising at their snorkel depth almost impossible. On the morning of August 25, an alarm indicated that ventilation was poor and hydrogen gas from the battery wells was rising to a dangerous level. Before corrective action could be taken, there was an explosion and fire and *Cochino* was forced to surface. Within minutes, the fire and gas forced the commander to order all hands forward and topside. Now the

problem was that the submarine was pitching wildly, battered by the storm, while 60 men had to occupy a space on or near the bridge, designed for only seven occupants. One of the men was unconscious, and five were barely able to help themselves because of injuries or grogginess from the gas. A further explosion was heard, and all the officers and men could do was hope that their SOS to the *Tusk* would bring about a quick rescue. In the meantime, 18 men were still below decks, several in the engine room fighting the fire and trying to cut off the flow of hydrogen.

It was more than an hour before the *Tusk* could maneuver into a position near the stricken boat, but even then her crew could do no more than put out a rubber boat with a line. By this time, the men on *Cochino* had managed to run a line across 100 feet of open deck to reach the after torpedo room hatch, from which the men trapped below could escape. In the process of trying to reach *Tusk* in a rubber raft to establish communications, two men were thrown into the raging waters, one of whom later drowned. A new problem arose when *Tusk* was forced almost a mile away by wind and waves. At this point, the commander, hearing further explosions below and with all systems dead, ordered all men below to come topside. Although they managed to do so, several were critically burned and others were injured. By this time—about mid-afternoon—the heroic attempts of the men who had remained below to restore power had partially succeeded, and *Cochino* was maneuverable enough, from the bridge and under auxiliary power, to move forward slowly. Since there was no rudder power, steering had to be done by using the engines and propellers—a dim prospect with the knowledge that the nearest land was 200 miles away!

At this point, *Tusk* came into view again, and this time maneuvered close enough so a plank could be put across as a makeshift bridge and the most seriously burned and injured transferred. Now it was apparent to *Cochino*'s commander and crew that there was no hope of prodding the crippled boat to port. Not only was her maneuverability almost zero, but it was evident that the explosions had opened seams and the boat was flooding, slowly going down at the stern. Just as the last man to dash across the plank to safety—the commander—reached the *Tusk*'s deck, the *Cochino* turned slowly and started to stand on end, with her bow pointed skyward. Now *Tusk* had to back away at emergency speed to avoid getting smashed in the death throes of the other boat. At 10:00 P.M., *Cochino* disappeared on her last patrol with a blast of spray.

Cod (SS-224)

A submarine of the Gato class, built by the Electric Boat Company and launched in June 1943. Assigned to the Pacific, she berthed at Brisbane, Australia, and on her first war patrol in October 1943 she penetrated the South China

Sea, but made only one enemy contact, with no results. On her second war patrol in the same area, she surfaced in mid-February 1944 to sink a sampan by gunfire and torpedo a Japanese merchantman. She sent another to the bottom several days later and then attacked a third target, only to be forced deep by a concentrated depth charge from an escort ship. In April, *Cod* sailed to the Sulu and South China Seas off Luzon for her third war patrol. Tracking a massive Japanese convoy heading for Subic Bay in the Philippines on the night of May 10, 1944, *Cod* maneuvered into firing position just after sunrise. She fired three of her four stern tubes at a Japanese destroyer before unloading all six of her bow tubes at two columns of cargo ships and troop transports. The first torpedo exploded under the destroyer's bridge, the ship started to sag in the middle, with both bow and stern rising, just as the second torpedo hit near the main mast causing the whole rear half of the destroyer to disintegrate. A minute later, all six of the bow shots hit targets among the columns of enemy ships. *Cod* submerged to her 300-foot test depth and ran at top underwater speed for 10 minutes to leave the immediate area, which was quickly saturated with aircraft bombs and depth charges. Between the explosions of enemy depth charges, *Cod's* sonar operators could hear the sounds of several Japanese ships breaking up and the distinct firecracker sound of an ammunition ship's cargo exploding. Within further minutes, a barrage of more than 70 Japanese depth charges shook her, some violently. *Cod* put to sea on her fifth war patrol in mid-September 1944, bound for Philippine waters. She made her first contact, a cargo ship, and sent it to the bottom. Two days later, she inflicted heavy damage on a tanker. Contacting a large convoy in late October, *Cod* launched several attacks without success; however, with all her torpedoes expended, she continued to shadow the convoy to report its position. In November she took up a lifeguard station off Luzon, ready to rescue carrier pilots making the series of air strikes on Japanese bases that paved the way for the invasion of Leyte later that month. After a three-month stateside overhaul, *Cod* sailed for the East China Sea in March 1945, on her sixth war patrol. Assigned primarily to lifeguard duty, she also sank a tug and its tow by gunfire, rescuing three survivors, and in late April launched an attack on a convoy, which resulted in the most severe depth charging of her career. The next day, she sent a minesweeper to the bottom. Shortly afterward, she was threatened by a critical fire in the aft torpedo room, but was saved by the heroism and skill of her men who brought the fire under control and manually fired a torpedo already in its tube before the fire could explode it. One man was lost overboard during the emergency.

After refitting at Guam in June 1945, *Cod* put out for the Gulf of Siam and the coast of Indochina on her seventh and final war patrol where she would carve a niche for herself, not by destroying enemy ships, but by performing a unique international submarine-to-submarine rescue. On the morning of July 8, 1945, *Cod* arrived at Ladd Reef in the South China Sea to aid the Dutch submarine *0–19*, which had grounded on the coral outcropping. Dismayed by two days of pulling, the captains of both vessels agreed there was no hope of freeing the Dutch sub from the grip of the reef. So, after removing the 56 Dutch sailors, *Cod* destroyed the *0–19* with two scuttling charges, two torpedoes, and 16 rounds from her three-inch deck gun. The *Cod* became home to 153 men for the two-and-a-half-day run to the recently liberated Subic Bay naval base.

Cod's next mission was to patrol an area off the coast of Vietnam, where she resumed boarding and sinking junks carrying enemy supplies. During one of these pirate operations, a five-man boarding party was stranded on a junk after *Cod* was strafed by a Japanese plane and forced to crash dive. It was several hours before *Cod* could surface to retrieve her boarding party. When she did, the horizon was littered with junks. After a two-day search involving several American submarines, the lost crewmen were recovered by the *Blenny*. (Highlights of the patrol, including the *0–19* rescue and return of the lost boarding party, were recorded in color movies made by Norman Jensen, a navy photographer who was assigned to film *Cod's* war patrol. The films were discovered in the National Archives in 1992.)

After the war, *Cod* returned to New London, where she was placed in reserve, then reactivated in 1951 to participate in NATO antisubmarine training exercises. Her cold war voyages took her to Newfoundland, as well as ports in Cuba and South America. During the 1950s and 1960s, she served as a Naval Reserve training vessel in Cleveland. In 1971, no longer useful as a training ship, *Cod* was stricken from the register of navy ships. Five years later, however, she began a new career as a floating memorial, and in May 1976 was opened for public tours and 10 years later designated a National Historic Landmark. *Cod* is credited with sinking eight enemy vessels totaling 26,985 tons, and damaging another 36,000 tons of enemy shipping. All seven of her war patrols were considered successful and she was awarded seven battle stars.

Columbia (SSN-771)

This submarine of the Los Angeles class, built by the Electric Boat Division of General Dynamics, was launched in September 1944, with a displacement of 6,900 tons (submerged), an armament of four torpedo tubes amidships, aft of the bow, and 12 vertical launching tubes (VTL) for *Tomahawk* cruise missiles, and an underwater speed of up to 30 knots. She carries a crew of 12 officers and 115 enlisted men. *Columbia* is a vital key in the navy's "Forward . . . from the Sea" doctrine, bringing to bear shallow-water operational capabilities, including mine warfare, coastal surveillance and intelligence gathering, and operations with special task forces. Her ability to strike targets at, below, or beyond the water's surface, strongly increases her capabilities for both peacetime and wartime operations. She is also designed with a stronger-than-usual sail and retractable bow planes for surfacing through the ice during polar missions.

See LOS ANGELES.

Columbus (SSN-762)

This submarine of the Los Angeles class was built by the Electric Boat Division of General Dynamics and launched in August 1992. For specifications and boats in this class, see LOS ANGELES.

Conger (SS-477)

A submarine of the Tench class, built by the Portsmouth Naval Shipyard and launched in October 1944. She tested new submarine equipment at New London until she departed July 21, 1945, for Pacific service. At sea between Balboa and Pearl Harbor upon the end of hostilities, she was ordered back to the Panama Canal Zone, and in early September arrived at Key West to provide services to the Fleet Sonar School until December, after which she sailed to her assigned home port at Cristobal, Canal Zone. She operated in the Caribbean until August 1947, when she sailed for a complete circuit of the South American continent on special hydrographic work, passing through the Straits of Magellan. She returned to Caribbean operations until June 1949 when her home port became Norfolk, Virginia, and she operated along the East Coast and in the Caribbean, assisting in the training of surface ships, taking part in fleet exercises, and perfecting her own readiness for action. She was again transferred in 1952, arriving at New London, her new home port, December 12. From that time through 1960, she continued her East Coast operations and frequently put to sea with Submarine School students on board. *Conger* was decommissioned in July 1963.

Congressional Medal of Honor

Between 1943 and 1945, seven submarine officers earned America's highest military honor. They are the following.

Captain John Cromwell was a senior officer aboard the *Sculpin* in November 1943, sent to attack Japanese shipping off the island of Truk, one of the enemy's largest naval bases during World War II. During an engagement with a Japanese destroyer, *Sculpin* was forced to the surface because of damage to her depth gauge. When the destroyer's deck guns pounded the submarine viciously enough for the officer on deck to order "Abandon ship!" Cromwell elected to go down with the submarine rather than be captured. As the commander, he knew that the

Japanese would torture him into finally giving up vital information—which he alone knew—about the location of U.S. submarines in this area of the Pacific. He was awarded the medal posthumously.

Commander Sam Dealey was a legend in the submarine navy. He was killed in August 1944, while commanding the sixth war patrol of USS *Harder*. In the 14 months between June 23, 1943, and August 22, 1944, the submarine better known as "Hit 'em Again *Harder*!" sank a total of 16 Japanese ships for a total of more than 50,000 tons. The feat was all the more remarkable because three of the victims were destroyers—the most deadly enemies against submarines—sunk because of Dealey's daring tactic of luring the enemy by exposing his periscope, then charging them down the throat, bow to bow, and unleashing a spread of three torpedoes. It is not known exactly where and how the *Harder* was lost, with all hands, that fateful August—possibly attacking another destroyer head on.

Commander Eugene Fluckey, skipper of the USS *Barb*, stalked two potential targets right into the Japanese harbor of Namkwan during the early morning hours of one memorable day in January 1945. Since the water was very shallow, he had to run on the surface as he entered the harbor where he found some 30 Japanese ships anchored in three columns. He fired 10 torpedoes at the clustered ships and then swung around to beat it out to deeper water at flank speed. It was a tense and potentially perilous hour and 20 minutes between the firing of the first torpedo and the *Barb's* reaching water deep enough in which to dive and hide. The Japanese never revealed the number of ships sunk, but observers on the *Barb* reported seeing every one of the 10 fish score a hit. This exploit, which became popularly referred to as "the Namkwan smashup," earned Fluckey the medal and his crew a presidential citation.

Commander Howard Gilmore, taking his submarine, the USS *Growler*, on her fourth war patrol in January 1943, located a convoy of Japanese ships under conditions of poor visibility. Before he knew it, a gunboat protecting the convoy turned and collided with *Growler* head on, at the same time raking her bridge with machine-gun fire. Gilmore, badly wounded, ordered every one topside to get below. Then, knowing he could not get below in time if his ship were to be saved, he gave his final order, "Take her down!" The *Growler* survived, but when she surfaced again half an hour later, with the hope of finding Gilmore afloat in the sea, there was no sign of life, or of the gunboat or any of the other enemy ships. For his supreme sacrifice, Gilmore received his medal posthumously.

Commander Richard O'Kane, skipper of the USS *Tang*, faced instant disaster at the end of October 1944, when a torpedo he had just fired in battle went wild, circled back, and exploded against its own submarine. Ironically, at the time, *Tang* led all other submarines in the number of ships sunk and had only a few days earlier hit seven ships in one convoy, and later had torpedoed a tanker and a troop transport and damaged a destroyer that was trying to protect the convoy. It was at the moment when O'Kane brought *Tang* to the surface to finish off the crippled troopship that the errant torpedo made its hairpin turn. Emergency efforts proved futile, the torpedo struck *Tang* in the stern, pitched those on deck into the sea, and sent its own submarine to the bottom in 180 feet of water. Unfortunately, O'Kane and a handful of survivors were pulled from the water by a Japanese destroyer escort, which was also rescuing survivors from ships that *Tang* had just sunk. The Japanese, angered by the loss of so many of their own troops, vented their fury by clubbing O'Kane and his eight surviving crewmen senseless before dragging them off to a prison camp where they were further tortured. Only O'Kane and a handful of his men survived the brutalities.

Commander Lawson "Red" Ramage, skipper of the *Parche,* earned his medal for one brilliant attack on July 23, 1944, when he spotted a large convoy of Japanese ships in the middle of the night and managed to maneuver his submarine into the very center of the supposedly well-protected fleet. Then, in a daring move, he surfaced *Parche* and let loose with bow and stern torpedoes every time a likely target loomed in his path. So much confusion reigned among the Japanese ships that some of the escorts, unable to spot the submarine in the darkness, began shooting their own ships. The "pigeon shoot" lasted about three-quarters of an hour, during which time *Parche* sank four ships and damaged at least one other. Ramage and his boat dove deep and slipped away without a scratch.

Commander George Street, taking command of a brand new submarine, *Tirante,* in the fall of 1944, set a record for enemy sinkings over a period of less than two months. He departed Pearl Harbor on his first war patrol on March 3 and returned April 25, after attacking 12 enemy ships and sinking half of them, as well as damaging others. But it was on April 14 that he earned recognition, steaming into a Japanese harbor and unleashing every torpedo left aboard at the enemy vessels moored there. On the way home, Street sank one more ship and picked up two downed Japanese aviators as prisoners of war.

In addition to these seven submariners, the Congressional Medal of Honor went to another submariner of another era, the only enlisted submariner to be so honored: Henry Breault, TM2. Breault and another mate, TM Brown, were in the torpedo room of the USS *0–5* (SS-6) in the Canal Zone when, on the morning of October 25, 1923, the submarine collided with the SS *Abangarez.* The *0–5* sank in less than a minute, but in that minute, Breault exhibited a supreme act of heroism. When he felt the boat starting to sink, Breault headed for the open torpedo room hatch and had just reached it when the water started to cascade in. Realizing that he could escape, but that Brown would be trapped in the flooded room, Breault pulled the hatch shut, thus blocking the water and headed back down to ensure the watertight door was shut. He did so with the realization that now both of them were trapped in the sinking boat, but in so doing he gave his shipmate the only chance to live. Fortunately, they were both rescued two days later when the bow was lifted clear of the water.

One other submariner also received the Congressional Medal of Honor, though not for a feat in a submarine. He was Ensign Paul F. Foster, who while serving aboard the USS *Utah,* was sent ashore to lead a detachment in a battle in Veracruz, Mexico. He was awarded the medal for distinguished service on April 21 and 22, 1914. "Fighting at the head of his company," said the commendation, "Ensign Foster was eminent and conspicuous in his conduct, leading his men with skill and courage." Later, Foster was transferred to the submarine service and given command of *AL-2* (SS-41). During World War I, while engaged off Bantry Bay, Ireland, he was credited with sinking a German submarine, *UB-65,* one of only three sunk in that war by the U.S. Navy. For this feat, he was awarded the Distinguished Service Medal for "exceptionally meritorious service." He was subsequently also awarded the Navy Cross for heroism exhibited during the October 1925 six-inch gun turret explosion and fire aboard the USS *Trenton* (CL-11).

Connecticut (SSN-22)

The second submarine of the Seawolf class, built by the Electric Boat Company and launched in September 1997, she has been described as "the most capable attack submarine ever built. With mission and growth capability far beyond previous submarines, the robust design uniquely supports missions such as surveillance, intelligence collection, special warfare, covert cruise missile strike, mine warfare, anti-submarine and anti-surface ship warfare." In addition to its formidable open ocean presence, the Seawolf class is also a highly capable shallow water warfare platform, setting the standard for submarine technology into the next century. Its inherent stealth, coupled with state-of-the-art sensors and advanced combat systems, makes it one of the world's most advanced weapons systems and a benchmark for undersea excellence. *Connecticut's* flexibility and impressive capabilities provide the navy with an undersea weapons platform to operate in any scenario against any threat, whether under arctic ice, in the deepest oceans, or even in shallow water. Armed with *Tomahawk* cruise missiles, she can safely conduct strike missions deep into enemy waters while submerged far off an enemy's coast. She also carries the Mark 48 advanced capability (ADCAP) torpedo, the most reliable torpedo in the world for use against surface ships and submarines. *Connecticut* has twice as many torpedo tubes as a Los Angeles-class submarine, and 30 percent greater weapons capacity.

continental shelf

Around each continent is an area, of varying distance from shore, that lies in water of relatively shallow depth. It is called the continental shelf. In some of these areas, river channels can be traced well out to sea. Submarine navigators use these submerged channels, which have been charted, as aids in navigation. The ocean currents of the world have also been charted, particularly in relation to the shelves and valleys of the oceans. Today, while the ocean floor is being charted in greater detail and at greater depths than ever before, it is also being studied as a means of determining where submarines of the future can venture during their operations and, in time of war, seek evasive action when attacked. Emphasis is also on plans for meeting the requirements of antisubmarine defenses. Electronic depth-finding instruments have produced much data for charts of the ocean floor.

Current methods of ocean navigation and communication involve very-low-frequency radiation, or hydronic radiation, the name given to electromagnetic waves having frequencies of 14 to 30 kilohertz, which travel through water much as radio waves travel through the atmosphere. These waves and methods of transmitting and receiving are especially useful in land-based communication with submarines. When transmitted from appropriate antennas, very-low-frequency waves have directional properties that are essential in underwater navigation.

Coral Sea, Battle of (May 7–8, 1942)

One of the key battles in the Pacific between Japanese and American naval forces during WORLD WAR II, in which Japan's drive south was forever halted. The battle was occasioned by a Japanese offensive designed to capture three targets in the Coral Sea: the Australian base at Port Moresby, New Guinea; the Louisiade Islands; and the port of Tulagi, Solomon Islands. A successful operation would have allowed the Japanese to launch air attacks on Australia and isolate it from its allies. The Japanese fleet included heavy cruisers, submarines, destroyers, and an invasion flotilla. In addition, there was a carrier strike group, which consisted of three aircraft carriers and 125 aircraft, to cover the entire operation. American intelligence soon learned of the Japanese plans, and an Allied task force was quickly assembled. It consisted of Task Force 11, Task Force 17, and Task Force 44, and included the carriers *Yorktown* and *Lexington* and a group of cruisers and submarines. On May 2, the Japanese landed on Tulagi, at which time American forces caused some damage to the Japanese and then regrouped to oppose the second Japanese invasion force, which was heading for Port Moresby. On May 7 American carrier planes located this force and sank the Japanese light carrier *Shoho,* causing the Japanese, with minimal air protection, to return to Rabaul. It was not until May 8 that the opposing carrier forces established their respective positions. The battle that followed—the first naval engagement in which the opposing warships remained out of sight—was conducted exclusively by carrier aircraft. In two attacks the Americans lost 33 aircraft but seriously damaged the Japanese carrier *Shokaku.* The Americans suffered heavier losses during a counterattack by 70 Japanese planes in which the carrier *Lexington* was lost and the *Yorktown* was damaged. Despite these losses, the battle of the Coral Sea represented a strategic victory for the U.S. Navy. The Port Moresby invasion force had to withdraw and Australia remained beyond the reach of Japanese bombers. The damage to Japanese ships and the heavy loss of naval aircraft weakened their position at the decisive battle of MIDWAY, which occurred a month later.

Corporal (SS-346)

This submarine of the Balao class was built by the Electric Boat Company and launched in June 1945, too late for active service during World War II. She was armed with a five-inch deck gun, six 21-inch torpedo tubes forward and four aft, and carried a complement of six officers and 60 enlisted men. *Corporal* was decommissioned in November 1973 and sold to Turkey, where she served as *Ikinci Inonu* until 1996.

Corsair (SS-435)

This submarine of the Tench class was launched in May 1946, and commissioned the following November for service initially as a training boat. In July 1949, she sailed with the rest of her group (SubDevGrp2) for exercises near northern Ireland, Portsmouth, England, and in polar waters. It was during this cruise that one of her group, USS *Cochino,* was tragically lost on August 24 from a battery explosion. *Corsair's* career thereafter was largely along the East Coast and in the Caribbean, participating in training and operational exercises until February 1963, when she was decommissioned and struck from the Navy list.

Corvina (SS-226)

A submarine of the Gato class, built by the Electric Boat Company and launched in May 1943. Venturing into enemy waters during World War II for her first time, she departed from Pearl Harbor in early November 1943. After topping off with fuel at Johnston Island, she proceeded to an area south of Truk, to attack enemy naval forces during the invasion of the Japanese-held Gilbert Islands. She was ordered to patrol as close to Truk as enemy antisubmarine measures would permit. In mid-December, she was to pass to the command of Task Force 72 and proceed to an eastern Australia port for refit and duty in the southwestern Pacific. When the major surface force operations in the Gilberts were finished, messages were sent to *Corvina* to comply with these orders and acknowledge them. The message was repeated three times on each of two successive nights, on December 2 and 3, but no acknowledgment was ever received. Because of the difficulty being experienced as a result of Japanese interference, *Corvina* was considered to have passed to Task Force 72, despite her failure to acknowledge. Thus, she was directed to proceed to Tulagi and rendezvous with a surface escort, but she did not appear. Again, transmissions directing answers were repeatedly sent, but were not fruitful. Since she had not appeared or been heard from since her departure from Johnston Island in November, *Corvina* was presumed lost. Japanese war records later indicated that she met her doom on November 16, 1943, when a Japanese submarine reported having sighted a surfaced American submarine in the vicinity where *Corvina* would have been on that day, and torpedoed her. Three torpedoes were fired and two were reported to have hit, causing a "great explosion sound."

Crevalle (SS-291)

A submarine of the Balao class, built by Portsmouth Naval Shipyard and launched in February 1943. Ordered on her first war patrol in late October 1943, to the South China Sea, she sank a passenger-cargo ship of almost 7,000 tons, and made two more attacks on merchant ships before returning to Fremantle, Australia, for refitting. Her second war patrol, in the South China Sea in January and February 1944, found her attacking a submerged Japanese submarine, only to know the frustration of premature torpedo explosion. In a hazardous special mission, she laid mines off Saigon in mid-January, and 10 days later sent a Japanese freighter to the bottom. In early April she again sailed for the South China Sea, where she sank a freighter and an oiler, and in mid-May surfaced off Negros Island in the Philippines on another daring special mission. She rescued 40 refugees here, including 28 women and children, and four men who had survived the Bataan Death March and made their escape. She also took off the family of an American missionary who then returned ashore to continue his ministry among the guerrillas. For her fourth war patrol, *Crevalle* returned to the South China Sea, as well as cruising off the northern Philippines, between mid-June and early August 1944. In company with three other submarines, she joined in an attack on a convoy, sinking one freighter, and polishing off another already crippled by one of her group. Two days later, she also inflicted heavy damage on another freighter.

Ten days out on her fifth war patrol in September 1944, after surfacing, the boat suddenly took a sharp down angle and submerged with the upper and lower conning tower hatches open, washing the officer of the deck and a lookout overboard. The flow of water through the upper hatch prevented anyone from closing it, until at a depth of 150 feet the hatch suddenly locked shut. The boat continued diving to 190 feet at an angle that reached 42 degrees down. With communications out, an alert motor machinist mate, Robert Yeager, saved the submarine by taking the initiative, and ordering "All backfull!" without orders. The pump room, control room, and conning tower flooded, and all electrical equipment was inoperative. When the boat was finally brought under control and had attained enough ballast to rise to the surface, the crew was able to open the hatch again and rescue the nearly drowned lookout from the water. Tragically, however, the officer of the deck, Lieutenant Howard T. Blind, was never located. It was determined that he had lost his life in a final act of sacrifice—closing the hatch cover to save the crew, but remaining on the surface as the submarine went down. In all probability, he had been sucked underwater and drowned before he could be rescued. *Crevalle* made her way back to Fremantle and was ordered to proceed to an overhaul at Mare Island Naval Shipyard.

Crevalle put to sea on her sixth war patrol from Pearl Harbor in mid-March 1945. Cruising in the East China Sea, she took up a lifeguard station during air strikes preparing for the Okinawa invasion, then made a hazardous three-day search for a minefield believed to be located near the southern entrance to the Tsushima Straits. After refitting, she sailed from Guam in late May for her seventh war patrol in the northeast section of the Sea of Japan. She sank a freighter a day on June 9, 10, and 11, and on June 22 inflicted heavy damage on an escort ship. The war ended before she could go on another patrol, and she was ordered back to Pearl Harbor and then, in March 1946, to New London, her new home port, where she was assigned to East Coast and Caribbean operations through 1960. All of *Crevalle's* war patrols, save the interrupted fifth, were designated successful, and the first four won her the Navy Unit Commendation for distinguished performance of duty as well as four battle stars. She had a wartime tally of nine vessels and 51,814 tons.

Croaker (SS-246)

A submarine of the Gato class, built by the Electric Boat Company and launched in December 1943. She put to sea on her first war patrol in July 1944, sailing to the East China and Yellow Seas. In a series of brilliantly successful attacks, which won her the Navy Unit Commendation, she sank a light cruiser and two freighters. During this patrol, she also served as lifeguard during air strikes on the Bonins. She then refitted at Midway, and in late September sailed in a wolf pack for the same area on her second war patrol. Again successful, she sank three freighters and damaged another with her last torpedo. Tubes empty, she returned to Midway to fuel, and pushed on to Pearl Harbor for refitting. *Croaker's* third war patrol, in the Luzon Straits and South China Sea in late 1944 and early 1945, found her making no contact with enemy shipping, but providing essential lifeguard service during strikes on Luzon preparatory to the invasion landings in Lingayen Gulf. Further patrols were unproductive and, at war's end, she was assigned peacetime missions out of New London until March 1953, when she was ordered to Portsmouth Naval Shipyard for conversion to a hunter-killer submarine (SSK). She then resumed local operations out of New London, with occasional cruises to distant ports until her retirement in 1971 and current service as a museum ship at Buffalo, New York. Along with the Navy Unit Commendation, *Croaker* received three battle stars for World War II, during which she sank six enemy vessels, for a total of 19,710 tons.

Cubera (SS-347)

A submarine of the Balao class, built by the Electric Boat Company and launched in July 1945. She received a GUPPY II conversion in 1948, becoming one of the first boats with greater underwater propulsive power. After her conversion, she was based in Key West, Florida, where she participated in training of both submarine and antisubmarine personnel, and was later assigned to Submarine Squadron Six in Norfolk, Virginia, operating in the Atlantic Ocean and Caribbean Sea. In May 1958 she became one of the original members of the new Task Group Alfa, the navy's famous first antisubmarine task group, part of a development effort to build knowledge, tactics, and strength in antisubmarine warfare. She made a Mediterranean deployment from October 1960 through March 1961, followed by numerous antisubmarine exercises and training periods in the western Atlantic. *Cubera* was one of the radar/sonar-picket boats assigned to patrol Cuba while Russia and Cuba tested the United States by sneaking in missiles. She was decommissioned in January 1972, sold to Venezuela, and ultimately scrapped.

Cusk (SS-348)

This submarine of the Balao class was built by the Electric Boat Company and launched in July 1945, and not commissioned until after World War II. However, she had a significant peacetime career. As a pioneer in the missile field, she was designated SSG-348 in January 1948, and became the first submarine to launch a guided missile from her deck—a forerunner of things to come. *Cusk* was later assigned to Pearl Harbor as her home port and from there continued her missile experiments for many years, until she was decommissioned in September 1969.

Cutthroat (LSV-2)

This boat, the navy's largest autonomous submarine, is described as the "next generation submarine stealth technologies test," and was constructed at the navy's Acoustic Research Facility in Bayview, Idaho. She is named for the West Slope cutthroat trout that lives in lakes and streams of northern Idaho and western Montana. The 111-foot-long unmanned vessel is a quarter-scale version of the navy's New Attack Submarine (NSSN) and is used as a demonstrator for the advanced technologies anticipated for submarines of the future. She applies advanced electric drive technologies to field the latest in permanent magnet propulsion motor and motor drive systems. High data rate sensor recording permits improved hydrodynamic experimentation. Advancements in control surface actuation and ballast tank solid port closure systems are also demonstrated. The autopilot and guidance and navigation control systems are the most sophisticated of their kind.

Cutlass (SS-478)

A submarine of the Tench class, built by the Portsmouth Naval Shipyard and launched in October 1944. Ordered from Kittery, Maine, to Pearl Harbor, she left on her maiden war patrol in mid-July, assigned to patrol in the area of the Kurile Islands. However, by the time she reached her destination, Japan had surrendered, and she was ordered to the Canal Zone and peacetime operations in the Caribbean, with occasional cruises to South American ports. *Cutlass* was converted to a GUPPY II submarine at Philadelphia Naval Shipyard in 1948. She was later assigned in succession to Key West, Florida, and Norfolk, Virginia, at which time she made cruises to the Mediterranean, visiting France, Greece, Turkey, North Africa, Gibraltar, Malta, and Spain: then sailed in Cuban waters to act as a target for destroyers and aircraft engaged in antisubmarine exercises. She joined in local operations, fleet exercises, and antisubmarine warfare training in the Caribbean until September 1956 when she departed for the Mediterranean and operations with NATO forces including the Sixth Fleet. She visited Italy, Greece, Crete, Majorca, Portugal, and England, returning to Norfolk in December. In 1958 she sailed on a north European cruise, visiting Rosyth, Scotland; Copenhagen and Korsor, Denmark; and passing through the Kiel Canal. She was decommissioned in December 1971 and sold to Taiwan for service in its navy as *Hai Shih* (791).

Cuttlefish (SS-11) (B-2)

The first to bear the name, *Cuttlefish* was built by the Fore River Shipbuilding Company and launched in September 1906. A tiny boat of only 173 tons (submerged), she had a complement of one officer and nine enlisted men and was armed with two torpedo tubes, forward. She reported to

Commissioned October 1907, the USS *Cuttlefish/B-2* (SS-11) remained on duty until December 1919 when she was used as a target and sunk near Corregidor. *(United States Navy)*

Submarine Flotilla 2, Atlantic Fleet, and operated along the Atlantic coast, running experiments, testing machinery and equipment, and conducting extensive training exercises. Reassigned, she served with the Atlantic Torpedo Fleet until joining the Reserve Torpedo Group at Charleston Navy Yard in May 1911. In December 1912, she was towed to Norfolk and placed on board a cargo ship for transfer to the Asiatic Station at Cavite, Philippine Islands. She remained on duty in the Philippines until decommissioned at Cavite in December 1919.

Cuttlefish [ex-V-91] (C-2) (SS-171)

A submarine of the Cachalot class, built by the Electric Boat Company and launched in November 1933. Assigned to San Diego, she sailed on torpedo practice and fleet tactics along the West Coast, as well as in the Hawaiian Islands, until June 1937, when she sailed for the Panama Canal, Miami, New York, and New London. She conducted experimental torpedo firing, sound training, and other operations for the Submarine School. She was later assigned to the Canal Zone and Hawaii, where, in 1939, she was based at Pearl Harbor on patrol duty, and also joined in battle problems and exercises in the Hawaiian area. With the outbreak of World War II, she put to sea on her first war patrol in late January 1942. On February 13 she performed a reconnaissance of Marcus Island, gaining valuable

information, and after patrolling in the Bonins, returned to Pearl Harbor and Midway, which she cleared in May on her second war patrol. She reconnoitered Saipan and the northern islands of the Marianas group, and attacked a patrol ship, and while maneuvering for a second attack, was detected. She was forced deep to endure four hours of severe depth charging, more of which came her way on May 24 when she challenged three enemy destroyers. The next day an alert enemy plane caught her on the surface and dropped two bombs as she went under, both of them misses. As it became obvious that the Japanese Fleet was out in strength, *Cuttlefish* was ordered to patrol west of Midway, remaining on station during the battle of Midway during the first week of June 1942. She returned to Pearl Harbor, and there and at Midway prepared for her third war patrol. Patrolling off the Japanese homeland, she attacked a destroyer in mid-August and received a punishing depth charge attack. Three days later she launched a spread of torpedoes, three of which hit a freighter and one of which hit an escort. Explosions were seen, but the sinking could not be confirmed. In early September she attacked a tanker, which, it is believed, she sunk. Too old for further war patrols, she was ordered to New London, where she served the Submarine School as a training ship from December 1942 until war's end. She was decommissioned in October 1945. *Cuttlefish* received one battle star for her third patrol and one for her service during the battle of Midway.

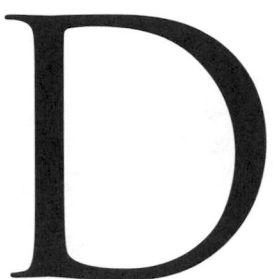

D

D-3 [ex-*Salmon*] (SS-19)

An early submarine built by the Fore River Shipbuilding Company and launched in March 1910. With a complement of one officer and 14 enlisted men, she joined the Atlantic Torpedo Fleet, based at Newport, Rhode Island. This pioneer submarine operated very actively in diving grounds in Cape Cod and Narragansett Bays, in Long Island and Block Island Sounds, in Chesapeake Bay, and off Norfolk, Virginia; on target ranges proving torpedoes; doing experimental operations; and conducting cruises along the East Coast of the United States. In April 1913, *D-3* cruised to the Caribbean and remained to serve with the forces operating in Mexican waters following the occupation of Vera Cruz. Later, she served as flagship of SubDiv2. She trained aspiring submariners at Newport and New London until being decommissioned in March 1922.

Dace (SS-247)

A submarine of the Gato class, with an impressive World War II record, *Dace* sailed on her first patrol in late October 1963 and on her very first contact with the enemy, severely damaged a freighter with torpedo hits. She made contacts and scored hits on another tanker during her second patrol, but without being able to confirm the results. On her third patrol, in March 1944, she made no attacks on the enemy, but landed commando parties and later made a rendezvous at sea with the badly damaged submarine, *Scamp,* and escorted her into Manus. On her fourth war patrol, between mid-June and mid-August 1944, she scored at least three hits on a large transport whose two escorts dropped a total of 43 depth charges, shaking the submarine up badly but causing little damage. A daring reconnaissance mission took her into Sarangani Bay in mid-July, and 10 days later, she began an epic chase. She pursued a smoke contact visible on the horizon for a full day, eight times being forced down to avoid detection by patrolling aircraft. That night after dark, she reestablished contact, and just after midnight on July 27 launched her attack, firing 10 torpedoes into a convoy of three merchantmen guarded by six escorts. She sent a tanker to the bottom, then was forced deep as one of the escorts tried to ram her and began its depth charge attack. Three days later, she sank a small freighter, and the next day received another severe depth charging after an attack on a well escorted freighter, at which time she had expended her last torpedo.

Dace cleared Brisbane September 1, 1944, on her fifth and most successful war patrol. In mid-October, she attacked a convoy of seven ships, sinking two and heavily damaging a third. She now joined *Darter* in a feat of skill and courage that brought both submarines the Navy Unit Commendation. On October 23 they contacted the Japanese Center Force approaching Palawan Passage for the attack on the Leyte landings, which developed into the decisive battle for Leyte Gulf. Since the location of this enemy force had been a mystery, the contact report flashed back by *Dace* and *Darter* was one of the most significant of the war. The two boats closed with the task force, and *Darter* attacked first, sinking the flagship, the cruiser *Atago.* Now *Dace* sent her torpedoes away, although heavy depth charges by the destroyers were beginning. She sank the heavy cruiser *Maga,* then went deep to avoid the counterattack. Continuing to track their target, hoping for a chance to finish off the cruiser *Takao* previously damaged

Grayling/D-2 (SS-18), *Narwhal/D-1* (SS-17), and *Salmon/D-3* (SS-19) three at right in photo, joined the fleet in 1909 as a class of three, which, at nearly 135 feet long, were the largest submarines at the time. *(United States Navy)*

by *Darter*, the two submarines worked through treacherous Palawan Passage. When *Darter* went aground, *Dace* took the entire crew off to safety, then fired torpedoes to destroy the stranded submarine. But before she could complete the job, she had to dive deep to avoid a patrolling Japanese aircraft, which obligingly bombed the abandoned *Darter*.

Dace left Fremantle, Australia, in early December 1944, on her sixth war patrol. With a mission to mine the Singapore/Hong Kong shipping lane and the channel between Palau Gambir and the mainland. Finishing her task two weeks later, she heard loud explosions from the mined area, an indication of a job well done. Three days later, while preparing to attack an eight-ship convoy, *Dace* was violently shaken by four depth charges. She went deep, hitting bottom, and while waiting for the escorts to break off their attack was bumped and scraped along the bottom by strong currents. Somehow the enemy did not detect all this noise, and she was able to surface later, repair minor damage, and sail on to patrol farther north. In late December she sank a

naval auxiliary and damaged a freighter in the same convoy. Her seventh war patrol racked up even more tonnage: two sailing ships, a large freighter, and an escort vessel. The war ended as she was preparing for her eighth war patrol, which marked the end of her active service, with a wartime record of six enemy vessels sunk for a total of 28,689 tons, and in February 1947 she was placed out of commission.

Dallas (SSN-700)

This submarine of the Los Angeles class was launched in April 1979, at the Electric Boat Division of General Dynamics, listed as having a displacement of 6,900 tons (submerged), armament consisting of four 21-inch torpedo tubes, amidships, aft of the bow, and a crew of 12 officers and 115 enlisted men. Dallas, with the capability of running at more than 30 knots submerged, has proven to be one of the top deterrent submarines.

See LOS ANGELES.

Daniel Boone (SSBN-629)

This submarine of the Lafayette class was launched in July 1963, at the Mare Island Shipyard and was listed as having a displacement of 8,251 tons (submerged), a fire power of four 21-inch torpedo tubes forward and 16 missile tubes, and a crew of 14 officers and 126 enlisted men. She served in the world's oceans as a deterrent force for three decades and was decommissioned and struck from the Navy list in February 1994.

See LAFAYETTE.

Daniel Webster (SSBN-626)

This submarine of the Lafayette class was launched from the Electric Boat Division of General Dynamics in April 1963, and served for three decades as a deterrent in the world's oceans. A boat of 8,251 tons displacement (submerged), and with 16 missile tubes and four 21-inch torpedo tubes forward, she had a complement of 14 officers and 126 enlisted men. She was decommissioned in February 1993, and converted to a dockside trainer.

Darter (SS-227)

A submarine of the Gato class, she was built by the Electric Boat Company and launched in June 1943. In October 1944, on her fourth war patrol, she sailed to the South China Sea with the *Dace* as a coordinated attack team, at which time she sank 9,900 tons of enemy shipping and damaged 19,900 tons. On the 24th of the month, both submarines contacted and tracked a large enemy force heading north through Palawan Passage en route to the battles for Leyte Gulf. They attacked while the enemy forces were unable to alter course appreciably, and in brilliant pre-dawn submerged attacks, sank two heavy cruisers and so severely damaged a third that she was useless for the rest of the war. While trying to finish off the stricken cruiser, *Darter* grounded on Bombay Shoal while cruising at 17 knots. Efforts to get off the reef were unsuccessful and a message was sent to *Dace* requesting assistance. After confidential gear had been smashed and classified matter burned, the men of *Darter* were transferred to *Dace*. When *Darter*'s demolition charges failed to explode, *Dace* used her remaining torpedoes in trying to destroy her without success, the torpedoes hitting the reef and exploding before they could reach their target. Two more submarines were called for assistance, *Rock,* which fired 10 torpedoes at *Darter,* with similar lack of success, and *Nautilus*, on her 13th patrol, which scored 55 six-inch-gun hits, effectively eliminating any possible use the Japanese would have for the lost boat. *Darter*'s final score during four patrols was 19,429 tons of enemy shipping sent to the bottom, and 30,000 tons damaged.

Darter (SS-576) represented the early postwar fleet of non-nuclear submarines, built by the Electric Boat Division of General Dynamics, with her keel laid in 1954. She carried a complement of eight officers and 75 enlisted men, and was armed with six 21-inch torpedo tubes forward and two aft. *(United States Navy)*

Darter (SS-576)

Launched in May 1956, *Darter* bore the same name as an earlier WORLD WAR II submarine with an enviable record in the Pacific and was among the last of the conventional submarines built by the Electric Boat Division of General Dynamics. She was a diesel-electric attack submarine, designed for a crew of eight officers and 75 enlisted men, and was armed with six 21-inch torpedo tubes forward and two aft. After long service with the fleet, she was decommissioned in December 1989.

dead reckoning

There are four methods of navigation at sea: piloting, dead reckoning, electronic navigation, and celestial navigation. In dead reckoning, the navigator estimates a ship's position by keeping a careful record of its movement. The initial point of departure for dead reckoning is usually the last fix the navigator obtains from objects on land at the start of a voyage. From this point, true courses steered and distances traveled (as recorded by log) are plotted on a chart. Points along the dead reckoning line, representing successive positions of the ship, are labeled with the appropriate time and the notation *DR*. Dead reckoning commonly begins anew each time bearings, celestial observations, or electronic aids provide an accurate fix. The dead reckoning line on a navigator's chart is important because it indicates at a glance the theoretical position of the ship, the track the ship should have followed, and the direction in which the ship is traveling.

Modern electronic devices are important aids in finding position at sea; for example, the navigator whose ship is equipped with a radio direction finder can determine the bearings of radio transmitting stations on shore. Special radio beacons for navigation are established at lighthouses, lightships, and prominent points along coasts. Radio bearings may be plotted on a chart to obtain a fix.

A variety of other electronic aids to navigation are in use or under development. Loran (long-range navigation) and shoran (short-range navigation) are among the most widely known. Radar is also of value, especially for a ship near the shore. Consol is designed for operation over relatively long ranges. A ship at sea can obtain a fix on its position from Consol shore stations with the use of an ordinary radio receiver.

decompression sickness

The bends, also known as decompression sickness and caisson disease, results from differences in underwater pressure. Because of the increased pressure under water, the nitrogen in the compressed air that is breathed is absorbed by the fluids and tissues of the diver's body. If a diver who has been in deep water comes up properly, as pressure is reduced, the nitrogen is released from the fluids and tissues, passes through the veins, is freed in the lungs, and is breathed out. Since the key to coming up properly is time, the United States Navy developed decompression tables to indicate the amount of time it takes for nitrogen to dissolve from the bloodstream. If a diver comes up too rapidly, bubbles can go into the bloodstream and lodge in the brain, lungs, or spinal cord. Severe cases can result in pain, partial or total paralysis, and death.

deep-ocean submersibles

Several submersibles are operated by the U.S. Navy to support search, rescue, research, and deep-ocean recovery activities. These crafts have also been employed to maintain sea-floor test range and acoustic surveillance equipment. In addition to the manned submersibles listed here, the navy also has several deep-ocean, tethered research and work vehicles. Some of these vehicles are surface controlled/supported, while others can be operated from submerged submarines. The Deep Submergence Rescue Vehicle (DSRV) is fitted with elaborate search and navigation sonars, closed-circuit television, and optical viewing

Sea Cliff (DSV-4). *(United States Navy)*

devices. It can be launched and recovered by a submerged attack submarine or by submarine rescue ships. It is fitted with a remote-control manipulator. DSRV can be transported via Air Mobility Command cargo aircraft to any crisis point in the world. Two C-141s, two C-17s, or one C-5 can be used to transport the DSRV, transport truck, and other equipment. The modified Alvin class is a small submersible used for deep-ocean research. The *Sea Cliff* is fitted with a titanium sphere; its 20,000-foot diving depth provides access to 98 percent of the ocean floor. A light, fiberglass outer hull is fitted to the spheres. The craft have closed-circuit television, external lights, sonars, cameras, and twin hydraulic, remote-control manipulators.

2 Deep Submergence Rescue Vehicles (DSRV)

Number	Name	Launched	Completed
DSRV-1	*Nxstic*	1970	1971
DSRV-2	*Avalon*	1971	1972

2 Research Submersibles—Modified Alvin Class

Number	Name	Launched	Completed
DSV-2	*Turtle*	1968	1969
DSV-4	*Sea Cliff*	1968	1969

1 Research Submersible—Alvin Class

Number	Name	Launched	Completed
DSV-2	*Alvin*	1964	1965

The *Alvin* is operated by the Woods Hole Oceanographic Institution for the Office of Naval Research, which sponsored its construction. After sinking in 5,051 feet of water in 1968, she was refitted with a titanium sphere and a remote-control manipulator. In 1988, *Alvin* aided in the location and photographing of the sunken ocean liner *Titanic*.

Dentuda (SS-335)

A submarine of the Balao class, built by the Electric Boat Company and launched in September 1944. She saw duty in the Pacific on a single war patrol in the East China Sea, during which she damaged a large freighter and sank two patrol craft. As a test vessel for Operation "Crossroads," *Dentuda* sailed for Bikini Atoll in May 1946. She underwent both atomic weapons tests with her crew safely away from their submarine, and returned to Pearl Harbor in September. She was decommissioned in December

Sea Cliff (DSV-4), submerged. *(United States Navy)*

1946 and stationed in the 12th Naval District for the training of members of the Naval Reserve. Her single war patrol was designated as "successful"; and she received one battle star for her contribution to the success of the Okinawa invasion.

Department of the Navy

This branch of the United States government consists of only two services: the U.S. Navy and the U.S. Marine Corps. However, in times of war or crisis, units of the Coast Guard (which is under the jurisdiction of the Department of Transportation) may be placed under the Department of the Navy. The operational forces of the navy are assigned to two major fleet commands; the Atlantic Fleet, headquartered at Norfolk, Virginia, and the Pacific Fleet, headquartered at Pearl Harbor, Hawaii. These fleet commands have both administrative and operational functions. In the administrative role, the commands are responsible to the chief of naval operations. Each fleet commander has six subordinate commanders:

Commanding General Fleet Marine Force
 Pacific/Atlantic

Commander Naval Air Force U.S. Pacific/Atlantic
 Fleet

Commander Naval Surface Force U.S. Pacific/Atlantic
 Fleet

Commander Naval Logistics Force Pacific/Atlantic
 Fleet

Commander Naval Submarine Force U.S.
 Pacific/Atlantic Fleet

There are five operating fleets, which report directly to the naval component commanders of unified commands. These are:

Area	Naval Component Commander	Operating Fleet
Atlantic	CINC U.S. Atlantic Fleet	Second Fleet
Mediterranean	CINC U.S. Naval Forces Europe	Sixth Fleet
Eastern Pacific	CINC U.S. Pacific Fleet	Third Fleet
W. Pacific/Indian Ocean	CINC U.S. Pacific Fleet	Seventh Fleet
Indian Ocean/Persian Gulf	CINC U.S. Naval Forces CENTCOM	Fifth Fleet

Ships rotate on a regular basis between the Second Fleet in the Atlantic and the Sixth Fleet in the Mediterranean, and the Third Fleet in the eastern Pacific and the Seventh Fleet in the western Pacific–Indian Ocean area. Ships are normally deployed to the Sixth or Seventh Fleet for six months, with a year's interval in overhaul, in their home port, or on local or area exercises.

The Second Fleet has a dual role as NATO Striking Force Atlantic, and operates in the North Atlantic (including the Norwegian Sea, North Sea, and Baltic Sea approaches), the Caribbean Sea and Gulf of Mexico, and the South Atlantic.

The Sixth Fleet, which also has a dual role as NATO Striking Force Southern Europe, is deployed in the Mediterranean and is subordinate to the U.S. European Command. Its surface combatants are drawn from the Second Fleet. Sixth Fleet units also make periodic excursions into the Black Sea.

The Fifth Fleet does not have any ships permanently assigned, but rather operates ships drawn from other fleets on a rotational basis. Fifth Fleet functions as the naval component of the U.S. Central Command. Fifth Fleet, headquartered in Bahrain, is responsible for operations in the Red Sea, Persian Gulf, Arabian Sea, and a portion of the Indian Ocean west of India and north of Kenya.

In the Pacific, the Third Fleet operates in the Bering Sea, the Gulf of Alaska, and the eastern and mid–Pacific Ocean areas.

The Seventh Fleet is normally deployed in the Western Pacific, off northeast and southeast Asia, and also operates in the eastern portion of the Indian Ocean.

Administrative control over the navy devolves from the secretary of defense to the secretary of the navy (SECNAV) and the chief of naval operations (CNO). The SECNAV and the CNO are responsible for logistics, maintenance, personnel management, procurement, and research and development. They are assisted in their work by extensive staffs. The principle administrative commands are:

Bureau of Medicine and Surgery
Bureau of Naval Personnel
Naval Air Systems Command
Naval Data Automation Command
Naval Doctrine Command
Naval Education and Training Command
Naval Facilities Engineering Command
Naval Intelligence Command
Naval Investigative Service Command
Naval Legal Service Command
Naval Meteorology Oceanography Command
Naval Safety Center
Naval Sea System Command
Naval Security Group Command
Naval Space Command
Naval Supply Systems Command
Naval Telecommunications Command
Naval Recruiting Command
Space and Naval Warfare Systems Command

There are 374 commissioned ships in the navy, including:

18 ballistic missile submarines
70 nuclear attack submarines
13 aircraft carriers
27 cruisers
89 destroyers
47 frigates
55 amphibious warfare ships
13 patrol craft
14 mine warfare ships
16 combat logistics ships
5 mobile logistics ships
4 fleet support ships
3 other auxiliaries

depth charge

A type of weapon used by surface ships or aircraft to attack submerged submarines. The first depth charges, developed by the British in World War I for use against German submarines, consisted of a canister filled with explosives that was rolled off the stern of a ship in the vicinity of the submerged submarine. The canister would sink through the water, and its explosive charge would be detonated at a preselected depth. The depth charge rarely exploded close enough to sink the submarine, but its shock waves could damage the submarine's systems and instruments, thus forcing it to the surface. An attacking ship would drop a pattern of depth charges around the expected location of a submarine to increase the chances of one exploding near enough to damage the sub. Later, devices were used to propel depth charges through the air over distances of 100 or more yards, thus widening the effective radius at which a ship could attack submarines. Another development was the Hedgehog, which consisted of a salvo of many small, high-explosive bombs that could be launched to a distance of 250 yards or more, and which exploded on contact. Other, more conventional depth charges weighing as much as 300 pounds were used in World War II.

depth finder

Also called fathometer and echo sounder, this is a device used on ships to determine the depth of water by measuring the time it takes a sonic pulse from the transducer to return, or echo, from the bottom of the body of water. Fathometer, though of varying types, are in operation on virtually all ships, whether in the navy or otherwise.

Devilfish (SS-292)

A submarine of the Balao class, built by Cramp Shipbuilding Company and launched in May 1943. After service in aiding the training program of the Fleet Sonar School at Key West, Florida, she sailed for the Pacific and between mid-January and the end of the war undertook four war patrols. On her second, patrolling an area in northern Nanpo Shoto, she was attacked by a kamikaze plane as she was trying to submerge, destroying the mast structure and causing serious leakage. On her third patrol, she sought targets off northern Honshu, and on June 16, in heavy seas, attacked an enemy submarine carrying a midget submarine on its deck, and later an escort ship, but in both cases the targets escaped. During this patrol she acted as lifeguard for strikes accompanying the Okinawa operation, and several times rendezvoused with other submarines to take off medical cases and previously rescued aviators. Her fourth war patrol was largely lifeguard duty for the Third Fleet raids on Japan. She was placed out of commission and in reserve in late September 1946, having received three battle stars for World War II service.

Diablo (SS-479)

A Portsmouth-built submarine of the Tench class, she was launched in December 1944, but set out on her intended war patrol too late to intercept any enemy ship before the

USS *Devilfish* (SS-292) seen here being used as target by USS *Wahoo* (SS-565) following a very active career (1943 to 1968).

end of hostilities. Her career in peacetime was first on the West Coast, based in the Canal Zone, making simulated war patrols off the South American coast. She later transferred to the East Coast, making training runs in the Caribbean and along the eastern coast of South America. Her training missions continued through the 1960s, and in 1964 she was decommissioned and sold to Pakistan. She served its navy as the *Ghazi* for six years, but was lost with all hands in 1970.

diesel submarine, components

The diagram below illustrates the structure of the submarine *Bonefish,* and others of its now outmoded diesel class, which is divided into three main watertight compartments, surrounded by the inner, or pressure hull. These compartments are the torpedo room, the midship compartment, and the machinery compartment. They are separated from each other by pressure bulkheads and a heavy watertight door. Each has its own deck hatch for access topside. The torpedo room is where the ship's main armament is stored. Forward of the torpedo room, in the free flooding bow, are the ship's sonar (hydrophone) arrays and transducer that are used to detect other ships and submarines when the submarine is submerged.

The midship compartment consists of three levels. The upper level contains the control room, where the ship is controlled and navigated, both surfaced and submerged, and the attack center, where information from the ship's electronic sensors is processed and sent to the torpedo fire control system in order to direct the torpedo to its target. Behind the attack center is the radio room, the wardroom,

OUTLINE OF A TYPICAL GUPPY SUBMARINE

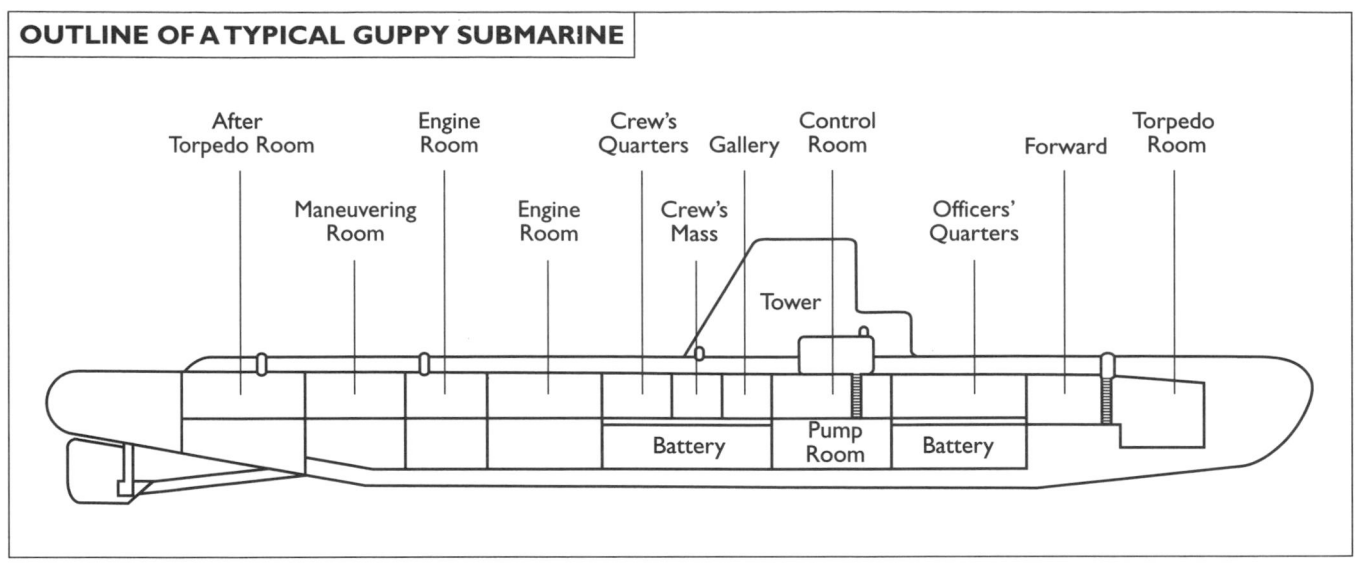

After Torpedo Room

Maneuvering Room

Engine Room

Engine Room

Crew's Quarters

Crew's Mass

Gallery

Control Room

Tower

Forward

Officers' Quarters

Torpedo Room

Battery

Pump Room

Battery

OUTLINE OF A BARBEL-CLASS DIESEL SUBMARINE

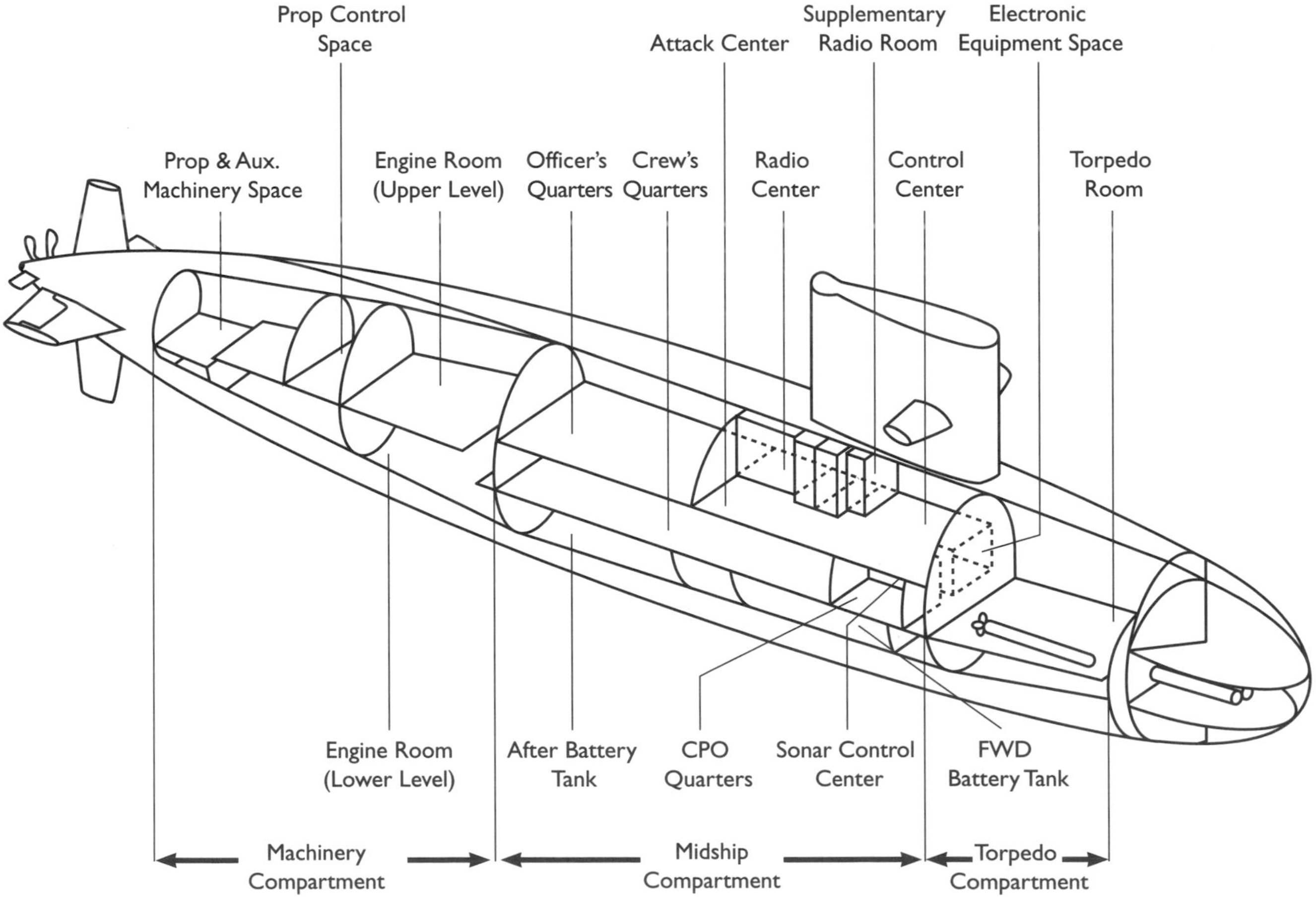

Prop Control Space

Attack Center

Supplementary Radio Room

Electronic Equipment Space

Prop & Aux. Machinery Space

Engine Room (Upper Level)

Officer's Quarters

Crew's Quarters

Radio Center

Control Center

Torpedo Room

Engine Room (Lower Level)

After Battery Tank

CPO Quarters

Sonar Control Center

FWD Battery Tank

Machinery Compartment

Midship Compartment

Torpedo Compartment

and the officer's staterooms. The next level in the midship compartment contains the sonar room, where information from the sonar arrays is processed, and chief petty officer and crew berthing. Aft of berthing is the crew's mess, which is also used for showing films and training sessions. The bottom level contains the main storage battery used for submerged propulsion.

The third compartment is the machinery compartment. The first section is the engine room, which contains the ship's three main propulsion diesel engines, whose air to run them comes through the ship's snorkel system. The engine exhaust leaves the ship through piping that ends slightly below the surface of the water, mixing with sea water to prevent detection. Each engine drives a large electric generator, which creates electrical power that is stored in the main battery. Also in the engine room is the ship's air conditioning and refrigeration equipment and the hydraulic power plant used to operate the rudder, diving planes, and major hull valves. In the after end are two distilling units for making fresh water from seawater. Just aft of the engine room is maneuvering, which contains all the main propulsion control equipment. Here the engines are controlled and electrical power directed from the main battery to the main motors that actually turn the ship's propeller. In the lower level are the two high-pressure air compressors that provide air for numerous purposes throughout the ship.

Diodon (SS-349)

A submarine of the Balao class, *Diodon* was launched in September 1945, and spent her first four years of service as a training vessel on the West Coast. In 1950, she sailed for the Far East and had the distinction of rescuing six downed airmen off Guam while in transit. She next had the assignment of training frigates in antisubmarine warfare for the Republic of Korea, after which she conducted simulated war patrols, particularly focusing on methods to use stealth in passing through sensitive combat zones undetected. Later, in the mid-1950s, *Diodon* engaged in training operations on the West Coast, before proceeding to Australia to participate in commemorations of the great victory of the Allies in the Battle of the Coral Sea in May 1942. She served again in the Far East before being decommissioned in January 1971.

displacement

Also known as "displacement tonnage." When referring to ships, this is a measure to define their size and weight. The term does not refer to the physical weight of the ship if it were to be placed on a gigantic scale, but instead to the weight of the volume of water displaced by a vessel, whether at anchor, docked, or seagoing. Submarines are unique in that they have not one, but two displacements. The first, and the lesser, is the measure used for a boat on the surface; while the second is the measure used for a boat that is completely submerged. Thus, a submarine of the Balao class, the most predominant in the Pacific during WORLD WAR II, might have a surface displacement of 1,870 tons, but a submerged displacement of 2,391 tons.

diving

Underwater diving and the capabilities of staying below for extended periods of time have long fascinated marine explorers. As far back as 1716, the English astronomer and mathematician Edmund Halley invented two types of diving bell. One was made of wood and looked like an upside-down wastebasket with "eyes" to let light in. Air was provided by two 36-gallon barrels that alternated from surface to bottom with cargoes of fresh air, and a flexible tube that transferred the air from the barrel to the bell and the diver inside. His second diving bell was made of lead and had a seat inside for several divers and an air-supply system essentially the same as for the first bell. Halley and four other daring divers reportedly stayed at 60 feet for an hour and a half in the lead bell. Their only problem, he reported, was a pain in the ears "as if a quill had been thrust into them." In those days the problems of increased pressure and depth were not yet understood.

Modern exploration of the undersea world had its beginnings in June 1943, when Jacques Cousteau made his first dive with a revolutionary breathing device he had developed with Emile Gagnan, a French engineer. Captain Cousteau, then a French navy gunnery officer, had not been satisfied with the superficial probing of the ocean surface; it was not enough that humans could stay underwater and look only as long as they could hold their breath. Since then, commercial diving technology has made significant strides in ushering in the age of undersea exploration. Dives have extended into deeper and deeper waters in part because of the growing needs of the offshore petroleum industry. After an oil platform is placed offshore, the subsea support structure must be maintained, serviced, and inspected periodically by divers.

Until the 1960s divers went to depths of only 300 feet or less, and in these depths diving practices have remained the same. Divers descend from the surface breathing mixed gas, rather than compressed air, to prevent the nitrogen narcosis problem. They are tied to the surface by hoses, which supply both breathing gases, and by the necessary communication lines. Frequently allied to these operations are submersible chambers, in which divers rest between dives during their underwater work periods. The chambers also serve for decompressing, or being brought back to surface pressure, at the end of a job. Very gradually, diving helmets and other gear are being perfected that will not only permit deeper and deeper dives, but will also protect divers from the bends—decompression sickness that can be fatal. Diving was greatly enhanced by the use of the self-contained underwater breathing apparatus, commonly known by its acronym as scuba, which made it possibly to dive and stay underwater for long periods of time with complete freedom and no dependency on air hoses or other oxygen supplies.

Dogfish (SS-350)

This submarine of the Balao class was launched in October 1945, and was initially assigned to local duties and training along the East Coast and in the Caribbean. She engaged in various other exercises and operations thereafter, not only along the East Coast but in European waters, the Mediterranean, and elsewhere in NATO anti-submarine warfare exercises. She was decommissioned in July 1972, and sold to Brazil where she served that nation's navy as *Guanabara* until 1983.

Dolphin (AGSS-555)

Dolphin was built by the Portsmouth Naval Shipyard and launched in August 1968. Displacing 800 tons on the surface and 950 tons submerged, she was designed to carry a complement of four officers and 30 enlisted men. At the time of construction, she was the navy's deep-diving submarine, designed to test advanced submarine structures, sensors, weapons, communications, and machinery systems. She also served as a scientific platform capable of operations at unprecedented depths greatly exceeding that of any known operational submarine. Three months after her launching, she set a depth record for operating submarines, and the next year launched a torpedo from the deepest depth that one had ever been fired. Utilizing a large payload and a highly versatile instrumentation suit, both civilian and naval activities utilized her for testing a multitude of technologically advanced and complex equipment. *Dolphin* set records, not only in deep diving, but also in acoustics, submarine-to-aircraft communications, laser communication, and advanced sonar systems.

Dolphin [ex-(V-7) (D-1)] (SS-169)

The first of two boats to bear this name was built by the Portsmouth Naval Shipyard and launched in June 1932 as the prototype of a class in the 1930s. Her early service was mainly on the West Coast, taking part in tactical exercises and test torpedo firings until March 4, 1933, when she got underway for the East Coast. By chance, she was stationed at Pearl Harbor on December 7, 1941, where she used her deck guns to fire on enemy bombers, after which she immediately got underway for a patrol in search of Japanese submarines off the Hawaiian Islands. She left Pearl Harbor in late December 1941, on her first war patrol, during which she reconnoitered in the Marshall Islands in preparation for later air strikes. *Dolphin* patrolled off the island itself during the critical battle of Midway in early June 1942, attacking a destroyer and a tanker with undetermined results. Her third war patrol, during October and November, was in the storm-tossed waters of the Kurile Islands, where she performed reconnaissance essential to the operations that were to keep Japanese bases there largely ineffective throughout the war. With newer submarines now available for offensive war patrols, *Dolphin* was assigned less dramatic, but still vital, service on training duty at Pearl Harbor, the Canal Zone, and New London until the end of the war, and was decommissioned in October 1945.

Dorado (SS-248)

A submarine of the Gato class, built by the Electric Boat Company and launched in May 1943, she sailed from New London, Connecticut, on October 6, 1943, for Panama. She did not arrive at Panama nor was she heard from at any time after sailing. The Commander in Chief, United States Fleet, in his comments concerning the court of inquiry covering the case, listed three possible causes for the loss of *Dorado*: operational casualties; enemy action; and attack by friendly forces. The standard practice of imposing bombing restrictions within an area 15 miles on each side of the course of an unescorted submarine making passage in friendly waters was carried out and all concerned were notified. It was learned that a patrol plane, which was assigned at Guantanamo to furnish air coverage on the evening of October 12, received faulty instructions as to the location of the bombing and attack restriction area in which *Dorado* was moving. The plane delivered a surprise attack of three depth charges on an unidentified submarine. About two hours later, the plane sighted another submarine with which it attempted to exchange recognition signals without success. This submarine fired upon the plane. A German submarine was known to be operating near the scene of these two contacts. Because of the lack of evidence, the court of inquiry was unable to reach definite conclusions as to the cause of the loss of *Dorado*.

Dragonet (SS-293)

A submarine of the Balao class, built by Cramp Shipbuilding Company of Philadelphia and launched in April 1942. She began her first war patrol, from Pearl Harbor, in November 1944, bound for the Kurile Islands and the Sea of Okhotsk. On the morning of December 15, 1944, while submerged south of Matsuwa, *Dragonet* struck an uncharted submerged pinnacle, which holed her pressure hull in the forward torpedo room. The space was completely flooded, and in order to surface the submarine, it was necessary to blow water out of the compartment with compressed air. When she surfaced, her position was only four miles from a Japanese airfield on Matsuwa, and she had to clear the danger area as quickly as possible. This necessitated entering the flooded compartment to rig the bow planes properly for underwater navigation, a very tricky and risky operation that was accomplished only by the daring and skill of her crew. She was further tested when she had to run through two days of storm to reach Midway Island for emergency repairs. Her next patrol entailed lifeguard duty south of the Japanese home islands, where she rescued four downed army pilots. Her third war patrol, between July 8 and August 17, 1945,

was a combination of lifeguard duty and attacks on Japanese shipping in Bungo Suido. At this late stage in the war, the remnants of the Japanese merchant marine provided few targets, and her last accomplishment was the rescue of a downed naval aviator near Okino Shima. In April 1946, she was decommissioned and placed in reserve.

Drum (SS-228)

This submarine of the Gato class was launched in May 1941, and by mid-April 1942 was action-bound on her first war patrol in the Pacific. Cruising off the coast of Japan, she sank a seaplane tender and three cargo ships before returning to her base at Pearl Harbor. Although

Drum (SS-228), one of the stars in the World War II Gato class, had an enviable battle record in the Pacific, completing 13 war patrols and earning 12 battle stars. *Drum* is now a museum ship in Mobile, Alabama. *(United States Navy)*

Early submarine dry dock, prior to World War I. Such docks were at sea level so boats could move in, after which a flood gate closed, the water was pumped out, and the entire hull was then available for repairs or improvements. *(United States Navy)*

discouraged by a lack of results during her second patrol, she made up for the paucity of action on her third sortie by knocking off three cargo ships and damaging two others. Her fourth patrol, though rendered hair-raising by severe damages from depth charging, resulted in extensive damage to a carrier and a large tanker. She later sank two freighters on her fifth patrol, a cargo ship on her sixth, and another on her seventh. Her actions were repetitious thereafter, and she ended up on her 13th and last patrol with an overall record of 15 enemy victims for a total of 80, 580 tons. *Drum* received 12 battle stars for her service in World War II.

dry docks

Found in most large ports, and particularly in ports large and small that are responsible for the construction and/or repair of ships, these docks are of two basic types: graving docks and floating dry docks. The former is a basin, commonly made of concrete, that forms three sides, with the fourth side being—at least in part—a watertight gate that can be closed after a submarine (or other vessel) has entered the dock. The water is then pumped out, or in some cases, where the dock is located in a tidal basin, allowed to run out with the tide. The vessel is held firmly in place, both by timbers beneath its hull ("keel blocks") and restraining cables, thus making it possible for workers to have access to portions of the hull that are normally underwater. A floating dry dock is mobile and is, in effect, a vessel in its own right that can be towed to locations at sea. It is constructed in such a fashion that it can be raised or lowered by increasing or decreasing the amount of water within its hollow sidewalls. Floating dry docks are routinely used for submarines.

E

E-1 [ex-*Skipjack*] (SS-24)

An early submarine built for the navy by the Fore River Shipbuilding Company and launched in May 1911. She was christened and launched as *Skipjack,* but renamed *E-1* six months later. She was a boat of less than 500 tons (submerged) and had a complement of one officer and 23 enlisted men. Six days after commissioning, *E-1* sailed from Boston for Norfolk, and off the Virginia Capes underwent tests before heading north again for operations off southern New England. In September 1912, she was installed with a Sperry gyrocompass, for which she became a pioneer underwater test platform. She also experimented with using radio equipment while submerged. Throughout his career, Admiral Chester W. Nimitz played a progressive and leading role in the incorporation into the navy of the vast scientific and technological developments of this century, many of them pioneered by the United States Navy. *E-1* continued important experimental development and training with the Atlantic Fleet for the next five years, until December 1917, when she left for the Azores and more hazardous duty. During January 1918, she patrolled between Ponta Delgada and Horta, protecting the Azores from German attack and their use as a haven by U-boats. After World War I, she returned to the New London base where she trained new submariners and tested the experimental underwater listening gear later to be known as SONAR. She was decommissioned in October 1921.

E-2 [ex-*Sturgeon*] (SS-25)

An early navy submarine, built by the Fore River Shipbuilding Company and launched in June 1911. She was christened and launched as *Sturgeon* and renamed *E-2* five months later, as she set out on training exercises. In April 1914, she cruised to Guantanamo Bay, Cuba, and the Gulf of Mexico. She returned to Newport on July 27 for training operations for the remainder of the summer, and, from February to May 1915, operated off the coast of Florida. She was the victim of a violent explosion and fire in January 1916, when hydrogen gas venting from her storage battery was ignited by a spark. Four men were killed and seven injured. After being placed out of commission for use as a laboratory for exhaustive tests of the Edison storage battery, she was reactivated and served in training and experimental work at the United States Naval Submarine Base in New London. In May 1918, she was ordered to Norfolk, Virginia, to prepare to operate against German submarine activity in the vicinity of Cape Hatteras, North Carolina. Between mid-May and late August, she made four war patrols against the U-boat threat. During War Patrol Number 4, she sighted a large U-boat for which she made extended submerged searches after the German submarine submerged. *E-2* was commended by the chief of naval operations for two of those antisubmarine patrols, which were exceptionally long for a submarine of her size and not in the calmest of waters. She made two more war patrols before the armistice was signed, and then returned to training student officers and qualifying men for duty in submarines. She was decommissioned in October 1921.

Electric Boat Company

The world's foremost designer and builder of nuclear submarines, whose ancestry extends back a century to 1899, when the company produced the first practical submarine for the United States Navy. It had its origins when the inventor, John Philip Holland, formed the J. P. Holland Company to begin building the submarines he was designing, but needed help in the form of more advanced facilities and financing. Shortly after the founding of Electric Boat, the company began its long experience building submarines under contract with the navy. In 1911, Electric Boat acquired the New London Ship and Engine Company in Groton, Connecticut, to build diesel engines and other machinery and parts for submarines and commercial ships. During World War I, it produced no fewer than 85 submarines for the U.S. Navy. The pace slacked off in the 1920s and through much of the 1930s, until World War II, when it supplied the navy with 74 submarines. Later acquired by General Dynamics, the company became the chief designer and builder of American submarines, establishing itself with unique capabilities in the early 1950s when it designed and built *Nautilus,* the world's first nuclear-powered submarine. Since then it has designed 15 of the 18 classes of nuclear submarine, including all ballistic-missile-firing classes. Other significant contributions to America's undersea power were the USS *George Washington,* which in 1960 embarked on the first strategic deterrence patrol carrying 16 Polaris missiles; the launching of *Sturgeon* in 1966 as the lead ship in a new class of attack submarines; the completion of *Ohio,* the first of an 18-ship class popularly known as Tridents, and the launching in 1995 of *Seawolf,* the most advanced class of attack submarine in the world.

electronic deception

The deliberate radiation, alteration, suppression, absorption, denial, enhancement, or reflection of electromagnetic energy in a manner intended to convey misleading information to an enemy or enemy weapon. Among the types of electronic deception are actions to convey misleading indicators that may be used by hostile forces, simulative electronic deception actions to represent friendly notional or actual capabilities so as to mislead hostile forces, and electronic deception imitating enemy emissions by introducing electromagnetic energy into enemy systems.

electronic navigation

Electronic devices are vital aids in finding positions at sea. Navigators whose submarines are equipped with radio direction finders can determine the bearings of radio transmitting stations on shore. Special radio beacons for navigation are established at lighthouses, marine bases, and other shore points, as well as at fixed vessels at sea, and from them radio bearings may be plotted on a chart to obtain a fix. A variety of other electronic aids to navigation are in regular use, such as Loran (long-range navigation) and shoran (short-range navigation). Loran-C was originally developed to provide radio navigation for U.S. coastal waters and was later expanded to include complete coverage of the continental U.S. and Alaska. Radar is also imperative. The AN/BPS 15 (H) Submarine Navigation Radar is carried on Ohio-class submarines, among others, and is used in conjunction with Electronic Chart Information Systems (ECDIS), which eliminate the former manpower-intensive requirement for paper navigation charts.

Today, the Global Positioning System (GPS) and Differential GPS (DGPS) are becoming the means of navigation and position determination. GPS is a satellite-based radio navigation system (SATNAV, using instant data from orbiting satellites) that permits submarines and other ships to determine their three-dimensional position, velocity, and time, 24 hours a day in all weather, anywhere in the world, in a manner that is continuously updated and recorded on electronic charting. Another increasingly important electronic navigation aid is the Submarine Inertial Navigation System (SINS), which makes it possible to guide intercontinental ballistic missiles from submarines to very distant targets.

Complex though these electronic navigation systems are, they can be linked in a compact Navigation and Data Management Center (NDMC) to other navigational controls, sonar and weapon guidance systems, the ship's technical control system, and data logging and evaluation facilities.

Entemedor (SS-340)

A submarine of the Balao class, built by the Electric Boat Company and launched in December 1944. Assigned to the Pacific, she put to sea for her only war patrol in late July 1945, but found no likely enemy targets. She was assigned to San Diego and participated in various fleet exercises in the eastern Pacific, with extended deployments to the Far East, operating out of Subic Bay in the Philippines. During the 1950s, she was stationed in New London and operated in the western Atlantic. She was converted to a GUPPY IIA-class submarine at the Electric Boat Company in 1952. During the 1970s, she also saw service in the Caribbean and participated in two NATO exercises off the western coast of the United Kingdom. She was decommissioned in July 1972 and a year later sold to Turkey where she served as *Preveze* (S-345) until 1987.

Ericsson, John (1803–1889)

A Swedish-born American naval engineer and inventor who built the first armored turret warship and developed the screw propeller, first used in 1837 on the *Francis B.*

Ogden, built in London. Captain Robert F. Stockton, of the U.S. Navy, ordered a small iron vessel, the *Princeton,* to be fitted by Ericsson with engines and screw; it reached New York City in May 1839. A few months later, Ericsson immigrated to the United States and lived the rest of his life in New York City, becoming a naturalized citizen in 1848. During the American Civil War, Ericsson's proposal to the Navy Department for a novel warship was accepted, and the *Monitor* was launched on January 30, 1862. Wholly steam-powered and with a screw propeller, the vessel, with its armored revolving turret, set a revolutionary pattern for warships that continued into the 20th century. On March 9 the *Monitor* fought the Confederate ironclad *Virginia* (formerly *Merrimack*), leading the federal government to place an order with Ericsson for many more Monitor-type vessels; these ships played an important role in the blockade of the Confederacy. In later years he developed a torpedo and investigated solar-powered motors.

escape devices—early developments

In the early days of submersibles, recruitment was a problem because of the claustrophobia associated with being confined underwater in a ship that offered no form of escape if it were to sink. The Confederate submarine, *Hunley,* had proven to be the graveyard of almost every crew that set out in her, and any number of inventors had died in test runs of sunken submarines. One of the first breakthroughs came in 1909, when Ensign Kenneth Whiting was put in command of the *Porpoise,* built in 1900, which was then docked at Cavite, in the Philippines. On April 15, Whiting and his crew took the *Porpoise* into Manila Bay, diving soon thereafter and leveling off at a depth of 25 feet, at which time Whiting announced he was going to try an experiment—an underwater escape. The young ensign, familiar with tragedies of men trapped in a sunken submarine, was convinced there was a method of escape that had never been tried: through the torpedo tube. After instructing his men, he squeezed into the bow tube, only 18 inches in diameter, and grasped the crossbar of the outer door. The second officer closed the inner door as instructed, and released the lock to the outer door. When water rushed into the chamber, Whiting held his breath, hung onto the crossbar, and pulled himself through to freedom. He then swam to the surface, in slightly more than a minute, and reported the incident to his flotilla commander, advising that crews be trained in this method of escape when there was no other alternative.

Every time there was a disaster in which crew members died when trapped in a sunken submarine, the navy made renewed efforts to develop practical escape methods. The situation came to a head with the sinking of the *S-4* just before Christmas 1927, after she had been rammed by a surface vessel and 42 men were lost. Although at least six men survived initially, trapped in the forward torpedo room, the lack of any escape capability resulted in their slow and tortured death, while family members waited in vain for their rescue. Following the *S-4* disaster, the navy worked on a plan to equip the submarine, after she was eventually raised, with an escape compartment near the conning tower. From this chamber, crews in a sunken submarine could escape through the overhead door and ascend slowly on a guideline released with a buoy to the surface, wearing an "escape lung" invented by Lieutenant C. B. Momsen, of the Navy Bureau of Construction and Repairs. Successful tests aboard the salvaged *S-4* just 13 months after her tragic sinking, proved that escapes could be made, though not without danger, from as far down as 200 feet below the surface.

Escape methods were put to the test during training exercises off Portsmouth, New Hampshire, on May 23, 1939, when the submarine *Squalus* went suddenly out of control after water flooded the engine room. Despite all attempts by the crew to blow the ballast tanks, the submarine slid stern first and settled on the bottom at a depth of 242 feet. When the commandant of the Portsmouth Navy Yard lost communication with *Squalus,* he ordered search vessels to comb the area. They picked up remote alarm signals and soon located the source from which they had come—one of two rescue-phone buoys stowed fore and aft in pockets on the submarine's deck for just such an emergency. On the buoy, painted bright yellow, was a metal plate with the inscription, "Submarine Squalus Sunk Here—bow buoy."

Now began a test of every state-of-the-art rescue device that could have been built into a submarine just prior to World War II. These included enough oxygen tanks and compounds for neutralizing poisonous carbon dioxide in stale air so the trapped crew members who had not drowned in the engine room could survive for up to a week; emergency salvage air connections on the deck that were easily accessible to divers; individual escape lungs that were modern improvements of the one invented by Momsen after the *S-4* disaster; and valves through which air could be pumped into ballast tanks by rescue crews to lighten the sunken vessel so it would rise to the surface.

When it was decided that the engine room was totally flooded and there was no way of raising the boat without weeks of effort, there was one more rescue device that could be used. This was a rescue chamber that could be lowered to a specially designed hatch cover and fitted tightly in place. The hatch could then be opened, permitting nine men to climb into the escape chamber, and eventually be raised safely to the surface, where the chamber was lifted out of the water and onto the deck of the rescue ship, *Falcon*. Although 26 officers and men, trapped in the flooded engine room, perished, the rest of the crew was saved in an operation that has gone down in the records as one of the most successful in submarine history. Since that time, many other more efficient rescue devices have been developed. Examples of the evolution of escape devices are the Momsen lung, Stanke hood, and the modern escape suits.

Escolar (SS-294)

A submarine of the Balao class, built by Cramp Shipbuilding Company, Philadelphia, and launched in April 1943. She was ordered to Pearl Harbor, from which she put out for her first war patrol in September 1944, along with two other submarines, *Croaker* and *Perch*, for a coordinated patrol in the Yellow Sea. On September 30, when *Escolar* was estimated to be north of the Bonin Islands, the following partial message was received from her: "This from Escolar attacked with deck gun boat similar to ex-Italian Peter George five . . ." Although no further transmissions were ever received by bases from *Escolar* which was forced to break off the transmission, *Croaker* had stated that she suffered no damage and was in frequent communication until October 17, 1944. *Perch* reported that on October 17 she had received a message from *Escolar* stating her position, but neither *Perch* nor *Croaker* could raise her by radio after this transmission was received. *Escolar* failed to make an expected rendezvous, and in late November she was presumed lost. No Japanese report after the war accounted for this boat; however, there were mines in the general area of *Escolar*'s predicted position, and the most likely explanation for her end is that she detonated a mine.

eternal patrol, U.S. submarines on

Eternal patrol is the term used by submariners for boats that have been sunk in battle or lost in tragic accidents at sea.

| USS *Shark* I | (SS-174) | Feb. 11, 1942 | 58 Lost |
| Japanese surface attack, Makassar Strait, Celebes Island | | | |

| USS *Grunion* | (SS-216) | July 30, 1942 | 70 Lost |
| Unknown causes off Kiska Island, Aleutians | | | |

| USS *Argonaut* I | (SS-166) | Jan. 10, 1943 | 105 Lost |
| Japanese surface attack in Java Sea | | | |

| USS *Amberjack* I | (SS-219) | Feb. 16, 1943 | 74 Lost |
| Japanese air/surface attack in Solomon Sea | | | |

| USS *Grampus* I | (SS-207) | Mar. 5, 1943 | 71 Lost |
| Japanese surface attack, Solomon Islands | | | |

| USS *Triton* I | (SS-201) | Mar. 15, 1943 | 74 Lost |
| Japanese surface attack off New Guinea | | | |

| USS *Pickerel* I | (SS-177) | Apr. 3, 1943 | 74 Lost |
| Japanese surface attack off Honshu, Japan | | | |

| USS *Runner* I | (SS-275) | June 1943 | 78 Lost |
| Possible Japanese mine between Midway Island and Japan | | | |

| USS *Pompano* I | (SS-181) | Sept. 1943 | 76 Lost |
| Possible Japanese mine off Honshu, Japan | | | |

| USS *Grayling* I | (SS-209) | Sept. 12, 1943 | 76 Lost |
| Unknown causes along approaches to Manila, P.I. | | | |

| USS *Cisco* | (SS-290) | Sept. 28, 1943 | 76 Lost |
| Japanese air/surface attack in Sulu Sea | | | |

| USS *Wahoo* I | (SS-238) | Oct. 11, 1943 | 80 Lost |
| Japanese air/surface attack in La Perouse Strait off Japan | | | |

| USS *Dorado* I | (SS-248) | Oct. 12, 1943 | 76 Lost |
| Air attack in Southwest Atlantic | | | |

| USS *Corvina* | (SS-226) | Nov. 16, 1943 | 82 Lost |
| Japanese submarine attack off Truk | | | |

| USS *Capelin* | (SS-289) | Dec. 2, 1943 | 78 Lost |
| Unconfirmed Japanese surface attack in Celebes Sea | | | |

| USS *Scorpion* I | (SS-278) | Jan. 5, 1944 | 76 Lost |
| Possible Japanese mine in Yellow Sea off China | | | |

| USS *Grayback* I | (SS-208) | Feb. 27, 1944 | 80 Lost |
| Japanese air/surface attack off Okinawa | | | |

| USS *Trout* I | (SS-202) | Feb. 29, 1944 | 81 Lost |
| Japanese surface attack in Philippine Sea | | | |

| USS *Gudgeon* I | (SS-211) | May 12, 1944 | 78 Lost |
| Japanese air/surface attack in northern Marianas | | | |

| USS *Herring* | (SS-233) | June 1, 1944 | 84 Lost |
| Japanese shore battery off Matsuwa Island, Kuriles | | | |

| USS *S-28* | (SS-133) | June 4, 1944 | 50 Lost |
| Foundered off Hawaiian Islands | | | |

| USS *Golet* | (SS-361) | June 14, 1944 | 82 Lost |
| Japanese surface attack off Honshu, Japan | | | |

| USS *Robalo* | (SS-273) | July 26, 1944 | 78 Lost |
| Possible Japanese mine off Palawan | | | 4 POWs |

| USS *Harder* I | (SS-257) | Aug. 24, 1944 | 79 Lost |
| Japanese depth charge attack off Luzon, P.I. | | | |

| USS *Seawolf* II | (SS-197) | Oct. 3, 1944 | 99 Lost |
| Unknown causes off Samar | | | |

| USS *Escolar* | (SS-294) | Oct. 17, 1944 | 82 Lost |
| Possible Japanese mine in Yellow Sea off China | | | |

| USS *Shark* II | (SS-314) | Oct. 24, 1944 | 87 Lost |
| Japanese depth charge attack off Formosa | | | |

| USS *Albacore* I | (SS-218) | Nov. 7, 1944 | 86 Lost |
| Japanese mine between Honshu and Hokkaido, Japan | | | |

| USS *Growler* I | (SS-215) | Nov. 8, 1944 | 85 Lost |
| Possible Japanese surface attack in South China Sea | | | |

| USS *Scamp* I | (SS-277) | Nov. 11, 1944 | 83 Lost |
| Japanese surface attack in Tokyo Bay area | | | |

| USS *Swordfish* I | (SS-193) | Jan. 12, 1945 | 89 Lost |
| Possible Japanese surface attack or mine off Okinawa | | | |

| USS *Barbel* I | (SS-316) | Feb. 4, 1945 | 81 Lost |
| Japanese air attack off entrance to Palawan Passage | | | |

| USS *Kete* | (SS-369) | March 1945 | 87 Lost |
| Unknown causes between Okinawa and Midway | | | |

| USS *Trigger* I | (SS-237) | Mar. 28, 1945 | 89 Lost |
| Japanese air/surface attack in East China Sea | | | |

| USS *Snook* I | (SS-279) | Apr. 8, 1945 | 84 Lost |
| Unknown causes off Formosa | | | |

| USS *Lagarto* | (SS-371) | May 4, 1945 | 85 Lost |
| Japanese surface attack in Gulf of Siam | | | |

| USS *Bonefish* I | (SS-223) | June 18, 1945 | 85 Lost |
| Japanese surface attack off Honshu, Japan | | | |

| USS *Bullhead* | (SS-332) | Aug. 6, 1945 | 84 Lost |
| Japanese air attack off Bali Coast | | | |

| USS *Thresher* II | (SSN-593) | Apr. 10, 1963 | 129 Lost |
| Accident during deep diving exercises off New England coast | | | |

| USS *Scorpion* II | (SSN-589) | May 22, 1968 | 99 Lost |
| Possible torpedo detonation off Azores | | | |

The following is a listing of boats lost taking portions of their crews on Eternal Patrol:

| USS *F-4* | (SS-23) | Mar. 25, 1915 | 21 Lost |
| Battery explosion off Honolulu | | | |

| USS *F-1* | (SS-20) | Dec. 16, 1917 | 19 Lost |
| Rammed off Honolulu | | | |

| USS *G-2* | (SS-27) | July 30, 1919 | 3 Lost |
| Foundered in Long Island Sound | | | |

| USS *H-1* | (SS-28) | Mar. 12, 1920 | 4 Lost |
| Foundered off Santa Margarita Island, California | | | |

| USS *O-5* | (SS-66) | Oct. 20, 1923 | 3 Lost |
| Rammed in Limon Bay, Canal Zone | | | |

| USS *S-51* | (SS-162) | Sept. 25, 1925 | 33 Lost |
| Rammed off Block Island, Rhode Island | | | |

| USS *Squalus* | (SS-192) | May 23, 1939 | 26 Lost |
| Foundered off Portsmouth, New Hampshire (boat salvaged and recommissioned under a new name) | | | |

| USS *O-9* | (SS-70) | June 20, 1941 | 33 Lost |
| Foundered off Isle of Shoals | | | |

| USS *Sealion* I | (SS-195) | Dec. 10, 1941 | 4 Lost |
| Japanese air attack, Cavite Navy Yard, P.I. | | | |

| USS *S-26* | (SS-131) | Jan. 24, 1942 | 46 Lost |
| Collision in Gulf of Panama | | | |

| USS *R-12* | (SS-89) | June 12, 1943 | 42 Lost |
| Foundered off Key West, Florida | | | |

| USS *S-44* | (SS-155) | Oct. 7, 1943 | 55 Lost |
| Japanese surface attack in Sea of Okhotsk | | | |

| USS *Sculpin* I | (SS-191) | Nov. 19, 1943 | 12 Lost |
| Japanese surface attack off Truk | | | 51 POWs |

| USS *Tullibee* I | (SS-284) | Mar. 26, 1944 | 79 Lost |
| Circular run of own torpedo off Palau Islands | | | |

| USS *Flier* | (SS-250) | Aug. 13, 1944 | 78 Lost |
| Japanese mine in Balabac Strait | | | |

| USS *Tang* I | (SS-306) | Oct. 24, 1944 | 78 Lost |
| Circular run of own torpedo in Formosa Strait | | | |

| USS *Cochino* | (SS-345) | Aug. 26, 1949 | 1 Lost |
| Battery explosion off Norway | | | |

The following boats have crewmembers on Eternal Patrol as a result of incidents that did not result in the direct loss of the boat:

| USS *S-49* | (SS-160) | Apr. 4, 1926 | 4 Lost |
| Battery explosion, Submarine Base, New London, Connecticut; boat survived | | | |

| USS *S-4* | (SS-109) | Dec. 17, 1927 | 40 Lost |
| Rammed off Provincetown, Massachusetts; boat salvaged | | | |

| USS *Seadragon* | (SS-194) | Dec. 10, 1941 | 1 Lost |
| Japanese air attack, Cavite Navy Yard, P.I.; boat survived | | | |

| USS *Bass* I | (SS-164) | Aug. 17, 1942 | 25 Lost |
| Flooding off Panama Canal; boat survived | | | |

| USS *Perch* I | (SS-176) | Mar. 3, 1942 | 6 POWs |
| Scuttled after Japanese depth charge attack | | | |

| USS *Grenadier* I | (SS-210) | Apr. 22, 1943 | 4 POWs |
| Scuttled after Japanese air attack, Malay Peninsula | | | |

| USS *Growler* | (SS-215) | Feb. 7, 1943 | 1 Lost |
| Surface action with Japanese vessel | | | |

| USS *Tusk* | (SS-426) | Aug. 26, 1949 | 6 Lost |
| Assisting USS *Cochino* off Norway; boat survived | | | |

| USS *Bonefish* II | (SS-582) | Apr. 24, 1988 | 3 Lost |
| Fire and explosion off Florida; boat decommissioned | | | |

Torpedo room on USS *Ethan Allen* (SSBN-608) showing torpedoes being loaded. *(United States Navy)*

Ethan Allen (SSBN-608)

Launched in July 1958, *Ethan Allen* was the first in the new class named after her, which consisted of five deep-diving boats whose maximum depth was in excess of 1,000 feet. The boats in this class had a displacement of 6,900 tons, on the surface, and 8,000 submerged, and were armed with 16 Polaris A-1 (later A-3) missiles. At the conclusion of their last Polaris patrols, the boats were modified as attack submarines, but suffered from their relatively large size, limited torpedo reloads (eight), lack of tactical missile capabilities, and slower speed compared with other, more recently built submarines.

The submarines in the Ethan Allen class also included:

Sam Houston (SSBN-609)

Thomas A. Edison (SSBN-610)

John Marshall (SSBN-611)

Thomas Jefferson (SSBN-618)

The *Houston* and *Marshall* were additionally converted to special-mission submarines, equipped to carry frogmen or commandos, and to conduct other special operations. Each could carry two dry deck shelters (DDS) to accommodate a swimmer delivery vehicle (SDV) or swimmers.

F

F-1 (SS-20)

On December 16, 1917, the *F-1,* known as the *Carp,* she collided with a sister ship, *F-3,* while maneuvering on the surface during an exercise off the California coast. *F-1* was struck on the port side, just forward of the engine room, and sank so quickly that only three of the 22 men in her complement were able to escape.

F-4 (SS-23)

The sinking of this submarine (also known as *Skate*) on March 25, 1915, was the first submarine loss and tragedy faced by the fledgling navy submarine service. *F-4* foundered approximately one-and-a-half miles off of Honolulu, while running submerged, when acid corrosion of the lead lining of the battery tank permitted seawater seepage into the battery compartment, causing loss of control. Efforts were made to find the sunken submarine and save her crew of 21, without success. There were no survivors. She was eventually located in 300 feet of water (her maximum depth was 200 feet), and raised in late August 1915, using cables suspended from pontoons that had been specifically designed and built for this purpose. She was declared a total loss and struck from the Navy Register on August 31, 1915.

At first, the navy had hoped that some of the crew might have survived, and made preparations for rescue. Two divers went down to 190 feet and later to 215 feet, at a location where an oil slick and air bubbles were sighted, but saw no sign of the sunken vessel. When the boat was finally located, an initial attempt to raise the hull by passing a sling around it was unsuccessful. The next attempt

Launched as *Skate* (SS-23) and renamed *F-4* in November 1911, *F-4* sank off Honolulu in March 1915 (crew of 21 perished). *(United States Navy)*

involved sweeping a wire under the submarine and trying to bring it up to the surface. This effort also failed. It then was clear that the submarine was full of water, and no one on board was left alive. Although rescue was no longer an option, the navy was determined to recover the submarine to see what caused the sinking. Using a pair of scows and a lifting apparatus, the salvage team moved *F-4* into shallow water by a series of short lifts. Although poor weather complicated the job, the hull rested in less than 50 feet of water by May 25. Pontoons (which would become an important element of later submarine salvage jobs) then were attached for buoyancy, and *F-4* made a final journey to a dry dock in Honolulu. An examination of the wreck showed that battery acid had eaten through rivets, and water had leaked in through the rivet holes. This finding resulted in vital design modifications for future American submarines. It also demonstrated how difficult it was for divers to work at any depth below 200 feet, and sparked research into improved diving techniques and equipment in anticipation of future submarine emergencies and in the hope of saving lives, if not boats.

fathom

In maritime usage, as a unit of depth measurement, one fathom is commonly interpreted as equivalent to six feet. In the past, however, the fathom's exact value varied considerably. In the age of sail, mariners defined it, for working purposes, as the span of a man's outstretched arms. Since a tall man's arm span was considerably greater than a small man's, one man's "fathom" might be as much as a foot longer or shorter than another's. Generally today, the standard six-foot value is used, and is a vital unit of measurement in undersea operations.

films

The following past and present popular films, from an unofficial Navy list published during the centennial of navy submarines in 2000, have covered the subject in many dramatic and often tragic ways.

- *Above the Waves* (1955)
- *Around the World under the Sea* (1966)
- *The Atomic Submarine* (1959)
- *The Bedford Incident* (1965)
- *Crash Dive* (1943)
- *Crimson Tide* (1995)
- *Das Boot* (1981)
- *Destination Tokyo* (1943)
- *Down Periscope* (1996)
- *Enemy Below* (1957)
- *Flying Missile* (1950)
- *Gray Lady Down* (1978)
- *Hell Below* (1933)

- *Hellcats of the Navy* (1957)
- *Hostile Waters* (1997)
- *The Hunley* (1999)
- *The Hunt for Red October* (1990)
- *Ice Station Zebra* (1968)
- *The Last U-Boat* (1990)
- *Monster from the Ocean Floor* (1954)
- *The Mysterious Island* (1961)
- *Mystery Submarine* (1950)
- *On the Beach* (1959)
- *Operation Pacific* (1951)
- *Operation Petticoat* (1959)
- *Run Silent, Run Deep* (1958)
- *The Sea Wolves* (1910)
- *Submarine Command* (1951)
- *Submarine D-1* (1937)
- *Submarine X-1* (1968)
- *Tomorrow Never Dies* (1997)
- *Torpedo Alley* (1953)
- *U-571* (2000)
- *Up Periscope* (1959)
- *Voyage to the Bottom of the Sea* (1961)
- *We Dive at Dawn* (1943)

Finback (SS-230)

Built at the Portsmouth Naval Yard as a Gato class submarine, *Finback* departed for the Pacific shortly after being commissioned in January 1942. She carried a crew of 82, was armed with six bow and four stern torpedo tubes, took on 24 21-inch torpedoes at the start of each war patrol, and achieved an enviable record of sinking 13 Japanese vessels for a total of 59,383 tons. She also was active in the Submarine Lifeguard League, established early in the war at the time of the Gilbert Islands campaign to rescue downed airmen. As a lifeguard boat, she rescued five airmen, the most noted being former president George H. W. Bush, then serving as a carrier pilot, who was shot down near the Bonin Islands. Bush, who narrowly escaped capture by a Japanese vessel before being rescued, spent almost a month aboard *Finback* before the submarine's return to port. During that time, *Finback* sank two enemy ships and was heavily depth-bombed. Many years later, Bush commented, "That experience was far scarier than an airplane bombing run. At least in the plane, you controlled your destiny to some extent . . . but there, under the water, all you could do was hope like hell the enemy wouldn't put an explosive on top of you."

Flasher (SS-249)

After *Flasher* was built by the Electric Boat Company and launched in September 1943, she was ordered to the Pacific and commenced her first war patrol in January 1944, when, off Mindoro, she sank her first target, sending a 2,900-ton gunboat to the bottom. Adding to what would be the greatest total of enemy tonnage credited to an American submarine in World War II, she then sank a freighter and two cargo ships off Manila and two more cargo ships of the same convoy 10 days later. On her second war patrol in April and May, she continued her route of devastation, knocking off a gunboat, a freighter, and a large cargo ship off the coast of Indochina before retiring to Fremantle, Australia, for refitting. On her third patrol, this time in the South China Sea in late June 1944, she contacted a heavily escorted convoy of 13 ships. She made a cautious approach, undeterred by the escort, and shortly after midnight June 29, broke into the convoy to sink a freighter and badly damage a large passenger cargo ship. Her next victim was a freighter and, 12 days later, a cruiser escorted by a destroyer. Within one more week, she also accounted for a destroyer, and the week after that a merchant tanker, before having to leave the scene with no more torpedoes left.

During her fourth war patrol, in the Philippines, *Flasher* headed a coordinated attack group that included two other submarines. Although she was on lifeguard station during the air attacks preliminary to the invasion of the Philippines during part of this patrol, *Flasher* managed to sink three more ships, including a light cruiser, a transport, and a cargo ship. Heading the same attack group, *Flasher* now sailed on her fifth war patrol in mid-November 1944, bound for Cam Ranh Bay. On December 4 one of her companions reported a tanker convoy, and *Flasher* set a course that would bring her to the target. As she made her approach in a heavy downpour, a destroyer suddenly loomed up before her, and *Flasher* launched her first spread of torpedoes at this escort. The destroyer was stopped by two hits, and began listing and smoking heavily. *Flasher* loosed a spread of torpedoes at a tanker before she was forced deep by a second destroyer, which dropped 16 depth charges. Rising to periscope depth, *Flasher* located the tanker, burning and covered by yet a third destroyer. Speedily reloading, she prepared to sink the destroyer and finish off the tanker; though almost blinded by rainsqualls, she did just this with a salvo of four torpedoes, two of which hit the destroyer, and two of which passed beneath her as planned to hit the tanker. Once more, counterattack forced *Flasher* down, and when she surfaced she found no trace of the two damaged destroyers, which later were confirmed as having sunk. The tanker, blazing away, was still guarded by three escorts until abandoned at sunset, when *Flasher* delivered a coup de grace with one torpedo. She contacted another well-guarded tanker convoy on the morning of December 21, 1944, and she began a long chase, getting into position to attack from the unguarded shoreward side. In rapid succession, *Flasher* attacked and sank three of the tankers, receiving no counterattack since the enemy commanders apparently believed they had stumbled into a minefield. One of these tankers was the largest she sank during the war; the other two, of the same displacement, were tied for third-largest.

In late January 1945, *Flasher* made her sixth war patrol off the coast of Indochina. Contacts were few, but in late February she sank a sea truck by surface gunfire and four days later a cargo ship with torpedoes. Bound for Guam on a seventh war patrol at the close of the war, *Flasher* was ordered back to New London, where she was decommissioned and placed in reserve in March 1946. Later, she received the Presidential Unit Citation for her brilliantly successful third, fourth, and fifth war patrols. For her six war patrols, she received six battle stars and was credited with having sunk 21 vessels, a total of 100,231 tons of Japanese shipping.

Flier (SS-250)

Built by the Electric Boat Company and launched in July 1943, this submarine of the Gato class was ordered to the Pacific, where she had a stroke of luck west of Luzon on her first patrol and sank four freighters, and damaged a fifth freighter and a tanker, for 19,500 tons sunk and 13,500 tons damaged. But her luck changed with a vengeance when she encountered difficulties on her second war patrol in mid-August 1944. As she transited Balabac Strait, south of Palawan, disaster struck when suddenly a terrific explosion, estimated to have been forward on the starboard side, shook the boat. Several of the men on the bridge were injured, including the commanding officer who was thrown violently to the after rail. Oil, water, and debris deluged the bridge. There was a strong smell of fuel, a fierce venting of air through the conning tower hatch, and the sounds of flooding and of screaming men below. Within half a minute, the submarine sank while still making 15 knots through the water, apparently the victim of a mine. The survivors, some of whom were wounded, and several of whom simply vanished in the water as they struggled to stay afloat, were now faced with a deadly decision—whether to try to swim to a nearby island occupied by the Japanese or to strike out for uninhabited coral reefs to the northwestward. The decision was to try for the latter, but several of the survivors fell behind—one of them having been blinded by burning oil—and were not seen again. Those few who were strong enough and less injured by the blast, were helped by fate when they reached a floating palm tree and used this to aid themselves in remaining afloat and pushing toward land. This group finally came ashore on Mantangule Island and were met by two others who had been strong enough to swim the distance. They then managed to construct a small lean-to and spend the night on the beach. In the days following, plans were laid to obtain food and water and to make contact with friendly natives. A raft was made of drifted bamboo lashed together, and the party began working from island to island, with Palawan the ultimate objective. On August 19 they contacted natives who led them to a U.S. Army Coast Watcher Unit on Palawan, which then made contact with naval forces and set up a plan for evacuation by submarine. On the night of August 30 the survivors from *Flier* embarked in two small boats, and, having made their way safely around a Japanese merchant ship anchored near the rendezvous point, were picked up by the submarine *Redfin* early in the morning of August 31.

Flounder (SS-251)

Launched in late August 1943, this submarine of the Gato class was ordered to New Guinea the first week in March 1944, and a week later embarked on her first war patrol, bound for the Palaus. Many planes were sighted, limiting her action, and few contacts were made. The second patrol fared little better, though she did sink two small transports in the Philippine Sea during the assault on the Marianas, for which the Japanese retaliated by pounding her into retreat with several small bombs that landed close aboard and inflicted moderate damage. The third war patrol fared little better. On her fourth war patrol in late October 1944, *Flounder* patrolled the South China Sea with two other submarines. North of Lombok Strait on November 10, she sighted what was first thought to be a small sailboat. When closer inspection revealed the target to be the conning tower of a submarine, *Flounder* went to battle stations submerged. She sent four torpedoes away, observing one hit and feeling another as the target submarine exploded and was enveloped by smoke and flame. Coming back to periscope depth a half-hour later, *Flounder* found nothing in sight. She had sunk, not a Japanese submarine, but the *U-537,* one of the German submarines operating in the Far East. The pickings were not only very few when *Flounder* set out on her fifth and sixth war patrols, but also she was plagued with a series of mishaps, including instrument malfunctions, an erratic torpedo that not only failed to hit the intended Japanese target but also did an about face and threatened to hit its sender, and a freak accident in which she and another submarine, the *Hoe,* brushed each other and caused a leak. Ordered back to the States, *Flounder* saw no more war service, was placed in reserve in New London, and was decommissioned in February 1947.

Flying Fish (SS-229)

After her launching at the Portsmouth Naval Shipyard in early July 1941, *Flying Fish* went through a series of trials as World War II began and in mid-May 1942 was ordered out to patrol west of Midway Island in the Pacific, where an expected Japanese attack would result in the battle of Midway the first week in June. A month later, she scored her first hit, on a Japanese destroyer off Taiwan. On her second patrol in mid-August, bound for a zone north of Truk, she sighted a Japanese battleship, guarded by two destroyers and air cover. Four torpedoes were launched at this prime target, and two hits were picked up by sound. Immediately the counterattack began, and the boat had to dive to maximum depth, amidst a barrage of depth charges. She closed Truk once more during the first week in September and, after a series of encounters and no sinkings, was considerably damaged by depth charges and forced to retreat to Pearl Harbor for repairs. Her fourth patrol was more successful, when, after doing reconnaissance of the Marianas and gaining much valuable intelligence, she damaged a freighter in Apra Harbor in late January 1943, hit a passenger-cargo ship, and sank another freighter. Her fifth war patrol, off the coast of Honshu in March and April, was highly successful—she sank three freighters and two cargo ships.

Flying Fish continued her successful runs, with the following results: a cargo ship on her sixth patrol; a merchant ship on her seventh; a cargo ship and tanker on her eighth; a merchantman, cargo ship, and freighter on her ninth; two passenger-cargo ships on her 10th; and two cargo ships during her 12th and last patrol. After the war, based at New London, she conducted training exercises and served the Underwater Sound Laboratory in sonar experiments. In February 1952, she made submarine history as she dived for the 5,000th time. *Flying Fish* was decommissioned in May 1954. Of her 12 war patrols, all save the 11th were designated "Successful," and she received 12 battle stars for World War II service. In all, she sank 15 vessels for a total of 58,306 tons.

Robert Fulton (1765–1815)

A noted American inventor known for his design of the steamboat *Clermont,* he also experimented with submarines. In 1800, while in France, he built the submarine *Nautilus* under a grant from Napoleon Bonaparte. It was constructed of copper sheets over iron ribs, and had a hand-turned propeller and the prototype of a conning tower fitted with a glass-covered porthole. The *Nautilus* submerged by taking water into ballast tanks, and a horizontal diving plane helped keep the craft at the desired depth. Fulton's boat contained enough air to keep four men alive and two candles burning for three hours underwater. *Nautilus* was intended to attach an explosive charge to the hull of an enemy ship in much the same manner as the *Turtle,* and was actually successful later in the experimental sinking of an old schooner. But France's interest in submarines waned, as did that of England, to whom Fulton next turned for sponsorship. Fulton then came to the United States and succeeded in obtaining congressional backing for a more ambitious undersea craft, which was to carry no fewer than 100 men and be powered by a steam engine. Fulton died before the craft, named *Mute,* was actually finished, and the hull was left to rot, eventually sinking at its moorings.

G

Gabilan (SS-252)

Submarine built by the Electric Boat Company and launched in September 1943. She was assigned to Pearl Harbor in March 1944, and spent her first war patrol scouting the Marianas and gathering information for the United States invasion of those islands. Her second war patrol, in July and August, took her to the south coast of Honshu, Japan, where, on the night of July 17, she made a daring radar chase through bright moonlight and phosphorescent water. Skirting dangerous reefs and shoals, she pressed home an attack that sank a 492-ton minesweeper. Her third war patrol, in September and October, took her south of the Japanese Empire in company with *Sugo* and *Ronquil* to detect the departure from Bungo Suido of any major enemy fleet units that might interfere with the campaign to liberate the Philippine Islands. The latter period of the patrol was an independent search of approaches to Kii Suido, where, in a dawn periscope attack in late October, *Gabilan* destroyed an auxiliary ship with a single torpedo. Her fourth war patrol was in the South China Sea in January and February 1945. She joined *Perch* and *Barbel* in a coordinated patrol off the southern entrance to Palawan Passage and the western approach to Balapac Strait, where two Japanese battleships were expected to appear en route to threaten American invasion forces in the Philippines. There were many quick dives to avoid aircraft, culminated by the appearance of a Japanese minelayer that made two deliberate attacks in shallow water, dropping 20 depth charges. *Gabilan* conducted the greater part of her fifth war patrol in April and May as a unit of a wolf pack, which began an epic four-day chase on April 4 with a morning contact on cruiser ISUZU and her four escorts. One of the escorts fell prey to *Besugo* and the elusive cruiser was spotted as she entered Bima Bay on the night of April 6. Word was flashed to *Gabilan,* already executing a daring surface attack that left the cruiser listing and down by the bow.

Gabilan outwitted three escorts to sink a small freighter, then scored hits on two cargo ships of another convoy. After a short stay off the coast of Hainan where she destroyed drifting mines, she returned to Pearl Harbor for refit. Her sixth and last patrol was on lifeguard station for American fliers off Tokyo Bay at the end of World War II. She first rescued six men, the crews of two torpedo bombers, then raced well inside Tokyo Bay, in easy range of shore batteries, to rescue another three-man crew. After the war, she joined the Atlantic Reserve Fleet and was decommissioned in December 1959. She received four battle stars for World War II service.

Gar (SS-206)

Built by the Electric Boat Company and launched in November 1940, she departed for San Diego just four days before the Japanese attack on Pearl Harbor and two months later embarked on her maiden war patrol deep into enemy territory at the entrance to the Inland Sea of Japan, where she sank a cargo ship, as well as compiling intelligence reports. During her second war patrol, in April and May, she scored hits on a freighter off Kwajalein atoll and a submarine decoy "Q-ship" west of Truk atoll, then terminated her patrol at Fremantle, Australia. Her third war patrol was uneventful, while her fourth patrol, in the fall of 1942, took her to the northernmost waters in the Gulf of Siam, where she laid 32 mines in one of the most

USS *Gar* (SS-206) on her 15th and final war patrol (December 1944). *Gar* landed 35 tons of supplies on the west coast of Luzon and returned to Pearl Harbor with urgent intelligence documents, including maps locating enemy gun emplacements, beach defenses, troop concentrations, and fuel and ammunition dumps on Luzon. *(United States Navy)*

important Japanese shipping lanes. On her next three patrols, she scored hits mainly on small ships, but also sank two cargo ships of about 4,000 tons. *Gar's* war career was a lengthy one, covering a total of 15 patrols, during the last few of which she sank two more cargo ships and damaged or sank many small ships in convoys, as well as saving American aviators while on lifeguard duty and performing valuable reconnaissance work off Surigao Strait. She also bombarded installations on Yap and ended her patrol at Brisbane, Australia. After the war, she was largely engaged in training duties before being decommissioned in May 1959. She received 11 battle stars for her service in World War II, during which she sank 8 vessels for a total of 20,392 tons.

Garfish [formerly *H-3*] (SS-30)

Built by Seattle Construction and Drydock Company and launched in July 1913, she was attached to the United

States Pacific Fleet and began operations along the West Coast of the United States. While engaged in operations off the northern California coast, she ran hard aground in heavy fog on Samoa Beach at Eureka, on the morning of December 16, 1916. Immediate efforts to get her free failed, so the United States Coast Guard removed her crew to safety by means of breeches buoy transfers. Subsequent attempts to free the submarine failed. After many further attempts it was decided to bring in one of the navy's cruisers, the USS *Milwaukee*, which had powerful 24,000-horsepower engines, thought to be more than ample to free the submarine. Many weeks went by, with the cruiser floundering in heavy surf every time an effort was made. It was a disaster, and the *Milwaukee* suffered so much damage—without even budging the stranded submarine—that the cruiser was declared a loss. Her hull broke in half and was later sold to salvage firms for scrap.

The irony of this debacle was that *Garfish* was finally refloated by a commercial salvage company and returned to the navy. She was refitted and relaunched in April 1917, and served as flagship of SubDiv7, operating along the West Coast until being decommissioned in October 1922.

Gato (SS-212)

The first of two boats to bear this name, she was built by the Electric Boat Company and launched in August 1941. She was the prototype for the Gato class, boats built during the 1940s, displacing 1,475 tons on the surface and 2,370 submerged, and carrying a complement of six officers and 54 enlisted men. She departed on her first war patrol in late April 1942, where she attacked a converted aircraft carrier but was driven off by the fierce depth charging of four destroyers off the Marshall Islands. On her second war patrol in July and August, she patrolled toward the Aleutian chain and obtained four torpedo hits with unconfirmed damage to an enemy ship. Her third patrol was unsuccessful, but on her fourth in January and February, she sank a transport and two cargo ships off New Georgia, Solomon Islands. On her fifth war patrol, in the spring of 1943, she landed an Australian Intelligence party at Toep, Bougainville, and evacuated 27 children, nine mothers, and three nuns. Shortly after bringing them to safety, she was shaken so violently by three exploding depth charges that she returned to Brisbane for temporary repairs. *Gato* landed more Australian commandos at Toep Harbor in May, transported more evacuees to Ramos Island, and then reconnoitered off Tarawa in the Gilbert Islands before putting in at Pearl Harbor.

On her sixth war patrol, in September and October, she attacked a convoy, scoring hits for unknown damage to two large cargo ships, and on her seventh sank two freighters and damaged a third. On her eighth, in February and March 1944, she sank a trawler, a transport, and a freighter. She conducted five more patrols, adding three more enemy ships to her credit, and was attacking a ship near Tokyo Bay when she received word of Japan's surrender. After the war, she served for a number of years as a Naval Reserve training ship before being struck from the Navy list in March 1960. She received 13 battle stars and a Presidential Unit Citation, having sunk nine enemy ships for a tally of 26,085 tons.

Gato (SSN-615)

A submarine designed for a complement of 12 officers and 115 enlisted men, built by Electric Boat Company and launched in May 1964, her armament consisted of four 21-inch torpedo tubes located amidship, with MK-37 and MK-48 torpedoes, MK-67 SLMM, UGM-84 Harpoon cruise missiles, and short-range ballistic missiles. She later

Garfish (H-3) hard aground off the northern California coast in December 1916, while engaged in operations during heavy fog. Although she was refloated and put back into service, a navy cruiser, the *Milwaukee,* was damaged beyond repair while trying to pull the stranded boat free. *(United States Navy)*

On August 15, 1945, USS *Gato* (SS-212) while on her 13th war patrol off the eastern coast of Honshu received word of "Cease Fire" while making an attack approach on an enemy vessel. *(United States Navy)*

had an extension to her hull for better habitability and buoyancy, and a sail modification, making it longer and wider. After the loss of *Thresher,* her class was the first to be upgraded under the Subsafe program. During the time from her commissioning in January 1968 to her decommissioning in the summer of 1995 (the last of her class to serve), she received many awards for her participation in fleet exercises, training, and missions in the oceans of the world, including more than 25 for excellence in battle maneuvers, communications, damage control, and humanitarian services.

George Washington (SSBN-598)

The first of a new class, built by the Electric Boat Company and launched in June 1959, the *George Washington* was originally the *Scorpion* (SSN-589), lengthened by the insertion of a 130-foot missile section. As modernized and recommissioned, she had a displacement of 5,959 tons on the surface and 6,709 submerged, and required a complement of 12 officers and 100 enlisted men, each in two crews. In late June 1960, she sailed for Cape Canaveral,

Florida, where she loaded two solid propellant Polaris missiles. Standing out into the Atlantic Missile Test Range, the nuclear submarine made history July 20, 1960, when she successfully launched the first Polaris missile from a submerged submarine. At this moment, her commanding officer sent President Eisenhower the historic message: "Polaris—from out of the deep to target. Perfect." This event led the navy to report "the free world everywhere had gained a weapon of utmost importance to the protection of civilization." Less than two hours later another missile from the submerged submarine homed in on the impact area 1,100 miles downrange, thus proving that a new and powerful weapon had been added to America's naval arsenal. After duplicating her earlier successes by launching two more missiles while submerged, the submarine got underway in late October for Charleston, South Carolina, to load her full complement of 16 Polaris missiles. There she was awarded the Navy Unit Commendation, after which she embarked on her first deterrent patrol. The submarine completed her first patrol after 66 days of submerged running in January 1961, and departed on her next patrol in mid-February. It was not until four years after her initial departure from the shipyard that the *George Washington* had to return to "refuel," having cruised some 100,000 miles—a far cry from the days when World War II war patrol submarines were limited to about two months at sea before requiring a complete refit. The *George Washington* continued her pioneering missions until January 1985, when she was decommissioned and struck from the Navy list. Her sail was removed prior to disposal and now resides at the Submarine Force Library and Museum in New London, Connecticut.

The other four submarines in her class were:

Patrick Henry (SSBN-599)

Theodore Roosevelt (SSBN-600)

Robert E. Lee (SSBN-601)

Abraham Lincoln (SSBN-602)

George Washington Carver (SSBN-656)

A submarine of the Benjamin Franklin class, built by Newport News Shipbuilding and Drydock Company and launched in August 1965, she was the 37th fleet ballistic missile submarine to join the navy. Two years later, she successfully launched three Polaris A-3 missiles in the ship's first strategic operational test. In 1971, *Carver* was converted to carry the Poseidon C-3 missile, which she launched for the first time in May 1973, on the range at Cape Canaveral, Florida. Two months later, she commenced her first post-conversion strategic deterrent patrol with the C-3 Poseidon missile system. By 1982, Carver had completed more than 50 strategic deterrent patrols, and in 1991, after having completed 73 strategic deterrent patrols, she began a new career as a fast-attack submarine for the Pacific Fleet. After more than 26 years of proud service, the *George Washington Carver* was decommissioned in March 1993 at the Puget Sound Naval Shipyard, Bremerton, Washington.

Gilbert Islands, capture of (November 1943)

These islands in the mid-Pacific were occupied by the Japanese in 1941 as they advanced across the Pacific at the start of World War II. The islands' recapture was a key American objective in the central Pacific campaign in 1943. The naval forces assigned to this campaign included a fast carrier force of six fleet carriers, five light carriers, and six battleships. On November 20, 1943, the two most westerly islands in the Gilbert group, Makin and Tarawa, were invaded from the sea. Makin was lightly defended and fell within four days, but Tarawa was much better protected. The landing, which was preceded by a heavy bom-

bardment from the sea and air, was complicated by the fact that Tarawa's coastal waters, which are enclosed by a coral reef, proved to be too shallow for landing craft. The U.S. Marine Corps had to wade ashore for several hundred yards under heavy fire. They faced determined Japanese resistance, which produced heavy losses on both sides but could not prevent the island from falling to the Americans on November 23. This victory allowed American naval forces to withdraw and to move on to the Marshall Islands, the next target in their "island-hopping" campaign against Japan.

Glenard P. Lipscomb (SSN-685)

Built by the Electric Boat Company and launched in August 1973, this attack submarine of a new class had a submerged displacement of 6,480 tons and was designed for a complement of 12 officers and 109 enlisted men. She and a sister ship, *Tullibee,* were built to experiment with

George Washington (SSBN-598), the first of a new class of nuclear submarines, was launched in June 1959. She successfully launched the first Polaris missile from a submerged submarine. *(United States Navy)*

the technology of electric drive, specifically a Turbine Electric Drive (TED) propulsion plant. Speed was sacrificed to reduce machinery noise. However, the electric motor and power conversion technology of the 1970s was not sophisticated enough to compete with the advances made in mechanical drive and as a result these early electric-drive submarines were more difficult to maintain. The *Lipscomb* provided valuable information for later submarines that in the 1980s and 1990s profited well from the experiments. The *Glenard P. Lipscomb* was homeported in Norfolk, Virginia, and was decommissioned and struck from the Navy list in July 1990. No additional submarines of this type were built because of a decision to make the faster Los Angeles (SSN-688) class in the standard SSN design.

The first *Grampus A-3* (SS-4), one of the navy's earliest submarines, cruising off San Diego. She had her keel laid down at the Union Iron Works in San Francisco in December 1900, but was not commissioned until May 1903, as the fourth to join the fledgling fleet. *(United States Navy)*

Glomar Challenger

An oceanographic drilling and coring vessel, she was constructed in the late 1960s by Global Marine, Inc. The only ship of its kind in the world, it is capable of drilling in water depths up to 6,000 meters (20,000 feet) and of bringing back core samples from depths as great as 750 meters (2,500 feet) below the seafloor. To maintain the extreme stability required for this operation under differing current, wind, and wave conditions, the vessel is equipped with a computer-controlled roll-neutralizing system. An automatic pipe-racking device helps handle the numerous lengths of drill pipe needed. A drilling derrick 43 meters (140 feet) high, mounted in the center of the vessel, lowers the drill through an opening 6 by 6 meters (20 by 20 feet) that extends through the bottom of the ship, which is 120 meters (400 feet) long and 20 meters (65 feet) wide. To prevent the roll and pitch of the ship from bending the string of the drill pipe too sharply, a flared structure on the ship surrounds the pipe. Living facilities are provided on board for 70 persons. Core samples gathered by the *Glomar Challenger* from 1968 to 1983 added much weight to the hypothesis of seafloor spreading, which played a pivotal role in the development of the theory of plate tectonics.

Golet (SS-361)

A submarine of the Gato class, she was built by the Manitowoc Shipbuilding Company, Manitowoc, Wisconsin, and launched in August 1943. Sent to the Pacific, she departed Pearl Harbor in March 1944 for her maiden war patrol off the Kurile Island chain, southern Hokkaido, and eastern Honshu, Japan. Severe combinations of fog, rain, and ice were encountered and she had no success. She left Midway on May 28, 1944, to patrol off northern Honshu, Japan. A door of silence closed behind her and *Golet* was never heard from again. In the reports covering Japanese antisubmarine attacks, made since the war's end, one is recorded as having been made on June 14, 1944, at a position where the lost boat may have been. This attack is considered to explain her loss, since the enemy, in his report, states, "On the spot of fighting we later discovered corks, raft, etc., and a heavy oil pool of 50 by 5,200 meters."

Eighty-two gallant men perished with *Golet*.

Grampus (SS-207)

A submarine of the Gar class, the second to bear the name, built by the Electric Boat Company and launched in December 1940, she was ordered to the Pacific where she began her first war patrol in early February 1942. She sank an 8,636-ton tanker, the only kill of her short career, and reconnoitered Kwajalein and Wotje atolls, later the scene of bloody but successful landings. Her second and third

Grayback (SS-208), launched in January 1941, departed Pearl Harbor one year later on the first of 10 patrols and sank more than 63,800 tons of enemy shipping. She was reported missing somewhere in the East China Sea and was declared lost in late March 1944. *(United States Navy)*

patrols were marred by a heavy number of antisubmarine patrol craft off Truk and poor visibility, as heavy rains haunted her path along the Luzon and Mindoro coasts. Taking aboard four coast watchers, the courageous men who were stationed on Japanese-held islands to radio back vital information on shipping, military buildup, and weather, *Grampus* sailed in early October for her fourth war patrol. Despite the presence of Japanese destroyers, she landed the coast watchers on Vella Lavella and Choiseul Islands while conducting her patrol. The next two patrols, during the height of the Guadalcanal campaign, took *Grampus* into waters teeming with enemy warships. Although escaping more than 100 depth charges, she was not credited with sinking any ships. In company with *Grayback,* she departed Brisbane in mid-February 1943 for her sixth war patrol, from which she failed to return. On March 5, two Japanese destroyers conducted an attack in Blackett Strait, where a heavy oil slick was sighted the following day, indicating that *Grampus* may have been lost there in a night attack against these two enemy ships.

The first *Grampus,* for which this boat was named, was launched in July 1902 as Submarine Torpedo Boat #4 in the U.S. Navy, and served on the West Coast and later in the Philippines, where she patrolled during World War I. She was struck from the Navy list in July 1921, and ended her career as a target ship.

Grampus (SS-523)

The third submarine to bear this name was built by the Boston Naval Shipyard and launched in December 1944. Her construction was uncompleted at the end of World War II, and she was not commissioned until late October

1949, and a year later converted to a GUPPY II. With new snorkeling equipment, which permitted her to remain submerged for periods far longer than the World War II fleet-class ships, *Grampus* served as a prototype for the GUPPY II-class submarines and also incorporated many features to appear later in nuclear submarines. She participated in a variety of exercises along the East Coast and in the Caribbean, including torpedo and attack exercises, snorkeling tests, and antisubmarine training. During the late 1950s and 1960s, *Grampus* operated out of Norfolk in the North Atlantic, and later in the North Atlantic participated in NATO ASW exercises. She was decommissioned in May 1972 and sold to Brazil.

Grayback (SS-208)

Launched in January 1941, she was attached to the Atlantic Fleet until just after the start of World War II, when she was ordered to Hawaii, leaving on the first of her many war patrols in mid-February 1942. After a deadly four-day game of hide-and-seek with an enemy submarine off Guam, she shook the other sub and drew first blood by sinking a 3,290-ton cargo ship. Her next three patrols were frustrated by bad weather conditions and an overabundance of enemy patrol boats. But on her fifth patrol, in January 1943, after sinking four Japanese landing barges with her deck guns, she attacked and sank the *I-18,* one of 25 Japanese submarines chalked up by American submarines. Two days later, *Grayback* served as beacon ship for the bombardment of Munda Bay and also indulged in some hair-raising rescue work. Lying off Munda early in the morning, she received word that six survivors of a crashed American bomber were holed up on the island. Her skipper sent two men ashore, then submerged at dawn to avoid enemy aircraft. The submariners located the downed aviators, three of whom were injured, and hid out with them in the jungle. As night fell, *Grayback* surfaced offshore and by coded light signals directed the small boat safely aboard with the rescued aviators. For this episode, her skipper, Edward C. Stephan, received the Navy Cross.

Grayback's sixth patrol was marred by a faulty radar, but on her seventh she sank two cargo ships, damaged two more, and damaged a destroyer. In September, at Midway, she joined *Shad* and *Cero* to form the first of the submarine force's highly successful wolf packs. The three submarines returned to base with claims of 38,000 tons sunk and 3,300 damaged. On her eighth patrol, *Grayback* accounted for two ships, a passenger-cargo vessel and a light cruiser, and assisted *Shad* in administering the coup de grace to a 9,000-ton transport. On her ninth war patrol, within five days of her first contact with Japanese ships, she had expended all her torpedoes in a brilliant series of attacks that netted four ships for a total of over 10,000 tons. *Grayback's* 10th patrol, her most successful in terms of tonnage sunk, was also to be her last. She sailed in late January 1944 for the East China Sea. On February 24, she radioed that she had sunk two cargo ships and damaged two others. On February 25 she transmitted her second and final report. That morning she had sunk one tanker and severely damaged another. With only two torpedoes remaining, she was ordered home from patrol. Due to reach Midway on March 7 *Grayback* did not arrive. By month's end, ComSubPac reluctantly listed her as missing and presumed lost with all hands. From captured Japanese records it became evident that a Japanese carrier-based plane had spotted a submarine on the surface in the East China Sea and attacked. According to Japanese reports, the submarine "exploded and sank immediately," but antisubmarine craft were called in to depth-charge the area, clearly marked by a trail of air bubbles; until at last a heavy oil slick swelled to the surface. Her career, so tragically ended, had been an illustrious one. She ranked 20th among all submarines in total tonnage sunk, with 63,835 tons, and 24th in number of ships sunk, with 14.

Grayback (SSG-574)

The second submarine to bear this name was launched in July 1957 as the first of the navy's guided missile submarines designed and built to carry the Regulus sea-to-surface missiles. She pointed the way to a revolutionary advance in the power of navies to attack land bases. She operated largely on the West Coast and in far Pacific waters. During nine patrols she spent more than 20 months at sea and logged well over 130,000 miles on deterrent missile strike missions. As more and more

Polaris submarines became operational, they assumed the deterrent functions previously assigned to *Grayback* and her sister ships. In the 1960s, *Grayback* was converted to a troop-carrying submarine (APSS). As such, she operated in the western Pacific for several years. She was decommissioned in June 1984 and was sunk as a target in or near Subic Bay, in the Philippines, in April 1986.

Grayling (SS-18) (Ex-D-2)

The first submarine of this name was built by the Fore River Shipbuilding Company and launched in June 1909. She joined the Atlantic Torpedo Fleet and operated in Cape Cod and Narragansett Bays, in Long Island and Block Island Sounds, in Chesapeake Bay, and off Norfolk, Virginia, on target ranges proving torpedoes, doing experimental operations, and conducting cruises along the East Coast of the United States. During the First World War, she trained crews and classes of officers and served in experimental work while based at New London, Connecticut. She was decommissioned in January 1922.

Grayling (SS-209)

The second submarine of this name was built by the Portsmouth Naval Shipyard and launched in September 1940. Her first war patrol, made in January and February 1942, was a reconnaissance of the northern Gilbert Islands. She went to the Japanese homeland for her second patrol, and sank a freighter and damaged a sampan. Truk was the scene of her third patrol, where she sank a large freighter. On her fourth patrol, this boat again went to Truk, and sank a medium tanker, while she damaged an aircraft transport. In January and February 1943, she patrolled the approaches to Manila on her fifth patrol. Here she sank two freighters and a medium freighter-transport. *Grayling* patrolled the lesser islands south of the Philippines on her sixth patrol, and sank two freighters, a small freighter-transport, and two schooners. She went to the area west of Borneo for her seventh patrol, and sank a medium freighter and two sampans. Damage was done to a large tanker. *Grayling* was listed at that point as 16 ships sunk, totaling 61,400 tons, and six ships damaged, for a total of 36,600 tons. *Grayling* departed Fremantle, Australia, on July 30, 1943, for her eighth war patrol, heading through Makassar Strait and thence to the Philippine area. On August 19, she reported having damaged a 6,000-ton freighter near Balikpapan, and the following day told of having sunk a small tanker by gunfire in Sibutu Passage, taking one man prisoner. This was the last report received directly from *Grayling*. However, four days later, she completed a special mission at Pandan Bay, Panay, delivering a cargo to guerrillas. This mission was relayed by guerrillas, who also reported that the submarine had intended to head for Tablas Strait, there to reconnoiter and patrol approaches to Manila until September 10, after which she was to return to Pearl Harbor for refit. Since she had not been heard from since August 19, by the end of September 1943, *Grayling* was reported as presumed lost. Interpreting postwar Japanese naval reports, it was deemed certain that *Grayling* was lost between September 9 and 12, 1943, either in Lingayen Gulf or along the approaches to Manila.

Greater Underwater Propulsion Power Program (GUPPY)

Following World War II, when it was recognized that there was a need for improvement in the speed, maneuverability, and submerged endurance of fleet submarines, this new technology program was gradually introduced. While not an exact acronym, GUPPY had a fishlike ring to it at a time when all submarines were then being named after undersea life. In the mid-1940s, after studying two high-caliber German U-boats, the U.S. Navy learned certain lessons about how to increase the battery capacity, streamline a boat's structure, add a snorkel, perfect the fire control system, and make other design improvements. This resulted in seven successive improvements, each one a little better or different than the previous refinement: GUPPY I, GUPPY IA, GUPPY IB, GUPPY II, GUPPY IIA, GUPPY III, and the Fleet Snorkel.

Although much of the information about the operation of the GUPPYs during the cold war still remains classified, it is well acknowledged that without the conversion of the fleet boats of World War II, many of the operations for which they were responsible would not have been possible. Such operations included maneuvers in extremely rough, cold, and treacherous seas, battling storms, and maintaining long periods of stealth by remaining just below the surface. The GUPPYs thus fulfilled vital assignments at a critical period in naval history before the development and launching of the later SSNs and SSBNS.

The GUPPY I program started with the conversion of the *Odax* (SS-484) and *Pomodon* (SS-486), which had been built at the Portsmouth Naval Shipyard at the end of World War II and consisted of such external improvements as the removal of deck guns; the streamlining of the entire conning tower fairwater "sail," including the bridge structure and enclosure of masts; the design of a streamlined hull superstructure, including a rounded bow (now to be referred to as the "GUPPY bow") and retractable deck cleats; and the placement of removable stanchions, railings, and other deck fixtures. Internally, among other improvements, battery power and capacity were increased, sonar was upgraded, open switchboards were enclosed, and the electrical system was modernized. The results

were evident when, in the early 1950s, the *Pomodon* set an underwater submarine speed record of 19.6 knots.

The GUPPY IA program carried the improvements further, with conversions for the *Atule, Becuna, Blackfin, Blenny, Caiman, Chivo, Chopper, Sea Poacher, Sea Robin,* and *Tench*. These refinements included the addition of a snorkel, two Sargo batteries, streamlining on the sail and superstructure, new masts, and various equipment upgrades and rearrangements. The GUPPY IB program was an interim conversion on five boats being transferred to foreign navies: the *Barb, Dace, Hawkbill, Icefish,* and *Jallao*.

The GUPPY II conversion was generally similar to that of the GUPPY I, the major difference being the addition of a snorkel system, four batteries, radar, and new masts and the streamlining of the entire superstructure. Some 24 boats were subject to this conversion, including the two with GUPPY I. This program started in 1947 and lasted five years.

The GUPPY IIA program included improvements in the sail and the bow, overall streamlining, the rearrangement of some of the interior apparatuses and equipment, and the installation of two Sargo batteries. A major change was the removal of one of the forward engines and the auxiliary engine, with the space then utilized for air-conditioning plants and refrigeration units. This conversion affected 16 fleet submarines that had been built in the mid-1940s.

The GUPPY III program addressed the problem in the mid-1950s of the increasing amount of electronic equipment that was being required on submarines. Nine boats that already had a majority of GUPPY conversion work completed and were in good condition were taken into the shipyard, cut in half, and lengthened with a 15-foot section at the forward end of the control room to create a new space for sonar. In addition, the conning tower was enlarged with an additional five-foot section to accommodate an MK-101 fire control system and MK 37 director. A "northern" sail was also added, which increased the height of the bridge, allowing it to be manned in the severe weather of northern seas. The GUPPY IIIs had two engine configurations: Some had three engines, and some had four.

Fleet Snorkel (FS) submarines are generally considered to be GUPPYs, although they are a special class of boat. Initially, 25 submarines were converted much like the GUPPYs but without some of the internal modifications. Basically, they were fleet boats with the snorkel system and a streamlined sail.

The net result of these conversions was that between 1945 and 1955, the submarine was transformed from a fast surface ship that could hide briefly underwater into a true underwater boat, able to cruise and operate for weeks on end without ever surfacing. As a result, they changed the way the navy made its long-ranging strategic planning for the use of submarines in peace and in war.

Generalized Guppy Conversion Characteristics (BY CLASS)

	GUPPY CLASS						
	I	IA	IB	II	IIA	III	FS
Streamlined hull superstructure, including GUPPY bow	X	X	X	X	X	X	
Streamlined conning tower and fairwater "sail" (low/high)	X	X	X	X	X	X	X
Snorkel systems		X	X	X	X	X	X
Engines	4	4	4	4	3	4*	4
Batteries	4	2	2	4	2	4	2
Upgraded sonar system	X	X		X	X	X	X
Upgraded fire control system	X	X		X	X	X	X
Lengthened hull and conning tower						X	

Tiru had only three engines.

Greeneville (SSN-772)

A submarine of the Los Angeles class, built by Newport News Shipbuilding and Drydock Company and launched in September 1994. She conducted shakedown operations in the western Atlantic during 1996, and in April 1997 was moved to the submarine base at Pearl Harbor, Hawaii, and conducted cruises to Japan, Korea, Guam, and New Caledonia. During the next three years, her operations were normal for an attack submarine until, on a fateful day in February 2001, she met disaster. At approximately 1:50 in the afternoon, she was cruising submerged some nine miles south of Diamond Head off Honolulu. She was demonstrating to 16 civilian visitors aboard how a submarine could rise abruptly and swiftly from the depths, when she collided with a Japanese vessel, *Ehime Maru,* on the surface directly above her. Within minutes, the stricken Japanese vessel, her hull ruptured, had plunged to the bottom. Despite desperate and immediate efforts by *Greeneville's* crew and units of the Coast Guard, which arrived promptly on scene, nine of the 35 crew members and passengers on the Japanese vessel were lost. This tragic accident, which touched off international repercussions, initiated one of the most intense investigations in submarine history, and yet left many questions unanswered relating to command decisions and procedures. Although *Greeneville's* skipper, Commander Scott Waddle, accepted the blame and apologized to the families of the victims and the Japanese nation, there was considerable doubt about where the blame should lie. He was thus spared a court-martial proceeding, but instead given an official letter of reprimand, which, in effect, ended his navy career.

Greenfish (SS-351)

A submarine of the Balao class, built by the Electric Boat Company and launched in December 1945, she started her career with fleet exercises in the Caribbean, during which she effected one of the first transfers of personnel from an aircraft carrier to a submarine by helicopter. In January 1948, she underwent a GUPPY II conversion at the Portsmouth Naval Shipyard. The conversion included the installation of snorkeling equipment to enable her to operate on diesel engines while submerged. In November 1949, she was attached to the Pacific Fleet, and spent most of the rest of her career in the Pacific, ranging from Hawaii to the mid-Pacific, the western Pacific, and Southeast Asia, until the Cuban missile crisis sent her to Japan to strengthen the Seventh Fleet. *Greenfish* was further converted to a GUPPY III at Pearl Harbor Naval Shipyard in 1961. *Greenfish* was decommissioned in December 1973 and subsequently sold to Brazil.

Greenling (SS-213)

A submarine of the Gato class, launched in September 1941, in early 1942 she sailed out of Pearl Harbor for her first war patrol in the Marshalls and Carolines. Her first battle was frustrating when she attacked a freighter four times but, due to faulty torpedoes, was not able to sink her. She finally recorded her first kill May 4 when she torpedoed a cargo ship amidships, breaking her in two. She departed on her second war patrol July 10, 1942. One of the first submarines to operate in the Truk area, she now joined in the undersea blockade of that important base, in an attempt to cut its supply lines to Japan. She succeeded this time in sinking two cargo ships with torpedoes and a trawler with her deck gun. Her third war patrol took her off the Japanese home islands, where she sank four cargo ships in rapid succession. Steaming into the Solomons-Truk area for her fourth war patrol, *Greenling* sank two cargo ships with torpedoes and two small boats with her deck gun. Her next four patrols were uneventful, except for landing intelligence agents on the coast of New Britain and sinking one small freighter. During her eighth patrol, in late December 1943, she sank another freighter. Not until her 11th patrol did she have further success, torpedoing an oiler, a transport, and a patrol boat—her last victim. Damaged by depth charges on her 12th patrol, she was ordered back to the Portsmouth Naval Shipyard, where she assisted in the training of reservists until March 1960, when she was placed out of service. *Greenling* received 10 battle stars for World War II service and a Presidential Unit

Citation for her outstanding performance in her first three war patrols, during which she sank 15 vessels for a total of 59,234 tons.

Grenadier (SS-525)

A submarine of the Tench class, built by the Boston Naval Shipyard and launched in February 1944. *Grenadier* displaced 2,416 tons (submerged), and was armed with one five-inch deck gun, six 21-inch torpedo tubes forward and four 21-inch torpedo tubes aft. She carried a complement of six officers and 60 enlisted men. She went into service too late for World War II combat patrols, but served on essential peacetime missions for almost 30 years. She was decommissioned and struck from the Navy list in 1973, after which she was sold to the Venezuelan navy.

Groton (SSN-694)

This submarine of the Los Angeles class was built by the Electric Boat Division of General Dynamics, launched in October 1976, and commissioned some two years later. She had a displacement (submerged) of 6,900 tons, was armed with four 21-inch torpedo tubes amidships, aft of the bow, and had a complement of 12 officers and 115 enlisted men. After serving for only 17 years, she was decommissioned and struck from the Navy list in October 1995.

Grouper (SS-214)

A submarine of the Gato class, launched in October 1941, she was ordered to join the Pacific Submarine Force and received more than her share of action when she was assigned to the submarine screen ringing the area where the American and Japanese fleets clashed in the decisive battle of Midway. On June 4, *Grouper* sighted two burning enemy carriers, but could not close for attack because of heavy air cover. On that day she was strafed by fighter planes and driven deep in a series of aircraft and destroyer attacks that saw over 170 depth charges and bombs dropped on the novice submarine. On her second patrol in September and October 1942, she sent two freighters to the bottom, and on her third knocked off a passenger-freighter headed for the Solomon Islands with troop reinforcements. Her next five patrols were relatively unproductive, but she gathered valuable intelligence, rescued a stranded aviator, and pinpointed several key Japanese radar installations in the Solomons. She also landed 50 men and 3,000 pounds of gear on New Britain Island to carry on guerrilla warfare and at the same time rescued another American aviator. On her ninth war patrol in May and June, she netted what was to be her last kill of the war, a ship that she

sank in a night surface attack. Later, she stood lifeguard duty during several air strikes and rescued seven downed aviators during raids on the Palaus in September 1944. After the war, she was involved in training and fleet exercises, during one of which she accomplished the first discharge and recovery of men from a submarine that was both submerged and underway.

In 1950, *Grouper* entered the Mare Island Shipyard for conversion to the navy's first "killer" submarine, after which she served in research on deadly submarine-versus-submarine warfare. For the next eight years, as a unit of Submarine Development Group 2, *Grouper* worked to develop concepts of hunter-killer antisubmarine warfare. In late 1959, her forward torpedo room was converted into a floating laboratory, additional berths for scientists were installed, and various types of sonar gear were added topside. Thus equipped, she embarked on a new phase of her long career, as a research vessel for the Naval Research and Underwater Sound Laboratories. She was decommissioned in December 1968. *Grouper* received 10 battle stars for World War II service, during which she sank four vessels for a total of 17,983 tons.

Growler (SS-215)

This submarine of the Gato class was launched in November 1941 and was ordered to the Pacific shortly after being commissioned. She went on her first war patrol at the end of June 1942, heading for Dutch Harbor, Alaska, where she sank one destroyer and damaged two more. On her second, and most successful, war patrol, in August and September near Taiwan, she sank a gunboat, a supply ship, and two cargo ships.

In January 1943, *Growler* was patrolling Truk-Rabaul shipping lanes when she sighted an enemy convoy and sank a cargo-passenger vessel. Later, she stealthily approached a gunboat for a night surface attack. The small, fast ship suddenly turned to ram. The skipper, Lieutenant Commander Howard Gilmore, standing on the bridge, took the only move he could to save his ship; he brought *Growler* left full rudder and rammed the enemy amidships at 17 knots. Machine-gun fire raked the bridge at point blank range. The courageous sub seemed lost. Gilmore ordered every one else to go below. Desperately wounded, he realized that he could not get below in time if his ship were to be saved. "Take her down!" he ordered; in sacrificing his life, he wrote another stirring chapter of inspirational naval history. For his heroic sacrifice to ship and crew, Gilmore was awarded the Congressional Medal of Honor.

Though severely damaged, *Growler* survived and escaped to undergo repairs and once again head for battle. Her next three patrols were relatively uneventful, in part because of heavy enemy air cover, a lack of target, typhoon weather, and generator problems, though she did sink one cargo ship. Her 10th war patrol was a wolf pack operation, in company with *Sealion* and *Pampanito*. In the Formosa Straits area, they were credited with a total of six enemy ships. *Growler* had sunk a destroyer and a frigate. The submarines had also rescued over 150 Allied prisoners from one of the torpedoed ships, which had served the Japanese as a prison ship. This difficult operation had been carried out despite rough seas caused by an approaching typhoon. In November 1944, *Growler* joined *Hake* and *Hardhead* in another wolf pack operation. In the early morning hours of November 8, while the three submarines were engaging enemy forces, both *Hardhead* and *Hake* heard explosions, which they could not confirm, but which sounded like torpedoes. *Growler* had earlier reported radar contact on an enemy target group, but all attempts by both *Hake* and *Hardhead* to contact *Growler* were unsuccessful, and she was never heard from again. Postwar Japanese records failed to suggest the time and place of *Growler's* last battle. She received eight battle stars for her sacrificial career, during which she sank ten enemy vessels for a total of 32,607 tons.

Growler (SSG-577)

A submarine of the Grayback class, *Growler* was built by the Portsmouth Navy Yard and launched in April 1958, designed for a crew of nine officers and 75 enlisted men. Her first assignments were in the Caribbean, where she trained in launching *Regulus I* and *II* guided missiles. In 1959, Growler was deployed to Pearl Harbor to serve as flagship of SubDiv 12, where she completed further training and exercises with guided missiles. She then undertook a series of silent, secret missions, each lasting two months or more, many times submerged—armed with nuclear warheads as deterrents during the cold war period. From May 1960 through December 1963, *Growler* completed nine such deterrent mission patrols. She was decommissioned in May 1964, and now serves as a museum ship in the USS *Intrepid* park in New York City.

Grunion (SS-216)

A submarine of the Gato class, she was launched two weeks after the attack on Pearl Harbor, and set out in late May 1942 to get revenge. As she transited the Caribbean for Panama, she rescued 16 survivors of USAT *Jack* torpedoed by a German U-boat, and conducted a fruitless search for other survivors before depositing her shipload of survivors at Coco Solo. On her first war patrol, *Grunion* proceeded to the Aleutian theater and patrolled westward from Attu on routes between the Aleutians and the Japanese Empire. In mid-July, *Grunion* radioed that she had sunk three destroyer-type vessels, but the message was gar-

bled to the extent that details of the attacks were never learned. The submarine had been ordered to the area near Kiska, where there was a strong concentration of enemy vessels, only a month and a half after the enemy had taken that island. On July 22, *Grunion* reported an attack on unidentified enemy ships six miles southeast of Sirius Point, Kiska. Her last transmission was received July 30, 1942. She reported heavy antisubmarine activity at the entrance to Kiska, and that she had 10 torpedoes remaining. On the same day, *Grunion* was directed to return to Dutch Harbor. She was not contacted or sighted after July 30, despite every effort to do so, and on August 16 was reported lost. Her fate remains an unsolved mystery, since no enemy minefields are known to have been in her area, and there were no Japanese reports of a submarine being torpedoed.

Guadalcanal, Battle of (August 1942– February 1943)

A series of World War II land and sea battles between Allied and Japanese forces on and around Guadalcanal, one of the southern Solomon Islands, in the South Pacific. Japanese troops had landed on Guadalcanal on July 6, 1942, and had begun constructing an airfield there. On August 7, in the Allies' first major offensive in the Pacific, 6,000 U.S. Marines landed on Guadalcanal and seized the airfield, surprising the island's 2,000 Japanese defenders. Both sides then began landing reinforcements by sea, and bitter fighting ensued in the island's jungles. The Japanese forces on the island reached a peak strength of 36,000 troops by October, but they were unable to overwhelm the Americans' defensive perimeter and retake the airfield. Six separate naval battles were also fought in the area as the navies of both sides sought to land reinforcements. By November, the U.S. Navy was able to land reinforcements on Guadalcanal faster than were the Japanese, and by February 1943, the Japanese, badly outnumbered, were forced to evacuate from Guadalcanal. The Japanese lost a total of 24,000 men killed in the battle of Guadalcanal, while the Americans sustained 1,600 killed and 4,200 wounded. The various naval battles cost each side 24 warships: the Japanese lost two battleships, four cruisers, one light carrier, 11 destroyers, and six submarines, while the Americans lost eight cruisers, two heavy carriers, and 14 destroyers. American submarines played a key role in these battles, not only as attackers of enemy ships, but also as rescuers of downed flyers and survivors of sunken vessels.

Guardfish (SS-217)

A submarine of the Gato class, launched in January 1942, she was ordered to the Pacific and began her first war patrol in the hitherto unpatrolled waters off northeast Honshu in early August 1942. She was unusually successful, sinking a trawler, three cargo ships, and a freighter. Her second patrol, two months later, resulted in two more prizes, ships of 4,000 tons and 6,362 tons. On her third war patrol, at the beginning of 1943, she sank a Japanese patrol craft and a cargo ship in the Truk area, and then polished off the destroyer *Hakaze*, which had attacked her while trying to protect the other two victims. Her next two patrols were relatively quiet, resulting in the sinking of one small freighter and damage to another. On her sixth patrol, in September and October, she landed two reconnoitering parties on Bougainville, sank a 5,460-ton Japanese vessel, and served as a lifeguard ship during air strikes on Rabaul. Her seventh war patrol resulted in the sinking of a 10,000-ton oiler and another destroyer. In July 1944, *Guardfish* joined submarines *Thresher*, *Piranha*, and *Apogon* to form the famous coordinated attack group known as the "Mickey Finns," which patrolled the shipping lanes around Formosa with spectacular success, *Guardfish* sinking 5,863-ton auxiliary *Mantai Maru*, 2,838-ton cargo ship *Hizan Maru*, and 5,215-ton cargo ship *Jinsan Maru* southwest of Formosa. After damaging another freighter, *Guardfish* sank 5,872-ton *Teiryu Maru* the next day, barely escaping the attacks of her escort vessels. She arrived at Midway for refit, and for her outstanding performance on the eighth patrol was awarded a second Presidential Unit Citation. Her ninth patrol—again as a member of a wolf pack—was less successful, resulting in a single small cargo vessel.

Guardfish had an unfortunate experience after she left for her 10th patrol in the South China Sea in January 1945. She recorded no sinkings during this cruise, but nearing Guam in the early morning darkness of January 24 she mistook *Extractor*, an American salvage ship, for an I-class Japanese submarine and torpedoed her. *Guardfish* succeeded in rescuing all but six of her crew of 79 from the sea, and brought them back to Guam two days later. Her 11th and 12th patrols were deep in enemy waters, largely spent watching for enemy fleet units attempting to escape from the Inland Sea of Japan by way of Kii Suido and acting as a lifeguard station for the ever-increasing air attacks on the Japanese mainland. She sank a small trawler with gunfire and arrived back at Pearl Harbor in late June, her patrolling days over as the war came to an end. After a brief tour with the training command, she returned to New London, serving her final days as a Naval Reserve training ship until being struck from the Navy list in June 1960. *Guardfish* earned 11 battle stars for her World War II service during which she sank 19 vessels for a total of 72,424 tons.

Guardfish (SSN-612)

A submarine of the Permit class, *Guardfish* was built by the New York Shipbuilding Corporation in Camden, New Jersey, and launched on May 15, 1965. She was armed with four 21-inch weapons tubes aft of the bow, displaced 3,500 tons (submerged), and was designed for a complement of nine officers and 76 enlisted men. Guardfish served some 27 years, on cold war, training, and technological missions, and was decommissioned and struck from the Navy list in February 1992.

Guavina (SS-362)

A submarine of the Gato class, she was built by the Manitowoc Shipbuilding Company, Manitowoc, Wisconsin, and launched in August 1943. She underwent training exercises in the Canal Zone and in early April 1944 sailed on her first offensive cruise. She sank two trawlers and a large *maru*, before encountering a seven-ship convoy. She aimed torpedoes at two merchant ships. One of them sank almost immediately; the second *maru* also exploded, although persistent depth charging prevented *Guavina* from staying around to observe the sinking. On her second war patrol in June and July, she sank two ships and rescued 12 downed aviators. Her third patrol, in August and September, took her along the Philippine coast off Mindanao where she sank two small coastwise steamers and later a large transport. Heading to the South China Sea for her fourth war patrol in November, she sank a merchant ship and two tankers. Working with a wolf pack, which included *Becuna* and *Blenny*, from late January to early March 1945, *Guavina*, on her fifth patrol, sank two large tankers in the South China Sea. After the second victory, however, she suffered one of the severest depth chargings of the war. With no room to run, she lay on the bottom at only 130 feet while Japanese escorts and planes dropped a total of 98 depth charges and bombs during the next few hours. Battered but undaunted, she sailed to the Fiji Islands, for a badly needed refit. Her sixth, and last, war patrol found no targets because, near the end of the war, there were few Japanese warships left on the open seas. During the next few years, *Guavina*, now converted to a submarine oiler (AOSS), saw service along the West Coast, the East Coast, the Caribbean, and the Mediterranean before being decommissioned in June 1967. *Guavina* received battle stars for six patrols, during which she sank six enemy vessels for a total of 24,366 tons.

Guitarro (SSN-65)

Named for a fish with a guitar-shaped body, this submarine of the Sturgeon class was launched in July 1968, after construction at the Mare Island Shipyard in Vallejo, California. She displaced 4,762 tons (submerged), was armed with four 21-inch torpedo tubes amidships, aft of the bow, and carried a complement of 12 officers and 95 enlisted men. She served almost 25 years and was decommissioned and struck from the Navy list in May 1992.

Guitarro I (SS-363)

A submarine of the Gato class, launched by the Manitowoc Shipbuilding Company in September 1943, she operated out of Balboa, Canal Zone, for several weeks and set out for Pearl Harbor in early April 1944. She departed on her first war patrol in May 1944, where, off Formosa, she sank a heavily escorted cargo vessel and later a frigate. On her second venture, she sank another frigate and a small coastal vessel, then proceeded to another war zone where she sank two tankers and a cargo ship. In company with *Bream*, *Guitarro* departed Fremantle October 8, 1944, for her third war patrol in Philippine waters. As the epic battle of Leyte Gulf developed, she played an important role. She sighted the Japanese Central Force under Admiral Kurita on the night of October 23–24 and tracked the ships through Mindoro Strait, unable to close for an attack. Her contact reports on the force were vital to the success of the ensuing engagements, which by October 26, virtually eliminated the remaining Japanese naval forces in the Pacific. A week later, she sank a cargo ship loaded with explosives and was driven down 50 feet by the force of the explosion. Later, she teamed up with the submarine *Bream* to sink a passenger-cargo ship. After *Bream*'s initial attack, *Guitarro* added four hits before diving to avoid escort vessels. The wolf pack next encountered a convoy that included the cruiser *Kumano*. *Guitarro* fired nine torpedoes and gained three hits, but failed to sink the cruiser. Pounded by torpedoes from the other boats, *Kumano* was finally stopped, towed ashore by one of her sisters, and eventually finished off by carrier aircraft. *Guitarro*'s fourth war patrol, in December and January, found no targets, although she made one attack with undetermined results on a convoy off Cape Batagan, before heading for Fremantle for refitting. The hard-working submarine again put out to sea in early April 1945, on her fifth war patrol, and was unsuccessfully attacked by aircraft and a patrol boat in Lombok Strait. She then made her way to the northeast coast of Sumatra, where she engaged in a new mission, the laying of mines off Behala Island. Battered and in need of repairs, *Guitarro* was ordered to San Francisco, where she was in reserve at the end of the war. She later underwent conversion to snorkel and was recommissioned, used for training Turkish sailors, and ultimately, in 1954, loaned to Turkey. She was awarded four battle stars for her war service, which included eight Japanese vessels sunk, for a total of 23,132 tons.

Gulf War (1990–1991)

Following a series of territorial disputes and disagreements over oil production, Iraq invaded the small, oil-rich Persian Gulf emirate of Kuwait and rapidly gained control of the country. There was a swift military response from the United States, Britain, and several other countries, which dispatched troops and naval units to the area in Operation Desert Shield to prevent an Iraqi invasion of Saudi Arabia. It soon became evident that, despite intense diplomatic activity and the introduction of economic sanctions, the Iraqis would not withdraw fully from Kuwait unless military action were taken. The remainder of the year was devoted to assembling the forces from 30 countries required to launch Operation Desert Storm on January 16, 1991, from land bases in Saudi Arabia and from ships in the Persian Gulf and other waters. The operation began with a massive air assault, which continued until February 24, on Iraqi positions in Kuwait and on the military and economic infrastructure of Iraq itself. The ground assault on Kuwait, which began on February 24, secured the country within a few days, with parts of the Iraqi army failing to put up any effective resistance. Before Operation Desert Storm had begun, the coalition had assembled an impressive array of naval units, including six carrier battle groups, in the Persian Gulf. The U.S. Navy was the dominant naval power and had deployed ships in the Red Sea and the Mediterranean as well as the Gulf. The small Iraqi navy was no match for the allied naval forces, which took complete control of the sea on their arrival. A major naval contribution to the operation was the use of Tomahawk cruise missiles fired from battleships, cruisers, submarines, and frigates, against targets deep inside Iraq that were too dangerous for manned aircraft to reach. It was the first wartime use of the cruise missile.

Gunnel (SS-253)

Launched in May 1942, this submarine of the Gato class embarked on her first war patrol in mid-October of that year, during which she participated in Operation Torch, the Allied invasion of North Africa. One of six submarines assigned to Admiral Hewitt's Western Naval Task Force, she made reconnaissance runs off Fedhala two days before the invasion, and on D-day, November 8, made infrared signals to guide the approaching fleet to the beachheads. Missions well accomplished, the submarine reached Rosneath, Scotland, one month later to terminate her first patrol. On her second patrol, in May and June 1943, she ranged waters west of Kyushu Island in the East China Sea, and returned with two torpedoed cargo ships to her credit. This was followed by her third patrol, off Honshu, when she sent a passenger-cargo ship to the bottom right in the heart of the Japanese homeland. Her next three patrols found no targets, but on her seventh, at the end of the year, in the South China and Sulu Seas, she sank a motor torpedo boat, passenger cargo ship, and a torpedo boat. On this same patrol, she evacuated 11 naval aviators at Palawan, after the fliers had been protected and hidden by friendly guerrilla forces for some two months. Although she conducted an eighth patrol in the Bungo Suido area, it was too near the end of the war to locate any likely targets, and she returned from the patrol after duty as a lifeguard ship for B-29s flying toward Japan on bombing missions. She had only a short peacetime career and was decommissioned in May 1946. *Gunnel* received five battle stars for World War II service, which tallied up to six vessels sunk for a total of 24,265 tons.

GUPPY See GREATER UNDERWATER PROPULSION POWER PROGRAM (GUPPY).

Gurnard (SS-254)

Launched by the Electric Boat Company in June 1942, this submarine of the Gato class had her initial assignment in a much different location than most boats sent by the navy to tackle the enemy. She was deployed to the Bay of Biscay where she lay off the Spanish coast awaiting German blockade runners bound for Spanish ports. The patrol was uneventful; no enemy ships were sighted and subsequently *Gurnard* was ordered to the Pacific where her second war patrol took her to Toagel Mungui Passage. There, in late June 1943, she saw action for the first time, damaging two Japanese merchantmen and surviving 24 depth charges thrown by an enemy destroyer. Varied damage was inflicted on other ships in these waters before *Gurnard* made her first kill, sinking a cargo ship before returning to port. Underway again in early September, she sailed to the South China Sea to begin her third war patrol. A five-ship convoy was sighted near midnight October 7, and *Gurnard* began her stalk, eventually sending to the bottom a cargo ship and a passenger-cargo ship west of Luzon. One month later she sailed on her fourth patrol to prowl off the southeast coast of Honshu and soon found good hunting. A convoy was sighted December 24, 1943, and the submarine sank two cargo ships and damaged a third.

Gurnard departed Pearl Harbor in mid-April 1944, bound for the eastern Celebes Sea. On this, her fifth patrol, she chalked up one of the highest single-patrol tonnage scores of the Pacific war, attacking a convoy and sinking a 6,886-ton cargo ship, a 6,995-ton passenger-cargo vessel, and a 5,824-ton passenger-cargo ship. Nearly a hundred depth charges rained down around her, but she eluded the hunters and escaped undamaged. This vital convoy carried 40,000 troops intended to oppose MacArthur in New Guinea, and the embarked units suffered losses of nearly 50 percent. She polished off this patrol by successfully torpedoing a 10,090-ton tanker. Her sixth through ninth patrols were a letdown, with little to report but damage to one merchantman and the sinking of a cargo ship. By this time, the war was ending and enemy vessels were hard to find. After the war, she was largely assigned to Naval Reserve submarine training before becoming inactive and eventually stricken from the Navy list in May 1961. *Gurnard* received six battle stars and the Navy Unit Commendation for service in World War II, during which she sank ten enemy vessels for a total of 57,866 tons.

Gurnard (SSN-662)

Launched in May 1967 at Mare Island Naval Shipyard, this submarine of the Sturgeon class, bearing the name of an illustrious World War II boat, had an unusual 25-year career, including WESTPAC missions, an award for Vietnam service, the search and rescue of a downed B-52 plane crew in the midst of Typhoon *Rita*, an under-ice operations record (with surfacing at the North Pole), deployment to the Indian Ocean in response to the Iranian Hostage Crisis, a cruise of 44 days under the ice, a record circumnavigation of North America, and records for refueling and potential enemy ship sinkings during simulated war games. During her service over a quarter of a century, she received, among other honors: seven awards for "Excellence" in different operating modes; three Navy Expeditionary Medals; three Meritorious Unit Commendations; one Navy Unit Commendation; and one Tactical Excellence Award for missiles. *Gurnard* was decommissioned in April 1995.

H

H-1 [ex-*Seawolf*] (SS-28)

Launched by Union Iron Works, San Francisco, in March 1911, *H-1* was a boat of 258 tons on the surface and 467 tons submerged, and carried a crew of two officers and 23 enlisted men. Armed with four 18-inch torpedo tubes in the bow, she was attached to the Second Torpedo Flotilla, Pacific Fleet, and operated along the West Coast out of the submarine base at San Pedro, California, on various exercises and patrols. During the First World War, she was transferred to New London, Connecticut, where she patrolled Long Island Sound, frequently with officer students from the submarine school on board. She sailed back to San Pedro in January 1920, and on March 12, while making her way up the coast, she suffered an onboard fire and was intentionally grounded off Santa Margarita Island, California. Four men, including the commanding officer, were killed as they tried to reach shore. USS *Vestal*, a repair ship, pulled *H-1* off the rocks in the morning of March 24, only to have her sink 45 minutes later in some 50 feet of water. Salvage was abandoned. Her name was struck from the Navy list on April 12, 1920, and her hulk was sold for scrap in June of that year, but never salvaged. Her hulk, now useless, was rediscovered by divers in 1992.

Other boats of the *H* class, of the same tonnage and crew and built at Puget Sound and launched in 1918, were: the *H-5, H-6, H-8,* and *H-9*. All participated in various training exercises and patrols, with SubDiv6 and SubDiv7, and all were decommissioned in October or November 1922. None were active in World War I patrols, since they were beyond the range of any U-boats or other enemy craft, and none suffered any accident.

During World War I, *H-1* (ex-*Seawolf*), frequently with officer students on board, patrolled Long Island Sound. An onboard fire and intentional grounding caused her to sink off the coast of California in March 1920. *(United States Navy)*

Hackleback (SS-295)

A submarine of the Balao class, built by the Cramp Shipbuilding Company and launched in May 1943. She engaged in sonar training and related exercises on the East Coast and in the Canal Zone during the remainder of 1943 and 1944, before being deployed to Pearl Harbor in late January 1945. She left on her first war patrol in March, but enemy shipping had been decimated by the Pacific Fleet, and *Hackleback* encountered no targets in any of her patrols. But on this first patrol, she did play a key role in the sinking of *Yamato*, the last of Japan's super-battleships.

When *H-1* went aground off Santa Margarita Island on March 12, 1920, *H-2* (above photo) stood by and sent rescue and search parties to look for survivors and helped to save all but four of her sister ship's crew. *(United States Navy)*

Patrolling the Bungo Suido area the night of April 6, she made radar contact on a fast group of ships at about 25,000 yards. She sent a stream of location reports back to Pearl Harbor, at the same time attempting to close with the task group. *Hackleback* three times came to within 13,000 yards of the force, but destroyers forced her out of range before she could get in position to fire torpedoes. *Yamato* was not to escape, however. The following morning, planes from Admiral Mitscher's famous TF 58 squadron, guided by *Hackleback's* contact location reports, struck the *Yamato* group. In four successive waves, the carrier planes accounted for the destruction of *Yamato,* the light cruiser *Yahagi,* and two destroyers, leaving only six destroyers of the Japanese task force to escape. On the submarine's second patrol, her primary mission was lifeguard duty off Saki Shima Gunto as the carriers mercilessly pounded the Japanese home islands. In late June she picked up a downed carrier pilot and also engaged in shore bombardment. After an air strike on Shokoto Sho Island in early July, she closed with the shore and fired 73 rounds of five-inch shells before returning to her base in Guam. Since her third and final patrol began only one day before the Japanese surrender in August, she was soon ordered to San Francisco where she operated on peacetime duties before

being placed on reserve and decommissioned in March 1946.

Haddo (SS-255)

Launched by the Electric Boat Company in June 1942, this submarine of the Gato class was deployed in April 1943 to Rosneath, Scotland, to join Submarine Squadron 50, which was assigned to patrol off Norway and Iceland and stand ready in case of a breakthrough of the German fleet from Norway. When it became clear after three patrols that targets were scarce in this region, *Haddo* and her sister submarines were sent back to the United States, and she was ordered to join the Pacific Fleet in November 1943, leaving for the Philippines on what was her fourth war patrol the following month. She encountered no targets until her fifth patrol, in waters off Borneo, Java, and Indochina, when, after a disappointing attack March 8 in which two torpedoes exploded prematurely, she made an attack on a tanker and escort a week later that produced unconfirmed results. Moving to the Indochina coast she sank a small craft with gunfire and damaged a freighter before returning to base at Fremantle. Her sixth patrol was disappointing, but on her seventh, in August 1944, she joined a coordinated attack group with five other submarines to cruise Philippine waters. Learning from *Harder* about the position of a Japanese convoy, *Haddo* closed for the attack. Launching six torpedoes at three targets, she had to dive deep to avoid air attack. Over 100 depth charges churned the sea. But *Haddo* had already sunk cargo ships *Kinryu Maru* and *Norfolk Maru*. The next day, she made an attack on a small convoy with escorts and sent one of them to the bottom. Following a lone destroyer and awaiting her opportunity, *Haddo* was suddenly turned upon by the Japanese ship. She launched a four-torpedo spread "down the throat" of the destroyer, which veered off and headed for Manila. Cruising off Cape Bolinao, she was about to torpedo a tanker close to shore when she detected a pursuing destroyer. With four torpedoes she ripped off the ship's bow. *Haddo* then maneuvered to finish off her antagonist, giving her another kill. *Haddo*'s eighth and ninth war patrols resulted in the sinking of an oiler, a cargo ship, and several small vessels. She departed on her 10th and last war patrol August 10, 1945, but it was soon terminated by the surrender of Japan. She then headed for Tokyo Bay, where her officers witnessed the signing of the surrender on board USS *Missouri* and departed for home. She was decommissioned and placed in reserve until being stricken from the Navy list in August 1958. In addition to a Navy Unit Commendation, *Haddo* received six battle stars for her World War II service, for sinking nine Japanese vessels, for a total of 21,618 tons.

Haddo (SSN-604)

This submarine of the Permit class was built by the New York Shipbuilding Corporation in Camden, New Jersey, and launched in August 1962. She had a displacement of 3,500 tons, was armed with four 21-inch torpedo tubes amidships, aft of the bow, and had a complement of nine officers and 76 enlisted men. Like others in her class, she had a submerged speed of 28 knots—almost twice her speed on the surface. She served for almost 30 years and was decommissioned and struck from the Navy list in June 1991.

Haddock (SS-231)

Launched by the Portsmouth Naval Shipyard in October 1941, this submarine of the Gato class was ordered to the Pacific and departed on her first war patrol in late July 1942, the first submarine to do so with the new SJ-type submarine surface radar, which added greatly to her ability to attack enemy ships in darkness or reduced visibility. Penetrating the East China Sea area, *Haddock* attacked a freighter on the surface, damaged her, and next day sank a transport of about 4,000 tons. In the Formosa Straits, she

The first *Haddock (K-1)* (SS-32) had the distinction of being one of the first American submarines to operate in European waters during World War I. *(United States Navy)*

missed with four stern shots at *Teinshum Maru* but sent the target to the bottom by swinging around hard for a shot from the bow tubes. Her second war patrol, in October and November, was carried out in the Yellow Sea, where she torpedoed *Tekkai Maru* and cargo ship *Venice Maru* east of the island of Honshu. On her third war patrol, *Haddock* operated south of Japan, departing in late December from Pearl Harbor. She was attacked by two destroyers raining depth charges, and when she finally surfaced to clear the area, she found herself surrounded by Japanese patrol craft, and had to speed out of the trap just in time to avoid destruction. A few days later, in mid-January 1943, she sank an unidentified freighter of 4,000 tons, and later detected six cargo vessels steaming in double column. Gaining attack position on the last ship, she scored two hits and sent her to the bottom.

Haddock departed Midway in early March 1943, for her fourth war patrol, and saw action when she encountered a transport protected by a corvette. She sank the transport, but had to dive, where depth charges from the corvette damaged her conning tower and radar enough to require a return to Pearl Harbor for repairs. Her next two patrols were largely discouraging, with some damage and "small game" sinkings to her credit. On her next four patrols, she damaged three transports and an escort carrier, and sank only one escort vessel. However, she played a significant role during the battle off Cape Engano, part of the epochal battle for Leyte Gulf on October 25, 1944, helping to force many of the Japanese warships away from the battle at critical times. Fitted out with extra deck guns for her 11th war patrol, in February and March 1945, *Haddock* sailed in company with two other submarines for the seas east of Japan. The boats made a diversionary sweep designed to pull early warning craft away from the intended track of a carrier group en route for air strikes against Tokyo. Gaining their objective with complete success, the submarines attacked the picket boats with gunfire, allowed them to send contact reports, and then sunk several, diverting Japanese efforts away from the undetected carrier group. Her final two patrols, from April 1945 until the end of the war, were spent on lifeguard station near Tokyo, standing by to rescue downed airmen after raids on Japanese cities. She returned to the submarine base at New London, Connecticut, where she was assigned duty as a reserve training ship for the Sixth Naval District until being struck from the Navy list in August 1960. *Haddock* received 11 battle stars for her service in World War II, sinking eight enemy ships for a total of 33,585 tons sent to the bottom.

Haddock (SSN-621)

A submarine of the Permit class, and the third to bear the name, *Haddock* was built by the Ingalls Shipbuilding Company in Pascagoula, Mississippi, and launched in May 1966. She first served on the West Coast, out of San Diego, and was then deployed to Pearl Harbor where she received a Meritorious Unit Commendation for significant undersea achievements. She was later deployed again to the West Coat, where she earned the coveted Battle Efficiency "E" Award for 1988. *Haddock* was the last boat of 13 to be commissioned in the format of the Thresher/Permit class, designed to detect, attack, and destroy enemy vessels. She served some 27 years, and was decommissioned and struck from the Navy list in April 1993.

Hake (SS-256)

Launched in July 1942 at the Electric Boat Company, this boat of the Gato class began her first war patrol from her first home port, New London, Connecticut, in April 1943. Her mission on this patrol was to search out and destroy German submarines in the North Atlantic, but no contacts were gained, nor on her second mission, off the Azores. She therefore was ordered to Pearl Harbor for her third war patrol in late December 1943, which proved to be more productive, sinking three transports and damaging a tanker, though suffering considerable damage on one attack. Her fourth patrol was also productive—damaging several ships and sinking a tanker in the South China Sea in March and April 1944. On her fifth patrol, starting in late May, *Hake* sank a destroyer and two transports in an area southwest of Mindanao. During her next two patrols, she made no hits but spent a harrowing 16 hours during the first week in November, counting nearly 150 depth charges and sustaining considerable damage. She was subsequently sent on a special mission to Panay Island, where she rendezvoused with Filipino guerrillas to bring on board 29 American aviators shot down in recent air attacks. Although she departed on two more patrols, in 1945, the areas in the South China Sea were now almost denuded of targets, and her missions were largely to act as a lifeguard ship during the terminal air strikes against Japan. During peacetime, she served largely as a training ship until being decommissioned and struck from the Navy list in April 1968. *Hake* received seven battle stars for her service in World War II, sinking seven enemy vessels for a total of 37,923 tons.

Halfbeak (SS-352)

This submarine of the Balao class was launched in February 1946, at the Electric Boat Company and, although she was initially a fleet boat of the type made famous in the Pacific during World War II, she was converted to a GUPPY II submarine at Electric Boat in 1948. *Halfbeak* was assigned to the Submarine Research and Development Group after her conversion, and was sent on an extended cruise to European waters on a sonar evaluation project. Assigned to Submarine Squadron 10 in 1954, she was deployed to the Mediterranean as a unit of the U.S. Sixth Fleet. She operated with U.S. forces in the Mediterranean during the Suez crisis, until January 1957, and was involved for the next few years in NATO exercises and a scientific information gathering trip to the far north for the International Geophysical Year, and later for ice familiarization exercises on her extended deployments. She also served in the Caribbean and Mediterranean Seas before being decommissioned in July 1971. She was awarded three Battle Efficiency "E" awards during her career.

Halibut (SS-232)

The first boat to bear the *Halibut* name was a submarine of the Gato class, launched in December 1941 and assigned to the Aleutian Islands in early August for her first patrol—and later for her second, during which she almost met an untimely end. Surfacing for a torpedo attack on what appeared to be a large freighter, she discovered almost too late that it was a decoy "Q-boat" equipped with concealed guns and torpedo tubes. The ship attacked *Halibut* with high-explosive shells and a torpedo, forcing her to take radical evasive action to escape the trap. Her third patrol, in late November off the northeast coast of Japan, was more to her liking. There she made several attacks, sinking three ships in a convoy. Her fourth and fifth patrols resulted in only one sinking, a freighter, but her sixth, in August and September 1943, was more successful, and two more freighters were scratched from the Japanese fleet.

She had little more to record until her ninth patrol. Cruising eastward of Okinawa in April 1944, she sank a passenger-cargo ship and fired six torpedoes to separate a convoy. Closing in on one ship separated from the group, *Halibut* sank it, then shifted her attack to a coastal minelayer, sinking her also. The submarine was then forced into evasive action as some 90 depth charges were dropped close aboard. Surfacing off the northeastern shore of Kume Shima at the end of April, she bombarded two warehouses and other buildings with her deck gun, and made an attack on a group or sampans with gunfire. With crewmen critically wounded in the gun battle, she returned to Pearl Harbor.

On her 10th war patrol *Halibut* joined a coordinated attack group with *Haddock* and *Tuna*. While proceeding to Luzon Strait, the submarines were ordered to set up scouting lines to intercept crippled units of the Japanese fleet retiring after the battle off Cape Engano. *Halibut* encountered the remnants of Admiral Ozawa's force in late October and attacked, inflicting some damage. Her next contact came when she attacked a convoy in Luzon Strait. She was immediately attacked in turn by planes using magnetic airborne detectors. A short, effective depth charge attack

directed by the aircraft left *Halibut* severely damaged but still under control. Her crew made temporary repairs, enough so she could reach Saipan. For this action, she received a Navy Unit Commendation. Later she made it to Pearl Harbor, and eventually to the yards at Kittery, Maine, where it was found that her damage was too extensive to justify repair. She decommissioned in July 1945, and received seven battle stars for World War II service. She sank 12 Japanese vessels totaling 45,257 tons.

Halibut (SSGN-587)(SSN-587)

Launched by Mare Island Naval Shipyard, Vallejo, California, in January 1959 as a new class of submarine, *Halibut* had the distinction of being the first nuclear submarine to be designed and built from the keel up to launch guided missiles. Intended to carry the Regulus I missile, she had her main deck relatively higher above the waterline to provide a dry deck when launching missiles at sea. Her missile system was a completely automated group of hydraulically powered machinery, controlled from one central command station. Departing for Australia for her shakedown cruise in early March 1960, with a crew of 12 officers and 99 enlisted men, *Halibut* became the first nuclear-powered submarine to launch a guided missile successfully. During the years that followed, she participated in numerous guided missile launching exercises and underwent intensive training. In 1964, *Halibut* joined eight other submarines in testing and evaluating the attack capabilities of the Permit-class submarines. After an overhaul, which configured the boat as a special mission submarine, and redesignation to an SSN in the 1960s, she returned to Pearl Harbor and operated with the Pacific Fleet and Submarine Development Group I out of Mare Island until decommissioning in 1976.

Halsey, William Frederick, Jr. (1882–1959)

American naval officer, one of the great World War II leaders, nicknamed "Bull" by the press for his pugnacious nature. The son of a navy captain, Halsey entered the Naval Academy in 1900 and served on battleships as part of the Great White Fleet's circumnavigation of the globe in 1907–09. Seeing service mainly in torpedo boats, he commanded a destroyer during the 1914 Mexican intervention. During World War I, he commanded destroyers operating from Queenstown, Ireland, on antisubmarine patrol duty, receiving the Navy Cross. After commands of destroyer squadrons, Halsey trained and earned his wings in 1935 at the age of 52. He became a fervent advocate of naval air power and of fast carrier task forces, for which he would gain his greatest fame. When the Japanese attacked Pearl Harbor, Halsey, who commanded the aircraft carriers of the U.S. Pacific Fleet, was returning to base after having delivered planes to Wake Island. From his flagship, *Enterprise,* he conducted the first major offensive operation of the war by attacking the Japanese-held Marshall and Gilbert Island chains as well as Wake and Marcus Islands early in 1942. He then led *Task Force 16* on the famous air raid on Tokyo, led by the Army Air Corps's Lieutenant Colonel James Doolittle from the *Hornet* in April 1942. He became commander of the South Pacific Force and Area, directing the victories in late 1942 and early 1943 off the Santa Cruz Islands and Guadalcanal. From 1943 and into much of 1944 he directed Allied efforts in the Solomons. Appointed commander of the Third Fleet in June 1944, he helped formulate plans for retaking the Philippines. Near war's end, his command participated in the Okinawa campaign and air attacks on the Japanese home islands. The surrender took place on the deck of his flagship, *Missouri,* in September 1945 in Tokyo Bay. Recipient of many medals and awards, foreign and domestic, Halsey was promoted to fleet admiral in December 1945, and retired in March 1947.

Hammerhead (SS-364)

Launched in October 1943 at the Manitowoc Shipbuilding Yard, this submarine of the Gato class was ordered to Pearl Harbor and left on her first war patrol in early June 1944, headed for the seas south of Formosa, where she sank a sampan with gunfire and damaged several ships of a convoy. This modest success was multiplied on her second war patrol in September and October in the Java and South China Seas. There she attacked a convoy, scored a total of six hits, and sent three of the cargo ships to the bottom. The morning of October 20, the submarine found still another six-ship convoy, and after evading one of the escorts delivered a six-torpedo attack. Two more cargo ships fell victim to *Hammerhead*'s marksmanship, and she was later awarded the Navy Unit Commendation for outstanding performance. Her third and fourth patrols were letdowns, with only one prize: a Japanese frigate. On her fifth war patrol in March 1945, she sighted a large convoy and broke an escort vessel in two with a single hit, as well as damaging other members of the group before retiring. Her sixth patrol, in the Gulf of Siam, earned credit for a tanker and a cargo ship; while her seventh (and last) patrol, in the same area, near the end of the war, gave her credit for several more ships. She went into reserve in 1946, but was activated again during the Korean conflict and engaged in training duty on the West Coast until May 1952, when she decommissioned. Two years later, *Hammerhead* was loaned to Turkey, where she served the Turkish navy as *Cerbe.* She received seven battle stars and a Navy Unit Commendation for World War II service, during which she rank 11 vessels for a total of 35,635 tons.

Harder (SS-257)

Launched in August 1942 at the Electric Boat Company, this submarine of the Gato class created so much havoc among Japanese shipping that she was dubbed "Hit 'Em Again *Harder*" and her record of daring battle exploits became legendary. Ordered to the Pacific theater, under the command of Lieutenant Commander Samuel D. Dealey, she departed on her first war patrol in June 1943. Cruising off the coast of Japan, the submarine worked her way inside a picket line, made a radar approach on the surface, and fired four torpedoes at the two-ship convoy, sinking one for her first kill. She began her second war patrol in late August, heading for the Japanese coast. While patrolling off Honshu, she attacked and sank *Koyo Maru* and later that night ran by an escort ship at a range of 1,200 yards without being detected. Two days later, she encountered a convoy and, after running ahead to improve her firing position, sank cargo ship *Yoko Maru* with a spread of three torpedoes. Continuing her patrol, *Harder* sighted two more ships in mid-September, but was forced to dive deep, and was kept down with a severe depth charge attack, which lasted for over two days and almost exhausted her batteries. After evading the Japanese ships, *Harder* detected her next target and torpedoed almost immediately. Though running in bad weather, she continued to find good targets, sinking a 4,500-ton freighter and, with her last remaining torpedoes, a 5,800-ton tanker off Nagoya Bay, before having to head for home.

For her third war patrol *Harder* teamed with *Snook* and *Pargo* to form a deadly and coordinated attack group. Two weeks after departing for the Marianas in late October, *Harder* encountered and promptly dispatched one ship with torpedoes and later surfaced to sink a trawler escort with gunfire. Heading toward Saipan, she sighted three *marus*, radioed her companions, and closed for attack. But she needed no help and handily dispatched all three, and later a fourth, and then, with no torpedoes left, headed for base. She departed on her fourth war patrol in late February 1944, heading for the western Caroline Islands, where she was assigned duty as a lifeguard ship for downed aviators. During American air strikes against Woleai, *Harder* received word of an injured pilot awaiting rescue from the beach of a small enemy-held island west of Woleai. Protected by air cover, she nosed against a reef, maintained her position with both screws, and sent a boat ashore through breaking surf. Despite Japanese snipers, boiling shoals, and the precarious position of the submarine, the daring rescue succeeded, and the submarine hastily returned to the open sea. In mid-April an enemy plane sighted *Harder* north of the western Carolines and reported her position to *Ikazuchi,* a patrolling destroyer. As the enemy ship closed to within 900 yards, *Harder* fired a spread of torpedoes that sank the attacker within five minutes. Commander Dealey's famous report was terse:

"Expended four torpedoes and one Jap destroyer." Four days later *Harder* spotted a 7,000-ton merchant ship, not only sinking this prize, but also damaging one of her destroyer escorts. Then, adding to the enemy's misery, she returned to Woleai where she surfaced on the morning of April 20 to end her patrol by delivering a shore bombardment under cover of a rain squall.

Harder departed for her fifth patrol in the Celebes Sea in late May 1944. She picked up coast watchers from northeastern Borneo, and gave a very valuable contact report on a major task force leaving Tawi Tawi anchorage, Sulu Archipelago, preparing to engage in the first battle of the Philippine Sea. On June 6 *Harder* entered the heavily patrolled Sibutu Passage in North Borneo and encountered a convoy of three tankers and two destroyers. She gave chase on the surface but was illuminated by the moon. As one of the destroyers turned to attack, she submerged, turned her stern to the charging destroyer, and fired three torpedoes at a range of 1,100 yards. Two struck and exploded; the destroyer sank within minutes. After attacking the second escort without success, *Harder* was held down by a depth charge attack while the convoy escaped. After surfacing, *Harder* spotted another destroyer searching the area for her. As the enemy closed the range, *Harder* took the initiative, firing three torpedoes at short range, one of which detonated the ship's magazine with a tremendous explosion, sending the destroyer immediately to the bottom. *Harder* continued her patrol by rendezvousing off the northeast coast of Borneo, where during darkness she picked up six British coast-watchers. Early the next day she headed once more for Sibutu Passage, where she sighted two enemy destroyers patrolling the narrowest part of the passage. After submerging, she made an undetected approach and at 1,000 yards fired four torpedoes at the overlapping targets. The second and third torpedoes blasted destroyer *Tanikaze;* she sank almost immediately, her boilers erupting with a terrific explosion. The fourth shot hit the second ship and exploded with a blinding flash. Within minutes *Harder* surfaced to survey the results, but both ships had disappeared. Soon afterward, she underwent the inevitable depth charge attack by enemy planes, then she set course for a point south of Tawi-Tawi to reconnoiter.

On the afternoon of June 10 *Harder* sighted a large Japanese task force, including three battleships and four cruisers with screening destroyers. An overhead plane spotted the submarine at periscope depth and a screening escort promptly steamed at 35 knots toward her position. Once again, *Harder* became the aggressive adversary. As the range closed to 1,500 yards, she fired three torpedoes on a "down the throat" shot, then went deep to escape the onrushing destroyer and certain depth charge attack. Within a minute two torpedoes blasted the ship with violent force just as *Harder* passed under her some 80 feet below. The deafening

explosions shook the submarine far worse than the depth charges and aerial bombs, which the infuriated enemy dropped during the next two hours. She then reconnoitered the area and transmitted her observations, which were of vital importance to Admiral Spruance's fleet prior to the decisive battle of the Philippine Sea. The important results of *Harder*'s fifth war patrol have been called the most brilliant of the war. Not only did she further deplete the critical supply of destroyers, but also her frequent attacks and a rash of enemy contact reports on this fleeting marauder so frightened Admiral Toyoda that he believed Tawi-Tawi to be surrounded by submarines and withdrew his fleet prematurely. This act upset the Japanese battle plans, and forced Ozawa to delay his carrier force in the Philippine Sea, thus contributing to the stunning defeat suffered by the Japanese in the ensuing battle.

Harder, accompanied by *Hake* and *Haddo,* departed Fremantle August 5 for her sixth and last war patrol. Assigned to the South China Sea off Luzon, the wolf pack headed northward, where they were joined by three other submarines for a coordinated attack against a convoy off Paluan Bay, Mindoro. The Japanese lost four passenger-cargo *marus,* possibly one by *Harder.* The next day, *Harder* and *Haddo* attacked and destroyed three coastal defense vessels off Bataan, then, joined by *Hake,* they headed for Luzon, searching for new targets. Before dawn on August 24 they sighted a Japanese minesweeper and a destroyer. As *Hake* closed to attack, the destroyer turned away, so she broke off her approach, turned northward, and sighted *Harder*'s periscope about 600 to 700 yards dead ahead. Swinging southward, *Hake* then sighted the minesweeper about 2,000 yards off her port quarter swinging toward them. To escape the charging minesweeper, *Hake* started deep and rigged for silent running. Later, she heard 15 rapid depth charges explode in the distance astern. She continued evasive action that morning, then returned to the general area of the attack shortly after noon. She swept the area at periscope depth but found only a ring of marker buoys covering a radius of one-half mile. The vigorous depth charge attack thus ended the career of *Harder,* and she went down with all hands. *Harder* received the Presidential Unit Citation for her first five patrols, and six battle stars. The resolute and resourceful Commander Sam Dealey, "a submariner's submariner," was posthumously awarded the Congressional Medal of Honor for his outstanding contribution to the war effort on *Harder*'s fifth patrol. *Harder* was credited with sinking at least 16 vessels for a total of more than 54,000 tons.

Harder (SS-568)

Bearing the same name as one of the most famous submarines of World War II, which was lost in the Pacific after sinking more than 54,000 tons of enemy shipping, this new Harder was also built by the Electric Boat Division of

General Dynamics in Groton, Connecticut. A submarine of the Tang class, she was launched in August 1952, had a displacement (submerged) of 2,700 tons, was armed with six 21-inch torpedo tubes forward and two 21-inch torpedo tubes aft, and was designed for a complement of eight officers and 75 enlisted men. *Harder* had a relatively short life—a little over 20 years—but continued in service after being decommissioned in January 1973 and sold to the Italian navy, where she was renamed *Romeo Romei*.

Hardhead (SS-365)

Launched in December 1943, this submarine of the Balao class departed on her first war patrol in late July 1944 and proceeded to her patrol area off the Philippines. Four weeks later, she detected a Japanese light cruiser east of San Bernardino Strait, and closed for a surface attack. The first well-directed salvo stopped the cruiser dead in the water; a second sent her to the bottom. During the remainder of her first patrol, *Hardhead* rendered lifeguard services during strikes by fleet aircraft on the Philippines and operated with a reconnaissance line during the Palaus operation. Her second patrol began in late October, as she set course for the Philippines. While steaming on the surface through the Sulu Sea, she discovered a life raft adrift. In it was Commander Bakutis, fighter squadron commander of the aircraft carrier *Enterprise,* who had been in the water for six days after being shot down during America's smashing victory in the battle for Leyte Gulf. Operating in a pack with submarines *Growler* and *Hake, Hardhead* sighted a large cargo ship with escorts. After being driven off in one attack, she aggressively gained a strategic position and sank the cargoman. It was during this attack that *Growler* was lost. *Hardhead* performed lifeguard duty off Subic Bay in November and on the 25th came upon an escorted merchant ship. She sank a coast defense vessel, damaged the merchantman, and evaded a retaliatory depth charge attack. Putting to sea again in late December 1944, she began her third war patrol in the South China Sea. Operating with sister ships *Besugo* and *Blackfin, Hardhead* damaged several ships before sinking one and, in February 1945, took up lifeguard duty for the B-29 strikes on Singapore. *Hardhead*'s fourth war patrol, in March and April, included a special mission, laying mines off French Indochina. She then entered the Gulf of Siam, where, after several attacks, she sank a cargo ship but found few contacts, since American submarines had by this time reduced Japanese merchant activity to a trickle. On her fifth war patrol, in late June in the Java Sea, she damaged a freighter with her deck guns and sank four coastal defense craft during an attack on Ambat Roads, but was forced to return to base because of the critical illness of her skipper. Her sixth and last patrol was cut short by the Japanese surrender, and she sailed to Mare Island, where she was put in reserve until 1952. Following a GUPPY IIA conversion at the Electric

Boat Company in 1953, including streamlining, installation of a snorkel breathing apparatus, and larger storage batteries, *Hardhead* joined the Atlantic Fleet for training exercises and tactical drills in the years that followed, operating mainly in the Caribbean and off the East Coast of the United States. She sailed for the Mediterranean September 7, 1956, to strengthen the Sixth Fleet during the Suez crisis. In July 1958, *Hardhead* joined SubDevGrp2, turning from fleet operations to research and testing of equipment and tactical doctrine. She operated off the East Coast and in the North Atlantic and by 1961 had won four consecutive "E" awards for her performance. She was struck from the Navy list in July 1972, at which time she was transferred to Greece, where she gave 21 more years of service as a training vessel under the name *Papanikolis*. She received six battle stars for World War II service, during which she sank nine vessels for a total of 20,146 tons.

Harpoon

A long-range, sea-skimming, antiship missile that became the most widely used of its type. The ship-launched version of the Harpoon was originally conceived as an air-to-surface missile that could be used to attack surfaced Soviet cruise missile submarines. The missile, since upgraded, is now deployed in surface ships, submarines, land-based coastal defense positions, and on aircraft. In configuration, it is a thick cylinder with pointed nose; cruciform trapezoidal wings at mid-body; and cruciform in-line swept cropped delta control fins at the tail. Wings and control surfaces fold for storage and pop-out after launch. These vary in size and design, according to the launch site—air, ground, or sea. Submarine-launched Harpoons are carried in a buoyant capsule that is launched from a standard 21-inch torpedo tube. The capsule's fins and elevators steer the missile toward the surface, veering away from the submarine's centerline if the tubes lie along the longitudinal axis. When the capsule's nose breaks the surface, the nose cap is blown off, the capsule tail section falls away, and the missile's booster ignites. From that point, the missile's flight is similar to that of a ship- or coast-launched Harpoon.

Hart, Thomas Charles (1877–1971)

The commander of the doomed U.S. Asiatic Fleet when the United States entered World War II. Born on June 12, 1877, in Michigan, Hart entered the U.S. Naval Academy in 1893, and reached the rank of admiral in 1939. During the Spanish-American War of 1898, he saw service at sea, participating in the battle of Santiago on July 3, 1898. During World War I, he commanded two U.S. submarine divisions, one based in the waters around the British Isles and the other in the Azores operating with British submarines against the German U-boat threat. As a submariner with great experience, in 1939 he became commander in chief of the Asiatic Fleet, headquartered at first at Shanghai and then at Manila, as war with Japan became more likely. Working with British, Dutch, and Australian forces, Hart was forced to move by submarine to the Dutch East Indies. With his pathetically small force he set about trying to stem the Japanese attack toward Southeast Asia and the Dutch East Indies. For political reasons as much as anything else, he was forced to relinquish command to the Dutch just before the disastrous battle of the Java Sea in February 1942. After retiring from the service, he was appointed to complete a vacated Connecticut seat in the U.S. Senate, 1945–47. He died in Connecticut on July 4, 1971.

Hawkbill (SS-366)

Launched in January 1944 at the Manitowoc Shipbuilding Yard, this submarine of the Balao class was ordered to the Pacific where, in late August, she departed Pearl Harbor for her patrol area in the Philippines in company with *Baya* and *Becuna*. In October she shifted patrol to the South China Sea and, while approaching two carriers, was forced down by violent depth charging by Japanese destroyers. Two days later, she attacked a 12-ship convoy with *Becuna,* damaging several of the ships. *Hawkbill* then transited heavily patrolled Lombok Strait, and terminated her mission at Fremantle, Australia. In mid-November, in company with *Becuna* and *Flasher,* she departed for her second patrol, bound for the area north of the Malay Barrier. Four weeks later, she encountered a convoy and sank a destroyer with six well placed torpedoes during a night attack. On her third war patrol in February and March, *Hawkbill* returned to Lombok Strait where she sank two submarine chasers and some small craft before turning for the South China Sea, where she detected a convoy and sank a 5,400-ton cargo ship with a spread of torpedoes. On her fourth patrol in May and June, she served on lifeguard station for a B-24 strike on the Kangean Islands north of Bali, and later encountered minelayer *Hatsutaka* heading south along the coast. She attacked and obtained two hits causing severe damage. The ship was observed next morning being towed to the beach. At a range of almost 5,000 yards, *Hawkbill* fired three more torpedoes into the shallow waters and broke the ship in half, sinking a familiar enemy of submarines operating on the Malayan coast.

Hawkbill departed for her fifth and last war patrol in mid-July 1945, returning to the coast of Malaya, where she attacked a convoy. Her first torpedoes missed, and an hour later a depth charge attack of unusual intensity began. *Hawkbill* was blown partially out of the water by a perfectly placed pattern and heavily damaged, but by hugging the bottom, she avoided almost certain destruction. After a stay at Subic Bay for repairs, she steamed to a rendezvous with Australian army officers off Borneo, where she destroyed two radio stations with her deck guns, landed commandos, and bombarded shore installations. Following the surrender of Japan, *Hawkbill* was placed in reserve. In April 1953 she was converted to a GUPPY IA at the Electric Boat Company and was loaned to the Netherlands under the Military Assistance Program. She received six battle stars for World War II service and a Navy Unit Commendation for her outstanding performance on patrols one, three, and four.

Hawkbill (SSN-666)

Sometimes called the Devil Boat because of a chapter in the Bible referring to beasts in the number of 666, *Hawkbill* was built by Mare Island Naval Shipyard and launched in April 1969.

A Sturgeon class fast attack submarine, she was the last of this breed, described by a submarine group commander as "the real work horses of the Cold War," which played "a significant role in our country's eventual victory in that potentially devastating conflict." *Hawkbill* deployed to the Western Pacific no fewer than 10 times and in addition undertook five missions in the polar regions, largely under ice. Vice Admiral Al Konetzni, deputy commander of the U.S. Atlantic Fleet and former commander of the Submarine Force in the Pacific, echoed this sentiment and spoke of Hawkbill's "heroic and sometimes harrowing service" during most of her career, with very little recognition until her last expedition at the end of some 30 years of service. She was decommissioned at the Puget Sound Naval Shipyard in March 2000.

Hedgehog

A British antisubmarine weapon of World War II vintage, it was later adopted and developed by the United States Navy. Used operationally for the first time in January 1942, the Hedgehog was a multistaved (barrel) launcher that fired a pattern of 24 depth charges ahead or off the bow of the attacking ship. The bombs were armed with a charge of 35 pounds and were positioned on the launcher in four rows of six each. The advantage of this system was that it permitted the attacking ship to remain in sonar contact with the target submarine as the charges were fired. This eliminated much of the guesswork associated with conventional depth charges. The Hedgehog did not have a hydrostatic fuse that would enable it to explode at a preset depth, but was designed so that it would explode only on impact against a submarine hull. Although this was considered by some to be a weakness, because there was no guarantee that the charge would hit the target, it actually increased the number of successful attacks on enemy submarines. Later, it was replaced by the Squid, which combined the advantages of the depth charge with the forward-throwing capability of the Hedgehog.

Herring (SS-233)

A submarine of the Gato class, she was launched in January 1942, at the Portsmouth Naval Shipyard and, after her shakedown cruise, was one of five submarines sent to the Mediterranean in November of that year to take station off the North African coast prior to Operation Torch, the invasion of North Africa. Reaching her position off Casablanca, she was engaged in spotting, but not attacking, likely targets. On the morning of November 8 as the invasion was launched, she had her chance, sinking a 5,700-ton cargo ship. *Herring* then returned to Rosneath, Scotland, from which she left on a second war patrol, which proved to be nonproductive. On her third patrol, however, *Herring* made up for the slump when she attacked and sank a marauding Nazi submarine, *U-163*, on March 21, 1943. The fourth war patrol, an antisubmarine sweep in Icelandic waters, and the fifth patrol, which took her back to the States in late July 1943, netted her no more kills. Heading for the Pacific in November 1943, on her sixth war patrol, to join the ranks of American boats systematically decimating Japanese shipping, she scored two kills for 3,948 tons in mid-December and 6,072 tons to celebrate New Year's Day 1944. Her next patrol was a frustrating one when, in late March, she stalked a large aircraft carrier but was detected by its escorts and driven deep before she could attack. *Herring*'s eighth war patrol was to be both her most successful and her last. Topping off at Midway on May 21, 1944, she headed for the Kurile Islands patrol area. Ten days later she rendezvoused with *Barb*, and was never seen or heard from again. However, Japanese records later proved that she sank two ships the night of May 30–31; *Herring*'s exact manner of loss was also determined from these records. Two more merchant ships were sunk while at anchor in Matsuwa Island, Kuriles, the morning of June 1, 1944. In a counterattack, enemy shore batteries scored two direct hits on the submarine's conning tower and, as the report concluded, "bubbles covered an area about 5 meters wide, and heavy oil covered an area of approximately 15 miles." On her last patrol, *Herring* had sunk four Japanese ships for a total of 13,202 tons. In all, she had sunk six *marus* totaling 19,959 tons, an Axis cargo ship, and a German U-boat. She received five battle stars for her service in World War II.

H. L. Hunley

A Confederate submarine, the *H. L. Hunley*, became the first submarine to sink a ship in wartime when she torpedoed the Union steam frigate *Housatonic* in 1864, during the American Civil War. Built in 1863, this boat was made from a steel cylinder that was tapered at both ends. She was about 40 feet long and was operated by a crew of nine: one man steered while the other eight turned a crankshaft that drove the propeller. She could obtain a maximum speed of about four knots. Her armament consisted of a single spar torpedo, which was fixed to a pole at the front of the boat. The *Hunley*, a member of the David class of Confederate boats, was named after her designer. Technically, she was a submersible or semi-submersible rather than a submarine in the modern sense, because she was unable to dive. Two ballast tanks enabled her to operate with only her hatchway above water. This provided air for the crew to breathe. She had a brief operational career, much of it disastrous. At least two of her nine-man crews had drowned during test runs, and for a time the idea of ever using her in battle was discarded. Her first intended victim was to have been the Union warship *New Ironsides* off Charleston, but that ship was anchored in water that was too shallow for the submarine to operate in. Her opportunity came in February 1864, when she attacked the Union blockade ship *Housatonic* off Charleston. The Yankee ship's crew reacted too slowly to the submersible's approach, and the *Housatonic* was hit below the waterline by a spar torpedo. She sank rapidly, but not before taking the *Hunley*, which had been caught by the effects of the blast, with her. For many years, there was great speculation as to just what had caused the submarine to sink, where she had gone down, and how much of her might be intact. During the 1990s, interest in the *Hunley* grew and her location was discovered by divers early in May 1995, lying off Sullivan's Island. The hull, which appeared to be in good condition, protected by mud and silt, was enclosed in a protective cage, and its condition monitored around the clock by the Coast Guard and navy. On August 8, 2000, she was raised from the sea floor, brought to the surface, and moved shoreward in a floating cradle and taken to the Warren Lasch Conservation Facility, located on the grounds of the old naval shipyard in Charleston, so that researchers could sift through the silt inside the hull, and remove the remains of the crew, their personal belongings, and equipment. The *Hunley* is probably the most priceless—and certainly the most unique—submarine artifact ever salvaged from the depths.

Hoe (SS-258)

This submarine of the Gato class was built by the Electric Boat Company and launched in September 1942. After being ordered to Pearl Harbor, she embarked on her first combat patrol in late May, and patrolled the Guam-Palaus area, where she damaged two freighters. Her second patrol, west of Truk, was marred by engine trouble, and she succeeded only in damaging a tanker. Her third patrol, in January and February 1944, was somewhat more successful. Patrolling between Mindanao and Halmahera, the submarine damaged one ship and then, in two separate attacks, sank a tanker. *Hoe*'s fourth, fifth, and seventh patrols, in the South China Sea, the vital Japanese sea supply line, were relatively unproductive, leaving behind her several damaged freighters. Her sixth patrol was more satisfying, when, in early September, she was designated as the leader of a coordinated attack group, along with *Aspro* and *Cabrilla*, to operate southwest of Lingayen Gulf. The pack of three accounted for some 38,000 tons of Japanese shipping in five surface attacks at night. *Hoe* was also credited with the sinking of a passenger-cargo ship. Her final war patrol knocked off an escort vessel, at a time when the pickings were getting slim indeed, and the war ended before she had another chance at the enemy. *Hoe* served her final days with the Atlantic Reserve Fleet, acting as a Naval Reserve training ship and was decommissioned in April 1960. She received seven battle stars for World War II service, during which she sank three vessels for a total of 13,999 tons.

Holland, John Philip (1840–1914)

The inventor of what was determined to be the first really successful submarine, was born in Ireland in 1840. He was a schoolteacher and the most unlikely person to think of in terms of challenging the deep. But he was an inventive genius and had fanatical determination and, when it came to fighting for something, an Irish heart. Conceiving the idea that a submersible vessel would assist the Irish in gaining their independence, Holland immigrated to the United States in 1873. Holland's idea received support in 1881 from the American Fenian Society to finance the construction of the Fenian Ram, "which embodied the chief principles of the modern submarine in balance, control, and compensation of weight loss in torpedo discharge." Until 1898, however, his designs for submarines to be constructed for the U.S. Navy were not adopted, principally because of the navy's dedicated emphasis on the battleship as the most important vessel in the fleet. However, the value of submarines was clearly demonstrated in 1898 with the successful and hugely influential *Holland* design, which provided the basis for all future developments. Built to John Holland's specifications, it was purchased by the Navy Department in 1900, thus initiating the hundred years of submarine service celebrated in the Navy Centennial of the year 2000.

Holland, USS (SS-1)

One of the earliest true submersibles, this boat was designed privately by John Philip Holland and represented a major step forward in the development of the submarine, providing a prototype for subsequent models. Built under his supervision by the Electric Boat Company of Connecticut, the *Holland*, which had a surface displacement of 64 tons and 74 submerged, was launched in 1897 and completed the following year. It was the first submarine to use an electric motor for propulsion underwater and an internal combustion engine for power on the surface. An earlier, less successful, Holland design, the *Plunger*, had

John P. Holland, inventor, self-taught engineer, Irish emigrant, and designer of the *Holland* (SS-1), launched May 17, 1897. *(United States Navy)*

combined a steam engine and an electric motor. The 45 horsepower gasoline engine powered the boat at eight miles per hour cruising on the surface, while the electric motor produced a maximum speed of five miles per hour underwater. She had a length of just under 54 feet and a beam of 10 feet 3 inches. She was also the first submarine to be equipped with horizontal rudders, which enabled it to do a controlled dive rather than merely sink when it wished to submerge. This was described as a "porpoising" principle, making it possible for the boat to run completely underwater even when it had slight buoyancy. The idea, explained Holland to the navy board reviewing the acceptance of this unfamiliar vessel of war, was that the submarine could dive down and remain under while approaching a target, but quickly and readily surface to launch the torpedo and then dive before any fire could be returned by the enemy. The U.S. Navy purchased her after extensive trials and she entered the service in October 1900, the first submarine commissioned by the navy. Although her armament was very limited, consisting of a

The *Holland* (SS-1) was consciously designed to imitate the sleek lines of a porpoise to enhance submerged performance, resulting in a low-in-the-water appearance when topside. *(United States Navy)*

single torpedo tube and a dynamite gun, the *Holland* was a key influence on later submarine design—and eventually on the makeup and strategies of the world's navies.

Hunley (AS-31)

A submarine tender, named after the famed Civil War submarine, launched in September 1961 as the first tender specifically designed to service Fleet Ballistic Missile (FBM) submarines. Three SSBNs could be serviced alongside simultaneously. Her sister ship, the *Holland* (AS-32), was launched in January 1963. As originally constructed, they could support the Polaris missile. The *Hunley* was modified in 1973, and the *Holland* in 1974, to support Poseidon-armed submarines, which carried 16 of these missiles. The tenders were built with a 32-ton hammerhead crane, fitted aft, and were each armed with two twin, three-inch, 50-caliber anti-aircraft guns. Both ships were employed as general-purpose submarine tenders during the last years of their service life, and were replaced by the later Simon Lake-class tender.

hydrography

The scientific study of the sea and other waters on the Earth's surface, hydrography dates back to the earliest explorations of the oceans of the world. The Arabs, who invented the compass and astrolabe, were the first to record systematically the results of their surveys of coastlines, harbors, sea depths, currents, and winds during the medieval period. Their charts and maps were made widely available to seafarers as they navigated the globe. The development of hydrography as a scientific study expanded as the oceans were explored and new instruments, including the sextant and quadrant, became available. The science gained further momentum during the 16th through 19th centuries when sailing navies required more accurate information that would enable them to navigate the oceans with much greater precision.

The French navy took an early lead, forming a hydrographic department in 1720, but the U.S. Navy did not follow suit for 100 years. Although the British equivalent was not formally established until 1795, the Royal Navy had played a key role in shaping knowledge about the world's oceans during the 18th century. During the 19th century it assembled comprehensive information on all aspects of the sea. Changes in the nature of naval warfare—especially in regard to undersea missions—have made new demands on naval hydrographic departments. For example, submarine warfare has stimulated the need for improved sonar-based information about sea depths. Another motivation has been the growth in amphibious operations, which have required more data about coastlines and how they might best be approached. These gaps are increasingly filled by the use of satellite surveys, which often provide valuable supplementary data.

I

Icefish (SS-367)

Launched in February 1942 at the Manitowic Shipbuilding Yard, this submarine of the Balao class was assigned to Vice Admiral Lockwood's *Task Force 17*. She joined "Banister's Beagles" with *Sawfish* and *Drum,* and departed in early September on her first war patrol, which took her into Luzon Straits and the South China Sea. October 1944 was a peak month in the war for American submarines, which sank 322,265 tons of Japanese shipping, almost one third of which consisted of tankers. In October *Icefish* and *Drum* together sank 26,901 tons of enemy shipping in "Convoy College," the code name for the area extending across the East China Sea from Luzon Strait to Formosa and the coast of China. *Icefish* sank a 4,000-ton cargo vessel on October 23 and on October 26 she was credited with sinking a transport of 10,000 tons, before terminating her first war patrol at Majuro, Marshall Islands. Although greatly revved up by this record, the officers and crew of *Icefish* were disappointed in the second patrol, near the end of the year, which lasted 43 days with no results, and she was forced to return to Pearl Harbor by engineering difficulties. The third war patrol began in late February when she again headed for the East China Sea, but by this time Japanese shipping had dwindled so acutely that she could find no targets. The same was true of her fourth and fifth patrols. However, *Icefish* put herself to good use when, in June 1945, she rescued six army aviators off the coast of Formosa and performed other useful lifeguard and reconnaissance duties. She joined the Reserve Fleet the next year and was transferred to the East Coast, where she served until February 1953, when she was decommissioned, converted to a GUPPY IB at the Electric Boat Com-

pany, and transferred to the Netherlands, where she served as *Walrus* for the next 18 years. She received four battle stars for World War II service.

Inchon Landing (September 15–25, 1950)

A large-scale amphibious landing by American forces at Inchon, Korea, that proved to be a turning point in the Korean War and saved the United Nations forces, headed by the United States, from possible defeat. This strategic operation was possible only because of the U.S. Navy's command of the sea, and the ability to support two American divisions in their landing at the port of Inchon, where they cut enemy supply lines and advanced successfully on Seoul. The North Korean forces then were caught in a dual movement by these forces; the American Eighth Army, which broke out from the Pusan perimeter to the south, and the invading forces advanced according to plan, with Seoul falling to the allies before the end of the month.

Inland Sea

This body of water, lying between the Japanese islands of Honshu, Shikoku, and Kyushu, was one of the most strategic mission destinations for American submarines during World War II. It is composed of five distinct basins linked together by channels. Its east-west length is about 270 miles, and its waters are easily navigable. The sea has an irregular coastline and is dotted with hundreds of small islands, the largest of which is Awaji Island in the east. Entrance to the Inland Sea from the Philippine Sea and the Pacific Ocean is afforded by the Bungo Strait and the Kii

Strait. The narrow Shimonoseki Strait at the western end leads to the East China Sea. Since the Inland Sea was a major transportation route, it was the obvious route taken by Japanese warships, coming and going, as well as for outgoing supplies and troop ships servicing Japanese bases in the Pacific. Though very heavily guarded by planes, surface ships, and submarines, it was a prime target area for American submarines, and particularly during the later stages of the war when Japanese defenses had been greatly weakened and American submarines could find relatively easy targets.

intelligence

This is known in more technical terminology as Information, Surveillance, and Reconnaissance (ISR). Naval forces always have made use of the intelligence gathered as a result of espionage activity or from more open sources, including photographic reconnaissance obtained by aircraft or satellite. High-quality intelligence collected, analyzed, and distributed by specialist agencies has played a vital part in the outcome of several major naval battles of the 20th century. Equally, the absence of relevant intelligence—or the failure to interpret it correctly—also has had major consequences. The establishment of permanent national intelligence organizations is a relatively recent development, dating to the late 19th century. Specialist naval intelligence services also originate from this time, although most remained underdeveloped and small-scale until the outbreak of the First World War necessitated a great expansion of the intelligence horizon. Early in World War I, the British obtained a copy of the German navy's code book. Unknown to the Germans, they were able to decode intercepted radio messages for the rest of the war. The British also achieved continuing success against the Germans in World War II, discovering a way to read messages encoded on the famous Enigma machine. As a result, British naval intelligence was able to produce valuable information bearing on U-boat operations. A similar American operation, code-named Magic, was created in 1939 to break Japanese military codes. While it failed to warn of the Pearl Harbor attack, it had a vital success in revealing the Japanese attack plan for the battle of Midway in 1942, a decisive American victory and a turning point in the Pacific war.

Although precise and accurate analysis of intelligence gathered from decoded messages is required if the correct conclusions are to be drawn, details need to be communicated within an appropriate time period to operational commanders. Pearl Harbor was an example of an intelligence weakness; the code-breaking experts had become aware of a possible Japanese attack, but failed to predict precisely when and where it would occur. This shortcoming was compounded by the fact that increasingly explicit indications of Japanese actions received in the days leading up to the attack on Pearl Harbor were not passed on to naval headquarters in Honolulu. In recent years, the perfection of intelligence methods, and lessons learned from World War II, have made it possible for American submarines to carry out very effective intelligence missions, particularly in monitoring Russian plans and the movement of that nation's submarines, other naval vessels, and fleet movements.

The Office of Naval Intelligence defines the role of intelligence as part of its overall operations as follows:

> As an integral part of naval forces, naval intelligence resources are forward deployed around the world. Because of this forward deployment, naval intelligence must always be at a high state of readiness, with unparalleled situational awareness of the operating theater. To maintain that awareness, naval intelligence operations in peacetime closely parallel those in war and in operations other than war. More than any other service, naval intelligence supports peacetime operational decisionmaking on a daily basis.
>
> Since its formal establishment in 1882, the Office of Naval Intelligence has been a major player in many successful operations that have meant the difference between ultimate victory and defeat. During World War II, an intensive cryptanalytic effort by the Navy's Communications Security Group—forerunner of today's Naval Security Group—led to the breaking of the Japanese Navy's code system and played a pivotal role in attaining final victory in the Pacific. The naval cryptanalytic efforts of World War II foreshadow similar cryptologic tasks that will be required for operations against future adversaries including signals search methodology, language skills, and signal access.

Intelligent Whale

A man-powered submersible, this early prototype of the submarine was purchased from its inventor by the U.S. Navy in 1870, but never placed in service because of its failure to perform during sea trials. Features included air purifiers, pressurized air to empty ballast tanks, and the ability to release a diver while submerged. The Intelligent Whale, while cumbersome, almost impossible to maneuver, and a likely coffin for any crew attempting to navigate her in battle, was credited with opening the eyes of the navy to future possibilities, and even inspiring John Holland to develop his more successful submarine.

Irex (SS-482)

This submarine of the Tench class was built by the Portsmouth Naval Shipyard and launched in January 1945; ordered to the Pacific after her shakedown cruises, she got no farther than the Canal Zone when the war ended. She was then ordered to Key West, where she joined SubRon4.

She spent the remainder of the year there and at Guantanamo Bay conducting exercises. By December 1946, the navy had completed plans for the modern telescopic snorkel, the device to enable diesel-powered submarines to run submerged for long periods of time, and *Irex* was ordered to Portsmouth Naval Shipyard in 1951 for installation and testing of this equipment subsequently known as a Fleet Snorkel conversion. After 10 years of service along the East Coast and in the Caribbean, she was deployed to the Mediterranean with units of the powerful Sixth Fleet. In the Mideast crisis that culminated in the nationalization of the Suez Canal in July 1956, and armed conflict between Egypt and the forces of France, Israel, and the United Kingdom, U.S. naval forces acted early to support America's policy. In February 1957, patrols in the Red Sea and along the Israeli-Egyptian border were established as a means of expressing our interest in the peaceful outcome of the crisis. Returning to New London, she resumed her operations, served as a training ship for submarine students, and participated in fleet exercises in the North Atlantic and the Mediterranean. She also aided in the development of anti-submarine warfare tactics, and was decommissioned and struck from the Navy list in November 1969.

Iwo Jima, invasion of (February 19– March 15, 1945)

Iwo Jima, an island in the western Pacific, five miles long and varying in width up to 2.5 miles, was under Japanese control as a military stronghold until early in 1945, when it became the scene of a fierce battle between Japanese and invading U.S. troops during the last phases of World War II. The island was strategically important because, if captured, it could serve as a base for U.S. fighter planes to accompany U.S. heavy bombers flying to Japan from bases on Saipan, an island 700 miles farther south that U.S. troops had taken in 1944. Two U.S. Marine divisions landed on Iwo Jima on February 19–21, 1945, and were soon followed by a third division. The island's Japanese defenders had entrenched themselves so effectively in caves that weeks of preliminary naval and air bombardment failed to weaken their ability to offer strong resistance to the landing. The struggle for possession of the island continued for almost a month before it was officially pronounced captured by the United States. More than 21,000 Japanese troops were killed, while U.S. forces counted almost 7,000 killed and more than 20,000 wounded.

Jack (SS-259)

A submarine of the Gato class, launched in October 1942, she was ordered to the Pacific and departed on her first offensive war patrol in June 1943. Taking part in a submarine offensive against Japan, she patrolled off Honshu, where she came upon a five-ship convoy and, in a series of five well-executed attacks, sank a 4,000-ton passenger-cargo ship and a 6,000-ton cargo ship. In attempting to torpedo a third ship, the submarine was shaken by an aerial torpedo; but the alert crew corrected her dangerous diving angle and effected repairs. On the Fourth of July, she began to track smoke on the horizon and soon detected a cargo ship with an escort. *Jack* then sent the cargo ship under with three torpedoes and returned to Pearl Harbor for repairs. *Jack's* second war patrol brought no opportunities for attack because of engineering difficulties that forced her to return prematurely to Pearl Harbor. Leaving on her third war patrol the submarine proceeded westward from Pearl Harbor to the South China Sea on January 16, 1944. Prowling the pivotal Singapore-Japan shipping lanes, she encountered five large oil tankers with three escorts and fired three torpedoes, scoring one hit. She then began a long circling maneuver designed to bring her in front of the remaining four tankers; and late in the afternoon of February 19 she was again ready to attack. Two torpedoes sank two more of the frantically zigzagging ships and *Jack* moved in on the trailing tanker. Her first spread of torpedoes missed and the tanker replied with a salvo from her 5" guns; but *Jack* returned three hours later to sink her with four well-placed torpedoes. In this remarkable series of attacks the submarine sank four tankers, all over 5,000 tons.

Departing Australia April 6, 1944, *Jack* returned to the South China Sea for her fourth war patrol. She chased a long convoy through the afternoon of April 25, and shortly after midnight next day attacked, sinking *Yoshido Maru* and damaging two others. She also sank a radio-equipped trawler with gunfire. For her fifth war patrol, in June and July, she again returned to the South China Sea where she spotted a large convoy and fired three torpedoes, sinking a large tanker, before being forced to retire by escorting aircraft. Five days later she came upon another large convoy, and by early on June 30 was in a position to attack. Three successive attacks sent two cargo ships to the bottom. For her highly successful and aggressive first, third, and fifth war patrols, the submarine was awarded the coveted Presidential Unit Citation, but that was not the end of her success. On her sixth war patrol, in the Celebes Sea in August, she sank a small minesweeper and another cargo ship; and on her seventh she accounted for two more cargo ships, after which she had to return to San Francisco for a major overhaul. By the time she returned to the Pacific theater of war, there were very few potential victims left, and her major job during her final three patrols was to act as lifeguard for the massive carrier strikes and bomber missions on the Japanese mainland. During the peacetime that followed, *Jack* was placed in the Atlantic Reserve Fleet, and in December 1957 she was loaned to the Royal Hellenic Navy where she served as HHMS *Amfritriti*. In addition to her Presidential Unit Citation, *Jack* received seven battle stars for World War II, during which she sank 15 enemy ships for a grand total of 76,687 tons.

Jack (SSN-605)

The second submarine to bear the name was of the Permit class, and was built by the Portsmouth Naval Shipyard and launched in April 1963, five years after the original *Jack* was transferred to the Greek navy. A submarine of 3,070 tons on the surface and 3,500 submerged, with a crew of nine officers and 76 enlisted men, she served in the fleet until being decommissioned and struck from the Navy list in July 1990.

Jallao (SS-368)

A submarine of the Balao class launched in March 1944, she was ordered to the Pacific and in October went on her first war patrol, operating with *Pintado* and *Tule* in a coordinated attack group (wolf pack) known as "Clarey's Crushers." At first the submarines proceeded toward Luzon Strait; but, during the battle for Leyte Gulf late in October, they were directed to take up scouting positions between the Philippines and Japan to cut off Japanese cripples struggling home after their devastating defeat at the battle of Cape Engano. On the evening of October 25, *Jallao* sighted a damaged light cruiser, *Tama*, and moved to attack. She fired seven torpedoes, three of which hit, although no sinking was confirmed. Her second war patrol, in January 1945, and her third, in April and May, yielded no targets, though she had an opportunity to brave shore batteries to move in and pick up five men in a raft, delivering them safely to Saipan. She then departed for the coast of Japan and more lifeguard duty, as American heavy bombers stepped up their attacks on the home islands. After advanced training in the Marianas, *Jallao* departed Guam at the end of July 1945 to patrol the Sea of Japan. On this, her fourth and final patrol, the submarine sank a 6,000-ton freighter just four days before the end of the war. After returning to Mare Island, she was placed in the Pacific Reserve Fleet. She was then transferred to New London, Connecticut in 1953, for a conversion to a GUPPY IB in which she was streamlined and equipped with snorkeling gear and new electric equipment, after which she operated along the East Coast, training with Canadian and American antisubmarine units. In January and February 1955, she took part in fleet exercises in the Caribbean, and later in the Mediterranean. *Jallao* was decommissioned, struck from the Navy list and sold to Spain in June 1974. She received four battle stars for World War II service.

Java Sea, Battle of the (February 27, 1942)

A strategic battle between Allied and Japanese forces in the Pacific during World War II, in which submarines played a vital role. By February 1942, Japanese plans for the invasion of the Dutch East Indies island of Java were well advanced; and Allied naval units based at Soerabaja were the only real obstacle. This mixed force of American, British, and Dutch warships included five cruisers and nine destroyers but had no air support. It had been operating, along with submarines of the three nations, against Japanese convoys off Sumatra and Java for some months. On the afternoon of February 27, an invasion force was detected some 80 miles northeast of Soerabaja in the Makassar Straits. Soon after, sightings were made on the Japanese escort, which consisted of two heavy and two light cruisers and 14 destroyers. The engagement began at 4:20 P.M. when the Japanese heavy cruisers opened fire at a range of some 16 miles. The Allied force closed in so that its light cruisers could attack the enemy destroyers. During a Japanese torpedo attack, the British cruiser *Exeter* was badly damaged and withdrew together with three other ships. An Allied counterattack resulted in the loss of two more Allied ships, forcing a retreat south to regroup. A destroyer was lost in a minefield and four American destroyers that had run out of torpedoes were sent back to port. Later in the evening, the Allies turned north again in a final bid to stop the invasion, but they lost two cruisers and later two more, which were attempting to escape western Java. Allied losses in men and ships were extremely heavy in this abortive attempt to stop the Japanese invasion of the island of Java.

Jimmy Carter (SSN-23)

The third, and final, submarine of the Seawolf class, launched in June 1995, she was named for former president Jimmy Carter, honoring him not only as the 39th president of the United States, but also as the only U.S. president ever to qualify in submarines. He was a 1947 graduate of the U.S. Naval Academy and served as an officer aboard submarines while in uniform, and, of course, served as commander-in-chief from 1977 to 1981 while in the Oval Office. The three submarines of the Seawolf class are the most capable, multimission submarines ever built. They combine speed, stealth, a large and varied weapons load, and the latest in high-tech electronics to provide unlimited flexibility while operating. These submarines have an overall length of 353 feet, a beam of 40 feet, displace 9,150 tons and carry a crew size of approximately 130. With mission and growth capability far beyond previous submarines, the design uniquely supports missions such as surveillance, intelligence collection, special warfare, covert cruise missile strike, mine warfare, and antisubmarine and antisurface ship warfare. In addition to its formidable open ocean presence, the Seawolf class is also a highly capable shallow-water warfare platform. Its inherent stealth, coupled with state-of-the-art sensors and advanced combat systems, make it the benchmark for underwater excellence, whether in deep seas, the shallows,

USS *John Adams* (SSBN-620), seen here being readied for an extended cruise of many weeks without surfacing, was constructed at the Portsmouth Naval Shipyard and commissioned in 1964. She spent more than 15 years submerged on deterrent patrol and traveled over 975,000 miles during her distinguished career. *(United States Navy)*

John C. Calhoun (SSBN-630) was commissioned in 1964 at Newport News, Virginia, and 16 years later converted to Trident ballistic missiles. This illustration dramatically shows the size of the sail on modern submarines, in contrast to the small conning towers of earlier diesel boats. *(United States Navy)*

or under the arctic ice. The Seawolf class is armed with *Tomahawk* cruise missiles, making it possible to conduct deep-strike missions while submerged far off an enemy's coast, and also carries the Mark 48 advanced capability torpedo (ADCAP), the most reliable torpedo in the world for use against surface ships and submarines.

John Adams (SSBN-620)

A submarine of the Lafayette class, built by the Portsmouth Naval Shipyard and launched in January 1963, she was a member of the Atlantic and Pacific fleets, and completed 32 Polaris deterrent patrols and an additional 43 Poseidon deterrent patrols. She was awarded the Atlantic Fleet Golden Anchor Award as a result of 100 percent retention for several years and the best personnel programs in the fleet, the Meritorious Unit Commenda-

tion, Battle Efficiency "E" and Engineering Red "E," and was the only submarine to receive an award for a flawless performance during an inspection of both Polaris and the Mark 45 nuclear torpedo. *John Adams* spent more than 15 years submerged on deterrent patrol and traveled over 975,000 miles during her distinguished career. She was decommissioned and was struck from the Navy list in March 1989.

John C. Calhoun (SSBN-630)

A submarine of the Lafayette class, the *John C. Calhoun* was launched in June 1963 at the Newport News Shipbuilding & Drydock Company, and began operational patrols two years later, armed with far-ranging Polaris missiles. She underwent a Poseidon missile conversion in the early 1970s and a Trident missile conversion in 1980 at the

Norfolk Naval Shipyard. As with the other boats in her class, she carried a large crew of 14 officers and 126 enlisted men, displaced more than 8,000 tons (submerged), could cruise at more than 21 knots underwater, and was armed with 16 missile tubes and four 21-inch torpedo tubes forward. She was decommissioned and struck from the Navy list in March 1994.

John Marshall (SSBN-611)

A submarine of the Ethan Allen class, built by Newport News Shipbuilding and Drydock Company and launched in July 1961, she joined the Atlantic Fleet 10 months later as a unit of SubRon14. She became the ninth operational fleet ballistic missile submarine, and began conducting deterrent patrols from Holy Loch, Scotland, later operating on missions from Rota, Spain. She was commended for the effectiveness and dependability of her fleet ballistic missile system, later upgraded to support the Polaris A-3 system. The *John Marshall* later saw service as an attack submarine in the Pacific, and after that was deployed to the Mediterranean. In September 1987, a special operational demonstration was conducted near Puerto Rico with a SEAL delivery vehicle team, while a year later marked the 1,000th dive of the boat, off Puerto Rico. On May 1, 1989, after conducting a variety of exercises with carriers and other submarines, the boat departed for its third Mediterranean deployment. This was the first time a submarine had deployed anywhere in the world with two dry deck shelters on board, adding a unique flexibility and endurance to the fleet commander for special warfare operations. The boat conducted three special warfare training exercises in the Caribbean Sea in 1990, including a highly successful exercise that featured the employment of submarine launched mobile mines. In September 1991, *John Marshall* served as flagship for the largest submarine/special warfare exercise, during which over 191 personnel, including three flag officers and navy SEAL and army special forces, embarked to conduct joint special operations during Exercise Phantom Shadow. She was decommissioned and struck from the Navy list in July 1992.

K

K-1 [ex-*Haddock*] (SS-32)

Built by the Fore River Shipbuilding Company, this K-class submarine was launched in September 1913 and a year later joined SubDiv4 of the Atlantic Torpedo Flotilla at Newport, Rhode Island. She continued operations along the East Coast of the United States for almost three years, aiding in the development of submarine warfare tactics. The techniques learned from these experiments were soon put into practice when German U-boats interfered with Allied shipping bound for Europe during the First World War. *K-1* and three of her sister ships were the first American submarines to operate in European waters during the war. Leaving the United States Naval Submarine Base at New London, Connecticut, in mid-October 1917, the four submarines, accompanied by submarine tender USS *Bushael,* set course for their new base at Ponta Delgada in the Azores. For over a year, these boats searched for the German U-boats and surface raiders reputed to be operating in the Azores area. However, no contacts with the enemy were ever made. With the war over, *K-1* transited to Philadelphia and began operating along the East Coast. From 1919 to 1923, when she was finally decommissioned, she cruised along the Atlantic coast of the United States, from New England to Florida, conducting experimental exercises. To her credit, it was stated that the development of submarines was greatly accelerated through the technology learned from these experiments. New listening devices, storage batteries, and torpedoes were tested; and their later adoption contributed greatly toward enhancing American submarine superiority and strength on the high seas.

K-5 (SS-36)

Similar in all respects to her prototype, *K-1,* this submarine was launched in March 1914, built at Fore River, and assigned to SubDiv4 of the Atlantic Torpedo Flotilla for experiments and exercises to develop the techniques of submarine warfare. She operated for almost three years along the Atlantic coast of the United States, from New England to the Gulf of Mexico, conducting underwater maneuvers, undergoing diving and torpedo firing practice, and training submariners. And, after the outbreak of World War I, she joined *K-1* in the same wartime mission. In January 1919, she was ordered to Key West, Florida, where she operated in the Gulf of Mexico and the Caribbean. Later she served along the eastern seaboard, from Cape Cod to the Florida Keys, participating in numerous experiments and maneuvers to improve the operational and tactical abilities of the submarine. Following further operations in Chesapeake Bay, she was decommissioned in December 1930.

K-6 (SS-37)

Following her launching at the Fore River Shipbuilding Company in March 1914, *K-6* joined SubDiv4 of the Atlantic Torpedo Flotilla and followed a career almost parallel to that of her sister submarine, *K-5,* ranging along the United States Atlantic coast from New England to the Caribbean. She conducted experimental dives and underwater maneuvers, to prove the value of submarines as an effective part of the United States Navy. She was decommissioned in Hampton Roads, Virginia, in May 1923.

USS *K-6* (SS-37), shown above, was one of four K-boats (*K-1, K-2, K-5*, and *K-6*) that were the first American submarines in European waters during World War I. With no reported contacts, they searched for German subs for over a year. *(United States Navy)*

K-7 (SS-38)

As a unit of the Pacific Torpedo Flotilla, *K-7* sailed out of San Diego in late December 1914, six months after her launching at the Union Iron Works in San Francisco, to commence shakedown and training along the California coast. She departed the West Coast of the United States on October 3, 1915, for experimental duty in the Hawaiian Islands. Arriving at Pearl Harbor 11 days later, she began conducting torpedo and diving tests and participated in operations developing the tactics of submarine warfare. *K-7* departed Pearl Harbor in late October 1917, for antisubmarine patrol duty in the Gulf of Mexico, since the United States was now an active participant in World War I. After the war, she resumed training and development operations near Key West and in the Caribbean. She then transferred to the United States Naval Academy at Annapolis, Maryland, for training missions, and for more than two years ranged the eastern seaboard of the United States, from Hampton Roads, Virginia, to Provincetown, Massachusetts, training submariners, conducting diving experiments, and practicing underwater warfare tactics. After further service in Chesapeake Bay, she was decommissioned at Hampton Roads in February 1923.

K-8 (SS-39)

Following much the same path as *K-7*, her sister boat, *K-8* was launched from the Union Iron Works in San Francisco in June 1914 and sailed in October 1915 for duty in the Hawaiian Islands. For more than two years she operated with *K-7* and two other sister subs, *K-3* and *K-4*, developing and perfecting submarine techniques in diving, torpedo firing, and underwater tactics. When the United States became an active participant in the First World War, she was ordered to return to the West Coast of the United States in October 1917, and from there to the United States Naval Station at Key West, Florida, where she was to conduct war patrols out of that port, and later from Galveston, Texas. Her further career was spent with operations in the Caribbean, in the Chesapeake, in training missions at the Naval Academy, and service as the "school boat" for the Submarine School at the United States Naval Submarine Base at New London, Connecticut. *K-8* was decommissioned at Norfolk, Virginia, in February 1923.

Kete (SS-369)

Launched in April 1944, from the Manitowoc Shipbuilding Yard in Manitowoc, Wisconsin, this submarine of the Balao class was ordered to the Pacific, where, in late October of that year, she set out on her first war patrol, heading for the East China Sea. Harassed by heavy weather and nonfunctioning bow planes, she returned and then made her war patrol north of Okinawa. Despite prolonged periods of heavy weather, she made lifeguard patrols off the central Ryukyus during January 1945, searching for American fliers downed during air strikes on the Ryukyus. Departing Guam on March 1, 1945, *Kete* headed for her second war patrol in the vicinity of the Nansei Shoto island chain. Ten days later, she reported having sunk three medium-sized freighters on the previous night, and later that she had fired four torpedoes, which missed a small enemy cable-laying vessel, and had only three torpedoes left. *Kete* was then directed to proceed to Pearl Harbor for refit, stopping at Midway en route for fuel. On March 19, she acknowledged receipt of these orders, and a day later her exact position. This was the last message received from her. At normal cruising speed she should have arrived at Midway about March 31, 1945. When she was neither sighted nor heard from by April 16, 1945, she was reported as presumed lost.

Japanese information concerning antisubmarine attacks gained at the end of the war gives no positive evidence to what happened to *Kete*. There were a few minefields in the Nansei Shoto Chain, but since *Kete* was already east of the islands at the time of her last message and was heading home, loss through a mine was considered highly improbable. It is now known that a number of enemy submarines were in the area through which she was required to pass en route to Midway. One Japanese submarine was sunk east of Okinawa by a U.S. destroyer on March 23, 1945, and two other Japanese submarines were sunk southeast of Okinawa near this date. Conditions attendant to *Kete's* loss suggest the likelihood that one of these submarines might have torpedoed and sunk her and been unable to report the attack before being sunk herself. Thus, *Kete* must be considered probably a loss due to an unreported enemy attack. She is credited with sending three medium freighters, totaling 6,881 tons, to the bottom on this last patrol.

King, Ernest Joseph (1878–1956)

The top-ranking American naval officer during World War II, King was born on November 23, 1878, in Lorain, Ohio. Appointed to the U.S. Naval Academy in 1897, he graduated fourth in his class, serving as battalion commander. After service during World War I, he began his association with submarines and with naval aviation. He purposely sought as wide a range of experience as possible in nearly every type of vessel and base installation. Although he never qualified as a submariner, he did command submarine squadrons as well as the New London, Connecticut, submarine base. Although he was only a year from retirement at the start of World War II, he was pressed into active service as commander of the Atlantic Fleet, and authorized to conduct defensive operations against Axis surface and undersea raiders. Within two weeks of the Pearl Harbor attack, King was elevated to the position of commander of the U.S. Fleet, and the following March he was made Chief of naval operations (CNO), becoming the first officer to combine these two key positions. As such he was in charge of and exercised complete control over the U.S. Navy, Marine Corps, and Coast Guard, and was thus second only to General George C. Marshall in the U.S. military hierarchy. His experience in submarine and aviation warfare fitted him for the task of commanding a naval war on two oceans. Despite his age, he continued to advise the president, as well as several secretaries of defense and secretaries of the navy until his death at Portsmouth, New Hampshire, in June 1956.

Korean War (1950–1953)

Following Japan's defeat at the end of World War II, Korea was partitioned between the communist north and the non-communist south, leading to border clashes and the invasion of South Korea by communist forces from the north on June 25, 1950. A United Nations force intervened, and its success in pushing back the North Koreans resulted in communist Chinese involvement in the war. With the balance of power turned in their favor, the communist forces advanced southward and captured Seoul, the South Korean capital. UN forces counterattacked and were able to push the North Koreans back across the 38th parallel, and the war settled into a bloody stalemate. By the end of the war, in 1953, the UN force had restored a fragile peace. Naval power made a vital but indirect contribution to the outcome of the war—providing UN ground forces with the necessary supplies and troops. In addition, the fleet prevented communist forces from being resupplied by sea. The U.S. Navy regularly supported land operations with air strikes and heavy shore bombardments, as well as in the mounting of amphibious operations. The navy also successfully evacuated 200,000 U.N. troops and civilians from the port of Hungnam in December 1950 in the face of Chinese offensive operations. The Korean War emphasized the key role of the navy in conventional warfare and ensured that it did not suffer drastic postwar reductions.

Kraken (SS-370)

Launched in April 1944 at the Manitowoc Shipbuilding Yard, this submarine of the Balao class was ordered to Pearl Harbor, from where she departed in December 1944 for her first war patrol, setting course for Indochina, where she maintained lifeguard duty in support of Third Fleet carrier strikes. While on station she rescued a carrier pilot from rough seas and evaded a strafing enemy plane by diving, but found no targets. Her second patrol was equally uneventful, but on her third, in May 1945, she sailed to the Java Sea where she bombarded Merak and riddled a coaster and a small ship with her deck guns. Three days later while chasing an eight-ship convoy, *Kraken's* torpedoes sank an oiler and a coastal steamer and her guns inflicted heavy damage on one of the Japanese submarine chasers in the convoy. Her fourth patrol was cut short by Japan's surrender, and she rendezvoused with Halsey's Third Fleet and formed a part of the honor escort as the admiral passed under the Golden Gate Bridge in the fleet's flagship, USS *South Dakota*. Ten days later, she returned to San Francisco where she was placed in reserve on May 4, 1946. Her peacetime service continued until October 1958, when she was decommissioned and transferred for loan to the Spanish government. She ended her career in service to the Spanish navy as *Almirante Garcia*. *Kraken* received one battle star for World War II service.

L

L-1 (SS-40)*

The first of a new class, *L-1* was launched in January 1915 at the Fore River Shipbuilding Company, and had a complement of two officers and 26 enlisted men. She was a boat of 548 tons (submerged) and was armed with a four 18-inch torpedo tubes forward. After trials and exercises in New England waters, she was assigned to the Atlantic Submarine Flotilla and operated along the East Coast of the United States. During World War I, she sailed to European waters to protect Allied shipping from German surface raider and submarine attacks. From 1919 to 1922, *L-1* operated along the Atlantic coast of the United States experimenting with new torpedoes and undersea detection

equipment. The technological advances through tests performed by *L-1* and her sister submarines during the post-World War I era added to the strength and quality of the U.S. Navy submarines that contributed so much toward the defeat of Japan during the Second World War.

L-4 (SS-43)

Launched in April 1915 from the Fore River Shipbuilding Company in Quincy, Massachusetts, this L-class submarine operated along the Atlantic coast of the United States, assisting in the development of new techniques in undersea warfare, until April 1917. She was then dispatched to European waters to protect the Allied shipping lanes between North America and Europe during World War I. While on patrol during April 1918, *L-4* twice encountered enemy German U-boats in British waters and chased them from the paths of friendly convoys. Following the Armistice, which ended the First World War on November 11, 1918, she operated along the East Coast of the United States, performing valuable experiments in developing the tactics of undersea warfare. She was decommissioned in April 1922.

L-11 (SS-51)

Launched in May 1916 from the Fore River Shipbuilding Company in Quincy, Massachusetts, this submarine of the

L-1 (SS-40), as the first of a new class, was ordered to World War I patrol duty shortly after her commissioning, and operated in British waters throughout America's involvement to thwart German U-boats from attacking Allied ships. *(United States Navy)*

---

* *L-2, 3, 5, 6, 7, 8, 9,* and *10* had routine careers, and are not included here because of lack of space.

L-boats (SS-42–SS-47) being readied for World War I patrols.
(United States Navy)

L-class was assigned to the Atlantic Submarine Flotilla and operated along the East Coast of the United States, developing new techniques of undersea warfare, until December 1917. Then she was ordered to the British Isles to join SubDiv5 in antisubmarine patrol off the United Kingdom, during the last year of World War I. For the next nine months *L-11* ranged the shipping lanes and sighted German U-boats on three occasions. On May 11, 1918, the submarine made a torpedo attack on an enemy submarine with inconclusive results. After the war, she operated off the East Coast of the United States, developing submarine warfare tactics, and was decommissioned in November 1923.

Lafayette (SSBN-616)

The prototype and namebearer of a class of nuclear-powered strategic ballistic missile submarines built in the early to mid-1960s to carry the Polaris submarine-launched ballistic missile (SLBM), with all subsequently being modified to carry the Poseidon C-3 missile. They were designed with 16 missile tubes and four torpedo tubes, with space for carrying 48 Mark 48 torpedoes. Twelve of the boats were upgraded, from 1979 to 1982, to fire the Trident C-4 missile. In effect, this class represented an enlarged and improved version of the previous Ethan Allen (SSN-608) class. As in the Ethan Allen class, the pressure hulls were constructed of HY-80 steel or better. The Lafayette-class had a deeper operating depth than that of the later Ohio (SSBN-726) class. Twelve of the Lafayettes also had quieter machinery installations and

other minor differences and were then officially designated as the Benjamin Franklin class. (For this reason, there are duplications in the list below and the one shown with the Benjamin Franklin-class grouping.) These submarines were designed for a 20-year service life and later upgraded—with improvements—to 30 years.

The submarines in the Lafayette class also included:

Alexander Hamilton (SSBN-617)
Andrew Jackson (SSBN-619)
John Adams (SSBN-620)
James Monroe (SSBN-622)
Nathan Hale (SSBN-623)
Woodrow Wilson (SSBN-624)
Henry Clay (SSBN-625)
Daniel Webster (SSBN-626)
James Madison (SSBN-627)
Tecumseh (SSBN-628)
Daniel Boone (SSBN-629)
John C. Calhoun (SSBN-630)
Ulysses S. Grant (SSBN-631)
Von Steuben (SSBN-632)
Casimir Pulaski (SSBN-633)
Stonewall Jackson (SSBN-634)
Sam Rayburn (SSBN-635)
Nathanael Greene (SSBN-636)

USS *L-11* (SS-51), one of seven L-boats, patrolled the waters surrounding the British Isles during World War I. L-boats made 20 contacts with German subs, but were credited with no kills. *(United States Navy)*

Decommissioning of this class began in 1986 with the *Nathan Hale* and *Nathanael Greene,* which were struck from the Navy list in 1986 to conform with the SLBM limitations of the SALT II agreement. All but one of the submarines—the *Alexander Hamilton,* which was deployed to the West Coast—were assigned to the Atlantic Fleet, operating out of New London, Connecticut, and Charleston, South Carolina. The remaining ships were all decommissioned by 1994.

Lafayette class

The following chart of Lafayette class submarines is only partial and is shown here to provide an overall view of this class, its origins, and the duration of service of the average boat in the class before being decommissioned and scrapped in the 1990s.

Nuclear-propelled Strategic Missile Submarines

Number	Name	FY	Builder	Launched	Commissioned	Status
SSBN 617	*Alexander Hamilton*	61	G	1962	1963	Scrapped
SSBN 624	*Woodrow Wilson*	61	M	1963	1963	Scrapped
SSBN 628	*Tecumseh*	62	G	1963	1964	Scrapped
*SSBN 629	*Daniel Boone*	62	M	1963	1964	Scrapped
*SSBN 630	*John C. Calhoun*	62	N	1963	1964	Scrapped
*SSBN 632	*Von Steuben*	62	N	1963	1964	Scrapped
*SSBN 633	*Casimir Pulaski*	62	G	1964	1964	Scrapped
*SSBN 634	*Stonewall Jackson*	62	M	1963	1964	Scrapped
*SSBN 640	*Benjamin Franklin*	63	G	1964	1965	Scrapped
*SSBN 641	*Simon Bolivar*	63	N	1964	1965	Scrapped
SSN 642	*Kamehameha*	63	M	1965	1965	conv**
*SSBN 643	*George Bancroft*	63	G	1965	1966	Scrapped
SSBN 645	*James K. Polk*	63	G	1965	1966	conv**
*SSBN 655	*Henry L. Stimson*	64	G	1965	1966	Scrapped
SSBN 656	*George W. Carver*	64	N	1965	1966	Scrapped
*SSBN 657	*Francis Scott Key*	64	G	1966	1966	Scrapped
*SSBN 658	*Mariano G. Vallejo*	64	M	1965	1966	Scrapped
SSBN 659	*Will Rogers*	64	G	1966	1967	Scrapped

*indicates *Trident* missile submarine conversion
**Converted to special operations transport submarine and later scrapped
Builders G = General Dynamics/Electric Boat, Groton, Connecticut
   M = Mare Island Naval Shipyard, California
   P = Portsmouth Naval Shipyard, Kittery, Maine
   N = Newport News Shipbuilding, Newport News, Virginia

Lafayette class submarines were built to carry the Polaris submarine-launched ballistic missile (SLBM), with all subsequently being modified to carry the Poseidon C-3 missile. Twelve submarines were later upgraded to fire the Trident C-4 missile. The Trident submarines indicated above (#) were converted to launch that missile from 1979 to 1982.

These submarines are enlarged and improved versions of the previous Ethan Allen (SSN-608) class. As in the Ethan Allen class, the pressure hulls are constructed of HY-80 steel. The Lafayette-class operating depth is probably deeper than that of the later Ohio (SSBN-726) class. The last submarines of this class have quieter machinery installations and other minor differences and are officially designated as the Benjamin Franklin class. These submarines were designed for a 20-year service life, but in the early 1980s the navy determined that they could operate successfully for 30 years.

STATUS

The *Francis Scott Key* made the first Trident C-4 deployment, beginning in October 1979. The *Mariano G. Vallejo* was credited with completing the 2,500th SSBN patrol in April 1987. Decommissioning of this 31-boat class began in 1986 with the *Nathan Hale* and *Nathanael Greene,* which were decommissioned in 1986 to conform with the SLBM limitations of the SALT II agreement.

All but one of the operational submarines were assigned to the Atlantic Fleet, operating out of New London, Connecticut, and Charleston, South Carolina. In February 1991, the navy closed the submarine base at Holy Loch, Scotland, and the tender USS *Simon Lake* and a floating drydock would eventually return to the United States. The remaining ships were all decommissioned by 1994.

The *Alexander Hamilton* shifted to the Puget Sound Naval Shipyard in 1987 for a two-year overhaul and refueling; she did not return to the Atlantic and was the only Lafayette-class ship assigned to the Pacific Fleet. In October 1992, the *Alexander Hamilton* was placed in reserve in lieu of decommissioning. The *Henry L. Stimson, Will Rogers,* and *George Washington Carver* were similarly placed in reserve pending decommissioning on November 2, 1992.

The *John Marshall* was decommissioned in July 1992, followed by the *Lewis and Clark* in August 1992, the *James Madison* in November 1992, the *Francis Scott Key* in February 1993, the *Lafayette* in February 1992, the *Tecumseh* in February 1993, the *George Bancroft* in March 1993, the *Benjamin Franklin* in April 1993, the *Von Steuben* in July 1993, and the *Daniel Boone* in July 1993. The rest of these vessels were stricken by the end of 1994 through the Submarine Recycling Program.

CHARACTERISTICS

Displacement:	6,650 tons light; 7,250 tons standard; 8,250 tons submerged
Dimensions:	
length	425 ft. (129.6 m) overall
beam	33 ft. (10.1 m)
draft	31 ft. 6 in. (9.6 m)
Propulsion:	2 steam turbines; 15,000 shp.; 1 shaft
Reactors:	1 pressurized-water
Speed:	approx. 20 kts. surface; approx. 25 kts.submerged
Manning:	143 (13 Off. + 130 Enl.)
Combat Systems:	
missiles	16 tubes for Poseidon C-3 in 10 submarines
	16 tubes for Trident C-4 in 12 submarines
torpedo tubes	4 21-in. (533-cm) bow Nk 65
torpedoes	Mark 48 torpedoes
radars	BPS-11/11A or 15 surface search
sonars	EDO passive
	Western Electric towed array
	Raytheon navigation
	Honeywell passive array
	Raytheon active/passive detection
EW	NLR-8 passive intercept
fire control	Mark 113 torpedo/missile FCS

VARIANTS

The Benjamin Franklin–class submarines *Kamehameha* and *James K. Polk* were converted to serve as transport submarines for special operations forces. They are fitted to carry troops, equipment, and delivery vehicles for covert insertion onto enemy-controlled shorelines.

Leyte Gulf, Battle of (October 23–26, 1944)

A decisive air and sea battle that crippled the Japanese Combined Fleet, permitted U.S. invasion of the Philippines, and gave the Allies control of the Pacific. The battle was precipitated by a U.S. amphibious assault on the central Philippine island of Leyte on October 20. The Japanese responded with a plan to decoy the U.S. Third Fleet north, away from the San Bernardino Strait, while committing three forces to Leyte Gulf to prevent the landing. As the Japanese forces moved into position southwest of Leyte, submarines of the U.S. Seventh Fleet discovered and sank two heavy cruisers on October 23. A series of almost continuous surface and air clashes followed, especially in the Sibuyen Sea, while the U.S. Third Fleet chased the Japanese decoy. Finally, on October 25, the three major engagements of the battle were fought, almost simultaneously. At the Surigao Strait, battleships and cruisers from the Seventh Fleet forced the Japanese to withdraw. Meanwhile, although a Japanese attack inflicted heavy damage on Seventh Fleet carriers off Samar, it withdrew unexpectedly just as it seemed ready to attack the landing operations. In the north, off Cape Engano, submarines and other warships of the Third Fleet sank the Japanese decoy carriers, while another part of the naval force moved south. American submarines proved to be a decisive factor in the battle of Leyte Gulf.

Lifeguard League

During the Gilbert Islands campaign in the Pacific in World War II, Rear Admiral Charles A. Pownall, commanding a carrier task force, foresaw that he could realistically expect a substantial number of casualties when his airmen were shot down by the enemy. He therefore proposed that a plan be put into operation for submarines to be on the lookout for survivors in life jackets or rubber rafts. The plan was approved and was soon known by participating submariners as the Lifeguard League. No one realized at the time how effective lifeguard duty would be for those submarines whose secondary—and sometimes primary—mission was to rescue downed airmen. From that time on during the war, American submarines rescued no fewer than 553 survivors from almost sure death or capture in the vast Pacific waters. Among the rescue leaders were *Tigrone*, with 31 saves; *Tang*, with 22; and *Ray*, with 21. Historically, the most publicized was the story of USS *Finback* (SS-230), which made a total of five rescues. As the war in the Pacific was drawing to a close and Japanese shipping had been decimated, more submarines became available for lifeguard duty. While patrolling near the Bonin Islands, *Finback* picked up a pilot who narrowly escaped capture before being rescued. He was former president George H. W. Bush, who in 1943 had become the youngest pilot to fly off a carrier and had been shot down on his last mission. Bush remained aboard the *Finback* for nearly a month before the submarine returned to base, during which time the boat sank two enemy ships and survived several severe depth-charge attacks. The former president was quoted as commenting, "That experience was far scarier than an airplane bombing run. At least in the plane you controlled your destiny to some extent . . . but there, under the water, all you could do was hope like hell that an enemy wouldn't put an explosive on top of you."

Lockwood and others. *(United States Navy)*

Lockwood decorated. *(United States Navy)*

Lockwood, Jr., Charles Andrew (1890–1967)

As the most noted American submarine commander in the Pacific Theater during World War II, Lockwood had a history as a career submariner. He entered the U.S. Naval Academy in 1908, and began his long career in submarines in 1914, commanding the Asiatic Fleet's first submarine division three years later. Much of his career was spent in outfitting, commissioning, and commanding new classes of submarines between the world wars. His shore assignments included submarine-related duty while at the office of chief of naval operations. Shortly after the U.S. entry into World War II, he became Commander, Submarines Southwest Pacific, based at Fremantle, Australia. Under orders to try to stem the tide of the Japanese advance, he operated with limited resources. In February 1943 he was based at Pearl Harbor as the new commander of submarines for the Pacific Fleet. In this post he coordinated the destruction of Japan's merchant fleet and much

of its navy during the American counteroffensive. He retired in 1947.

Loggerhead (SS-374)

A submarine of the Balao class, she was launched at the Manitowoc Shipbuilding Yard in August 1944 and deployed to Hawaii, where she embarked on her first war patrol in mid-May 1945, headed for the Luzon Straits and the South China Sea where she mainly performed lifeguard duty, but also bombarded a Japanese radar installation south of Hong Kong, causing severe damage to the tower. The end of hostilities found *Loggerhead* two days out of Fremantle heading for the Gulf of Siam on her second war patrol. She returned to base and a month later was reassigned to San Francisco. She was placed in the Pacific Reserve Fleet, and in December 1962 was reclassified an auxiliary submarine, AGSS, and placed in service as a reserve training submarine until June 1967, when she was decommissioned and struck from the Navy list.

logistics

Historically, the problems of logistics—the science of dealing with the procurement, supply, and maintenance of equipment, and the provisions for personnel—have been factors in the success of naval operations and major sea battles. During the long reign of the sailing ship, the absence of a fuel requirement was a major factor in the superior mobility of fleets over armies. The shift to steam, though it brought speed and mobility and the absence of dependence on the winds, brought logistical problems of another kind: the inordinate amount of space that had to be allocated to carry wood or coal, which seriously inhibited the usefulness of early warships. For modern navies, the importance of bases goes far beyond the need for periodic replenishment of fuel, although this remains essential. Within limits, these needs can be filled by specialized auxiliary ships either accompanying naval forces at sea or stationed at predetermined rendezvous points. Naval operations in World War II saw a proliferation of these auxiliary vessels—so much so that by 1945 only 29 percent of the U.S. Navy consisted of purely fighting ships. By using auxiliaries and by rotating ships and personnel, as well as having facilities for preserving food and other perishables, modern fleets can remain at sea indefinitely, especially if not engaged in combat. One of the greatest advances in the field of submarines has been nuclear propulsion, making it possible for modern boats to remain on missions for many weeks on end and cover thousands of miles before ever having to return to port or be serviced by auxiliary vessels. Although the basic logistic function of replenishing fuel may eventually disappear, submarines in battle will still face the logistics problem of running out of missiles and other forms of ammunition.

Long Lance torpedo

A Japanese weapon, the Long Lance was regarded by many military experts as the most successful weapon of its kind in use in World War II. This 24-inch weapon had a liquid-oxygen-powered engine and was equipped with a 1,000-pound warhead. Noted for its reliability, it had a maximum speed of 49 knots and a range of some 11 miles, with the capacity of traveling almost twice that distance at a lower speed of 36 knots. The high-performance Long Lance torpedo first was used to great effect in the battle of the Java Sea in February 1942, and in many subsequent surface engagements of the Pacific War.

Long-term Mine Reconnaissance System

Known as LMRS, this is a clandestine mine reconnaissance system that employs unmanned underwater vessels capable of launch and recovery from SSN-688- and later-class submarines. The system was designed to provide an early, rapid, accurate means of surveying potential minefields in support of proposed amphibious operations, other battle group operations, and for safe ship transit around mined waters. Six new and improved initial LMRS systems are planned for deployment in both Los Angeles- and Virginia-class submarines beginning in 2004. Each system is comprised of two unmanned underwater vehicles, a recovery system, and onboard handling equipment and support electronics. A shore-based facility will maintain and store the system between deployments. Unlike an earlier system, LMRS features autonomous operation without the use of fiber-optic cables. An underwater vehicle—launched, recovered, and maintained from existing U.S. submarines—will have the ability to transit to an area, search it, and report back to the submarine via satellite every 12 hours over several days.

Loran (A, B, and C)

This long-range system was developed for marine and air navigation, in which lines of position are determined by noting differences in time of reception of synchronized pulses from widely spaced transmitting stations. A master station broadcasts an uninterrupted series of pulses of fixed duration and at a fixed rate, while a slave station, 200 to 300 miles away, automatically transmits its own signals, maintaining a frequency and pulse duration in accord with those of the master station. The slave station maintains a fixed time difference between its reception of the master signal pulse and the sending out of its own. The noted time difference of arrival of the two pulses locates the craft somewhere on a curve every point of which differs in distance from master and slave station by the same amount. Tuning in a second slave station locates the craft on another curve, or hyperbola, so its exact position can be fixed at the intersection of the two.

Los Angeles (SSN-688)

Launched in November 1974, this nuclear-powered attack submarine was the prototype for the class listed in her name—launched between that year and through the 1980s and into the 1990s. As a class, these boats displaced 6,000 tons on the surface and 6,900 submerged, and carried a crew of 12 officers and 115 enlisted men. They were initially developed to counter the Soviet *Victor* class fast-attack submarines, and were about five knots faster than the earlier Sturgeon class. Not until 1984 were these boats equipped with missiles, when the 12-tube Tomahawk vertical launch system (VLS) was introduced in the design of their bows. Later boats also had the capabilities for deploying mines. The Los Angeles class was the largest class of submarine built by any nation since World War II, except for the Soviet diesel-electric Whiskey class, and, with 62 submarines built in all, represents the world's largest class of nuclear-propelled boats.

The navy lists the submarines in this class as follows:

39 Nuclear-propelled attack submarines

23 Improved nuclear-propelled attack submarines

Number	Name	FY	Builder*	Launch	Commissioned	Status
SSN-688	*Los Angeles*	70	N	1974	1976	Pacific
SSN-689	*Baton Rouge*	70	N	1975	1977	Scrapped
SSN-690	*Philadelphia*	70	G	1974	1977	Atlantic
SSN-691	*Memphis*	71	N	1976	1977	Atlantic

SSN-692	Omaha	71	G	1976	1978	Stricken
SSN-693	Cincinnati	71	N	1977	1978	Stricken
SSN-694	Groton	71	G	1976	1978	Stricken
SSN-695	Birmingham	72	N	1977	1978	Stricken
SSN-696	New York City	72	G	1977	1978	Stricken
SSN-697	Indianapolis	72	G	1977	1980	Stricken
SSN-698	Bremerton	72	G	1978	1981	Pacific
SSN-699	Jacksonville	72	G	1978	1981	Atlantic
SSH-700	Dallas	73	G	1979	1981	Atlantic
SSN-701	La Jolla	73	G	1979	1981	Pacific
SSN-702	Phoenix	73	G	1979	1981	Stricken
SSN-703	Boston	73	G	1980	1982	Atlantic
SSN-704	Baltimore	73	G	1980	1982	Stricken
SSN-705	City of Corpus Christi	73	G	1981	1983	Atlantic
SSN-706	Albuquerque	74	G	1982	1983	Atlantic
SSN-707	Portsmouth	74	G	1982	1983	Pacific
SSN-708	Minneapolis-Saint Paul	74	G	1983	1984	Atlantic
SSN-709	Hyman G. Rickover	74	G	1983	1984	Atlantic
SSN-710	Augusta	74	G	1984	1985	Atlantic
SSN-711	San Francisco	75	N	1979	1981	Pacific
SSN-712	Atlanta	75	N	1980	1982	Atlantic
SSN-713	Houston	75	N	1981	1982	Pacific
SSN-714	Norfolk	76	N	1981	1983	Atlantic
SSN-715	Buffalo	76	N	1982	1983	Pacific
SSN-716	Salt Lake City	77	N	1982	1984	Pacific
SSN-717	Olympia	77	N	1983	1984	Pacific
SSN-718	Honolulu	77	N	1983	1985	Pacific
SSN-719	Providence	78	G	1984	1985	Atlantic
SSN-720	Pittsburgh	79	G	1984	1985	Atlantic
SSN-721	Chicago	80	N	1984	1986	Pacific
SSN-722	Key West	80	N	1985	1987	Atlantic
SSN-723	Oklahoma City	81	N	1985	1988	Atlantic
SSN-724	Louisville	81	G	1985	1986	Pacific
SSN-725	Helena	82	G	1986	1987	Pacific
SSN-750	Newport News	82	G	1986	1989	Atlantic

SSN-755	Miami	84	G	1988	1990	Atlantic
SSN-756	Scranton	85	N	1989	1991	Atlantic
SSN-757	Alexandria	85	G	1990	1991	Atlantic
SSN-758	Asheville	85	N	1990	1991	Atlantic
SSN-759	Jefferson City	85	N	1990	1992	Atlantic
SSN-760	Annapolis	86	G	1991	1992	Atlantic
SSN-761	Springfield	86	G	1992	1993	Pacific
SSN-762	Columbus	86	G	1992	1993	Atlantic
SSN-763	Santa Fe	86	G	1992	1994	Atlantic
SSM-764	Boise	87	N	1991	1992	Atlantic
SSN-765	Montpelier	87	N	1991	1993	Atlantic
SSN-766	Charlotte	87	N	1992	1994	Atlantic
SSN-767	Hampton	87	N	1992	1993	Atlantic
SSN-768	Hartford	88	G	1993	1994	Atlantic
SSN-769	Toledo	88	N	1993	1993	Atlantic
SSN-770	Tucson	88	N	1994	1995	Pacific
SSN-771	Columbia	89	G	1994	1995	Pacific
SSN-772	Greeneville	89	N	1994	1996	Atlantic
SSN-773	Cheyenne	90	N	1995	1996	Pacific

* Builders: General Dynamics/Electric Boat and Newport News Shipbuilding

Losses

IMPROVED LOS ANGELES CLASS

Number	Name	FY	Builder	Launch	Commissioned	Status
SSH-751	San Juan	83	G	1986	1988	Atlantic
SSN-752	Pasadena	83	G	1986	1988	Pacific
SSN-753	Albany	84	N	1987	1990	Atlantic
SSN-754	Topeka	84	G	1988	1989	Pacific

SUBMARINES LOST DURING PEACETIME OPERATIONS

Name	Date of Loss	Cause of Loss
USS F-4 (SS-23)	March 25, 1915	Foundered
USS E-2 (SS-25)	January 15, 1916	Explosion
USS F-1 (SS-20)	December 16, 1917	Collision
USS H-1 (SS-28)	March 12, 1920	Grounding
USS S-5 (SS-110)	August 1, 1920	Foundered
USS S-48 (SS-159)	December 7, 1921	Foundered
USS S-38 (SS-143)	July 17, 1923	Flooding
USS O-5 (SS-66)	October 29, 1923	Collision
USS S-48 (SS-159)	January 29, 1925	Grounding
USS S-51 (SS-162)	September 23, 1925	Collision
USS S-4 (SS-109)	December 17, 1927	Collision
USS Squalus (SS-192)	May 23, 1939	Foundered (renamed Sailfish)
USS O-9 (SS-70)	June 20, 1941	Foundered
USS Bass (SS-164)	August 17, 1942	Fire
USS R-12 (SS-89)	June 12, 1943	Foundered
USS S-28 (SS-132)	June 4, 1944	Foundered
USS Lancetfish (SS-296)	March 15, 1945	Flooded
USS Cochino (SS-345)	August 26, 1949	Explosion

USS *Stickleback* (SS-415)	May 30, 1958	Collision
USS *Sargo* (SSN-583)	June 14, 1960	Explosion (repaired)
USS *Grayback* (SSG-574)	August 27, 1963	Fire (repaired)
USS *Thresher* (SSN-5931)	April 10, 1963	Foundered
USS *Scorpion* (SSN-589)	May 21, 1968	Foundered
USS *Ray* (SSN-653)	September 20, 1977	Grounding
USS *Nathanael Greene*	March 13, 1986	Grounding
USS *Bonefish* (55582)	April 24, 1988	Fire
USS *Baton Rouge*	February 11, 1992	Collision
USS *Dolphin* (AGSS-555)	May 21, 2002	Fire

lost boats

The hazards of submarine service are apparent in the statistics: more than 10 percent of all the navy submarines in service have been lost, including:

CATEGORY I
LOST WITH ALL HANDS
(44 SUBMARINES)

USS *F-4* [ex-*Skate*] (SS-23) was lost on March 21, 1915, with the loss of 19 officers and men when it foundered off Honolulu Harbor.

USS *S-4* (SS-109) was lost on December 17, 1927, with the loss of 34 officers and men when it was sunk after being rammed by USCG *Paulding*.

USS *O-9* (SS-70) was lost on June 20, 1941, with the loss of 34 officers and men when it foundered off Isle of Shoals, 15 miles from Portsmouth, New Hampshire.

USS *Shark* (SS-174) was lost in February 1942 with the loss of 59 officers and men when it was sunk in the area of Menado, Celebes.

USS *Grunion* (SS-216) was lost on August 1, 1942, with the loss of 70 officers and men when it was sunk near the entrance to Kiska (Alaska) Harbor.

USS *Argonaut* (SS-166) was lost on January 10, 1943, with the loss of 84 officers and men when it was sunk off Rabaul.

USS *Amberjack* (SS-219) was lost on February 16, 1943, with the loss of 72 officers and men when it was sunk off Rabaul. Last Contact at 5'05'S 152'37'E.

USS *Grampus* (SS-207) was lost on March 5, 1943, with the loss of 72 officers and men when it was sunk in the Blackett Strait, possibly in Vella Gulf.

USS *Triton* (SS-201) was lost on March 15, 1943, with the loss of 74 officers and men when it was sunk at 0009'N 144055'E.

USS *Pickerel* (SS-177) was lost on April 3, 1943, with the loss of 74 officers and men when it was sunk near Shiramuka Light off Honshu.

USS *R-12* (SS-89) was lost on June 12, 1943, with the loss of 42 officers and men when it foundered off Key West at 24-24'30"N 81-28'30"W.

USS *Runner* (SS-275) was lost on July 1, 1943, with the loss of 78 officers and men when it was sunk somewhere between Midway Island and Hokkaido.

USS *Pompano* (SS-181) was lost on September 1, 1943, with the loss of 76 officers and men when it was sunk off the northeast coast of Honshu.

USS *Grayling* (SS-209) was lost on September 9, 1943, with the loss of 76 officers and men when it was sunk in or near Tablas Strait, Philippine Islands.

USS *Cisco* (SS-290) was lost on September 28, 1943, with the loss of 76 officers and men when it was sunk in the Sulu Sea west of Mindanao at 9'47N 12 1'44'E.

USS *Wahoo* (SS-238) was lost on October 11, 1943, with the loss of 79 officers and men when it was sunk in or near La Perouse Strait.

USS *Dorado* (SS-248) was lost on October 12, 1943, with the loss of 78 officers and men when it was sunk in the western Atlantic, possibly near Cuba.

USS *Corvina* (SS-226) was lost on November 16, 1943, with the loss of 82 officers and men when it was sunk just south of Truk as the result of an attack at 151 '1 O'E 5'5 ON.

USS *Capelin* (SS-289) was lost on December 1, 1943, with the loss of 76 officers and men when it was sunk off the Celebes, possibly off Kaoe Bay, Halmahera.

USS *Scorpion* (SS-278) was lost on February 1, 1944, with the loss of 77 officers and men when it was sunk in the East China Sea.

USS *Grayback* (SS-208) was lost on February 26, 1944, with the loss of 80 officers and men when it was sunk near 25'47'N 128'45'E.

USS *Trout* (SS-202) was lost on February 29, 1944, with the loss of 79 officers and men when it was sunk near 22-40'N 131-45'E, middle of Philippines Basin.

USS *Gudgeon* (SS-211) was lost on May 12, 1944, with the loss of 80 officers and men when it was sunk off Saipan near Maug Island.

USS *Herring* (SS-233) was lost on June 1, 1944, with the loss of 80 officers and men when it was sunk within shore battery range of Point Tagan, Matsuwa Island, in the Kuriles.

USS *S-28* (SS-133) was lost on June 4, 1944, with the loss of 50 officers and men when it foundered off Hawaii, while operating with USCGC *Reliance*.

USS *Golet* (SS-361) was lost on June 14, 1944, with the loss of 82 officers and men when it was sunk near 41004'N14?013'E.

USS *Growler* (SS-215) was lost on July 8, 1944, with the loss of 84 officers and men when it was sunk in the South China Sea.

USS *Robalo* (SS-273) was lost on July 26, 1944, with the loss of 84 officers and men when it was sunk two miles off west coast of Palawan.

USS *Harder* (SS-257) was lost on August 24, 1944, with the loss of 80 officers and men when it was sunk off Caiman Point near Bataan.

USS *Escolar* (SS-294) was lost on October 1, 1944, with the loss of 82 officers and men when it was sunk somewhere east of 33'44N 127'33'E, heading for 33'44N 124'06'E.

USS *Shark* (SS-314) was lost on October 24, 1944, with the loss of 90 officers and men when it was sunk in channel midway between Hainan and Bashi Channel at 20'4 1'N II 8'27'E.

USS *Seawolf* (SS-197) was lost on October 3, 1944, with the loss of 102 officers and men when it was sunk just north of Morotai between the Philippines and Indonesia, by USS *Rowell*.

USS *Albacore* (SS-218) was lost on November 7, 1944, with the loss of 86 officers and men when it was sunk near 4 1'49'N 14 1'1 1'E in channel between Hokkaido and Honshu.

USS *Scamp* (SS-277) was lost on November 16, 1944, with the loss of 83 officers and men when it was sunk off Inubo Saki near Tokyo Bay.

USS *Barbel* (SS-316) was lost on February 4, 1945, with the loss of 81 officers and men when it was sunk in southern entrance to Palawan Passage at 7'49.5'S 11 6'47.5'E, SW of Palawan.

USS *Swordfish* (SS-193) was lost on February 15, 1945, with the loss of 90 officers and men when it was sunk near Yaku Island off Kyushu.

USS *Kete* (SS-369) was lost on March 1, 1945, with the loss of 87 officers and men when it was sunk somewhere between 29'38'N 130'02'E and Midway Island.

USS *Trigger* (SS-237) was lost on March 28, 1945, with the loss of 91 officers and men when it was sunk in area bounded by 32'16'N 127'50'E (perhaps near 32'16'N 132'05'E).

USS *Snook* (SS-279) was lost on April 8, 1945, with the loss of 84 officers and men when it was sunk within 100 miles east of 18'40'N 11 1'39'E, near Hainan Island.

USS *Lagarto* (SS-371) was lost on May 30, 1945, with the loss of 88 officers and men when it was sunk off Malay Coast in or near the Gulf of Siam at 7'55N 102'00'E.

USS *Bonefish* (SS-223) was lost on June 18, 1945, with the loss of 86 officers and men when it was sunk in Toyama Wan near Suzu Misaki at 37'18'N 137'25'E.

USS *Bullhead* (SS-332) was lost on August 6, 1945, with the loss of 84 officers and men when it was sunk in west end of Lombok Strait.

USS *Thresher* (SSN-593) was lost on April 10, 1963, with the loss of 129 officers and men when it sank while on sea trials near Isle of Shoals.

USS *Scorpion* (SSN-589) was declared lost on June 2, 1968, with the loss of 99 officers and men when it sank west of Azores while in transit from Mediterranean Sea.

CATEGORY 2
SUBMARINE LOST WITH SOME OF THE CREW AS SURVIVORS
(15 SUBMARINES)

USS *F-1* [ex-*Carp*] (SS-20) was lost on December 17, 1917, with the loss of 19 officers and men when it was sunk after collision with *F-3* off San Clemente.

USS *H-1* (SS-28) was lost on March 12, 1920, with the loss of four officers and men when it grounded in Magdalena Bay, Mexico, and sank in 9 fathoms of water while being towed off.

USS *O-5* (SS-66) was lost on October 18, 1923, with the loss of 2 men when it was sunk after collision with SS *Abagarez* (United Fruit Co.) off Panama Canal.

USS *S-26* (SS-131) was lost on January 24, 1942, with the loss of 46 officers and men when it was sunk after being rammed by USS *PC-460* in the Gulf of Panama.

USS *S-51* (SS-162) was lost on September 25, 1925, with the loss of 32 officers and men when it was sunk after collision with SS *City of Rome* off Block Island.

USS *Squalus* (SS-192) was lost on May 23, 1939, with a loss of 26 officers and men when it flooded and sank off Portsmouth, New Hampshire.

USS *Sealion* (SS-195) was lost on December 10, 1941, with the loss of 5 officers and men when it was scuttled in Manila Bay after damage at Cavite.

USS *Perch* (SS-176) was lost on March 3, 1942, with the loss of 8 officers and men when it was sunk off Java. (60 officers and men were taken prisoner; 52 survived the war.)

USS *Grenadier* (SS-210) was lost on April 23, 1943, with the loss of 4 officers and men when it was sunk near Penang (61 officers and men were taken prisoner; 57 survived the war.)

USS *S-44* (SS-155) was lost on October 7, 1943, with the loss of 56 officers and men when it was sunk one day out of Attu. (2 men were taken prisoner; both survived the war.)

USS *Sculpin* (SS-191) was lost on November 19, 1943, with the loss of 40 officers and men when it was sunk near Truk. (42 officers and men were taken prisoner; only 21 survived the war.)

USS *Tullibee* (SS-284) was lost on March 26, 1944, with the loss of 79 officers and men when it was sunk north of Palau. (One man was taken prisoner and he survived the war.)

USS *Flier* (SS-250) was lost on August 13, 1944, with the loss of 80 officers and men when it was sunk in Balabac Strait. (Eight of the crew were taken prisoner; all survived the war.)

USS *Tang* (SS-306) was lost on October 25, 1944, with the loss of 83 officers and men when it was sunk in Formosa Strait. (Nine of the crew were taken prisoner; all survived the war.)

USS *Cochino* (SS-345) was lost on August 26, 1949, when it was sunk in Norwegian Sea after onboard fire. (One man from *Cochino* and 6 men from USS *Tusk* were lost.)

CATEGORY 3
SUBMARINES LOST WITH ALL
THE CREW AS SURVIVORS
(7 SUBMARINES)

The Civil War submarine *Alligator* was lost in 1863 when it was sunk off Cape Hatteras while it was being towed south to aid Union efforts in forcing entrance into Charleston.

USS *S-5* (SS-110) was lost on September 1, 1920, when it foundered off Delaware Capes at 40 miles offshore. All the crew escaped through a hole cut in the hull in the tiller room.

USS *S-36* (SS-141) was lost on January 20, 1942, when it was destroyed after grounding on Taka Bakang Reef in Makassar Strait, Dutch East Indies. The entire crew was rescued.

USS *S-27* (SS-132) was lost on June 19, 1942, when it grounded off Amchitka Island, 400 yards off St. Makarius Point. The entire crew was rescued.

USS *S-39* (SS-144) was lost on August 1, 1942, when it was destroyed after grounding on reef south of Rossel Island, Louisade Archipelago. The entire crew was rescued.

USS *Darter* (SS-227) was lost on October 24, 1944, when it became grounded on Bombay Shoal off Palawan, then was destroyed. The entire crew was rescued by USS *Dace*.

USS *Stickleback* (SS-415) was lost on May 30, 1958, when it sank off Hawaii while under tow after collision with USS *Silverstein*. The entire crew was taken off prior to sinking.

CATEGORY 4
SUBMARINES LOST WHILE IN
FOREIGN SERVICE
(6 SUBMARINES)

USS *S-25* (SS-130) was lost on November 4, 1941, with the loss of all hands when it was sunk by Allied escorts off Norway.

USS *R-19* (SS-96) was lost on June 21, 1942, with the loss of all hands after being rammed by HMCS *Georgian* while on lease to England.

USS *Blower* (SS-325) was lost with all hands when, as a Turkish submarine, it was sunk in the Dardanelles after collision with Swedish ship *Naboland*.

USS *Diablo* (SS-479) was lost with all hands in 1970 when it was sunk in Bay of Bengal (as Pakistani submarine *Ghazi*), possibly due to mine explosion.

USS *Catfish* (SS-339) was lost on July 1, 1981, with the loss of an unknown number of officers and men when sunk (as Argentinian submarine *Santa Fe*) during Falklands war.

USS *Atule* (SS-403) was lost with an unknown number of officers and men when it was sunk (as Peruvian submarine *Pachocha*) after being rammed by a Japanese merchantman off Callao, Peru.

CATEGORY 5: SUBMARINES LOST UNDER SPECIAL CIRCUMSTANCES (3 SUBMARINES)

ex-USS *G-2* (SS-27) was lost on July 30, 1919, when it sank with 3 crewmembers as a test vehicle for explosive tests. Sank in Two Tree Channel, a quarter-mile off Pleasure Beach, Connecticut; counted here due to loss of life.

USS *Bonefish* (SS-582) declared functional loss and decommissioned after onboard fire off Florida coast in which 3 crewmen lost their lives.

USS *Nathanael Greene* (SSBN-636) decommissioned instead of repairing after grounding (to conform to SALT agreement).

Luzon Strait

The scene of many submarine missions and naval battles, this is a strait extending for more than 200 miles between the islands of Taiwan (north) and the Philippines' Luzon (south). It connects the South China Sea (west) with the Philippine Sea (east). The strait is a series of channels, dotted with islands in its southern reaches, especially the Batan and Babuyan island groups. The main channels are Bashi (north), Balintang (central), and Babuyan (south). It is on a main shipping route.

M

M-1 (SS-47)

Built by the Fore River Shipbuilding Company, Quincy, Massachusetts, and launched in September 1915, this M-class boat weighed in at 488 tons on the surface and 676 tons submerged. She carried a crew of two officers and 26 enlisted men, and had four 18-inch torpedo tubes in the bow. Following commissioning, M-1 was assigned to Sub-Div2, and was homeported at Newport, Rhode Island. For the next three years, she operated off the East Coast, providing training for the new generation of submariners who would contribute to the defeat of the Japanese navy in World War II. During her last year of active service, she was under the operational control of SubDiv5 and SubDiv3. She was decommissioned in Philadelphia in March 1922.

M-1 (SS-47), seen cruising at what was then a remarkable speed of more than 11 knots, was launched from the Fore River Shipyard in Quincy, Massachusetts, in September 1915, and operated largely as a training vessel until being decommissioned in 1922. *(United States Navy)*

Macabi (SS-375)

Built by Manitowoc Shipbuilding and launched in September 1944 this submarine of the Balao class was ordered to Pearl Harbor for final training where she left on her first, and only, war patrol in mid-July, heading for the Caroline Islands. She went on lifeguard station off Truk, arriving July 21, but 10 days later was forced to dive to avoid two aerial bombs off Moen Island, was damaged, and had to put in at Apra Harbor, Guam, for repairs. Although she was repaired and sent out again to continue her patrol, it was only two days before the end of the war and she was ordered back to Pearl Harbor. *Macabi* was inactivated in the spring of 1946, put into reserve, decommissioned, and then transferred to Argentina in August 1960, where she served for 10 years under the name *Santiago del Esterow.*

Mackerel (SS-204) (M-1)

Built by Electric Boat and launched in September 1940 as the first of a class under the Mackerel name, this was a boat of 900 tons on the surface and 1,179 tons submerged, and carried a crew of five officers and 54 enlisted men. Unlike the new submarines being built under high priority at the beginning of the 1940s, she saw no war patrols, but was assigned throughout World War II to SubRon1 at New London, Connecticut, her basic mission being to train the navy's rapidly expanding submarine force. Designed as an experimental submarine, she provided support services to the Underwater Sound Laboratory and training services to the Submarine and the Prospective Commanding Officers Schools at New London, in addition to training Allied surface vessels and aircraft in antisubmarine warfare. Although most of her time was spent in the New London area, she steamed as far north as Casco Bay and as far south as Chesapeake Bay to conduct antisubmarine training exercises. During the course of the war, *Mackerel* made only one contact with the enemy. Having departed New London in mid-April 1942, she proceeded, on the surface, to Norfolk, Virginia, to conduct antisubmarine training exercises for army and navy aircraft. On the night of the 14th her lookouts sighted the wakes of two torpedoes heading for the submarine. Evasion maneuvers proved effective and *Mackerel* launched two torpedoes—both unsuccessful—at a surfaced enemy submarine. The following morning, the enemy submarine was again sighted, but was able to outdistance her intended attacker and escape. At the end of the war, *Mackerel* was ordered to Boston, where she was decommissioned in April 1947.

magnetic anomaly detection (MAD)

As early as 1917, alternatives to the detection of submarines by hydrophones were being studied. One such area for consideration was the use of magnetism. In 1918, the United States experimentally tried out a ship-towed magnetic detection device. This device was found to have too limited a detection range and also suffered from the presence of the magnetic signature of the towing ship. For the time being, magnetic detection was abandoned as impractical.

With the outbreak of World War II, renewed interest occurred in alternative detection systems for antisubmarine warfare. For aircraft there was a pressing need to devise a means for them to be able to detect a submerged submarine. One of the devices that received renewed attention was the use of magnetic anomaly detection.

As early as 1941, magnetic detection devices (which measure changes in the Earth's magnetic field) had been developed in both Britain and the United States. The first airborne use of these devices was in American K-type blimps. This was followed by much wider installation of MAD devices in ASW patrol aircraft. By 1943, most ASW aircraft were equipped with MAD.

Initially, the United States thought that MAD would be a primary means of detecting submerged submarines, but it was found to be a system of limited usefulness. This was due to its very limited range and its inability to distinguish between sources of magnetic variance. Frequently, wrecks or local magnetic disturbances were classified as submarines. This was particularly true earlier in the war before experience with the system had discovered its limitations.

By late war, MAD in combination with sonobuoys proved more useful. The pairing allowed MAD on an aircraft to localize a contact made with sonobuoys, and the sonobuoys, in turn, provided confirmation that the contact was indeed a submarine. In this combination MAD became the secondary system to the sonobuoy, the reverse of what was originally expected.

magnetic mine

Developed prior to World War II, this is the term applied to any mine designed to respond to the magnetic field of the target. The change in the local magnetic field generated by a moving target is detected within the mine either by search coils or magnetometers. Search coils, which detect changes in a single axis, are used in bottom mines, while magnetometers, which detect changes in three axes, are normally used in moored mines. The firing mechanism contains software and sensitive responders that are designed to screen out decoy devices, which can explode them with no harm to the enemy vessels they are designed to damage or sink. Most U.S. Navy mines have firing mechanisms that can be triggered not only by magnetic influence, but by pressure and acoustic changes as well.

Manta (SS-299)

Built by the Cramp Shipbuilding Company, Philadelphia, and launched in December 1944, this submarine of the Balao class was deployed to the Kurile Islands for her first war patrol, where she found no enemy ships within range, and had barely begun her second patrol when the war ended. Placed temporarily in reserve, she was ordered to Key West, Florida, in the fall of 1949, and redesignated auxiliary submarine AGSS-299. For the next four years, she operated as a target ship for experimental antisubmarine warfare projects of Operational Development Force, Atlantic Fleet. She was struck from the Navy list in June 1967, and ended her career as a target, sunk off Norfolk, Virginia, in July 1969.

Mariana Trench

A submarine trench in the floor of the western North Pacific Ocean, situated east of the Mariana Islands. It is the deepest such trench known. An arcing depression, the trench stretches for more than 1,580 miles, with a mean width of 43 miles. There is a smaller, steep-walled valley on the floor of the main trench. In 1899 Nero Deep (31,693 feet) was discovered southeast of Guam. This sounding was not exceeded until a 32,197-foot hole was found in the vicinity 30 years later. In 1957, during the International Geophysical Year, the Soviet research ship *Vityaz* sounded a new world record depth of 36,056 feet (later revised to 36,201 feet). In January 1960, the French-built/U.S. Navy-operated bathyscaphe *Trieste,* with the inventor's son, Jacques Piccard and U.S. Navy lieutenant Don Walsh aboard, made a record dive to 35,800 feet in the trench.

Marlin (SS-205) (M-2)

Launched in January 1941, *Marlin,* like her sister submarine *Mackerel,* devoted her career to training officers and men for wartime duty and training new escort vessels in antisubmarine warfare. In July 1944, while making a submerged practice approach on USS *Chaffee* (DE-230), there was a collision that caused slight damage to both ships. She was deployed briefly on patrol duty along the East Coast, but was ordered to Boston and decommissioned at the Boston Navy Yard in November 1945.

Marshall Islands, occupation of (January/February 1944)

This island group in the central Pacific was occupied by the Japanese at the beginning of World War II, and was the site of several airfields and a fleet anchorage. By the latter part of 1943, the American central Pacific offensive was underway and plans for the invasion of the Marshall Islands were made. They were in themselves relatively unimportant, but their capture would put the U.S. Navy within striking distance of Truk, headquarters of the Japanese Combined Fleet, 1,000 miles away. The navy's attack was split in two—the first group was to go to Roi and Namur islands, while the second was to hit Kwajalein. Accompanying the amphibious units were four carrier task forces of the U.S. Fifth Fleet, which were to deal with any local opposition from adjoining islands and to meet any threat from the main Japanese fleet. Following three days' bombardment, landings began on January 31 and U.S. forces took Majuro, the first Japanese possession captured in the war. Other islands, including Kwajalein, fell after fierce fighting. Confident after the quick success of this operation, the Americans decided to bring forward the attack on Truk. On February 17–18 the Fifth Fleet attacked Truk and caused the loss of two enemy cruisers and four destroyers. By the end of February 1944, the Eniwetok island group had finally fallen, completing the U.S. occupation of the Marshall Islands.

Medregal (SS-480)

Launched in December 1944 as a boat of the Tench class, and built by Portsmouth Naval Shipyard she departed New London, Connecticut, in June 1945, and steamed to participate in final operations in the Pacific against the Japanese. But emergency repairs at Portsmouth delayed her arrival in the Pacific until after the cessation of hostilities, and she was deployed to Key West to train reserves, support activities of the Fleet Sonar School, and take part in antisubmarine warfare exercises. Her cruises sent her along the East Coast from Florida to Virginia, into the Gulf of Mexico and the Caribbean, and to operating areas in the western Atlantic. Periodically she deployed to Guantanamo Bay and Havana, Cuba, as well as to Puerto Rico and islands of the West Indies, and in late 1952 underwent conversion to a Fleet Snorkel submarine at Charleston, South Carolina. She participated in missile evaluation projects in the Caribbean off the Virgin Islands and in the Atlantic out of Puerto Rico. In the summer of 1959, she was ordered to the Pacific, where she served in Hawaiian waters, the Far East, Japan, and the Philippines, and then along the West Coast. Later she steamed to Australia and participated in the commemoration of the battle of the Coral Sea. She was decommissioned and struck from the Navy list in August 1970.

Merrimack

Although in no way a "submersible," this Confederate warship, which fought a much-recounted duel with the Union armored warship, *Monitor,* on March 9, 1862, was an early vessel in a line of experimental ones that presaged the torpedo boat and later the submarine. She was originally a wooden-hulled, steam-powered Union frigate, armed with 40 guns, that had been scuttled by the North when the navy abandoned its base at Norfolk, Virginia. The Confederates subsequently raised her from the sea bed, converted her into an ironclad by covering her topside entirely with armor plates, more than doubled her fire power, and fitted her with an iron ram. She enjoyed initial success, destroying two Union ships of a blockade at Hampton Roads. However, the *Merrimack/Monitor* battle was a draw, after four hours of useless gunfire, and the Confederate hopeful never went into battle again. Still, the engagement marked an important turning point in naval history because it established the importance of armor and the turreted gun.

midget submarines

As the term is associated with warfare, this type of undersea craft has been little cultivated by the U.S. Navy. Developed for the most part during World War II, it was used by several of the principal naval powers for attacking ships in harbor. The midget sub arose from the concept of the human torpedo, such as one developed and used successfully by the Italian navy during World War I; it was operated by a two-man crew, with a detachable warhead. In a turnabout operation, the British devised the *Chariot,* based on Italian designs, and used it in the Mediterranean during World War II to destroy three cruisers. The Royal Navy improved on this with the introduction of the X-craft, which was a class of true midget submarines, designed to attack enemy warships in heavily defended anchorages that were beyond the range of land-based aircraft. Operated by a crew of four, the X-craft was armed with explosive charges that were released under the target and detonated by a timing device. The X-craft were involved in a number of successful operations, including heavy damage to the German battleship *Tirpitz,* and later to the Japanese cruiser *Takao* in Singapore Harbor, on July 31, 1945. Despite these successes by other nations, the American Navy has used midget submarines only sparingly, and then mostly for undersea research.

Midway, Battle of (June 3–6, 1942)

One of the decisive engagements of World War II, fought almost entirely with aircraft, in which the United States destroyed Japan's first-line carrier strength and most of its best-trained naval pilots, and ended the threat of further Japanese invasion in the Pacific. Despite a setback in May 1942, in the indecisive battle of the Coral Sea, the Japanese had continued with plans to seize Midway Island and bases in the Aleutians. Seeking a naval showdown with the numerically inferior U.S. Pacific Fleet, the Japanese com-

mitted the bulk of their fleet, including four heavy and three light aircraft carriers, with orders to engage and destroy the American fleet and invade Midway. U.S. intelligence, however, had broken the Japanese naval code, and the Americans were ready when three heavy aircraft carriers of the U.S. Pacific Fleet were mustered. Whereas the Japanese had no land-based air support, the Americans from both Midway and Hawaii could commit about 115 land-based planes, as well as those on the carriers.

The battle began on June 3, 1942, when American bombers from Midway struck at the Japanese carrier strike force. Early the next morning, Japanese planes from the strike force attacked and bombed Midway heavily. However, as the morning progressed, the Japanese carriers became overwhelmed by the challenge of simultaneously sending a second wave of bombers, zigzagging to avoid the bombs of attacking U.S. aircraft, and trying to launch more planes to sink U.S. warships that had come in sight. Although one wave of American torpedo bombers was all but wiped out by enemy defensive fire, carrier-launched U.S. dive-bombers reversed the onslaught by catching the Japanese carriers while their decks were cluttered with armed aircraft and fuel. U.S. planes quickly sank three of the enemy's aircraft carriers and one heavy cruiser, and later disabled the fourth heavy carrier. But the U.S. carrier *Yorktown* became a casualty when she was fatally torpedoed, along with a destroyer, by a Japanese submarine. The Japanese, however, appalled by the loss of their carriers, as well as another cruiser, had already begun a general retirement on the night of June 4–5, without attempting to land on Midway. The successful defense of Midway marked the turning point of the naval struggle between the two nations.

mine

The earliest forms of mines were explosives placed under shallow ground, or otherwise hidden, in places where they could be triggered by soldiers on foot, and, in later developments, to damage ground vehicles and wound or kill personnel in them. Such mines were initially detonated by the actions of the victims, but later rigged so they could be detonated by timing devices or remote controls. In naval mine warfare, mines were used initially as deterrents, to surround vessels in a harbor so they could not readily be attacked on the surface by enemy ships. With the advent of the submarine as an attacking vessel of war, mines were developed so they could take forceful action against undersea craft when they submerged in order to escape surface guns or shallow-draft torpedoes. Technically, the term does not include devices attached to the bottoms of ships or to harbor installations by divers or those devices that explode immediately at a predetermined time after being laid in position.

minelayer

A specially built or modified warship used for laying mines, first introduced in the middle of the 19th century, but not of much consequence in naval warfare until the First World War, at which time they were produced more and more frequently by the Allies as a means of trying to combat the attacks of German U-boats. By the end of the war, the nations involved were beginning to produce submarines, which could lay mines all but undetected—and during daylight hours as well as at night. Minelaying submarines have proved to be better in many respects, and are often considered to be the quickest and cheapest method of laying mines without revealing one's position or course of action to an enemy.

Mine Neutralization System (MNS)

This system is a remotely piloted, unmanned, mine-hunting submersible, a common version of which is called the SLQ-48, and which has a torpedo-like hull. Unlike some systems, which use batteries, it is powered by the parent ship through a 3,500-foot-long umbilical, rather than by on-board batteries, thus providing almost unlimited endurance. The hull has a wedge-shaped cross-section with a rounded upper body and a rectangular lower section. The sonar is carried in the nose, and is well protected by a bottle-nose dome. Below the sonar is a television camera and two cable cutter claws, which release underwater mines so they float to the surface where they can readily be exploded from a distance by gunfire. Farther aft is a horizontal tunnel fitted with a thruster unit, below which is the bay for an explosive charge, often a small magnetic mine that can be used to explode mines underwater rather than release them to the surface. In practice, the parent ship's sonar provides initial detection and localization. The *MNS*'s high-resolution sonar refines the contact and homes in on the target, where it then has the option of cutting the cable or placing the explosive charge and moving out of harm's way.

minesweeper

This category of navy ship covers a wide variety of vessels capable of sweeping and/or exploding mines of all kinds, whether in shallow coastal waters or on the high seas. Early minesweepers conducted mainly hit-or-miss patrols, trailing long, serrated cables that would catch a mine's anchor chain and sever it so the captured mine would float to the surface where it could be exploded safely at a distance by gunfire. During World War I, the system was improved by using two minesweepers operating together, with a cutting wire extended between them, thus enabling the sweepers to clear a wider area of minefields in a single operation. Later, the addition of a net increased the chances of capturing more mines than in the past. However, as new and different types of mines were invented, the techniques to clear them became more complex, and new minesweeper designs were called for. The mission became even more difficult when different types of mines were mixed in the same field and anti-sweeping devices were added to them. Pressure mines, activated by the pressure waves of a passing vessel, are the most difficult to locate and disable. Sonar equipment is one method for pinpointing them successfully. Acoustic mines are detonated by simulating a ship's noise and attracting them to a location, or to set off a premature explosion. When seeking magnetic mines, a system was devised whereby two minesweepers would be employed, with two electric cables, known as "sweeps," stretched between them. When electric current was passed along the cables, it would create magnetic fields that would detonate any magnetic mines positioned between the two ships. Since World War I, oceangoing minesweepers have played a crucial role in naval defense systems.

minesweeping boats (MSB)

Following World War II, the navy retained very few minesweeping boats in service during peacetime, locating them in a handful of strategic ports around the world, and sometimes placing them on loan to friendly nations seeking to eliminate from their waters existing mines of present or previous conflicts. During the Vietnam War, wooden-hulled MSBs, armed with machine guns and a raised gun tube aft, were designed to be carried to assault areas aboard amphibious ships. In August 1987, four MSBs were placed aboard the *Raleigh,* an amphibious transport ship, for minesweeping duties in the Persian Gulf. By the beginning of the 21st century, the navy had decommissioned or inactivated many of its minesweepers, retained four in port in Panama, one in Florida, one in Texas, and seven that form Mine Division 125, at Charleston, South Carolina. Two others were loaned to the National Oceanic and Atmospheric Administration (NOAA), and a few others are used in various navy ports as utility and training craft.

Mingo (SS-261)

Launched in November 1942 and built by the Electric Boat Co. as a submarine of the Gato class, she was ordered to the Pacific and departed on her first war patrol in June 1943, during which she damaged three Japanese merchant ships and bombarded enemy-held Sorol Island off the Palaus. Her second war patrol, in October and November, took her to the Marshalls, Carolines, and Marianas, during which she damaged a Japanese cruiser. Her third patrol, in the South China Sea, was unproductive, but on her fourth, she attacked a high-speed Japanese convoy off Luzon and sank a 2,100-ton destroyer in early June. The mission on her fifth war patrol, starting at the end of August, was lifeguard duty in support of 13th Air Force strikes on the Philippines and Borneo, but on the way to her assigned area she sank four coastal freighters. *Mingo* performed well in her job as lifeguard, too, since she rescued 16 Liberator fliers shot down off Borneo, six from rubber boats in Makassar Strait and the others from a beach at Celebes Island. Her sixth war patrol, assigned as reconnaissance duty, was west of Borneo. In late December, she made a night torpedo attack on a Japanese convoy off Singapore, damaged an escort gunboat, and she sank a 9,486-ton tanker. *Mingo* took station at the South China Sea for her seventh and last war patrol, but tragedy struck when she was caught in a hurricane the second week in February, lost two men, and was forced to head for Fremantle to repair damage. She was able to perform only restricted patrol duty, and while en route to Hawaii for refitting received word of the war's end. After a short stay at Pearl Harbor, she sailed for the West Coast to serve with the Pacific Fleet until May 1955, when—ironically in light of her war record—she was transferred on loan to Japan under the Military Assistance Program and renamed *Kurushio*. She then served the Japanese navy until being decommissioned in March 1966, when she was returned to U.S. control. *Mingo* received five battle stars for World War II service. Her World War II record indicates 2 vessels for 11,586 tons.

Minuteman Missile

Designated as an ICBM, this weapon was an intercontinental ballistic missile that constituted the majority of the land-based nuclear arsenal of the United States from the 1960s, in three generations. Minuteman I, three-stage and 56 feet, was the first ICBM to use solid fuels (considered safer than the more volatile liquid fuels) and the first to be based in underground silos, rather than on above-ground launch pads. Between 1966 and 1973 this prototype was replaced by the Minuteman II, whose improved propulsion gave it a longer range of about 8,000 miles. Its reentry vehicle, carrying a thermonuclear warhead, was equipped with electronic jammers and other devices designed to penetrate radar-directed antiballistic missile defenses. The third generation of this Minuteman III ICBM was deployed between 1970 and 1975 with two or three independent reentry vehicles, each carrying a thermonuclear warhead. In the 1980s three enhanced warheads were installed on some Minuteman IIIs, along with a more accurate guidance system. Beginning in 1986, some Minuteman IIIs were replaced by the new Peacekeeper missile.

missions

THE ROLES OF SUBMARINES AT THE START OF THE 21ST CENTURY

The basic developments and technological innovations in the U.S. submarine force just since the end of the Cold War have initiated major shifts in submarine warfare concepts and doctrines, both aggressively and defensively. The emphasis on deterrence of global war, for example, has become a strong point in the missions of the submarines of the U.S. Navy, as well as the support of America's national interests in regional crises and conflicts. Antisubmarine warfare (ASW) orientation and training has also been of primary concern, with the development and perfection of methods to neutralize nuclear-powered submarines intent on aggression against the United States. These changing operational contexts have influenced all elements of U.S. submarine operations, from peacetime presence to strategic deterrence.

The transitions in the submarine force follow directly from the transitions in the world order and the evolving nature of the U.S. Navy. The world order has shifted from a bipolar superpower alignment to a multipolar collection of interests. While the likelihood of global conflict is greatly reduced, there is an increasing chance of regional conflict. The composition and operational posture of the U.S. Navy reflects this, having changed from a blue-water emphasis to a littoral emphasis. For the submarine force this has meant several changes in roles: prior to the end of the Cold War, antisubmarine warfare was the major role for U.S. attack submarines. Now U.S. submarines are more multi-mission oriented. Today, the primary roles and missions for the U.S. submarine force are:

- peacetime engagement
- surveillance and intelligence
- special operations
- precision strike
- battle group operations
- sea denial
- deterrence

MK 48 torpedo

A highly capable submarine-launched weapon, the MK 48 can be used against surface ships or submarines, and has been test fired under the Arctic ice pack and in other arduous conditions. The advanced capability (ADCAP) version, in comparison with earlier Mark 48 torpedoes, has improved target acquisition range, reduced vulnerability to enemy countermeasures, reduced shipboard arming and reactivation time, and enjoys a greater effectiveness against surface ships. The torpedo is propelled by a piston engine with twin, contra-rotating propellers, and uses a liquid monopropellant fuel. Although the torpedo has a conventional, high-explosive warhead, it employs a sophisticated guidance system that makes possible a variety of attack options. As the torpedo leaves the submarine's launch tube, a thin wire spins out, electronically linking the submarine and torpedo. This enables an operator in the submarine, using the submarine's ultra-sensitive sonar systems, to guide the torpedo initially toward the target. This procedure enhances the torpedo's ability to avoid decoys and jamming devices that might be deployed by the enemy. During the final phase of the attack, the wire is severed and the torpedo's own high-powered sonar guides it precisely to the target. Torpedoes are carried internally in U.S. submarines and launched through fixed torpedo tubes. The torpedo tubes in American submarines, varying from 21 inches to 30 inches, can also launch missiles and mines.

mobile mines

Most attack submarines can carry and lay mines, which are launched through torpedo tubes and replace torpedoes or cruise missiles generally on a two-for-one basis. The navy employs two principal types of mine to be launched from submarines: the mobile mine (SLMM) and the encapsulated torpedo (CAPTOR). The SLMM is a self-propelled, torpedo-like weapon that travels underwater after leaving the submarine and comes to rest on the seafloor at the end of the run. The mine is then activated and can attack passing surface ships or submarines. This is the navy's only self-propelled mine, with an electric motor providing a range of some 17,000 yards. The CAPTOR is the navy's principal antisubmarine mine. It can be laid by aircraft or submarine in medium-depth and deeper waters. When laid, the CAPTOR is anchored to the ocean floor and floats in the water column. It can detect the acoustic signatures of passing submarines while ignoring surface ships. Upon detecting a hostile submarine, the CAPTOR then launches an MK 46 torpedo that zeroes in on the enemy submarine.

Moccasin (SS-5) (A-4)

Built by the Crescent Shipyard, Elizabethport, New Jersey, she was launched in August 1901 as a submarine of the A class. She was very small, only 123 tons submerged, had an 18-inch torpedo tube in the bow, and was designed to carry a crew of one officer and six enlisted men. Originally designated "Torpedo Boat #5," she was assigned to duty at the Naval Torpedo Station at Newport, Rhode Island, and operated locally on training and experimental missions until assigned to the Reserve Torpedo Flotilla at Norfolk, where she remained inactive for the next five years. In the summer of 1909, she was shipped by cargo vessel, along with her sister submarine, *Adder,* to the Philippines where they were both assigned to the First Submarine Division, Asiatic Torpedo Fleet. During World War I, they patrolled the entrance to Manila Bay and convoyed ships moving out of local waters. *Moccasin* was decommissioned at Cavite in December 1919.

Monitor

This vessel, unique in history as well as design, was about the closest a warship could be to a submarine without actually submerging. Except for its revolving turret, it was flat on the water and designed for use in shallow harbors and rivers to blockade the Confederate states during the Civil War. Built by a noted Swedish naval engineer, John Ericsson, for the U.S. Navy, it contained many innovations supporting the essential attack and defense features of its design. Its minimal exposure above the waterline, which made it almost impossible to hit with any naval weapons then in existence, and its protective armor plate—five inches in the hull and one inch in the deck—made the *Monitor* almost unsinkable by enemy fire. The need to aim her guns when the ship could not be maneuvered, as in a harbor, led to the development of the revolving turret. Swiveled by steam power, her armored turret contained two 11-inch cannons, which could shoot 360 degrees in whatever setting was called for.

On March 9, 1862, *Monitor* engaged the Confederate ironclad *Merrimack* in a much recounted, though inconclusive, battle that attracted international attention and resulted in construction of similar vessels for the U.S. Navy. The original *Monitor* was not seaworthy, and met its end in December 1862, when it went down off Cape Hatteras with a loss of four officers and 12 men. Convinced, however, that this class of ship was useful to its fleet, the navy for many years commissioned similar—though more seaworthy—vessels, which were employed in battle during the Civil War with mixed results. Though quite effective against other vessels and, hence, valuable in maintaining blockade, Monitors were not effective in attacking fortified harbors. The last of the Monitors—four in all, which were commissioned in 1902 and 1903—were used as submarine tenders during World War I.

multiple independent reentry vehicle (MIRV)

This nomenclature refers to any of several types of nuclear warheads carried on a "buss" on the front end of a ballistic missile in such a manner that they can be sent on their independent ways after the main propulsion stages of the missile launch have shut down. The warheads can be released from the ballistic missiles at different speeds and on different trajectories. MIRV technology was first developed by the United States, but its systems were copied, and by the late 20th century both the United States and the Soviet Union had many intercontinental and submarine-launched ballistic missiles equipped with MIRVs.

Muskallunge (SS-262)

Launched in December 1942 and built by Electric Boat as a submarine of the Gato class, *Muskallunge* was deployed to the Pacific and cleared Pearl Harbor in early September 1943 for her first war patrol, taking station off the Palau Islands. She carried the first electric torpedoes (MK-18) to be fired in the war by a U.S. submarine. She made two attacks on Japanese convoys, and, although plagued by malfunctioning torpedoes, she managed to damage a passenger freighter and a cargo ship. Her second war patrol, at the end of the year, was conducted in the western Carolines and south of Guam. During this patrol, she scored hits on a tanker and two freighters, sinking one, before returning to base. On her third war patrol in June, she joined eight other submarines in an operation designed to intercept enemy forces approaching the Marianas, which the navy was invading. In the ensuing battle of the Philippine Sea, two of these submarines landed fatal blows on Japanese carriers, and American naval aircraft wiped out the Japanese fleet's air arm in a one-sided melee known as "the Marianas Turkey Shoot." In company with a sister boat, *Flier,* she left on August 1 for her fourth patrol, heading for the South China Sea, where she sank a 7,163-ton passenger-cargo ship before being severely depth charged. Her fifth and sixth patrols, during which she did lifeguard duty, netted her no victims. Her seventh and last war patrol started only two weeks before war's end, when there were few Japanese warships in action any longer. She attacked and damaged several small ships in a dense fog, in enemy waters, but lost one crew member and two men wounded from enemy fire before learning of the Japanese capitulation and heading for Tokyo Bay for the surrender ceremonies on the battleship *Missouri.* She joined the Atlantic Reserve Fleet in January 1947, and 10 years later was loaned to Brazil under the Military Assistance Program, where she served for another 10 years as *Humaita* (S-14) until being returned to the United States for decommissioning. *Muskallunge* received five battle stars for World War II service.

N

Narwhal (SS-17) (D-1)

Built by the Fore River Shipbuilding Company, Quincy, Massachusetts, and launched in April 1909, this early submarine had a complement of one officer and 14 enlisted men, and was armed with two 18-inch torpedo tubes in the bow. She joined the fleet as lead boat of a class of three, which, at nearly 135 feet, were the largest American submarines at the time. Narwhal's 13-year operational life, confined to the East Coast except for one cruise to the Caribbean and Gulf of Mexico, was fairly unremarkable. Perhaps her biggest claim to fame was the assumption of command by Lieutenant Chester W. Nimitz. As an ensign, he commanded SubFlot1 and, concurrently, the submarine Plunger and, later, Skipjack. After that, on his road to the highest post in the navy, he established the position of Commander Atlantic Submarine Flotilla, the forerunner of ComSubLant. Narwhal was decommissioned in February 1922.

Narwhal (SS-167) (N-1)

Built by the Portsmouth Naval Shipyard, Kittery, Maine, and launched in December 1929, the second submarine to bear the Narwhal name, she was assigned to San Diego and the the West Coast where she had the distinction of completing the first submarine rescue of a downed naval aviator, taking aboard a victim of engine failure by a biplane floatplane off Coronado in March 1935. She shared another "first" when, after war broke out in December 1941, she and the Tautog shot down a Japanese torpedo plane. For an aging submarine, her wartime exploits were remarkable during no fewer than 15 war patrols. Her first

three patrols accounted for four merchant ships sunk and another damaged, and included a reconnaissance of Wake Island and participation as a scout to the east of the island in the decisive battle of Midway. Narwhal's fifth patrol saw her land half a company of army scouts on Japanese-held Attu in the Aleutians in preparation for the major assault that dislodged the enemy from those U.S. islands. She was also involved in shore bombardment with her six-inch guns on an air field on Matsuwa in the Kurile Islands. This attack at the Empire's doorstep, besides its salutary psychological effect, diverted the enemy's attention to permit safe withdrawal of the navy's first penetration, by three

USS Narwhal (SS-167), during Pearl Harbor attack. Having World War II patrol exploits, Narwhal shared a first kill with USS Tautog (SS-199) and a nearby DD: a Japanese torpedo plane. (United States Navy)

submarines, of the Sea of Japan. On her sixth patrol, she conducted a torpedo run to the Marshall Islands and brought one more merchant kill to her credit. Her remaining patrols, all from Australia, featured 19 special missions in support of guerrilla warfare in the Philippines: deliveries of guns, ammunition, equipment, saboteurs, spies, and coast-watchers were made by rubber boat across beaches, or by transfer to other craft, in basically uncharted waters in Japanese-held areas. On her 11th patrol, she bombarded an oil refinery in the East Indies on the way to another anything-but-routine support mission. Later in the same run, she shot up a coastal freighter and a gunboat. By the time of her last run, it was evident that age and the heavy operating schedule were catching up with her, and she was transferred back to the states and berthed in Philadelphia.

She had some unusual design features. Not readily visible on *Narwhal* were the "deck-firing" torpedo tubes, which she put to good use during the war. She was equipped with only six submerged tubes but also carried four pressure-proof surface-only tubes in the superstructure half-deck amidships. Adjacent to each was a storage tube to provide one reload, and one-third of her torpedos were carried topside.

Narwhal sank seven vessels during World War II for a total of 13,829 tons.

Narwhal (SSN-671)

Launched in September 1967, the third submarine to bear the *Narwhal* name was literally in a class by herself. She was not only the quietest of submarines at the time of her commissioning, but also displaced 1,500 tons more than her predecessor, submerged, and was broader and shorter. Her quiet performance was the result of a superb engineering plant powered by a revolutionary natural circulation reactor, which set the standards to which U.S. submarine designers work to this day. Her Sturgeon-class state-of-the-art combat capabilities were the best in the world as she entered the fleet. Cold war stories (at least those that can be revealed) are not usually as dramatic as those of undersea attacks against Japan during World War II, but *Narwhal*'s singular exploits were an exception. Sixteen extended deployments to foreign seas marked her active operating cycles. She garnered a Navy Unit Commendation for a 1972 deployment and Meritorious Unit Commendations for similar operations in 1971, 1977 and 1979. Five Battle Efficiency "Es," four Engineering "Es," and awards of the Antisubmarine Warfare "A," the Communications "C," and the Supply "E" attest to her readiness over the years. She also received the Edward F. Ney Memorial Award for food service excellence, the first submarine to be so honored in the five-year history of the "Golden Anchor Award," and was the only boat to receive the ComSubLant "Silver Anchor Award" for six consecutive years, from 1990 through 1995. Although *Narwhal* never fired a single shot in anger, she was a crucial member of the historic, select championship team that won the cold war.

National Maritime Alliance (NMA)

Founded in the late 1980s, this organization is dedicated to preserving the values and traditions of American seafaring in every facet of its history, from early nautical skills to every kind of vessel, waterfront buildings, harbors, and the personnel devoted to maritime affairs. Membership in NMA represents a diverse group, including: maritime museums, historic ships, lighthouses, boat yards, canals, shipbuilders, historic preservation groups, sailing schools, marine unions, naval officers and crews, and many others who share like interests. The alliance is committed to helping America preserve maritime artifacts, establish programs to improve public knowledge about maritime affairs, attract new supporters, and fund nonprofit institutions in this subject field. It is also engaged in coordinating local, regional, and national efforts to enact legislation for assistance in the maritime heritage field. An example of an important advance in this category was the passage of the National Maritime Heritage Act of 1994, which is designed to provide an ongoing national competitive grants program for worthy maritime projects.

NATO (North Atlantic Treaty Organization)

The North Atlantic Treaty, signed in Washington on April 4, 1949, created an alliance of 10 European and two North American independent nations committed to each other's defense. Four more European nations joined the alliance between 1952 and 1982, bringing the number of members to 16. The admission of the Czech Republic, Hungary, and Poland on March 12, 1999, brought the number of members to 19. NATO's members are Belgium, Canada, the Czech Republic, Denmark, France, Germany, Greece, Hungary, Iceland, Italy, Luxembourg, the Netherlands, Norway, Poland, Portugal, Spain, Turkey, the United Kingdom, and the United States.

The North Atlantic Treaty, itself a very simple document, conforms to the spirit of the charter of the United Nations and derives its legitimacy from the charter. In the treaty, member countries commit themselves to maintaining and developing their defense capabilities, individually and collectively, providing the basis for collective defense planning. One article of the treaty provides the framework for consultations between the member countries, whenever one of them feels that its security is at risk. Another article refers to the right to collective self-defense, stating that an armed attack on one or more members of NATO will be deemed an attack against them all. In other articles of the treaty, each member country undertakes to contribute to the development of peaceful and friendly international relations in a number of ways, including by strengthening their free institutions and promoting conditions of stability and well-being. The treaty also provides for efforts to eliminate conflict in the international economic policies of member countries and to encourage cooperation between them.

NATO is an alliance committed to the collective defense of its member countries as the basis for preserving peace and ensuring future security, and has become a catalyst for extending security and stability throughout Europe. The transformation of NATO, following the end of the cold war, is aimed at generating a higher degree of cooperation and mutual trust, from which the whole of Europe will benefit.

Nautilus (SS-29) (H-2)

The first U.S. Navy submarine to bear the *Nautilus* name officially was built in San Francisco by Union Iron Works in March 1911. She was only 358 tons on the surface and 467 when submerged, had four 18-inch torpedo tubes in the bow, and carried a crew of two officers and 23 enlisted men. She was attached to the United States Pacific Fleet, and operated along the West Coast of the United States, usually in company with other boats of her class, then designated "H" boats. In October 1917, she was transferred to the East Coast of the United States, as a unit of the Atlantic Fleet, and cruised in the Caribbean in search of enemy U-boats, until the end of World War I. After a brief tour training student officers from the submarine school, she headed back to San Francisco in company with *H-1*, which went aground off Santa Margarita Island on March 12, 1920. *H-2* stood by and sent rescue and search parties to look for survivors and helped to save all but four of her sister ship's crew. She conducted drills and exercises with the Pacific Fleet and Submarine Division Seven until reassignment to Hampton Roads, Virginia, from which she ranged the Caribbean until being decommissioned in October 1922.

Nautilus (SS-168)

The second submarine to bear the *Nautilus* name was built by Electric Boat and launched in March 1930 and was a giant compared with the first one—displacing almost 10 times that of her predecessor, and with a crew of eight officers and 80 enlisted men. She operated out of New London initially, but was transferred to the West Coast in the mid-1930s. Modernized and upgraded just before the start of World War II, she was transferred to Pearl Harbor and in May 1942 left on her first war patrol, destination Midway, with her mission being to help repel an expected

attack by the Japanese fleet. In early June, while approaching the northern boundary of her patrol area near Midway, she sighted masts on the horizon, but was attacked by Japanese planes and had to dive deep. After surfacing, she again sighted enemy vessels, and was again forced to dive. When the attack ceased, *Nautilus*, planed up to periscope depth. Ships surrounded her. Sighting on a battleship, she fired twice, but again had to dive and suffer a relentless series of depth charges. Later, upon once more surfacing, she found the battleship and two of the cruisers were now out of range, but shortly thereafter she sighted a damaged carrier with two escorts. An hour later, *Nautilus* had moved into attack position and fired three torpedoes at the carrier, then less than 3,000 yards away. Flames appeared along the length of the ship, and she was abandoned by her crew. Near the end of June, *Nautilus* was again on the attack, this time off Honshu, where she damaged a destroyer guarding the entrance to the Sagami Sea. Within the next week, she sank a destroyer and a sampan and damaged an oil tanker and a cargo ship, but was so badly shaken up by depth charges that she had to retreat to Pearl Harbor for repairs.

Nautilus departed Hawaiian waters August 8 on her second patrol, a special troop transport mission of three weeks' duration. Sailing with *Argonaut* and carrying marines of the Second Raider Battalion, she arrived off Makin on August 16 to stage an attack to divert Japanese attention from the Solomons. Early the following morning, she sent the Raiders ashore on Little Makin in rubber boats rigged with outboard motors. She provided gunfire support against enemy positions, and then shelled enemy ships in the lagoon, sinking two, a troop barge and a patrol boat. Soon afterward, enemy planes attacked, and two landed in the lagoon to discharge troops. About 35 of the reinforcements made it to shore to fire on the Americans. The marines began to withdraw, but many were unable to clear the breakers without the aid of their damaged outboards. Only seven rubber boats and less than 100 men made it to the submarine that night. The remainder, less nine who were later captured and executed, discovered there were no Japanese left to fight and so crossed to the lagoon side, whence they headed for the submarine after nightfall on the 18th.

On her third war patrol, in September and October, *Nautilus* returned to Japanese waters to join the submarine blockade chain stretched from the Kuriles to the Nansei Shoto. Despite heavy seas, which precluded periscope depth operations and torpedo firing during much of the patrol, and mechanical breakdowns, which impeded approaches to targets, she torpedoed and sank three marus and three sampans to add over 12,000 tons to her scorecard. On October 12, however, the patrol became one of her more perilous missions. On that day she took a heavy depth charging and the next day the crew noticed a slight

Shown above in port, *Nautilus V-6* (SS-168) expended five torpedoes and survived 42 depth charges in her efforts to successfully destroy a Japanese carrier on June 4, 1942. *(United States Navy)*

oil slick in her wake. The hindering seas now protected her by breaking up the trace. Within the next few days the oil leak had enlarged considerably—leaving a clear trail for Japanese defense patrols. Moving to a quieter area, with less aerial activity, she continued her patrol until the 24th when she sank her third maru of the patrol, then headed for home.

During her fourth patrol, conducted in the Solomons from mid-December 1942 to early February 1943, *Nautilus* rescued 26 adults and three children from Toep Harbor, then added a cargo ship to her kills and damaged a tanker, a freighter, and a destroyer. After disembarking her passengers in Brisbane, she headed for Dutch Harbor, Alaska, and

commenced instructing Seventh Army scouts in amphibious landings. She then embarked 109 scouts and on May 1 headed for Attu, where she landed them only five hours before the main assault. Her sixth patrol, starting in mid-September, was a photo reconnaissance of the Gilberts, concentrating on Tarawa, Kuma, Butaritari, Abemam, and Makin, resulting in much of the most useful intelligence gathered of the area. Her seventh patrol continued with reconnaissance and troop missions. Her eighth war patrol, conducted west of the Marianas in February and March 1944, netted one cargo ship, with damage inflicted on three others. On her ninth patrol, starting at the end of May, she carried ammunition, oil, and dry stores to Mindanao, and later to Negros, where she embarked evacuees for Darwin. During her 11th patrol, in July, she landed a reconnaissance party and 12 tons of stores on North Pandan Island, then delivered supplies to Leyte and Mindanao. During her 12th, 13th, and 14th patrols, she returned to the central Philippines, landed personnel and supplies at various points on Mindanao and Luzon, and carried evacuees to Australia. On September 25, during the first of these three patrols, she grounded on Luzon Shoal. Forced to lighten her load, her evacuees, mail, captured documents, and cargo were sent ashore. All secret materials were burned. Her reserve fuel tanks were blown dry, variable ballast was blown overboard, and ammunition jettisoned. With the blowing of her main ballast tanks, she was finally able to get off the reef, despite a receding tide, and clear the area by dawn before she could be spotted by enemy planes.

Nautilus completed her 14th, and last, patrol at Darwin, at the end of January 1945, after which she was routed to Philadelphia, judged to be too aging and too battle-scarred to continue combat patrols in the Pacific. She was decommissioned in June 1945, with a bottle of champagne for her long service. She earned the Presidential Unit Citation for her aggressive war patrols in enemy-controlled waters where she sank six vessels for 21,149 tons. *Nautilus* received 14 battle stars for her service during World War II.

Nautilus (SSN-571)

Although the third submarine to bear the *Nautilus* name, this historic boat holds the distinction of being the worlds first nuclear submarine, initiating an entirely new concept of undersea operations, whether in war or peace. Built by the Electric Boat Company and launched in January 1954, she displaced 3,533 tons on the surface and 4,092 submerged, and was designed to carry a crew of 13 officers and 92 enlisted men. In addition to its three submarines, the navy has a long history of preference for this unique seashell, first popularized by author Jules Verne as the name of his fictional submarine in *Twenty Thousand Leagues Under the Sea*. It first appeared on the Navy list as a schooner of 12 guns, seeing battle with Commodore Preble's squadron in the Mediterranean during the campaign against the Tripolitan pirates. *Nautilus* next appeared as a schooner, which was commissioned in 1847 and played a role in the war with Mexico. It was also assigned to a navy patrol boat that saw duty as an escort during World War I. And it was the name of several early submersibles— one by Robert Fulton—considered, but rejected, by the American military in the 19th century.

Construction of the nuclear *Nautilus* was made possible by the successful development of a nuclear propulsion plant by a group of scientists and engineers at the Naval

Reactors Branch of the Atomic Energy Commission, under the leadership of Captain Hyman G. Rickover, USN. On the morning of January 17, 1955, the ship's first commanding officer, Commander Eugene P. Wilkinson, ordered all lines cast off and signaled the memorable and historic message "Underway on Nuclear Power." Over the next several years, *Nautilus* would shatter all submerged speed and distance records. One of her major exploits occurred in July 1958, when she conducted "Operation Sunshine," the first crossing of the North Pole by a ship. After a long overhaul and testing, she was ordered two years later to deploy to the Mediterranean Sea to become the first nuclear submarine assigned to the U.S. Sixth Fleet. Over the next six years, *Nautilus* participated in fleet exercises while steaming over 200,000 miles. In the spring of 1966, she again entered the record books when she logged her 300,000th mile underway. During the following 12 years, she was involved in many developmental testing programs while continuing to serve alongside the more modern nuclear-powered submarines she had preceded. She was decommissioned in March 1980, after an illustrious career spanning 25 years and almost half a million miles. In recognition of her pioneering role, *Nautilus* was designated a National Historic Landmark by the secretary of the interior in May 1982, and now resides in Groton, Connecticut, at the Submarine Force Museum, open to the public as the first and finest exhibit of its kind in the world.

Naval Historical Center

The Naval Historical Center, located at the Washington, D.C., Navy Yard, is the official repository of extensive information regarding the U.S. Navy, its origins and past and present activities. One of its vital features is the Photographic Section, which houses massive reference files on all aspects of naval history. Its own collections are the principal sources of photographs and other illustrations of U.S. Navy subjects made prior to 1920, and contain a wide selection of unique photography from later years. The center also holds thousands of references to naval photographs held by other repositories. It maintains an on-line library of selected images, a readily accessible picture index to some of the Photographic Section's images. Although the center provides limited research services to the public, to assist in locating graphics relating to maritime history and specific vessels, it does not provide photographic reproductions directly, but rather directs inquiries to other sources.

Naval Submarine League (NSL)

The league is an organization whose members, both civilian and military, recognize the need for a strong and continuing submarine force in the U.S. Navy, and are dedicated to providing information and promoting an awareness to the public at large. NSL members consist of individuals and groups whose objective is to keep alive all aspects of submarine history, assist in attacking problems relating to navy submarines, personnel, and operations, and help to influence and guide the growth and future of undersea craft in the service of the U.S. Navy. Membership is open to civilians, as well as members of the armed forces, entitling members to four issues of *The Submarine Review* each year, an annual *Directory of Members,* and a biannual *Fact and Submarine Anecdote Book.* The *Review* contains articles authored by a variety of experts on submarine history, current operations, and the requirements of the future. Additional benefits include membership in a local chapter of NSL, attendance at the annual league symposium in June, and special consideration to attend engineering symposiums on submarine technology, if desired. The latter are specialized in nature, exploring the leading edge of submarine advanced research and development.

Naval Submarine School

Established by the U.S. Navy on January 1, 1917, the Submarine School is—and always has been—located at the submarine base in New London, Connecticut. Its mission is to train officers and enlisted sailors in the basic knowledge and skills upon which operational submarine commands in the Atlantic and Pacific can build competence and proficiency in operating and maintaining submarines and all their systems. It also provides functional, refresher, advanced, and team training to submarine and submarine support personnel in order to increase and maintain their knowledge and proficiency in specific skills. In more recent years, it has established equipment, models, visual materials, and specialists to provide updated state-of-the-art information and data about developments and capabilities of new undersea craft and weaponry, to ensure maximum operational effectiveness on the part of officers and crews who are already in service. The Submarine School maintains a staff of more than 550 officers and enlisted personnel and 15 civilians, and during normal semesters may have more than 1,200 students in training. One program of the school is devoted to coping with high-risk situations, using special trainers that simulate accidents, enemy attacks, and other emergency situations, such as fire, flooding, critical leaks, acute pressure changes, and lack of oxygen—all requiring immediate action and damage control. A vital program is also devoted to the escape trainer, simulating a modern submarine escape trunk, as well as other means of evacuating from a sunken submarine. Every section and component of submarines is reproduced in replica, as well as

on-board training on the various types of submarines in the navy undersea fleet.

naval warfare

Five centuries ago, there was no concept of naval warfare of the kind that would evolve later. Fighting at sea was based on the same strategies as land battles in that warships were little more than floating battlefields that carried soldiers as well as seamen to sail them. Fleets of such ships would close in on each other and then engage in hand-to-hand combat, in much the same manner as on a land battlefield, until one side gained a victory. Not until the 16th century, when the first naval cannons were conceived and mounted on ships, did warfare really go to sea. A step forward was the addition of gun ports, which were cut in the upper hulls of men of war, and the enlargement of the hulls so that a new breed of ship, called the galleon, could have two or three tiers of gun ports—and obviously a great deal more fire power in battle than was possible with single-deck ships. Naval strategy thus had to conform to the ultimate fire power available, and train the crews of warships to maneuver in every way possible to deliver raking fire and broadsides against enemy ships. Later, improved communication devices and methods made it possible to coordinate ship movements and positions in a fleet to take advantage of the user's strengths and the enemy's weaknesses. This was evident during the Napoleonic Wars (1792–1815), as English warship captains developed innovative new tactics to defeat the French. Harnessing the power of new gun designs, the English fleet concentrated the fire of several ships on the center and rear, with the aim of breaking the enemy line before other warships had an opportunity to intervene.

The traditional tactics remained in place until armored ships, breech-loading guns, and explosive shells forced radical changes in naval warfare in the 1860s. The introduction of these more powerful weapons meant that naval combat at close quarters came to an end. Exchanges of gunfire took place at increasingly long range, enhanced both by improvements in gunnery and developments in armor protection—making the risks of close-in fighting more apparent. The appearance of the submarine, at the end of the 19th century, along with the development of torpedoes and mines, changed the entire spectrum of naval warfare. Further changes were wrought as communications—especially the radio—came into play, along with improvements in all forms of weaponry. By World War I, it was becoming evident that the days of the battleship and the big guns were numbered, as the MINE, aircraft, and submarine made their impact.

The full potential of the submarine as an instrument of economic, as well as conned, warfare was felt in the battle of the Atlantic (1915–17), which almost brought Britain to its knees before the introduction of the convoy system. By World War II, direct combat between large surface units was rare; and the main threat to surface ships came from the submarine and from the air, as the aircraft carrier replaced the battleship as the capital ship of war. The submarine has been the dominant naval unit of the postwar period, with the nuclear-armed types playing a major strategic role in nuclear deterrence. The capabilities of the U.S. Navy have been heavily devoted to improved means of both protecting and hunting these submarines, using guided missiles, improved detection systems, and state-of-the art communication methods.

navigation

From the Latin words *navis* (ship) and *agare* (to direct), this term originally applied only to the guidance of ships across the seas. Today, it applies not only to the sea, whether on the surface or at great depths, but also to land, air, and outer space. Travel and exploration of any kind are practical only to the extent that current directions and positions can be precisely identified and future locations accurately estimated. Such data can be determined in various ways. In cases where external references, such as stars or radio and satellite beacons, are unavailable, inertial navigation, which relies on a stable gyroscope for determining position, is normally used, and is more accurate than the old technique of dead reckoning, which depended on knowledge of a ship or plane's original position, coarse and speed and the effects of winds and currents on the course. Another position-fixing method is LORAN (long-range navigation), a system that determines position by measuring the differences in the time of reception of synchronized pulses from widely spaced transmitting stations. Satellite navigation has proved to be the most accurate method of locating geographical position, in which location and position are calculated relative to a set of satellites whose orbits are known by measuring the change in the frequency of a *received* signal from that of a *transmitted* signal. The system originally suffered from a limited number of system satellites, as well as variations of frequencies, particularly in the tropics. But the system is being improved to provide nearly continuous positioning capability worldwide, and is known as the Global Positioning System, which can provide fixes anywhere on Earth to an accuracy within less than 100 feet.

navigational lights and buoys

Light stations and lightships, as well as many forms of buoys, are maintained along coastlines to warn approaching ships of potential dangers such as off-lying shoals, sunken wrecks, rocks, and other hazards. Most lights use on-and-off cycles, the length of time required for a light to complete a full cycle of changes being referred to as "the period of the light." Lights that are off longer than they are on are called "flashing lights," while those that are on as long as, or longer than, they are off are called "occulting lights." Floating navigational aids, other than lightships and weather ships, which are anchored or moored, are called buoys. United States waters are marked for safe navigation by the lateral system of buoyage. Simple arrangements of colors, shapes, numbers, and lights are employed to indicate the side of a buoy on which a ship should pass when moving in a given direction.

N Boats

During 1917, the navy contracted with the Seattle Construction and Drydock Company, Seattle, Washington, and the Lake Torpedo Boat Company, Bridgeport, Connecticut, to build seven submarines in a new class to be designated "N." These boats displaced 348 tons on the surface and 414 tons submerged. They were each armed with four 18-inch torpedo tubes forward, and had complements of two officers and 26 enlisted men. Four of the submarines had short careers and were decommissioned in 1922. The other three, *N-1*, *N-2*, and *N-3*, remained in service until 1930. All of the boats saw service during World War I, patrolling along the New England coast in search of German U-boats. They made no contacts, but *N-5* nearly met disaster when she was mistaken for a U-boat and fired upon. The N boats were used largely for training missions and testing experimental weapons, such as radio-controlled torpedoes. Although they all served well and helped the navy to strengthen its budding undersea service and attract qualified officers and men to the submarine school in New London, Connecticut, their careers were relatively uneventful. Several boats played important roles in weapons development, and the *N-3* had the distinction of being one of the first submarines ever to navigate the St. Lawrence River and the Great Lakes.

Nearterm Mine Reconnaissance System (NMRS)

This system utilizes a submarine-launched, unmanned underwater vehicle (UUV) that provides minefield reconnaissance in water of any depth. The NMRS incorporates torpedo tube technology, guided by active search sonars, and a guidance system monitored and controlled from within the parent submarine. The NMRS system consists of two reusable underwater vehicles, launch and recovery equipment, including a winch and drogues; and shipboard control, processing, and monitoring equipment. A typical UUV is slightly shorter than a Mark 48 torpedo and is launched and recovered via a standard torpedo tube. The

N-1 (SS-53) was the first of a class of seven boats that were built prior to, and served during, World War I. Several of the *N*-boats played important roles in weapons development. *(United States Navy)*

vehicle carries a highly accurate sonar system that can pinpoint and classify mine-like objects, and is battery-powered, both for propulsion and the operation of its on-board electronic systems. The vehicle's speed, depth, status, and sonar data are continuously relayed back to the host submarine via a fiber-optic cable, thereby allowing continuous monitoring of the vehicle during its search and attack missions in mined areas. Should the cable break for any reason, the UUV vehicle is programmed to return automatically, and under its own power, to a pre-set rendezvous point for recovery by the parent submarine.

Newport News (SSN-750)

Built by Newport News Shipbuilding and Drydock Company and launched in March 1986 as a boat of the Los Angeles class, she was the eighth vessel to bear the name of the Virginia shipbuilding city. Three previous ships, including a heavy cruiser that saw service in both the Korean and Vietnam wars, have been in the navy; two were brought into the military for only short periods of time to provide transportation for troops and carry supplies overseas; and the remaining four plied commercial waters, carrying either passengers or freight. The *Newport News* was built with the latest sound quieting features and is one of only a handful of submarines equipped with 12 vertically launched *Tomahawk* cruise missiles mounted in her bow. She operated in many areas with the fleet. Partic-

ularly noteworthy was her wartime deployment in support of *Operation Desert Storm* in January 1991, for which she was awarded the Southwest Asia Service Medal with one bronze star. In October 1994, she was again called to the Persian Gulf region, becoming the first carrier battle group submarine ever to transit the Suez Canal. Bringing her formidable strike capabilities to bear within hours of the crisis, *Newport News* played a key role in the restoration of regional stability and proved the versatility of the fast-attack submarine. Her consistently outstanding performance earned her the SubRon8 Engineering "E" Award for 1992 and 1993 and the Battle "E" for 1993, an award reserved for the squadron's top performing submarine.

Nimitz, Chester William (1885–1966)

Commander of the U.S. Pacific Fleet during World War II, and one of the navy's foremost administrators and strategists, he commanded all land and sea forces in the Pacific area. A 1905 graduate of the U.S. Naval Academy at Annapolis, Nimitz served in World War I as chief of staff to the commander of the U.S. Atlantic Submarine Force, a tour of duty that convinced him of the effectiveness of submarine warfare. He held a variety of posts at sea and on shore until 1939, when he was appointed chief of the Bureau of Navigation of the U.S. Navy. After the Japanese attack on Pearl Harbor on December 7, 1941, Nimitz was elevated to commander in chief of the Pacific Fleet, a command that brought both land and sea forces under his authority. By June 1942, he had proudly announced decisive victories at the battles of Midway and the Coral Sea, where enemy losses were 10 times greater than those of the United States at Pearl Harbor. In succeeding years, the historic battles of the Solomon Islands (1942–43), the Gilbert Islands (1943), the Marshalls, Marianas, Palaus, and Philippines (1944), and Iwo Jima and Okinawa (1945) were fought under his direction. The Japanese capitulation was signed aboard his flagship, the USS *Missouri,* in Tokyo Bay on September 2, 1945. In December 1944, Nimitz had been promoted to the navy's newest and highest rank—that of fleet admiral (a five-star admiral). After the war, Nimitz served as chief of naval operations (1945–47). Always active in navy affairs after retirement, he died near San Francisco on February 20, 1966.

NR-1

This vessel, a nuclear-powered research submersible, entered navy service in 1969, designed primarily to locate and recover underwater objects, such as sunken Soviet submarines or missiles. Her secondary mission was to engage in deep submergence research. *NR-1* is 140 feet long and 12 feet in diameter, displaces 400 tons submerged, and is designed to carry a crew of two officers, three enlisted men, and two scientists. She is equipped with a pressurized water reactor that drives two externally mounted motors with propellers and four thrusters for maneuverability. While this submersible does not have to be as quiet as a combat submarine or able to withstand as much shock during operations, she meets the same standards of reactor safety and reliability as any other nuclear submarine in the fleet.

oceanographic research submarines

The submersibles used for oceanographic research bear little resemblance to military vessels, in design, size, capabilities, and other characteristics. Because most research submarines are constructed primarily to operate on the floor of the ocean, they tend to be relatively small, and with limited power or speed. However, they do have high maneuverability, being able to move in any direction and at any angle, and to hover in place during the research and photographic missions for which they are employed. They are also designed and built to withstand tremendous water pressure and maintain their equilibrium and capabilities over extended periods of time, even at the greatest depths. Although such craft can move as described along or near the ocean floor, they are usually dependent on supporting surface ships for descending and surfacing.

O-class submarines

The O boats consisted of 16 submarines (SS-62 through SS-77) that were launched just prior to, and during, World War I, built mainly by Fore River Shipbuilding Company, in Quincy, Massachusetts, but also by several other shipbuilders on the East and West Coasts. They ranged from 566 to 629 tons (submerged), had four 18-inch torpedo tubes in the bow, and were designed to be crewed by two officers and 27 enlisted men. They had relatively uneventful careers, some seeing service in patrols off the East Coast during World War I, and most employed for training and testing during peacetime. A number of the boats, including the *O-2, O-3, O-4, O-6, O-7, O-8,* and *O-10,* were upgraded and actually served in World War II, though only as training boats for the

increasing numbers of submariners needed for the war in the Pacific.

Three boats were involved in accidents. *O-5* (SS-66) was struck by the merchant steamer *Abangarez* in Limon Bay, Panama, on October 28, 1923, as she was preparing to transit the Panama Canal, and sank in less than a minute. Three crew members were killed outright, while 16 others escaped. Two of them had been trapped in the forward torpedo room, which they sealed against the water flooding the boat. Fortunately, local engineers and divers were able to rig cranes and lift the bow high enough so it broke the surface, exposing a hatch that led to the compartment where the two men were trapped.

O-13 lived up to her unlucky number when, prior to her commissioning and during test runs, she rammed and sank *Mary Alice,* a patrol boat that was accompanying her during her submerged trials in Long Island Sound on October 5, 1919. Although *Mary Alice* sank within minutes, *O-13* was able to rescue the entire crew.

Far less fortunate was *O-9* (SS-70), which had been used for training and then recalled for service at the outbreak of World War II. On June 19, 1941, she departed New London, Connecticut, with other *O* boats, for tests off the Isle of Shoals, near the New Hampshire coast. One day later, after the other submarines had successfully completed their tests, she submerged to conduct deep submergence trials. Somehow, she went below her limit and her hull was crushed by the pressure of the water at a depth of more than 400 feet. She went to her grave 15 miles off Portsmouth, in the area where the *Squalus* had foundered two years earlier. Rescue ships and divers converged on the scene, but it was too late. The boat was lost, along with all 34 officers and men aboard her.

O-1 (SS-62), seen shortly after repairs at the Portsmouth Navy Yard, was the first of 16 submarines launched prior to, and during, World War I. Several were upgraded enough during the 1930s to see service in World War II as training boats. *(United States Navy)*

One of the boats, *O-12* (SS-73), had a unique history. After a 13-year career as a training boat, winning awards for gunnery and torpedo exploits, she was transferred from the navy to the U.S. Shipping Board for conversion by the Philadelphia Navy Yard for use by Sir Hubert Wilkins, a famous World War I flier and world explorer, the first to make an exploratory flight in the Antarctic. He was forming an arctic expedition with the intention of using a submarine to cruise under the ice pack to the North Pole to make meteorological and other scientific observations. Unfortunately, the aging submarine—despite improvements and alterations for Sir Hubert's plan of operation—was by no means up to the task. Repeated engine breakdowns and other problems forced even the indomitable Wilkins to abandon the attempt

and return to base. The submarine, which had been renamed *Nautilus*, was returned to the Navy Department which sunk her in November 1931, in a Norwegian fjord.

USS *Octopus* (C-1) (SS-9)

Built by the Fore River Shipbuilding Company and launched in October 1906, this early submarine of the C class displaced 238 tons on the surface and 275 submerged, was armed with two 18-inch torpedo tubes forward, and had a complement of one officer and 14 enlisted men. Assigned to the Second Submarine Flotilla, she operated out of Newport, Rhode Island, and New York for two years, and until 1913 was the subject of numerous tests and experiments with both submarine design and the tactical use of her type of boat. She was then reassigned to the First Submarine Group, Torpedo Flotilla, Atlantic Fleet, operating out of Guantanamo Bay, Cuba. She served in Panamanian waters in training, and later, on patrol during World War I. In August 1919, she was decommissioned at Coco Solo in the Canal Zone.

Odax (SS-484)

Built by Portsmouth Naval Shipyard and launched January 10, 1945, *Odax*, a Tench class, was selected for GUPPY I conversion in September 1946. The conversion was completed in August 1947, making *Odax* the first of the GUPPY submarines. In 1951 a snorkel system was added at Portsmouth shipyard and *Odax* was redesignated a GUPPY II. Until 1955, she spent time providing services to the Operational Development Force and Fleet Sonar School in Key West and the Fleet Sonar Group in Guan-

O-13 (SS-74) was one of the last boats built by the old Lake Torpedo Boat Company. She fell victim to her "unlucky number," when she rammed and sank a patrol boat, but through quick action was able to rescue the entire crew. *(United States Navy)*

tanamo Bay, reporting to Charleston Naval Shipyard in 1956 to receive equipment of improved design. From Charleston, *Odax* was sent to the North Atlantic to operate with the British fleet in order to train submariners in the latest tactics of undersea warfare.

Deployed to the Mediterranean Sea in September 1958, she transited the Suez Canal, participating in a Baghdad pact in the Arabian Sea and returned to Charleston, her new home port, in August 1959. After returning to the North Atlantic for barrier patrol, there was a visit to Glasgow, Scotland in August 1960, exercises conducted with naval units from various South American countries, and then a return to Charleston in December to resume local operations. In August 1964 she deployed again to South America for combined operations while circumnavigating the continent.

Operating out of Charleston from 1965 to 1967, *Odax* was then deployed to northern Europe and upon returning received the coveted battle efficiency "E" for fiscal year 1967. Resuming coastal operations in October 1967, *Odax* was decommissioned on July 8, 1972 and sold to Brazil.

Ohio class

NUCLEAR-PROPELLED STRATEGIC MISSILE SUBMARINES

Number	Name	FY	Launched	Commissioned	Status
SSBN-726	Ohio	74	1979	1981	Pacific
SSBN-727	Michigan	75	1980	1982	Pacific
SSBN-728	Florida	75	1981	1983	Pacific
SSBN-729	Georgia	76	1982	1984	Pacific
SSBN-730	Henry M. Jackson	77	1983	1984	Pacific
SSBN-731	Alabama	78	1984	1985	Pacific
SSBN-732	Alaska	78	1985	1986	Pacific
SSBN-733	Nevada	80	1985	1986	Pacific
SSBN-734	Tennessee	81	1986	1988	Atlantic
SSBN-735	Pennsylvania	83	1988	1989	Atlantic
SSBN-736	West Virginia	84	1989	1990	Atlantic
SSBN-737	Kentucky	85	1990	1991	Atlantic
SSBN-738	Maryland	86	1991	1992	Atlantic
SSBN-739	Nebraska	87	1991	1992	Atlantic
SSBN-740	Rhode Island	88	1993	1994	Atlantic
SSBN-741	Maine	89	1994	1995	Atlantic
SSBN-742	Wyoming	90	1995	1996	Atlantic
SSBN-743	Louisiana	91	1996	1997	Atlantic

These are the largest submarines ever built in the United States, utilizing a conservative design with the bow sonar dome and amidships torpedo tubes of later attack submarines (SSN). They are the only 24-tube strategic missile submarines in the world, designed to use the latest models of the Trident. They have the capability to conduct 70-day patrols interrupted by 25-day upkeep/replenishment/crew relief periods. Under this schedule, the submarines undergo a lengthy overhaul and reactor refueling every 10 years. Submarines in this class have three large 36-inch logistic hatches, which include escape trunks that can be temporarily removed while in port to provide large resupply and repair access points.

CHARACTERISTICS

Displacement:	16,764 tons standard; 18,750 tons submerged
Dimensions:	
length	560 ft. overall
beam	42 ft.
draft	36 ft. 5 in.
Propulsion:	2 steam turbines 60,000 shp.; 1 shaft; 1 Magnetek auxiliary prop motor
Reactors:	1 pressurized-water reactor S8G
Performance:	
speed	28 kts. surface; approx. 30 kts. submerged
Manning:	163 (15 officers + 148 enlisted) (14 officers in first six) (two crews)
Combat Systems:	
missiles	24 tubes for Trident C-4 SLBM 24 tubes for Trident D-5 SLBM in later units
torpedo tubes	4 21-in. (533-mm) amidships Mk 68
ASW weapons	Mark 48 or Mark 48 ADCAP dual purpose torpedoes
radars	BPS-15A surface search BPS-16A (in 741–743 only)
sonar	BQQ-6 bow-mounted passive BQS-13 spherical array BQS-15 ice avoidance BQR-15 towed array BQR-19 active navigation BQS-13 active search BQQ-9 TASPE
fire control	CCS Mk 2 Mod 3 1 Mk 98 missile FCS 1 NK 118 torpedo FCS
EW	WLR-8 (V)5 WLR-10 8 launchers for Mark 2 torpedo decoys

(United States Navy)

Okinawa, invasion of (March–June 1945)

The massive American amphibious assault on Japanese-occupied Okinawa, an island in the Ryukyu group north of Formosa, was designed to provide a forward base for the projected invasion of Japan. The island was defended by 100,000 troops of the Japanese 32nd Army, against which the Americans planned on landing 154,000 troops on the southwest of the island, using an invasion force of 1,300 ships. Well in advance, American submarines made reconnaissance missions to determine the nature and strength of all Japanese naval units within range of Okinawa, and chart their movements. Air support was provided by Task Force 58 and a British carrier force, both of which were under constant attack from kamikaze pilots. In the days following the first landing on April 1, heavy ground fighting was matched by further major action at sea. On April 6 some 700 Japanese aircraft mounted a kamikaze raid on the Allied fleet, resulting in damage to 13 American destroyers. The Japanese navy also mounted a suicide attack using its last remaining battle squadron, but this was destined to fail from the start: the Japanese fleet was sighted and destroyed by American aircraft a considerable distance from its intended destination. The destruction of the battle squadron and its supporting units marked the effective end of the Japanese navy as a fighting force. The island finally fell to the Americans on June 21, 1945.

Oklahoma City (SSN-723)

Built by Newport News Shipbuilding & Drydock Company, Newport News, Virginia, and launched in January 1984, this submarine of the Los Angeles class has a displacement of 6,000 tons on the surface, and 6,900 tons submerged. She is designed for a complement of 12 officers and 115 enlisted men.

USS *Orcal* (K-3) (SS-34)

Built by the United Iron Works, San Francisco, and launched in March 1914, *Orcal* was a K-class boat of 392 tons on the surface and 521 tons submerged. She carried a crew of two officers and 26 enlisted men and mounted four 18-inch torpedo tubes in the bow. She joined SubDiv3 of the Pacific Torpedo Flotilla in December 1914, and operated along the California coast developing underwater warfare tactics and coordinating the use of underwater craft with the fleet. The submarine arrived in Hawaiian waters a year later to perform similar exercises in light of increasing emphasis on submarine warfare, especially as World War I saw German U-boats taking command of the seas. *Orcal* was dispatched to Key West in January 1918, and conducted war patrols along the Florida coast while training men in underwater techniques. When peace came, she continued operations along the East Coast, testing new devices such as listening gear, improved types of storage batteries, and torpedoes. She was decommissioned in February 1923.

Orion (P-3)

Orion is the U.S. Navy's long-range maritime patrol and antisubmarine warfare (ASW) aircraft, some of which have been adapted to electronic intelligence (ELINT) collection and special reconnaissance roles. Powered by four turboprop engines, fitted in nacelles on the wing, it is propeller-driven and is noted for its impressive takeoff performance and maneuverability. In addition to a complex, state-of-the-art communications system, the *Orion* has an internal weapons bay and 10 external stations for carrying a mix of ASW torpedoes, depth bombs, and Harpoon antiship missiles. The internal weapons bay can accommodate a variety of depth bombs and mines or up to eight lightweight ASW torpedoes. Sonobuoys can be launched from external pods or from a set of tubes located internally aft of the weapons bay. The navy is modernizing the P-3s from their initial antisubmarine role to a broader antisurface warfare role as well. Approximately 25 percent of the fleet will carry out a primary role of intelligence, surveillance, and reconnaissance, although some craft will also have strike capability.

P

Paddle (SS-263)

Launched in December 1942 and built by the Electric Boat Company, as a submarine of the Gato class, *Paddle* was based at Pearl Harbor during her first two war patrols, between which she trained destroyers in antisubmarine warfare. Her first patrol, July 20–September 12, was conducted south of Japan. She scored a hit on a large freighter in her first attack, but was damaged later by enemy search planes, which dropped seven bombs as she patrolled submerged off the coast of Japan. She repaired the damage quickly and struck back, sinking a passenger-cargo ship before returning to port. During her second war patrol, October 17–November 9, 1943, *Paddle* took station off Nauru to provide continuous weather reporting for the carrier task force attacking the Gilberts and Marshalls to cover the Tarawa landings. By radio, she also guided army bombers in to raid Tarawa. During this engagement, she attacked an enemy tanker off Eniwetok, though escorting destroyers forced her down before she could observe the damage inflicted. *Paddle* sailed for her third war patrol in mid-March, bound for the Dutch East Indies and the southern Philippines. In a brilliant night attack, she sank two of a three-ship convoy guarded by four escorts, and then attacked a tanker, which had joined the group, and engaged escorting destroyers and aircraft.

Paddle's fourth war patrol took place in June and July 1944, with reconnaissance of the eastern approaches to Davao Gulf, guarding against a Japanese sortie during the U.S. landings on Saipan. Damaged by bombs in the Celebes Sea, she made repairs and then attacked a small convoy, twice hitting a large freighter, and sinking a destroyer before being forced down by other escorts. On

her fifth and sixth patrols, in the Sulu Sea area, she encountered few contacts, but even so, she damaged a cargo ship and sank another cargo ship and three small vessels. Her seventh patrol, in the South China Sea, resulted in damage to an enemy destroyer and the sinking of a tanker. After an overhaul at San Francisco, *Paddle* returned to the Yellow and East China Seas for her eighth and last war patrol in May and June 1945. Finding few substantial targets—she and her sisters having by this time almost annihilated Japanese shipping—she turned her attention to the sinking of floating mines with gunfire, and sank eight schooners and picket boats. After the war, *Paddle* was transferred to the East Coast, where she conducted training cruises, until August 1956, when she was loaned to Brazil under the Mutual Defense Assistance Program to serve in that country's navy as *Riachuelo*. *Paddle* received eight battle stars for World War II service. Her tally is five vessels for 18,798 tons.

Pampanito (SS-383)

Launched in July 1943 and built by Portsmouth Naval Shipyard, this Balao-class boat narrowly escaped doom during her first two war patrols. While attacking an enemy convoy on the first patrol, *Pampanito* was severely depth charged and damaged. On her second patrol, off the coast of Japan, her lookouts spotted two torpedo wakes approaching—luckily, in time to avoid them. Two days later another wake was sighted. Evasive measures were taken and the torpedo crossed her bow, missing by only a few yards. During her third patrol she operated as part of a wolf pack consisting of *Growler* and *Sealion*. On the morning of September 12, 1944, the pack attacked a convoy carrying war production materials. Unknown to the submarine skippers, the convoy also carried over 2,000 British and Australian prisoners of war. Many of the ships in the convoy were sunk by the pack, including the two carrying the POWs. *Sealion* sank the *Rakuyo,* which carried over 1,300 POWs, and *Pampanito* sank the *Kachidoki* with 900 POWs. The three subs then steamed away to pursue the scattered ships in the convoy. Later, *Pampanito* moved back to the area of the original attack and spotted men clinging to rafts. As she closed in, the men were heard to be shouting in English—they were the survivors of *Rakuyo,* sunk four days earlier by *Sealion. Pampanito* was able to pick up 73 men and called in three other subs in the area. *Sealion* rescued 54 men, *Queenfish* 18, and *Barb* 14. Of the 1,300 men on *Rakuyo Maru* sunk by *Sealion,* 159 were rescued by the four subs. The Japanese rescued an additional 136 men for a total of 295 survivors. Of the 900 men on the ship sunk by *Pampanito,* 656 men were rescued by the Japanese and taken to camps in Japan, of which over 500 were released by U.S. troops at war's end. *Pampanito* made three more successful patrols during the war before being retired from service. Following the war she served as a training boat and was eventually transferred to the National Maritime Museum in San Francisco, California for public display.

Parche (SS-384)

Built by the Portsmouth Naval Shipyard, Kittery, Maine, and launched in July 1943, this submarine of the Balao class had one of the most dramatic attack records of any vessel in the navy. Under the leadership of Commander Lawson P. Ramage, she departed Pearl Harbor in late March 1944, along with sister ships *Tinosa* and *Bang* for her first war patrol. The three reached the sea lanes south of Formosa, and on April 29 *Bang* reported a large convoy 50 miles away; the wolf pack attacked, *Parche* getting one hit. Five days later, *Tinosa* reported a seven-ship convoy and *Parche* headed north at full speed to intercept. An hour after midnight she was in position and scored three torpedo hits on the leading ship and two hits on the second freighter, sinking both. *Parche* then scored two hits on the third freighter, which settled by the stem and began to list to port. Postwar records credited the trio of submarines with five sinkings and 30,542 tons, *Parche* getting credit for three cargo ships and returning to Midway after making a thorough photo reconnaissance of military installations on the Japanese-held island of Ishi Gaki Jima.

Parche's second patrol was again south of Formosa, forming with submarines *Hammerhead* and *Steelhead* as a coordinated attack group. In late June, *Parche* sighted and sank a patrol vessel with gunfire. In late July, *Parche* and *Steelhead* joined in an attack that sank a 4,471-ton cargo ship and a 10,238-ton tanker. During this daring night surface action, *Parche* barely avoided being rammed by one ship, and then collaborated with *Steelhead* in sinking an 8,990-ton transport. *Steelhead* then sank two other ships, a transport and a cargo vessel. Another tanker and a cargo ship were damaged. For this action *Parche* received the Presidential Unit Citation.

On her third war patrol, September 10 to December 2, one of the longest of the war, *Parche* did not encounter any targets. But on her next patrol, starting at the end of December 1944, she discovered a freighter and a tanker at anchor in Naze Ko, firing six bow tubes at the tanker for five distinct hits and four stern tubes at the freighter for two possible hits. A week later, she sighted and sank a 984-ton cargo ship. Japanese shipping, decimated by continual submarine and air attacks, was becoming increasingly difficult to find. When *Parche* left Pearl Harbor in mid-March 1945, she headed directly for the east coast of Honshu, Japan, where she sank an escort vessel, followed by a coastal freighter and a number of small boats, using her deck guns. Two Japanese planes caused her to dive, leaving all her guns loose and much of her ammunition exposed. A heavy explosion shook her on the way down, but inflicted no damage. She finished off the patrol by sinking two more small tankers.

Parche got underway in late May for her sixth and last patrol, joining the "Lifeguard League" south of Honshu. Her first torpedo contact came June 21 when she sighted a gunboat, soon joined by a subchaser and then by a freighter. Picking the freighter as the best target, *Parche* fired four torpedoes from her forward tubes for one hit, which threw up a veil of dense white smoke. Later, she attacked and sank several more small ships by gunfire. Two days later, she sighted three large ships and six escorts headed north along the coast, one of the most tempting convoys seen for some months in Japanese home waters. After *Parche*'s attack the escorts shook the sub up considerably with depth charges for four and a half hours, before she managed to work away and resume her patrol, leaving an ex-gunboat sunk and another ship badly damaged. After another round of lifeguard duty for the carrier planes of Task Force 38, she rendezvoused with submarine *Cero* to take aboard three fliers before heading back to Pearl Harbor in late July. A navy yard overhaul kept the ship in port until after the Japanese surrender. In 1946, she was assigned to Operation Crossroads, as a target ship for the atomic bomb tests at Bikini. *Parche* survived both the air burst and the underwater burst, coming through relatively undamaged. After decontamination, she proceeded to Mare Island. She was then assigned to Naval Reserve training duty, and served as an auxiliary submarine until being decommissioned and struck from the Navy list in November 1969. She received five battle stars for World War II service and was responsible for sinking 8 vessels for 31,696 tons. In recognition of his leadership and especially his boldness in pressing one particular attack against an overwhelming enemy force, *Parche's* skipper, Commander Lawson Paterson Ramage, was honored with the following navy citation:

For conspicuous gallantry and intrepidity at the risk of his life above and beyond the call of duty as commanding officer of the U.S.S. Parche in a pre-dawn attack on a Japanese CONVOY, 31 JULY, 1944. Boldly penetrating the screen of a heavily escorted convoy, Commander Ramage launched a perilous surface attack by delivering a crippling stern shot into a freighter and quickly following up with a series of bow and stern torpedoes to sink the leading tanker and damage the second one. Exposed by the light of bursting flares and bravely defiant of terrific shellfire passing close overhead, he struck again, sinking a transport by two forward reloads. In the mounting fury of fire from the damaged and sinking tanker, he calmly ordered his men below, remaining on the bridge to fight it out with an enemy now disorganized and confused. Swift to act as a fast transport closed in to ram, Commander Ramage daringly swung the stern of the speeding Parche as she crossed the bow of the onrushing ship, clearing by less than 50 feet but placing his submarine in a deadly crossfire from escorts on all sides and with the transport dead ahead. Undaunted he sent three smashing "down the throat" bow shots to stop the target, then scored a killing hit as a climax to 46 minutes of violent action with the Parche and her valiant fighting company retiring victorious and unscathed.

Parche (SSN-683)

The second submarine to bear this name was built by Ingalls Shipbuilding and launched in January 1973. It was designed for a complement of 12 officers and 95 enlisted men. A member of the Sturgeon class, *Parche* displaced 4,762 tons submerged and was initially assigned to the Atlantic Submarine Force before being transferred to the Pacific Fleet in 1976. In 1990, during extended overhaul at the Mare Island Shipyard, *Parche* was modified for research operations, with a 110-foot extension added to her hull, and was then assigned to Submarine Development Squadron 5, with her home port at Bangor, Washington. Like all Sturgeon class submarines, *Parche* was of ice-strengthened construction, with reinforced sail and diving planes strong enough to avoid damage when the boat crashes through ice to surface during northern research missions. In her "second life," she was designed for a larger complement of men—179, including 22 officers—and had her submerged displacement increased to 7,800 tons. *Parche* has a defense capability equal to that of other submarines in her class, with four 21-inch torpedo tubes amid-

ship, capable of firing MK-48 torpedoes or Harpoon or Tomahawk missiles.

Pargo (SS-264)

A submarine of the Gato class built by Electric Boat and launched in January 1943, she was ordered to the Pacific, where the first of her eight war patrols began in mid-August, taking her into the East China Sea where she twice attacked the enemy, inflicting undetermined damage to several ships before returning to Pearl Harbor. After refitting, she sailed at the end of October in company with sister ships *Snook* and *Harder* in a wolf pack. The efforts of the three were well directed against the open sea area northwest of the Marianas where *Pargo* sank two freighters totaling 7,810 tons, in late November. On her third patrol, beginning in late March 1944, she sank a net tender, but on her fourth she found few targets while roaming the Celebes Sea, but did manage to damage several ships and sink a 5,236-ton cargo ship. During September and October, *Pargo* ranged the South China Sea, pressing her attacks to damage several Japanese ships and to sink two more, including a minelayer. In late October, she sailed from western Australian waters in company with sister ship *Haddo,* for her sixth patrol. From Exmouth Gulf she continued alone into the South China Sea where she found that increased Allied air activity had further diminished use of the shipping lanes. She sank a tanker off Brunei Bay in late November. Following this action she received the worst depth charging of her career but escaped without serious damage, and returned to Australia. Her seventh patrol, off the Indochina coast, was successful. In late January 1945, she launched a night torpedo attack that damaged several ships. Ten days later she again engaged the enemy and blew up a destroyer. *Pargo's* eighth and final patrol spanned the 42-day interval from July 14 to September 9. Transiting the minefields of Tsushima Strait, she entered the Sea of Japan where she attacked a six-ship convoy. She made her last sinking on August 8, a passenger-cargo ship, to total nine vessels for 27,983 tons for the war. After Japanese capitulation, *Pargo* remained in the mine-filled waters until the peace terms were signed and then sailed for Guam. Returning to Pearl Harbor with the knowledge that she had contributed materially to the victory in the Pacific, she assumed postwar duties as part of the squadron based there. Later she was assigned to train Naval Reservists until June 1960, when her name was struck from the Navy list. *Pargo* received eight battle stars for World War II service.

Patrick Henry (SSBN-599)

A submarine of the George Washington class built by Electric Boat and launched in September 1959, *Patrick*

Henry was designed to carry a crew of 12 officers and 100 enlisted men. Manned alternately by two crews, blue and gold, to maximize her submerged operations, this second fleet ballistic missile submarine (FBM) commenced her first deterrent patrol in December 1960. Between December 1960 and December 1964, *Patrick Henry* conducted 17 deterrent patrols while remaining continuously deployed overseas, operating out of Holy Loch, Scotland. When she surfaced to Holy Loch on March 8, 1961, she had set a record for her type, cruising submerged 66 days and 22 hours. In December 1964, she returned to Electric Boat Division of General Dynamics, Groton, Connecticut, where she remained for 18 months to complete extensive overhaul and repair operations, including refueling of the reactor plant and modifications to permit the handling of Polaris A-3 missiles. After shakedown in mid-1966 off Puerto Rico and Cape Kennedy, Florida, *Patrick Henry* departed Charleston in December for patrol #18, equipped with Polaris A-3 missiles and assigned to SubRon14. In March 1968, she completed her 22nd patrol at Holy Loch. She remained with the Atlantic Fleet into the 1970s. In 1982 she was reclassified and finished her career as an SSN and was decommissioned in May 1984.

Pearl Harbor, attack on (December 7, 1941)

This surprise attack by Japanese carrier-based aircraft on the Pacific fleet at its base at Pearl Harbor, Hawaii, on a Sunday morning at dawn brought the United States immediately into World War II. At the time of the attack, some 75 warships, including three aircraft carriers, were

Crew members loading a torpedo into the forward torpedo room of a submarine of World War II vintage at Pearl Harbor. *(United States Navy)*

based in the harbor, most of them gathered there specifically in case they were required to respond to any acts of Japanese aggression in the Pacific region. The planning for this operation had begun almost a year earlier under the direction of Admiral Isoroku Yamamoto, commander in chief of the Japanese Imperial Navy. His objective was to destroy the bulk of the American fleet in a single decisive blow, thus leaving the Japanese free to extend their rule across large areas of Southeast Asia. The plan reflected the view of many senior Japanese naval officers that they did not have the resources to fight an extended war with the United States, and that an effective sneak strike was their best option. The basic strike force consisted of two battleships, three cruisers, nine destroyers, and six carriers, whose combined wings included 104 high-level bombers, 135 dive-bombers, and 80 fighter aircraft. Leaving the Kurile Islands on November 26, the strike force moved into position so that by dawn on December 7, when the first attack was launched, it was some 275 miles north of Oahu Island, the location of Pearl Harbor. The first bombs were dropped on the American fleet at 7:55 A.M., sinking three battleships, the *Arizona, West Virginia,* and *California,* and critically damaging a fourth, the *Nevada.* The Japanese attacked five airfields, destroying some 200 aircraft on the ground. There was a supporting operation by Japanese midget submarines. A second wave of enemy aircraft followed some 45 minutes later and continued the destruction, although smoke rising from damaged warships was actually so heavy as to seriously impair pilot visibility.

American ground defenses, which were totally unprepared for the attack and in many cases did not even have anti-aircraft weapons at the ready, offered little effective response, and Japanese losses were thus correspondingly small: 100 casualties, 29 aircraft, and five midget submarines. By contrast, the American naval and military forces suffered heavily: 2,400 lives lost, 1,300 wounded, and another 1,000 missing. Although 18 American warships were destroyed or damaged, along with virtually all of the U.S. combat planes on the ground and many aircraft facilities, the Japanese victory was far from complete. The most notable survivors were the U.S. fleet's three aircraft carriers—the *Enterprise, Lexington,* and *Saratoga,* which were at sea at the time of the attack, and the harbor installations, which also escaped serious damage. Another strong point in America's favor was the intense public reaction that followed and the determination now to bend every effort to beat the enemy. The following day the United States declared war on Japan.

In the long run, the Japanese decision to attack Pearl Harbor was a disastrous one. The U.S. fleet had not been destroyed and, as some Japanese admirals had predicted, Japan was not able to survive a prolonged war with the United States.

Sub Base, Pearl Harbor, circa World War II. *(United States Navy)*

Perch (SS-176) (P-5)

Built by Electric Boat and launched in March 1936, *Perch* was the first of a new class of submarine, seeing several years of peacetime duty before the start of World War II. She was ordered to Port Darwin, Australia, where she embarked on her first two patrols in early 1942. At this time the Japanese campaign to secure the Dutch East Indies was at its height. The Philippines had been effectively neutralized by that time, and their fall was only a matter of time. The Japanese were forcing their way down the Strait of Makassar, and an invasion of Borneo or Java was imminent. From February 8 to February 23 *Perch* was sent several reports concerning enemy concentrations near her area, and was directed to patrol or perform reconnaissance in various positions near the islands of the Java Sea. On February 25 she was directed to go through Salajar Strait and patrol along the 100-fathom curve northeast of the Kangean Islands as part of the force then attempting to defend Java. On February 25 she reported two previous attacks with negative results, and stated that she had received a shell hit in her conning tower, which,

damaging the antenna trunk, made transmissions uncertain, but she could receive. On February 27, she sent a contact report on two cruisers and three destroyers. No further reports were received from her and she failed to arrive in Fremantle, her home port. The following account of what happened to *Perch* is taken from a statement made by her surviving commanding officer, who was repatriated at the end of hostilities, having been held by the enemy.

The last station assignment was given *Perch* on February 28, 1942, in the Java Sea. A large enemy convoy had been cruising about for several days, waiting to land on Java; now the objective had been discovered and submarines were to disregard their areas and attack at the landing point. Shortly after surfacing on the night of March 1, *Perch* sighted two destroyers, and dove. The commanding officer ordered 180 feet. At 90 to 100 feet, the destroyer passed over and dropped a string of depth charges; shortly thereafter *Perch* hit bottom at 147 feet. During the depth charge attacks that followed, the ship lost power on her port screw, but she managed to pull clear of the bottom and surface when depth charging had ceased. Shortly before dawn two Japanese destroyers again were sighted, and once more *Perch* went to the bottom, this time at 200 feet. Efforts to move from the bottom were unsuccessful, and the attackers continued depth charging until after daylight.

At dusk on March 2 *Perch* again surfaced, after an hour of effort. There was no enemy in sight. Reduction gears were in bad shape, there were serious electrical grounds and broken battery jars, and the engine room hatch leaked badly, so arrangements were made to scuttle if necessary. On trying to dive before sunrise on March 3, 1942, it was found that, due to the severe depth charge attacks she had been through, water poured in from conning tower and engine room hatches, and from leaks in the hull. Nothing the crew did seemed to help the leakage and, while further attempts were being made to repair the boat, three enemy destroyers came in sight and opened fire. The submarine's gun was inoperative and torpedoes could not be fired. Enemy depth charges had caused three of *Perch's* torpedoes to run in their tubes, and the heat, exhaust gases, and mounting nervous tension aggravated already extremely difficult conditions. The decision was made to abandon and scuttle her. The entire crew got into the water safely, and all were picked up by Japanese ships. The state of Japanese antisubmarine capabilities was made apparent by Lt. K. G. Schacht, a survivor of *Perch*, when stating "loss of air and oil during attacks caused both previous enemy groups to believe their target had been destroyed." Most of the personnel of *Perch* were taken to the illegal questioning camp at Ofuna, Japan, and then to the Ashio mines, where they were forced to work until the close of the war. Fifty-three of their number were received from the Japanese at the war's end. *Perch* was credited with sinking a 5,600-ton enemy freighter on her first patrol, conducted west of the Philippines.

Perch (SS-313)

Built by Electric Boat, *Perch* (SS-313) was the second submarine to bear this name. She was of the Balao class and was launched in September 1943. Many of the fleet submarines from World War II had long and useful lives following the war. More powerful batteries, streamlined conning towers and hull shapes, snorkel systems, and improved radar and sonar equipment extended the useful life of submarines built in the middle 1940s into the cold war years of the 1960s and 1970s. In addition to the GUPPY (Greater Underwater Propulsive Power) modernization programs, new or special missions sometimes required major modifications to the basic fleet boat, such as the addition of deck storage containers, missile launching equipment, or the removal of torpedo tubes and deck guns. *Perch* is just one example of fleet subs built during

World War II that continued their active service well into the era of the nuclear-powered submarine. Having fought in the 1940s, these boats once again found themselves on patrol in unfriendly waters during the major conflicts of the cold war, Korea and Vietnam.

First commissioned in January 1944, *Perch* operated out of Hawaii and Australia during World War II and was one of only two submarines to receive the Submarine Combat Patrol insignia during the Korean War. In the 1960s, *Perch* conducted special operations in Vietnam for which she again earned the Combat Patrol pin. She was decommissioned and struck from the Navy list in January 1971. She was named after the first *Perch*, which was lost on March 3, 1942, north of Surabaya during the navy's futile attempt to slow Japanese expansion at the beginning of the war.

Perch arrived in Hawaii in spring 1944 and completed five war patrols out of Pearl Harbor, in missions that took her to the Luzon Straits, the Philippine Sea, the East China Sea, the Java Sea, and the home waters of the Japanese Empire. Like many other "latecomer" boats in the Pacific theater, she found few targets this late in the war and was not credited with any sinkings.

Decommissioned on January 15, 1947, *Perch* underwent a dramatic conversion that would extend her usefulness to the navy for many years. She was stripped of all her torpedo tubes, and main engines one and two were removed. The forward engine room and the forward and aft torpedo rooms were now converted to berthing and equipment areas for up to 110 troops. Topside, on the afterdeck, a large, cylindrical watertight locker was added for storing inflatable boats and other equipment. All topside armament except two 40 millimeter cannon and two .50 caliber machine guns were removed, and the after deck was lengthened to provide more room for troop staging when on the surface. Recommissioned as a transport submarine, she looked so ungainly that she was derisively called the "Pregnant Perch." Her new mission: the transportation, landing, and recovery of an amphibious landing force. On June 25, 1950, the North Koreans invaded South Korea, and the cold war was suddenly hot. Korea was a long war. There was little enemy naval or air opposition. Even so, the role of the navy was as vital as ever. For the submarines assigned to Submarine Group, WESTPAC, there were no targets, no depth charge attacks as in the previous war. Submarine operations in support of the Korean War consisted primarily of shipping surveillance patrols, reconnaissance missions, limited amphibious landings and raiding operations, a few special missions, and ASW services to the fleet. During the Korean War, *Perch* was involved in commando and demolition raids along the coast.

With the beginning of America's involvement in the Vietnam War, *Perch* was readied once again for duties with the landing of reconnaissance, survey, or special forces teams, and thus became the first U.S. submarine ever to see active service in a third war! Given her special capabilities, *Perch* was very active during her tour of duty with Submarine Flotilla Seven (SUBFLOTSEVEN). Operating out of Subic Bay, in the Philippines, she was assigned various missions in support of underwater demolition team detachments. She carried out several covert beach reconnaissance missions in the Ben Goi area of South Vietnam in preparation for the amphibious landings of Operation Dagger Thrust, the first in a series of special operations that she would conduct through 1972.

Perch's active service spanned 27 years. Her participation in three wars, though exceptional, was not unique, for a handful of other boats, having survived World War II, found themselves on patrol in dangerous waters again during Korea and Vietnam. It was *Perch*'s special abilities that brought her "up close and personal" with the enemy. One boat, three wars—not a bad score.

Permit (SS-178)

Built by Electric Boat and launched October 5, 1936, *Permit* joined SubRon6 on December 18, 1937, spending the next 22 months cruising the eastern Pacific Ocean from southern California to the Aleutian and Hawaiian Islands.

After valuable training during peacetime operations, *Permit* conducted her first World War II war patrol December 11–20, 1941, off the west coast of Luzon. With the exception of embarking members of Admiral Hart's Asiatic Fleet staff and evacuating them to Java, her second and third war patrols were uneventful. On the fourth war patrol, beginning February 22, 1942, *Permit* rendezvoused off Corregidor, and on March 15–16, she enlisted men and landed ammunition on Corregidor and took onboard 40 officers. War patrols five and six passed uneventfully; number seven resulted in *Permit* attacking a nine-ship convoy off the coast of Honshu, Japan, sinking a 2,742-ton cargo ship. *Permit*'s eighth war patrol resulted in no sinkings; however, during number nine, she sank two more cargo ships.

In total, *Permit* had 14 war patrols. The last ended at Pearl Harbor. She was then refitted and sailed to the continental United States on January 29, 1945, to serve as a school boat for the Submarine School at New London/Groton, Connecticut.

Permit was decommissioned November 15, 1945, and sold to A. G. Schoonmaker of New York City on June 28, 1958, for $162,850 for subsequent scrapping.

Permit received 10 battle stars for her World War II service.

Permit (SSN-594)

The first of a new class of nuclear-propelled attack submarines, *Permit* (and her sister ship, *Thresher*) had a deep-diving capability (achieved with the use of HY-80 steel), quiet machinery, and large, bow-mounted sonar with their torpedo tubes amidships. The boats in this class had a displacement of 4,250 tons on the surface and 4,465 tons submerged, ranged from 278 to 292 feet in overall length, and carried crews of 13 officers and 114 enlisted men. They were armed with Harpoon SSM missiles, had four 21-inch torpedo tubes amidships, and were capable of laying mines.

Originally a class of 14 submarines, after the loss of the *Thresher* (SSN-593) these submarines were officially renamed the Permit class. The later submarines of this class were delayed for inspection and modification after the loss of *Thresher*. The *Dace* (SSN-607) was decommissioned in February 1988 and stricken in March 1989. The *Pollack* (SSN-603) was decommissioned in November 1988 and stricken in early 1989. The *Plunger* (SSN-595) was decommissioned in January 1989 and struck in January 1990. The *Barb* (SSN-596) and *Jack* (SSN-605) were stricken by the end of 1990. In October 1990, the navy decommissioned the *Permit* (SSN-594) and *Haddo* (SSN-604), and the *Tinosa* in January 1992. Other 1992 retirements were *Guardfish* (SSN-612), *Flasher* (SSN-613), *Greenling* (SSN-614), and *Haddock* (SSN-621). The *Gato*, last of the class, was decommissioned in April 1996.

Permit class (SSN)

NUCLEAR-PROPELLED ATTACK SUBMARINES

Number	Name	FY	Launched	Commissioned	Status
SSN-614	*Greenling*	60	1964	1967	Scrapped
SSN-615	*Gato*	60	1964	1968	Scrapped
SSN-621	*Haddock*	61	1966	1967	Scrapped

DESCRIPTION

These submarines established the basic design for subsequent U.S. Navy SSNs and SSBNs, having a deep-diving capability (achieved with the use of HY-80 steel), quiet machinery, and large, bow-mounted sonar with their torpedo tubes amidships. This class and later nuclear submarines have their turbines and related gearing mounted on a sound-isolated "raft" to reduce self-generated noises. While the concept is successful, it does increase the volume required for machinery and, hence, overall submarine size, with a resulting loss of speed. This class was credited with an operating depth of 1,300 feet, the same as the later Sturgeon class. In an effort to reduce underwater drag, the sail structure was kept to a minimum size, resulting in a reduction of masts and intelligence-collection capabilities.

CHARACTERISTICS

Displacement:

surface	3,780 tons
SSN-605	4,000 tons
SSN-613–615	4,250 tons
submerged	4,465 tons
SSN-613–615	4,770 tons

Dimensions:

length	278 ft. 5 in. overall
SSN-605	297 ft. 4 in.
SSN-613–615	292 ft. 3 in.
beam	31 ft. 8 in.
draft	28 ft. 10 in.

Propulsion:	2 steam turbines
Reactors:	1 pressurized-water S5W
Speed:	approximately 15 kts. surface
	approximately 30 kts. submerged
Manning:	127 (13 officers and 114 enlisted men)

Combat Systems:

missiles	Harpoon SSM launched from torpedo tubes
torpedo tubes	4 21-inch amidships Nk 63
ASN weapons	Mk 48 torpedoes
mines	capable of laying mines
radars	BPS-15 navigation/surface search/fire control

Sonars:	BQQ-5 bow-mounted
	BQS-11 active
	BQS-14 under ice/mine detection
	BQR-15 towed array
Fire control:	Mk 117 torpedo fire control

The *Thresher,* the lead ship of this class, was lost during post-overhaul deep-diving trials off the New England coast on April 10, 1963. All 112 naval personnel and 17 civilians on board were lost in what remains history's worst submarine disaster, as well as the first nuclear submarine loss.

Peto (SS-265)

Built by the Manitowoc Shipbuilding Company and launched in April 1942, this submarine of the Gato class had the unique experience of being loaded on a barge and transported to sea down the midwestern waterways to New Orleans. She was ordered to join the Pacific Fleet and arrived in Brisbane, Australia, in March 1943, leaving for her first war patrol two weeks later. This mission found no targets, but on her second patrol, in June and July, she sank an enemy auxiliary craft and caused severe damage to a tanker, and on her third, sank two freighters. In November and December, in the Solomons, she sank an escort vessel and transported marines to an embattled island; in February 1944, in the same region, she sank a transport and later a cargo ship. *Peto* had no more hits until September, when, assigned to the Yellow Sea region, she damaged one enemy vessel and sank two others. In November, she racked up three more victims, which proved to be her last. On her ninth and 10th patrols—her last—she was largely engaged in lifeguard duty, rescuing 12 downed pilots in all, one of them severely wounded. After the war, for which she received eight battle stars, *Peto* became a Naval Reserve training submarine and was decommissioned in August 1960. *Peto* was responsible for sinking seven vessels for 29,139 tons.

Philippine Sea, Battle of the (June 19–20, 1944)

A major naval battle of World War II, between the Japanese Combined Fleet and the U.S. Fifth Fleet. It accompanied the U.S. landing on Saipan and was known as "the greatest carrier battle of the war," ending in a complete U.S. victory. It began on the morning of June 19, when the Japanese sent more than 400 planes in four waves against ships under the command of Admiral Raymond Spruance. The result for the Japanese was a disaster. During the first day alone, the Japanese lost more than 200 planes and two carriers. Then, as their fleet retired northward toward safe harbor at Okinawa, it lost another carrier and nearly 100 more planes. During the two days of battle, U.S. losses totaled 130 aircraft and some damage to ships. One of the major weaknesses by the Japanese was the command decision to send into action many pilots who had only a few months of training, whereas many U.S. pilots had spent two full years in training. Another problem was that the Japanese planes, while highly maneuverable and more long-range than U.S. planes, were inferior in that they had inadequate armor protection and a lack of self-sealing fuel tanks. U.S. submarines played a major role by undertaking reconnaissance missions that provided U.S. commanders with intelligence of enemy movements and strategies for attacking and sinking Japanese ships.

Pickerel (SS-22) (F-3)

Built by Seattle Construction and Drydock Company and launched in March 1912, this submarine of the F-class was a boat of only 435 tons (submerged), armed with two 18-inch torpedo tubes in the bow and carrying a complement

During nine war patrols USS *Peto* (SS-265), shown above being launched, was credited with sinking seven large enemy ships totaling nearly 30,000 tons. *(United States Navy)*

of one officer and 21 enlisted men. She completed her trials in the Puget Sound area before reporting for duty with the First Submarine Group of the Pacific Torpedo Flotilla. The flotilla operated along the coast of California, conducting constant exercises and experiments to develop the techniques of submarine warfare and, from August 1914 to November 1915, carried out similar operations in the Hawaiian Islands. During maneuvers conducted on December 17, 1917, she collided with another submarine, *F-1, Carp* (SS-20) which sank almost immediately. *Pickerel,* along with other submarines with whom she was operating, rescued several *F-1* crew members. But 19 of *F-1's* crew went to the bottom with that ill-fated submarine. *Pickerel* suffered a cracked bow cap in that collision. After

repairs at the Mare Island Navy Yard, she was assigned operations in cooperation with a civilian motion picture company in experiments with underwater photography. From 1919 through 1921, she served at San Pedro as a training ship, and in March 1922 was decommissioned.

Pickerel (SS-177)

Built by Electric Boat and launched July 7, 1936, *Pickerel* was the first submarine to be lost in the central Pacific area. Setting out from Pearl Harbor on March 18, 1943, she topped off with fuel at Midway on March 22 and headed for her seventh war patrol off the eastern coast of Honshu. *Pickerel* was never heard from again and, to this

Pickerel (SS-524), a submarine of the Tench class, was launched in December 1944, but arrived in the Pacific too late for participation. She was one of the first submarines, however, to enter the Korean conflict, and was later loaned to the Italian navy. *(United States Navy)*

day, continues to be lost. It is likely that *Pickerel* was sunk by enemy depth charges. During her first six war patrols, *Pickerel* is credited with sinking eight enemy vessels and damaging 20 others.

Pickerel (SS-524)

Launched in December 1944, this submarine of the Tench class was assigned to the Pacific Fleet but arrived at her base after the war had ended and thus saw no enemy action. However, after deployment in the western Pacific, in 1949, *Pickerel* was converted to a GUPPY II at Portsmouth Naval Shipyard. She spent four months in the Korean War zone, one of the first submarines to enter the Korean conflict. Returning to Pearl Harbor in the spring of 1951, she operated in the Hawaiian area, undergoing tests of maximum capabilities and conducting intensive training until she returned to the Far East in July 1953. One of her tests, which gave light to a much publicized and highly dramatic photograph, was surfacing from a depth of 250 feet at flank (top) speed so that her bow broke the water with a surge of waves and spray at an angle of 48 degrees. (This was one of the forerunners of similar surfacing exploits, including the tragic one in which the nuclear submarine *Greeneville* collided with the hull of a Japanese vessel off Pearl Harbor on February 9,

2001, with the loss of nine lives in the stricken vessel, which sank within minutes.)

In 1962, *Pickerel* was converted to a GUPPY III at Pearl Harbor Naval Shipyard. In the fall of 1966 her duties were broadened to include operations in the Vietnam combat

The USS *Pickerel* (SS-524), conducting a large angle surfacing demonstration. *(United States Navy)*

zone. She was decommissioned and loaned to Italy in August 1972, where she served the Italian navy as *Primo Longobardo* (S-501).

Picuda (SS-382)

Built by Portsmouth Naval Shipyard and launched in July 1943 as a Balao-class submarine, *Picuda* got under way from Pearl Harbor for her first war patrol in mid-February 1944, setting course for waters off the Caroline Islands, and not far from Truk sank a 2,672-ton gunboat. In March, off Yap Island, she sent a 1,504-ton freighter to the bottom with two torpedo hits. Eleven days later, *Picuda* closed with two freighters under escort of two destroyers off the western coast of Yap and let go five torpedoes at the largest merchantman. The first hit stopped the target dead in the water and a second torpedo tore off the port quarter to capsize the 5,873-ton cargo ship. In early May, she joined *Perch* and *Peto* to form a wolf pack in waters off Formosa. She sank a 1,200-ton river gunboat and severely damaged a 3,172-ton cargo ship with the same salvo. On June 2, she closed with a convoy of 12 ships hugging the coast of Formosa, slipped between two of the three leading escorts, and pressed home an attack on a large tanker. Three hits were heard as all escorts made for *Picuda* and she had to dive deep and live out repeated depth charges from no fewer than eight enemy vessels.

Picuda in a wolf pack with *Spadefish* and *Redfish* departed Pearl Harbor for her third war patrol in late July, in waters of the Luzon Straits, and four weeks later spotted 10 ships hugging the coast. Slipping past five escorts, and with three enemy patrol planes overhead, she sent six torpedoes streaking to sink a 1,943-ton cargo ship, then maneuvered for a down-the-throat shot that sank a 1,270-ton pursuing enemy destroyer. She probed deeper in the Luzon Strait, in mid-September, for a daylight attack on an eight-ship convoy, guarded by three destroyers and air cover. She sank a 5,975-ton cargo ship and scored hits for unknown damage to two other freighters. Searching the southern border of her assigned patrol area, *Picuda* found another convoy hugging the north coast of Luzon a week later, and sent a 1,948-ton freighter to the bottom.

After forming a new wolf pack in late October 1944, *Picuda* set course to range over the northern waters of the East China Sea, where she sank a 9,433-ton passenger-cargo ship, and later a 6,933-ton cargoman and a 5,296-ton passenger-cargoman. In late December, she put to sea for fifth war patrol in the Formosa Straits and the East China Sea, where she closed with a convoy in the Straits of Formosa to inflict severe damage with four torpedo hits on a 10,045-ton tanker. In early January, she attacked another convoy and slipped between two escorts to pick out two large passenger-freighters. Three bow tubes fired at each target resulted in one hit on each. She swung and

fired stem shots at a tanker, then discovered an escort dead ahead, distance 700 yards, and so was forced to clear the area. A 2,854-ton coastal tanker, hit by both *Picuda* and *Barb,* which had joined her, was disabled and ran aground. Another freighter had a similar experience, and severe damage was inflicted on a 6,600-ton freighter, as well as on a 6,516-ton coastal tanker. *Picuda* then set course for lifeguard station in support of the Third Fleet air strikes on Formosa. In the early morning darkness of January 29, she made out at least three large ships in the rain and commenced tracking, finally getting another kill—a 5,497-ton passenger-cargo ship. In March and April 1945, *Picuda* spent much of her sixth war patrol on lifeguard station off the coast of China, where she assisted in rescuing five members of an army B-29 bomber.

Picuda received six battle stars for her war services, and was assigned to the East Coast for patrols and training. She was converted to GUPPY IIA in 1953 at Portsmouth Naval Shipyard, and assigned to the Atlantic Fleet, subsequently seeing duty in the Caribbean, the North Atlantic, the Mediterranean, and other areas. In 1972, she was decommissioned and sold to Spain, where she served under the name *Narciso Monturiol*. *Picuda* is credited with sinking 12 vessels for 49,539 tons during World War II.

Pike (SS-6) (A-5)

A submarine of the A-class and built by Union Iron Works, she was launched in January 1903—a small boat of 123 tons (submerged), with a single 18-inch torpedo tube in the bow and a crew of only one officer and six enlisted men. She was classified as a "submarine torpedo boat." She operated out of the Mare Island Naval Shipyard, and, following the earthquake in San Francisco on April 18, 1906, members of *Pike's* crew took part in the relief efforts in the wake of the disaster. She was assigned to the Pacific Torpedo Flotilla, operating off the Pacific coast, until the spring of 1915, when she was transferred aboard a collier to the Philippines, where she joined the Asiatic Fleet. During World War I, she patrolled the waters of Manila Bay. Although she had an accident when her main ballast tank leaked and she sank at her mooring, she was raised, refitted, and put back into service until July 1921, when she was decommissioned, ending her days as a target vessel.

Pike (SS-173)

Launched in September 1935, this submarine of the Porpoise class was the last full, double-hull, riveted submarine built for the navy and had old-style berthing and messing arrangements in the same space. The all-electric propulsion plants suffered from growing pains; the main motors flashed-over under load and had to be restricted to partial power until the generators and motor armatures could be rebuilt or replaced. The engines broke down frequently, and were ultimately replaced. In addition to other improvements, the "P" boats were also equipped with a fire control device, the Mark I Torpedo Data Computer (TDC), receiving data from the periscope or sonar on the enemy's bearing, range, and angle on the bow. The TDC automatically plotted the course of the target relative to the course of the submarine and computed and set the proper gyro angle in the torpedo. *Pike* was first assigned to San Diego, then Pearl Harbor, and then to the Philippines, where she joined the Asiatic Fleet in Manila, in December 1939. When World War II began, she was already in the heart of the action, having patrolled along the coast of China, as well as in the Philippines.

Pike got under way on her first war patrol on the very first day of the war, departing Manila Bay for the China Sea off Hong Kong. During the patrol no aircraft were sighted, although several junks were encountered and avoided. One enemy ship was sighted, but a submerged torpedo attack failed to damage her. *Pike* got under way from Manila Bay in late December 1941, on her second war patrol, and although enemy ships were sighted, they were either too distant or too well protected by air cover to make an attack. Her third patrol was equally fruitless, jeopardized somewhat by the problem of recognizing which foreign vessels were friendly or enemy. During this patrol, *Pike* suffered damage from depth charges dropped by a Japanese destroyer and returned to her base at Fremantle. Her fourth war patrol resulted in no sinkings, and on her fifth patrol, north of the Hawaiian Islands in late May 1942, she helped to guide American bombers to Wake Island during the battle of Midway. Afterward, *Pike* was ordered to the Mare Island Shipyard in California for badly needed overhaul and extensive modernization, so she did not return to Pearl Harbor until the end of December 1942, for her sixth war patrol, off the coast of Honshu Island. While preparing for an attack on three ships, she herself was attacked by a destroyer and forced to dive deep. She was then subjected to an extremely severe depth charge attack, which forced her to return to Pearl Harbor. Her seventh war patrol was more successful when, off Truk Island, she attacked a convoy and was credited with damaging 7,000-ton and 5,000-ton freighters. But, once again, a depth charge attack inflicted so much damage on *Pike* that she was forced to return to port for repairs. Her eighth war patrol resulted in the sinking of a 2,022-ton Japanese cargo ship, after which *Pike* spotted the enemy aircraft carrier *Otaka* the first week in August. A submerged torpedo attack was made and two torpedoes were heard to hit. A resulting depth charge attack by a destroyer prevented verification of the hits and of any damage made. Two weeks later, she scored two hits on a ship in a convoy, but again, a forced dive made it impossible

to judge whether the enemy vessel had been sunk. Later, however, *Pike* was credited with sinking one passenger-cargo vessel of 2,022 tons and damaging an auxiliary aircraft carrier of 22,500 tons, a freighter of 1,992 tons, and a second freighter of 4,000 tons.

Upon completion of her eighth war patrol, *Pike* was considered to have done more than her share of action for a submarine of her vintage, and she was deployed to New London, Connecticut, in November 1943 to serve as a training boat for future submariners. She later was deployed to Baltimore, Maryland, as a Naval Reserve training ship, and was decommissioned in February 1956.

Pilotfish (SS-386)

A submarine of the Balao class and built by Portsmouth Naval Shipyard she was launched in August 1943 and deployed to the Pacific, where she embarked on her first patrol in company with sister ships *Pintado* and *Shark,* in the area west of the Mariana Islands. After a week the group sailed to an area south of Formosa and patrolled across a probable route of reinforcement or retirement of the Japanese force engaged in the battle of the Philippine Sea. *Pilotfish* departed on her second war patrol, to the Bonin Islands area, in late July, mainly on lifeguard duty, and on her third patrol, in the same area, torpedoed and damaged a 4,000-ton cargo ship. She completed three more patrols before the end of the war, mainly on lifeguard duty, and rendezvoused with other navy ships in Tokyo harbor to participate in the initial occupation of Japan and the formal surrender ceremonies. She saw little peacetime service and was decommissioned in August 1946. *Pilotfish* received five battle stars for World War II service.

Pintado (SS-387)

Built by the Portsmouth Naval Shipyard and launched in September 1943, this submarine of the Balao class was deployed to the Pacific in the spring of 1944 and on her first war patrol, served as flagship of a wolf pack, which also included the submarines *Shark* and *Pilotfish.* Departing Pearl Harbor in May and headed for waters west of the Marianas and south of Formosa, they formed a scouting line in search of a convoy reported by submarine *Silversides.* After sparring with the convoy's escorts, *Pintado* fired a spread of six torpedoes at overlapping targets, destroying a 4,716-ton cargo ship. She then daringly came within 700 yards of an escort while bringing her stem tubes to bear on another merchant ship. Although explosions suggested that some of the second spread of torpedoes had scored, no second sinking has been confirmed. On June 4, *Pintado* spotted smoke from a Japanese convoy heading toward Saipan. She and her sister subs headed for the enemy, and soon *Shark* sank a 6,886-ton cargo ship before slipping away from a heavy depth-charge attack. The U.S. submarines continued to shadow the convoy, and early the next day *Shark*'s torpedoes accounted for two more cargo ships.

Pintado made her kills shortly before noon of June 6 (D-day in Normandy), with a spread of torpedoes at overlapping targets. An awesome explosion tore one ship apart, her bow and stem both projecting up in the air as she sank. The stem of a second was underwater before she was swallowed by smoke and flame. These victims were later identified as a 5,652-ton and a 2,825-ton marus. An airplane and five escorts tried to box in the submarine and dropped more than 50 depth charges, but she escaped damage. *Pintado* and her sisters in the wolf pack had all but destroyed the convoy, which was attempting to reinforce Japanese defenses of the Marianas before heading back to base.

Her second war patrol took the submarine to the East China Sea. On August 6, she sank a 5,401-ton cargo ship and damaged another target in a Formosa-bound convoy before escaping a downpour of exploding depth charges. On August 22, *Pintado* spotted an 11-ship convoy guarded by three escorts. After dark she moved into the center of the convoy, passing a scant 75 yards from an escort, to attack a former whale factory ship. Two spreads of torpedoes from the submarine left the monster ablaze and sinking, and damaged two other tankers. One victim, *Tonan Maru* was one of the largest merchant ships sunk by an American submarine during World War II. Following lifeguard station duty off Japan, *Pintado* returned to Pearl Harbor on June 14.

Pintado's third war patrol was again a wolf pack operation that this time included sister ships *Atule* and *Jallao*. The group departed Pearl Harbor in early October 1944, heading for the South China Sea. Meanwhile, General MacArthur was preparing to return to the Philippines. When his troops landed on Leyte, the Japanese navy struck back with all its force in a "go-for-broke" attempt to smash the invasion. The result was the decisive Battle of Leyte Gulf. As the U.S. Navy turned back the three prongs of the Japanese offensive, the wolf pack sped toward Luzon Strait to attack the Northern Japanese Force which Admiral Halsey's fleet had engaged off Cape Engano. On the night of October 25, *Jallao* made radar contact with a bomb-damaged light cruiser fleeing from Halsey, launching seven torpedoes, and the light cruiser broke up and went to the bottom. In early November, a bonus came when *Pintado*'s periscope revealed "the largest enemy ship . . . ever seen"—apparently an oiler in the support group for the Japanese carriers. *Pintado* fired six bow torpedoes at the huge target, but an enemy destroyer crossed their path before they could reach their target. The destroyer disintegrated in a tremendous explosion that provided an effective smoke screen protecting the

original target until the two remaining Japanese escorts forced the submarine to dive and withdraw to escape exploding depth charges. *Pintado* joined submarine *Halibut* on November 14 and escorted the damaged submarine to Saipan, arriving five days later. After a week in port, she resumed her war patrol south of Saipan, sinking two enemy landing craft and an unidentified ship before heading for port in Brisbane. In late January 1945, she departed Brisbane but found no targets as she patrolled the Singapore-Saigon shipping lanes. Throughout the patrol, she played hide-and-seek with Japanese aircraft and on February 20, barely escaped when a plane appeared from the clouds and dropped two depth charges that jarred the submarine. She made temporary repairs and continued to patrol until returning to Fremantle at the end of March. *Pintado* sailed to Pearl Harbor before getting underway the first week in June for her fifth war patrol on lifeguard station for bomber raids on Tokyo. On June 26, just south of Honshu, a smoking B-29 bomber crossed her bow at about 2,000 feet, dropped a dozen parachutes, and exploded. In less than an hour, the submarine had rescued the entire crew, whom she took safely to Guam two weeks later. Her sixth and last war patrol was cut short, off Tokyo Bay, when the war ended. Her peacetime career was that of an auxiliary submarine in the Pacific Reserve Fleet, where she served until being struck from the navy in March 1967. *Pintado* received five battle stars for her war service, during which she sank eight vessels for a total of 42,956 tons.

Pintado (SSN-672)

Launched in August 1969 and built by Mare Island Naval Shipyard the second navy ship to bear the name, *Pintado* was an attack submarine of the Sturgeon class. She began her first operational deployment to the U.S. Seventh Fleet in the western Pacific in late October 1972, and later became the first submarine to launch the Harpoon missile. From September to November 1978, she operated under the polar ice, surfacing at the North Pole. A year later, she deployed to the Indian Ocean and supported Carrier Battle Groups Alpha and Bravo during the early weeks of the Iranian hostage crisis. She again deployed to the western Pacific from February to August 1991. Three years later, she returned to the Arctic Ocean, operating under the polar ice from September to November 1984, in company with the *Gurnard* (SSN-662), where they became the third pair of submarines to surface together at the North Pole. From July 1985 to January 1986, she completed her fifth operational deployment to the United States Seventh Fleet, during which she steamed over 33,000 miles and conducted numerous fast-paced and highly successful operations. *Pintado* surfaced at the North Pole for the third time in June 1987, during arduous Arctic operations extending from May to July. Five years later, she conducted her fourth arctic operation, also marking her 1,000th dive. She surfaced at the North Pole for an unprecedented fourth time in September 1992, and returned to Pearl Harbor in November after circumnavigating North America and steaming over 20,000 miles. In 1996, *Pintado* conducted her sixth and final deployment to the western Pacific. She was decommissioned and struck from the Navy list in February 1998.

Pioneer

A Confederate submarine, *Pioneer* was designed to attack Union shipping. Construction began late in 1861, and within a few months *Pioneer* underwent trials in Lake Pontchartrain, Louisiana, during which she managed to sink a barge with a bomb towed behind the submarine. *Pioneer* never went into action against Union shipping, however, because she was scuttled when New Orleans was evacuated. *Pioneer* was some 20 feet long, six feet wide, and four feet deep. A stern propeller, cranked by hand, provided propulsion. She was the handiwork of a team that included James R. McClintock, Baxter Watson, and Horace L. Hunley, who also collaborated on two other submarines for the Confederacy. After the loss of *Pioneer,* the three men began work on a submarine equipped with a battery-powered electrical engine. The technology of the 1860s was inadequate for building such a system, however, and so the design had to be changed in favor of a clumsy hand-powered drive. This vessel was swamped and sank while under tow. After several other failures, they devised another hand-powered submersible, which later was to be referred to as the *Hunley.* She was a death trap and drowned several crews before going on to glory and sinking the Union corvette *Housatonic* off Charleston on February 17, 1864.

Pioneers

(As listed by the Naval Historical Center)

John Holland   Holland, a schoolteacher born in Ireland, designed the navy's first submarine, the *Holland VI,* which the navy purchased on April 11, 1900, and commissioned as USS *Holland* (SS-1) on October 12, 1900.

Simon Lake   Lake competed with John Holland to build the navy's first submarine. Although the navy did not purchase Lake's submarine, *Protector,* it used some of Lake's inventions in its submarines.

Charles A. Morris   Morris, a New Jersey engineer, helped John Holland design the *Holland VI.* He served as shipyard superintending engineer during the construction of the *Holland VI.*

Rear Admiral William W. Kimball, USN (Retired)   Kimball was one of the first officers assigned to the Naval Torpedo Station, Newport, Rhode Island. As an ordnance lieutenant, he worked to bring Holland's submarine plans to the attention of senior navy officials.

Elihu Frost   Frost provided the early financial backing that allowed Holland to build his prototype submarine. He helped incorporate the Holland Torpedo Boat Company.

Isaac Rice   Rice was president of the Electro-Dynamic Company, which made the batteries for *Holland VI.* He merged the Electro-Dynamic Company with the Holland Torpedo Boat Company, to form the Electric Boat Company.

Arthur L. Busch   Busch was chief constructor at the Crescent Shipyard in Elizabethport, New Jersey, when he met John P. Holland in 1896. Busch became construction supervisor for the building of *Holland VI,* and subsequently supervised construction of *Fulton,* the prototype for the A-class submarines.

August Busch   Busch, a St. Louis industrialist, bought the American rights to Rudolf Diesel's engine patents. His Busch-Sulzer Company made most of the navy's early diesel engines.

Charles Creecy   Creecy, a Washington attorney, was legal counsel to the Holland Torpedo Boat Company. His lobbying efforts helped win submarine construction contracts for the company.

Frank Cable   Cable, a Philadelphia engineer, served as test captain for the submarine *Holland* during her initial sea trials. Cable repaired the *Holland V's* motors after she sank at pierside in 1897.

Captain John T. Lowe, USN (Retired)   Lowe helped navigate the submarine *Holland* during the final series of tests that persuaded the navy to purchase the submarine. He then wrote the final test report recommending that the navy purchase the submarine. He also spent 15 hours submerged during an endurance test.

Commander Harry H. Caldwell, USN (Retired)   Caldwell, the navy's first submarine commanding officer, assumed command of USS *Holland* (SS-1) on October 6, 1900. Caldwell also served on the staff of Admiral George Dewey.

Lawrence York (L.Y.) Spear   Spear was superintendent of construction at the Crescent Shipyard where the navy's first five submarines were built. He graduated from the U.S. Naval Academy and served six years before resigning his commission. He was president of the Electric Boat Company during World War II.

Rear Admiral Yates Stirling, Jr., USN (Retired)   Stirling was chairman of the navy's Submarine Standardization Board in 1917 when the navy designed its first mass production of submarines, the S-class. He played a major role in submarine design and construction during the 1920s.

Admiral Thomas C. Hart, USN (Retired)   Hart, director of submarines in the office of the chief of naval operations after World War I, chaired the postwar U-Boat Plans Committee. The committee called for building long-range cruiser submarines capable of operating in the Pacific Ocean. These ideas were the genesis of the World War II fleet boat submarines.

Vice Admiral Emory S. Land, USN (Retired)   Land, a naval architect, specialized in submarine construction. He was vice chairman of the post–World War I U-Boat Plans Committee and played a major role in designing the S-class submarines during World War I.

Rear Admiral Thomas Withers, USN (Retired)   Withers proposed in February 1928 that U.S. submarines should be independent raiders, rather than operating with the battle fleet, during any war in the Pacific. He was the first commander of Submarine Force Pacific Fleet, following the Japanese attack on Pearl Harbor.

Rear Admiral Allan R. McCann, USN (Retired)   McCann developed the submarine rescue chamber or diving bell that was used to rescue 33 crewmen from the sunken USS *Squalus* (SS-192) in May 1939. McCann commanded a submarine squadron during World War II.

Vice Admiral Charles B. Momsen, USN (Retired)   Momsen invented the "Momsen lung" submarine escape apparatus that allowed submariners to escape from sunken submarines. More than eight submariners used their "Momsen lungs" to escape from the USS *Tang* (SS-306) in the East China sea in October 1944. Momsen commanded two submarine squadrons during World War II.

Vice Admiral Charles A. Lockwood, USN (Retired)   Lockwood was commander of Submarine Force Pacific Fleet from 1943 to 1945. He provided the leadership to a submarine force that sank more than 50 percent of Japan's merchant ships and warships during World War II.

Admiral Hyman G. Rickover, USN (Retired)   Rickover, an engineering duty officer, served as director of naval reactors from 1949 to 1982. He provided the major impetus behind the development of nuclear-powered submarines and surface ships.

Vice Admiral William F. Raborn, Jr., USN (Retired)   Raborn, a naval aviator, directed the Polaris submarine-launched ballistic missile program. Raborn accomplished his mission in five years, rather than the expected 10 years.

Vice Admiral Eugene P. Wilkinson, USN (Retired)   Wilkinson was the first commanding officer of the USS *Nautilus* (SSN-571), the world's first nuclear-powered submarine. He developed many of the early tactics for nuclear-powered submarines. He was awarded the Silver Star during World War II.

Captain William Anderson, USN (Retired)   Anderson commanded the submarine USS *Nautilus* (SSN-571) during the submarine's epic voyage from the Pacific Ocean to the Atlantic Ocean under the North Pole in 1958. Anderson was awarded the Bronze Star during World War II.

Captain Edward L. Beach, USN (Retired)   Beach commanded the nuclear-powered submarine USS *Tilton* (SSN-586) during her 83-day submerged voyage around the world. Beach has written many histories and novels about the navy and submarine warfare. He was awarded the Navy Cross during World War II.

Vice Admiral James F. Calvert, USN (Retired)   Calvert commanded the nuclear-powered submarine USS *Skate* (SSN-578) when she surfaced at the North Pole in February 1959. He pioneered many arctic submarine tactics during his command of the *Skate*. Calvert was awarded the Silver Star and the Bronze Star during World War II.

Pipefish (SS-388)

A submarine of the Balao class built by the Portsmouth Naval Shipyard and launched in October 1943, she was ordered to join the Pacific Fleet, and left on her first war patrol in late May 1944. Cruising west of the Marianas, as a rescue submarine for pre-invasion carrier strikes on Saipan, she saved an American pilot and also cruised in the Surigao Straits sector to block Japanese escape from the battle of the Philippine Sea. On her second war patrol, in August and September, she patrolled off the southeastern coast of Honshu, sinking one enemy ship, but also barely avoiding disaster when, trying to evade escorts after that attack, she struck bottom three times before escaping. Her third through sixth patrols, off Taiwan and

China, resulted in only one small sinking, though she provided rescue capability for B-29 strikes, and saved eight aviators in May and June. After the war, she joined the Pacific Reserve Fleet, and was struck from the Navy list in March 1967. *Pipefish* received six battle stars for World War II service.

Piper (SS-409)

Although built late in World War II by the Portsmouth Naval Shipyard and launched in June 1944, this submarine of the Balao class was able to complete three successful war patrols before the cessation of hostilities, operating as a lifeguard for plane strikes and as an advance picket for fast carrier task forces. She began her war career in late January 1945, when she slipped out of Pearl Harbor as the leader of a five-ship wolf pack. The mission was an antipicket boat sweep in preparation for carrier strikes on Honshu. After a short stop at Saipan, the pack arrived in the assigned area south of Iwo Jima February 10. Three sweeps from February 10 to 13 revealed no picket boats. *Piper* spent February and March off the south and southeast coasts of Honshu serving alternately on independent patrol and lifeguard duty for the intensive B-29 and carrier strikes against Japan. On the night of February 25, she found her first target and, in a night surface attack, sank a 2,000-ton Japanese vessel. The last four days before departure were spent guarding the approaches to Bungo Suido against a possible Japanese sortie on the American aircraft carrier USS *Franklin,* which had been damaged by enemy action. *Piper* departed in late April for her second war patrol in another wolf pack, this time in the Sea of Okhotsk, making concentrated surface shipping sweeps of the area. In late May, she got her first chance on this patrol when she sighted two small merchantmen with two escorts in Boussole Channel. Working her way through a heavy fog, she launched a surface torpedo attack, sinking one 4,000-ton merchantman. In mid-July 1945, she departed on her third war patrol, accounting for two small vessels and rescuing six American prisoners of war, just a day before Japan capitulated. During the next few years, *Piper* served on the East Coast, out of New London, and in the Caribbean except for tours of duty with the U.S. Sixth Fleet in the Mediterranean. In 1951, *Piper* was converted to a Fleet Snorkel submarine at Charleston Naval Shipyard. She was also fitted with an AN/BQR-4 passive sonar. In the fall of 1962 she was deployed in the Caribbean area during the Cuban Missile Crisis. She later saw duty again in the Mediterranean and in other European waters. By the spring of 1967, she was decommissioned finally, having made 13,724 dives, a record for commissioned submarines. She received four battle stars for service in World War II.

Piranha (SS-389)

Built by the Portsmouth Naval Shipyard and launched in October 1943, this submarine of the Balao class was ordered to the Pacific and made her first war patrol in June and July 1944, along with sister boats *Guardfish, Thresher,* and USS *Apogon.* The coordinated attack group prowled waters west and north of Luzon, striking with notable success at Japanese convoys. *Piranha's* victims were two passenger-cargo ships, one of 6,504 tons, and another of 5,773 tons, sunk four days later. For the first part of her second patrol, she joined nine other submarines in offensive reconnaissance covering the Third Fleet during the assault on Peleliu in September. When that base, essential for the liberation of the Philippines, had been seized, *Piranha's* group dissolved and she searched for targets westward, but found no more targets. During her third war patrol, again with an attack group, besides seeking targets in the East China Sea from mid-November to mid-January 1945, she served as lifeguard during B-29 strikes on Kyushu and scored two hits on a merchantman. In mid-February she sailed for her fourth war patrol, a classic exhibition of submarine versatility. With her attack group she sought targets on the convoy lanes from Luzon to Formosa and Hong Kong, spent 17 days on lifeguard during air strikes on Formosa, sank an enemy vessel serving as an aircraft spotter, and bombarded a Japanese naval base with 100 five-inch shells. With the decimated Japanese merchant marine hugging its own coast, *Piranha* was frequently frustrated by shallow water and omnipresent escorts in her attacks. Hair-raising encounters with submarine chasers and aircraft were rendered more dangerous by being fought so close offshore where she had little water depth for maneuver. But her persistence and courage paid off; she heavily damaged a freighter, sank a coastal tanker, and destroyed three trawlers by gunfire. Her final patrol lasted only one day, aborted when the Japanese surrender was announced. She had little peacetime service, being placed in reserve and finally, in March 1967, being decommissioned. Her conning tower is preserved at the Fleet Admiral Chester W. Nimitz Memorial Naval Museum at Fredericksburg, Texas. *Piranha* received five battle stars for World War II service.

Plaice (SS-390)

Built by the Portsmouth Naval Shipyard and launched in November 1943, this submarine of the Balao class was underway for the Canal Zone in mid-April 1944 when, while submerged off the Virginia Capes, a series of distant underwater explosions was heard. A dispatch then arrived telling of the sinking of a Victory ship in the vicinity. On the following day, while making a routine dive, the officer of the day sighted a periscope and the soundman reported echo ranging. The crew hustled to battle stations but no further contact was made. This was believed to be an enemy submarine and the first contact of many with the enemy. After arriving in Pearl Harbor and completing a two-week training period, *Plaice* departed to meet the enemy on June 3, 1944, heading for an area off Chichi Jima. There she was successful in sinking two freighters for a total of 8,000 tons, one transport at 9,500 tons; and one destroyer at 1,360 tons. She had a successful second patrol as well, accounting for 10,600 tons of enemy shipping and damaging 36,400 tons, including an enemy battleship. She then damaged two enemy destroyers on her third patrol in November 1944, and a 4,400-ton cargo ship on her fourth, in March 1945. Her fifth and sixth patrols were too close to the end of the war to net anything but small vessels, but she did rescue five downed air force pilots. She was placed in reserve until 1963 when she was sold to the Brazilian navy for training in submarine warfare. Her name was changed to *Bahia* and she retired from active service in the Brazilian navy in 1973 at which time she became a museum ship in Santos, Brazil. *Plaice* was awarded five battle stars for her service during World War II.

Plunger (A-1)

The second submarine built by John Holland for the U.S. Navy, she was built by the Crescent Shipyard in Elizabethport, New Jersey, and commissioned in 1903. She was cigar-shaped, like earlier Holland designs, was 85 feet long by 12 feet in diameter at her widest girth, displaced only 168 tons, and was armed with five Whitehead torpedoes, which could be fired through either of two forward tubes. She was too unreliable, however, and could be held on course only with difficulty; she never saw active service in the navy. By contrast, a later *Plunger* (SSN-595) was a navy submarine of 3,500 tons (submerged), built by the Mare Island Naval Shipyard, where she was commissioned in

Polaris (A-1) submarine-launched ballistic missile (SLBM) surfacing after being launched from the nuclear submarine, *Abraham Lincoln*, in tests that showed its capability of zeroing in on targets more than 1,000 miles away. *(United States Navy)*

November 1962, and was designed for a complement of nine officers and 76 enlisted men.

Plunger (SSN-595)

A submarine of the Thresher/Permit class, and named after one of the navy's very early submarines (1903), Plunger was built at the Mare Island Shipyard and launched in December 1961. She had a displacement (submerged) of 3,500 tons, was armed with four 21-inch torpedo tubes, and was designed for a complement of 100 officers and enlisted men. She had an active career in the Pacific without incident until a fateful winter day when, on December 1, her captain, Commander Alvin B. Wilderman, was swept overboard from the bridge, off San Francisco. Since he had cleared the bridge of other officers and men, who were endangered, to stand duty alone in freezing high seas, he was posthumously awarded the Meritorious Service Medal. *Plunger* served for 29 years and was decommissioned in January 1990.

Polaris

The U.S. Polaris submarine-launched ballistic missile (SLBM) was the product of a successful navy weapons

The USS *A-1* (SS-2), was originally laid down as USS *Plunger* (Submarine Torpedo Boat #2). *(United States Navy)*

Polaris (A-1) launch circa 1960. *(United States Navy)*

development program. Although succeeded by the Poseidon and Trident SLBMs, the Polaris was a giant step forward in the perfection of undersea weaponry. Its development began in late 1955 after the navy had attempted to join the U.S. Army in the perfection of the liquid-propellant Jupiter missile for shipboard use. The Polaris design was based on the availability of improved solid-propellant motors and small nuclear warhead technology. The development of the Polaris was especially remarkable for the short time it took to perfect the new missile, submarine inertial navigation systems, and operational concepts. The initial Polaris A-1 missile was deployed for the first time in November 1960, in the submarine *George Washington,* followed by 40 additional submarines, each carrying 16 missiles, being deployed by 1967. The successive A-2 and A-3 missiles provided additional range, with the A-3 carrying a multiple reentry vehicle (MRV) payload with three warheads that could be shotgunned onto the same target to increase damage.

Pomfret (SS-391)

A submarine of the Balao class and built by Portsmouth Naval Shipyard, *Pomfret* was launched in October 1943 and left Pearl Harbor on her first patrol, heading for East Kyushu and Bungo Suido, in July 1944, but scored no hits until her second patrol in October, when she sank a 6,962-ton passenger-cargo vessel in the South China Sea. After refit and training, *Pomfret* reentered the same patrol area in November as part of a wolf pack and sank two passenger-cargo vessels, one of 7,347 tons and another of 5,271 tons (and later another of the same size). She began her fourth patrol in late January 1945, in another wolf pack. The mission was a picket boat sweep ahead of a carrier task force soon to strike the Tokyo-Nagoya area. After completing the sweep without encountering any picket boats, she

moved south of Honshu for lifeguard work, where she rescued a pilot from the aircraft carrier *Hornet* and, the next day, one from the carrier *Cabot.* That day she also captured two prisoners and in late March returned to her base at Midway. Her next sortie had few results and she departed on her final patrol the first week in July. After lifeguard duty south of Honshu, she began patrol in the East China Sea. On July 19 she sank the first of 44 floating mines. On July 24, she shelled the Kuskaki Jima lighthouse and radio installations, and on July 26 she destroyed a three-masted junk and a small schooner. On August 8 she rescued the entire five-man crew of a B-25 bomber. *Pomfret* continued to shell small craft and pick up Japanese and Korean survivors until the cessation of hostilities, August 15, and the same day headed for Guam to deliver the survivors. After the war, she was involved in the Philippines in antisubmarine warfare exercises, and then along the West Coast until February 1951, when she was called upon to participate in the Korean action. *Pomfret* was converted to a GUPPY IIA at Mare Island Naval Shipyard in 1953, after which she was again involved in antisubmarine warfare exercises in the late 1960s. She was struck from the Navy list and transferred to Turkey in July 1971. *Pomfret* received five battle stars for World War II service and is credited with sinking four vessels for a total of 20,936 tons.

Pomodon (SS-486)

A submarine of the Tench class, she was launched in June 1945, too late to see action in World War II. She was deployed to the Panama Canal Zone for training and, in July 1947, to San Diego to begin operations in the area as part of Task Forces 52 and 56. She was converted to a GUPPY I submarine at Mare Island Naval Shipyard in 1947 and upgraded to a GUPPY II in 1951, the first of its type in the Pacific Fleet. At the outbreak of hostilities in Korea in July 1950, *Pomodon* was deployed to Pearl Harbor, and in November 1951 ordered on a six-month deployment with the United Nations Forces resisting communist aggression in Korea, followed by operations in the San Diego area. During the next decade, *Pomodon* made six more deployments, bolstering the forces of freedom in the Far East. Her next major deployment was with the Seventh Fleet, from June through November 1966, which took her to Vietnamese waters where she operated with American destroyers and the carrier USS *Kearsarge.* Training operations on the West Coast and overhaul at Hunter's Point Division, San Francisco Naval Shipyard, filled 1967. She again headed west across the Pacific for her ninth deployment in May 1968. *Pomodon* was equipped with the unique prototype "silent snorkel" engine in the late 1960s. She operated in Japanese waters, off Okinawa, and in the Philippines before entering the Vietnam combat zone in mid-August. She was decommissioned and struck from the Navy list in August 1970.

Pompano (SS-181)

A submarine of the Perch class and built by Mare Island Naval Shipyard, she was launched in March 1937, and in the years preceding World War II operated out of Mare Island, California, ranging the West Coast of the United States, training her crew, and patrolling in a constant state of readiness. Although *Pompano* was awarded a battle star for the Pearl Harbor raid, she had not yet arrived from Mare Island. Reaching port shortly after the disastrous strike, she sailed December 18, 1941, for her first war patrol, devoted mainly to reconnoitering the eastern Marshall Islands for a carrier raid in January. Planes from the American flattops bombed the submarine by mistake, but she escaped damage. Soon afterward, she sighted several large enemy ships protected by patrol craft in the harbor at Wotje. On January 13, one of the large vessels came out. *Pompano* fired four torpedoes, scoring two hits, and the vessel broke up. Four days later, when one of the patrol boats steamed out of the harbor, *Pompano* worked her way between this enemy and the channel. Both torpedoes exploded prematurely, foiling her first attack. On her next patrol, undertaken in Japanese home waters, *Pompano* was able to attack five vessels successfully, sinking a total of 16,500 tons. On her next patrol, in April and May, she ranged the steamer lanes west of Okinawa and in the East China Sea. Shipping was scarce, but on May 24 she caught a large sampan and sent it down with gunfire. On the next day, she torpedoed a tanker, which exploded and sank. As she shifted her patrol to the main route between Japan and the Indies, she sighted and sank a large, 7,983-ton transport. In mid-July, she headed for Japan on her third war patrol, and began patrolling within four miles of the coast. After being depth charged so severely that she was springing leaks in the engine room, she eventually escaped, and sank an attacking destroyer and freighter. Later she ran close enough to the enemy coast to sink a Japanese patrol boat with gunfire, before returning to base. Her fourth war patrol started in mid-January 1943, during which she damaged three tankers. Her next two patrols were unsuccessful, partly because of severe weather conditions, but mainly because of a lack of targets.

Pompano left Midway August 20, bound for the coasts of Hokkaido and Honshu. She was never heard from again. When no transmission was received from her, especially just prior to her expected arrival at Midway the first week in October, she was reported as presumed lost in enemy waters. The Japanese knew that she was in their area, however, for two ships fell to her torpedoes during September: a 5,600-ton cargo-carrier on September 3, and a 2,958-ton cargo carrier on September 25. Japanese information available showed no attack on a submarine in her estimated location. So, in view of the evidence given, it is considered probable that *Pompano* met her end by an enemy mine. She received seven battle stars for service in World War II and is credited with sinking 5 vessels for 21,443 tons.

Pompon (SS-267)

Built by Manitowoc Shipbuilding Company this submarine of the Gato class was launched in August 1942 and was ordered to Brisbane, Australia, from which she departed on July 10, 1943, to conduct her first war patrol in the Truk area. Only a few days out, a Japanese submarine fired two torpedoes at her, both passing ahead. Besides patrolling off Truk, she formed a scouting line with other submarines to cover Seventh Fleet operations. In late July she torpedoed a 5,871-ton cargo ship, and damaged a second transport and a smaller transport. Her second through fourth patrols were relatively uneventful, resulting in the sinking of two small vessels and the mining of enemy waters southwest of Cochin, China. On her fifth patrol, off the coasts of Kyushu, Shikoku, and Honshu in June 1944, she sank a cargo ship, and on her sixth and most successful patrol, operating from the eastern coast of Honshu to the Sea of Okhotsk, she sank a 300-ton armed trawler with gunfire. Then on August 12 she spotted a Japanese convoy off the coast of Russian Sakhalin. In the wild night surface action that followed, an 8,000-ton tanker was badly damaged by two torpedoes, a 2,718-ton transport was sunk, and a hit was possibly obtained on one of two hotly pursuing escort vessels. During this melee, *Pompon* was almost sunk by one of her own torpedoes. While she was surfaced, with the enemy bearing down, one of her own "fish" perversely circled and just missed the stern. She was driven down by gunfire and then depth charged, but managed to escape without damage. Her seventh patrol was almost a disaster. While sailing with a wolf pack in the Yellow Sea in January 1945, she assisted other submarines in making kills, but had none of her own. Then, while making a morning trim dive, the conning tower hatch failed. Before the dive could be halted, *Pompon* reached a depth of 44 feet, partially flooding the conning tower and control room, and completely flooding the pump room. She had to creep homeward, having to run awash on the surface until the flooding could be lessened. While struggling along in this condition, she blundered into an enemy convoy and was sighted. The escorts forced her to dive despite her dangerous condition, but she miraculously escaped. Fortunately a sister ship, *Pogy,* helped to divert the enemy, and then led her safely to a base at Midway. *Pompon*'s last two patrols were largely engaged in lifeguard duty, during which she transported 10 survivors from a downed plane to safety and found the hunting poor just as the war ended. She was ordered to the East Coast and placed in the Atlantic Reserve Fleet, then reassigned to the Sixth Fleet in February 1954. In the 1950s she was converted to a Migraine III radar picket submarine. She operated in the Atlantic, the Caribbean, and the Mediterranean, and was decommissioned and struck from the Navy list in April 1960. *Pompon* earned four battle stars for World War II service and is credited with sinking three vessels for 8,772 tons.

Porpoise (SS-7) (A-6)

Built by the Crescent Shipyard, Elizabethport, New Jersey, and launched in September 1901, this early submarine of the A class displaced only 123 tons (submerged), had a single 18-inch torpedo tube in the bow, and carried a crew of one officer and six enlisted men. Assigned initially to the naval torpedo station at Newport for experimental torpedo firing work, she was later assigned to the First Torpedo Flotilla in March 1907, and then to the Naval Academy for instruction of future naval officers. In April 1908, partially disassembled, she was loaded on the after well deck of a collier for a voyage to the Philippine Islands as deck cargo along with her sister ship *Shark.* In April 1909, Ensign Kenneth Whiting, a future naval aviation pioneer, became *Porpoise's* commanding officer. On April 15, Whiting and his crew of six took the submarine out for what was to be a routine run. *Porpoise* moved out into Manila Bay, diving there and leveling off at a depth of 20 feet. Only then did Whiting reveal his intentions. Convinced that a man could escape from a submarine through the torpedo tube, Whiting determined that he was going to try and test his theory with himself as a guinea pig. Squeezing into the 18-inch diameter tube, he clung to the crossbar which stiffened the outer torpedo tube door, as the crew closed the inner door. When the outer door was opened and water rushed in, Whiting hung onto the crossbar that drew his elbows out of the tube's mouth, and then muscled his way out using his hands and arms, and swam to the surface. *Porpoise* surfaced soon thereafter, picked up its wet skipper, and returned to its dock. Reticent to speak about the incident in public, Whiting nevertheless informed his flotilla commander, who submitted a report on how the feat had been accomplished. In *Porpoise's* log that day, Whiting had simply commented: "Whiting went through the torpedo tube, boat lying in (the) water in (a) normal condition, as an experiment . . ."

Becoming a unit of the First Submarine Division, Asiatic Torpedo Fleet, in December 1909, *Porpoise* continued her routine of local operations out of Cavite for the next decade. During World War I, she patrolled the entrance to Manila Bay and convoyed vessels out of port. She was decommissioned in December 1919.

Porpoise (SS-172) (P-1)

Launched in June 1935 from Portsmouth Naval Shipyard as the first in a new class and the second to bear this name, *Porpoise* joined the Pacific Fleet at San Diego in September 1936. She was sent to Pearl Harbor and later, in November 1939, to Manila to join the Asiatic Fleet. At the outbreak of the war with Japan, she was at Olongapo undergoing a refit. With all four main engines being overhauled and her entire battery out, the required work was accomplished in

record time. By December 22, she was en route on her first war patrol in Lingayen Gulf and the South China Sea, and although she tracked two enemy ships, she returned empty-handed. Conducting her second war patrol in the Dutch East Indies in February and March 1942, she sank a cargo ship, but failed to make a hit during her third patrol, although she did rescue five airmen off the enemy-held island of Ju before heading back across the Pacific. Her fourth patrol was dry, but her fifth resulted in the sinking of a 2,024-ton cargo ship, in early April 1943, and her sixth scored two hits on cargo ships near the Marshall Islands, and the torpedoing of a 2,718-ton passenger-cargo ship, in mid-July.

Because of engineering problems, including leaky fuel oil tanks, she was transferred in September 1943 to New London, Connecticut, where she was to be used as a training sub. *Porpoise* was later transferred to Houston, Texas, as a training ship for the Naval Reserve, and was decommissioned in August 1956. She earned five battle stars for World War II service and is credited with sinking three ships for 9,741 tons.

Poseidon

The Poseidon submarine-launched ballistic missile (SLBM) was derived from the earlier Polaris SLBM. It was the first strategic missile of any nation to carry a multiple independently targetable reentry vehicle (MIRV) warhead, a refinement that greatly increased Poseidon's strike capability. The Poseidon could carry up to 14 MIRVs, which could be directed to specific targets within the limits of the missile's range. However, this range was reduced as larger numbers of MIRVs were carried. The development of the Poseidon was first made public in January 1965. After several years of testing and development, the navy awarded the Poseidon contract to what was then the Lockheed Missile and Space Company. Initial operational capability was achieved in March 1971 aboard the USS *James Madison.* All Lafayette-class ballistic missile submarines replaced their Polaris missiles with Poseidons from that date to 1978. No longer in production, the Poseidon missile was retired from use by 1994.

postage stamps (commemorative, year 2000)

In March 2000, the United States Postal Service unveiled five new stamps to honor the navy's submarine force during its centennial year. A dramatic moment occurred immediately thereafter when a bell was tolled for the 52 submarines lost in World War II and in the postwar era. The five stamp designs depict different periods in submarine history and include the USS *Holland,* the first submarine acquired by the navy, as well as boats of the S, Gato, Ohio, and Los Angeles classes.

Protector, one of Simon Lake's few operational submarines. *(United States Navy)*

propulsion, advanced

In the early days of the submarine, electric power was dominant because it could function quietly, with no danger of fumes and with increasing efficiency, as larger and longer-lasting batteries were invented. Many submarines in smaller navies continue to use diesel-electric dual-propulsion systems because they are less expensive. Electric motors have the advantage of being extremely quiet and drawing their energy from storage batteries. They are adequate for smaller, coastal missions where underwater range is not a significant factor. For oceangoing submarines, however, nuclear propulsion is far more advantageous. Nuclear power plants, using the tremendous heat generated by atomic reactors, create a continuous supply of steam to drive powerful turbine engines at high speeds. Refueling is accomplished in port by replacing the uranium core of the reactor, though modern nuclear submarines have the capability of traveling more than 500,000 miles before such replenishment is necessary.

propulsion, steam turbines

Although weapons were the driving force in the development of ships of war down through the ages, changes in propulsion would become increasingly important. In 1890, propulsion was exclusively by reciprocating piston steam engines, which were limited in power and tended to vibrate. To escape these limits, warship designers adopted steam turbines, which ran more smoothly and had no inherent limits. Turbines were used most successfully in destroyers at the turn of the century, and then in large battleships during the decade prior to World War I. One drawback of turbine propulsion was that turbines ran too fast to drive propellers efficiently, a problem that was solved by reducing turbine speeds to acceptable propeller speeds through reduction gearing. By the 1920s, single-reduction gearing was commonplace, as well as a refinement adopted by the U.S. Navy, double-reduction gearing, which permitted even higher turbine speeds without requiring propellers to run any faster. In the field of submarines, while the improvements in weaponry have always motivated the designs and capabilities, propulsion was in the past—and still is—a dominant factor.

Protector

Built by Lake Torpedo Boat, this early submarine was designed by Simon Lake and sold to Russia in 1904 for its navy at the time of war with Japan. She was the first of seven submarines designed by Lake for Russia, and was a tiny vessel of only 130 tons. Unable to proceed very far at sea, she was shipped to Russia on a cargo vessel and then carried on a specially built railway car some 6,000 miles across Siberia to her destination. There is no record of her service during the Russian-Japanese War, but Lake enjoyed considerable publicity for his submarine design and construction.

Puffer (SS-268)

Built by Manitowoc Shipbuilding Company and a submarine of the Gato class, Puffer was launched in November 1942 and was deployed to Australia, leaving on her first war patrol in the Celebes Sea area in September and October 1943, which resulted in several damaged ships but no sinkings. Her second patrol was more fruitful when, in the Sulu Sea and the approaches to Manila, she sank a destroyer and a 6,707-ton freighter in late December. On her third and fourth patrols, she sank a 15,105-ton transport in February in the South China Sea and a freighter and tanker in the Sulu Sea. In May and June, while also acting as lifeguard for the first Allied carrier strike on Soerabaja, she earned a Navy Unit Commendation. In mid-July *Puffer* departed for her fifth war patrol, in the Makassar Straits and in the Celebes, Sulu, and South China Seas, where she sank a 5,113-ton tanker. On her sixth war patrol, in early 1945, she sank a coastal defense vessel in the Nansei Shoto area, and damaged a destroyer, three freighters, and a tanker. Her last three patrols were relatively unproductive from the standpoint of enemy shipping destroyed or damaged, but she did lifeguard duty, bombarded Japanese land bases and harbor installations, and knocked off a number of small vessels with gunfire before the war ended. During the peace that followed, *Puffer* served largely as a training vessel until being decommissioned in the fall of 1960. She earned nine battle stars for World War II service and is credited with sinking eight vessels for 36,392 tons.

Puffer (SSN-652)

This submarine of the Sturgeon class was built by the Ingalls Shipbuilding Company in Pascagoula, Mississippi, and launched in March 1968. She displaced (submerged) 4,762 tons, was armed with four 21-inch torpedo tubes amidships, aft of the bow, and was designed for a complement of 12 officers and 95 enlisted men. After more than 28 years of service, in cold war operations, as a training ship, and in fleet exercises, she was decommissioned and struck from the Navy list in July 1996.

Queenfish (SS-393)

A submarine of the Balao class and built by Portsmouth Naval Shipyard, she was launched in November 1943, at a time when submarine warfare had reached a fever pitch in the Pacific. By the time she was commissioned a little over seven months later, the U.S. Navy had overcome its initial aversion to wolf pack operations. Fleet-type submarines had become plentiful enough to concentrate multiple units in areas where Japanese supply lines provided a wealth of targets. Departing Pearl Harbor in early August 1944, *Queenfish* teamed up with *Barb* and *Tunny* in Luzon Strait. In about two weeks "Ed's Eradicators" (after pack commander Captain Edward R. Swinbume in *Barb*) dispatched to the bottom six confirmed merchantmen in three separate convoys, despite *Tunny's* withdrawal after a week on station with hull damage from aircraft bombs. *Queenfish* nailed three of the victims for an official 15,000 tons (an estimate probably only half of the real tonnage destroyed). *Queenfish* and *Barb* had just finished dealing with convoy #2 when ComSubPAC ordered them to assist the adjacent pack in rescue work. On the way, the "Eradicators" paused for a couple of hours to attack their third convoy. *Queenfish* fired her last four torpedoes for damage only, while *Barb* recorded two large kills. They then raced away to the rescue scene. The Japanese had picked up their own survivors from the wreckage of two large transports sunk by the adjacent pack, but made no attempt to save any survivors from among the 2,100 British and Australian prisoners of war who had been aboard the stricken transports. The attackers managed to pull 127 men out of the water, all that could be safely taken aboard. The "Eradicators" searched for two days, *Queenfish* rescuing 18 men and her

companion 14. An approaching typhoon terminated the hunt and the patrol, as the submarines had to return to base in the Marshall Islands for refit after 59 days at sea.

Although the first *Queenfish* patrol was not unusual from the wolf pack aspect, it was highly successful. The two packs accounted for 13 ships of more than 89,000 tons. The hazards of so many submarines working in small areas, communication difficulties, and nuances of change of command were being steadily overcome. When *Queenfish* departed on her second patrol in late October 1944, her skipper had pack command as well as ship command. They had scarcely arrived in their area on the busy shipping lanes between Shanghai and southwest Korea when *Queenfish* drew first blood, sinking two freighters, while *Barb* sank a merchant ship and light cruiser. Two days later, *Queenfish* attacked a strongly defended convoy in heavy seas, damaging one ship before being blasted with 50 depth charges. She surfaced after this barrage to alert *Barb,* which then sank one of the larger cargo ships in the group. The pack continued the fight by hitting the convoy farther on, sinking one ship and damaging two others. Both packs were then alerted to the approach of a large convoy heading for the Philippines. Besides the usual tankers and freighters, it included a carrier and a large aircraft ferry loaded with planes for Manila, plus several troop transports. Once again, *Queenfish* made the first contact and sent the 9,200-ton ferry to the bottom. In the next 48 hours, the two packs destroyed eight ships, including the 21,000-ton carrier and the largest troop transport. One Japanese army division and its equipment never reached the Philippines, making General MacArthur's battle that much easier. The two packs sank four more loners and, torpedoes expended, headed for Guam. *Queenfish* accounted for four ships in the total bag of one of the most successful wolf-pack operations of the war—19 ships and 110,000 tons.

Queenfish was under way again in late December 1944, once more leading the pack, which took up station in the north Formosa Strait, close to the mainland where convoys holed up at night and hugged the coast by day. Almost immediately *Barb* spotted a big convoy and all three submarines attacked. *Queenfish* unleashed an all-tube load of torpedoes at three targets, but all 10 missed. After reloading, she assisted in jointly attacking and sinking a tanker. Two shots from the stern tubes at a charging destroyer missed. *Queenfish* successfully evaded the counterattack, while *Picuda* and *Barb* pressed new attacks. The former leveled a 10-shot salvo that damaged three ships, then sank a tanker with reloads. *Barb* put at least three ships on the bottom. All told, the pack eliminated five ships from the convoy and severely damaged three others. For the rest of the patrol, *Queenfish* and her sisters operated independently. She expended her last torpedoes and headed for home. Some days later, *Picuda* expended her last weapons more successfully and sank a transport. Both concluded their patrols while *Barb* remained, entered an enemy harbor, shot up the garrison, and saw her commanding officer, Eugene Fluckey, earn the Medal of Honor.

When *Queenfish* departed Hawaii again, it was as a member of "Post's Panzers," named after Commander W. S. Post in *Spot*, who also had *Sea Fox* in his wolf pack. The three proceeded to the Formosa Strait, where *Spot* netted one kill and shared another with a navy aircraft, then left to get more ammunition. The pack command was now transferred to Commander Loughlin, skipper of the *Queenfish*. Almost two weeks of fruitless patrolling ended when *Sea Fox* attacked a small convoy, damaged one vessel, and alerted the pack commander. What occurred that night, April 1, 1945, has been the subject of dozens of articles and of entire chapters in several books. *Queenfish* sank a lighted, marked Japanese ship that had been granted safe conduct by the Americans to carry supplies for Allied prisoners-of-war. A tragic combination of circumstances and errors engulfed *Queenfish* and her skipper, including missed communications, unclear messages, near-zero visibility, concern for counterattacking destroyers, and unfortunately, as it turned out, perfect accuracy with four radar-aimed torpedoes. The ship, *Awa Maru*, sank within minutes. When the lone survivor picked up by *Queenfish* told his story, skipper Loughlin immediately reported to ComSubPAC and the commander of the Pacific Fleet. *Queenfish* was ordered into port, and Loughlin was relieved of command, tried by court-martial, and convicted of one of three charges: negligence in obeying orders. It seemed like a sad ending for an illustrious career—both for the submarine and its skipper. However, after the war it was discovered and confirmed that the Japanese ship, *Awa Maru,* far from being an innocent conveyor of supplies for Allied prisoners of war, was loaded with munitions and contraband. Loughlin was properly exonerated, and survived to continue an illustrious career that led to flag rank. *Queenfish* made one last patrol, under a new skipper, but by this time there were no enemy targets left. She did, however, conduct lifeguard duty and rescued 13 pilots from downed aircraft. Later she was force flagship, and after that served during the Korean conflict and on the West Coast as an auxiliary submarine. She was decommissioned in 1963, and, as a navy commendation reported, "Instead of being scrapped, she was saved for a nobler end. She rests at the bottom of the Pacific, where she spent all her adult life, sunk as a target for more modern weaponry." *Queenfish* is credited with sinking eight vessels for 40,767 tons.

Queenfish (SSN-651)

Built by Newport News Shipbuilding & Drydock Company and the second to bear this now illustrious name, *Queenfish* was launched in February 1966 as a Sturgeon-class attack submarine. Interestingly, she was actually commissioned earlier than the *Sturgeon* (SSN-637), as the navy's 64th nuclear sub and the first single-screw submarine specifically designed for under-ice missions. In February 1966, she exercised her under-ice capability, surfacing in the arctic winter, marginal ice zone in the Davis Strait. Her Atlantic test completed, she headed for the Pacific and was assigned to Pearl Harbor, which remained her home port for the rest of her days. Before the year was over, *Queenfish* began the first of 10 deployments to the western Pacific, a region in which she would spend almost a quarter of her nearly 24-year operational life. In addition to the usual stops in Japan, Okinawa, and Guam, she also worked the Vietnam war zone, a not very historic mission in that pre-Tomahawk-missile era. More than three years elapsed between her first and her second trip under the polar ice cap in 1970. Following the precise track of *Nautilus* in 1958, she surfaced at the North Pole where ice thickness and shallow ocean depth frequently provide clearance of only 25 feet above and below the boat. Her third trip to the Pole in 1985 included a joint surfacing with *Aspro,* and her fourth and final run to the top of the world included a surfacing with two other boats on the 30th anniversary of the pioneer *Nautilus* visit to the pole. In 1981, she performed the sad duty of burying at sea Commander Milo P. Daughters, who had previously been her skipper for three years.

Queenfish recorded many "firsts," including those for her polar performances, her commendations, and her length of service without overhauls. But unfortunately, she became one of the early casualties of the cold war victory—a victory in which she had played a key role. The twin factors of reduced naval requirements and intensified economic needs accomplished what no enemy could. In September 1990, *Queenfish* was deactivated, and a year later was decommissioned and struck from the Navy list.

Quillback (SS-424)

Launched in October 1944 and built by Portsmouth Naval Shipyard, this submarine of the Tench class was first assigned to the submarine base at New London, Connecticut, and then to an experimental ordnance project at the naval station at Key West, Florida. By the time she was deployed to the Pacific, she would experience only a single war patrol, off the coast of Kyushu in June and July 1945, during which she was attacked by, and destroyed, a Japanese suicide motorboat, and rescued one aviator from the water only a half-mile from the heavily armed shore. Peacetime duties returned *Quillback* to New London as a unit of Submarine Squadron 2. From 1945 to 1951, she operated in a training capacity as a "school boat" for the Submarine School, and also became involved in experiments with the nearby Naval Underwater Sound Labora-tory. She was one of 16 submarines in a 1952 program that provided for conversion of fleet-type submarines to GUPPY submarines. The modifications included stream-lining the superstructure deck and conning tower, installing a snorkel system, engine renovations, and new sonar equipment. *Quillback* was converted to a GUPPY IIA submarine in 1953 at Portsmouth Naval Shipyard. When reactivated, *Quillback* was 306 feet in length over-all; had a maximum beam of 27 feet; had a normal displacement of 1,840 tons when on the surface and 2,445 tons when submerged; had accommodations for eight officers, five chief petty officers, and approximately 70 enlisted men; was armed with 10 21-inch torpedo tubes 6 forward and 4 aft; and could make 18 knots on the surface and 15 knots submerged. From Key West, *Quillback* conducted local operations from the naval station; made occasional trips to Guantanamo Bay, Cuba, to provide services for the fleet training group working on antisub-marine warfare projects, participated in major fleet and NATO exercises in the North Atlantic, and participated in experimental torpedo research and development projects. She continued a wide range of operations until being decommissioned in March 1973.

R

R-1 (SS-78)

Built by the Fore River Shipbuilding Company, she was launched in August 1918, the first submarine in the R class, with a displacement of 569 tons on the surface and 680 submerged. She was designed for a complement of two officers and 27 enlisted men, and armed with four 21-inch torpedo tubes in the bow. Assigned to SubDiv9 of the United States Atlantic Fleet, she was initially based in New London, Connecticut, where she ranged the East Coast and the Gulf of Mexico. She was ordered to Pearl Harbor and, for the next eight years, she trained submarine crews and developed submarine tactics. She was later transferred back to the East Coast, and was at the submarine base on the day the Japanese attacked Pearl Harbor; she was immediately ordered to patrol the sea lanes leading to New England and to join sister submarines in the hunt for German U-boats preying on maritime traffic along the North American coast. Although limited in cruising range, the R-boats continued their patrols through the Nazi submarine offensive of early 1942. In mid-April 1942, while on patrol some 300 miles northeast of Bermuda, *R-1* sighted, attacked, and probably damaged a surfaced German U-boat. She continued these patrols until December 1944, when she underwent an extensive conversion to enable her to participate in the development of antisubmarine warfare (ASW) equipment and tactics. She then operated largely out of Key West, Florida, until November 1945, when she was decommisioned and struck from the Navy list.

R-1 (SS-78), commissioned in 1918, was the first of a class of 27 submarines and, though antiquated at age 24, was renowned for having attacked, and probably damaged, a German U-boat in the Atlantic in April 1942, during her World War II service. *(United States Navy)*

USS *R-12* (SS-89) left, and tied up, right, alongside the *R-18*, was launched in August 1919 and remained in active service until May 1943 when she was lost in a tragic accident off Key West, Florida. The submarine flooded and sank. Although the six men on the bridge at the time, including the commanding officer, survived, 42 others were lost. *(United States Navy)*

radar (ballistic missile detection radar)

The systems for detecting and tracking ballistic missiles are much larger than those for aircraft detection because the ranges are longer. Such radars have ranges of 2,000 to 3,000 nautical miles—much farther and with more powerful transmitters than for the average radars designed for aircraft detection. Antennas for this application have dimensions of as much as 100 meters or more, and are electronically scanned, phased-array antennas capable of steering the radar beam without moving large mechanical structures. Radar systems so equipped are commonly found at the lower frequencies. The use of radio waves to detect a metallic object beyond the range of vision by reflecting them back to their source dates back to experiments conducted by the Germans well before World War I. It was the British, however, who first produced radar— radio detecting and ranging—in a practical form when they established a chain of radar stations along Britain's southeast coast in 1939. This development was soon followed by the invention of the magnetron, a device that produced short radio waves and provided the basis for the development of modern radar.

radar-picket submarines

Based on experiences during the late stages of World War II, the U.S. Navy laid plans for placing early-warning radar equipment aboard submarines. The need was dramatically emphasized during the invasion of Okinawa, during which severe losses were felt when surface picket ships bore the brunt of the increasing attacks by Japanese kamikaze (suicide) planes. The USS *Requin* (SS-481) and the USS *Spinax* (SS-489) became the first radar-picket submarines, capable of carrying out a threefold mission: to control friendly aircraft defending against attacking enemy aircraft, to direct planes outbound on missions, and to provide an early-warning capability to the surface fleet. Strategically, these radar-picket submarines operated in pairs but some distance apart. Thus, if one boat had to dive to avoid enemy attack, the other could pick up the coverage until the first boat could surface again and resume coverage.

At the start, the persistent problem was overcrowding, since the picket submarines did not shed their torpedo tubes and other armament but retained most of the accoutrements of fighting ships as well as the radar equipment. This untenable situation was solved with the introduction of the Migraine program (so called because of the "big headache" caused by the internal cramming). Thus it was that both *Requin* and *Spinax* underwent conversion from their dual-purpose roles to the more simplified radar role. Eight other radar-picket submarines were designed from the beginning for this purpose, including *Burrfish, Pompon, Rasher, Raton, Ray, Redfin, Rock,* and *Tigrone.*

The Migraine program had four phases, I, II, and III. The first, which included *Requin* and *Spinax,* included a snorkel system, the removal of the four stern torpedoes, and the conversion of the after torpedo room into a combat information center (CIC). The second, involving the other boats listed above, added a snorkel system, a streamlined step sail, and a 24-foot additional hull section to house a combat information center. The third phase saw the construction of two submarines, *Sailfish* (SSR-572) and *Salmon* (SSR-573) from the keel up as specifically designed radar-picket submarines, and the fourth involved only one submarine, *Triton* (SSRN-586), which was built as a two-reactor nuclear-powered radar-picket submarine. This boat, on her shakedown cruise in 1960, set a record by completing the first submerged circumnavigation of the globe.

Radar-picket Submarines

	Migraine	Missile Guidance
Requin	pre & II	X
Spinax	pre & II	X
Tigrone	I	X
Burrfish	I	X
Pompon	III	X
Rasher	III	X
Raton	III	X
Ray	III	X
Redfin	III	X
Rock	III	X
Sailfish		X
Salmon		X
Triton		

radar responders

In marine navigation, these are also referred to as racons, which transmit only in response to an interrogation signal from a ship's radar, at the time when the latter's rotating scanner bears on it. During this brief period, the racon receives multiple radar pulses, in reaction to which it transmits back a coded reply pulse that is received and dis-

played on the ship's radar screen. A racon can greatly increase the strength of the echo from a poor radar target, such as a submarine periscope, and is also helpful in ranging on and identifying positions on inconspicuous and featureless coastlines or open waters, where there may be small buoys, mine markers, or other objects of interest to navigating submarines.

Rasher (SS-269)

Built by Manitowoc Shipbuilding Company and launched in December 1942, this submarine of the Gato class was deployed to Brisbane, Australia, where, in late September 1943, she operated in the Makassar Strait-Celebes Sea area during her first war patrol and sank a passenger-cargo ship in a submerged attack at dawn. Four days later, off Ambon Harbor, she spotted a convoy of four merchantmen escorted by two destroyers and a seaplane, fired two salvos of three torpedoes each, and crash-dived to avoid the destroyers and bombs from the scout plane. A freighter broke up and sank, while the escorts struck back in a vigorous but vain counterattack. *Rasher*'s next victim was a tanker, and a later attack on a second convoy resulted in a hit on a tanker; but vigorous countermeasures by enemy destroyers prevented any assessment of damage. Following refit, *Rasher* commenced her second war patrol in mid-December 1943 and stalked Japanese shipping in the South China Sea off Borneo. She fired at a target while submerged, and heard the explosions rip into a tanker's hull, but was unable to confirm a sinking. She pursued another tanker, firing a spread of four fish; a mushroom of fire arose as the last two torpedoes struck, and the target sank, leaving only an oil slick and scattered debris. During this patrol, *Rasher* also planted mines off the approaches to Saigon harbor. Her third war patrol, from February 19 to April 4, 1944, was conducted in the Java-Celebes Sea area. She attacked a Japanese convoy off Bali, sinking two cargo ships, destroyed another in the Celebes Sea, and ended her run with another cargo ship in early March. Her fourth patrol, in the spring of 1944, resulted in the sinkings of a freighter, a gunboat, and a cargo ship.

Her fifth patrol, from July 22 to September 3, was spent largely with *Bluefish* in the South China Sea west of Luzon, where she fired a spread of five torpedoes at the largest ship in a three-ship convoy. Diving to avoid being rammed, she heard the sounds of a ship breaking up as it went down. On the dark, stormy night of August 18, *Rasher*'s radar picked up a large convoy, protected by destroyers and air cover. The first target, a tanker loaded with gasoline, exploded into a column of flame 1,000 feet high. The escorts fired wildly and laid depth charge patterns two miles astern of *Rasher*, which then fired a second spread, sinking a cargo-transport and scoring hits on a second vessel. *Rasher* resumed the attack on the shattered convoy, sinking a transport and a carrier. *Bluefish* intercepted the remaining ships, sinking two tankers. Then *Spadefish* joined the wolf pack and scored hits on two of the surviving transports. All torpedoes expended, *Rasher* then set course for Midway. Her sixth patrol, also in a wolf pack, starting in late January 1945, was a restful one, with no suitable targets in sight except small patrol craft. Her seventh patrol, in April and May, was little more rewarding. On lifeguard station off Honshu, she riddled two small craft with gunfire, and returned to Midway. The war ended as she proceeded to the Gulf of Siam, and she returned to the Philippines.

During the peacetime that followed, Rasher was converted to a Migraine III radar-picket submarine (SSR) and saw service on the East Coast and West Coast as a picket submarine. In January 1956, she deployed to the Seventh Fleet, where she operated with U.S. and SEATO naval units. In late 1959, she departed for the Far East to participate in exercise Blue Star, a large-scale American-Nationalist Chinese amphibious exercise. In May 1960, she took part in the Black Ship Festival at Shimoda, Japan, commemorating Admiral Perry's landing. She returned to San Diego on June 20, 1960. After further service, which included amphibious and antisubmarine warfare (ASW) training support for Republic of Korea, Nationalist Chinese, and Thai units, as well as operations with the Seventh Fleet off Vietnam, she spent the remainder of her career providing training services off the coast of California to underwater demolition team and ASW units. She was decommissioned in May 1967, and later was towed to Portland, Oregon, where she served as a training submarine for Naval Reservists until struck from the Navy list in December 1971. *Rasher* was awarded the Presidential Unit Citation for outstanding performance in combat during World War II patrols one, three, four, and five, and received seven battle stars in World War II service and two battle stars for service off Vietnam. *Rasher* was credited with sinking 18 vessels for 99,901 tons.

Raton (SS-270)

Built by Manitowoc Shipbuilding Company and launched in January 1943, this submarine of the Gato class was ordered to Brisbane, Australia, from whence she departed on her first war patrol in November in the Solomon Islands. While patrolling west of Massau, *Raton* sighted two Japanese cargo-type ships, with two destroyers and a floatplane. She trailed the convoy and that night made a torpedo attack, sinking one of the cargomen, but the aggressive countermeasures of the escorts thwarted four attempts to sink the remaining freighter. A week later, she sighted a convoy of five cargo ships with two escorts. In a submerged attack, *Raton* sank two ships, dove deep to escape heavy pounding by the escorts, and then remained in the area for a return bout. In a night attack, she heavily damaged a third freighter, and called for assistance, since her torpedoes were nearly expended. Her sister boat *Gato* joined the attack, only to be jumped by the two Japanese destroyers. *Raton* surfaced and raced at flank speed to draw the escorts away and succeeded, allowing *Gato* to sink the damaged freighter. *Raton* departed on her second war patrol from mid-December to late January 1944, for the Mindanao-Celebes area, where she made an attack on four merchantmen and two destroyers, sinking one of them and damaging an auxiliary aircraft carrier. On January 2, she encountered two tankers, escorted by a destroyer on the Palau shipping lane. She scored hits on one tanker, but the efficient countermeasures of the Japanese escort interrupted the attack. Her third patrol, from mid-February to mid-April, was conducted in the Java Sea, the Karimata Strait, and the South China Sea, where she sank the only two ships she contacted.

Raton's fourth patrol, from May 19 to June 23, 1944, in the South China and Java Seas, provided good hunting. The first week, she intercepted two small intercoastal freighters, sinking both with her deck gun. That same evening she contacted a fast convoy of three transports and four destroyers. She sank one of the destroyers and damaged a transport. On May 28, she tracked a Japanese submarine, but missed because of an unfavorable firing angle. She next made contact with a large convoy of 11 ships, with four escorts. One frigate was blown apart by three hits, but *Raton* received a severe pounding from prolonged depth charge attacks before making her escape. Later, a boarding party from the submarine captured a sailing vessel, taking 11 prisoners and scuttling the craft. Four days later, she sighted a small freighter, sinking it with one torpedo and rescuing nine survivors, after which she headed for Fremantle to deposit her catch and refit. Her fifth patrol resulted in a lone tanker in the Philippines, but her sixth patrol, in October and December 1944, was more fruitful, taking her to the South China Sea where, on the night of October 18, she slipped into the center of a nine-ship convoy for a surface attack. She fired torpedo tubes, fore and aft, accounting for two ships sunk and two damaged. With her torpedo supply running low and a typhoon approaching, *Raton* pulled into Mios Woendi, for more fuel and torpedoes with which to finish the patrol, and later headed seaward to encounter an enemy task group of two heavy cruisers and five escort vessels. In a submerged attack, she scored three hits on a Mogami-class cruiser but did not put the heavy vessel out of action. A week later, *Raton*, joined by *Ray*, attacked a four-ship convoy guarded by three escorts. In a surface action, *Raton* sank two targets with four torpedoes. Then, both submarines fired torpedoes at the remaining auxiliaries with unconfirmed results.

In mid-March 1945, after an overhaul, *Raton* sailed for the Yellow Sea for her seventh war patrol. On May 2, she blew up a loaded tanker in a night torpedo attack off Shantung Peninsula, despite gunfire from two Japanese escorts. That same day, she sank a cargo ship in a submerged torpedo approach, and two weeks later, she made a submerged attack on two transports, sinking the larger one. *Raton* sailed on June 22 for her final patrol, lifeguard duty off Hong Kong; but with the war ending, she found neither downed planes nor enemy ships. She received orders to return to New London, where for the next few years she was engaged in training exercises in the North Atlantic and the Caribbean. In July 1952, she was converted to a Migraine III radar-picket submarine (SSR), and during the 1950s and 1960s saw service on the East Coast, the Far East, and the West Coast. She was decommissioned in June 1969. *Raton* was awarded six battle stars for services during World War II and credited with sinking 13 vessels for 44,178 tons.

Ray (SS-271)

The first to bear the name *Ray,* this submarine of the Gato class was built by Manitowoc Shipbuilding Company and launched in February 1943 and ordered to Brisbane, Australia, from whence she departed on her first war patrol, in November, in an area north of the Bismarck Archipelago. On the New Hanover-Truk shipping lane, she made radar contact with a three-ship convoy, escorted by three patrol craft. Attacking just before dawn she scored three hits on one of the freighters. Then, after evading the escort's countermeasures, she followed the convoy and sank a converted gunboat with a spread of torpedoes. Before ending her patrol in December, *Ray* twice unsuccessfully attacked another convoy. Her second patrol, starting in mid-December, was in the Celebes-Ambon-Timor area. Near midnight on December 26 she sighted an unescorted tanker standing out from Tioro Strait. When the enemy ship reached open water, *Ray* fired a spread of torpedoes, which stopped the tanker dead in the water and sent a huge mushroom of flame into the night sky as it disintegrated. On January 1, 1944, *Ray* intercepted two ships with escorts in the mouth of Ambon Bay, Java, and sank a converted gunboat with three hits. The accompanying cargo ship tried to ram the submarine, and a combined aerial attack by patrol bombers and a sustained depth charge attack forced *Ray* to run deep. The third patrol, in February and March, in the South China and Java Seas included the laying of a minefield off Saigon, Indochina. On the evening of March 2, *Ray* intercepted a nine-ship convoy, and early on the 3rd came within firing range. A spread of four torpedoes damaged a tanker; unfortunately, at that moment the submarine *Bluefish* crossed *Ray's* line of fire, preventing a coup de grace. Two weeks later, *Ray* intercepted two destroyers and a patrol craft, fired six torpedoes, and dived deep, at which time an explosion was heard.

Ray departed Fremantle in late April 1944, for her fourth patrol, assigned to the Davao Gulf-Molucca Passage area. Three weeks out, she spotted a nine-ship convoy escorted by surface ships and seaplanes. *Ray* surfaced that night, pursued the convoy, and attacked early the next morning. She fired six torpedoes, sinking a transport and damaging a freighter. A spread fired from her stern tubes resulted in hits on a tanker, and possibly a minelayer. During the ensuing confusion, *Ray* escaped by running at flank speed on the surface. Overtaking the disorganized convoy during a tropical squall the next day, *Ray* fired on two radar contacts, scoring hits. When the weather cleared, *Ray* saw one ship whose stack was going under and whose bow was rising from the water. The second was enveloped in a cloud of smoke and her decks awash. During her fifth patrol, in July and August 1944, in the South China Sea, she sank a tanker before the mission ended. In her next patrol, at the south entrance to Makassar Strait, *Ray* first sank two cargo ships and damaged a transport. Then, in mid-August, off northern Balabac Strait, Philippines, she closed with a large convoy that was protected by surface escorts and planes, fired six "tin fish" at a tanker, and dived as a destroyer raced in to counterattack. Heavy explosions were heard, and a three-hour depth-charge pounding followed. During the action, *Ray* heard another violent explosion and the sounds of a ship breaking up, as a tanker went down. The submarine surfaced that evening and pursued the convoy into Palawan Bay. Air cover prevented a daylight attack, but the wolf pack of *Ray, Harder,* and *Haddo* waited for the ships to come out. *Ray* fired her four remaining torpedoes at a passenger-cargo ship. Three fish missed, but the fourth hit the target amidships. The escorts forced *Ray* to dive, but she heard the 7,000-ton cargo vessel break up.

Ray's war patrol of September 23 to December 8 took her to the familiar waters of the South China Sea. During the first week in October, she twice torpedoed a tanker, inflicting undetermined damage. Five days later, she destroyed a cargo ship with two direct hits and escaped a subsequent depth charge attack. On October 14, while making a crash dive to escape a Japanese patrol plane, *Ray's* conning tower was flooded by an improperly secured hatch. Although she was brought under control before reaching 85 feet, the damage forced *Ray* to put into Mios Woendi for emergency repairs. On November 1, *Ray* closed a five-ship convoy, sinking a cargo ship and damaging a small tanker. Escaping the escorts, she landed men and supplies on the west coast of Mindoro, Philippines, picking up two downed navy fliers, two army POWs escaped from Corregidor, and an escaped Filipino political prisoner. On the night of November 4, the sub sighted a cargo ship with its superstructure aflame, from an earlier attack by *Bream*. She fired two torpedoes, scoring a hit amidships and blowing away the bow. On November 6,

Ray intercepted a convoy of two heavy cruisers and several transports, protected by surface and air escorts. She fired six torpedoes at the cruiser, damaged earlier by *Raton,* was forced to dive to escape aerial and surface attack, and grounded in shoal water, shearing off her starboard sound head, damaging the torpedo room, and starting to flood. To prevent further flooding, she came to periscope depth where she saw the bowless cruiser being towed away by a transport. But her own damage and the Japanese escorts kept *Ray* from following up the attack. On the night of November 14, *Ray* made a surface attack on a three-ship convoy, blowing up a frigate with a direct hit. Two days later she fired two torpedoes at a grounded transport, but could not complete the attack because of minefields and shoal water. Five days after that, she rescued a downed pilot from aircraft carrier USS *Cowpens* (CVL 25) before heading home.

Ray cleared Guam for her seventh war patrol in May and June 1945. The first week, while on lifeguard duty off Kyushu, she rescued 10 fliers from a drowned B-29, and a week later 10 crewmen of a PBM Mariner patrol bomber, which was foundering in heavy seas. She transferred the rescued crews to *Lionfish* and USS *Pompon* and continued her patrol. On May 19, she intercepted three small freighters, which turned out to be a disguised hunter-killer group, and which converged on the area where *Ray* had dived, laying a depth charge pattern. But *Ray,* counting on surprise, suddenly surfaced and fired her deck gun at her pursuers as she dashed away at flank speed. The remainder of the patrol was devoted to attacking patrol craft and coastal vessels with gunfire until it ended at Midway in mid-June. Her eighth and final wartime patrol took *Ray* to the Gulf of Siam, where she sank 16 small craft by gunfire and sent boarding parties to burn seven junks at anchor. She was heading to a base for more ammunition when the war ended. Her peacetime assignments, out of New London, consisted of training exercises along the East Coast and in the Caribbean, service as a Migraine II radar-picket submarine (SSR), and fleet exercises. Deploying to the Mediterranean in 1956, she operated with NATO and U.S. Navy units, and later off Scotland, France, and Portugal. She was decommissioned in September 1958. For her World War II service, *Ray* was awarded seven battle stars and the Philippine Presidential Unit Citation and credited with sinking 12 vessels for 49,185 tons.

Ray (SSN-653)

As the second submarine to bear the name, this boat of the Sturgeon class was launched in June 1966, after Congress authorized the building of 14 submarines: six Polaris fleet ballistic missile submarines and eight Sturgeon-class attack submarines. She served first in SubRon6, home-ported at Norfolk, Virginia, and the remainder of her career as a unit of SubRon4 in Charleston, South Carolina. In over 25 years of commissioned service, *Ray* successfully completed numerous deployments to the Mediterranean Sea and the North Atlantic, Central Atlantic, and Arctic Oceans. Many of these deployments were missions of great importance to the safety and security of the United States. For her actions, she was awarded five Navy Unit Commendations and six Meritorious Unit Commendations. When she was inactivated on July 24, 1992, *Ray* was the most decorated submarine in the Atlantic Fleet.

Razorback (SS-394)

A submarine of the Balao class, launched January 27, 1944, and commissioned April 3, 1944. She was built by Portsmouth Naval Shipyard. *Razorback* proceeded to Pearl Harbor, Hawaii, from whence she left on her first war patrol in late August, heading for Luzon as a member of an offensive group in support of the Palau landings. Although she found no targets, she was rewarded on her second patrol in mid-November, in company with *Trepang* and *Segundo.* Operating with these submarines in the Luzon Straits, *Razorback* damaged a 6,933-ton freighter, sank a destroyer, and damaged another freighter at the end of her run. Her next two patrols resulted in little battle action, though she sank some small vessels, took aboard three Japanese prisoners, and rescued four B-29 pilots and a fighter pilot before retiring to Midway to end that patrol, and refit. Her final patrol, in the Sea of Okhotsk, was equally short of targets as the war ended, though she sank eight small cargo vessels in surface gun actions and performed lifeguard duty. After the war she remained active with the Pacific Fleet, serving off Japan and China in early 1948 and again in late 1949. In August 1952 she converted to a GUPPY IIA submarine, and took up duty on the West Coast. She was involved in antisubmarine exercises and spent much of her time in the western Pacific, where she earned her first Vietnam Service Medal. She continued to operate on the West Coast out of San Diego thereafter, with cruises to the western Pacific, until being decommissioned in November 1970. She was then transferred to the Turkish navy where she was recommissioned *Murat Reis.* *Razorback* earned five battle stars for World War II service and four stars for Vietnam service. *Razorback* was credited with sinking one vessel for 820 tons.

R boats (SS-78 through SS-97)

This was a class of 27 submarines constructed during the World War I period (1918–19) by three shipyards—largely Fore River Shipbuilding Company, but also Union Iron Works and Lake Torpedo Boat Company. The first 20 were of 680 tons (submerged), and the remaining seven slightly smaller—598 tons. They were all designed for a crew of two officers and 27 enlisted men, and were armed with four 21-inch torpedo tubes in the bow. They all saw initial postwar service operating out of New London as a base, and ranging the East Coast, the Caribbean, and the Gulf of Mexico. Most of them also saw service in Panama in the 1920s, where they engaged in fleet exercises off Central America, along the West Coast, and on occasion ranging along the west coast of South America. Most of them were also deployed to Pearl Harbor, Hawaii, for short tours of duty.

Seven of the boats, *R-21* through *R-27,* had short careers, and were all struck from the Navy list in May 1930 and sold for scrap. The others, with several exceptions, had long careers, remaining in service until late 1945, patrolling the East Coast sea lanes leading to New England during World War II, looking for German U-boats. During the winter of 1942, the submarines established a patrol line between Bermuda and Nantucket Island, Massachusetts. On that patrol line, some 300 miles northeast of Bermuda, *R-1* sighted, attacked, and probably damaged a surfaced German U-boat on April 16, 1942.

Two of the boats, *R-5* and *R-6,* had the distinction of being used in the filming of the Fox motion picture, *The Eleventh Hour* (1923). The latter also had the distinction of being one of the few submarines of her generation to be equipped with an experimental installation of a folding-mast snorkel, permitting her to run her diesel engines when submerged.

One boat, *R-3,* was transferred to England in late 1941 as HMS *P5–1,* a training submarine for that country during World War II.

Another boat, *R-14,* had a unique experience. Assigned to Pearl Harbor, she was assisting in a search for a lost sea-going tug, *Conestoga,* in May 1921, when she ran out of fuel southeast of Hawaii. Her ingenious crew fashioned makeshifts sails from blankets and sheets, and she made her way to Hilo, Hawaii, on May 15 after five days under sail.

Two of the 27 *R* boats were lost at sea in tragic accidents. On June 21, 1942, while operating in the western Atlantic, on loan to Britain's Royal Navy, *R-19* was rammed and sunk by HMCS *Georgian,* a unit of the Canadian navy, and went down with all crew members on board. None were saved. The other accident occurred when *R-12* was underway on the surface while off Key West, Florida, shortly after noon on June 12, 1943. While making preparations to dive for a torpedo practice approach, the forward battery compartment started to flood. The alarm was sounded, and her skipper, Lieutenant Commander E. E. Shelby, who was on the bridge, immediately ordered all hatches shut and main ballast tanks blown. But those actions were not enough to save the boat, which went down in a matter of seconds. The six men on the bridge, including the commanding officer, were the only ones res-

cued, while 42 others were lost. Tragically, *R-12* had more than its usual complement of two officers and 27 men aboard, and included two Brazilian navy officers and others who were there to observe a special torpedo firing exercise. The boat sank in 600 feet of water, too deep for rescue or salvaging—or even investigation—in those days.

reactors

In a modern submarine, a nuclear reactor provides the heat that generates the steam that powers a steam turbine, which in turn drives the propellers. Commonly, in this type of propulsion, uranium in a reactor produces heat by nuclear fission. In the reactor, the uranium is surrounded by a moderator, which is required to slow the reaction neutrons so they will interact more efficiently with the uranium. In most reactors the moderator is water, which is also used to carry away the heat of reaction. Pressurized to prevent it from boiling, it runs through a heat exchanger, in which the heat is passed to a secondary, water circuit, which provides the steam that actually turns the turbine. Another type is the liquid metal-cooled reactor, which operates on the principle that molten metal can carry much more heat than water, so that a more compact turbine can be used. However, despite that advantage, molten metal can become highly radioactive, so that leaks, which are dangerous enough in a pressurized-water plant, become much more so, with possibly catastrophic results. This type of reactor was used, but replaced later, in *Seawolf* (SSN-575).

Redfin (SS-272)

A submarine of the Gato class, *Redfin* was built by Manitowoc Shipbuilding Company, launched in April 1943, and in January of the following year conducted her first war patrol in the South China Sea and north of Australia to defend against a possible Japanese attack. On her second war patrol in March and April, she sank a 1,900-ton Japanese destroyer off Zamboanga, Mindanao, and later two enemy passenger cargo ships for 4,621 tons and 3,807 tons. On the night of April 22–23, she landed four of her crew near Dent Haven, Borneo, to evacuate a British reconnaissance party. Attacked by the Japanese, the landing party returned to *Redfin,* but the British agents were later evacuated by an Australian officer and transferred to the submarine *Harder.* On her third war patrol, May 26 to July 1, she landed six Philippine guerrillas on a small island near Balabac Strait. Then, proceeding to scout the enemy naval base at Tawitawi, she sank a 5,142-ton Japanese tanker on the 11th. She also warned American forces in the Marianas of the departure from Tawitawi of the Japanese task force that was later defeated in the battle of the Philippine Sea. Operating off Leyte on the 24th, she sank a

3,028-ton Japanese passenger-cargo ship before returning to Fremantle. Her next assignment was to lay a minefield off the west coast of Borneo, rescue eight survivors of the submarine *Flier* at Palawan Island on August 30, and conduct lifeguard duty. During her fourth patrol, she sank a 15,226-ton Japanese tanker west of the Philippines on November 8. Completing her fourth war patrol on January 7, 1945, she proceeded to Mare Island Naval Shipyard, San Francisco, where she received special mine detection gear. Underway from Pearl Harbor May 30 to July 10, and later from July 30 to September 5, she made mine surveys first off Honshu and Hokkaido, and later off Kyushu, Japan. After the war, *Redfin* was converted to a Migraine III radar-picket submarine in the early 1950s, and later became a laboratory and training ship for the testing of inertial navigation systems used in Polaris submarines. She preceded the first ballistic missile submarine *George Washington* as flagship of SubRon14. After searching for the lost submarine *Thresher* in April 1963, she was reclassified AGSS, and operated in the Atlantic, where she continued to assist in special research and development projects, including the Polaris A-3 missile, until she was decommissioned in May 1967, to become a Naval Reserve training ship. *Redfin* received six battle stars for World War II service and is credited with sinking six vessels for 23,724 tons.

Redfish (SS-395)

A submarine of the Balao class, she was built at Portsmouth Naval Shipyard and launched in January 1944 and deployed to Pearl Harbor, where she embarked on her first war patrol in late July of that year and a month later sank a 5,953-ton Japanese cargo ship, and a 7,311-ton tanker and a 8,506-ton transport a few weeks later—all off Formosa—before arriving at Midway for refitting. Departing Saipan in early November, she sank a 2,345-ton Japanese transport during the night of the 23rd. Then, in early December, she joined *Sea Devil* to inflict heavy damage on the Japanese aircraft carrier *Hayalaka*, putting her out of action for the remainder of the war. Continuing her round of success, *Redfish* sank the newly built 18,500-ton Japanese aircraft carrier *Unryu*, bound for Mindoro, on December 19. After diving to 232 feet, she rose to the surface and raced to escape Japanese pursuit. Sent to the Portsmouth (N.H.) Naval Shipyard for repairs in February 1945, she returned to Pearl Harbor in late July and remained there until the end of the war. After duty at Guam from September 1945 to January 1946, she operated off the West Coast and Hawaii until ordered to Korea in February 1951, in support of UN forces. In the early 1950s, Redfin was one of the first boats to be involved in early underice exploration. Returning to San Diego on July 3, she operated off the West Coast, and in the spring of 1954 became a "movie queen" when she participated in the Walt Disney produc-

tion of Jules Verne's *Twenty Thousand Leagues Under the Sea*, following up in September 1957 with the motion picture *Run Silent, Run Deep*. After more usual duties for the next few years, including training cruises to the western Pacific, she was decommissioned in June 1968 and subsequently sunk as a target vessel. *Redfish* received two battle stars for World War II service and is credited with sinking five vessels for 42,615 tons.

Regulus

This guided cruise missile was the U.S. Navy's first nuclear-armed cruise missile (SSM-N-8A) in the mid-1950s and at that time was adapted for use on diesel-powered submarines. The concept of the guided cruise missile, which is self-propelled and flies like an aircraft for much of its flight, originated with the German V-1 "buzz bomb" during World War II. The navy's first version was the Loon, copied in part from the V-1. Using a pulse jet engine, it had a range of about 150 miles and was tracked by radar and controlled by radio. The earliest submarines to use the Regulus missile were *Tunny, Barbero, Grayback, Growler,* and *Halibut,* all of which were originally attack boats converted to SSGs, except *Halibut.* Basically, the system required teamwork between a launch boat, which sent the missile on its way, and a guidance boat, closer to the target area, which would then control the flight of the missile to the target itself.

Remora (SS-487)

This submarine of the Tench class was launched in July 1945, too late for service in World War II. She operated out of New London, Connecticut, as a training submarine until January 1947. She was converted to a GUPPY II submarine at Mare Island Naval Shipyard to increase her power and efficiency. She was then ordered to San Diego, her new home port. For the next two years, she remained in the eastern Pacific operating primarily off California but ranging as far north as the Aleutians. In May 1950, *Remora* was deployed to Yokosuka, Japan, where she conducted ASW training exercises with units of Naval Forces Far East. Two weeks later the Korean War began. As a unit of TF-6, Naval Forces Japan, she patrolled Soya Strait, between Hokkaido and Sakhalin in July and early August. Later in the month, she headed back to San Diego, where she underwent overhaul, provided services for the Line School at Monterey, and conducted training exercises. She went back to the western Pacific in early 1953. Arriving at Buckner Bay in mid-March, she continued on to Japan in April and at mid-month rejoined TF-96. In June she was back in Okinawan waters for patrols and exercises, after which she returned to Yokosuka. After the fighting in Korea ended, *Remora* remained based at San Diego and through the decade continued to alternate training exercises and patrols in the western Pacific with similar First Fleet operations off the West Coast and in Hawaiian waters. She remained in the eastern Pacific during 1956 to 1958, but, during the spring of the latter year, was engaged in extended exercises off Alaska. In 1962 after being transferred to Pearl Harbor, she underwent a GUPPY III conversion, which lengthened her hull by 15 feet and her conning tower by 5 feet. She was employed to evaluate antisubmarine sonar in Hawaiian waters, and then continued deployments to the western Pacific until 1969 when she returned to Charleston, operating along the Atlantic seaboard, in the Caribbean, and in the Gulf of Mexico, until being decommissioned in October 1973. She was then transferred to Greece where she served the Hellenic navy as *Katsonis*.

Requin (SS-481)

This boat of the Tench class was built by the Portsmouth Naval Shipyard and launched in January 1945, although deployed to Hawaii to join the Pacific Fleet, she arrived just too late for her intended first war patrol when Japan surrendered. In 1946, *Requin* was sent to Portsmouth Naval Shipyard to undergo the first of three conversions to become the first U.S. Navy radar-picket submarine. She operated in the Caribbean, along the East Coast, and north of the Arctic Circle, and in 1949 sailed for her first deployment with the Sixth Fleet, for five years of service in the Mediterranean. In June 1959, she reported to Charleston Naval Shipyard for conversion to a Migraine II Fleet Snorkel radar-picket submarine, after which she was again deployed to the Mediterranean. In September 1963, *Requin* completed her 5,000th dive. She continued operations with the Sixth Fleet until May 1964 when she resumed her duties with the Second Fleet until the fall of 1966, when she began an extended deployment for operation UNITAS VIII, cruising around the South American continent on exercises with various navies. In late 1968, she was sent to St Petersburg, Florida, and served there as a Naval Reserve trainer until 1971 when she was decommissioned. However, she enjoyed an afterlife—when she was assigned to the city of Tampa, Florida, to become an educational attraction for visitors; in 1990, she was towed up the Mississippi and Ohio Rivers to Pittsburgh where she was dedicated as a public memorial to the submarine service.

research missiles

In the last stages of World War II, American troops captured the underground factory where Germany's V-2 rockets had been manufactured. Later, immense carloads of rocket parts were shipped to the United States for study and development for America's future weapons needs.

Some 75 V-2 rockets were reassembled (some with manufactured parts) and were then fired in tests at the newly established White Sands Proving Ground in New Mexico. Later, a special V-2 panel of the Naval Research Laboratory was formed for the purpose not only of testing, but also creating new control instruments and training military personnel in the handling and use of such missiles. After some failures, the White Sands rockets soon reached heights of more than 100 miles. The scientific instruments were hooked up with an automatic radio transmitter, as well as cameras, and data were recorded on the ground while the rocket was in flight. It was during these tests that other rockets were developed. One of them, the Navy's Vanguard, was as tall as the V-2, but slimmer and lighter. It went as high as 135 miles. In a later, and very important development, a U.S. Navy ballistic missile was launched from a submerged submarine. This led to the perfection of the navy's Subroc, which could be launched underwater against enemy submarines or other underwater targets.

There are two main groups of missiles. The first is the type that has wings and can in effect fly through the air, as airplanes do. These "cruise" missiles were capable of carrying either a nuclear or a conventional warhead, the cruise missile was designed to be difficult for radar to observe and to fly close to the ground while traveling at a relatively slow speed to its target. The second type is the ballistic missile, which is wingless and not supported by air. These follow ballistic trajectories, just as bullets do. Since they are powered by rockets, ballistic missiles can reach higher altitudes than can missiles powered by air-breathing engines. Ballistic missiles are of three general classes. Short-range missiles, which can travel about 200 miles; intermediate-range, about 1,500 miles; and intercontinental, about 7,000 miles.

Guided missiles are so named because they are controlled throughout the time they are in motion. Many winged missiles, and some wingless ones, can be guided into contact with a moving target. As the target changes its direction, the path of the missile can be changed accordingly. A ballistic missile is also aimed at its target but is guided only during the brief powered phase of its flight. Surface-to-air missiles need continuous, precise guidance. There are three principal systems. One system uses two radar beams. One beam follows the target; the second beam follows the missile. The point of interception is computed, and electronic signals guide the missile to the target. A second, one-beam system uses a missile called a beam-rider. It travels in a radar beam pointed at the target. If the missile leaves the beam, its built-in sensing system puts it back on course. The third system is referred to as "homing." The missile is fired in the general direction of the target. It carries a device that responds, for guidance, to a reflected radar beam or to the heat or noise of the target's engine. Modern cruise missiles are guided by an inertial navigation system that was updated during flight by a technique called Tercom (terrain contour matching), using contour maps stored in the system's computerized memory.

Rickover, Hyman George (1900–1986)

Rickover was a U.S. naval officer whose foresight and dedication to the submarine service eventually gained him unique recognition as the "father" of the navy's nuclear propulsion program following World War II. Born on January 27, 1900, in Makov, Russia, he immigrated to the United States at an early age, graduated from the U.S. Naval Academy in 1922, and later earned an advanced degree in electrical engineering from Columbia University before beginning his long association with submarines. During World War II, he headed the electrical section of the Bureau of Ships, and in the peace that followed became involved with nuclear energy as a source of ship power in the future. Despite what has been frequently described as "an increasingly cantankerous and unorthodox manner that made him widely unpopular with other officers," he began a vigorous personal campaign to develop nuclear-powered submarines. In command of the Bureau of Ships' nuclear power divisions, his efforts and oftentimes abrasive manner pushed the projects he believed in to the fore, and eventually resulted in the launching, in 1954, of the first nuclear-powered craft, the attack submarine *Nautilus*. He also worked on the Polaris missile system for submarines and served as assistant chief of the Bureau of Ships and on the Atomic Energy Commission. Still on active duty but transferred to the retired list by President Lyndon Johnson in 1964, Rickover remained on active duty until 1982 as deputy commander for nuclear propulsion, naval sea system command, in that year he was retired as an admiral after 64 years on active duty, the longest in the history of the U.S. Navy. He remained controversial and outspoken right up to the time of his death on July 8, 1986, in Arlington, Virginia.

Robalo (SS-273)

Built by Manitowoc Shipbuilding Company this submarine of the Gato class was launched in March 1943 and ordered to the Pacific where, on her first two patrols, she damaged a large freighter and a 7,500-ton tanker. Her third patrol took her to the South China Sea in the vicinity of the Natuna Islands. After traversing Makassar and Balabac Straits, she was to arrive on station the first week in July and operate there for one month. On July 2 a contact report stated that *Robalo* had sighted a Fuso-class battleship with air cover and two destroyers for escort just east of Borneo. No other messages were received from *Robalo*, and when she did not return from patrol, she was reported as presumed lost.

The following information (now available in the Ship's History Section of the Office of Naval Records and History) was received via Philippine guerrillas and a U.S. Navy enlisted man who was a prisoner of war at Puerto Princesa Prison Camp in the Philippines:

On 2 August, 1944, a note dropped from the window of the prison cell in which survivors from Robalo *were held was picked up by an American soldier in a work detail and given to Yeoman H.D. Hough, USN, another prisoner. On 4 August, Hough contacted Mrs. Trinidad Mendosa, wife of guerilla leader Dr. Mendosa, who furnished further information on the survivors. From these sources, he put together the following facts:* Robalo *was sunk 26 July 1944, two miles off the western coast of Palawan Island as a result of an explosion of her after battery. Four men swam ashore, an officer and three enlisted men: Samuel L. Tucker, ENS; Floyd G. Laughlin, QMI; Wallace K. Martin SM3; and Mason C. Poston, EM2. They made their way through the jungles to a small barrio northwest of the Puerto Princesa camp. They were captured there by Japanese Military Police, and confined in the jail. They were held for guerilla activities rather than as prisoners of war, it is said. On 15 August 1944, they were evacuated by a Japanese destroyer, and nothing further is known of their destination or whereabouts.*

The prisoners from *Robalo* may have been executed by the Japanese or the destroyer may have been sunk. At any rate, they were never recovered and their note stated that there were no other survivors. There is doubt that a battery explosion could be sufficiently violent to cause the sinking of the boat, and it is more likely that *Robalo* struck an enemy mine. *Robalo* earned two battle stars for World War II service.

Rock (SS-274)

Built by Manitowoc Shipbuilding Company this Gato-class submarine was launched in June 1943 and deployed to the Pacific where, on her first patrol, in late February 1944, she contacted a large enemy convoy en route to Truk. While making a night surface approach on the convoy, she was detected by an enemy destroyer while on the surface, fired a salvo of four torpedoes, all of which missed, and then came under fire from the destroyer's five-inch guns. *Rock* then submerged and experienced four hours of random depth charge attacks, which damaged her periscope and forced a retreat to Pearl Harbor after an unsuccessful 34-day war patrol. Her second patrol found no likely targets, and she began her third in late June 1944, in company with sister submarines *Tilefish* and *Sawfish*, heading for Majuro as a wolf pack. In mid-July, in the Luzon Straits, *Rock* contacted a Japanese convoy of seven large ships and three escorts, firing 10 torpedoes, six of which hit their mark. She was subsequently depth charged, but escaped undamaged. On July 21, another enemy convoy was contacted, consisting of six large ships and four escorts. *Rock* fired four torpedoes, two of which were hits. The remainder of the time on station was uneventful, with the exception of weathering a severe typhoon and witnessing the sinking of a Japanese submarine.

In early September 1944, *Rock* headed for the South China Sea for her fourth war patrol, and in late October attacked a tanker, which had three escorts. She fired a salvo of six torpedoes and scored three hits. A few days later, she had the unique experience of firing nine torpedoes at a sister submarine, *Darter,* which had been stranded on Bombay Shoal, to prevent the Japanese from examining her. Unfortunately, because of shallow water, the torpedoes did not find their mark, and *Rock* sailed to Fremantle, Western Australia, for her refit. Another uneventful patrol was her fifth, though she rescued a downed pilot. Her sixth patrol, to the Indian Ocean, saw more action, starting with the rescue of 15 merchant seamen, whose ship had been torpedoed, and who had been adrift in a lifeboat for 32 days. Shortly after landing the survivors at an Allied base and returning to sea, *Rock* was bombed by a fighter plane and that night was struck by a dud torpedo. Neither event caused any critical damage. In late March 1945, she sank an enemy destroyer escort (834 tons) in a night action, and in mid-April joined forces with the submarine *Tigrone* in the bombardment of Bataan Island, where they left the Japanese radio station in ruins. Forced to sail to San Francisco for an overhaul, *Rock* proceeded to Pearl Harbor and readied for a seventh patrol, which was canceled as the war ended. In early 1951, after a period in mothballs, *Rock* was converted to a *Migraine III*-type radar-picket submarine (SSR). She was bisected at the forward bulkhead of the control room, and a new 24-foot section was inserted to house the electronic equipment necessary in fulfilling her new mission. In late July 1954, she headed for the western Pacific area to operate as part of a carrier strike force in defense of the Formosa Straits. Throughout the rest of the 1950s and 1960s, *Rock* participated in normal training exercises, conducted operations off the Pacific coast, and conducted operations in support of fleet training in the Hawaiian operating areas. She was decommissioned in September 1969. Rock earned four battle stars for World War II service.

Ronquil (SS-396)

A submarine of the Balao class, she was built by Portsmouth Naval Shipyard and launched in January 1944. *Ronquil* was ordered to join the Pacific Fleet, sailing on her first war patrol in August and September in the northeastern Formosa area, where she sank two attack cargo ships of 4,646 tons and 5,969 tons. *Ronquil's* second war patrol,

in October and November, was carried out in two phases. She first operated with a coordinated submarine attack group in the Bungo Suido area, and then joined six other submarines to carry out an antipatrol ship sweep off the Bonin Islands. Her third and fourth war patrols, in 1945, brought her no worthwhile enemy targets but resulted in the rescue of 10 army aviators from a B-29 bomber downed between the Bonins and Japan. Her fifth and last patrol, from mid-May to the end of July 1945, took her into the East China Sea and the Yellow Sea. She proceeded to San Diego in the fall of 1945 and engaged in training exercises off the California coast. In January 1947, *Ronquil* departed San Diego for her first peacetime western Pacific deployment. This cruise lasted 114 days and took the submarine to Tahiti, the Carolines, the Marianas, Japan, and the Yellow Sea. On her return to San Diego, she resumed local operations before beginning a three-year period of intensive training in offensive and antisubmarine warfare, embodying lessons learned during World War II, as well as new postwar developments. In 1953 she was converted to a GUPPY IIA at Mare Island Naval Shipyard. During GUPPY modernization, her superstructure and sail were streamlined for greater submerged speed, and she received new, increased-capacity batteries for underwater endurance, and a snorkel that enabled her to use her diesels at periscope depth. New electronics, including improved sonar and fire control systems, were installed, and in June 1953 she departed for Japan, participating in antisubmarine operations in the waters near Japan. This was to set the pattern for most of her later deployments. She returned to San Diego, where she engaged in Naval Reserve training and fleet exercises and other operations off the West Coast. During the summer of 1960, she participated in extensive antisubmarine exercises in the eastern Pacific with United States and Canadian forces, and in the early fall of 1961 again sailed for the Far East, returning in March 1962. Late in 1964 *Ronquil* began preparations for deployment to the Vietnam area, and in February 1965 she sailed for Southeast Asia and a five-month deployment. On her return to San Diego, she briefly participated in the filming of the motion picture *Ice Station Zebra*. She shuttled back and forth on assignments in the western Pacific, the eastern Pacific, and on the West Coast, with the Seventh Fleet, and in July 1971 was decommissioned and sold to Spain. Renamed *Isaac Peral,* the submarine served the Spanish navy until being stricken in 1982. *Ronquil* earned six battle stars for World War II service and is credited with sinking two vessels for 10,615 tons.

Runner (SS-275)

Launched in May 1942 and built by Portsmouth Naval Shipyard, this submarine of the Gato class was ordered to the Pacific Fleet and was sent on her first patrol in mid-

January 1943, to the area between Midway and the Palau Islands. Five Japanese cargo ships were torpedoed on this patrol, but none was confirmed as being sunk. In making the last attack of the patrol on a freighter off Peleliu, *Runner* was damaged by a near miss from a bomb dropped from a patrol bomber. The concussion knocked out her sound gear and the power supply for both periscope hoists. She made her escape by a deep dive, the crew made emergency repairs, and the ship returned to Pearl Harbor for overhaul. On her second patrol, April 1 to May 6, *Runner's* primary mission was to lay a minefield off Pedro Blanco Rock. Successful in this mission, she proceeded to Hainan Straits, off the Chinese mainland. One freighter was torpedoed, and the sound of a ship breaking up was heard over her sound gear, but again the kill could not be confirmed, and the boat returned to Midway. In late May, *Runner* left Midway to proceed to her third war patrol, and was to have reached an area south of Hokkaido and east of the northern tip of Honshu, where she was to patrol until

the Fourth of July. She was never heard from following her departure from Midway. After futile attempts to sight the submarine or reach her by radio, she was reported as presumed lost. A summary of Japanese antisubmarine attacks received since the close of the war uncovered no mention of an attack that could explain the loss of *Runner.* Thus her loss must be ascribed to an enemy minefield, of which there were at least four in the area to which she was assigned, to an operational casualty, or to an unreported enemy attack. Destruction by a mine is considered the most likely of these possibilities. *Runner* was awarded one battle star for World War II service and credited with sinking two vessels for 6,274 tons.

Runner (SS-476)

A Tench-class submarine, *Runner* was built by Portsmouth Naval Shipyard and launched in October 1944. *Runner* was deployed to Pearl Harbor, from which she departed in late

(United States Navy)

May 1945 for her first war patrol, off Honshu, Japan, where her primary mission was to scout for the presence of defensive minefields guarding the Japanese home islands. In early July, while on patrol in the Sea of Japan, she intercepted two worthwhile targets, a tanker and a minesweeper. The tanker and her two escorts escaped the spread of torpedoes fired at them, but the minesweeper was splintered by three of *Runner*'s torpedoes. Before departing station, she took aboard 16 downed aviators from submarines *Gabilan* and *Aspro* for transfer to Guam. The eagerness of the crew to effect a second successful combat mission was balked when, immediately after arriving on station off the east coast of Honshu, peace was announced. After a short stint at Pearl Harbor and New London, *Runner* was based in Panama for the next three years, and then at Norfolk, Virginia, for the following seven. *Runner* was converted to a Fleet Snorkel submarine in 1952 at Charleston Naval Shipyard. She subsequently participated in NATO exercises, visiting ports in France and England, then moved to San Juan, Puerto Rico, for a year, operating in the Caribbean as a Regulus missile guidance submarine. Returning to Norfolk in July 1959, she operated with the fleet along the Atlantic coast for the next three years. She deployed to the Mediterranean in early 1962, operating with United States and NATO units. The remainder of 1962 was taken up with local ASW exercises; throughout 1963 and 1964, she engaged in antisubmarine warfare exercises in the western Atlantic, then saw service in the Great Lakes, training Naval Reservists, and was later deployed to the Mediterranean with the Sixth Fleet. In 1969, *Runner* was towed to the Great Lakes Naval Training Station, where she was redesignated AGSS-476 and served as a Naval Reserve training vessel until decommissioned and struck from the Navy list in December 1971. *Runner* received one battle star for World War II service and was credited with sinking one vessel for 630 tons.

S

Sailfish (SS-192)

The name has historically caused some confusion in the records, since this submarine was originally the *Squalus*, and was renamed after her disastrous sinking in May 1939, salvage, and commissioning as a new vessel a year later. *Sailfish* went on to have a very successful war record in the Pacific, sinking or damaging enemy ships for a total of more than 83,000 tons. She was finally decommissioned in October 1945, but her conning tower was on display at the Washington Navy Yard for many years. (See also *SQUALUS*.)

Sailfish (SS-572)

Launched in September 1955, this boat was built by Portsmouth Naval Shipyard and the first of the class bearing her name and was 3,160 tons on the surface, and carried a complement of 10 officers and 85 enlisted men. *Sailfish* was the first submarine built expressly for radar-picket service, and was also the largest conventionally powered submarine in the U.S. Navy built after World War II. She began her first extended deployment with the Sixth Fleet in the Mediterranean, and after five years of service was refitted and reclassified as an attack submarine. After five more years of service, she was again modernized and upgraded to a GUPPY III and assigned to SubRon8 and joined the submarines of SubDiv82, specialists in antisubmarine warfare. At the end of the 1960s, *Sailfish* was ordered to the Pacific and assigned for deployment with the Seventh Fleet in the western Pacific, where she operated out of Yokosuka, Japan. In January 1970, she participated in Allied exercises off Taiwan and Okinawa; in February, she conducted joint training operations with Republic of Korea navy units; and in March, she operated with units of the Japanese Maritime Self Defense Force. She experienced two more tours of duty in the western Pacific (WesPac) before being assigned to the West Coast, where she operated until being decommissioned in September 1978. She is credited with sinking seven vessels for 45,029 tons. (See also *SQUALUS [SS-192].*)

Salmon (SS-182)

Launched in June 1937 and commissioned in 1938, *Salmon* was the first to bear her name, which was also the name of her new class. She joined SubDiv15 at Kittery, Maine, as flagship of her division, and operated along the Atlantic coast until the division was shifted to the West Coast at San Diego. In 1940, she was transferred with her division and the submarine tender *Holland* to the Asiatic station in Manila to bolster defenses in the Philippines as tension was growing because of Japanese militarism. *Salmon* was conducting a patrol along the west coast of Luzon at the time of the surprise air raid by the Japanese against the Philippine bases and Pearl Harbor. Having been on defensive deployment since November 27, in a wait-and-watch posture, she commenced war patrolling immediately upon receiving word of the attacks. On December 22, while on the surface in the Lingayen Gulf, she encountered two Japanese destroyers and pressed home an attack that seemed to bewilder the reluctant enemy. She succeeded in damaging both targets, catching them as they veered course in opposite directions. In January 1942, she moved south to operate in the Gulf of Davao and off the southern tip of Mindanao and thence proceeded to Manipa Strait in the Molucca Islands. In February, she patrolled the Flores Sea from north of Timor to Lombok Strait in the Sunda Islands, then put into Tjilatjap on the south coast of Java on the 13th. When this harbor was threatened by the Japanese, she moved her base of operations to Exmouth Gulf, Australia, on February 20, 1942, and set out on her second war patrol, which found no targets. Her third patrol was more successful, when she established a barrier along the south coast of Java to intercept Japanese shipping. In early May, she torpedoed and sank an 11,441-ton repair ship; and, on the 28th, she sank a 4,382-ton passenger-cargo vessel. Her fourth patrol, in the South China–Sulu Seas area, was highlighted mainly by numerous sightings and reports of shipping movements to sister subs in the vicinity.

Salmon's fifth war patrol sent her to the seas off Corregidor and Subic Bay. On November 17, along the approach to Manila Bay, she sighted three vessels and maneuvered for attack. She fired torpedoes at each of the ships and succeeded in damaging two and sinking a 5,873-ton salvage vessel before heading for the West Coast and refitting. Her sixth patrol found her assigned a special mission that took her to the coast of Honshu, Japan, where she damaged two freighters. Her next three missions took her to the Kuriles to help cut Japan's Aleutian supply route, where she sank a coastal patrol vessel and a passenger-cargo vessel and damaged three freighters. In April 1944, *Salmon* departed from Pearl Harbor en route to Johnston Island in company with *Seadragon*, assigned a special photo reconnaissance mission for her 10th patrol, which would assist in preparing plans for gaining control of the Caroline Islands. She conducted a reconnaissance of Ulithi and two other strategic atolls, which resulted in much valuable information that was utilized in last-minute changes to the American military assault strategy.

Salmon's 11th and last war patrol, beginning in late September, was conducted in company with submarines *Trigger* and *Sterlet* as a coordinated attack group in the Ryukyu Islands. In late October, *Salmon* attacked a large tanker that had been previously damaged by *Trigger*. This tanker was protected by four antisubmarine patrol vessels cruising around the stricken ship. *Salmon* fired four torpedoes and made two good hits, but was forced to dive deep under a severe depth charge attack by the escorts. She leveled off at 300 feet but was soon forced to nearly 500 feet—way beyond her maximum depth—because of damage and additional pounding of the depth charges. Unable to control leaking and maintain depth level, she was forced to surface to fight for survival. Although she was a sitting duck, the enemy seemed wary and held their distance while sniffing out the situation—just long enough to give *Salmon*'s crew precious time to repair some of the most threatening damage. When the Japanese vessels finally

began to close, *Salmon* took an aggressive stance, turned on the attackers and, passing within 50 yards down the side of one, raked it with her deck gun. Apparently killing the topside personnel of the patrol escort, which came to a stop, *Salmon* then exchanged fire with a second enemy escort, which again seemed to hesitate at some distance for reinforcement from two others heading for the battle scene. *Salmon* used another strategy and began radioing directions in plain language for all other subs in the vicinity to attack. This bold action apparently discouraged the Japanese commanders who, fearing other submarines in the vicinity, began milling around and pinging on sound gear, while temporarily ignoring *Salmon* as a target. Shortly thereafter, *Salmon* took advantage of a rain squall and slipped away. Other than the damage caused by depth charges, *Salmon* suffered only a few small-caliber hits from the enemy vessels. Escorted by her sister subs, she made it to Saipan and was later given one-third credit for a 10,500-ton tanker. But her war patrol days were over, and she was ordered to the Portsmouth, New Hampshire, Navy Yard for repairs and overhaul, and then assigned as a training vessel. After the war's end, deemed too badly damaged for further overhaul, she was decommissioned on September 24, 1945. *Salmon* was awarded the Presidential Unit Citation for extraordinary heroism against enemy surface vessels during her eleventh war patrol in restricted, enemy-held waters of the Pacific, and she earned nine battle stars for World War II service in the Asiatic-Pacific area. *Salmon* is credited with sinking four vessels for 24,107 tons.

Salmon (SS-573)

Built by the Portsmouth Naval Shipyard and launched February 25, 1956, *Salmon* was the second of a class of radar-picket submarines and the largest and most powerful conventional-powered submarine built after World War II.

Salmon was sent to San Diego, California, in late May 1957, by way of the Panama Canal to Callao, Peru, and then on to San Diego, arriving on July 25, 1957. Her first western Pacific deployment came in September and *Salmon* joined the Seventh Fleet, returning to San Diego on April 19, 1958.

Undergoing overhaul and limited conversion at Mare Island Naval Shipyard, *Salmon* gave up a large radom from her superstructure but gained instrumented missile guidance capability and improved, longer-range sonar. Again she operated with the Seventh Fleet in Allied training exercises, returning to San Diego on February 14, 1960. Through 1961 *Salmon* operated along the western coast of the United States, was reclassified SS-573, and in November was reassigned to SubDiv52. During the 1960s *Salmon* earned five consecutive Battle Efficiency "E"'s.

During the latter part of 1962, *Salmon* had her third WesPac deployment, operated with hunter-killer groups in fleet exercises, became flagship of SubFlot1, was the first submarine to earn and be awarded the Golden "E," and won hashmarks signifying retention of that status during 1963 and 1964. During June 1964, *Salmon* was modernized to GUPPY III status and commenced her fourth WesPac deployment on August 23. *Salmon's* fifth deployment to the western Pacific was from March 20 to October 4, 1967.

Overhaul at San Francisco took place during the spring of 1968 to prepare *Salmon* for support of the DSRV (Deep Submergence Recovery Vehicle) program. On June 1, 1968, she was redesignated AGSS-573 and on October 25 sailed for her sixth WesPac deployment. *Salmon* had three more WesPac deployments; however, on her ninth the deployment was cancelled upon arrival in Pearl Harbor due to damage to her number three and number four main engines. Overhaul was begun on November 26 at Mare Island Naval Shipyard.

Salmon was decommissioned and struck from the Navy list on October 1, 1977. She was converted to a shallow water sonar target in 1992 and sunk near Hudson Canyon, south of Long Island on June 5, 1993.

Sam Houston (SSBN-609)

Launched in February 1961, this nuclear-powered submarine of the Ethan Allen class was the nation's seventh Polaris submarine. She contained 16 missile tubes and four 21-inch forward torpedo tubes, and carried a complement of 10 officers and 100 enlisted men. *Sam Houston* embarked on her first patrol in October 1962, and later made several historic deployments abroad, including a rendezvous with NATO forces in the Mediterranean. She completed 17 Polaris deterrent patrols prior to entering the Portsmouth Navy Yard in the fall of 1966 for a complete overhaul, which gave the boat the latest developments in submarine operational capability. A remarkable statistic revealed that she had spent over 70 percent of her life at sea submerged, ready to perform her mission of deterrence. She was decommissioned and struck from the Navy list in June 1991.

Sandlance (SS-381)

A submarine of the Balao class, *Sandlance* was launched in June 1943 at the Portsmouth Naval Shipyard, was ordered to join the Pacific Fleet, and in February 1944 departed on her first war patrol, in the Kurile Islands. En route, she passed through two typhoons and encountered fields of ice, which damaged her number one periscope. Nevertheless, she succeeded in sinking two cargo ships and damaging others. In mid-March, she came up to periscope depth and found herself in the midst of a Japanese convoy, consisting of five merchantmen and three heavily-armed war-

Sam Houston (SSBN-609), seen steaming out of port, was commissioned in March 1962, and was later adapted to service for the transportation and support of navy SEAL units. *(United States Navy)*

ships. Near the end of her mission, she had only six torpedoes remaining, but she put them to good use, loosing four from the stern tubes and two from the bow. Two of the four stern torpedoes hit a merchantman and the other two ripped into a light cruiser, while the two from the bow smashed into another freighter. At least two of the ships went to the bottom. For her nastiness, *Sandlance* underwent a 16-hour, 100-depth charge pounding from the accompanying destroyers before she could finally escape and head home. Her second patrol was in the Marianas, at the start of the American invasion of those islands. She contributed heavily to the success of that campaign by knocking out of action no fewer than five of the Japanese cargo ships that were carrying supplies and ammunition to the Japanese land forces. Her next patrol, to the Molucca and Celebes Seas in July, found her running into trouble. She started out well, sinking a gunboat and damaging two other ships. But in early August, while she was stalking several small freighters, aircraft bombs exploded just astern of her with enough force to lift her several feet and damage her port shaft. She was then attacked by enemy escorts and, to add to her misery, was further damaged in the stern when one of her torpedoes exploded prematurely, only seconds after being launched. Unable to repair the damage at sea, she limped to the nearest Allied port, Fremantle, on one shaft. After extensive repairs, she put to sea again but her remaining two patrols were relatively quiet, the first knocking off a small coastal freighter and the second curtailed by the Japanese surrender on August 15. After the war, *Sandlance* remained inactive until designated for loan to the Brazilian navy under the terms of the Military Assistance Program. She was later sold to Brazil, where she operated as *Rio Grande do Sol* (S-11) in the 1970s. *Sandlance* earned five battle stars and a Presidential Unit Citation for World War II service and is credited with sinking 10 vessels for 37,368 tons.

Sargo (SS-188)

Designated the first of a new class bearing her name, *Sargo* was launched in June 1938, commissioned a year later and assigned for duty with the Pacific Fleet. She operated in the eastern and mid-Pacific for the next two years, including a practice, 40-day war patrol between Midway and the Marshall Islands in the fall of 1941, and was stationed in Manila when Japan attacked Pearl Harbor. The next day, she got underway for her first war patrol, which took her along the coast of French Indochina and to the Dutch East Indies. She made eight separate attacks on enemy shipping, but the depth control and firing mechanisms of her Mark 14 torpedoes malfunctioned, permitting her targets to escape unharmed. On January 20, 1942, she assisted in the rescue of the crew of *S-36* after that submarine had run aground on Taku Reef in the Makassar Strait. *Sargo* remained surfaced, relaying distress messages to friendly aircraft and surface ships. After the rescue by a Dutch merchant ship, *Siberole*, *Sargo* headed for Java, where she offloaded her remaining torpedoes and took aboard one million rounds of .30 caliber ammunition desperately needed by Allied forces in the Philippines. After delivering her vital cargo to Mindanao, she returned to Java with 24 aircrew men from Clark Field on board. In late February 1942, *Sargo* headed for Australia and was one day out of Fremantle when she was attacked by an Allied plane that mistook her for a Japanese ship. Although a near-miss by the plane's bomb caused minor damage, she arrived safely at Fremantle with 31 passengers from Java.

In early June, *Sargo* put to sea for her fourth patrol, in the Gulf of Siam off Malaya. She attacked only one target, a small tanker, but failed to score before returning to Australia eight weeks later. During her next four patrols, she sank a freighter, a tanker, and a cargo ship, and had an unconfirmed sinking of another cargo ship. On her ninth and 10th patrols, she had better luck: a cargo ship and two passenger-cargo vessels. She conducted two more missions during 1944, sinking one more cargo ship and damaging trawlers with her deck gun, far into enemy waters, before being pulled off war patrol duty and assigned to training

submarine crews. *Sargo* was awarded eight battle stars for her service in World War II and received the Philippine Presidential Unit Citation. She is credited with sinking seven vessels for 32,777+ tons. *Sargo* was decommissioned June 22, 1946.

Sargo (SSN-583)

Built by Mare Island Naval Shipyard, she was the second submarine to bear the *Sargo* name and was of the Skate class and launched in October 1957. From the start, she was designated for arctic exploration. Following a 19,000-mile Pacific shakedown cruise, scientific instruments were installed to assist her in navigating under the shifting polar ice with its potentially hazardous submerged pressure ridges; in locating open leads and thin ice through which to surface; and in gathering oceanographic and hydrographic data. November and December 1959 brought intensive training programs and the embarkation of scientific specialists; and, on January 18, 1960, *Sargo* cleared Pearl Harbor and headed north to make a submerged exploration of the arctic basin. By the 25th, *Sargo* had reached the vicinity of St. Matthews Island where she found ice, in packs and blocks, and made her first stationary dive while surrounded by ice. On February 9, she arrived under the North Pole. Making her first pass under the pole, she began a clover leaf search for thin ice and surfaced 25 feet from the pole. By March 1960, *Sargo* had covered more than 11,000 miles, 6,003 under ice, taking many oceanographic and hydrographic findings. Later she participated in many other assignments, including exercises to enhance the antisubmarine warfare readiness of hunter-killer groups and actions to support operations resulting from the Gulf of Tonkin incident. *Sargo* was decommissioned in February 1988.

Saury (SS-189) (S-8)

Launched in August 1939, this submarine of the Sargo class and built by the Electric Boat Company had one of the lengthiest—and in some ways most frustrating—war service of any boat in the navy's history, and an unusual taste of World War II before it even happened. After service along the East Coast, in the Caribbean, and off the West Coast, she sailed to Hawaii in April 1940 to participate in Fleet Problem XXI, an eight-phased problem simulating an attack on the defenses of the Hawaiian area and the destruction of one fleet prior to the concentration of another. In October 1941, she was ordered to the Philippines, where she was operating out of Cavite at the time of the Pearl Harbor attack. She steamed out on her first patrol on December 8, moving north to search for and intercept ships of the expected Japanese invasion force. Lack of emergency identification systems and radio problems complicated her job. During the next two weeks, she patrolled near Vigan and on December 21 was ordered into Lingayen Gulf in response to a report from submarine *Stinger* of Japanese forces there. For the next month, she ranged the seas looking for enemy targets, unable to close in because of attacks by Japanese destroyers, and suffering many very threatening depth charges. In early February, *Saury* departed Soerabaja for her second war patrol, heading east along the north coasts of the Lesser Sundas. On the night of the 19th, she received word of the Japanese landing on Bali, sighted her first enemy ships of the patrol, and commenced 18 hours of submerged evasive tactics to avoid destroyer depth charges. Despite all further attempts to engage the enemy, she had little to report but frustrations and incessant depth charging.

Further patrols proved equally unsuccessful, in part because of counterattacks by destroyers, but also because of mechanical and weapons problems. Finally, on August 24, 1942, in Manila Bay, she sank a small tanker, and two weeks later, off Makassar City, she sent off three torpedoes and dispensed with a 8,606-ton aircraft ferry. On her fifth patrol, she made 27 enemy contacts, but scored only one hit, which at the time could not be confirmed. Leaving in early May 1943 on her sixth patrol, she had more luck. After battling a typhoon, she sighted a five-ship convoy near the Japanese island of Kyushu and sank a cargo ship, and by the end of the month another two cargo ships and a tanker.

Saury's seventh war patrol, starting in mid-July 1943, was almost a disaster. One week after departing Pearl Harbor, her number four main engine broke down and remained inoperative for the rest of the mission. Then, at the end of the month, while trying to intercept two large warships and a destroyer, she was forced by depth charges to dive deep. But the charges did part of their work, jolting her into a dangerous list and knocking her two periscopes and both radars totally out of commission. After limping back to Pearl Harbor, she at least had the satisfaction of learning that she had been given credit for damaging an enemy destroyer. During repair and refit, *Saury* was given an enlarged conning tower, new periscopes, and new radar equipment. Her number four engine was completely overhauled, and in early October, she was ready for sea.

On her eighth and ninth war patrols, October 4 to November 26, 1943, and December 21, 1943, to February 14, 1944, she inflicted no damage. Much of the latter patrol was spent in fighting extremely bad weather in the East China Sea, during which proper navigational positions were unobtainable. At the end of that patrol, one day out of Midway, she was swamped by an oversized swell while her hatches were open. The wave overtook *Saury* from the quarter, pushed her over to a 40-degree list to port, turned her 140 degrees from her course, and sent green water through two of her hatches. Electrical equip-

ment grounded out, small fires were started, and she was out of action for almost a day before emergency repairs could be completed.

In late June 1944, *Saury* departed on her 10th war patrol, soon to be marred by a cracked engine cylinder. But she continued on to her assigned area, San Bernardino Strait in the Philippines, where she was again unsuccessful in finding targets before being forced to return to base. From September 20 to November 29, 1944, *Saury* conducted her 11th and last war patrol. She patrolled in the Nansei Shoto area, rescuing a downed pilot but sinking no enemy ships, as she hunted in the wake of the fast carrier forces. After stopping at Saipan for refitting, she proceeded on the second phase of her mission: an antipatrol vessel sweep north of the Bonins. Extremely poor weather again interfered, but on the 18th, she damaged a Japanese tanker before returning to Pearl Harbor. For the remainder of the war, *Saury* served in the Hawaiian area as a target and training submarine. As soon as the war ended, she was ordered to San Francisco, where she was decommissioned in June 1946. *Saury* earned seven battle stars during World War II and was credited with sinking five vessels for 28,542 tons.

Sawfish (SS-276)

Launched in June 1942, this submarine of the Gato class got underway for the first of her 10 war patrols at the end of January 1943, leaving Pearl Harbor and heading for waters off southwestern Japan where she attacked several targets and reported, though unconfirmed, that she had sunk or damaged some. The same problem of nonconfirmation stalked her on her third patrol (after sinking only a gunboat on her second), when she attacked a convoy of nine ships in the East China Sea and concluded that she had scored several hits. Finally, early on the morning of July 27, 1943, her luck changed when she attacked a convoy escorted by a minelayer. *Sawfish* fired a spread of four torpedoes from a range of only 750 yards, finished off the minelayer, and then ducked deep for an hour to escape retaliation. Her next three patrols were frustrated by defective torpedoes, which failed to find their mark, but she ended up with one kill—a 3,267-ton passenger-cargo ship, before returning to Midway. She claimed two other hits, but they were unconfirmed.

During her seventh war patrol, *Sawfish* joined submarines *Rock* and *Tilefish* for wolf-pack operations in the Philippines. On July 18, she damaged a tanker and, on the 26th, fired a spread of four torpedoes at a surfaced Japanese submarine, which exploded and sank. For her eighth patrol, *Sawfish* joined another wolf-pack mission, this time with *Drum* and *Icefish,* and, from time to time, other submarines, in waters south of Formosa where the submarines took a heavy toll on enemy shipping. *Sawfish* herself accounted for a 6,521-ton tanker on October 9 and a 6,838-ton seaplane tender two weeks later. During the patrol, she also served on lifeguard station in support of carrier raids, and rescued a pilot who had survived four-and-one-half days at sea in a small rubber boat without food, water, or sunshade. *Sawfish* spent her last two war patrols mainly on lifeguard duty off Formosa, where she rescued a pilot, and off Nansei Shoto supporting air strikes, and preparing for and covering the conquest of Okinawa. She returned to Pearl Harbor in late April 1945, and was ordered to San Francisco for overhaul in the Bethlehem Steel Company yard there. She was ready for action and heading toward Hawaii on August 15 when hostilities ended. She reached Pearl Harbor on the 22nd but soon headed back to the West Coast for duty as a training ship for the West Coast Fleet Sound School. She later served as a Naval Reserve training ship, and was decommissioned in June 1946. *Sawfish* received eight battle stars for service during World War II and was credited with sinking six vessels for 22,504 tons.

S boats

The 51 submarines in this class were launched during a period from 1918 through 1922, and were built by a number of shipyards, including Lake Torpedo Boat Company, Fore River Shipbuilding Company, Union Iron Works, and Portsmouth Naval Yard. They varied in tonnages from 1,062 to 1,230 on the surface, and were designed to carry a crew of four officers and 34 enlisted men. For armament, they had four 21-inch torpedo tubes forward, and some of the later boats also had a 21-inch torpedo aft. All were equipped with deck guns, and a few were able to lay mines or release depth charges. Although most of the S boats were decommissioned prior to World War II, 22 of them—despite their age—saw service on war patrols in the

Pacific, several with enviable records of enemy ships sunk. Those with the most auspicious or interesting records are the following.

S-18 served in the Aleutians and was credited with one battle star. However, like many of the other S boats that were urgently ordered to enemy waters, she suffered from aging and had the disadvantages of mechanical breakdowns, outdated communications equipment, and malfunctioning torpedoes.

S-23, also assigned to the Aleutians, was deployed on six war patrols, two of them in such stormy weather that crew members were injured when 20-foot waves broke over the bridge, causing serious injuries and broken bones. Most of her operations were in support of American bombardments of Japanese-held islands. She was awarded one battle star.

S-27 was stationed at Mare Island, California, at the outbreak of the war and in May 1942, after being refitted, she was ordered to patrol the Aleutians. On June 18, while on patrol near Kiska, she grounded on rocks off St. Makarius Point. After all efforts to free her failed and she was badly pounded by heavy seas, causing flooding, the crew members were evacuated by rubber rafts and lines rigged to the shore. Everything portable was taken from the stricken boat and all equipment on board was destroyed, leaving nothing but the hulk. There were no casualties.

S-28 was stationed in San Diego when the war started, and in May 1942 was sent to Dutch Harbor for patrol duty in the Aleutians. Although she made seven war patrols, she was plagued by slow speed, mechanical failures, and bad weather and succeeded in sinking only one enemy ship, a 1,368-ton gunboat. In October 1943, she was ordered to Pearl Harbor, and on July 4, 1944, was conducting anti-submarine warfare exercises with a Coast Guard vessel, the *Reliance,* in Hawaiian waters. Late in the afternoon, she dived about four miles distant from the *Reliance,* which

S-1 (SS-105), shown with a floatplane on her afterdeck in 1923, served as an experimental vessel to explore the potential for using submarine-borne observation and scouting aircraft. The plane was housed, collapsed, in the cylindrical pod mounted abaft the conning tower, and quickly assembled and launched by ballasting the boat until the decks were awash. (United States Navy)

USS *S-21* (SS-126) through USS *S-24* (SS-129), with crews on board, standing ready. *S-21, S-22,* and *S-23* were launched in 1920 and scrapped in 1945, while *S-24* was launched in 1922 and intentionally destroyed in August 1947. *(United States Navy)*

soon lost contact with her. At no time were there any distress signals or sounds indicating any explosion. Despite searches by other vessels during the next two days, the only trace ever found was an oil slick made by diesel fuel. Because of the extreme depth in the area of the exercises, salvage operations were impossible. The ultimate conclusion was that *S-28* had lost depth control, and gone so deep that she was crushed by the ocean pressure.

S-30 had a taste of war prior to Pearl Harbor when she completed four patrols along the East Coast looking for German U-boats. She was later transferred to Dutch Harbor, Alaska, and in August 1942, departed on her first of five war patrols in the Pacific. Although constantly plagued by mechanical, engineering, and communication problems, she managed during her wartime career to dispatch a large sampan, a 5,228-ton cargo ship, and a 7,000-ton merchantman. She was awarded two battle stars.

S-31 was also assigned to Alaska, starting her first war patrol in July 1942, where she too suffered foul weather,

mechanical breakdowns, and such poor communications that she was twice attacked by American patrol planes and almost sunk. Yet she managed, on her fifth patrol, to sink a 2,864-ton cargo ship. Transferred to Hawaii in early 1943, she left for her sixth patrol in March, heading for Kwajalein Atoll, for her seventh patrol to the New Hebrides, and for her eighth and last to Rabaul and New Guinea.

S-32 received orders to Alaska in July 1942, where she patrolled the Kuriles during one mission and ran aground while trying to approach two enemy ships at anchor, yet still managed to set one afire with torpedoes. In March 1943, she attacked two enemy submarines. The first was never confirmed, but the second was seen, with smoke pouring from her conning tower, heading for the nearest beach, and then disappearing from view. During her next patrol, she sighted two small ships and fired four torpedoes. Two explosions were seen and both ships disappeared from the radar screen. At this point, her war career was cut short by repeated engineering breakdowns, radar

S-36 (SS-141), which was built in the early 1920s, was one of several S-boats called into service when America faced World War II with a shortage of submarines. Despite her age, plagued by equipment failures, and often battling Pacific storms, *S-36* undertook war patrols, sank a transport, and finally ran hard aground on Taka Bakang Reef and was damaged beyond repair and abandoned. *(United States Navy)*

failings, and other problems and she was ordered back to Mare Island, California, and decommissioned. *S-32* received five battle stars.

S-33 joined her sister ships at Dutch Harbor in July 1942, where she undertook eight war patrols and earned one battle star before being put on reserve and placed on training status in 1944. She sank two enemy sampans.

S-34 had a similar record, constantly faced with equipment failures, storms, and ice, but undertook six war patrols, sank one freighter and received one battle star.

S-35 was deployed to Dutch Harbor and set out on her first war patrol in mid-April 1942. In mid-December, while on patrol near Amchitka and after a tough battering by heavy seas, which caused injuries to several crew members, she suffered a series of fires in her control room and forward battery, which not only threatened personnel but also could eventually have caused explosions and sunk the boat. In June, returning to the Aleutians after repairs at the Puget Sound Navy Yard, she engaged and sank a 5,430-ton Japanese ship. Although she embarked on more patrols, she was sent to Pearl Harbor early in 1944 and assigned to training duties. She received one battle star.

S-36 was stationed in the Philippines at the outbreak of war and, in early January 1942, was sent on patrol near Verde Island, where she sank a small transport. Soon afterward, faltering because of engine problems, she was spot-

ted by a Japanese destroyer and severely damaged by depth bombs. She was forced to run at one-third speed, began losing depth control, and was further threatened by engine bearings that began to smoke and a failing trim pump. The destroyer finally left the scene, but *S-36* was still in critical condition and faced now with an engine fire. She limped along to Makassar Strait where on the morning of January 20, she ran hard aground on Taka Bakang Reef. After radioing for aid, she was approached by a Dutch launch, which took off all crew members. The fight to save the submarine was abandoned. Her equipment was destroyed and she was flooded, to prevent any possible salvage by the enemy.

S-37 was in Manila Bay as war began and left on her first war patrol a day later, taking up station near Mindoro, and providing intelligence information about Japanese movements. She made no attacks, but on her second patrol, on February 8, she attacked a convoy protected by four destroyers and sank one of them with a single torpedo. Limited in speed, slightly damaged from depth charges, and with engine problems, she put in at Surabaya Navy Yard for repairs, but had to leave prematurely when the Japanese began moving forces on Java. On February 28, with the battle of the Java Sea raging, she sighted a 50-foot open boat carrying Allied survivors; *S-37* took aboard as many as she could, supplied the others with provisions,

The damaged conning tower of the *S-4* (SS-109) after being raised from the bottom, following her tragic sinking near Portsmouth, New Hampshire, on December 17, 1927. Despite heroic efforts by divers in icy waters to save six men trapped in one compartment, all aboard perished. *(United States Navy)*

and contacted other Allied vessels for assistance. On her fifth patrol, in early July, though plagued by mechanical and electrical failures, she sighted and sank a 2,776-ton submarine chaser. Her sixth patrol resulted in damage to the last destroyer in a column of four, after which a fuel shortage and further mechanical failures forced her to head for Pearl Harbor. She was then placed in reserve as an anti-submarine warfare training boat until being decommissioned in February 1945. *S-37* earned five battle stars.

S-38, stationed in the Philippines at the time of the attack on Pearl Harbor, went on active war patrols, sank two Japanese vessels, damaged a third, and earned three battle stars.

S-39 was patrolling off southern Luzon during November 1941; when war broke out she was deployed to San Bernardino Strait to impede Japanese mining of the waters there. On December 13, she contacted and sank an enemy freighter. In early March, on her second war patrol, she sank a 6,500-ton tanker in the Java Sea. Her fifth patrol, in August 1942, turned out to be a nightmare. The first time she started, she had to turn back with major engine breakdowns. After repairs, she proceeded toward the Louisiade Archipelago where on August 13, 1942 she struck a submerged reef off Rossel Island, and listed 35 degrees, constantly jolted by heavy following seas that broke over her decks. All efforts to dislodge her not only failed but also seemed to make her position even worse, as well as dam-

aging her screws and over-depleting the batteries. Confronting these problems, and with ballast tanks ruptured by the rocks, the commander contacted Australia for help and was informed that a rescue ship, HMAS *Katoomba,* was in the area and would arrive the following morning to lend aid. When the ship listed even farther and threatened to roll over, life lines were strung to the shore to evacuate the crew. By the time *Katoomba* arrived, the situation was desperate. But all crew members reached safety. No attempt was made to shell *S-39,* since she was already breaking up in the pounding surf and it was obvious that she would be of no use to the enemy if later found.

S-40 was also stationed in the Philippines at the start of the war and was immediately deployed, with other vessels, to intercept a Japanese force reportedly bound for the Lingayen Gulf. Later, in February 1942, she was ordered to Makassar Strait and the Flores Sea. Further patrols that year took her to New Britain, the Solomons, and Papua, but she was unable to score any hits against enemy ships. After a long period of inaction and refitting, she headed for the Aleutians in June 1943, where she served until being deployed to San Diego to conduct training operations and then was decommissioned right after the war.

S-41, stationed in Manila in the fall of 1941, went into action immediately after the declaration of war, headed toward the Dutch East Indies. In mid-February 1942, she made her first kill, in Makassar Strait—a Japanese transport. Later, in May 1943, stationed in the Aleutians, she sank an enemy schooner and later a cargo ship in a night surface attack. She earned four battle stars.

S-42 saw service in the Coral Sea where, in May 1942, she sank a 4,400-ton enemy ship. Later, she was deployed

Collision of the USS *Silverstein* (DE-534) with the USS *Stickleback* (SS-415) on December 17, 1927. *(United States Navy)*

Launched in March 1923 and scrapped in November 1946, USS *S-43* (SS-154) was plagued by mechanical failures throughout her career—including being fired upon by an Allied merchant ship on March 18, 1945. *(United States Navy)*

She was attacked by a Japanese destroyer in the northern Kuriles and so severely damaged that she could not submerge. After taking more hits—in the control room, the forward battery, and the conning tower—she began to sink and the "Abandon Ship!" order was given. Only eight men escaped as *S-44* went down.

S-45 saw combat service, mainly defensive patrols off Panama early in the war, and then in several areas of the Pacific, and finally in the Aleutians. But she was more often attacked than attacking, suffering considerable damage and often coping with mechanical and other problems.

S-46 was ordered to Panama at the start of the war to undertake defensive patrols in the Canal Zone. She was then deployed to various ports in the Pacific theater, and finally in the Aleutians. She made seven war patrols, sank one enemy ship, and was awarded one battle star.

S-47 moved to Brisbane from the Canal Zone and, during a series of patrols off New Britain, Rabaul, and the Solomons, among others, damaged two Japanese warships, despite constant problems with her torpedo electrical firing circuits. She concluded her wartime service in the Aleutians, and was awarded three battle stars.

In addition to wartime sinkings and damage, four of the S-boats were lost during peacetime accidents:

S-4 served with the Asiatic Fleet, in the Canal Zone, and on the West Coast during the 1920s, and then was assigned to New London in May 1927, operating for the rest of the year off the New England coast. On December

to the Solomons and, in November, fired four torpedoes at a destroyer. Explosions were heard, but depth charge attacks made the sinking impossible to substantiate. She later served in the Aleutians and New Guinea. She earned one battle star.

S-43 was ordered to the Pacific and deployed to Australia, where she left Moreton Bay on her first war patrol in May 1942. She experienced three more patrols, and though she sank no enemy ships she was active in transferring agents and scouts to and from difficult areas of operation in the Pacific war zones.

S-44, serving in Panama as the war started, was ordered to Brisbane, Australia, from which she departed on her first war patrol in early May 1942. On the 12th, off Cape St. George, she sank a 5,000-ton salvage vessel. She was next deployed to Guadalcanal, where she sent a Japanese gunboat to the bottom. In August, back on patrol in the same area, she sighted a formation of four heavy cruisers. Firing four torpedoes at the rear ship, she sank the cruiser *Kako*, but suffered some damage. On her fourth patrol, in October, she damaged a destroyer off New Georgia, but suffered severe leaking after intense depth charging and had to effect temporary repairs and head back to port. Not until September 1943 was she back in action, this time departing Attu, in the Aleutians, on her final war patrol.

On June 7, 1942, an enemy plane dropped a bomb that exploded close enough to USS *S-44* (SS-155) to bend the conning tower hatch. Thirty gallons of seawater leaked in, doing considerable damage, and No. 1 periscope was thought to be damaged as well. Upon surfacing for repairs, a Japanese seaman's coat was found wrapped around the periscope head. *(United States Navy)*

17, 1927, having been refitted at Portsmouth Navy Yard, she was completing a submerged test run off the New Hampshire coast, but when she surfaced, she was rammed by the U.S. Coast Guard vessel, *Paulding*, whose lookout spotted her coming from below too late to avoid disaster. With a large hole in her hull, *S-4* heeled to port and started down by her bow. The real tragedy was not so much that of the men who died quickly in flooded compartments, but of the one officer, Lieutenant Graham Fitch, and five of his men who survived. They were trapped and able to tap signals in Morse code that could be heard by an heroic diver, Thomas Eadie, who risked his own life, and the lives of his fellow divers, in the icy waters again and again to go down into the depths and try in vain to determine a way for a rescue vessel, the *Falcon*, to raise the *S-4*. In the end, all efforts failed, and the doomed men died as the oxygen supply dwindled; it was not until mid-March 1928 that the submarine was finally raised and towed to the Boston Navy Yard with its cargo of dead heroes. The tragedy of the *S-4* was not in vain, for it immediately led to an intensive effort to redesign future submarines with escape devices, and to develop oceangoing cranes to raise them.

S-5 launched in November 1919, had barely finished builder's trials, outfitting, and crew training when, on August 30, 1920, while cruising off the Delaware Capes, it made a test dive. Something went horribly wrong, causing the boat to dive at too steep an angle and pouring water into her through an induction valve that had not properly closed. By the time corrections could be made, the torpedo room began flooding. All men inside it escaped quickly and bolted the door to prevent the flood from spreading into other compartments. However, despite all efforts to

blow ballast, trim ship, and otherwise prevent disaster, *S-5* settled to the bottom in 170 feet of water, 50 miles off the Delaware Capes. The situation was gloomy; with no marker buoy, no escape lungs, and no way to replenish air that would steadily diminish, the crew could be doomed. The skipper, Lieutenant Commander Charles Cooke, evaluated the situation and came up with a wild idea. The boat was 231 feet long; if the stern could be raised 75 degrees, a small portion of the tail would project above the surface of the water—which had been relatively calm that day. The steel hull was not quite an inch thick. If a hole could be drilled at the farthest possible point of the tail, it would provide air for survival longer than what was estimated to be a 72-hour limit. Cooke's idea was to blow all fuel and ballast tanks and at the same moment put the engines in

On November 3, 1942, USS *S-45* (SS-156) was sighted by an enemy destroyer that swung left to ram; *S-45* swung right, submerged, rigged for depth charging, varied her depth and course, and successfully outmaneuvered the enemy. *(United States Navy)*

S-45 (SS-156) saw combat service off Panama during World War II, as well as in the far Pacific and the Aleutians. However, her age was against her and mechanical problems were too chronic to give her a competitive edge over the enemy. *(United States Navy)*

emergency reverse. If all went as hoped for, the bow would be slightly loosened from the sea bed; the stern would rise, and the tail might even be sighted by a passing ship, whether or not the drilling could succeed. For a few moments after the engines vibrated fiercely, the tail rose so fast that several men were injured by flying objects. But it worked. Now the captain and engineering personnel rotated unceasingly as they took turns with an electric drill, cramped in a tiny compartment known as the tiller room, accessible through a manhole for inspection of the rudder gear. They could actually hear small waves lapping outside and thus estimated where the water level was.

It took 17 hours to break through the tough steel of the hull and then make a triangular-shaped hole about four inches at its longest dimension. Unfortunately, this did not help the air supply. Cooke became excited, however, when on one of his shifts he sighted smoke from a ship on the horizon. If they could only signal for help! Too late—it disappeared, but later another was sighted, considerably closer. Cooke called for the longest piece of narrow pipe

that could be found below and something to serve as a flag. Poking the pipe, with a white skivvy shirt at the top, he waved it back and forth frantically. The ship disappeared, no matter how much he and others waved in rotation. But within 20 minutes, they heard approaching engine sounds and then the swish of a small boat approaching. In communication through the hole, Cooke learned that, unfortunately, the ship's radio was out of commission. However, the ship, the *Alanthus,* sent up puffs of black smoke and distress signals, which attracted the attention of another ship the *Goethals,* which had not only a radio, but also a doctor and an engineer. While the radio operator reached the navy for help, the doctor advised Cooke about preventing asphyxiation from fumes, and the engineer brought every tool he had on board to widen the hole to provide a little more air to the trapped crew. The chief engineer of the *Goethals* worked with as much effort to make a hole as though he himself were trapped in the boat. He was spurred on by the fact that several crew members of the *S-5* were already in a bad way

On January 29, 1925, USS *S-48* (SS-159) grounded off Jeffery Point, New Hampshire, during a heavy snowstorm. Salvage operations began February 1 and a week later the S-boat was freed. *(United States Navy)*

from fumes and lack of oxygen. Finally, seven hours after he and his men had started their gargantuan labors—and 38 hours after the boat had plunged to the seabed—they had made the hole large enough to be able to bend back part of the section of steel plate with a crowbar, and provide enough space for a man's body to fit through. Immediately, crew members from the merchant ship began lifting men out onto a bos'n's chair, rigged from the deck of the *Goethals,* starting with several who were unconscious and others with injuries. So weak were the other crew members that it took almost four hours to complete the evacuation, ending with the last man—the skipper.

Although all 37 crewmen and four officers were saved, *S-5* was never to sail again. When the navy tried to secure towing cables around the protruding stern and tow her toward shallow water, she parted the cable and sank. Salvage attempts were made several times that year and again the following year. In 1921, the navy gave up and struck *S-5* from its list. It was never necessary to speculate what might have happened to her crew if the ingenious drilling plan had not been followed, or if the two rescue ships had continued on their way and had not stopped to investigate a tiny piece of white cloth fluttering at the end of a pole not far above the surface of the sea.

S-26, launched in October 1922, served along the East Coast, the West Coast, and the Canal Zone, largely on training duties and fleet exercises, until the start of World War II, at which time she was based in New London, Connecticut. She was then deployed to Coco Solo in the Canal Zone, preparatory to being refitted for wartime duty in the Pacific. On January 24, in the Gulf of Panama, 14 miles west of San Jose Light, she was proceeding to an assigned patrol position in company with sister submarines *S-21, S-29,* and *S-44,* along with an escort vessel, USS *PC-460.* As darkness approached, the escort vessel transmitted a visual message to the three submarines, proceeding on the surface, that she was leaving the formation and they were to proceed on the duty assigned. However, *S-21* was the only boat to receive the message; because of a mix-up in communications, *S-26* remained unknowingly in the path of the escort vessel's new course and was struck by her on the starboard side of the torpedo room. She sank within a matter of seconds. There were only three survivors—the skipper, another officer, and one enlisted man—all of whom were on the bridge at the time of the accident. Salvage operations started immediately, but were not successful.

S-51 was launched in August 1921, and then based in New London, Connecticut, as a unit of Submarine Division Four, operating off Block Island and in New England waters. Following deployment in 1924 to the Canal Zone to participate in fleet maneuvers, she returned to New London. On the night of September 25, while cruising on the surface 14 miles east of Block Island in Long Island

Looking into the torpedo room of USS *S-4* (SS-109).
(United States Navy)

Sound, she was rammed by a cargo-passenger ship, *City of Rome.* She sank in seconds. Only three men survived, while 33 perished. Desperate attempts were made to dive on the submarine to rescue the men trapped inside. All efforts failed, and it was not until June 1926 that she was raised and the dead officers were removed from their steel tomb and given proper funerals and burials. The heroic efforts to reach the trapped men were dramatically documented in *On the Bottom,* the personal account of Commander Edward Ellsberg, who was in charge of diving operations, and who, with his men, risked his and their lives to try in vain to bring the sunken submarine to the surface.

Scabbardfish (SS-397)

Built by Portsmouth Naval Shipyard and launched January 27, 1944, *Scabbardfish* completed advance training and final outfitting before reporting as a unit of Submarine Force, Pacific Fleet, Pearl Harbor on July 24, 1944. *Scabbardfish* sighted her first enemy ships on August 31 and fired two spreads of three torpedoes, but all missed. While patrolling the seas southeast of Honshu, she sank a 2,100-ton interisland steamer on November 16; sank an 875-ton target and damaged a 4,000-ton freighter on November 22; and sank a Japanese submarine on November 28. In late February 1945, she engaged 12 luggers and a trawler with her deck gun but was forced to submerge by an enemy plane. *Scabbardfish* was assigned to the Lifeguard League during the summer of 1945 and rescued seven pilots before spending a month at Eniwetok for ASW training duties. She then operated along the West Coast until March 17, 1947, when she returned to San Francisco Naval Shipyard for her second overhaul. After a simulated war patrol and visits to the Palau Islands, Hong Kong,

Shanghai, Tsingtao, and Okinawa, *Scabbardfish* returned to San Diego on December 11, 1947, and on to Mare Island, where she was berthed until being transferred to the Greek navy on February 26, 1965. *Scabbardfish* received five battle stars for World War II service.

Scamp (SS-277)

Built by the Portsmouth Naval Shipyard and the first to bear her name, *Scamp* was launched in July 1942, was ordered to join the Pacific Fleet, and began her first war patrol on March 1, 1943. She stopped at Midway Island on March 5, debarked a passenger, Rear Admiral Charles A. Lockwood, Jr., Commander, Submarine Force, Pacific Fleet, and then headed for the coast of Honshu. *Scamp*'s first two attacks on the enemy were doomed to failure by faulty magnetic detonators in her torpedoes. Nevertheless, she later scored two hits, one on an unidentified target on the night of March 20 and the other the next morning. Her second patrol resulted in the sinking of an airplane tender in late May near the Bismarck Archipelago. On her third patrol, in the same area, she scored a hit on a Japanese tanker in late July, and on the same day began a hit-and-run battle with a Japanese submarine. She had to dive to 220 feet to avoid a torpedo attack, but 10 minutes later returned to periscope depth to engage her adversary. *Scamp* launched four torpedoes and the submarine erupted in a tremendous explosion.

After almost a month in port at Brisbane, *Scamp* stood out on her fourth war patrol. She again patrolled off the Solomons and into the Bismarck Sea. In mid-August, she attacked a three-ship convoy and crippled one of them. Another changed course and avoided her torpedoes. *Scamp* passed close under the stricken enemy, trying to evade her escorts, and for a time lost the undamaged quarry in a rain squall. But she later returned to finish off the 8,614-ton passenger-cargo ship. On the morning of September 21, she spotted a heavily guarded convoy and began to stalk it. After dark, she moved in for the kill and, after launching three torpedoes, heard two double explosions. Her second attack was foiled by a severe rain squall. However, she hounded the convoy all through the day and finally unleashed four torpedoes at the convoy. While still maneuvering to attack, she passed through the wreckage and came upon an empty boat containing the sunken ship's logs and other documents. These were taken on board and later turned over to Intelligence. She made one more attempt against the convoy, but was driven off by planes and kept down by aerial bombs, at which time she was ordered to terminate her patrol and return to Brisbane.

Scamp cleared port again on October 22 and began her fifth mission in support of the Treasury Island invasion, later moving to her patrol area, between Kavieng and Truk. On November 4, she launched three torpedoes at a passenger-cargo ship. One exploded prematurely, but one reached its mark. Six days later, she sank a 6,481-ton target; then, after evading the escorts, pumped three more torpedoes into the listing target, and on November 12, she damaged a light cruiser. In mid-December, *Scamp* headed back to the Bismarck Archipelago for her sixth war patrol. In mid-January 1944, she slipped by two destroyers to launch six torpedoes at an enemy tanker. The 9,975-ton target sank as *Scamp* made her escape, racing south to act as lifeguard for B-24 bombers before putting in to Milne Bay, New Guinea, for refit.

Scamp spent her seventh war patrol, starting in early March, searching the shipping lanes between New Guinea, Palau, and Mindanao in the Philippines. In early April, south of Davao Gulf, she encountered six cruisers escorted by destroyers and planes. She dived and the destroyers passed overhead without noticing her presence a scant 100 feet below the surface. She returned to the surface at 14:05 but was forced down by a plane. A little later, she tried to surface again but was attacked by a diving floatplane. As she crash-dived to escape the enemy plane, an aerial bomb exploded. All hands were knocked off their feet by the explosion and all power was lost. *Scamp* began to take an up angle and started to settle rapidly. At just below 300 feet, she began to hang on, then started up. The diving officer reported that the hydraulic controller had been jarred to "off" in the attack and that the hydraulic plant started closing all the main vents as fire started filling the maneuvering and after torpedo rooms with a thick, toxic smoke. Fortunately, the sub caught at 52 feet, the decision having been made to surface and slug it out with the deck gun if she could not be held below 50 feet. *Scamp* "seesawed" three times before power was regained, and she could level off at 150 feet. She released oil and air bubbles to appear to have sunk and then, listing badly and with limited power, headed for the Admiralty Islands.

Leaving Pearl Harbor in mid-October 1944 after repairs, *Scamp* headed for her assigned eighth patrol area, in the Bonin Islands. On November 9, she received orders to stay clear of a certain area during B-29 raids, and she acknowledged, giving her position and reporting that she had made two torpedo attacks. This was the last communication received from *Scamp*, despite follow-up orders to her five days later and further attempts to make contact with her during the rest of the month. On November 29, 1944, information was received of an enemy minefield in the vicinity of *Scamp*'s patrol area, and by mid-December, she was reported as presumed lost on war patrol in enemy waters. Following the end of the war, Japanese sources indicated that a patrol plane had bombed what appeared to be oil trails left by a submarine, in the area where *Scamp* might have been, and that a coast defense vessel was led to the scene by the plane and dropped some 70 depth charges in three runs on the target, whereupon a large oil pool appeared. No further evidence was ever found. *Scamp* earned seven battle stars for World War II service and was credited with sinking five vessels for 34,108 tons.

Scamp (SSN-588)

This submarine of the Skipjack class was launched in September 1960 at the Mare Island Naval Shipyard, designed for a complement of nine officers and 76 enlisted men. For the first two years, she ranged from the West Coast to Hawaii on training and operational missions before being deployed to the western Pacific. After further assignments along the West Coast, she was ordered again to the western Pacific, in 1967, participating in fleet operations off the Vietnamese coast.

Durng the next few years, she operated largely out of San Diego. In 1971, she was again ordered to the western Pacific, operating with the Seventh Fleet in Far Eastern waters. She also served in the Mediterranean on special duty during the Libyan crisis in 1980–81, where she earned a Battle "E" for her performance. Several years later, during a major storm in the Atlantic, she made rescue attempts of seamen on a floundering Panamanian freighter. Although she was partially successful, she received such extreme damage to her sail and other exterior parts that she had to limp back to port with outside aid. *Scamp* never fully recovered from this accident and was decommissioned and struck from the Navy list in April 1988. She received three battle stars for service in the Vietnam War.

Scorpion (SS-278)

Built by Portsmouth Naval Shipyard, the first to bear the name and a member of the Gato class, this boat was launched in July 1942 and ordered to Pearl Harbor, where she underwent the installation of a bathythermograph, a new oceanographic instrument to enable her to locate and hide in thermal layers of the ocean that minimized detection by enemy sonar. She departed on her first war patrol in early April 1943, assigned to the east coast of Honshu, where she laid mines and sank her first enemy ships—a gunboat and four sampans. Later she sank a patrol vessel and a 6,380-ton merchant ship. However, she received her first casualty when one of her officers, Lieutenant Commander R. M. Raymond, was hit and killed by gunfire. On her second war patrol, during June and July, she was cornered by enemy vessels, forced to hit bottom in shallow water, and battered with depth charges. She not only escaped this trap, but also sank a 3,890-ton freighter and a 6,112-ton passenger-cargo ship. Her third war patrol, in October and November, was marred by bad weather, and she almost encountered dis-

aster at the hands of a "Q" ship, a warship disguised as a merchantman, before returning to base.

Departing Pearl Harbor on December 29, 1943, *Scorpion* headed for her fourth patrol, assigned to the northern East China and Yellow Seas. On the morning of January 5, *Scorpion* reported that one of her crew had sustained a fracture of the upper arm and requested a rendezvous with the submarine *Herring,* which was returning from patrol and was near her. The rendezvous was accomplished, but heavy seas prevented the transfer. *Herring* reported this fact on January 6, but *Scorpion* was never seen or heard from again after her departure from that rendezvous. After the war, Japanese records showed no indication that *Scorpion*'s loss was the result of enemy antisubmarine tactics, and in the end the most reasonable assumption was that she had hit a mine. *Scorpion* earned three battle stars for her World War II service and was credited with sinking four vessels for 18,316 tons.

Scorpion (SSN-589)

A submarine of the Skipjack class, and the second to bear the name, *Scorpion* was built by Electric Boat Division, General Dynamics Corporation, launched in December 1959 and assigned to SubRon5, in New London, Connecticut. She was later assigned to Norfolk, Virginia, where she specialized in the development of nuclear submarine warfare tactics. During the late winter and early spring of 1966, and again in the fall, she was deployed for special operations. Following the completion of those assignments, her commanding officer received the Navy Commendation Medal for outstanding leadership, foresight, and professional skill, and other officers and men were cited for meritorious achievement.

But, for the second time for a submarine named *Scorpion,* tragedy was in the offing. *Scorpion* got underway in mid-February 1968, for a Mediterranean deployment, operating with the Sixth Fleet into May and then heading west. On May 21, she indicated her position to be about 50 miles south of the Azores. Six days later, she was reported overdue at Norfolk. An intensive search was initiated; but, by the end of the month the submarine and all hands were declared "presumed lost." The search continued, however, and, at the end of October, the navy's oceanographic research ship, *Mizar,* located sections of *Scorpion*'s hull in more than 10,000 feet of water about 400 miles southwest of the Azores. Subsequently, a court of inquiry was reconvened and other vessels, including the submersible, *Trieste,* were dispatched to the scene. Despite the myriad of data and pictures collected and studied, the cause of the loss remains a mystery. Deep-sea photographs show the wreckage of *Scorpion* in two major sections. The forward hull section, including the torpedo room and most of the operations compartment, is located in a trench that was formed by the impact of the hull section with the bottom. The sail is detached. The aft hull section, including the reactor compartment and engine room, is located in a separate trench that was formed by the impact of the hull section with the bottom. The aft section of the engine room is inserted forward into a larger-diameter hull section in a manner similar to a telescope.

Later, a study of recordings from the navy's secret undersea listening network turned up evidence of what had happened to the ill-fated boat. The system had recorded what appeared to indicate an underwater implosion—the noise of a ship being crushed by water pressure—at a depth of approximately 2,000 feet, some 400 miles southwest of the island of San Miguel in the Azores. This was the boat's location immediately after her last radio transmission. What had caused *Scorpion* to sink, or go into an uncontrollable dive? In 1993, the navy released a report indicating that one of the submarine's torpedoes had somehow been activated; after being expelled from its tube, it had homed in on *Scorpion,* striking and sinking her before any evasive action could be taken. The sinking of *Scorpion* was one of two mystifying losses of American nuclear submarines in the 1960s. The other was the loss of *Thresher* off the New England coast in 1963.

Sea Devil (SS-400)

Built by the Portsmouth Naval Shipyard and launched February 28, 1944, *Sea Devil* went on her first war patrol on September 3, 1944, sinking an I-58 class submarine off the south coast of Honshu. By November 19, 1944, when *Sea Devil* was sent on her second war patrol, so much of the Japanese merchant tonnage was on the bottom there was little left to shoot at; however, on December 2, her torpedoes found a 6,859-ton freighter and a 9,467-ton passenger-cargoman off southwest Kyushu, resulting in additional tonnage on the bottom. Then, on December 9, 1944, a high-speed task force was contacted, and in a midnight submerged attack, the large carrier *Junyo* was sunk and a light cruiser was damaged, rendering Japanese shipping almost nonexistent in home waters.

In April 1945, a Japanese convoy, consisting of four merchant ships and three escorts blundered into *Sea Devil* who launched a 15-torpedo surface attack in foggy weather conditions; two freighters and three escorts were sunk.

Sea Devil patrolled the Yellow Sea area where she destroyed 58 drifting mines between August 17 and 18, 1945.

Sea Devil was decommissioned on February 17, 1964, struck from the Navy list April 1, 1964, and sunk as a target off the coast of southern California. She received the Navy Unit of Commendation, earned five battle stars, the Navy Occupation Service Medal, and the Asia and the China Service Medal.

Sea Dog (SS-401)

Built by Portsmouth Naval Shipyard and launched March 28, 1944, *Sea Dog* had her first war patrol on September 17, 1944, entering the Nansei Shoto area on September 28. On October 19, 1944, after unsuccessful patrols in the areas of Kikai Jima, Amami O Shima, and Okinoyera Jima, *Sea Dog* headed into the likely traffic lanes to Naha and Unten Ko. Remaining west of Okinawa, she took an armed trawler under fire and left it burning. On November 22, 1944, she sighted a convoy, and both of its cargomen were sunk by *Sea Dog.* Joining forces with USS *Guardfish* and USS *Sea Robin* to form a coordinated attack group (wolf pack) with the commander of *Sea Dog* in charge, the group patrolled the South China Sea. On April 16, 1945, *Sea Dog* sank a medium-sized cargo ship between Hachijo Jima and Mikua Jima.

During *Sea Dog*'s last foray into Japanese home waters she was made flagship for the nine-submarine Japan Sea Patrol Pack (TG-17.21). On June 9, 1945, *Sea Dog* sank a small cargo ship and a merchant ship, and on June 11 she fired one torpedo at a coastal freighter for a direct hit and another sinking to *Sea Dog*'s credit. On June 12, she sighted another Japanese convoy and fired on a freighter breaking it in two. On June 15 *Sea Dog* sighted a passenger/cargo ship standing south past the northern end of Oga Hanto and fired a torpedo, which hit just forward of amidships, sinking the target in four minutes. She cleared the area to allow small craft to pick up survivors. On June 17 *Sea Dog* sighted three merchantmen moving northward along the coast of Hokkaido. She fired on two, sinking one before being forced to submerge by an enemy plane.

Reentering Pearl Harbor on July 5, 1945, *Sea Dog* remained there until August 13 when on her way to her fifth war patrol she received orders to cease hostilities, reversing course back to Pearl Harbor. Conducting training operations in the Hawaiian Islands for the remainder of August, *Sea Dog* headed west on September 6 to join SubRon5 and for the next three-and-a-half months operated out of Subic Bay. Through 1947 she remained in the eastern Pacific. There were various assignments including one to the Bering Sea to collect hydrographic and oceanographic information, before returning to Pearl Harbor on June 15, 1948, where she resumed a schedule of local training exercises.

Upon returning to Pearl Harbor from a deployment to the western Pacific in January 1950, *Sea Dog* received orders to join the Atlantic Fleet headed for the East Coast. The fleet arrived in Norfolk in early July. On November 7, 1952, *Sea Dog* intercepted a distress signal from a damaged blimp and proceeded to pick up 11 survivors, who were later transferred to a surface ship. *Sea Dog* remained based at Key West into the fall of 1955, when she was ordered to New London for inactivation. *Sea Dog* earned two battle stars during World War II.

Seadragon (SS-194)

Built by the Electric Boat Company and launched as the first in a new class and the first to bear the name, *Seadragon* was ordered to the Philippines to serve with the Asiatic Fleet. Moored alongside her sister ship, *Sealion,* at the Cavite Navy Yard on December 10 and being readied for her first war patrol, she was bombed during a Japanese air raid, which ripped off part of her bridge, pierced her conning tower, killed one officer, and wounded five other crew members. The same raid demolished *Sealion.* Following repairs, some at Cavite and some at the Dutch port of Soerabaja, she set out on her first mission, on December 30, heading for the South China Sea to intercept Japanese shipping off the coast of Indochina. After numerous encounters with enemy ships, she damaged two of them in late January and sank a third, a troop ship, before returning to base. In mid-March, *Seadragon* again headed for the Indochina coast for her second war patrol, encountering a number of enemy ships but—more often the attacked than the attacker—made no hits. On her third patrol, June 11 to August 2, 1942, *Seadragon* returned to the South China Sea, where she sank two more ships. On her fourth patrol, she sank one more and damaged one. Her fifth patrol proved also to be successful. She not only damaged two cargo ships, but also engaged in a duel with a Japanese submarine, firing three torpedoes and sending her to the bottom with the last one. However, the second torpedo almost proved fatal to *Seadragon.* It exploded prematurely just after leaving the bow tube, with such force that it knocked down and injured crew members in the forward torpedo room and, worse yet, tripped the starting lever of a torpedo in an adjoining tube, which would have exploded inside the submarine had not the crew been able to force it to launch. Even so, depth control was temporarily lost and *Seadragon* was in an emergency mode.

After returning to base, *Seadragon* was ordered to Mare Island for repairs and refitting, and did not get back into action until mid-May 1943, when she headed west on her sixth war patrol in the Caroline Islands. She later damaged a freighter off Kwajalein Island, but had to cut short her mission to return to base with a damaged steering gear. In July and August, she conducted her seventh war patrol. Of the 44 days, 31 were spent on station near Wake and in the Marshalls where increased enemy air activity again hindered hunting and limited her score to five freighters damaged. Her next two patrols, in the same area, faced similar problems, and she returned home with only three cargo

ships damaged to her credit. On April 1, 1944, she cleared Pearl Harbor for the Japanese home islands and her 10th war patrol, but found the hunting to be very poor and was unable to do more than damage a freighter and sink an armed trawler in a surface attack.

In early September 1944, *Seadragon* departed on her 11th war patrol, a coordinated mission with submarines *Shark* and *Blackfish* in the northern China Sea. *Seadragon* accounted for a cargo ship and two passenger-cargo vessels during the patrol, but these successes were marred by the loss of *Shark,* which failed to respond to radio contacts. Later, it was determined that she had been sunk while attacking one of the wolf packs' targets on the night of October 21. Five days later, *Seadragon* headed toward Luzon, searching en route for downed aviators. Arriving at her destination on November 8, she commenced refit; and on December 3, 1945, she headed west for her 12th war patrol, which took her back into Japanese waters where she hunted enemy shipping and searched for downed aviators. In May, she was transferred back to the Atlantic Fleet and for the final months of the war, provided training services at Guantanamo Bay and Key West. She was transferred to Boston, where she was berthed as a unit of the Atlantic Reserve Fleet until being decommissioned in April 1948. *Seadragon* earned 11 battle stars during World War II and was credited with sinking 10 vessels for 43,450 tons.

Seadragon (SSN-584)

This submarine of the Skate class was built by the Portsmouth Naval Shipyard and launched in August 1958, designed for a complement of eight officers and 76 enlisted men. Following a Caribbean shakedown, she was deployed to the Pacific in August 1960, ordered to head there through an unusual route: the Northwest Passage. En route, following a guide journal written by explorer Edward Parry in 1819, she collected oceanographic and hydrographic data, transiting, among other bodies of water, Barrow Strait, Viscount Melville Sound, and McClure Strait. Another highlight in this voyage, following her completion of the first submarine transit of the Northwest Passage, was a period of completing scientific experiments in cooperation with scientists on ice island "T-3," and a transit of the North Geographic Pole. For this experimental project, she was awarded the Navy Unit Commendation. After service at her initial home port, Pearl Harbor, Seadragon was deployed on her second Arctic cruise in 1962, accomplishing numerous scientific missions and, unexpectedly, rescuing 12 survivors from a downed seaplane. In August 1964, *Seadragon* sailed west in response to the Gulf of Tonkin crisis, remaining in that region until the following March when she returned to Pearl Harbor. The remainder of her career was spent largely with deployments to the Seventh Fleet in the western Pacific, interspersed with training and evaluation exercises off the West Coast. She was decommissioned in June 1984.

Seahawk (SH-60)

The Seahawk is a multipurpose U.S. Navy tactical transport helicopter developed for antisubmarine warfare (ASW) and search and rescue (SAR) missions. It is designed so that the four rotor blades can be folded for storage, whether on an aircraft carrier or other war ship. It is noted for its automatic flight control system (AFCS), which includes an automatic control for altitude and hovering. The Seahawk's two turboshaft engines are mounted over the fuselage, separated from each other by the rotor drive train and transmission. The engines are especially processed to resist corrosion, and the airship can refuel from the hover in a process known as HIFER (helicopter in-flight refueling). The landing gear and systems of approach and descent are such that, when necessary, the Seahawk can land on a very small deck or other platform. As for weaponry, the helicopter is equipped with a 25-tube pneumatic sonobuoy launcher, in the port side of the fuselage, and machine guns in both cabin doors. The electronics equipment is such that the Seahawk can act as both "eyes" and "ears" in searching for enemy vessels, as well as having the weapons to sink them.

Seahorse (SS-304)

Built by Mare Island Naval Shipyard and launched in January 1943, this submarine of the Balao class was assigned to Pearl Harbor and set out on her first war patrol in early August 1943; she scored three hits on a transport in the Palaus, but was damaged and later expended the rest of her torpedoes in an unsuccessful attack on a large tanker. Her second patrol, in November, racked up two kills: a 7,809-ton cargo ship and a 5,859-ton cargo ship. Two weeks later, she fired four torpedoes from periscope depth, and sank a cargo ship. On November 26, the submarine contacted another enemy convoy and began to close the range. Determined to mount an attack before the targets entered the mined Tsushima Strait, the submarine fired four torpedoes at long range, quickly sinking a cargo ship and then, dodging enemy escorts, let go four stern shots at a second target. The results seemed disappointing until a sudden blast sent flames and debris mushrooming high into the air, completely destroying a 7,309-ton tanker. *Seahorse* expended the last of her torpedoes at an enemy convoy. However, one torpedo exploded just after it left the tube, and the entire convoy opened fire on the vicinity of the submarine. With so many explosions around her, it was impossible for *Seahorse* to determine whether any torpedoes had hit. Low on fuel and out of torpedoes, the submarine returned to Pearl Harbor on December 12 from a successful second patrol, with five ships and three trawlers sunk. In mid-January 1944, while on her third war patrol and en route to the Palaus, she destroyed a 784-ton cargo ship and five days later a 3,025-ton cargo ship and a 3,156-ton passenger-cargo ship. She ended the run at the end of the month with another cargo ship on her record.

On her fourth patrol, in the Marianas, *Seahorse* intercepted a large enemy convoy on April 8. After nightfall, she fired four torpedoes at overlapping targets, sinking a converted seaplane tender and, shortly thereafter, a cargo ship. Although a counterattack by escorting destroyers drove the submarine from the vicinity, she quickly regained contact and continued the chase into the following day, sinking a second cargo ship. She then took up lifeguard station for the carrier air strikes on Saipan and, while west of that island, sighted and sank a Japanese submarine. Not content with these victims, she concluded her mission by polishing off a 5,244-ton cargo ship. *Seahorse* put to sea for her fifth war patrol on June 11, 1944, patrolling between Formosa and Luzon. Two weeks later, she sank a tanker and damaged two other enemy vessels, and then, before returning to base, she sank a cargo ship and a passenger-cargo ship. Her sixth and seventh patrols, however, were letdowns. She had little to show for them except a frigate and a junk. Worse yet, she was attacked by two patrol boats, which left her interior a shambles of broken glass, smashed instruments, and spilled hydraulic oil. Her eighth, and final, patrol was cut short by the end of the war, and she was placed in reserve until being decommissioned in March 1946. She received nine battle stars for World War II service and was credited with sinking 20 vessels for 72,529 tons.

Seal (SS-183)

Built by the Electric Boat Company and launched in August 1937 as a submarine of the Salmon class, *Seal* operated along the East Coast and in the Canal Zone. She was then assigned to the Philippines, her home port at the start of World War II, from which she departed in mid-December for her first patrol. She netted one victim, a 3,500-ton Japanese freighter, and enjoyed similar success on her second patrol, and also on her third patrol, when she sank a 7,000-ton tanker off the coast of Indochina. On her fourth and fifth patrols at the end of 1942, in the waters of the South China Sea, she damaged another freighter and sank a third, but was almost put out of action herself when she was rammed by one of the ships in the convoy and had so much damage inflicted on her periscope that she was forced to proceed to Pearl Harbor for repairs. Her sixth war patrol concluded after a 10,200-ton tanker was torpedoed and sunk off the Palau Islands. *Seal's* seventh war patrol looked hopeful when, in late June 1943, she spotted likely targets right in the heart of the Japanese homeland, off Honshu. But she was so severely depth-charged by the escorts of a convoy there that she suffered a major fuel leak that could not be repaired at sea and had to return to base. She was plagued again by operational problems when, on her eighth mission, this time in the Sea of Okhotsk, the failure of the conning tower hatch to close during a dive resulted in flooding and such extensive electrical damage that *Seal* again had to return to port with no record of success against the enemy after 50 days at sea. Her ninth and 10th patrols, in late 1943 and early 1944, were mainly for photographic reconnaissance and produced much valuable information about Japanese operations in the Marshall Islands, which the Americans were about to invade, and Ponape.

Since the boat's engines, conning tower, and other major components were now considered old and obsolete, she was ordered back to the States for a long period of overhaul. But in early August 1944, fit and trim again, she headed for the Kurile Islands, where she proved her mettle by sinking two freighters and critically damaging three others before returning to Midway after 40 days at sea. In October, she again made a beeline for the Kuriles where, despite stormy weather and fog, she succeeded in sinking two more enemy freighters of 6,000 and 4,000 tons. This ended her fighting career, and she spent the rest of the war operating in the Hawaiian area as a training submarine, and later in the same capacity with the Submarine School, New London, Connecticut. Two months after the war, she was decommissioned. *Seal* sank a total of seven vessels, almost 30,000 tons of Japanese shipping, and was awarded 10 battle stars.

Sea Lance

The Sea Lance was originally designed as a rocket-boosted, ballistic antisubmarine weapon, a solid-fuel missile enclosed in a capsule with a Mark 50 torpedo as its warhead. It weighed slightly over 3,000 pounds and was just over 20 feet in length. Initially it was planned that this weapon could be fired vertically from surface ships, or horizontally from standard 21-inch submarine torpedo tubes. Later, it was decided that Sea Lance would be deployed only on submarines. A successor to the SUBROC missile, it was designed for longer range to work with several ASW sensors, including the Light Airborne Multipurpose helicopter-based sensor system.

Sealion (SS-195) (S-14)

Built by the Electric Boat Company and launched in May 1939, in the Seadragon class, *Sealion* had the unfortunate distinction of being the first submarine victim of enemy action in World War II, under Lieutenant Commander R.

G. Voge. The start of the war found her, along with *Seadragon,* in the last stages of overhaul at the Cavite Navy Yard in the Philippines. On the afternoon of December 10, 1945, 54 Japanese planes were sighted heading for the Navy Yard. With the exception of one officer, Lieutenant Albert L. Rabom, and three men, all personnel were below decks. The first stick of bombs landed some 100 to 200 yards astern of *Sealion,* and at that time, Voge, seeing that the planes were going to bomb from a high altitude where machine-gun fire could not reach them, ordered all hands below. It was a most fortunate decision. On the next bombing run, only a few minutes later, two bombs hit *Sealion* almost simultaneously. One struck the after end of the conning tower fairwater, completely demolishing the machine-gun mount, which had just been vacated, the main induction, the battery ventilation, and the after conning tower bulkhead. It exploded outside the hull; had it entered the hull before exploding, the majority of the crew would have been lost, as most of the personnel were in the compartment struck. A fragment from this bomb pierced the conning tower, instantly killing Ensign Sam Hunter stationed there, the first submarine casualty of the war. Other fragments from this bomb pierced the hull, inflicting minor wounds on three seamen in the control room. At almost the same instant another bomb exploded in one end of the after engine room, killing four men working in that compartment: Electrician Mates Foster, O'Connell, and Paul, and Machinist Mate Ogilvie. With this explosion, the after engine room flooded immediately and *Sealion* settled by the stern in the mud. The forward engine room and the after torpedo room flooded slowly through bomb fragment holes in the bulkheads. Personnel in these compartments, as well as in other parts of the ship, escaped through the hatches, which were all still above water. *Sealion* finally settled down by the stern with about 40 percent of the main deck underwater and a 15 degree list to starboard.

Although *Sealion* might eventually have been repaired, the bombing that wrecked her also demolished the navy yard, and the closest repair facilities were at Pearl Harbor, 5,000 miles away. Thus, after removing all gear of value, such as gyro, radio, and sound equipment, she was destroyed with three depth charges to prevent her from falling into enemy hands.

Sealion (SS-315)

Built by the Electric Boat Company and launched in October 1943 as a submarine of the Balao class, and the second to bear her name, *Sealion* joined *Tang* in June 1944 to enter the East China Sea and take up stations in the Osumi Gunto, an island group to the south of Kyushu. After *Sealion* unsuccessfully conducted her first attack, she underwent her first depth-charging. The submarines moved toward the Korean Peninsula. On the 28th, *Sealion* caught and sank a Japanese naval transport and two days later used her deck guns to sink a sampan. On the morning of July 6, she intercepted a convoy south of the Four Sisters Islands and sank a cargo ship, and five days later, she conducted several attacks, sinking two freighters. On her second war patrol, she damaged one tanker and sank a second. In mid-September, she was ordered back to the scene of the action to rescue Australian and British prisoners of war who had been on one of the tankers at the time of the sinking. *Sealion* picked up 54 of the survivors, all of whom were coated with crude oil and were in poor health, suffering from malaria, malnutrition, other diseases, and exposure. Four of them died before the submarine could transport them to the army hospital at Tanapag Harbor. She departed again on October 31 and, with sister ship *Kete*, headed west to patrol in the East China Sea. Two weeks later, despite a battery explosion, she sighted four enemy warships and sank a destroyer and damaged a cruiser, which she followed and later sank. On her fourth patrol, in February 1945, she sank a supply ship, and on her fifth and sixth patrols was largely occupied with rescuing downed pilots. After the war, she was converted to a troop carrier, later a transport submarine, and was active in exercises with the marines, underwater demolition teams, and beach jumper units. She was decommissioned in 1960. *Sealion* was awarded a Presidential Unit Citation and five battle stars. She was credited with sinking 11 vessels for 68,297 tons.

SEALs, U.S. Navy

With the name derived from "sea," "air," and "land," this distinguished unit has been described as "the most feared and respected commando force in the U.S. Military, if not the world—the most elite and highly trained force on the face of the Earth, as well as the most flexible." Formed in 1962 by President John F. Kennedy as a maritime counterpart to the U.S. Army Special Forces (the Green Berets), the SEALs have amassed a remarkable history of successes and have become legendary in their exploits both on and off duty. The teams have operated in every hellhole known to modern warfare, and come away with many casualties, but also victories and a history of achievements. Few SEAL missions are known to the public, and even then not until long after their completion. The men who make up this organization are trained to operate in small units—from just two or three in a squad to a platoon strength of 16. Most missions are clandestine in nature, planned in meticulous detail, and executed with precision and swiftness. During peacetime, SEALs experience the same rigorous training as during wartime or a major crisis. During the Vietnam War, SEAL Teams One and Two amassed a combined kill ratio of 200 to one, with only 46 deaths in their ranks. The SEALs have also seen service during Operation Urgent Fury in Grenada, Just Cause in Panama, Desert Shield/Storm in Iraq, as well as in other global hotspots such as Somalia, Haiti, and Bosnia, and most recently Operation Enduring Freedom in Afghanistan.

Sea Owl (SS-405)

Sea Owl was built by Portsmouth Naval Shipyard. Although this submarine of the Balao class was not launched until May 1944, and did not see action in the Pacific until November, she established a fine record during a short wartime career. Her first victim was a Japanese escort destroyer in the East China Sea; her second was an enemy submarine of the RO-35 class, off Wake Island; and her third, in May in the East China Sea, was another destroyer. She also rescued six downed aviators on this, her third—and final—patrol. In 1951, *Sea Owl* was converted to a Fleet Snorkel submarine at Philadelphia Naval Shipyard. She enjoyed a long peacetime service as well, roaming the globe on many missions and finally being decommissioned in November 1969, after more than 25 years of dedicated service. *Sea Owl* received five battle stars for her World War II operations and was credited with sinking two vessels for 1,689 tons.

Sea Poacher (SS-406)

Built by Portsmouth Naval Shipyard and launched in May 1944, this submarine of the Balao class was ordered to Pearl Harbor in October to join the Pacific Fleet. Although her first two war patrols were unproductive, during the third, conducted in the Kurile Islands area, she torpedoed and sank a Japanese trawler and, four days later, sent two fishing boats to the bottom in a surface attack. During the latter action, three crewmen were injured when the 20 mm gun exploded. Because of the seriousness of their injuries, the patrol was terminated ahead of schedule, and the submarine returned to Midway. After conducting her fourth war patrol off the eastern coast of Honshu, she was undergoing refitting at Pearl Harbor when the war ended. She was later based in the Canal Zone, and then in the Key West and Caribbean areas, providing services to various units of the Atlantic Fleet, with time out for tours of duty with the Sixth Fleet in the Mediterranean and various exercises with NATO forces. On July 10, 1952, while operating in the Key West area, the submarine had the unique experience of rescuing a blimp, which had suffered an engine casualty and was floating helplessly in the water. *Sea Poacher* was converted to a GUPPY IA at Charleston Naval Shipyard in 1952. In July 1959, *Sea Poacher* concluded her service with a three-and-one-half month deployment to the eastern and northern Atlantic areas to participate in antisubmarine training exercises with units of the Spanish and Portuguese navies. She was placed in reserve and finally decommissioned in November 1969. *Sea Poacher* received four battle stars for her service during World War II.

Searaven (SS-196) (S-15)

Built by Portsmouth Naval Shipyard and launched in June 1939, this submarine had enough changes in design to be listed as a new "Searaven" class. During the two years preceding America's entry into World War II, she operated in Philippine waters conducting training and maneuvers. At the outbreak of war, she was at the Cavite Navy Yard in Manila Bay. During her first two war patrols in December 1941 and the spring of 1942, she ran supplies to the American and Filipino troops besieged on the Bataan Peninsula and Corregidor Island. In a night action in the Molucca Strait on February 3, 1942, she torpedoed a Japanese destroyer and claimed her first victim of the war. *Searaven* conducted her third war patrol, in the Dutch East Indies, from April 2 to 25, 1942. On the 18th, she rescued 32 Royal Australian Air Force men from enemy-held Timor. Five days later, fire broke out in her main power cubicle, immobilizing her completely, and she was fortunate, even with the assistance of the submarine *Snapper*, to be able to reach port in Australia, before the Japanese found and destroyed her as a sitting duck. *Searaven's* fourth war patrol was a quiet one. However, after returning from her fifth, she reported 23,400 tons sunk and 6,853 damaged—a claim that could not be confirmed because of enemy attacks that drove her too deep, and for too long, to take tallies.

In early January 1943, on her sixth patrol, she claimed the sinking of a minelayer in the Banda Strait, but again could not confirm the victory. However, two weeks later, she pumped four torpedoes into a freighter and collected her first confirmed victory. After hitless seventh and eighth patrols, she set out on her ninth patrol in the Carolines in November, during which she got her second confirmed kill, sending a 10,052-ton tanker to the bottom. During her 10th and 11th patrols she claimed two more sinkings—again unconfirmed—but on her next she had more luck, knocking off a freighter, two trawlers, and eight sampans—all confirmed because they were in surface duels, where the results were readily apparent. Then she concluded her final patrol, terminating one Japanese transport and an oiler. *Searaven* ended her career in an unusual way, as one of the target ships in the 1946 atomic bomb test, Operation Crossroads, at Bikini Atoll. She escaped the tests with only negligible damage, but was decommissioned in December 1946, sunk as a target in September 1948, and struck from the Navy list. *Searaven* earned 10 battle stars for World War II service and was credited with sinking three vessels for 20,492 tons.

Sea Robin (SS-407)

A submarine of the Balao class, *Sea Robin* was built by Portsmouth Naval Shipyard and launched in February 1944 and sailed for Luzon Strait and her first war patrol, where, on January 6, 1945, she torpedoed and sank her initial victim of the war, a 5,000-ton Japanese tanker. Her second patrol proved to be her most productive. On March 3, while patrolling in the Java Sea, the boat evaded a Japanese escort ship and torpedoed a cargo ship. After several unsuccessful attempts to rescue survivors, the submarine finally hauled three prisoners of war on board and continued her patrol. Two days later, *Sea Robin* contacted a troop-laden convoy of two cargo ships, a converted gunboat, and several escorts. The gunboat was the first to be sent to the bottom, the victim of three torpedo hits. After evading the suddenly active escort vessels, the submarine commenced an end run and, several hours later, was again in firing position. The first of the two cargo vessels was zigzagging radically but was unable to avoid the three torpedoes that *Sea Robin* fired at her. She took one hit below her bridge and settled quickly by the bow. *Sea Robin* then fired a spread of three torpedoes at the remaining cargo ship, but the target zigged and they missed. On the second attempt, the ship was not so fortunate—the submarine fired three more torpedoes that broke her in half and sent her rapidly to the bottom. On her third patrol, in the South China Sea, she rescued a downed airman, but was unable to find any targets except two Japanese fishing vessels, taking three prisoners of war and, on the following day, taking on board 10 more Japanese, survivors of a foundering trawler that had been worked over by Allied aircraft. *Sea Robin's* third and final war patrol was conducted in the Yellow and East China Seas. After sinking a small patrol craft on July 9 and taking one prisoner, she torpedoed and sank a cargo ship. Shortly thereafter, while attempting to sink a large sampan, *Sea Robin* was caught on the surface by a Japanese plane, which dropped two bombs close aboard the submarine. Although it was not discovered until the end of the patrol, the submarine's bow tubes were severely damaged, causing numerous torpedo misses throughout the remainder of the patrol. With the exception of several trawlers sunk in surface attacks, the remainder of the patrol was unproductive. She was converted to a GUPPY IA at Portsmouth Naval Shipyard in 1951. *Sea Robin's* peacetime career included service in South America, where she circumnavigated the continent and became the first submarine to round Cape Horn; in the Canal Zone; in Europe; and on the East Coast. After her 12,920th, and final, dive, in October 1970, she was decommissioned and struck from the Navy list. *Sea Robin* received three battle stars for World War II service and was credited with sinking six vessels for 13,172 tons.

Seasprite (SH-2)

The Seasprite class is composed of antisubmarine warfare (ASW) helicopters, with watertight hulls, a pilot cabin, and a main cabin, which holds the ASW system operator's station and sonobuoy rack. The aircraft can carry three passengers, two litters, or an instructor's seat, and is fitted with a 4,000-pound external cargo hook and a 600-pound rescue hoist over the starboard door. The retractable main landing gear struts have two-wheel units and extend to the sides when lowered, retracting inward and forward into exposed wells; the fixed tail wheel is located well forward of the tail pylon. For hangar stowage, the main rotor blades fold back and the nose compartment splits into two folding halves. These craft are equipped with surveillance radar in a drum-like ventral radome located below the cockpit, and also contain smoke markers that can be dropped from a forward bay to port of the radome. A stores station on either side carries a single ASW torpedo or a drop tank.

Seawolf (SS-197) (S-16)

Built by Portsmouth Naval Shipyard and the first to bear her name, *Seawolf* was a submarine of the Searaven class, launched in August 1939 and assigned to the Pacific at the start of World War II. She is one of those submarines on "Eternal Patrol," whose fate will probably forever remain a mystery. *Seawolf,* under the command of Lieutenant Commander A. M. Bontier, left Brisbane on September 21, 1944—a war-scarred veteran on her 15th war patrol—and arrived at Manus eight days later. Leaving Manus on the same day, she was directed to carry certain stores and army personnel to the east coast of Samar. On October 3, *Seawolf* and *Narwhal* exchanged radar recognition signals, and later the same day an enemy submarine attack was made in the area, which resulted in the sinking of the *Shelton*. Since there were four friendly submarines in the vicinity of this attack, they were directed to give their positions. Three did, but *Seawolf* was not heard from. A day later, *Seawolf* was directed again to report her position, but failed to do so.

USS *Rowell* and an aircraft attacked a submarine in the vicinity of the attack on *Shelton*, having at that time no knowledge of any friendly submarines in the area. Is it possible that *Seawolf*—and *not* a Japanese submarine—was the submarine attacked? The battle report from *Rowell* indicates that an apparently lethal attack was conducted in conjunction with a plane, which marked the spot with dye. *Rowell* established sound contact on the submarine, which replied with long dashes and dots that bore no resemblance to the existing recognition signals. Later, a small amount of debris and a large air bubble were seen. After the war, it was confirmed that the Japanese submarine *RO-41*, which sank *Shelton* on October 3, had been able to return to Japan, and therefore was not the victim of the attack by *Rowell* and the American plane. The only other alternatives to the *Seawolf*'s

loss are that she was lost to an operational casualty or as a result of an unrecorded enemy attack. Destruction by a mine was apparently ruled out, since this area was not known to be heavily mined at that time.

The loss of *Seawolf* was a big blow to the navy, since, during her first 14 patrols, she had sunk 27 enemy ships and damaged 13. These included cruisers, transports, freighters, tankers, cargo ships, destroyers, and smaller vessels, for a total tonnage for ships sunk and damaged of 108,600 and 69,600, respectively. She also conducted photographic reconnaissance, rescued a number of downed aviators, and delivered cargo to guerrilla forces in the Philippines. She was awarded battle stars for 15 missions, as well as Navy Unit Commendations and credited with sinking 18 vessels for 71,609 tons.

Seawolf (SSN-575)

Seawolf, the world's second nuclear submarine, was built by the Electric Boat Division of General Dynamics and launched July 21, 1955. From September 3 to 25, she steamed across the North Atlantic, participating in NATO exercises and not surfacing until she was off the coast of Newport, Rhode Island, a distance of 6,331 nonstop miles.

After cruising to the Caribbean for an exercise in November, she participated in exercises along the East Coast until August 7, 1956, at which time she submerged and did not resurface again until October 6, logging more than 13,700 nautical miles and demonstrating to the world the ability of a nuclear-powered submarine to remain independent.

Seawolf returned to General Dynamics on December 12, 1958, for refueling and to convert her power plant from a sodium-cooled to a pressurized water–cooled reactor. On April 28, 1964, *Seawolf* departed from New London to the Mediterranean Sea and a three-and-one-half-month deployment with the Sixth Fleet. She was part of the world's first nuclear task force.

Seawolf was converted and operated under Command Submarine Development One as a "Special Mission" submarine from 1972 to 1987, except for a stand-down for a refueling/overhaul from 1978 to 1981. *Seawolf* was decommissioned on March 30, 1987, and struck from the Navy list on July 10, 1987.

Seawolf III (SSN-21)

Launched in June 1995, this submarine was built by the Electric Boat Company and was the first in the new SSN class, with a displacement of 8,600 tons on the surface and 9,137 tons submerged. She was designed near the end of the cold war, to counter the once rapidly increasing capabilities of the Soviet submarine force, which had been projected for the 1990s and beyond. She was described as "quiet, fast and well-armed with advanced sensors . . . capable of deploying to forward ocean areas to search out and destroy enemy submarines and surface ships and attack land targets. The many new features of this submarine represent a dramatic improvement over earlier designs." Her flexibility provided the navy with an undersea weapons platform that could operate in any scenario against any threat, with mission and growth capabilities that far exceeded the Los Angeles-class submarines, enabling her to perform a variety of crucial assignments from underneath the arctic icepack to littoral regions anywhere in the world. Its missions include surveillance, intelligence collection, special warfare, covert cruise-missile strike, mine warfare, and antisubmarine and antisurface ship warfare. *Seawolf*'s stealth characteristics made it the world's quietest submarine—so much so, in fact, that it was said to be "quieter at tactical speed than a Los Angeles-class submarine at pier side."

The other submarines in the Seawolf class were:

Connecticut (SSN-22)

Jimmy Carter (SSN-23)

Segundo (SS-398)

Built by the Portsmouth Naval Shipyard and launched February 5, 1944, *Segundo* stood out of New London on June 26 en route to the Pacific war zone. She arrived in Pearl Harbor July 25, was combat loaded on August 19 and 20, and sailed the next day for her first war patrol. *Segundo* formed a wolf pack with *Seahorse* (SS-304) and *Whale* (SS-239), and the trio, after refueling in Saipan on September 3, departed for their patrol area in the Philippines. Finding no worthwhile targets, *Segundo* ended her patrol on October 21 without having fired a shot.

A second patrol (November 16, 1944–January 5, 1945) with sister ships *Trepang* (SS-412) and *Razorback* (SS-394) had greater success. A convoy of seven escorted merchant ships was sighted, and all merchantmen were sunk.

Patrolling the East China Sea with *Razorback* and *Sea Cat* (SS-399) on February 1, 1945, three torpedo attacks were made on unescorted ships near the Korean coast. Three torpedoes fired during the first attack missed. Four torpedoes fired four days later during a second attack all missed. The third attack, against a cargo ship on March 11, included two torpedoes fired. The first blew the stern off and the second hit amidship, sinking the cargo ship in two minutes.

Segundo was assigned to a lifeguard station until May 16, 1945, when she departed for the East China Sea. She sank 12 ships of varying tonnage between May 16 and June 11 and sailed for Midway for upkeep.

In the Sea of Okhotsk, *Segundo* captured a Japanese submarine on August 29, 1945, deposited the crew in Tokyo and departed for Pearl Harbor and then San Diego. *Segundo* supported United Nations forces in Korea from July to September 1950, then returned to San Francisco Naval Shipyard to be converted to a "Fleet Snorkel." She operated out of her home port of San Diego for the next 16 years and was decommissioned August 1, 1970, struck from the Navy list August 8, 1970, and scuttled as a target by *Salmon* (SS-573). *Segundo* received four battle stars for World War II service and one for Korean service.

Sennet (SS-408)

Built by Portsmouth Naval Shipyard and launched in February 1944 as a member of the Balao class, this submarine held training exercises and torpedo tube testing off the coast of Connecticut and Rhode Island, off Maryland, and in the Canal Zone for almost a year before being ordered to join the Pacific Fleet. So she did not depart on her first war patrol until the end of January 1945, when she roamed the Bonin Islands and successfully attacked two Japanese picket boats, followed by a minelayer on her second patrol, and a cargo vessel and repair ship on her third. Her most profitable patrol was from July 1 to August 9 in the Sea of Japan. During the patrol, she sank one passenger-cargo ship, two cargo vessels, and one tanker, totaling 13,105 tons. When the war ended, *Sennet* was assigned to the Atlantic Fleet and operated from New London, Connecticut. From early December 1946, to mid-March 1947, she participated in Operation Highjump, the third Byrd Antarctic Expedition. In 1952, she was converted to a Fleet Snorkel submarine at Philadelphia Naval Shipyard. She also served in the Canal Zone, Key West, the Caribbean, and Charleston, South Carolina. She was decommissioned in December 1968. *Sennet* received four battle stars for World War II service and was credited with sinking seven vessels for 17,726 tons.

Shad (SS-235)

A submarine of the Gato class, she was built by Portsmouth Naval Shipyard and launched in April 1942 and, following shakedown off the New England coast, departed on a special patrol as a unit of SubRon50, to a point off the coast of French Morocco, to conduct reconnaissance in preparation for Operation Torch, the Allied invasion of North Africa. Upon completion, she sailed to Roseneath, Scotland, for repairs and further training. Her second war patrol was conducted in the Bay of Biscay and in Spanish coastal waters with other units of SubRon50 under British command. Although the majority of the vessels she sighted were neutral Spanish ships, the submarine sank an enemy trawler and a barge, and severely damaged a destroyer escort before she returned to Rosneath for refit in mid-February 1943. *Shad* departed Scotland in early March, heading for the Bay of Biscay on her third war patrol. During this mission, the submarine damaged a blockade runner, but made no successful contacts during her fourth patrol, conducted in Norwegian waters, or on her fifth, en route back to the United States. She was then ordered to the Pacific, where she departed from Pearl Harbor, on September 28, 1943, for her sixth war patrol, and her first against the Japanese, returning home with a record of one possible sinking (unconfirmed) and damage to three transports and a freighter. On her seventh war patrol in waters surrounding the Japanese home islands, she attacked a heavily laden freighter escorted by two small patrol craft. Although there was evidence of one hit, exact results were unknown because of the severe counterattack that forced the submarine to leave the area. But she later damaged a large transport and sank a frigate. Her eighth and ninth war patrols were uneventful, but on her 10th, operating as part of a coordinated attack group with *Balao, Dragonet,* and *Spikefish* in the East China Sea, in mid-May, she contacted a large freighter and two escorts; fired three torpedoes; and quickly got out of range. One torpedo hit forward on a freighter, blowing her bow completely off, and she settled quickly to the bottom. Later, *Shad* destroyed a small junk by gunfire and then attacked and sank a 1,370-ton cargo ship. Her final war patrol was cut short by the war's end, and she remained in service as a training vessel until being struck from the Navy list five years later. *Shad* earned six battle stars for World War II service and is credited with sinking three vessels for 6,209 tons.

Shark (SS-174) (P-3)

Built by the Electric Boat Company and the first of three submarines to bear the name, and the first in a new class so designated, *Shark* was launched in May 1935. She was assigned to San Diego as a training vessel, and in 1938 ordered to join the Pacific Fleet at Pearl Harbor, then transferred to Manila. At the start of the war, her first mission was to embark Admiral Thomas C. Hart, commander-in-chief of the United States Asiatic Fleet (ComSubAF), for transportation to Soerabaja, Java. After having transported Hart and other officials to Surabaya, *Shark* departed on January 5, 1942, for her second war patrol, ordered to reconnoiter a major enemy move south through Molucca Passage. On February 2 *Shark* reported to Surabaya that she had been depth-charged 10 miles off Tifore Island and that she had missed on one torpedo attack. Five days later, she reported an empty enemy cargo ship heading northeast, but when Surabaya tried to make contact again, no further messages were received from *Shark.* By the end of the first week in March she was reported as presumed lost. A postwar Japanese report of antisubmarine attacks recorded at least three that might have been against *Shark,* in the Celebes area, where Dutch and English submarines were also operating. *Shark* was credited with two missions during World War II.

Shark (SS-314)

Built by the Electric Boat Company and the second to bear her name, *Shark* was launched in October 1943 and the next year assigned to the Pacific Fleet. She was ordered to Saipan, in the Marianas, and departed on her third war mission in early October 1944, as part of a wolf pack with *Sea Dragon* and *Blackfish,* to conduct a coordinated patrol in the vicinity of Luzon Strait. On October 22, *Shark* reported having contacted four large enemy vessels, and two days later *Seadragon* received a message from her stating that *Shark* had made radar contact with a single freighter, and that she was going in to attack. This was the last message received from *Shark.* However, on November 13, 1944, a dispatch originated by Commander Naval Unit, 14th Air Force, stated that a Japanese ship en route from Manila to Japan with 1,800 American prisoners of war had been sunk on October 24 by an American submarine in a torpedo attack. No other submarine reported the attack, and since *Shark* had given *Seadragon* a contact report only a few hours before the sinking, and could not be raised after that by radio, it was assumed that *Shark* made the attack described and perished during or after it. Five prisoners who survived and subsequently reached China stated that conditions on the prison ship were so intolerable that the prisoners prayed for deliverance from their misery by a torpedo or bomb. *Shark* may well have been sunk trying to rescue American prisoners of war. During her first two patrols, *Shark* was credited with sinking five ships, totaling 32,200 tons and damaging two, for 9,900 tons. She was awarded three battle stars and credited with sinking four vessels for 21,672 tons.

ship classifications

Where do submarines fit in the overall picture of American fighting ships? The U.S. Navy maintains its ship-classification listings in four sections—Combatant Ships, Combatant Craft, Support Craft, and Auxiliary Ships.

COMBATANT SHIPS

Aircraft Carriers

All ships designed primarily for the purpose of conducting combat operations by aircraft, which engage in attacks against airborne, surface, sub-surface, and shore targets:

Aircraft Carrier	CV
Aircraft Carrier (nuclear powered)	CVN
Obsolete	CVA/CUS

Coastal Patrol Ships

Smaller vessels that can cruise in shallow waters:

All types	PC

Surface Combatant

Large, heavily armed, surface ships that are designed primarily to engage enemy forces on the high seas:

Battleships	BB
Gun Cruisers	CA
Guided Missile Cruisers	CG
Guided Missile Cruisers (nuclear powered)	CGN
Destroyers	DD
Guided Missile Destroyers	DDG
Frigates	FF
Guided Missile Frigates	FFG

Submarines

All self-propelled submersible types regardless of mission:

Attack Submarines	SS
Submarines (nuclear powered)	SSN
Ballistic Missile Submarines (nuclear powered)	SSNB

Patrol Combatant

Combatants whose mission may extend beyond coastal duties and whose characteristics include adequate endurance and capability to provide a capability for operations exceeding 48 hours on the high seas without support:

Patrol Ships	PC
Patrol Combatant	PG
Guided Missile Patrol Combatant (Hydrofoil)	PHM

Amphibious Warfare Ships

All ships having organic capability for amphibious assault and that have characteristics enabling long-duration operations on the high seas:

Amphibious Helicopter/ Landing Craft Carriers	
Amphibious Assault Ship (General Purpose)	LHA
Amphibious Assault Ship (Multipurpose)	LHD
Amphibious Assault Ship (Helicopter)	LPH
Amphibious Transport Dock	LPD
Landing Craft Carriers	
Amphibious Cargo Ship	LKA
Amphibious Transport	LPA
Tank Landing Ship	LST

Combat Logistics Ships

Ships that have the capability to provide underway replenishment to fleet units:

Ammunition Ship	AE
Store Ship	AF
Combat Store Ship	AFS
Oiler	AO
Fast Combat Support Ship	AOE

Mine Warfare Ships

All ships whose primary function is mine warfare on the high seas:

Minesweeper, Ocean	MSO
Mine Countermeasures Ships	MCM
Minehunters, Coastal	MHC

COMBATANT CRAFT

Patrol Craft

Surface patrol craft intended for use relatively near the coast or in sheltered waters or rivers:

Patrol Boat	PB
Patrol Craft (Fast)	PCP
Mini-armored Troop Carrier	ATC
River Patrol Craft	PBR

Amphibious Warfare Craft

All amphibious craft that have the organic capacity for amphibious assault and are intended to operate principally in coastal waters, or may be carried aboard larger units:

Landing Craft, Air Cushion	LCAC
Landing Craft, Mechanized	LCM
Landing Craft, Personnel, Large	LCPL
Landing Craft, Utility	LCU
Landing Craft, Vehicle, Personnel	LCVP
Amphibious Warping Tug	LWT
Side Loading Warping Tug	SLWT
Light SEAL Support Craft	LSSC
Medium SEAL Support Craft	MSSC
Swimmer Delivery Vehicle	SDV
Special Warfare Craft, Light	SWCL
Special Warfare Craft, Medium	SWCM

Mine Warfare Craft

All craft with the primary function of mine warfare that are intended to operate principally in coastal waters and may also be carried aboard larger units:

Mine Countermeasures Craft	MCC
Minesweeping Boat	MSB

SUPPORT CRAFT

Service Craft

A grouping of navy-subordinated craft designed to provide general support to either combatant forces or shore-based establishments:

Dry Docks (Non-self-propelled)

Auxiliary Floating Dry Dock	AFD
Auxiliary Repair Dry Dock	ARD
Harbor Tug	YTB
Fuel Oil Barge	YO
Harbor Utility Craft	YFU
Aircraft Transportation Lighter	YCV
Gasoline Barge	YON
Oil Storage Barge	YOS
Deep Submergence Rescue Vehicle	DSRV
Deep Submergence Vehicle	DSV
Submersible Research Vehicle	NR
Torpedo Trials Craft	YTT
Floating Crane	YD
Diving Tender	YDT
Salvage Lift craft	YLC
Dredge	YMN

AUXILIARY SHIPS

Mobile Logistics Ships

Ships that have the capability to provide direct material support to other deployed units operating far from home base:

Destroyer Tender	AD
Repair Ship	AR
Submarine Tender	AS

Support Ships

A grouping of ships designed to operate in the open ocean in a variety of sea states to provide general support to either combatant forces or shore-based establishments:

Salvage Ship	ARS
Submarine Rescue Ship	ASR
Fleet Ocean Tug	ATF
Salvage and Rescue Ship	ATS
Auxiliary Crane Ship	ACS
Deep Submergence Support Ship	AGDS
Missile Range Instrumentation Ship	AGM
Oceanographic Research Ship	AGOR
Ocean Surveillance Ship	AGOS
Surveying Ship	AGS
Auxiliary Research Submarine	AGSS
Hospital Ship	AH
Cargo Ship	AK
Vehicle Cargo Ship	AKR
Gasoline Tanker	AOG
Transport Oiler	AOT
Transport	AP
Cable Repairing Ship	ARC
Repair Ship	ARL
Aviation Logistic Support Ship	AVB
Guided Missile Ship	AVM
Auxiliary Aircraft Landing Training Ship	AVT

Simon Lake (AS-33)

A submarine tender, 634 feet long and 83 feet in beam, the *Lake* was launched in February 1964 and decommissioned in September 1999, then held in reserve. She and her sister ship, *Canopus,* were designed to service fleet ballistic missile (FBM) submarines with up to three SSBNs moored alongside simultaneously. In addition to regular capabilities, FBM submarine tenders also store ballistic missiles. These ships were originally built to support the Polaris missile. The *Simon Lake* was modified in 1971 and the *Canopus* in 1970 to support the Poseidon missile, equipped with side-by-side 30-ton cranes over the 16 vertical cells for the missiles. The *Lake* was later modified to handle the Trident C-4 missile. After having her missile support capabilities removed, she was used exclusively to service nuclear attack submarines.

Sims, William S. (1858–1936)

Sims became noted when his persistent efforts to improve ship design, fleet tactics, and naval weaponry marked him as one of the most influential officers in the history of the

U.S. Navy. He entered the Naval Academy in 1876, and after graduation in 1880, served almost continuously on sea duty for the next 17 years. During this time he wrote a navigation text that was long used by both the navy and the merchant marine. Sims served as naval attaché to the U.S. embassies in Paris and St. Petersburg from 1897 to 1900. His observations of foreign navies convinced him of the comparative inferiority of the U.S. Navy, despite its recent victories in the Spanish-American War. While serving in the U.S. Asiatic Fleet at the turn of the century, he learned from a British officer, Captain Percy Scott, of a successful new gunnery technique described as "continuous-aim firing." After writing reports to the Navy Department setting forth the technique, along with his criticisms of American naval marksmanship, and receiving little response, he went over the heads of his superiors and sent his opinions to President Theodore Roosevelt, who immediately understood the problems and personally ordered him to Washington as inspector of naval target practice. After seven years in this post Sims returned to sea duty, having effected remarkable improvements in the state of naval gunnery. Sims was promoted to rear admiral and became head of the Naval War College in 1917. When America entered World War I, he was promoted to vice admiral in command of the U.S. fleet that operated with Britain's Royal Navy in European waters. He played a major role in securing the adoption of the convoy system to protect Allied merchant ships against German submarine attack. After the war he resumed his post as president of the Naval War College, while continuing to agitate for reforms in the Navy Department. He retired in 1922.

Sirago (SS-485)

A boat of the Tench class, she was built by Portsmouth Naval Shipyard and launched in May 1945, too late to see action in World War II. However, she did participate in an unusual way. Deployed to Provincetown, Massachusetts, as a member of Submarine Squadron (SubRon) 8, in January 1946 she participated in the destruction of two German submarines. On return to New London, *Sirago* commenced duties that included training services for Submarine School and for the fleet's destroyer force; experimental exercises to evaluate new techniques and equipment; and fleet exercises that took her from Davis Strait into the Caribbean. In December 1948, she entered the Philadelphia Naval Shipyard for a GUPPY II conversion, and on July 25, 1949, she left the yard for Norfolk where, as a modernized high-speed attack submarine, she joined Sub-Ron6. Attached to SubRon6 for the next 22 years, *Sirago's* primary mission was antisubmarine warfare. During the 1950s she deployed to the Mediterranean where she operated as a unit of the Sixth Fleet. She was decommissioned in June 1972.

Skate/F-4 being inspected while under construction in Seattle, Washington, prior to commissioning in 1913. *(United States Navy)*

Skate (SS-23) (F-4)

Launched in January 1912, and the first of three submarines to bear her name, *Skate* joined the First Submarine Group, Pacific Torpedo Flotilla, and participated in the operations of that group along the West Coast and, from August 1914 on, in Hawaiian waters. During submarine maneuvers off Honolulu on March 25, 1915, she sank in 51 fathoms, a mile and a half from the harbor. Despite valorous efforts of naval authorities at Honolulu to locate the missing boat and save her crew, all 21 perished. A diving and engineering precedent was established with the navy's raising of the submarine in August 1915. Courage and tenacity marked the efforts of divers who descended to attach cables to tow the boat into shallow water; while ingenuity and engineering skill characterized the construction and use of specially devised pontoons. The investigating board ruled that corrosion of the lead lining of the battery tank had permitted seepage of sea water into the battery compartment, thereby causing the commanding officer to lose control during that last fatal dive.

Skate (SS-305)

The second submarine to bear the name *Skate* was built by Mare Island Naval Shipyard and launched in March 1943, and six months later was assigned to Pearl Harbor, from which she set out on her first war patrol, headed toward Wake Island to perform lifeguard duty for aircraft carriers during air strikes against that Japanese-held island. At

Three boats of the nuclear Skate class, *Sargo, Sea Dragon,* and *Swordfish* cruising in surface formation. *Skate* (SSN-578) was built by the Electric Boat Division of General Dynamics and commissioned in 1957 and was noted for her pioneering operations under the North Pole and the surrounding ice packs. *(United States Navy)*

dawn on October 6, the submarine was strafed by enemy aircraft, mortally wounding one of her officers as he attempted to assist wounded airmen from a life raft. The next day, *Skate* closed to within 5,000 yards of the beach, in the face of heavy enemy bombardment, to rescue two downed aviators. While searching for a third, she was attacked by a Japanese dive-bomber and was forced to dive to escape. On her second war patrol, conducted off Truk in the Caroline Islands in late November, she sighted five warships but, after firing a spread of torpedoes at overlapping aircraft carriers, was forced down by depth charging from the escort ships. In late December, she sank a cargo ship. Then, during a rain squall on Christmas Day, she made a daring attack that damaged the battleship *Yamoto*, the pride of the Japanese fleet. During her third patrol, again in the Wake Island area, she sank a Japanese light cruiser and, during her fourth, dispatched a cargo ship, sank an enemy sampan in a surface attack, and took three prisoners of war. Her fifth war patrol, in July 1944, was successful, knocking off a destroyer and two cargo ships.

Although *Skate*'s sixth patrol was largely photographic reconnaissance, with no sinkings, her seventh was very productive. Leaving Pearl Harbor on April 11, 1945, to form a coordinated attack group with other submarines, she sailed to the Sea of Japan where she encountered a Japanese submarine on the surface and returning to port.

As the enemy crossed her bow, *Skate* made two torpedo hits that quickly sank the submarine. Two days later, she enjoyed her most productive day of the war. While off the Nanto Peninsula, she evaded gunfire of enemy ships and an attack by enemy escort ships to sink three cargo vessels. Her eighth war patrol cut short by word of the Japanese surrender, she operated along the West Coast until May 1946, when she departed for Bikini Atoll, Marshall Islands, to be used as a target ship in Operation Crossroads, the atomic bomb tests. Although considerably damaged by the first of the tests, the submarine survived and was towed back to Pearl Harbor, where she was moored in an isolated berth. She was later towed to Mare Island, California, where she was inspected, decommissioned, and destroyed and sunk off the California coast in October 1948. *Skate* received eight battle stars for World War II service and was credited with sinking 10 vessels for 27,924 tons.

Skate (SSN-578)

Built by the Electric Boat Company and the third submarine to bear the name, *Skate* was also designated as the name of a brand new class of SSN nuclear boats when she was launched in May 1957. In late 1958, after operating in the Caribbean and waters off England, *Skate* steamed to the arctic where she operated under the ice for 10 days.

During this time, she surfaced nine times through the ice, navigated over 2,400 miles under it, and became the second ship to reach the North Pole. In the following months, as the first ship of her class, she conducted various tests in the vicinity of her home port. In early March 1959, she again headed for the arctic to pioneer operations during the period of extreme cold and maximum ice thickness. She steamed 3,900 miles under pack ice while surfacing through it 10 times. On March 17, she surfaced at the North Pole to commit the ashes of the famed polar explorer, Sir Hubert Wilkins, to the arctic waste. When the submarine returned to port, she was awarded a bronze star in lieu of a second Navy Unit Commendation for demonstrating " . . . for the first time the ability of submarines to operate in and under the Arctic ice in the dead of winter . . ." In the fall of 1959 and during 1960, *Skate* participated in exercises that were designed to strengthen American antisubmarine defenses. After the loss of *Thresher* in 1963, *Skate* became the first submarine to finish a major conversion program to overcome the problems that had caused the fatal sinking. *Skate* operated several more times in record-breaking polar maneuvers under the ice, and was decommissioned in September 1986.

Other submarines in the Skate class were:

Swordfish (SSN-579)

Sargo (SSN-583)

Seadragon (SSN-584)

Skipjack (SS-24) USS *E-1*

Built by Fore River Shipbuilding, *Skipjack* was launched on May 27, 1911, and renamed *E-1* on November 17, 1911. Arriving in New York on September 28, 1912, *E-1* underwent repairs, alterations, and installation of a Sperry gyrocompass and became an underwater test platform initiating experiments using radio equipment while submerged. *E-1* conducted tests of these and other important developments under the direction of Commander, Submarine Flotilla, and United States Atlantic Fleet. She patrolled the Azores from January 12, 1918, through September 1918 arriving back at New London/Groton, Connecticut, for overhaul, additional training, and testing of underwater listening gear later known as sonar. *E-1* was decommissioned on October 20, 1921, and sold on April 19, 1922.

Skipjack (SS-184)

Built by the Electric Boat Company and launched in October 1937 as a member of the Salmon class, the first of two boats bearing the *Skipjack* name spent her prewar years in many ports, ranging from the Caribbean and South Atlantic to California, Hawaii, and the Philippines, where she was undergoing repairs at the Cavite Navy Yard when America declared war on Japan. On December 9, *Skipjack* departed Manila on her first war patrol, with unfinished repair work still being completed by her crew, en route to a patrol area off the east coast of Samar. She conducted two torpedo

Skipjack/E-1 (SS-24) shortly after joining the fleet in 1912. The tent-like structure over the conning tower was typical of protections devised during hot weather when most long-range cruising was done on the surface. (United States Navy)

Britain. Operations began in August 1942, when the Americans landed on Guadalcanal and established a beachhead—as a first step in cutting Japanese supply lines on regular runs of their ships (the "Tokyo Express") from Rabaul to Guadalcanal through the channel between the eastern and western Solomons. The opposing navies met in fierce fighting on six separate occasions, not only in the Solomons and at Guadalcanal, but also at Cape Esperance, the Santa Cruz Islands, and Tassafaronga before the issue was resolved after six months. During these battles, 24 ships were lost, and the Japanese suffered the loss of as many as 600 naval pilots. After the American forces solidified control of Guadalcanal, they turned their attention to the remaining islands in the group. In a further series of seven naval battles they progressively seized more territory, including Kula Gulf, Vella Lavella, and Cape St. George, and completed operations in the Solomons with the capture of Bougainville on November 1, 1943.

sonar

This term, a contraction of "sound navigation ranging," refers to a technique for determining the distance and direction of underwater objects by detecting sound waves reflected from an object, such as a ship or plane, and analyzing them for the information they can provide. Three basic sonar systems are in use: The first, referred to as active, is one in which an acoustic projector generates a sound wave that spreads outward and is reflected back by a target, using a receiver to pick up and analyze the reflected signal to reveal the range, bearing, and motion of the target. The second, called passive, consists of receiving sensors that pick up the noise produced by the target, and evaluate the wave forms for identifying characteristics and direction. The third category of sonar devices are acoustic communication systems, which require a projector and receiver at both ends of the acoustic path.

Sonar, in its primitive stages, goes back as early as World War I, when a passive system, consisting of towed lines of microphones, was used to detect submarines. Subsequent developments included the echo sounder, fathometer or depth detector, rapid-scanning sonar, and side-scan sonar. The uses of sonar expanded when it was applied to an increasing number of systems used to detect, identify, and locate submarines, and was then applied also to acoustic homing torpedoes, acoustic mines, mine detection, mapping of the sea bottom, and acoustic locating for divers. Some sonar systems are also placed on the seabed, often in large arrays, to provide continuous surveillance.

sound surveillance system

The U.S. Navy operates several seafloor sound surveillance systems (SOSUS) in various parts of the Atlantic and Pacific Oceans, as well as across the Strait of Gibraltar and North Cape, off the northern coast of Norway. The system is composed of a series of fixed, passive arrays used to detect transiting submarines; in wartime, it would be used to direct air, surface, and submarine antisubmarine warfare forces to areas of suspected submarine contacts. During World War II, the Americans, British, and Russians installed limited-capability acoustic arrays on the ocean floor near harbors. Immediately after the war, the U.S. Navy began development and testing of deep-ocean arrays, and by 1951 the first ones were implanted off the East Coast, followed by arrays in the western Atlantic by the end of 1956 and in the Pacific by 1958. Also installed were a number of naval facilities (NAVFAC) to serve as the shore terminals, located along both U.S. coasts, in the Caribbean, Iceland, and Japan, and at other overseas locations. Other facilities were reported to have been located also in the Aleutian Islands, Canada, Denmark, Iceland, Turkey, Spain, South Korea, the Philippines, and the United Kingdom. The entire SOSUS program was upgraded during the Cold War when it was felt necessary to be more aware of Russian transgression. Despite the rapid shrinkage of the Soviet submarine force for which the system was first designed, this type of sonar is deemed to be of continuing value in view of growing Third World submarine forces.

Spadefish (SS-411)

Built by Mare Island Naval Shipyard and launched January 8, 1944, *Spadefish* spent a month at Pearl Harbor and got underway for her first war patrol on July 23, 1944. Her late entry into World War II activities did not deter her performance, as *Spadefish* is credited with sinking 21 ships and numerous trawlers and inflicting damage to many others. This performance got off to a quick start as it was only August 19, 1944, when *Spadefish* encountered and sank a 9,589-ton, passenger-cargo ship and the first of what was to become a lengthy list. *Spadefish* was decommissioned on May 3, 1946, reclassified on November 6, 1962, and struck from the Navy list and scrapped on April 1, 1967.

Spanish-American War (1898)

Toward the end of the 19th century, there was a growing concern in the United States about the widespread violation of human rights in the Spanish colony of Cuba. Anti-Spanish feeling in the United States was greatly increased when the battleship *Maine* exploded and sank in Havana harbor on February 15, 1898, with the loss of 260 crew. Although later inquiries concluded that a faulty boiler, and not a Spanish mine, was responsible, the United States increased its support for dissident Cubans and, on April 25, 1898, declared war on Spain. The U.S. Navy, unlike American ground forces, was prepared for war and went into action immediately. In the Pacific, the U.S. Asiatic Squadron entered Manila Bay in the Philippines, a Spanish colonial possession, and on May 1 attacked a larger enemy squadron, completely destroying it and blockading Manila until August 13, when American troops arrived to capture the city. In the Atlantic, the U.S. Atlantic Fleet blockaded the harbor at Santiago de Cuba from May to July, waiting for American ground troops, and by July 1 U.S. forces dominated the area around Santiago. When the Spanish fleet tried to escape, it came under heavy fire from superior American naval forces, and at the battle of Santiago Bay (July 3, 1898) the Spaniards were totally defeated. An armistice was agreed upon, and, by the terms of the Treaty of Paris (December 10, 1898), Spain relinquished control of Cuba and ceded Puerto Rico, Guam, and the Philippines to the United States. The outcome of the war recognized the emergence of the United States as a world power and the increasingly global role of its navy.

Spearfish (SS-190) (S-9)

This submarine of the Sargo class was built by the Electric Boat Company, launched in October 1938 and assigned later to Pearl Harbor, and then to the Philippines, where she was docked at the start of World War II. She left immediately on her first war patrol—as did most of the other American boats in the Philippines—heading into the South China Sea, near Saigon and Cam Ranh Bay, French Indochina, and off Tarakan and Balikpapan, Borneo. On December 20, she encountered a Japanese submarine, made a submerged attack, and fired four torpedoes—but all missed the target. Her second war patrol was equally disappointing, but on her third, in April and May in the Sulu Sea, she sank an enemy cargo ship of approximately 4,000 tons and, later, a 6,995-ton freighter. On the night of May 3, the submarine slipped into Manila Bay and picked up 27 passengers from Corregidor to be evacuated to Fremantle. She was the last American submarine to visit that beleaguered fortress before it surrendered. In July and August, she scouted the South China Sea for enemy shipping and, in October and November, searched the west coast of Luzon where she damaged two freighters. After several unproductive missions, she sailed on her eighth war patrol, in the Japanese home waters south of Bungo Suido, where on the night of September 10–11, 1943, she made a submerged torpedo attack on a convoy of seven freighters escorted by one destroyer and two torpedo boats. She fired torpedoes at four ships and damaged two. A week later, she attacked another convoy of seven ships with their escorts, sinking two and damaging one. After photographic and reconnaissance missions, Spearfish left on her 10th war patrol, south of Formosa, in January and February 1944, where she made two torpedo attacks on a convoy of three merchantmen and two escorts. She sank

an escort and a passenger-cargo ship, and in later attacks sank a transport and damaged three freighters. During her next patrol, in April and May in the East China Sea, she sank a freighter and, the following day, a cargo ship. Spearfish's last war patrol took place from mid-November 1944 to late January 1945. On the first part of the patrol, she made photographic reconnaissance surveys of Iwo Jima and of Minami Jima, then spent the second part in the Nanpo Shoto area on lifeguard duties and offensive patrols. She also rescued seven survivors of a crashed B-29, and later sank a sampan, taking on board three Japanese prisoners. Spearfish spent the rest of the war as a training vessel out of Pearl Harbor and was awarded 10 battle stars for World War II service. She was credited with sinking four vessels for 17,065 tons, decommissioned June 22, 1946, struck from the Navy list July 19, 1946, and sold for scrapping May 14, 1947.

special-purpose submarines

Through a century of ship designing, building, modifying, and converting, there have always been submarines that were either planned from the beginning or altered after being launched to undertake special-purpose missions. The following are characteristic examples.

Cargo submarines (SSA), such as Barbero (SSA-317). Originally in service in World War II, with a good record of enemy sinkings, Barbero was converted as a cargo ship in an experimental program in the 1950s.

Oiler submarines (AOSS), as represented by Guavina (AOSS-362). She too had an excellent World War II record before her conversion in the 1950s to a seaplane tender and a whole new kind of service until her decommissioning in the late 1960s.

Transport submarines (APSS/LPSS), such as Grayback (APSS/LPSS-574), which served as a troop transport in the western Pacific during the 1960s, as well as Perch, Sealion, and Tunny.

Auxiliary submarines (AGSS), which were terminated from their basic assignments and allocated to locations and organizations having special needs. Archerfish is a good example, a submarine of the Balao class, which had an outstanding World War II record and was assigned to meteorological research operations during peacetime, before being decommissioned in 1968. Another case is that of Chopper, which had an impressive record of peacetime operations from the mid-1940s until the 1960s. After suffering a control failure that forced her to sink far below her rated depth, she was too badly damaged for repairs; however, she served as a valuable salvage and rescue training hulk for a number of years thereafter.

Cruiser submarines (SC), such as Cachelot, Cuttlefish, and Dolphin, which finished their careers as training ships, cruising the oceans with new breeds of submariners.

Target submarines (SST) whose mission is to act as a target for training antisubmarine forces. *Mackerel* and *Marlin* are two such examples, along with two former K boats, *Barracuda* and *Bass*.

Minelayer submarines (SM) are exemplified by *Argonaut* (SM-1), with mine-laying, and sometimes mine destruction, as a primary function.

Miscellaneous special-purpose ships that do not fit these categories are classified IXSS.

Two other special-purpose boats, radar-picket submarines (SSR) and submarines for antisubmarine warfare (ASW) are covered separately in this volume as their primary mission.

Spikefish (SS-404)

A submarine of the Balao class, *Spikefish* was built by Portsmouth Naval Shipyard and launched in April 1944, was assigned to the Pacific Fleet, and left Pearl Harbor on her first war patrol in mid-November, headed for the Sea of Okhotsk. She encountered no enemy shipping during the patrol, which ended at Midway Island. In late January 1945, she sailed for the Ryukyus and began patrolling westward of that group. In late February, she made a submerged attack on a convoy of six cargo ships with four escorts. She fired six torpedoes at two of the freighters, three of which were heard to hit, but results were not observed because she was forced to go deep and weather out a four-hour attack of more than 80 depth charges. She sighted another convoy on March 5 and expended six torpedoes in a fruitless attack, which led to another pounding by escorts. Her next two patrols found no targets, but on her final patrol, in July and August 1945, she was more fortunate. Operating in the Yellow Sea and near Shanghai, she bombarded Surveyor Island, off the China coast, in an attempt to destroy an enemy radar station; sank an enemy cargo ship, taking aboard three survivors; and tracked down a Japanese submarine, which sank in a cloud of fire and smoke. The sole survivor, who was taken prisoner, identified the submarine as *I-873*. Barely a day later, she received word that the war was over. She delivered her prisoners to Saipan, and shortly after that was ordered to New London, Connecticut, where she operated until being decommissioned in April 1963. On March 18, 1960, *Spikefish* became the first United States submarine to record 10,000 dives. She received three battle stars for World War II service and credited with sinking one vessel for 1,660 tons.

Spinax (SS-489)

This submarine of the Tench class was built by Portsmouth Naval Shipyard, launched in November 1945, and assigned to Submarine Force Atlantic Fleet a year later. In January 1948, *Spinax* was designated a radar-picket sub-marine and reclassified to SSR. She operated throughout the Caribbean during the first part of 1948, returning in May to Portsmouth Naval Shipyard for an overhaul that lasted until the end of October. This overhaul upgraded *Spinax* to Migraine II, radar-picket destroyer status. *Spinax* deployed to the Mediterranean from January 3 to March 3, 1949, as the first postwar submarine unit of the Sixth Fleet. Upon her return to New London, she was assigned to SubRon6, based at Norfolk. This was the first time since WWI that submarines had been scheduled to operate from that base. She conducted operations along the East Coast until again being deployed to the Sixth Fleet from January 6 to May 13, 1950. She returned to Norfolk until June 12, when she was transferred to the West Coast.

The submarine arrived at San Diego on June 29 and proceeded up the coast to the San Francisco Naval Shipyard for an overhaul. She made a cruise to Pearl Harbor from August 17 to October 16, 1951, and returned to San Diego. She became a unit of SubDiv53 on January 1, 1952, and resumed her routine duties. *Spinax* was overhauled at Mare Island from April through early August and returned to San Diego on August 7, 1952.

Spinax operated out of that port until November 1, 1954, when she sailed for an extended tour in the Far East. The submarine operated with the Seventh Fleet and then visited the Philippines, Hong Kong, Formosa, and Japan before returning to San Diego on May 7, 1955. Overhaul at Mare island from June through October 1956 was followed by refresher training in the San Diego area. She was deployed to WesPac from January 4, to July 1, 1957, and again from July 3 to December 16, 1958.

Emphasis in antisubmarine warfare resulted in *Spinax* being converted to a Fleet Snorkel submarine. This was accomplished at Mare Island from April 13 to September 11, 1959. All radar except search and fire control were removed; the communication facility was reduced to that of a regular submarine; and the combat information center was converted into living quarters. The ship received improved sonar and fire control equipment, and modifications were made in her hull. On August 15, she resumed the designation of "SS." When the conversion was completed, the submarine conducted refresher training and local operations until early 1960.

Spinax departed San Diego on May 3, 1960, for a tour in the western Pacific with the Seventh Fleet that lasted until November 3, when she returned to her home port. Thereafter, except for four deployments to WesPac, her West Coast operations were interrupted only by yard overhauls. *Spinax* was deployed from June 27 to December 17, 1962; from August 18, 1965, to March 15, 1966; from January 6 to June 25, 1967; and from February to August 13, 1969, when she last returned to Mare Island. In September 1969, *Spinax* was declared unfit for further naval service. She was decommissioned and struck from the

Navy list on October 11, 1969. Her hulk was sold for scrapping on June 13, 1972.

Spot (SS-413)

Built by Mare Island Naval Shipyard and launched on May 19, 1944, *Spot* moved to San Diego and then on to Pearl Harbor, arriving on November 14, 1944. *Spot, Balao* (SS-285) and *Icefish* (SS-367) formed a hunter-killer group that patrolled the Yellow Sea where *Spot* sank 10 vessels. Additionally, *Spot's* record reflects two sinkings and one damaged vessel, plus the bombardment of an oil refinery and radio station while conducting a reconnaissance of the island of Kokuzan To off the coast of Korea. Her last war patrol on June 2 records two more sinkings by gunfire.

Spot was decommissioned on June 19, 1946, and attached to the Pacific Reserve Fleet. She was modernized in January 1961 and loaned to the Chilean government in January 1962, where she served until December 1982. *Spot* received four battle stars for World War II service.

Springer (SS-414)

Built by Mare Island Naval Shipyard and launched August 3, 1944, *Springer* was sent to the Ryukyus on her first war patrol on February 17, 1945. She made radar contact with three ships and sank the largest of the three before returning to Guam on March 25 to be refitted.

Springer, Trepang I (SS-412) and *Raton* (SS-270) sailed to the Yellow Sea as a wolf pack. While checking Tomei Harbor on Fukue Shima, *Springer* was unsuccessful in her attempt to close on two ships that were hugging the coast, however, she encountered an escort when leaving the harbor, sinking it with three torpedoes. Four more vessels were sunk as a result of this war patrol.

In Guam when the hostilities with Japan were over, *Springer* was attached to the Mare Island Group, Pacific Reserve Fleet during September 1945. She was modernized in April 1960 and transferred to the Chilean government on January 23, 1961, after being decommissioned. *Springer* received three battle stars for her World War II service.

Spruance, Raymond Ames (1886–1969)

An American naval officer, he was especially known for his achievements as the commander of American naval forces at the decisive battle of Midway in June 1942, during World War II. He was a graduate of the U.S. Naval Academy (1907), after which he served in engineering assignments, both at sea and ashore, as an instructor in strategy at the Naval War College, and as an officer at the Office of Naval Intelligence. When the United States entered World War II, he was commander of a cruiser division, participating in the early 1942 raids on the Marshall and Gilbert Islands and in the famous Doolittle Raid on Tokyo in April of that year. Relieving Admiral William Halsey, who was ill, Spruance assumed command of Task Force 16 on board the USS *Enterprise* and was thus subordinate to Admiral Frank J. Fletcher at the time of the Japanese advance toward Midway. However, the events of the battle were such that Spruance, though not an aviator himself, became the real hero of the navy's decisive victory over the Japanese at Midway. Later, as chief of staff, he helped to coordinate the central Pacific drive. In 1943 he commanded that campaign, then headed the Central Pacific Force. Promoted to the rank of full admiral in March 1944 and designated commander, Fifth Fleet, his forces conducted the invasions of the Marianas and engaged the Japanese navy at the battle of the Philippine Sea in June 1944. He also participated in the campaigns against Iwo Jima, Okinawa, and the Japanese home islands. At the end of the war he briefly commanded the Pacific Fleet before serving as president of the U.S. Naval War College. Retiring in 1948, he served as U.S. ambassador to the Philippines in the early 1950s.

Squalus (SS-192)

Launched in September 1938, this submarine of the Sargo class had two lives—first as *Squalus,* and later, refitted for wartime service, as *Sailfish,* recommissioned in May 1940. As *Squalus,* she was—and is—one of the best known American submarines in history, because of her tragic sinking and the dramatic, intensive efforts made to save members of her crew and later raise her from the depths. On May 23, 1939, she was cruising in a test run some 15 miles southeast of Portsmouth, New Hampshire, near the Navy Yard where she had been built, when a valve failed. She was barely underwater, at a depth of 40 feet, when water, without warning, flooded the engine room. There was a moment in which the intercom resounded with a squawked warning, "Water flooding . . .," and then went dead. Forward motion stopped as the boat, badly out of trim, nosed down, heavy and now out of control, to the bottom. Within seconds, her 299-foot-long hull lay motionless 242 feet down and in the mud. No emergency procedures, such as racing the propellers and trying to blow ballast, had any results. The struggle to increase buoyancy ceased as air spurted from the muddy valves. Unable to communicate in any other way, the commander ordered release of one of the rescue phone buoys, which had been built into the new submarine for just such a purpose. It read, "SUBMARINE SQUALUS SUNK HERE—BOW BUOY." He also released another new emergency device, a smoke bomb, which would send up clouds of smoke when chemicals within it were activated at the surface.

When *Squalus* failed to make expected communications or return to base on schedule, a search was instituted. Her sister ship, *Sculpin*, was the one to spot the smoke, locate the buoy, and make contact with the trapped survivors through the built-in phone. The hours went by as those below tried to assess the extent of the damage, and those in the submarine above sent out the most urgent calls for rescue vessels and equipment and a plan of action. The submarine *Falcon* arrived, along with a flotilla of other vessels and salvage equipment, which had been designed and perfected after the tragic sinking of the *S-4* some 12 years before. The first plan, to put down lines to blow air into the flooded engine compartment and provide enough buoyancy to float *Squalus*, failed, leaving the next best alternative: to lower a newly designed rescue chamber (loosely referred to as a "diving bell"), which could be attached to an escape hatch—but only if the angle of the sunken boat was not too severe!

The *Falcon*'s first action was to throw out a circle of anchors to maintain its position over the wreck, and then lower a diving stage with divers going below to inspect the hull and determine the feasibility of using the rescue chamber. In the end, the rescue chamber did work, rescuing survivors a few at a time. The nation—and indeed, the world—followed this emotionally charged and highly suspenseful story on radio and through regular press reports, almost minute by minute. Except for the unfortunate crew members in the flooded engine room—all of whom died within minutes of the boat's plunge to the bottom—every man not lost at the time of the accident was saved. *Squalus*, repaired, refitted, and equipped with the latest in communication equipment and weaponry, was renamed *Sailfish* in May 1940, and went on to a brilliant record against the Japanese in the Pacific. However, one last tragedy was still in store for her place in history. When she torpedoed and sank, as one of her several enemy victims, the Japanese aircraft ferry, *Chuyo*, she unwittingly sealed the doom of all but one of the 21 American prisoners of war aboard her, who were being taken to a prison camp. They were crew members who had been plucked from the sea by the Japanese after they had sunk an American submarine, the *Sculpin*.

SSBN patrol pin

The submarine service has long had a tradition of encouraging the use of patrol pins, one of which is the silver Polaris patrol pin, which is worn by SSBN crew members and former members—both officer and enlisted. It recognizes their sacrifice and hard work in completing strategic patrols. One gold star marks each patrol completed. A silver star marks five patrols. Upon completion of 20 patrols, a gold patrol pin is authorized. It has become traditional for the person on active duty with the most deterrent patrols to be presented with the Neptune Award, in an appropriate ceremony. That person retains the award either until some other submariner attains more patrols than the current holder or until the holder retires from the service, at which time it goes to the submariner with the next highest number of patrols.

Steelhead (SS-280)

A submarine of the Gato class, built by Portsmouth Naval Shipyard and launched in September 1942, *Steelhead* left Midway Island on her first war patrol in February 1943, during which she planted mines off the Japanese mainland and bombarded a steel plant. Her second and third patrols resulted in unconfirmed damage when she fired 10 torpedoes at an enemy task force and damaged a tanker, which was later sunk by a sister submarine, *Tinosa*. On her next patrol, she operated off Bungo Suido from late December 1943 to early March 1944, where she torpedoed and sank a 6,795-ton converted salvage vessel. Her fourth patrol, off Formosa from early April to May 23, provided no targets worthy of torpedo fire, but she sank a trawler by gunfire. On June 17, she sortied from Midway Island with *Hammerhead* and *Parche* to patrol south of Formosa. On July 31, she made three successful attacks in which one ship was damaged and two were sunk. *Parche* also sank two from the convoy. Routed to the West Coast for overhaul, she was out of action for many months after she suffered a serious fire that required the installation of a new conning tower. Not until April 1945 did she depart on her next— and final—mission. She performed lifeguard duty in the Caroline Islands and later patrolled in the Tokyo Bay area. She made no torpedo attacks but sank two trawlers by gunfire. The patrol ended at Midway Island on August 5, and 20 days later she sailed for the West Coast. Assigned as a training vessel and later placed in reserve, she was decommissioned in June 1946. *Steelhead* received six battle stars for World War II service and is credited with sinking three vessels for 22,159 tons.

Sterlet (SS-392)

In October 1943, *Sterlet*, accompanied by *Pomfret* and *Queenfish*, performed the first triple launch in submarine construction history at Portsmouth Naval Shipyard, Kittery, Maine. After an intensive training period at Key West, Florida, the boat departed for Pearl Harbor to join the Pacific Fleet and conducted her first war patrol in the vicinity of the Bonin Islands, just south of the main Japanese island of Honshu. Successful attack were made on enemy shipping, which resulted in the sinking of four ships totaling 14,200 tons. A prisoner was taken from a raft after carrier planes had destroyed an enemy convoy north of the Bonins. Departing Midway on September 18, 1944, for her second war patrol, *Sterlet* proceeded to the Nansei Shoto Islands. During the first carrier strike on Okinawa, she rescued six carrier airmen. Five torpedo attacks and two gun attacks were also carried out, resulting in the sinking of one large freighter, one small freighter, and a fishing vessel. She later sank a submarine chaser. On her third patrol, in early 1945, *Sterlet* added another large freighter and tanker to her record. Her fourth patrol, in May, was also successful, resulting in the sinking of a freighter and damage to another. *Sterlet* narrowly escaped disaster herself when another supposed freighter turned out to be a "Q" ship—a heavily armed warship in disguise. Her fifth, and final, patrol, in July and August 1945, was cut short by Japan's surrender before she could add any more enemy ships to her hit list. However, she did rescue two British carrier pilots and got her final assault on the enemy by making a daylight bombardment on the main island of Honshu and destroying oil storage tanks and a power plant. As a result of their actions, the officers and crewmen of *Sterlet* were awarded a total of 25 decorations: one Navy Cross, four Silver Stars; seven Bronze Stars; and 13 Letters of Commendation with Ribbon. *Sterlet* was converted to a Fleet Snorkel submarine at San Francisco Naval Shipyard in 1951 and subsequently configured with a major sonar upgrade. She remained in the Pacific, home-ported in Pearl Harbor. *Sterlet* conducted a number of deployments to the Western Pacific and remained active until January 1969 when she was sunk as a target by USS Sargo. *Sterlet* is credited with sinking 4 vessels for 15,803 tons.

Stingray (SS-186) (S-5)

A member of the Salmon class, this submarine was built by Portsmouth Naval Shipyard and launched in October 1937 and saw prewar service along the West Coast, in Hawaii, and in the Philippines, where she was stationed at the time of the Pearl Harbor attack, and where she made her first war patrol. On her second patrol, after sinking a transport ship as her initial victim, she was ordered to Fremantle, Australia. Her early patrols were unproductive, except for a gunboat, but on the seventh patrol she sank a cargo ship, and on her 10th another cargo ship. The rest of her patrols were largely on special missions, doing lifeguard duty, rescuing downed airmen, and transporting landing parties to key positions in the enlarging attack on Japan. In all, *Stingray* made 16 war patrols in the Pacific and received 12 battle stars for World War II service. *Stingray* was decommissioned on October 17, 1945, and credited with sinking four vessels for 18,558 tons.

strategic deterrent submarines

Popularly known in the service as the "boomers," the navy's ballistic missile submarines (SSBNs) have conducted their patrols and missions with less fanfare than the attack submarines (SSNs). At the end of World War II, the U.S. Navy found itself with a submarine force that was strong and capable, as evidenced by its stellar performance from 1941 through 1945, but with little strategic clout. Developments starting in the late 1940s saw the planning of submarines for the new cruise missile program. In a sense, this developed because of the success in several instances of submarines, late in World War II, which undertook rocket attacks on enemy shore facilities. A prime example of this was that of the *Barb* (SS-220), which for the first time in submarine history, successfully employed rockets against the towns of Shari, Shikuka, Kashaiko, and Shiritori. German World War II successes with long-range missiles and Soviet developments in this field motivated the United States to experiment with launching strategic missiles from submarines. One of the first ventures involved the Loon, a ramjet missile patterned in part after the German V-1. The submarine-launched turbojet-powered missiles made their appearance a few years later, notably with Regulus I, first launched at sea in March 1953 by the converted *Tunny* (SSG-282). Some five years later, both *Grayback* (SSG-574) and *Growler* (SSG-577) had been commissioned as the first boats to be designed specifically for launching Regulus missiles, each carrying two in a bow hangar.

"When USS *Grayback* (SSG-574) slipped its moorings and headed into the Pacific Ocean in September 1959," according to the Dictionary of American Fighting Ships "it began an era of submarine history that would go unrecognized for almost 40 years." This referred to the missions of five strategic deterrent submarines that deployed in no fewer than 41 deterrent patrols under the earth's oceans over the course of five years, thus establishing a vital new phase in submarine history.

Sturgeon (SS-187) (S-6)

The first to bear the name, this submarine of the Salmon class was built by Mare Island Naval Shipyard and launched in March 1938, was assigned to training operations for two years, and was moored in Mariveles Bay when the Japanese attacked Pearl Harbor. She put to sea the next afternoon to patrol an area between the Pescadores Islands and Formosa. Although she tracked several targets and fired a torpedo spread, she scored no hits and returned to base. On her second patrol, she attacked the enemy on several occasions, scoring at least three hits, but was unable to confirm them. In mid-March 1942, deployed to patrol off Makassar, she sank a cargo ship and a frigate and damaged another vessel. On her next patrol, in June, west of Manila, she caught up with a nine-ship convoy, fired three torpedoes at the largest ship, and heard explosions. After some 21 depth charges were dropped by the escorts, she managed to escape with only a few gauges broken, and shortly afterward sank a 7,267-ton transport. Her fifth war patrol in the Solomon Islands area, resulted in an important kill: an 8,033-ton aircraft ferry. Her sixth and seventh patrols were unrewarding, but her eighth and ninth were better: two ships sent to the bottom and two damaged. On her 10th and last patrol, in June 1944, she closed out her war patrol days with one more victory, knocking off one of the enemy vessels in an eight-ship convoy. After refitting, she was deployed to New London, Connecticut, to serve as a training vessel. She was decommissioned in 1948 and received 10 battle stars for World War II service and is credited with sinking nine vessels for 41,350 tons.

Sturgeon (SSN-637)

The third ship of the line to bear the name, she was the lead ship of 37 nuclear fast-attack submarines of the Sturgeon class. She was built by the Electric Boat Company and launched in February 1966, displaced 4,229 tons on the surface and 4,672 tons submerged, was armed with four 21-inch launching tubes amidships, aft of the bow, and was designed for a complement of 12 officers and 96 enlisted men. In September 1967, she conducted the first of her many extended submarine operations and, upon return to port, was transferred to Development Group Two. Four months later, she began a five-week antisubmarine exercise to evaluate the relative effectiveness of the Sturgeon- and Permit-class submarines.

In late May and early June 1968, she joined in the search for the lost submarine *Scorpion* in the vicinity of the Azores. She then participated in three months of tests and evaluations of a new sonar detection device, with accompanying training for her crew, and later spent several weeks aiding and evaluating aircraft antisubmarine warfare tactics and equipment. During the 1970s and 1980s, *Sturgeon* conducted many special operations, explored the waters of the arctic, supported a multinational task group engaged in amphibious strategies and tactics in the eastern Atlantic and Norwegian Sea, worked with the SEALs to support diver operations and develop new techniques for rendezvous and recovery, and developed operational procedures for employment of new types of mines and torpedo fire control systems. The year 1988 was highlighted by *Sturgeon*'s passing of a surprise operations test with superior performance, and she was judged as one of the outstanding submarines of the Atlantic Fleet. During her career, she was given numerous awards for outstanding performance in a number of categories. *Sturgeon* remained in active service until being deactivated in Charleston, South Carolina, in January 1994 and decommissioned six months later. In September 1995, her sail was transported to the Naval Undersea Museum in Keyport, Washington, where it is now on permanent display.

The other submarines in the Sturgeon class are:

Whale (SSN-638)

Tautog (SSN-639)

Grayling (SSN-646)

Pogy (SSN-647)

Aspro (SSN-648)

Sunfish (SSN-649)

Pargo (SSN-650)

Queenfish (SSN-651)

Puffer (SSN-652)

Ray (SSN-653)

Sand Lance (SSN-60)

Lapon (SSN-61)

Gurnard (SSN-662)

Hammerhead (SSN-663)

Sea Devil (SSN-664)

Guitarro (SSN-665)

Hawkbill (SSN-666)

Bergall (SSN-667)

Spadefish (SSN-668)

Seahorse (SSN-669)

Finback (SSN-670)

Pintado (SSN-672)

Flying Fish (SSN-673)

Trepang (SSN-674)

Bluefish (SSN-675)

Billfish (SSN-676)

Drum (SSN-677)

Archerfish (SSN-678)

Silversides (SSN-679)

William H. Bates (SSN-680)

Batfish (SSN-681)

Tunny (SSN-682)

Parche (SSN-683)

Cavalla (SSN-684)

L. Mendel Rivers (SSN-686)

Richard B. Russell (SSN-687)

Submarine Force Museum

This major submarine information resource is located, in New London near the submarine base in Groton, Connecticut, the site of the original submarine library and museum, and close to the shipyard where most of the navy's early submarines were designed and built. It was established by the United States Navy, with support from many manufacturers and organizations interested in the history, development, and operation of submarine fleets, to provide both those in naval service and the public with in-depth information. The main exhibit area contains two mini-theaters, each showing continuous programs, one on the history of submarines and the other providing a visual tour of the *Nautilus,* America's first nuclear submarine. Related films are also shown, such as *Steel Boats, Iron Men,* depicting life on board a modern submarine. On display in the main area is a full-scale replica of David Bushnell's *Turtle,* a tiny, barrel-shaped vessel that unsuccessfully attacked a British ship in New York harbor in 1776. Suspended from overhead nearby is a 50-foot-long, one-third scale, cutaway model of the submarine USS *Gato,* which belonged to the primary class of attack submarines used by the U.S. Navy during World War II. Torpedo and weaponry displays include torpedoes, a missile, and a deck gun carried by submarines for use against small surface ships or to ward off attacks by enemy aircraft. Other displays are dedicated to pioneers in submarine development; the design, construction and launching of submarines; World War II operations in battles around the globe; and the use of these undersea vessels to protect the nation's security in time of peace, as well as war. The *Nautilus* room contains numerous photographs, drawings, artifacts, and other materials associated with the USS *Nautilus* (SSN-571), as well as displays outlining the history of this noted submarine from construction to her journey under the polar icepack and final decommissioning.

submarine-launched ballistic missile

These missiles, known familiarly as SLBMs since their initial appearance in undersea weaponry in 1960, have been an increasingly important part of the world's armory of nuclear weapons. Deployed not only by the United States, but also by the Soviet Union, China, France, and Britain, among others, they are more difficult to identify and destroy than other nuclear weapons. They were a key element in maintaining the "balance of terror" between the United States and the Soviet Union (Russia) during the latter stages of the Cold War in the 1970s and 1980s. The successful introduction of the Polaris ballistic missile in particular escalated a technological race between America and the Soviet Union in the further development of SLBMs, the latter country unable to match the Polaris for almost seven years. Then the United States took the lead with the Poseidon in the 1970s, which was equipped with multiple independently targeted warheads—a marked increase in weapons capability. The Soviets also developed a multiple warhead variant, the SSN-18, which had a

longer range (4,800 miles) than its American equivalent; but within a few years, the navy's new Trident missile could travel a similar distance. During the 1980s, the missile race narrowed, and eventually planned increases in strategic nuclear arsenals were phased out, following the decline of the Soviet Union and the end of the cold war.

submarine rocket

This form of weapon, termed SUBROC, was a rocket-propelled antisubmarine nuclear depth bomb with a range of about 30 miles that could be launched from standard 21-inch submarine torpedo tubes while the boat was submerged. After being launched, the missile could streak to the surface, leave the water, and travel on a ballistic trajectory for a predetermined time. Then, the booster would separate and fall away and the bomb would reenter the water at supersonic speed, detonating at a present depth. SUBROCs were designed in the late 1950s, placed in operation in the mid-1960s, and phased out at the beginning of the 1990s, when they were considered inferior to new types of submarine missiles designed to replace them.

Submarine World Network

This website which is linked to more than 30 subpages is described by its producer as "the World's Largest Submarine Directory listing 1,000+ links to submarines of all nations and all periods of history." It is used as a major communication network for submarine veterans and historians, and is closely allied to United States Submarine Veterans, Inc. (USSVI), which also has its own communications network and website. The Submarine World Network on-site coverage includes news briefs on submarines and submariners, some 325 links to submarine home pages, information for navy veterans, listings of courses, seminars, conventions, reunions, and other topical events, descriptions of home ports, bases, and naval memorials, an on-line submarine bookstore, listings for ordering patches, caps, bumper stickers, insignia, videotapes, and other submarine-oriented merchandise, chat pages, and links to sources of information for assistance of many kinds. Submarine World Network is particularly valuable for veterans and former and present submariners who are trying to locate shipmates from the past or obtain other kinds of personalized information. And it can be used to track information and data of almost any kind about submarines and related subjects.

submersible

This term is used in general for any undersea craft capable of diving to great depths and withstanding tremendous pressures. However, it is seldom applied to submarines designed as ships of war but rather to other underwater craft designated for more peaceable pursuits. Submersibles go back further in history than naval submarines and have been used to explore the seabed, investigate shipwrecks, aid in salvage work, provide recreational sub-sea tours, and supply observational details that remote video equipment could not provide. Among the most famous submersibles is *Alvin,* of the Woods Hole Oceanographic Institution in Massachusetts. *Alvin* was used to explore the wreck of the British liner *Titanic* after the wreck was located by a joint French-American expedition in 1985. On its visits to *Titanic, Alvin* utilized a tethered, mobile camera system called "Jason junior" to enter the wreck and photograph portions of its interior. Despite the tremendous amount of information and striking photo images they may yield, submersibles are not used extensively to explore shipwrecks, partly because of extensive demand for their services and because operating such craft is very expensive. However, through the use of submersibles, such as *Alvin,* there is no place beneath the surface of the ocean that can't be reached.

Sub Pride

An unofficial submarine website that is popular with submariners and submarine buffs because it makes available at nominal fees—almost at cost—individual photographs and other illustrations, as well as CDs containing either specialized picture collections of vessels, historical sequences, customized selections, or as many as 1,000 submarine photos on a single disk. Images can be downloaded at no cost from the Sub Pride website (*http://www.subpride.com*). Further information and answers to questions about obtaining pictures of specific submarines or related subjects can be obtained from the organization via e-mail (*subpride@aol.com*).

Subsafe

When the nuclear submarine USS *Thresher* (SSN-593) was lost at sea with all persons aboard during a deep test dive

in April 1963, it was concluded that a flooding casualty in the engine room, resulting from a piping failure in a salt-water system, was the most probable cause for the disaster. Out of that tragedy and the lessons learned grew the Subsafe (Submarine Safety) program. Through that program, every submarine in the U.S. fleet, every pressure hull integrity–related system aboard those boats, and every pressure-related part within those systems must be certified as 100 percent reliable before the boat can leave its dock. "The goals," according to the Navy's Mission Statement, Level One/Subsafe, "are to provide maximum reasonable assurance that the integrity of the material used on the ship can operate at design test depth to ensure that seawater is kept out of the submarine and, in the event of a casualty, the ship and its crew can recover." To expedite the implementation of Subsafe, the navy established certain basic controls relating to the selection and construction of materials, the methods used during the building or renovation of submarines, and the design of critical elements that in the past have been prone to accidents, such as the ballast tanks, valves, electrical systems, high pressure air and gas components, and vents. Through the Subsafe program, all equipment involved with the submarine's pressure hull (designed and constructed to withstand pressures from the surrounding seawater down to a calculated safe depth) and that allows recovery from flooding undergoes intense design reviews at several levels by the Naval Sea Logistics Center. In addition, the program makes certain that all vital equipment to which crew members would need instant access in the event of an emergency is clearly marked, easily accessible, and able to be activated within seconds at the click of a switch.

Sunfish (SS-281)

This submarine, the first of two to bear her name, was a member of the Gato class and was launched at Mare Island Shipyard in May 1942. Six months later, she stood out to sea en route to the Pacific war zone, and embarked on her

USS *Columbus* (SSN-762) seen doing an "emergency blow," a process by which high-pressure air is rapidly introduced directly into the submarine's main ballast tanks. An emergency blow makes the submarine positively buoyant, allowing sufficient momentum to clear the surface and then settle back down to a normal surfaced position. This system was instituted as part of the Subsafe program following the loss of USS *Thresher*. (United States Navy)

first patrol in November, which was largely to the heart of enemy waters in order to lay a minefield at the entrance to Iseno Imi off the coast of Japan. On her second patrol, in February and March 1943, she sank three enemy ships in the East China Sea. Her third patrol found no targets, but on her fourth, in waters off Formosa, in August and September, *Sunfish* sank a tanker, a gunboat, and a cargo ship. After a disappointing fifth patrol, she sailed in mid-January 1944 to prowl the shipping lanes between the Caroline and Mariana Islands. She made a photographic reconnaissance of enemy positions in the islands, and in late February made four determined attacks on a convoy and sank two ships for a total of 9,437 tons of enemy shipping. Her seventh patrol was equally satisfying, when she roamed the waters of the Kurile Islands in July and August, sinking a passenger-cargo ship and a 6,284-ton cargo ship with torpedoes, and destroying a fleet of 14 sampans and trawlers with her deck guns.

Sunfish's eighth war patrol, in the Yellow Sea in September, resulted in two sinkings and several ships damaged. *Sunfish* then returned to the Yellow Sea, in late October, as part of a wolf pack that included *Peto* and *Spadefish*. Three weeks later, *Sunfish* sighted a convoy of eight ships, led by a 21,000-ton escort carrier. When the carrier passed out of range, word was flashed to the other two members of the pack. *Sunfish* attacked the remaining ships of the convoy and sank two. *Spadefish* caught the escaping carrier with four torpedoes and sent her under. The running battle continued, and *Peto* sank two marus, while *Spadefish* added a submarine chaser to the score, and later another maru. *Sunfish* then concluded the patrol by sending a transport to the bottom. When *Sunfish* roamed the East China Sea again, in mid-January 1945, she had the misfortune to collide with an unsighted ice floe that bent both periscopes, forcing her to make for Apra Harbor, Guam, on the 27th, for refit and repairs. *Sunfish* began her 11th and last war patrol in early April, off Honshu and Hokkaido. She damaged one ship, which managed to make it to a protected harbor. But the submarine ended her wartime career by sinking a transport and a frigate, and bagging two more ships with her last torpedoes before returning to Pearl Harbor and then departing for Mare Island, California, two days later. *Sunfish* went out of commission and in reserve until she was struck from the Navy list in May 1960; she was awarded nine battle stars for World War II service and credited with sinking 16 vessels for 59,815 tons.

Swordfish (SS-193)

The first *Swordfish* to bear the name was a submarine of the Sargo class, built by the Portsmouth Naval Shipyard and launched in April 1939. She had a long career operating in a number of assignments until, at the start of World War II, she was ordered to join the Pacific Fleet. She com-

Steaming over 35,000 miles during her first year in commission, with over 80 percent of them submerged, USS *Swordfish* (SSN-579) was the second nuclear-powered submarine to join the Pacific Fleet—USS *Sargo* (SSN-583) being the first. *(United States Navy)*

pleted 12 war patrols and succeeded in the sinking of Japanese ships in her assigned battle areas. She left Pearl Harbor on December 22, 1944, to carry out her 13th patrol, in the vicinity of Nansei Shoto. She topped off with fuel at Midway on December 26 and left that day for her area. In addition to her regular patrol, *Swordfish* was to conduct photographic reconnaissance of Okinawa, to provide valuable information to American forces then being committed to fighting for control of Okinawa and a possible last stage in defeating the Japanese Empire close to its homeland. On January 2, *Swordfish* was ordered to delay carrying out her assigned tasks in order to keep her clear of the Nansei Shoto area until completion of carrier-based air strikes that were scheduled. She was directed to patrol an assigned area until further orders were received. In the last communications received from *Swordfish*, she acknowledged receipt of these orders on January 3. On January 9, 1945, *Swordfish* was directed to proceed, finally, to the vicinity of Okinawa to carry out her special mission. It was estimated that the task would not take more than seven days after arrival on station, which she should have reached on January 11. Upon completion of her mission, *Swordfish* was to proceed to Saipan, or to Midway if she was unable to transmit by radio. Since neither place had seen her by February 15, and repeated attempts to raise her by radio had failed, she was reported as presumed lost, the victim of unknown causes. *Swordfish* is credited with sinking 12 vessels for 47,928 tons.

Swordfish (SSN-579)

The second *Swordfish* to bear the name, she was a member of the Skate class, built by the Portsmouth (N.H.) Naval Shipyard and launched in August 1957. After sea trials along the East Coast, she was assigned a home port in Pearl Harbor, the second nuclear-powered submarine to join the Pacific Fleet, joining *Sargo*. Assigned to SubRon1, *Swordfish* ranged over 35,000 miles during her first year in commission—over 80 percent of them submerged. She deployed to the western Pacific in 1960, as the first nuclear submarine in that area. During this time, President Chiang Kai-Shek, of the Republic of China, and later-president Carlos P. Garcia of the Philippines were taken aboard for undersea demonstrations. During her entire career, *Swordfish* was based largely in Pearl Harbor and in West Coast ports, ranging on operational and training cruises throughout all parts of the Pacific. She was decommissioned in June 1989, and her name was struck from the Navy list in January 1990.

T

T-1 (SS-52)

Built by Fore River Shipbuilding Company and launched in July 1918, this submarine, the first of the new "T" class, had a displacement of 1,482 tons (submerged) and was designed for a complement of four officers and 50 enlisted men. Her service, however, lasted less than three years. She operated out of Hampton Roads, Virginia, training crews and conducting maneuvers along the East Coast of the United States with other units of the United States Atlantic Fleet. Throughout the entire period, she remained a unit of SubDiv15. However, during her service, flaws in her design and construction—particularly in her propulsion plant—became apparent, and in December 1922 she was placed out of commission.

The next two "T" boats also had very short careers because of problems with their propulsion plants and other defects of design.

T-1 (AA-1) (SS-52), launched in July 1918, was the first of only three boats in her class, all of which had short service lives and were decommissioned because of serious flaws in their design and construction. *(United States Navy)*

tactical towed array sonar

Known as TACTAS, this is a passive hydrophone array deployed from cruisers, destroyers, and frigates. It was developed as a component subsystem of a surface antisubmarine warfare combat (SQQ-X) system. The sonar provides for long-range detection of submarines, using a towed array or "tail," which positions the sonar far away from the tow ship's generated noises, which could otherwise mask a target's acoustic signals. The sensitive section of the array is about 900 feet long and consists of vibration isolation modules, a telemetry drive module, heading, depth, and temperature units, and acoustic modules of varying degrees of frequency. The modular construction of the array permits hydrophone components that fail or are damaged to be replaced onboard the ship. The array can be effective at relatively high ship speed and in moderately rough seas.

Tambor (SS-198)

Built by the Electric Boat Company and launched in December 1940, this is the lead submarine of a new class bearing her name and was stationed in the Pacific and was engaged in a routine peacetime patrol of Wake Island when war with Japan broke out, but was forced to return to Pearl Harbor with engine problems. She began her second war patrol in mid-March 1942, to reconnoiter the areas around Wake, Truk, New Ireland, New Britain, and Rabaul. Her only luck was a single torpedo hit on a tanker, which could not be confirmed. Her third patrol was even less fortunate, ending with a depth bombing that damaged both her periscopes and forced a return to base. Her next patrol, in August and September, resulted in a net tender and a freighter, and damage to a tanker. Her fourth patrol, in Hainan Strait in October and November, knocked off another freighter and a sampan. Her next two missions were disappointing, resulting in just one hit on a freighter, but she did carry out a special mission in the Philippine Islands, landing a small navy party—with 50,000 rounds of .30-caliber ammunition, 20,000 rounds of .45-caliber ammunition, and $1 million in currency—on southern Mindanao.

Tambor's seventh patrol took her north of the Malay Barrier in May and June 1943, where she registered hits on a freighter and several cargo ships, but sadly was never able to confirm them. Her next patrol was equally disappointing, including more unconfirmed sinkings and one frustrating experience where three of her torpedoes struck a large freighter and bounced off without exploding. She began her ninth war patrol in early January 1944, in the East China Sea. She sighted a convoy of nine ships heading north and fired two torpedoes at a cargo ship in a surface attack. Both hit and it went down by the bow. When an escort headed straight for the submarine and ramming

seemed inevitable, *Tambor* opened fire with her aft 20 mm gun and turned hard to port, causing the escort to pass 20 yards astern. Later, after escaping destruction, she began tracking two ships and fired two torpedoes at a cargo ship, which both hit amidships. She directed two more at a tanker, and one hit forward of the target's stack. Ten days later, she encountered another three-ship convoy and sank a passenger-cargo ship.

After repairs at Pearl Harbor, *Tambor* put to sea in early April en route to the Marianas, where she sank a trawler and a cargo ship, and on her next patrol, in July and August, a freighter and a cargo ship. Her next missions reported numerous torpedo actions and explosions, but no verification of sinkings, except for a patrol boat during a surface battle. *Tambor* was ordered to Puget Sound, Washington, at the end of 1944, and was then assigned stateside training operations, which she continued after the war until being decommissioned in September 1959. *Tambor* received 11 battle stars for World War II service and is credited with sinking 11 vessels for 33,479 tons.

Tang (SS-306)

Built by Mare Island Naval Shipyard and launched in August 1943, this submarine of the Balao class had one of the most illustrious, yet strangest, records of any submarine in battle during World War II. Ordered to the Pacific, she embarked on her first war patrol in late January 1944, under the command of Lieutenant Commander Richard H. O'Kane. Heading for the Caroline-Mariana Islands area, she sighted a convoy and sank a freighter, then later two cargo ships. As she proceeded deeper into enemy territory, she sank another freighter, two more cargo ships, and a tanker before putting into Midway Island for refit. Her second patrol, beginning in mid-March, took her to waters around the Palaus, to Davao Gulf, and to the approaches to Truk. She made only five surface contacts and had no opportunity to launch an attack before she was assigned to lifeguard duty near Truk. *Tang* rescued 22 downed airmen and transported them to Hawaii at the conclusion of the patrol.

Tang's third war patrol was one of the most devastating carried out against Japanese shipping during the war. Leaving Pearl Harbor in early June, she hunted enemy targets in the East China Sea and Yellow Sea areas. On the 24th, southwest of Kagoshima, she contacted a convoy of six large ships guarded by 16 escorts. In a daring surface attack, she sank two cargo ships and two freighters, for a total of 16,292 tons of enemy shipping. A week later, not satisfied with these kills, she went on to sink another tanker, a freighter, and two more cargo ships, for an additional total of more than 39,000 tons. On her fourth war patrol, conducted from July 31 to September 3 in Japanese home waters off the coast of Honshu, she knocked off two freighters, two patrol boats, a tanker, and an escort vessel.

Commanded by Richard O'Kane, *Tang* (SS-306) was launched in August 1943, destroyed numerous Japanese ships during war maneuvers between the northwest coast of Formosa and the China coast, and was sunk by her own torpedo during a night surface attack. *(United States Navy)*

Tang set out from Pearl Harbor on September 24, 1944, to begin her fifth war patrol, heading for an area between the northwest coast of Formosa and the China coast. On the 27th, she topped off with fuel at Midway Island, and was never heard from again. But the saga was not finished. The incredible story of her sinking comes from the report of her surviving commanding officer. A night surface attack was launched on October 24, 1944, against a transport that had been stopped in an earlier attack. The first torpedo was fired, and when it was observed to be running true, the second and last was loosed. It curved sharply to port, broached, and circled. Emergency speed was called for and the rudder was thrown over, but that was not enough to prevent disaster. The errant torpedo headed right back at *Tang*. Although the quick evasive maneuver prevented a strike amidships, the torpedo hit the stern. The explosion was violent, and crewmembers as far forward as the control room received broken limbs. The boat went down by the stern with the after three compartments flooded. Of the nine officers and men on the bridge, including Commander O'Kane, three were able to swim through the night until picked up eight hours later. One officer escaped from the flooded conning tower, and was rescued with the others.

The submarine came to rest on the bottom at 180 feet, and the men in her crowded forward as the after compartments flooded, assembling in the forward torpedo room to attempt an undersea escape. The escape was delayed by a Japanese patrol, which dropped charges and started an electrical fire in the forward battery. Thirteen men escaped from the forward room, using the Davis submarine escape apparatus, and by the time the last one made his exit, the heat from the fire was so intense that the paint on the bulkhead was scorching. Of the 13 men who escaped, only eight reached the surface, and of these only five were able to swim until rescued. When the nine survivors were picked up by a destroyer escort, there were Japanese victims of *Tang*'s previous sinkings on board, and they inflicted tortures on the Americans.

The nine captives were retained by the Japanese in prison camps until the end of the war, and were treated by them in typical fashion. The loss of *Tang* by her own torpedo, the last one fired on the most successful patrol ever made by a U.S. submarine, was a stroke of singular misfortune. *Tang* received four battle stars and two Presidential Unit Citations for battle service. Her skipper, O'Kane, received the Congressional Medal of Honor for *Tang*'s final action. Tang is credited with sinking 24 vessels for 93,824 tons.

Tang (SS-563)

Built by Portsmouth Naval Shipyard and the second to bear this illustrious name, *Tang* was also the first of a new class of fast-attack submarine designed for the 1950s. The design was an adaptation of design features of the German Type XXI submarine. She was launched in June 1951 and fittingly sponsored by Mrs. Richard H. O'Kane, wife of the skipper of the original *Tang*, of World War II fame. From her base at Pearl Harbor, *Tang* operated in the Hawaiian Islands, providing services to surface and air antisubma-

Tarantula/B-3 (SS-12), one of four new submarines built at the Fore River Shipyard and delivered to the navy in 1907. She carried a complement of one officer and nine enlisted men, and was armed with two torpedo tubes. *(United States Navy)*

rine warfare (ASW) forces. She also cruised to the western Pacific, Alaskan waters, and Far Eastern waters, where she provided training services to units of the Japanese Maritime Self Defense Force, the Nationalist Chinese Navy, SEATO naval forces, and the U.S. Navy. In 1959, she cruised to the northwestern coast of North America, where she tested a newly developed snorkel system and conducted training with Canadian naval forces in British Columbia. During the 1960s, she operated largely in Pacific waters, and in the 1970s was also deployed to South American waters for special exercises, particularly with surface units and submarines of the American, Chilean, and Peruvian navies. At the end of her career, she engaged in a new primary mission, training Iranian navy personnel, as well as providing service to units of the Atlantic Fleet. She was decommissioned in February 1980 and sold to Turkey, where she served as *Piri Reis* through the 1990s. *Tang* also earned four battle stars for service in Vietnamese waters.

Tarantula (SS-12) (B-3)

Built by Fore River Shipbuilding Company and launched in 1907 and listed as a member of the "B" class of submarine, *Tarantula* displaced only 173 tons, submerged, was armed with two 18-inch torpedo tubes in the bow, and carried a complement of one officer and eleven enlisted men. She operated along the Atlantic coast with the First and Second Submarine Flotillas on training and experimental exercises, and later served with the Atlantic Torpedo Fleet. In April 1912, she was shipped aboard a cargo vessel to the Philippines where she served with SubDiv4, Torpedo

Flotilla, Asiatic Fleet, until being decommissioned and struck from the Navy list at Cavite in July 1921.

Tarawa, Battle of (November 1943)

A coral atoll of the Gilbert Islands, Tarawa lies in the west-central Pacific Ocean, 2,800 miles northeast of Australia, and is the most populous atoll in the Gilberts. The atoll was the scene of fierce fighting during World War II, when, in 1943, U.S. Marines retook it from Japanese occupation forces. Tarawa resulted in far greater American casualties than had been expected, and served as an object lesson for the navy: its submarines had to undertake strong advance reconnaissance missions to help determine enemy positions and strength, and planes and surface ships had to plan much heavier bombardments in order to weaken imbedded defense systems—even on atolls as small and as low to the sea as the islands of the Gilberts.

Tarpon (SS-175)

Tarpon was built by the Electric Boat Company, used the same name as an earlier "C" boat that was built in 1909 and saw service on the East Coast and then in the Philippines. This *Tarpon* was launched in September 1935 and assigned first to San Diego and then Pearl Harbor. In 1939, she was transferred to the Philippines, augmenting the six old S boats at Manila. Two days after the Japanese attacked Pearl Harbor, 18 submarines departed the Philippines to begin their first war patrol, *Tarpon* being assigned an area off southeastern Luzon. Although *Tarpon*'s second patrol recorded a freighter, she was severely jolted by depth charges that knocked out her bow planes and instrumentation, and left her temporarily grounded on the shallow bottom before she could back off and return to base. Her

The crew of the USS *Tarantula/B-3* (SS-12) in a photo taken shortly after the end of World War I. *(United States Navy)*

next missions were fruitless, but on her sixth war patrol, in Japanese home waters south of Honshu, she sank a 10,935-ton passenger-cargo ship and a 16,975-ton transport, loaded with troops. Her seventh patrol produced no ship contacts, and her eighth, though mildly successful, resulted in no sinkings, but damage to two cargo ships and a freighter. Her ninth patrol was unusual, in that she sent to the bottom a German warship, the *Michel,* which had been preying on Allied shipping in both the Atlantic and the Pacific, and was described as "the first German raider sunk by a U.S. submarine in the Pacific." Her next patrols were largely involved with reconnaissance and lifeguard duty, after which she was determined to be too old for further battle missions and, in January 1945, was ordered to the East Coast of the United States to serve as a training vessel, in which capacity she served until being decommissioned in September 1956. *Tarpon* received seven battle stars for World War II service and is credited with sinking two vessels for 27,910 tons.

Tautog (SS-199)

Built by the Electric Boat Company and launched in January 1940, *Tautog* was a boat of the Tambor class, and in April 1941 was deployed to Hawaii, where, in late October, she and the submarine *Thresher* stood out to sea, under sealed orders, to begin a 45-day, full-time, simulated war patrol in the area of Midway. For 38 consecutive days, the two submarines operated submerged for 16 to 18 hours each day, returning to Pearl Harbor on December 5. *Tautog* was thus at the submarine base when the Japanese attacked Pearl Harbor. Within minutes of the first enemy bomb explosions on Ford Island, her gun crews went into action and downed a Japanese torpedo plane as it came over Merry Point. Her first war patrol was largely reconnaissance duty off Kwajalein Island, later the site of a successful invasion of Japanese bases. Her second war patrol was unusual, when she again headed for the Marshalls and sank the Japanese submarines *RO-30* and *I-28,* and either damaged or sank a third submarine, which was not confirmed. She ran out of torpedoes near Truk, using her last ones to sink one cargo ship and damage another before returning to base.

After sinking one more ship on her third patrol, *Tautog* headed out of Fremantle, Australia, on October 8, 1942, loaded with mines for a combined attack and mining mission. She completed both, recording one more victim—a passenger-cargo ship. However, a severe depth charging caused extensive damage and she returned to base for repairs and refit. Her fifth war patrol, from December 15, 1942, to January 30, 1943, took *Tautog* to the Java Sea, where she sank a freighter and then did battle with a Natori-class cruiser, causing some damage, but then being forced to dive under a barrage of heavy fire. She concluded

the mission by sending one more freighter to the bottom. Her sixth war patrol, in Makassar Strait in March and April, racked up some more victims: a tanker, the destroyer *Isonami,* and three small vessels. Her seventh added two cargo ships, and her eighth, a submarine chaser and damage to a tanker and three cargo ships.

Tautog's ninth war patrol, starting in December 1943, took her to Japanese home waters, where she sank a freighter and a cargo ship and damaged another. Her 10th patrol, in March, took her to the Kuriles, where she was credited with a destroyer and a passenger-cargo ship. Returning to the Kuriles in April and May, she sank a large cargo vessel and a 5,973-ton army cargo ship. Her next patrol resulted in a small freighter, a coastal steamer, and a cargo ship, near Honshu. She phased out her battle missions in January 1945, on her 13th and last patrol, in the East China Sea, by polishing off a loaded troopship and a motor torpedo boat and damaging a tanker. She was then assigned to training duty on the West Coast. She was decommissioned in December 1945, but kept in reserve at a Naval Reserve training center for the next decade. *Tautog* received 13 battle stars and the Navy Unit Commendation for World War II service and is credited with sinking 26 vessels for 72,606 tons.

Tautog (SSN-369)

A submarine of the Sturgeon class, *Tautog* was built by the Ingalls Shipbuilding Company in Mississippi. Designed for a complement of 12 officers and 96 enlisted men, she was armed with four 21-inch torpedo tubes amidships, aft of the bow. She was commissioned in August 1968 and decommissioned and struck from the Navy list in March 1997, after almost 30 years of service.

Tench (SS-417)

Launched in July 1944, *Tench* was described as "the first submarine of a new class whose design incorporated the experience gleaned from two years of tough but highly successful submarine warfare. There was more horsepower, faster and deeper diving, longer cruising, more shooting with a bigger deck gun, and additional torpedoes to destroy the diminishing Japanese tonnage at sea." Perhaps more than any other submarine yet being readied for war patrols, *Tench* was prepared for battle. She had made 172 dives, 109 practice attacks, fired 66 torpedoes, and had held three gunnery practices. Her crew was trained to a high degree of perfection, their morale high. The submarine departed Pearl Harbor, February 7, 1945, on her first war patrol, in a wolf pack that included *Sea Devil, Balao,* and *Grouper,* to patrol in the China Sea west of Kyushu and then into the Yellow Sea. The pickings were poor, and after finding no targets, *Tench* was ordered to take up lifeguard station on the west coast of Kyushu when Fifth Fleet carrier planes were raiding Nagasaki. While investigating Akune Bay, *Tench* was caught in shallow water where she could not dive, just as a flight of enemy planes was sighted. Just when the situation looked bleakest, suddenly the sky was full of another group of planes, but these were from a U.S. Navy carrier returning from the Nagasaki raid, which chased the enemy and averted disaster. In the end, *Tench* had only an escort ship and two steam trawlers to report as her first battle victims. Her hopes for success were dimmed even further when an enemy task force that was supposedly heading the way of the wolf pack, was diverted by an opposing American force. Her second war patrol, in June 1945, was somewhat more successful. Off Esan Saki, she sank a freighter and off Skiriya Saki, a tanker hugging the coastline. Another attack, near Shiriua, sent a heavily laden island freighter to the bottom with one hit amidships, and later a small tanker. Low on torpedoes, *Tench* attacked a destroyer during the evening of June 20 on the surface and ended up its own target as one of the six fish she fired began to run erratically and make a circular run back at the submarine. Only quick evasive action kept *Tench* from being destroyed by her own torpedo. During the remaining days of the second patrol, *Tench* sank a motor trawler with her deck gun and retrieved six prisoners, to conclude a patrol that added 16,300 tons to her tonnage record.

Tench departed Midway Island July 12 for her third war patrol, in the East China Sea and the Yellow Sea, where she rode out a full-fledged typhoon and conducted a shore bombardment of a Japanese harbor, destroying four schooners and damaging five others, plus a trawler, sea truck, and a cluster of warehouses. But further battle action was denied when, on the night of August 14, a Chungking broadcast was picked up indicating a Japanese surrender. After one year in commission with 80,000 miles logged, she was credited with 22,150 tons of enemy shipping sunk during her three war patrols. In 1951, after the war, *Tench* was converted to a GUPPY IA submarine at Portsmouth Naval Shipyard and enjoyed more than two decades of service, for the most part conducting training operations off the East Coast. She was struck from the Navy list in August 1971 and subsequently sold to Peru. *Tench* is credited with sinking four vessels for 5,069 tons.

Tennessee (SSBN-734)

This submarine of the Ohio class was built by the Electric Boat Division of General Dynamics, launched in December 1986, and commissioned with a life expectancy of at least a quarter of a century. She was designed for a complement of 15 officers and 142 enlisted men (each in two crews). She has a displacement of 18,750 tons (submerged), has a length of 559 feet, and is armed with 24 missile tubes and four 21-inch torpedo tubes forward. *Tennessee* has all the

most advanced capabilities for sea-based deterrent systems, and incorporates state-of-the-art quiet machinery that cannot be installed in other fleet ballistic missile submarines because of space and weight constraints. Her design incorporates additional growth potential to accommodate future technology as it becomes available, both in ship systems and missile development. All of her missions—past, present, and future—are classified. (See also the entry for OHIO CLASS since many of these characteristics are true of the other boats, most of which are named after American states.)

Thornback (SS-418)

Built by Portsmouth Naval Shipyard and launched in July 1944, this submarine of the Tench class was selected as the lead ship of a wolf pack nicknamed "Abe's Abolishers," leaving June 30, 1945, bound for the Japanese home islands. By this point in the war, American and British task forces had steamed within easy gun range of Japanese coastal targets with near impunity. Japan's merchant marine and navy had dwindled, and Allied submarines and aircraft had taken an ever increasing toll. Moving ahead of Third Fleet task forces, the "Abolishers" made antipicket boat sweeps in the Tokyo-Yokohama area before proceeding to hunting grounds off the east coast of Honshu and south of Hokkaido. Roaming an area that had recently seen a series of devastating carrier raids by Admiral Halsey's Fast Carrier Task Force 38, *Thornback* found only straggling merchantmen and small patrol craft hugging the barren coasts. During the last days of July, she sank a number of small enemy vessels and patrol craft with her five-inch deck gun and one escort vessel with torpedoes. Her final battle of the war, the first week in August, consisted of little more than small targets and the shelling of Japanese shore positions, heavily damaging a factory and power plant. The submarine was on her way back to base at Midway Island when word was received of the Japanese surrender. In 1953, during peacetime, she was converted to a GUPPY IIA submarine at Charleston Naval Shipyard and served on a variety of training and fleet assignments on the East Coast and in the Caribbean, with deployments to the North Atlantic, the Mediterranean, and Cuba. She was decommissioned in July 1971 and turned over to the Turkish navy, where she remained in service as *Ulic Ali Reis. Thornback* received one battle star for her World War II service.

Thrasher (SS-26) (G-4)

Built by Cramp Shipbuilding Company and launched in August 1912, this submarine, with a displacement of 457 tons submerged, was designated as being in the "G" class, and was designed for a complement of one officer and 23 enlisted men. She was assigned for service with SubDiv3 of the United States Atlantic Submarine Flotilla in Long Island Sound, and later served as a schoolship for students of the Submarine School at Groton, Connecticut, while taking part in pioneering work to advance the capabilities of submarine and antisubmarine warfare. *Thrasher* assisted in experiments and tests with underwater sound apparatus in the Thames River in Long Island Sound, and in Narragansett Bay in Rhode Island. During the last year of World War I, she test-fired the Mark VIII torpedo, which was supplied later to N-class and O-class submarines. *Thrasher* continued her training and experimental duties until being decommissioned in September 1919, and she ended her career as a target for depth charge and ordnance tests.

Threadfin (SS-410)

Built by Portsmouth Naval Shipyard and launched in June 1944 as a member of the Balao class, this submarine was assigned to the Pacific Fleet, and reached her first assigned patrol area in the waters just south of Kyushu in January 1945. In late January, she sank a 2,000-ton coastal freighter, but could not verify that result visually because the escorts drove her deep with a persistent depth charge attack. She next had a chance at a Japanese R060-class submarine. However, the enemy's course changes kept *Threadfin* from gaining an advantageous attack setup; and the Japanese submarine disappeared into the distance. Further frustrations occurred when enemy escort vessels thwarted her strike at two large freighters, and again when she launched six torpedoes at a minesweeper and, despite excellent fire-control indications, all six missed. *Threadfin* embarked on her second war patrol on March 14, 1945. She sank a destroyer escort and damaged four small vessels, and then received orders to join submarines *Hackleback* and *Silversides* near Bungo Suido, the primary entrance to the Japanese Inland Sea, which separates Honshu from Kyushu and Shikoku. The new attack group's primary assignment was to guard against an undetected sortie of the remainder of Japan's fleet during the Allied assault on Okinawa. On the evening of April 6, *Threadfin* picked up the Japanese force at five miles, and excitement ran high as it became evident that it contained what would have been the biggest prize: the carrier *Yamato*. *Threadfin*'s orders were to report first and then attack. She closed to four miles and reported the force by radio, giving approximate composition, course, and speed—22 knots. By the time this was accomplished, *Yamato* had opened to 10 miles and there was no hope that *Threadfin* could catch up. However, the contact report from the submarine was later called "brilliant" by Vice Admiral Lockwood, Commander Submarine Force, and for good reason: the next day, as a result of the report, Task Force 58, which had moved northward from Okinawa, was able to intercept the big carrier, sinking not only *Yamato*, but also the *Yahagi* and

two of the destroyers, and damaging two others so badly that the Japanese sank them before fleeing to the nearest friendly port.

During her third, and final, patrol, *Threadfin* was assigned to the Yellow and East China Seas in June and July. But by this time, Japanese shipping had been so decimated that the submarine found nothing but small fish, although she did finish her battle career by sending two small cargo ships to the bottom, as well as rescuing three survivors from a downed American flying boat. She was awarded three battle stars for her wartime service. The balance of *Threadfin*'s 28-year career in the United States Navy proved to be routine in nature. Initially, she operated out of the U.S. naval submarine base at New London. Later she was one of 16 submarines in a 1952 program that provided for conversion of fleet-type submarines to GUPPY submarines. *Threadfin* was converted to a GUPPY IIA submarine in 1953 at Portsmouth Naval Shipyard. During her remaining years of service, she operated in the North Atlantic, the Caribbean, and the Mediterranean. In August 1972, *Threadfin* was placed out of commission and transferred to Turkey as a loan. There she was renamed *Birinci Inona*, and served the Turkish navy until the end of the century—a remarkable lifespan for a submarine of some 55 years. *Threadfin* is credited with sinking three vessels for 3,394 tons.

Thresher (SSN-593)

Built by Portsmouth Naval Shipyard and launched in July 1960, this nuclear fast-attack submarine took part in special nuclear submarine exercises off the northeastern coast of the United States in September 1961 and again in March 1962, operations designed to improve the tactical capabilities of nuclear submarines. She proceeded to Florida for SUBROC tests. However, while mooring at Port Canaveral, the submarine was accidentally struck by a tug that damaged one of her ballast tanks. After repairs, the boat returned south for more tests and trials off Key West. *Thresher* then returned northward and remained in dockyard through the early spring of 1963. In company with the submarine *Skylark*, *Thresher* put to sea on April 10, 1963, for deep-diving exercises. In addition to her 16 officers and 96 enlisted men, the submarine carried 17 civilian technicians to observe her performance during the deep-diving tests. Some 15 minutes after reaching her assigned test depth, the submarine communicated with *Skylark* by underwater telephone, apprising the submarine rescue ship of difficulties. Suddenly, listeners in *Skylark* heard a noise "like air rushing into an air tank, followed by silence."

Efforts to reestablish contact with *Thresher* failed, and a search group was formed in an attempt to locate the boat. The rescue ship *Recovery* subsequently recovered bits of debris, including gloves and bits of internal insulation. Photographs taken by the bathyscaphe, *Trieste,* proved that the boat had broken up, taking all hands on board to their deaths in 1,400 fathoms of water (approximately 8,500 feet), some 220 miles east of Boston. The photos indicate she was in six major sections on the ocean floor, with the majority of the debris in an area about 400 yards square. *Thresher* was officially declared lost on April 10, 1963. The loss of *Thresher* was ultimately attributed to mechanical failure, but because of the lack of evidence that could be obtained at that depth, this was largely theoretical. According to one theory, for example, a small leak could have developed when the boat was submerged, causing an electrical failure that resulted in the inability to prevent her from descending too far, and thus collapsing under the tremendous water pressure after she sank below her crush depth.

Tigrone (SS-419)

Built by Portsmouth Naval Shipyard and a submarine of the Tench class, *Tigrone* made news when, during her initial training period off the Isle of Shoals in New Hampshire, she made contact with and shadowed a German submarine that was attempting to land spies in the United States during World War II. Her timely reporting of the contact led to the immediate capture of the spies when they landed on Long Island, New York. Shortly thereafter, in January 1945, she was ordered to the Pacific, and three months later she joined the submarines *Bullhead, Blackfish,* and *Seahorse* to scout the South China Sea in hopes of intercepting Japanese shipping. Her first two war patrols recorded few hits on the enemy, mostly sinking or damaging small craft. However, during periods when she was ordered to lifeguard duty in the Philippine Sea, she made numerous rescues and managed to save a total of 30 airmen who had been downed in the sea. This was a new record. Her third mission was also for lifeguard duties, departing from Guam on July 31 and heading for Honshu. But the war ended shortly after she had run close to shore and bombarded a Japanese radio station and lighthouse tower. Though she sank no ships, she was officially cited by the chief of naval operations as having "fired the last shot of World World II." In 1948, *Tigrone* was converted to Migrane I and had her designation changed to SSR, radar-picket submarine, and thereafter had a long career in many seas around the world. She was finally decommissioned, after several more conversions, in June 1975, as the oldest submarine in the navy still on active duty. But she had one more distinction, relating to her wartime lifeguard service: in July 1953, she rescued the entire crew of a navy Skyraider that had been forced down at sea. *Tigrone* received two battle stars for World War II service.

Tilefish (SS-307)

Built by Mare Island Naval Shipyard and launched in October 1943 as a boat of the Balao class, *Tilefish* departed Pearl Harbor for her first war patrol in early April 1944, setting course for the Japanese home islands. She found very few targets, but managed to sink a troop ship, after which she made a hair-raising dive to 580 feet, well below test depth, to escape depth charges. On her second patrol, in June and July, she sank a freighter and a destroyer in Luzon Strait, and in waters east of Formosa, ambushed and sank an enemy submarine—located because the Americans were able to break the Japanese code. In September and October, in the Sea of Okhotsk and off the Kurile Islands, *Tilefish* sank a trawler and two small cargo vessels, a large cargo ship, and an antisubmarine vessel. Her fourth patrol was a battle of endurance in mid-winter in the Kurile Islands, where she was battered by hurricane-force winds, mountainous waves, and sleet that made the periscope almost impossible to use, but did make one kill: a torpedo boat. In February and March 1945, she was ordered to the Marianas to support planned strikes on Okinawa, where she sank two small enemy vessels and a minesweeper, and performed lifeguard duty. But this was her last patrol, since she had to return to San Francisco for repairs and overhaul, and did not reach the war zone again until just before the Japanese surrender. *Tilefish* operated largely out of California ports after the war, was decommissioned in May 1960, and sold to the Venezuelan navy, where she served as the *Carite* into the 1970s. *Tilefish* received five battle stars for World War II service, and was awarded one battle star for Korean service. *Tilefish* is credited with sinking two vessels for 1,019 tons.

Tinosa (SS-283)

Built by Mare Island Naval Shipyard and launched in October 1942, *Tinosa* was a boat of the Gato class, first seeing battle service in May and June in waters east of Kyushu, Japan, where she damaged three enemy ships. Although her second patrol was marred by a faulty torpedo firing mechanism that limited her record to one tanker damaged, over the next two years she completed 12 war patrols in the Pacific and was credited with sinking 16 enemy ships, totaling 64,655 tons. In September and October 1943, prowling the Carolines, she sank a tanker, three cargo ships, and a troop-cargo vessel, at the same time being damaged by depth charges. After sailing in early January 1944 for the South China Sea, *Tinosa* landed an intelligence team and its supplies at Labian Point, North Borneo, under cover of darkness before proceeding to the Flores Sea. Later, she sank four enemy ships and damaged a fifth. In April and May, off the Ryukyus, she made six major attacks, sinking a trawler and two more cargo ships, and in June and July, in the East China Sea, accounted for two troop-cargo ships.

Credited with sinking 16 enemy ships, *Tinosa* (SS-283) was launched in October 1942 and struck from the Navy list in September 1958—during which time she saw action in World War II and Korea. *(United States Navy)*

After repairs and refitting at Hunters Point, California, *Tinosa* spent 58 days at sea testing new FM sonar equipment in locating Japanese mines, and did not get back into battle action until March 1945, when she proceeded to the Nansei Shoto area and resumed testing the mine-detecting capabilities of her FM sonar. She also observed Japanese shipping, took reconnaissance photographs, and bombarded Japanese shore installations before ending the patrol. In June, she headed for the Sea of Japan, where she sank four Japanese vessels and damaged a fifth. Shortly thereafter, Japan's capitulation ended her wartime actions, and she was deployed to the West Coast for duty, later being placed in reserve. The Korean War precipitated her recommissioning in January 1952; she was decommissioned in December 1953, and her name was struck from the Navy list in September 1958. *Tinosa* received nine battle stars for World War II service, and the Presidential Unit Citation for her fourth, fifth, and sixth war patrols.

Tinosa (SSN-606)

This submarine of the Permit class was built at the Portsmouth Naval Shipyard, Kittery, Maine, and launched in December 1961. She displaced 3,500 tons, was designed for a complement of nine officers and 76 enlisted men, and was armed with four 21-inch torpedo tubes amidships, aft of the bow. After some 30 years of service on training, operational, and technological missions, she was decommissioned and struck from the Navy list in January 1992.

Tirante (SS-420)

Built by Portsmouth Naval Shipyard and launched in August 1944, this submarine of the Tench class was assigned training duties and did not get into battle action until March 1945, when she prowled Japanese home waters and the approaches to Nagasaki. She had good hunting. She sank a tanker, a freighter, a lugger, and a 2,800-ton cargo freighter loaded with a deck cargo of oil drums. Having broken the Japanese codes, American naval intelligence was able to anticipate Japanese movements. When one intercepted enemy message told of a convoy heading *Tirante's* way, she ambushed two targets, sinking one of them, a 5,500-ton transport, and damaged an escort ship. A second intelligence report led her near the mouth of the Yangtse River, where she located two escort vessels and a 4,000-ton transport, dispatching all three in a running battle. She concluded her patrol by bringing back to base three captured Japanese airmen. In recognition of her prowess, *Tirante* was awarded a Presidential Unit Citation, and her captain, Cmdr. George L. Street, a Medal of Honor. On her next patrol, in the Yellow and East China Seas, she pressed a successful, but never confirmed, attack on a cargo freighter, and the next day, crept into Ha Shima harbor, only seven miles from Nagasaki, and picked out a 2,200-ton target moored alongside a colliery. Three torpedoes dispatched this prize, though *Tirante* had to beat a hasty retreat as shells from shore guns fell around her. She also played havoc with small shipping between Korea and Japan, destroying junks carrying supplies from Korea to the Japanese home islands, bagging a dozen and destroying two heavily armed picket boats with surface gunfire. The war ended before she could depart on a third patrol, and she was later assigned to the East Coast. Subsequently converted at Portsmouth Naval Shipyard in 1953 to greater underwater propulsive power (GUPPY) IIA configuration, *Tirante* continued in operation for two more decades, mainly in the North Atlantic, Caribbean, and the Gulf of Mexico. The ship participated in joint exercises with NATO forces; sometimes served as a target for antisubmarine warfare (ASW) exercises; and, on occasion, assisted the Fleet Sonar School at Key West, Florida, in the development of ASW tactics and weapons. *Tirante* was decommissioned in October 1973, and received two battle stars and a Presidential Unit Citation for her World War II service. *Tirante* is credited with sinking eight vessels for 15,886 tons.

Tiru (SS-416)

Built by Mare Island Naval Shipyard and launched in September 1947, *Tiru* was stationed in Hawaii at the start of her career, and sailed for the Far East and her first western Pacific (WesPac) deployment in support of United Nations forces engaged in combating communist aggression in Korea. *Tiru* was converted to a GUPPY II in 1948 at Mare Island and between 1952 and 1959, *Tiru* conducted four more WesPac deployments and at the end of this time returned to Pearl Harbor for a major overhaul and a fleet rehabilitation and modernization (FRAM) conversion to a GUPPY III at Pearl Harbor Naval Shipyard in 1959. In the course of the work, her hull was lengthened by 12 feet; she acquired a new conning tower, five feet longer than its predecessor; and a fiberglass sail. Internally, increased sonar and ordnance equipment greatly enhanced the ship's capabilities. In the 1960s, she deployed again to the western Pacific and also participated in ASW exercises in the Coral Sea with warships of the Australian, British, New Zealand, and U.S. navies. She later saw service in Japan and in the Vietnam war zone, and participated in Exercise Sea Rover, with U.S. and Australian naval units. In 1970, she was transferred to the Atlantic Fleet and then operated in the Caribbean and off the lower East Coast of the United States, with two deployments to European waters. She was decommissioned in July 1975.

Tomahawk Cruise Missile

The Tomahawk is a long-range cruise missile that can be used against surface ships or land targets; it employs several different types of warheads. Weighing 3,450 pounds and 19 feet long, this missile was first used in submarines in 1983, and can be launched from standard 21-inch torpedo tubes or vertical launch tubes. The missile demonstrated its effectiveness in the 1991 Persian Gulf conflict when almost 300 Tomahawks were launched at enemy targets, including 12 launched by two attack submarines, underscoring the submarine's ability to participate in multiforce strike operations. When launched from a submarine, this missile rises to the surface, deploys small wings, and activates a turbofan engine that propels it toward the target. The small size of the Tomahawk gives it a low radar image, and its low level of flight makes it difficult to intercept. When launched from the water, it can also be directed to cross over land and attack enemy positions on shore, where it is accurate to a matter of just a few feet.

Toro (SS-422)

Built by Portsmouth Naval Shipyard and launched in August 1944, this submarine of the Tench class was ordered to the Pacific and embarked on her first war patrol in early May 1945, assigned to patrol and lifeguard duty south of Shikoku and east of Kyushu. She made few enemy contacts, but was able to rescue survivors from a downed B-29. Her second patrol, starting in mid-July, almost ended in disaster when ships in an American task force sweeping the seas of the enemy mistook her for a Japanese vessel. *Toro* attempted to establish her identity by using a flare, smoke bombs, and sonar; but the ships were still firing when she had to dive deep—down below her limit—and rigged for depth charges. The surface vessels, thinking that they had sunk a Japanese picket boat, remained in the area for half an hour searching for survivors without discovering that their target had been a friendly submarine. After her narrow escape, *Toro* continued on lifeguard duty and rescued three British and three American aviators. Placed in reserve, she was later reactivated and served in numerous regions, including the arctic, the East Coast, the Caribbean, and the Mediterranean. She was decommissioned in March 1963, and received two battle stars for World War II service.

Torsk (SS-423)

Built by Portsmouth Naval Shipyard, a submarine of the Tench class, launched in September 1944, *Torsk* got underway from Pearl Harbor for her first war patrol in May 1945, along the east coast of Honshu, but found potential targets either illusive or nonexistent. On her second patrol in August, she was somewhat more successful, sinking two coastal freighters and two frigates, and rescuing seven Japanese merchant seamen. As the war ended, she was credited with having sunk the last enemy vessel of World War II. For the next seven years, she operated out of New London, Connecticut, as a training ship, participating in exercises and tests, and occasionally making naval reserve training cruises. *Torsk* was converted to a Fleet Snorkel

Toro (SS-422) had to dive deep to avoid disaster when she was mistaken for a Japanese vessel by an American task force. *(United States Navy)*

submarine at Portsmouth Naval Shipyard in 1952 and later served along the East Coast, in the Caribbean, and in the Mediterranean. During the Cuban crisis in the fall of 1962, she patrolled in support of the island's blockade. *Torsk* was decommissioned in March 1968 and received two battle stars for World War II service. She is credited with sinking three vessels for 2,473 tons.

Trepang (SS-412)

Built by Mare Island Naval Shipyard and launched March 23, 1944, *Trepang*'s first war patrol, on September 13 south of Honshu, included the sinking of a 750-ton freighter, a questionable second sinking, and the sinking of a 1,000-ton transport. On October 12, 1944, *Trepang* acknowledged four pips on the radar screen, fired a full spread of six torpedoes toward their targets, and claimed success when explosions rumbled across the water and flames lit up the night sky. Four more torpedoes from her stern tubes proved less successful, missing their targets.

Leading a wolf pack that included *Segundo* (SS-398) and *Razorback* (SS-394) off Luzon, she detected a group of seven large ships. Shooting straight and true, *Trepang*'s torpedoes sent a freighter and two cargo ships to the bottom. A fourth sinking was claimed but not confirmed. On February 24, 1945, *Trepang* sank an 875-ton freighter and blew the bow of a smaller coastal vessel. For these efforts, *Trepang* received a seven-hour barrage of depth charges from the Japanese. Then, while patrolling a "hazardous duty" Yellow Sea area, *Trepang* bagged a 1,000-ton landing

craft on April 28, a 4,667-ton heavily laden freighter two days later, and on May 4 a minesweeper, which blew sky-high with a hit on her magazine.

Trepang had an unusual occurrence when en route to a rendezvous with *Devilfish* (SS-292). She sighted a troop laden freighter and sank the ship with her deck guns. A dozen or so Japanese soldiers from the flaming vessel refused to be picked up and taken prisoner and so were left to drown.

Patrolling off the eastern coast of Honshu, *Trepang* spotted a coastal convoy of three ships and torpedoed and sank the lead ship. The other two took evasive action and sped away.

Trepang was decommissioned on June 27, 1946, remaining in reserve at Mare Island into the 1960s. She was struck from the Navy list on June 30, 1967, and subsequently sunk as a target on September 16, 1969, by the combined gunfire of destroyers *Henderson* (DD-785) and *Fechteler* (DD-870). *Trepang* received five battle stars and a Navy Unit Commendation for World War II service.

Trepang (SSN-674)

A submarine of the Sturgeon class, *Trepang* was built by the Electric Boat Division of General Dynamics and launched in September 1969. With a displacement of 4,762 tons (submerged), she was 292 feet in length, carried four 21-inch torpedo tubes amidships, aft of the bow, and had a complement of 12 officers and 95 enlisted men. After almost 30 years of service on training, operational, and technological missions around the globe, she was deactivated in January 1999.

Trident I (C-4)

This is a submarine-launched ballistic missile (SLBM) developed to replace the Poseidon missile in strategic missile submarines and to arm the Ohio-class SSBNs. The C-4, first deployed in 1979, is a long-range, multiple-warhead missile to be launched from submerged submarines. Depending upon the number of warheads carried, it has almost double the range of the previous Poseidon missile. The C-4 is a three-stage solid-fuel missile that is powered only during the initial phases of flight. When the third stage is exhausted, the missile follows a ballistic trajectory. When the first stage motor ignites, an aero spike extends from the missile's nose, cutting the friction of the air flowing past the missile, thus extending its range. The third stage includes the unit ("BUS") that aims and dispenses the warheads at separate targets.

Trident II (D-5)

This submarine-launched ballistic missile (SLBM) is a significantly more capable version of the Trident I C-4 and was the first SLBM to have a hard-target kill capability—as high as an 88 percent probability of striking a target. Although more accurate than any previous SLBMs, Trident II shares some of the limitations of its predecessors. The difficulty of submarine communications and the dormant guidance system of the missile, which takes several minutes to activate, significantly affect reaction time. The range of this missile is dependent on the type and number of warheads carried, ranging from 4,000 to 6,000 nautical miles.

Trigger (SS-237)

Built by Mare Island Naval Shipyard and launched in March 1942, this submarine of the Gato class had a record of 12 war patrols, during which she sank a total of 27 ships for 180,800 tons and damaged 13 for a total of 102,900 tons. Her first patrol was in the Aleutians, her second through fifth in the heart of the Japanese homeland, and her sixth and seventh in the East China Sea, where she sent nine enemy ships to the bottom. Her eighth and ninth ranged the Caroline Islands, where she sank six more and damaged four. Her 10th and 11th were not up to par, mainly because Japanese shipping was becoming harder and harder to locate.

In mid-March 1945, Trigger departed from Guam on her 12th war patrol, heading for the Nansei Shoto area to provide rescue services for carrier-based aircraft, as well as to carry out a normal offensive patrol. She reported her first action, the sinking of a freighter and damage to another. Moving toward an area considered "restricted" because of the heavy presence of mines, she was ordered to provide as much data as possible about the movement of a Japanese convoy in these waters, after which she was told to proceed at best speed to join a wolf pack known as "Earl's Eliminators." She never did send an acknowledgment, but did transmit a weather report from the area—her last message, after which she was never heard from again. Members of the wolf pack attempted communications, but in vain. After many attempts to contact her by radio had failed, Trigger was ordered on April 4 to proceed to Midway. When she failed to arrive by the end of the month, she was reported as presumed lost in enemy waters on her 12th patrol, after a long and illustrious career. Postwar Japanese reports on submarine actions revealed the detection of a large oil slick in a position where Trigger was likely to have been. She received credit for her devastating record against the enemy, for 12 patrols, as well as a Presidential Unit Citation for three of her patrols.

Trigger (SS-564)

This submarine of the Tang class was built by the Electric Boat Division of General Dynamics and launched in June 1951. She had a displacement of 2,700 tons, was armed with six 21-inch torpedo tubes forward and two 21-inch torpedo tubes aft, and carried a crew of eight officers and 75 enlisted men. She served on many missions—training, operational, and technological—in the oceans of the world over a period of some 22 years. She was decommissioned and struck from the Navy list in February 1974.

Triton (SS-201)

Built by Portsmouth Naval Shipyard and launched in March 1940 as a member of the Tambor class, Triton had an enviable record during her first five World War II patrols, in which she sank 16 enemy ships, totaling 64,600 tons, and damaged four more for an additional total of 29,200 tons. Her patrols ranged from the East China Sea and the Solomon Islands to the Aleutians. In mid-February 1943, she left her base in Brisbane, Australia, and headed for enemy targets in the Rabaul area. Moving westward, and in contact with two other submarines, Snapper and Trigger, she reported the speed and course of a Japanese convoy and successful hits against three escort vessels. The last word from Triton came on March 11, 1943, when she reported, "Two groups of smokes, 5 or more ships each, plus escorts . . . Am chasing." She was ordered to stay south of the Equator, and was informed that Trigger was operating in an adjacent area. On the morning of March 13, she was told that three enemy destroyers had been sighted in her area on a northerly course, and three days later was ordered to change her area slightly to the east, where two other submarines, *Tuna* and *Greenling,* were also operating. Twelve days later, she was told to clear her area and return to Brisbane. When she failed to make her report or respond in any other way by the April 10, she was officially reported as lost.

Information made available by the Japanese after the end of the war, shows that *Triton* was, without a doubt, sunk by the enemy destroyers of which she was given information on March 13, since they saw "a great quantity of oil, pieces of wood, corks and manufactured goods bearing the mark 'Made in U.S.A.'" In addition, *Trigger,* in whose area this attack occurred, reported that on March 15 she made two attacks on a convoy of five freighters with two escorts. At this time she was depth charged, but not seriously, and she heard distant depth charging for an hour after the escorts had stopped attacking her. Since she was only about 10 miles from the reported Japanese attack cited above, it is presumed that she heard the attack that sank *Triton*. Triton was awarded six battle stars for World War II service, and was credited with having sunk two freighters on her last patrol.

Triton (SSBN/SSN-586)

Built by the Electric Boat Company and the second to bear her name and the prototype for the first generation of a new class of nuclear-powered radar-picket submarines employing a unique two-reactor engineering plant, *Triton* was launched in August 1958 and in mid-February 1960 embarked for the South Atlantic on a history-making voyage, Operation Magellan. Having remained submerged since her departure from the East Coast, *Triton* continued on south toward Cape Horn, rounded the tip of South America, and headed west across the Pacific. After transiting the Philippine and Indonesian archipelagoes and crossing the Indian Ocean, she rounded the Cape of Good Hope and arrived at her destination 61 days after her initial departure. Only once did she surface in all that time, when she transferred a sick sailor to the USS *Macon* off Montevideo, Uruguay, on March 5. She arrived back at Groton on May 10, having completed the first submerged circumnavigation of the Earth. Her globe-girdling cruise proved invaluable, not only enhancing America's prestige at sea but also demonstrating the submerged endurance and sustained high-speed transit capabilities of the new class of nuclear-powered submarines. During the early 1960s,

The first generation of a new class of nuclear submarines, *Triton* (SSN-586) employed a unique two-reactor engineering plant that allowed her to be the first submarine to circumnavigate the Earth. *(United States Navy)*

Triton served as a radar-picket submarine and conducted operational patrols and training exercises with the Atlantic Fleet. During this period, the rising threat posed by Russian submarine forces increased the navy's demands for nuclear-powered attack submarines with antisubmarine warfare (ASW) capability, and thus *Triton* was converted to an attack submarine. In April 1964, *Triton* became the flagship for the Submarine Force, Atlantic Fleet, and served in that role until June 1967. She was decommissioned in May 1969, and received both a Presidential Unit Citation and a Navy Unit Commendation for her service with the fleet.

Trout (SS-202)

A submarine of the Tambor class, *Trout* was built by Portsmouth Naval Shipyard and launched in May 1940 and later assigned to the Pacific Fleet, arriving at Pearl Harbor on August 4, 1941. She was conducting a simulated war patrol off Midway Island when she received word of the Japanese attack on Pearl Harbor. That night, the submarine observed two enemy ships shell Midway, but was unable to close in on them before they left the area. In her first 10 patrols, *Trout* sank 23 enemy ships, giving her 87,800 tons sunk, and damaged six ships, for 75,000 tons. Her first patrol resulted in no enemy damage, but her second was most unusual: the delivery of ammunition from Pearl Harbor to Corregidor in January 1942. To compensate for the weight of ammunition delivered, she brought back to Pearl Harbor as ballast 20 tons of gold, silver, and securities for safekeeping. *Trout* also sank a freighter and a patrol craft. From mid-March to mid-May 1942, she conducted her third patrol in the Empire, sank a large tanker, three freighters, and a gunboat, and damaged a large freighter. Her fourth patrol was in defense of Midway, with no successful attacks, but on her fifth, south of Truk, she sank a transport and damaged an aircraft carrier. After a no-hit sixth patrol, she had more luck on her seventh: a freighter, a tanker, and two sampans, and damage to two large tankers. In the same general area on her eighth patrol, *Trout* sank two sampans and damaged an auxiliary; on her ninth, added two tankers, a freighter, and two small schooners, and also damaged a freighter; and on her 10th a freighter, a transport, a sampan, and a submarine, the *I-182*, thought to have been destroyed in Surigao Strait.

With this record on the books, *Trout* left Pearl Harbor on February 8, 1944, en route to her 11th patrol; she topped off with fuel at Midway and left eight days later, never to be heard from again. Postwar Japanese records indicated that, on February 29, 1944, the *Sakito Maru* was sunk and another ship badly damaged. Since *Trout* was the only U.S. submarine that could have attacked at this time in this area, but did not report the action, it is assumed she was lost during or shortly after this attack. *Trout* received 11 battle stars for World War II service and the Presidential Unit Citation for her second, third, and fifth patrols.

Trout (SS-566)

A submarine of the Tang class, and the second to bear the *Trout* name, she was built by the Electric Boat Company and launched in August 1951 and operated out of New London as a unit of SubRon10 from 1952 to 1959. During this period, she conducted training and readiness operations with ships of the fleet and NATO nations, and engaged in sonar evaluation tests, practice ASW exercises, and submerged simulated attack exercises. She was deployed to the Sixth Fleet in September 1959 for her first Mediterranean cruise. Four months later, while returning home, she represented the United States at Bergen, Norway, during the 50th anniversary celebrations commemorating the birth of the Norwegian navy's submarine arm. During the 1960s, *Trout* made three more Mediterranean deployments, and participated in training and developmental exercises off the East Coast and in the Caribbean. In July 1970, she was assigned to the Pacific Fleet, making two deployments to the western Pacific and providing submarine services during ASW exercises conducted by warships of the U.S., South Korean, and Nationalist Chinese navies. Between these deployments, the submarine participated in antisubmarine warfare exercises and conducted local operations off the southern California operating areas, punctuating this service with weapons tests in the Pacific Northwest, out of Puget Sound.

She was decommissioned in December 1978 and sold to Iran, but, when the American hostages were seized at the U.S. Embassy in Iran, she was seized as an Iranian asset and later decommissioned again. *Trout*, though out of commission, remains in the navy inventory and is being considered for reactivation as a target submarine.

Trutta (SS-421)

Built by Portsmouth Naval Shipyard and launched in August 1944 as a member of the Tench class, this submarine was ordered to join the Pacific Fleet; she departed from Saipan on her first war patrol and an attempt to intercept a Japanese naval force that had sortied from Bungo Suido. The Allies feared that this enemy task force, headed by *Yamato*, the world's largest battleship, would interrupt the American assault on Okinawa. Although *Trutta* did not intercept the Japanese ships because they changed their course. The Japanese force never reached Okinawa because on that day aviators from the aircraft carriers of Task Force 58 sank the *Yamato*, the light cruiser *Agano*, and a destroyer, and inflicted damage to three other destroyers, which the Japanese scuttled. She encountered few enemy ships, but did sink one freighter and damaged another before returning to base. In early June, she started on her next patrol in company with *Queenfish* to undertake lifeguard duty for air strikes on Kobe, rescuing a downed army aviator who had been adrift in a small rubber boat for nearly a week and had weathered a typhoon. As air raids against the cities of the Japanese homeland intensified, *Trutta* manned a lifeguard station south of Kyushu, made patrols just off Bungo Suido, and conducted visual and photo reconnaissance of Tori Shima, approaching to within about one mile of the island. Although she encountered no big game, she dispatched an enemy tug and a whole fleet of armed schooners. Her third patrol was cut short by the Japanese capitulation, and she received two battle stars for her service in World War II. In 1953, *Trutta* was converted to a GUPPY IIA at Charleston Naval Shipyard. During peacetime, she saw service on the East Coast, operating largely out of Key West, with occasional deployments to the Mediterranean. Her long career ended in 1972, but she continued an entirely new life after being sold to the Turkish navy and renamed the *Cerbe*.

Tullibee (SS-284)

This submarine of the Gato class was built by Mare Island Naval Shipyard and launched in November 1942 and assigned to the Pacific Theater, where she got underway for the western Caroline Islands and her first war patrol in mid-July 1943. In early August, she attacked three freighters with four torpedoes, but missed when one of her targets abruptly turned and rammed her, damaging her number one periscope. Later, she attacked another convoy, sinking a passenger-cargo ship and damaging a freighter. In late September, she headed for the East China Sea on her second patrol, where she sank a passenger-cargo ship, damaged two other ships, and had the unique experience of sighting a Japanese military barracks on an island and plastering it with 55 shells from her deck gun. On her third patrol, leaving in mid-December 1943 for the Marianas, she damaged a Japanese escort carrier and sank a net tender. On March 5, 1944, *Tullibee* departed Pearl Harbor to start her fourth war patrol. She stopped at Midway to top off with fuel, and after leaving on March 14, she was not heard from again. The patrol area assigned to *Tullibee* was an open sea area north of Palau, and she was to cooperate with surface forces in the first carrier strike on Palau. After a number of orders and instructions failed to elicit any acknowledgments, she was presumed lost on May 15, 1944.

It was not until after the war that the story of *Tullibee*'s loss was told—not by Japanese records but by the incredible account of a lone survivor of her crew, C. W. Kuykendall, a gunner's mate. He reported that the submarine arrived on station on March 25, and the next night began tracking an enemy convoy consisting of a large troop and cargo ship, two medium-sized freighters, two escort vessels, and a large destroyer. *Tullibee* made several surface runs on the large transport, but held fire because of difficulty sighting the target in squally weather. Then, without warning, a terrific concussion shook the boat, and Kuykendall, who had been on the bridge, soon found himself struggling in the water. For about 10 minutes, he heard other survivors in the dark water around him, but the sounds diminished and he realized he was the sole survivor—without much hope of rescue. Around 10 the next morning, however, an escort vessel located him, and after firing on him with machine guns, came in and picked him up. He learned that the transport *Tullibee* had fired at had sunk. His captivity in Japanese hands was brutal, with beatings, starvation, and illness, and forced labor in the copper mines of Ashio. But somehow he survived, until being rescued the first week in September 1945. His boat, *Tullibee*, received three battle stars for World War II service and is credited with sinking three vessels for 10,579 tons.

Tullibee (SSN-597)

Built by the Electric Boat, *Tullibee* was the second submarine to bear the name. *Tullibee* was also the prototype of a new class when she was launched in April 1960. During the 1960s, she engaged in sonar evaluations and nuclear submarine tactical exercises, and deployed to numerous areas around the globe, including the East Coast, the Caribbean, and the Mediterranean, where she took part in NATO and Sixth Fleet exercises and made port visits to Greece, Italy, and Spain. She was decommissioned in June 1988, and received a Meritorious Unit Commendation for her service with the Sixth Fleet.

Tuna (SS-27) (G-2)

Built by Newport News Shipbuilding and Drydock Co. and launched in January 1912, *Tuna* displaced only 516 tons, submerged, and had a complement of one officer and 21 enlisted men, and was armed with four 18-inch torpedo tubes in the bow. She joined SubDiv3 of the Submarine Flotilla and cruised to Norfolk, Charleston, New York, Newport, and Provincetown. She engaged in numerous experimental exercises and training, and conducted defensive war patrols during June and July 1918, maintaining a listening and periscope watch for enemy German submarines in the vicinity of Block Island, Rhode Island, during the latter phase of the First World War. She later experimented with magnetic detectors and the Very system signal device and tested the strength of her hull against depth charge explosions before being decommissioned in April 1919. Her end was unfortunate. Designated as a target for testing depth charges and ordnance nets in Niantic Bay, Connecticut, she suddenly flooded during an inspection by a six-man maintenance crew on July 30, 1919, and sank at her moorings near Niantic Bay. She went down in 81 feet of water, drowning three of the inspection crew.

Tuna (SS-203)

This submarine of the Tambor class, built by Mare Island Naval Shipyard and launched in October 1940, was assigned to the Pacific Fleet and was in dry dock at Mare Island, California, when the Japanese attacked. In late January 1942, she ranged the East China Sea and made her first kill, a 4,000-ton cargo ship, followed by a second, a small cargo ship, on her second patrol. Her next missions bore little fruit, and it was not until her sixth patrol that she had any luck, sinking a 4,600-ton merchantman in the Admiralties. Her seventh patrol found no targets and her next was almost her undoing when, on July 29, 1943, as she set out from Brisbane on her eighth patrol, a Royal Australian Air Force patrol bomber attacked her, dropping three bombs close aboard and necessitating almost three weeks of major repairs. However, in mid-December, on her ninth patrol, she ranged the Java and Flores Seas and sent a 5,484-ton cargo ship to the bottom. War patrol number 10, in May 1944, resulted in only one small sinking, a trawler. However, it turned out that this ship was bound for Wake Island with classified documents on board, many of which were retrieved and turned over to American Intelligence. *Tuna* phased out her war experience after two more patrols, both of which were dogged with bad luck and lack of enemy contacts. She was then assigned to San Francisco for training and security duties, and after the war was again deployed to Pearl Harbor, where she was later selected as a target vessel for the upcoming atomic bomb tests at Bikini Atoll in the Marshall Islands. After decommissioning in December 1946, she was retained as a radiological laboratory unit and subjected to numerous structural studies at Mare Island, California. In September 1948, *Tuna* was sunk in 1,160 fathoms of water off the West Coast. She received seven battle stars for her World War II service and is credited with sinking four vessels for 14,986 tons.

Tunny (SS-282)

Built by Mare Island Naval Shipyard and launched in June 1942, this submarine of the Gato class departed Pearl Harbor in mid-January 1943 for her first war patrol, during which she sank an unidentified ship and a 5,000-ton cargo ship. In mid-March, she departed for Wake Island on a battle mission that the Commander, Submarine Force, Pacific Fleet, later would describe as belonging "in that exceptional category of one of the outstandingly aggressive patrols of the war." In late March, she sank two cargo ships, then headed north where, on April 4, she sent an 8,000-ton cargo-passenger ship to the bottom, and four days later an auxiliary carrier. Although it was impossible to determine how many hits *Tunny* made during this patrol because of her aggressive attacks and the frequent necessity of diving deep to escape depth charges, she played havoc with numerous Japanese convoys. Her third patrol, starting in late May 1943, took her first to Eniwetok, and later toward Truk, where she damaged a transport in mid-June and later sank a gunboat and an armed trawler. Her next patrol resulted in a series of close calls and severe depth charging that left her unfit for battle, and forced her return to base with extensive damages to the bow, diving planes, communication system, torpedo room, radar, hull plating, sonar, and other critical areas.

After extensive repairs and refitting, *Tunny* departed Pearl Harbor for her fifth war patrol in late February 1944. A month later, she damaged two heavily loaded cargo ships and sank a Japanese submarine. On the afternoon of March 29, she observed a large formation consisting of a 63,000-ton Japanese battleship, one light cruiser, and three destroyers. After a daring approach, she fired six torpedoes at the battleship from her bow tubes. The torpedoes passed directly under an alert destroyer, which immediately hoisted flags to warn the battleship, then swung parallel to the torpedo tracks, and made a run on the submarine. *Tunny* went deep, while the destroyer dropped 38 depth charges in a concentrated counterattack. Toward sunset, the submarine lost contact with the formation. Later that night, she encountered the same force and was held down for two hours by one of the escorting ships. Hits by two of her torpedoes had damaged, but failed to sink, the powerful battleship. After return to base, *Tunny* began patrolling in the Marianas in mid-May, where she scored her sixth confirmed kill—a 4,900-ton cargo ship—and later dispatched an armed sampan with gunfire. Her next patrol, in August 1944, proved to be disastrous. Not only did she fail to hit any targets, but also suffered so much damage from depth charges that her commanding officer was forced to discontinue the mission. Often having to run on the surface where she was a sitting duck, she barely made it back to Pearl Harbor—flooding, with sheared off bolts, all three radio antennas down, fractured gauges, and leaks in her pressure hull.

After repairs and refitting, *Tunny* departed Pearl Harbor once again, in early February 1945, for her eighth war patrol, headed for the Ryukyus to assist in the planned American invasion of Okinawa, one of Japan's few remaining strongholds, and to do lifeguard duty. Her ninth patrol saw considerable action, but resulted in no sinkings, since Japanese shipping was becoming more and more scarce. Because of the many beatings she had taken and damages sustained, she was ordered to Mare Island, California, for the duration of the war. In 1952, she was converted as a Regulus-missile submarine, serving in that capacity for nearly 12 years. *Tunny* was subsequently converted to a troop-carrying submarine (APSS/LPSS) and operated out of Subic Bay in the Philippines. She was assigned to various missions in support of UDT detachments. She carried out several covert missions during the Vietnam conflict. She was decommissioned in June 1969. *Tunny* received nine battle stars and two Presidential Unit Citations for her World War II service. She received five battle stars for her operations during the Vietnam War and the Deterrent Patrol Pin for eight successful Regulus deterrent patrols. *Tunny* is credited with sinking six vessels for 26,837 tons.

Tunny (SSN-682)

This submarine of the Sturgeon class was built by the Ingalls Shipbuilding Company and launched in June 1972. With a displacement (submerged) of 4,762 tons, a length of 302 feet, and a width of almost 32 feet, she was designed for a complement of 12 officers and 95 enlisted men. She carried four 21-inch torpedo tubes amidships, aft of the bow, and was capable of 25 knots underwater. She embarked on a multitude of missions at home and abroad and was decommissioned and struck from the Navy list in March 1998, after more than 25 years of service.

Turbot (SS-31) (G-3)

Launched in December 1913, this early navy submarine was built by the Lake Torpedo Boat Company, had a displacement of only 460 tons, submerged, and was designed for a complement of two officers and 23 enlisted men. For armament, she had four 18-inch torpedo tubes in the bow, and she could travel at a top speed of 14 knots on the surface and 10 submerged. *Turbot* spent the greater part of her entire career operating out of the U.S. naval submarine base at New London, Connecticut, as a training boat. In addition, she carried out pioneering work that included: experimental submarine net operations, testing diving bells, submerged sound and magnetic detection experiments, and the testing of depth charges. When enemy German submarines appeared off the eastern seaboard of the United States during the First World War, she patrolled the coast of Long Island Sound. *Turbot* was decommissioned in May 1921.

Turtle

Recognized as the first American submarine ever to go into battle against an enemy, the *Turtle* was a tiny, hand-powered submersible that was designed and built by David Bushnell, a Connecticut inventor, in 1775. The *Turtle,* shaped like a huge egg standing on end, floated upright in the water and could be partially submerged when two internal water tanks were filled. Power was provided by a propeller that was hand-cranked by the lone occupant. Her only weapon was a detachable explosive charge, which was meant to be wedged against the hull of an enemy warship, and then triggered by a cord after the *Turtle* backed away to a safe position. This first-recorded submarine attack took place on September 6, 1776, during the American War of Independence when the *Turtle* ventured out into New York harbor, where Admiral Lord Howe's flagship, the *Eagle,* was blockading the Hudson River. The attack failed because the explosive charge could not be attached to the *Eagle's* copper hull. Although this strange little craft was detected as it moved back toward shore, she managed to escape intact.

Tusk (SS-426)

Built by the Cramp Shipbuilding Company and launched in July 1945, this submarine of the Tench class completed her shakedown cruise in the southern Atlantic just after the end of World War II, with a round of goodwill visits to Latin American ports. For the next year, she conducted operations along the East Coast, and later engaged in oceanographic work along the Atlantic shelf in conjunction with Columbia University and the Woods Hole Oceanographic Institute. Converted to GUPPY II in 1948 at Portsmouth Naval Shipyard, she also underwent numerous modifications to improve her underwater performance characteristics and streamlining, as well as her range while submerged. *Tusk* participated in exercises with other U.S. and NATO forces, and ranged from the Caribbean Sea in the south to above the Arctic Circle in the north. *Tusk* was an unfortunate participant in a major submarine disaster while operating with a unit that also included the submarine *Cochino*. While steaming through a gale off the coast of Norway, *Cochino* suffered an explosion in one of her batteries. *Tusk* rushed to the aid of the stricken submarine, providing medical supplies for the injured by way of life rafts. One such raft capsized in heavy seas, sending a *Cochino* officer and a civilian employee of the Bureau of Ships into the icy Arctic waters. Both were recovered, but during the administration of artificial respiration on board *Tusk,* another wave broke over her deck washing away the civilian and 11 *Tusk* crewmen. Only five sailors were subsequently rescued. After those tragic events, *Tusk* and the limping *Cochino* headed for Hammerfest, Norway. Along the way, another explosion erupted in *Cochino's* after battery, sealing her doom. Water poured through her battered hull. *Tusk* came alongside in heavy seas and lashed herself to the sinking submarine. Under the worst possible conditions, she saved all of *Cochino*'s crew. Minutes later *Cochino* took her final plunge; and *Tusk* headed for Hammerfest.

In the early 1950s, *Tusk* returned to the United States to resume East Coast operations out of New London in support of the Submarine School, and later to conduct fleet exercises and to participate in training exercises with NATO forces in the northern Atlantic. She rounded out the final year of her career with normal operations along the eastern seaboard, primarily in the New England vicinity. She was decommissioned in October 1973, and transferred, by sale, to the Taiwan navy where she served as *Hai Pao*.

U

Ulysses S. Grant (SSBN-631)

Built by Electric Boat Division of General Dynamics and launched in November 1963 as a member of the Lafayette class, this fleet ballistic missile submarine was deployed to Guam, in the Marianas, and operated from there until 1970. In mid-1965 *Grant* became the first SSBN to conduct an OT (operational test) of a Polaris A-3 missile in the Pacific Ocean. The test, involving the firing of five missiles, was highly successful. She conducted 18 deterrent patrols before returning to the East Coast of the United States, departing the western Pacific in December 1970. After an overhaul at Charleston, South Carolina, she was deployed to Holy Loch, Scotland, and operated in the European area until September 1975, after which she was based with the Atlantic Fleet on deterrent patrols into 1980. She was decommissioned and struck from the Navy list in December 1992.

undersea warfare

This periodical is the professional magazine of the undersea warfare community, whose purpose is to educate its readers on undersea warfare missions and programs, with a particular focus on American submarines. It also draws on the Submarine Force's rich historical legacy to instill a sense of pride and professionalism among readers and to enhance their awareness of the increasing relevance of undersea warfare for America's defense. *Undersea Warfare* is published quarterly by the chief of naval operations, under the Department of the Navy. A typical issue contains news, technological information, personal biographies of noted submariners, notifications of awards and honors, history, and essays.

underwater archaeology

This is a branch of study that has developed during the past century along with submarine exploration of the depths. It involves some of the same techniques of observation, discovery, and recording that are the basis of archaeology on land, but adapted to the special conditions of working underwater. An important development was that of the French scientist Jacques-Yves Cousteau, who invented the self-contained underwater breathing apparatus known as the scuba, of which the most commonly used type is the Aqua Lung. Cousteau's work near Marseille was a pioneer underwater excavation, as was the work of the Americans Peter Throckmorton and George Bass off the coast of southern Turkey. In 1958 Throckmorton found a graveyard of ancient ships at Yassi Ada and then discovered the oldest shipwreck ever recorded, at Cape Gelidonya—a Bronze Age shipwreck of the 14th century B.C. George Bass of the University of Pennsylvania worked on a Byzantine wreck at Yassi Ada from 1961 onward, devising new techniques for the mapping of wrecks, and using a two-man underwater vessel, the *Asherah,* the first submarine ever built for archaeological investigation.

underwater demolition team (UDT)

A working unit of personnel especially trained and equipped for making hydrographic reconnaissance of approaches to prospective landing beaches and for effecting demolition of obstacles. The navy has incorporated such teams in its SEAL organization. They are involved, among other duties, with clearing mines in certain areas; locating, improving, and marking safe channels; the acquisition of information during pre-assault operations; and the performance of other combat underwater and surface tasks within their capabilities.

underwater navigation

Ever since submarines were first commissioned by the United States Navy at the beginning of the 20th century, underwater navigation has been vital in their operation and cruising. Advanced oceanographic exploration in recent years has also focused on the need to navigate the ocean depths more accurately and effectively. The losses of submarines at sea present the opportunity to use new and advanced navigational vehicles and devices. Since 1963 the United States and the Soviet Union/Russia have lost nuclear-powered submarines in very deep ocean waters. To locate an object at such depths requires a highly specialized form of navigation. At some time in the future it will even become possible to locate the remains of some of the 52 American submarines that were sunk in the Pacific depths during World War II. By combining the navigational efforts and techniques of researchers from France and the United States, the wreck of the sunken *Titanic* was found in September 1985, when underwater video images were obtained from a remotely controlled search vehicle. Ocean navigators will eventually be called upon to locate sunken treasures and mineral deposits and to establish useful bases of many kinds on the ocean floor.

United States Naval Academy

This outstanding institution of higher education, located in Annapolis, Maryland, is established by the Department of the Navy for the purpose of providing the naval service with leaders of character who will serve the nation in peace and war, and women to enter the lowest commissioned ranks of the United States Navy and the Naval Academy, it was founded on October 10, 1845, by Secretary of the Navy George Bancroft, who was also an historian and educator, to improve the unsatisfactory methods of instructing midshipmen. For the first five years, the course required only two years at the school, the other three being spent on board ships on active service. The school was reorganized in 1850–51 as the United States Naval Academy, with the four-year course of study that is now in practice. During the Civil War the academy was temporarily moved to Newport, Rhode Island; over the years, steady improvements have been made to the curriculum. During the Civil War, Spanish-American War, and World Wars I and II, the officer-training courses were abbreviated to provide more officers more quickly for combat duty. The academy is organized into an executive department, headed by the commandant of midshipmen

who is charged with interior discipline, drills, and all military and professional training; and an academic department, headed by the dean in charge of the faculty and academic programs. Education is provided in such subjects as naval engineering, navigation, weaponry, seamanship, tactics, military law, electronics, and leadership. Graduates are awarded the degree of bachelor of science and a commission as ensign in the navy or as second lieutenant in the Marine Corps.

United States Naval Institute (USNI)

The Naval Institute is a professional organization composed of nearly 70,000 men and women, both military and civilian, who are united by a common interest in free and independent discussion of issues facing the nation's military forces. Since 1873, the Naval Institute and its publishing arm, The Naval Institute Press, have served as the cutting-edge source of information for those interested in maritime history, reference, and the analysis of current affairs—through its magazine, *Proceedings,* numerous books, and its premier reference work, *The Naval Institute Guide to Combat Fleets of the World.* The institute also hosts naval seminars and expositions, and maintains an insignia collection, an oral history program, and photographic archives that rank as one of the world's largest collections of naval and maritime photographs.

United States Naval Observatory (USNO)

Since its beginning in 1833, this institution has been the official source for measuring celestial objects for purposes of timekeeping and navigation, working in coordination with the National Institute of Standards in Washington, D.C. Time signals for the public were first given in 1844 by the dropping of a ball from a staff on an observatory building. In 1904, the observatory broadcast the world's first radio time signals. The observatory makes use of reflecting telescopes in other geographical locations, such as Arizona, Florida, and Argentina, where the atmospheric conditions are conducive to clear readings. The USNO is specifically responsible for standard time, time interval, and radio-frequency standards for use by the U.S. Department of Defense and its contractors, and it broadcasts time and frequency information at intervals on a 24-hour basis.

United States Navy

When the Americans decided to fight for freedom in the War of Independence they faced England, then the greatest naval power on Earth, with no navy. The early battles at sea were fought by privateers, armed ships that were privately owned by patriots, sailing either on their own or on commission from one or more of the colonies. It was not until October 1775 that what was known as the Continental Navy was strong enough to make successful attacks against the British merchant fleet. However, this small naval force could not have had much success against the Royal Navy without the help of the French navy, which seized the opportunity to coordinate forces in striking back at France's longtime enemy. One example was the second battle of the Chesapeake, during which the French victory set the stage for the surrender of the British army at Yorktown.

Although the end of the war saw the Continental Navy disbanded, America was in need of a new naval force when its merchant ships began falling victim to the armed vessels of the Barbary pirates, who roamed the shipping lanes of the Mediterranean. To take action against this new enemy, Congress approved the construction of six frigates, in March 1794, as the basis of a new American naval force. Four years later, Congress established the Department of the Navy, just as the new ships were seeing action, fighting several successful duels with French warships, now in a nonwar against French interference in American and Caribbean waters.

The War of 1812 saw American ships once again pitted against the British, battling on inland waterways as well as on the high seas. Although the American forces were small compared with those of the British, the new frigates had some remarkably successful engagements, notably the famous victory of the *Constitution* over the British frigate, *Guerriere.*

By the beginning of the Civil War, the navy was at a low ebb, with only 42 warships. But the war saw a rapid expansion of the Union Navy, which was involved in blockading the South, capturing blockade runners, and moving troops into strategic locations. The Confederate Navy was weak and ineffectual, except in the interception of Union merchant shipping and in the design and construction of several new types of warships never before seen in battle. One of these was the submarine *Hunley,* which attacked and sank a Union blockade ship, the *Housatonic,* off Charleston, South Carolina.

In 1883, Congress authorized an upgrading and enlargement of America's fighting ships, which saw results in the navy's successes against a new enemy during the Spanish-American War. Then, during World War I, another modernization and expansion program provided the navy with what it needed to make a major American contribution to the defeat of Germany's U-boat threat during the Battle of the Atlantic. During World War II, despite its initial devastation at Pearl Harbor, the navy embarked on far-flung operations that could never have been anticipated a generation earlier. In 1941 it had 16 battleships, seven aircraft carriers, 37 cruisers, and 114 submarines, as well as a large number of smaller war-

ships, a fleet that greatly expanded during the next four years. After the battle of Midway, in 1942, which was a turning point in the naval war in the Pacific, American offensive operations decimated the Japanese fleet to the point of extinction by the time of the battle of Leyte Gulf in October 1944.

Although the U.S. Navy concentrated many of its operations in the Pacific, it also played a major role in the Battle of the Atlantic, the Normandy landings, and many amphibious missions in European waters. During the half-century following World War II, the U.S. Navy has functioned as the largest naval power in the world, fending off a surge in the modernization and expansion of the Soviet Russian fleet during the cold war, particularly in the area of missile power and undersea developments.

United States Navy Submarine School

The submarine school, located in New London/Groton, Connecticut, on Long Island Sound, is the basic educational institution for the training of officers and enlisted sailors in the knowledge and skills necessary for submarine service in all its branches. Founded in 1916, the school was then composed of a handful of buildings, offering students only six months of instruction about submarines, engineering, torpedoes, and electricity. Today, the curriculum provides functional, refresher, advanced, and team training to both submarine and submarine support candidates with the goal of increasing and maintaining knowledge and proficiency in specific skills relating to submarines and their technological systems. Its staff normally consists of some 570 officers and enlisted personnel and about 20 civilians with Civil Service qualifications. By contrast with the first year of operation, the school now graduates nearly 40,000 submariners annually. The location of the school is ideal, since it is adjacent to the submarine base, where many of the boats on duty are used for training cruises, as well as for operational cruises. Many of the graduates are assigned directly to submarines at the base.

United States Submarine Veterans Inc. (USSVI)

This organization's creed is "to perpetuate the memory of our shipmates who gave their lives in the pursuit of their duties while serving their country. That their dedication, deeds, and supreme sacrifice be a constant source of motivation toward greater accomplishments. Pledge loyalty and patriotism to the United States Government." USSVI was started by a group of United States submarine veterans of World War II who shared a belief in the need for an organization open to all submariners, from the very beginning of the submarine service through to the present and into the future, and not limited to those who served so ably in World War II. They wanted to make it known that those lost on submarines, in the line of duty for their country, would never be forgotten. The oldest members served on the small S boats of the 1920s, and the newest are submariners of the 21st century. They are from every state in the Union and belong to one of more than 70 local chapters; many participate in USSVI's annual convention, held in different locations each year, and in regional and district convention meetings throughout the year. The organization also publishes a national magazine, *The American Submariner.*

V

Vella Gulf, Battle of (August 5–6, 1943)

In their struggle to hold the Solomon Islands in the Pacific, the Japanese had been largely successful in maintaining their supply lines, but the battle of Vella Gulf would change that. Six American destroyers commanded by Commander F. Moosebrugger intercepted a Japanese squadron consisting of four destroyers in Vella Gulf. During this night-time action, American gunfire and torpedoes had a deadly effect: three of the four enemy destroyers were sunk and over 1,500 Japanese soldiers were drowned. The Japanese had been unprepared for the attack, and none of their torpedoes hit an American target. Operations in the Solomons were to continue for another three months and would include the battle of Vella Lavella,

USS *Argonaut* (SS-166), shown with tugs in the early 1920s, was one of several boats built when the navy began to design its so-called V class, after letting out no new contracts with private boat yards, like Electric Boat, for more than a decade. *(United States Navy)*

October 6–7, and the American capture of Bougainville on November 1, 1943. Throughout these engagements, American submarines contributed in three critical ways: (1) making reconnaissance/espionage cruises to determine the positions and strength of enemy forces (mainly naval, but some by landings and shore patrols to detect enemy land forces); (2) attacking enemy ships; and (3) doing lifeguard duty to rescue downed Allied fliers and survivors of sunken ships.

Viking (S-3)

The *Viking* is a carrier-based antisubmarine warfare (ASW) aircraft, with one eight-plane squadron serving on board each deployed aircraft carrier. The design incorporates the need to cruise at patrol speeds for long periods of time, to carry a comprehensive set of sensors and weapons, to take off and land on a carrier deck, and to occupy as little deck and hangar space as possible. Therefore, the aircraft has folding wings that facilitate on-ship storage. The boxy fuselage has a sturdy keel on the centerline that divides the weapons bay in half. The four crew members fly in individual ejection seats forward of the wing. Below the wing is the mission avionics bay and the weapons bay. The weapons bay can hold up to four 500-pound bombs or mines or four torpedoes. The two wing pylons can carry mines, rocket pods, or bombs. The *Viking* can also launch Harpoon antiship missiles.

Viper (SS-10) (B-1)

Built by the Fore River Shipbuilding Company in Quincy, Massachusetts, and launched in March 1907, this small submarine, with a submerged displacement of only 173 tons, had two 18-inch torpedo tubes in the bow and was designed to carry a crew of one officer and nine enlisted men. For two years, she cruised along the Atlantic coast on training and experimental exercises, after which she served with the Atlantic Torpedo Fleet and the Reserve Torpedo Group at the navy yard at Charleston, South Carolina. In April 1914, she was transported to the Philippine Islands on a cargo ship, where she was assigned to SubDiv1, Torpedo Flotilla, Asiatic Fleet, and later served with SubDiv2 in Manila Bay. She was decommissioned in December 1921.

Virginia (SSN-774)

The first of a new class of nuclear fast-attack submarines, which includes the *Texas, Hawaii,* and another in the planning stage. *Virginia* was designed to be smaller and less costly than the Seawolf class, but more flexible and capable of operating near shore. Compared with the Los Angeles class, the Virginias were designed to be longer, displace more water, have a larger weapons payload, greater displacement and feature many non-acoustic stealth measures. Although they have no additional launch tubes over other attack submarines they have more weapons storage and can deliver a wide variety of weapons. The *Virginia's* design also incorporates a special operations force (SOF) support capability. This includes the ability to land some of the weapons, and to make berths for, a 40-person SEAL team. Nine persons at a time can covertly leave or reenter the submarine through a chamber, and mini-submarines can ride piggyback to action sites. Production on the *Virginia* started in February 2000, with as many as 12 of her class scheduled for completion by 2012.

Volador (SS-490)

A submarine of the Tench class, she was built by Portsmouth Naval Shipyard and launched in May 1948. Following her commissioning as a GUPPY II boat, *Volador* was deployed to the West Coast to conduct various training exercises and in the 1950s, she saw service in the Far East, where she was on reconnaissance patrols to detect any Soviet or Chinese communist seaborne or airborne activity; conducted operations in the Puget Sound area; completed Alaska and arctic exercises; ranged the western Pacific; and again did reconnaissance in the Far East. In 1963 *Volador* was converted to a GUPPY III submarine at San Francisco Naval Shipyard and conducted a special assignment with the Pacific Fleet, which earned her a commendation for outstanding performance, and participated in missions to Japan, New Zealand, Hong Kong, and Korea. In 1970 *Volador* transferred from the Pacific Ocean to the Atlantic Ocean and in 1971, she deployed to the Mediterranean, after which she was decommissioned. In August 1972 *Volador* transferred to Italy where she served the Italian navy as *G. Gazzana Priaroggia* into the 1980s. *Volador* earned three campaign stars for service during the Vietnam War.

Von Steuben (SSBN-632)

A submarine of the Lafayette class, the *Von Steuben* (named after a Revolutionary War hero born in Russia) was built by the Newport News Shipbuilding and Drydock Company of Virginia and launched in October 1963. She displaced 8,251 tons (submerged), extended 425 feet in length, and carried 16 missile tubes and four 21-inch torpedo tubes forward. She was designed for a complement of 14 officers and 126 enlisted men (each in two crews). *Von Steuben's* career spanned more than 30 years and a profusion of missions. She was decommissioned and struck from the Navy list in February 1994.

W

Wahoo (SS-238)

This submarine of the Gato class was built by Mare Island Naval Shipyard and launched in February 1942. In late August of that year she departed for her first war patrol in the Caroline Islands, where she sank a freighter. During her second patrol, in the Solomons, she sank another freighter, and during her third, in the Palau area, sent two more freighters to the bottom, along with a troop transport, a tanker, and an escort vessel. In addition, she entered a harbor on the north coast of New Guinea and seriously damaged a destroyer, which had to be beached. Wahoo's fourth war patrol, in March 1943, proved to be a field day for the boat. Ranging the Yellow Sea, west of Korea, she polished off no fewer than eight

Wahoo (SS-238), shown returning from one of her seven successful patrols, has been cited as one of the most destructive submarines in history, having sunk 27 enemy ships and damaged two more. She was awarded seven battle stars and a Presidential Unit Citation. *(United States Navy)*

freighters, as well as a tanker, a patrol boat, and two sampans. Heading for the Kurile chain of islands for her fifth patrol, she added to her score two more freighters and a large tanker, and also damaged another freighter and a 15,600-ton aircraft transport ship. It may have been expecting too much that such a record could continue, and the sixth patrol was one of complete frustration. During 28 days on patrol, in part in the Sea of Japan, she expended 10 torpedoes in nine attacks without a hit. Her discouraged skipper returned prematurely to Pearl Harbor to have her torpedoes and tubes checked for problems, and requested permission for *Wahoo* to return to the Sea of Japan, where it was obvious that there were many likely enemy targets.

On September 9, 1943, *Wahoo* again departed Pearl Harbor, with her seventh patrol, scheduled as requested, for the Sea of Japan. She topped off with fuel at Midway and left on September 13, followed shortly thereafter by *Sawfish,* heading for the same waters. *Wahoo* was scheduled to pass through two straits between Hokkaido and Karafuto, and enter the Sea of Japan about September 20, with *Sawfish* arriving some three days later, assigned an area slightly north of her sister boat. No communication was received from *Wahoo,* either by a shore base or by *Sawfish,* nor was she sighted by *Sawfish* in the patrol area. *Wahoo* had orders to leave the Sea of Japan no later than October 21, and to report by radio after passing through the Kurile Island chain en route to Midway. By the end of October, with no sightings and still no report from *Wahoo,*

an aircraft search along her expected course was ordered. When this proved ineffective, the submarine was reported missing and presumed lost.

Although no transmission was ever received from *Wahoo,* the results of one of her attacks became known via a Tokyo broadcast, which reported that on October 5, a Japanese ship was sunk by an American submarine off the west coast of Honshu near the Straits of Tsushima. The submarine could have been none other than *Wahoo,* the only one that could possibly have been operating in that area. Information from Japanese sources after the war reported that an antisubmarine air attack was made in *Wahoo*'s assigned patrol area on October 11, 1943, to the effect that "our plane found a floating sub and attacked it, with 3 depth charges."

Wahoo's record during only seven patrols was one of the most impressive in submarine battle history, making her a legend. She sank 27 ships, totaling 119,100 tons, and damaged two more, making 24,900 tons, in the six patrols completed before her loss. It is probable that this remarkable record was not even complete. Japanese records now reveal that the following ships were sunk in the Sea of Japan shortly before *Wahoo*'s loss; *Taiko Maru* (2,958 tons) on September 25; *Konron Maru* (7,903 tons) on October 1; *Kanko Maru* (1,288 tons) on October 6; and *Kanko Maru* (2,995 tons) on October 9. *Wahoo* was the only submarine that could have sunk these ships. *Wahoo* was awarded seven battle stars and a Presidential Unit Citation for her World War II service.

Wahoo (SS-238) was known for her daring exploits during record-breaking missions against the Japanese in World War II, sinking or damaging some 145,000 tons of enemy shipping during a relatively short period of war patrols. She was reported "missing with all hands" somewhere in the Kurile Islands in October 1943, while on her seventh patrol. *(United States Navy)*

Wahoo (SS-565)

The second boat to bear the illustrious *Wahoo* name was of the Tang class, launched in October 1951 and assigned to the Pacific theater of operations. During the 1950s, and 1960s, she ranged from Hawaii to Hong Kong, Taiwan, Japan, the Philippines, and other ports in the western Pacific and Far East. In 1964, she was called to two tours of duty in the waters off Vietnam as the war intensified. In the 1970s, *Wahoo* was deployed to San Diego for operations along the California coast, but with frequent missions again to the western Pacific and Far East. One deployment brought with it a visit to Korea and a period of combined operations with units of the South Korean navy. Later in the cruise, she visited Taiwan and participated in bilateral ASW exercises with units of the Taiwan navy. She later participated in bilateral exercises with the South Korean and Nationalist Chinese navies. She also joined units of the Japanese Maritime Self-Defense Force in ASW training operations. In September 1977, she departed San Diego to transfer to the Atlantic Fleet, where she conducted exercises along the East Coast and in the Caribbean. She was decommissioned in March 1980, and earned three battle stars for service in the Vietnam conflict.

Wake Island, Battle of (December 1941)

Wake Island is a small atoll in the central Pacific, in December 1941 it was occupied by U.S. Marines and civilians and was the site of a half-completed U.S. air and submarine base. The Japanese first attacked Wake with 36 bombers at noon on December 8, a few hours after the Pearl Harbor attack. A Japanese naval task force that included cruisers and destroyers appeared on December 11, but was repulsed with considerable loss by the island's coastal-defense guns and aircraft, as well as by submarine attacks. Thereafter, however, the Japanese had the atoll under almost continuous air attack, and a U.S. relief force failed to reach the area before the Japanese returned on December 23 with a much more powerful force and in five hours forced the surrender of the American forces. Altogether 1,616 Americans were captured, and most of them were evacuated to China and Japan. The Japanese fortified the atoll heavily, but repeated attacks by U.S. aircraft during the remainder of the war devastated it completely.

Walrus (SS-35) (K-4)

Built by the Electric Boat Division of General Dynamics and launched in March 1914, this submarine of the K class had a displacement of 521 tons, submerged, was armed with four 18-inch torpedo tubes in the bow, and carried a complement of two officers and 26 enlisted men. Considered fast for her day, she could make more than 10 knots underwater and 14 knots on the surface. Joining the Pacific Torpedo Flotilla, *Walrus* operated along the coast of California, conducting experiments to develop the techniques of submarine warfare. She was then assigned for two years to operations in the Hawaiian Islands. In 1917, she was transferred to Key West, Florida, for patrol duty along the coast and in the Caribbean during the First World War. Later, she operated along the East Coast of the United States, training officers and enlisted men, until being decommissioned in May 1923.

War of 1812 (1812–1815)

This war between Britain and the United States was fought in part to defend the doctrine of freedom of the seas. The Royal Navy, which regularly violated the maritime rights of neutral nations, was seizing merchant ships flying the U.S. flag and impressing thousands of American seamen into its service in the war against Napoleonic France. Both sides imposed economic blockades, which severely disrupted trade across the Atlantic and led to the seizure of some 1,500 American merchant ships. On June 19, 1812, Congress declared war. Despite early setbacks, the American Navy won a key battle when it defeated a British fleet on Lake Erie. At sea the war was characterized by individual duels between American and British warships; despite its small size, the U.S. Navy achieved good results in its campaign against enemy merchant ships, deploying its well armed frigates to good effect. The Royal Navy imposed a blockade on the eastern ports of the United States that badly affected trade, although many privateers successfully evaded it. In 1814, fighting continued along the Canadian border until the war escalated with the arrival of more British troops from Europe. Combined British naval and land forces took the offensive on Lake Champlain and in Chesapeake Bay. In the north they eventually retreated to Canada following the decisive battle of Lake Champlain, September 11, 1814, but farther south the British captured Washington, D.C., and burned the White House. The combined force advanced toward Baltimore, which British troops attacked on September 12–14, while a naval force attacked Fort McHenry. The operation failed, inspiring Francis Scott Key to write "The Star-Spangled Banner." Operations continued in the New Orleans area, but a combined British naval and land force was defeated there early in January 1815, some two weeks after the war had been formally ended by the Treaty of Ghent.

West Virginia (SSBN-736)

This submarine of the Ohio class was built by the Electric Boat Division of General Dynamics and launched in

October 1989, with an expected service life of at least two decades.

See OHIO CLASS for specifications and TENNESSEE as a sister ship.

Whale (SS-239)

Built by Mare Island Naval Shipyard and launched in March 1942, this submarine of the Gato class, and the first to bear her name, departed Pearl Harbor in October of that year, on her first war patrol, to plant mines in the eastern entrance to the Inland Sea of Japan. Three minefields were planted successfully, and Whale spent several days in these waters attacking targets and obtaining periscope photographs of military installations along the coast, sometimes from a distance of only 500 yards offshore. During this dangerous procedure, she almost met her end when a patrol craft blasted the boat with her first severe depth-charging, flooding the induction valves and sending her plunging toward the bottom at a 20-degree angle before the crew could correct the situation and return the boat to normal several hours later and make it back to port. After extensive repairs, Whale departed in January for her second patrol, off the Marshall Islands, where she sank a freighter and two troop ships and damaged a tanker. Four freighters were sunk and a seaplane tender was damaged by Whale on her third and fourth patrols in the Mariana Islands. In August 1943, Whale conducted her fifth patrol, again in the Marianas, and sank the 7,149-ton aircraft ferry Maruto Maru. On her sixth patrol, off the Bonin Islands, she netted two more freighters. On her seventh, eighth, and ninth patrols, Whale continued to inflict heavy damage on the Japanese merchant fleet. On completion of her 10th patrol, a photo reconnaissance off Okinawa was conducted in preparation for the forthcoming invasion of that heavily defended island. In the late spring of 1945, after overhaul, Whale headed for the heartland of the enemy islands to conduct lifeguard services off Japan in support of carrier and B-29 strikes. She rescued 15 downed aviators, and was still at sea when the war ended, having racked up an enviable record of 9 vessels for 57,716 tons of Japanese shipping sunk. She was decommissioned in June 1946 and awarded 11 battle stars for her World War II service.

Whale (SSN-638)

Built by Bethlehem Steel and the second boat to bear her name, Whale was a fast-attack nuclear submarine of the Sturgeon class launched in October 1966. Located first in Charleston, South Carolina, she was later assigned to participate in arctic exercises and on April 6, 1969, achieved notoriety by surfacing at the North Pole 60 years to the day after Admiral Robert E. Peary had arrived there. In January 1970, she successfully demonstrated the capability of her class of boat to conduct underwater demolition team (UDT) operations, and the next month she conducted her second successful test of the SUBROC missile. During the 1970s, Whale was deployed to the Mediterranean to support the Sixth Fleet during the Jordanian conflict, and later ranged over the seas from Germany to Spain, Scotland, Greece, Italy, and other Mediterranean ports, before returning to duty on the East Coast. In the mid-1980s, she was transferred to the West Coast, where she served for most of her remaining career until being decommissioned at the Puget Sound Shipyard in Bremerton, Washington, in July 1996.

William H. Bates (SSN-680)

A submarine of the Sturgeon class and built by Ingalls Shipbuilding Company, she was launched in December 1971 as a fast-attack nuclear submarine. She was initially based in New London, Connecticut, operating in the eastern Atlantic, with several deployments to European waters, including extensive operations in the Mediterranean, and engaging in several international exercises with NATO and numerous foreign nations. During the 1970s, she operated from ports in the Atlantic until moving to San Diego in May 1978 for service in the Pacific Fleet—along the West Coast and then in Hawaiian waters. She currently operates from her home port, Pearl Harbor.

Will Rogers (SSBN-659)

This submarine of the Benjamin Franklin class was built by the Electric Boat Division of General Dynamics and launched in July 1966. With a displacement of 8,251 tons (submerged) and a length of 425 feet, she was designed for a complement of 14 officers and 126 enlisted men (each in two crews). Will Rogers was armed with 16 missile tubes and four 21-inch torpedo tubes forward and could cruise at underwater speeds of more than 20 knots. She was decommissioned in April 1993.

See BENJAMIN FRANKLIN for details about specifications, missions, and sister ships.

wolf pack

Although the term is said to have originated with packs of German U-boats that ranged European waters during World War I, and was used widely during the Battle of the Atlantic, 1939–45, it was adapted by American submariners during World War II, especially in the Pacific. American wolf packs were generally small in number, no more than three or four, under prevailing circumstances. The strategic theory was that a single submarine detecting a convoy could usually sink only one or two enemy vessels at best, leaving the rest to escape, whereas a wolf pack could coordinate a series of attacks, in order, and sometimes wipe out most of the convoy. As the war progressed, improved communication facilities made it possible for the commanders to work closely as a team, moving from one position to another to intercept the individual ships of an enemy convoy. American wolf packs often used the name of the commander of the lead submarine to designate themselves as combat teams, such as "Russel's Raiders" or "Ben's Blasters" or "Cliff's Hangers."

Woodrow Wilson (SSBN-624)

This submarine of the Lafayette class was built by the Mare Island Naval Shipyard, and launched in February 1963. With a displacement of 8,251 tons (submerged) and a length of 425 feet, she was designed for a complement of 14 officers and 126 enlisted men (each in two crews). She was armed with 16 missile tubes and four 21-inch torpedo tubes forward, and otherwise fitted for deterrent patrols, particularly in the western Pacific, during her lifetime of some 30 years. *Woodrow Wilson* was decommissioned and struck from the Navy list in September 1994. The submarine's sail and rudder have been preserved in "Deterrent Park" at the submarine base in Bangor, Washington, as a tribute and memorial to the "Forty-One for Freedom" boats—the first Polaris Ballistic Missile Submarines. See also the entry for LAFAYETTE.

World War I (1914–1918)

The advent of war in Europe was not unexpected, since rival groups of nations had been making alliances for many years and fomenting conflicts over land boundaries and populations. Europe was divided into two major camps, with Germany, Austria-Hungary, and the Ottoman turks on one side, and England, France, and Russia on the other.

Captured German U-boat *88* as it appeared in an American port after being navigated back from Europe by Commander Harold Travis Smith, USN, for examination of its weaponry and other components. Commander Smith, then an engineering officer and later to be in charge of several navy shipyards constructing submarines, also served in World War II and retired as a rear admiral. *(Courtesy of Commander Harold Travis Smith, Jr., USN (Retired).) (United States Navy)*

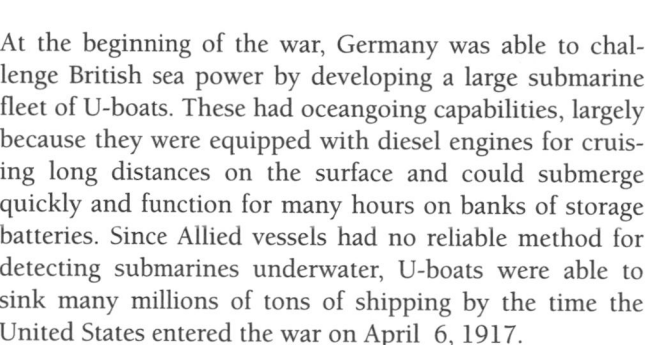

Captured U-boats. *(United States Navy)*

Nazi submarine sinking. *(United States Navy)*

At the beginning of the war, Germany was able to challenge British sea power by developing a large submarine fleet of U-boats. These had oceangoing capabilities, largely because they were equipped with diesel engines for cruising long distances on the surface and could submerge quickly and function for many hours on banks of storage batteries. Since Allied vessels had no reliable method for detecting submarines underwater, U-boats were able to sink many millions of tons of shipping by the time the United States entered the war on April 6, 1917.

Even before the United States entered the war, Germany temporarily cut back on U-boat attacks on merchant ships because of America's protests over civilian deaths, and particularly the sinking of the *Lusitania* and the *Arabic*, with the loss of many lives, including women and children. However, these reductions were short-lived, as Germany suffered more and more losses at sea.

Shortly after the United States entered the war, the American Navy began sending submarines to European waters, and Britain instituted a convoy system to protect fleets of its merchant ships at sea. Although few American submarines had opportunities to make attacks against enemy shipping, their increasing presence was a factor in Germany's eventual capitulation. World War I gave the United States Navy an opportunity to reevaluate the importance of submarines in warfare and to improve many technological designs. For this purpose, the navy also brought a number of captured U-boats to the United States for disassembly and study.

World War II (International relations and the turning point, 1942)

Within a year after American entry into the war, Axis power crested and then began to ebb as critical battles were fought in every major theater. The year also saw the forging of a Grand Alliance among the United States, Britain, and the U.S.S.R. and the first sign of disagreement on strategy and war aims. After Pearl Harbor, Prime Minister Churchill requested a critical conference with President Roosevelt, meeting for three weeks at the Arcadia Conference in Washington. They reaffirmed the Allied strategy and conceived a plan for Anglo-American landings in North Africa. They also issued, on January 1, 1942, the United Nations Declaration in the spirit of the Atlantic Charter. But the Russians were not happy with the plan, and Stalin complained that the Atlantic Charter was more directed against him than Hitler. The Soviets also made the first of what were to become their incessant demands that the Allies open a second front in France to take the pressure off the Red Army. President Roosevelt opted for a cross-channel invasion, but the British deemed it impossible. Russia was appeased by an Anglo-Soviet alliance, and, in late June 1942, Churchill and Roosevelt met again in Washington and confirmed plans for a joint operation in Africa despite the misgivings of American generals, who suspected the British of being more concerned for the defense of their empire than the rapid defeat of Hitler. In the end the British won, and the Allies approved *Torch*, a combined invasion of North Africa planned for the autumn. Although the Russians continued to complain, they had to be satisfied when, by December 1942, the German advance into the Soviet Union had been stopped, though at enormous cost.

The Allied landings in North Africa, where British forces had finally turned back the German Afrika Korps at el-Alamein, were targeted for Casablanca, Oran, and Algiers. Now the French stepped into the picture, unhappy with the choice of a French leader by the Allied command, and France promptly severed diplomatic relations with Washington and ordered French forces in North Africa to resist. Brief but serious fighting resulted at Oran and Casablanca. The Allies had been seeking a French leader with the prestige and willingness to rally French Africa against the Axis, but the nominal commander was Admiral Francois Darlan, an ardent collaborationist in the Vichy cabinet. The Americans soon escaped the embarrassment of having bargained with a leading fascist when a French royalist shot Darlan and General De Gaulle was able to become leader of Free French forces. Meanwhile, in the Pacific, the naval battle of Midway in June, the landing of U.S. forces on Guadalcanal in August, and the creation of an "island-hopping" strategy against Japan's sudden and far-flung empire similarly blunted the string of the early Axis victories. Meanwhile, General Douglas MacArthur rallied Allied forces in Australia, but was almost set back when a Japanese invasion force landed near Gona at the southeastern end of New Guinea in July 1942 and drove Australian troops back to within 32 miles of Port Moresby. Then MacArthur executed a series of landings behind the Japanese and secured the entire Papuan coast by late January 1943. Thenceforth Japan, too, went on the strategic defensive.

Wyoming (SSBN-742)

This submarine of the Ohio class was built by the Electric Boat Division of General Dynamics and launched in April 1979, almost eight years after the laying of her keel. Then, because of advanced designing, testing, and modifications, she was not ready for commissioning until July 1996. With a displacement of 18,750 tons, and a length of 559 feet, she is designed for a complement of 15 officers and 142 enlisted men (each in two crews), and is well qualified for the most advanced deterrent patrols and far-reaching operations. See the OHIO CLASS entry for information on this highly complicated and advanced submarine and her sister ships.

Z

Zumwalt, Elmo Russell, Jr. (1920–)

An American naval officer, who was chief of naval operations during the Vietnam War and revitalizer of the U.S. Navy during the 1970s. He graduated from the U.S. Naval Academy in June 1942, and saw duty during the Guadalcanal landings in 1942 and in the Aleutians in the spring of 1943. He also saw action at Saipan, Tinian, the Surigao Strait, Indonesia, the Philippines, and at the battle of Leyte Gulf. During the Korean War, he served as navigator of the battleship *Wisconsin*. Serving in important staff positions as well as commands at sea, he steadily rose in rank, and in July 1965, at the age of 44, was promoted to rear admiral, the youngest American naval officer to reach flag rank. From September 1968 to the spring of 1970, he served as commander of U.S. Naval Forces in Vietnam, and in July 1970, at the age of 49, he was appointed chief of naval operations, the youngest ever to hold that office. As the navy's top officer, he introduced radical reforms in the service to curb racial disharmony and to raise the standard of living for enlisted personnel. Zumwalt retired in July 1974.

APPENDIXES

APPENDIX I
CHRONOLOGY

APPENDIX II
LEADING INDIVIDUAL SUBMARINE SCORES

APPENDIX III
UNITED STATES NAVY SUBMARINES, 1900–2000

APPENDIX IV
SUBMARINE MUSEUMS

APPENDIX V
WEBSITES

APPENDIX VI
ACRONYMS

GLOSSARY

SELECTED BIBLIOGRAPHY

APPENDIX I

CHRONOLOGY

September 7, 1776
Turtle, a one-man submarine built by 34-year-old Yale graduate David Bushnell, unsuccessfully tries to attach a torpedo to the hull of HMS *Eagle* anchored off New York Harbor.

July 3, 1801
Robert Fulton's submarine *Nautilus* dives to a depth of 25 feet and remains there for more than an hour.

February 17, 1864
The Confederate submarine *H. L. Hunley* is the first to sink an enemy ship in combat when it rams its spar torpedo into the hull of the Union screw sloop USS *Housatonic* off Charleston, South Carolina. The concussion wave sank the *Hunley.*

1888
Bureau of Construction and Repair design competition brings inventor John P. Holland a contract to build *Plunger.*

August 7, 1897
Plunger, a steam-powered submarine, launches but fails to pass acceptance tests.

August 11, 1900
John P. Holland sells his internal combustion, gasoline-powered submarine, *Holland VI,* to the navy for $160,000 after demonstration trials off Mt. Vernon, Virginia, marking the official birth date of the U.S. Navy's submarine force.

October 12, 1900
USS *Holland* (SS-1), the former *Holland VI,* is commissioned.

1903
The U.S. Navy commissions the seventh and last boat of the original *Holland* A class, USS *Shark* (SS-8)

1909
The U.S. Navy imitates the diesel propulsion of French submarine *Aigrette* when the Electric Boat Company begins building the F Class (SS 20 through 23) and the E class (SS 24 and 25) at Fore River Shipyard.

March 5, 1912
The secretary of the navy establishes the Atlantic Submarine Flotilla, commanded by Lieutenant Chester W. Nimitz.

February 14, 1914
USS *Skipjack* (SS-24), the first U.S. submarine to run on diesel engines, is commissioned.

1916
USS *Skipjack* (SS-24) is the first U.S. submarine to cross the Atlantic under her own power. The Bureau of Construction and Repair and the Bureau of Steam Engineering produce the faster 15-knot, 800-ton, S-class submarines with the assistance of Electric Boat and Lake corporations.

June 19, 1916
Submarine Force U.S. Atlantic Fleet is established.

August 29, 1916
The revolutionary and hotly contested Appropriations Act of 1916 creates the Council of National Defense to take stock of domestic industrial capability to wage war. The navy begins building ships and submarines in much larger numbers; Congress specifically includes a provision in the bill to construct 30 new submarines.

January 1, 1917
The submarine school is established at the submarine base at New London, Connecticut.

March 4, 1917
The Appropriations Act of 1917 adds 18 more boats to the submarine construction program. The navy uses resources from the Naval Emergency Fund for 20 more.

June 28, 1917
Submarine Force U.S. Pacific Fleet is established.

December 12, 1918
The American submarine force in Europe borrows four captured U-boats from the British and takes them to Portland, England, for almost three weeks of tests and inspection.

December 17, 1927
While running submerged off Provincetown, Massachusetts, USS *S-4* (SS-109) is rammed by the Coast Guard cutter *Paulding,* sinks, and 42 men are lost. Although at least six men survived initially, trapped in the forward torpedo room, nonexistence of a rescue capability resulted in their death. This accident leads to the development of the Momsen Lung, which for the first time allows escape from a sunken submarine; the McCann rescue diving bell; and telephone buoys, which allows crews trapped inside a submarine to communicate with rescue ships on the surface.

1933
The Washington Navy Yard makes 20 sets of quartz steel, echo-ranging equipment, a major development in SONAR (SOund Navigation and Ranging) technology.

October 27, 1933
USS *Porpoise* (SS-172) is the first U.S. submarine to have electric reduction gear and high-speed diesel engines.

1935
The importance of submarine operations in the Pacific, Caribbean, and the South Atlantic leads the Navy Department to install the first air-conditioning system on board USS *Cuttlefish* (SS-171), in spite of space constraints.

May 23, 1939
USS *Squalus* (SS-192) sinks during a practice dive off the coast of Portsmouth, New Hampshire. By using a rescue chamber, 33 men are saved.

January 1, 1941
The first radar for submarines becomes operational.

December 7, 1941
Submarines are spared during the Japanese attack on Pearl Harbor, making the submarine force indispensable. "When I assumed command of the Pacific Fleet on 31 December 1941 our submarines were already operating against the enemy, the only units of the Fleet that could come to grips with the Japanese for months to come. It was to the submarine force that I looked to carry the load until our great industrial activity could produce the weapons we so sorely needed to carry the war to the enemy. It is to the everlasting honor and glory of our submarine personnel that they never failed us in our days of great peril." (Admiral Chester W. Nimitz)

December 31, 1941
Admiral Chester W. Nimitz, a qualified submariner, is sworn in as commander, Pacific Fleet, aboard USS *Grayling* (SS-209)

January 27, 1942
USS *Cudgeon* (SS-211) is the first U.S. submarine to sink an enemy submarine, the Japanese *I-173.*

1945
World War II ends. Fleet consists of 6,768 active units; 232 are submarines. The defense budget is $83 billion, representing 89.5 percent of federal spending. U.S. Navy begins study of German U-boat technology and future anti-submarine warfare (ASW) problems. Begins work on new sonar, weapons, and propulsion systems. Admiral Ernest J. King is the chief of naval operations (CNO), James V. Forrestal is secretary of the navy. Fleet Admiral Chester Nimitz replaces King as CNO.

September 2, 1945
By V-J Day, U.S. submarines have sunk five million tons of Japanese naval and merchant shipping at a loss of 52 U.S. submarines and more than 3,500 valiant men.

1946
Captain Hyman G. Rickover arrives at Oak Ridge to begin study of atomic energy. Greater Underwater Propulsive Power (GUPPY) program for World War II fleet boat modernization begins.

1947
James Forrestal becomes the first secretary of defense.

First two GUPPY submarines, USS *Odax* (SS-484) and USS *Pomodon* (SS-486), are commissioned.

USS *Irex* (SS-482), first fleet snorkel submarine, enters service.

1948

Bureau of Ships forms Nuclear Power Branch and Captain Rickover chosen as head.

Westinghouse signs contract with the Atomic Energy Commission to build the Bettis Atomic Power Laboratory, beginning the submarine thermal reactor (STR) design using pressurized water.

Submarine Squadron 6 in the Canal Zone conducts tests with USS *Tusk* (SS-426), concluding that submarines are the best ASW platform against snorkeling submarines. Charleston Naval Shipyard enters the submarine overhaul business.

January 20, 1948

USS *Cusk* (SS-348, later redesignated SSG-348) is the navy's first guided-missile submarine.

1949

USS *Cochino* (SS-345) lost at sea.

1950

President Harry S. Truman authorizes the construction of the first nuclear-powered submarine.

Bureau of Ships begins design work on swimmer delivery vehicles (SDV).

1951

Bureau of Ships signs contract with Westinghouse and Electric Boat for USS *Nautilus*, first nuclear-powered submarine.

1952

Keel laid for USS *Nautilus* (SSN-571) at Electric Boat, Groton, Connecticut.

1953

Admiral Robert B. Carney becomes CNO.

Fleet consists of 1,122 active units, including 110 submarines (all diesel). The defense budget is $52.8 billion, representing 69.3 percent of federal spending.

First submarine thermal reactor prototype reaches initial criticality.

Atomic Energy Commission approves the submarine fleet reactor (SFR) project. This will result in the S3W and S4W reactor designs.

Keel laid for USS *Seawolf* (SSN-575), the second nuclear-powered submarine, at Electric Boat. This submarine is designed with the submarine intermediate reactor (SIR) using liquid sodium as primary coolant.

USS *Albacore* (AGSS-569) is commissioned to test new submarine technology. Her most important innovation is her teardrop-shaped hull form.

May 8, 1953

USS *Tunny* (SS-282), prototype SSG conversion, is recommissioned. She is the first U.S. submarine equipped to fire surface-to-surface Regulus missiles.

September 30, 1954

USS *Nautilus* (SSN-571), the world's first nuclear-powered ship, is commissioned.

1955

The *X-1*, the U.S. Navy's first midget submarine, is placed in service.

January 17, 1955

Commander Dennis Wilkinson, aboard the USS *Nautilus* (SSN-571), sends the historic message, "Underway on nuclear power," signaling a new era in both submarine warfare and maritime propulsion.

December 3, 1956

The navy terminates participation in the U.S. Army's Jupiter missile program and begins pursuing development of the Polaris missile submarine.

1957

USS *Skate* (SSN-578), the first submarine to be powered by the submarine fleet reactor, is commissioned. This class introduces Portsmouth Naval Shipyard and Mare Island Naval Shipyard to nuclear-powered submarine construction.

Regulus missile program terminated to free funds for the Polaris project. SSGNs on order are recast as SSN-593-class attack submarines. Existing Regulus submarines continue operations.

August 3, 1958

USS *Nautilus* (SSN-571) is the first ship to pass beneath the North Pole, on a four-day, 1,830-mile voyage from the Pacific to the Atlantic.

1959

USS *Triton* (SSRN-586) commissioned as a radar-picket submarine. She is the first and only dual reactor submarine in the U.S. Navy.

USS *Skipjack* (SSN-585) is commissioned, the first submarine combining nuclear propulsion with the Albacore hull form. The first submarine powered by the S5W reactor. This reactor plant will become the workhorse of the nuclear-powered submarine force for more than 30 years. This class introduces Newport News Shipbuilding and Ingalls Shipbuilding to nuclear-powered submarine construction.

USS *George Washington* (SSBN-598), the first of the "41 for Freedom" fleet ballistic missile (FBM) submarines, is commissioned.

1960

USS *Halibut* (SSGN-587), the first and only nuclear-powered, Regulus guided missile submarine, is commissioned.

Polaris A-2 missile becomes operational.

May 10, 1960

USS *Triton* (SSG-586) completes the first submerged circumnavigation of Earth, following Ferdinand Magellan's route and covering more than 41,000 miles in just 84 days.

July 20, 1960

While submerged off the coast of Cape Canaveral, Florida, USS *George Washington* (SSBN-598) successfully fires two Polaris A-1 missiles with a range of 1,200 miles. This year she will depart Charleston, South Carolina, on the first operational strategic patrol with the Polaris missile system.

August 25, 1960

USS *Sea Dragon* (SSN-584) charts the Northwest Passage and surfaces at the North Pole where the crew plays baseball.

1961

USS *Thresher* (SSN-593) is commissioned at Portsmouth Naval Shipyard, the first unit of what will be a class of 14 submarines. This is the first new-design submarine for which Electric Boat is not the lead yard.

July 9, 1961

USS *Robert E. Lee* (SSBN-601) sets a new continuous underwater patrol record of more than 68 days.

November 8, 1962

USS *Ethan Allen* (SSBN-608) sets a missile record by firing six Polaris A-2 missiles with a range of 1,500 miles.

1963

USS *Sam Houston* (SSBN-609) is the first Polaris submarine assigned to the Mediterranean patrol.

USS *LaFayette* (SSBN-616), the third class of SSBN, is commissioned.

Polaris A-3 missile becomes operational.

April 10, 1963

USS *Thresher* (SSN-593) is reported overdue and presumed lost during a test dive 220 miles east of Boston. SUBSAFE program initiated as a result of this accident.

1964

USS *Halibut* (SSGN-587) makes the last Regulus patrol. With Polaris on line, Regulus submarines are phased out.

August 21, 1964

USS *Daniel Boone* (SSBN-629) is the first fleet ballistic missile submarine permanently assigned to the Pacific.

January 18, 1965

President Johnson announces plans to develop Poseidon, a more powerful missile than the Polaris A-3.

February 2, 1966

USS *George Washington* (SSBN-598), after long deployment on many submerged patrols, completes her initial overhaul and is refit to carry the 2,500-mile-range Polaris A-3 missile.

December 6, 1966

USS *Queenfish* (SSN-651) is the first Sturgeon-class attack submarine to be commissioned.

1967

USS *Sturgeon* (SSN-637), the lead ship of a 37-unit class, is commissioned. This class introduces General Dynamics to submarine construction. New York Shipbuilding Corporation drops out of submarine construction while building USS *Pogy* (SSN-647); she is towed, to Ingalls Shipbuilding in Pascagoula, Mississippi, to be completed.

April 1, 1967

USS *Will Rogers* (SSBN-659) is commissioned. This completes the building of the "41 for Freedom" FBM submarines, two years ahead of schedule.

1968

At the height of the Vietnam War, the fleet consists of 932 active units, including 156 submarines (diesel and nuclear). Puget Sound Naval Shipyard, Bremerton, Washington, enters the nuclear-powered submarine overhaul business.

June 5, 1968
USS *Scorpion* (SSN-589) is reported overdue and presumed lost during her transit from the Mediterranean to Norfolk.

August 17, 1968
USS *Dolphin* (AGSS-555), a small diesel-powered research and development submarine, capable of operating at depths in excess of any other known submarine, is commissioned.

1969
NR-1, the navy's only nuclear-powered research submarine, is commissioned.

April 5, 1969
The 100th Polaris patrol in the Pacific is completed when USS *Stonewall Jackson* (SSBN-634) returns to Apra Harbor, Guam.

1970
The first deep submergence rescue vehicle (DSRV), designed for quick deployment in the event of a submarine accident, is launched.

Poseidon missile conversions begin on SSBN-616-class submarines.

1971
Portsmouth Naval Shipyard drops out of the nuclear-powered submarine construction business. Overhaul business continues.

1972
Design work begins on the Tomahawk cruise missile. This is the U.S. Navy's first cruise missile since Regulus.

Design work begins on a submarine-launched version of the Harpoon antiship missile. Mare Island Naval Shipyard drops out of the nuclear-powered submarine construction business. Overhaul business continues.

February 16, 1973
The secretary of the navy announces Bangor, Washington, as the initial base for *Trident* submarine operations.

1974
Ingalls Shipyard drops out of the nuclear-powered submarine construction business. This action leaves only General Dynamics, Electric Boat, and Newport News Shipbuilding as the U.S. Navy's only sources of new construction, nuclear-powered submarines.

1975
USS *Tigrone* (SS-419), last of the World War II fleet submarines, is decommissioned.

November 13, 1976
USS *Los Angeles* (SSN-688) is commissioned at Newport News, Virginia, as the first of a new class of attack submarine. She is outfitted with the S6G reactor plant.

1977
The U.S. Navy consists of 523 active ships, including 118 submarines (three diesels, 115 nuclear). The defense budget is $95.1 billion, representing 23.4 percent of federal spending.

1978
Submarine base established at Kings Bay, Georgia, for Atlantic fleet Trident submarine operations.

1979
Ten SSBN-616-class submarines begin upgrades for Trident C-4 missile systems.

March 3, 1980
USS *Nautilus* (SSN-571) is decommissioned at Mare Island Naval Shipyard.

1981
USS *Theodore Roosevelt* (SSBN-600) and USS *Abraham Lincoln* (SSBN-602) are decommissioned. The remaining SSBN-598-class submarines are converted to SSNs. John Lehman becomes secretary of the navy. He plans a 600-ship navy with 100 attack submarines.

June 27, 1981
Upon return to port, USS *James K. Polk* (SSBN-645) completes the submarine force's 2,000th fleet ballistic missile deterrent patrol.

November 11, 1981
USS *Ohio* (SSBN-726), the first Trident-class submarine, is commissioned. She is outfitted with the S8G reactor plant.

February 1, 1982
Admiral Rickover is relieved by Admiral McKee.

March 1, 1982
The navy's last Polaris fleet ballistic missile submarine, USS *Robert E. Lee* (SSBN-601), is redesignated SSN-601, marking the end of the Polaris system after 21 years of service.

1983

Tomahawk cruise missile becomes operational.

USS *Sam Houston* (SSBN-609) and USS *John Marshall* (SSBN-611) begin conversion as swimmer delivery platforms.

Design work begins on the SSN-21 class to succeed the SSN-688, Los Angeles class. Introduction of the dry deck shelter, a modular housing capable of being fitted onto the deck of a submarine for swimmers and swimmer delivery vehicle (SDV) lockouts. This is the first real tasking of SSNs to special operations support. Long-hull SSN-637s and converted SSBNs are given capability to carry the shelters.

May 6, 1986

For the first time, three submarines surface together at the North Pole, USS *Archerfish* (SSN-678), USS *Hawkbill* (SSN-666), and USS *Ray* (SSN-653).

1987

U.S. Navy consists of 594 active units, including 139 submarines (three diesels, 136 nuclear). The defense budget is $274 billion, representing 27.3 percent of federal spending.

1988

USS *Tennessee* (SSBN-734), the first Trident submarine employing the D-5 missile system, is commissioned.

USS *San Juan* (SSN-751), the first improved 688 submarine, is commissioned. Improvements include a strengthening of the sail and the relocation of the fairwater planes to the bow. This gives the class an arctic operations capability.

1989

USS *Memphis* (SSN-691) is withdrawn from active service to become a research platform to test advanced submarine technology such as optronic non-hull-penetrating masts, unmanned underwater vehicles (UUV), and large-diameter torpedoes.

March 21, 1989

The first submerged test launch of the eight-warhead *Trident II* missile is made aboard USS *Tennessee* (SSBN-734) off Cape Canaveral, Florida.

1990

USS *Scamp* (SSN-588) becomes the first nuclear-powered submarine to be dismantled as part of the U.S. Navy's Submarine Recycling Program at Puget Sound Naval Shipyard. This program leads to a safe and effective process for disposing of decommissioned nuclear-powered submarines.

USS *Blueback* (SS-581), the last non-nuclear-powered attack submarine in the U.S. Navy inventory, is decommissioned.

The last of the SSN-585 (USS *Skipjack*) class submarines are decommissioned.

1991

The U.S. Navy consists of 529 active units, including 121 submarines (all nuclear-powered).

USS *Louisville* (SSN-724) fires the first Tomahawk cruise missile from a submarine in a combat situation during Operation Desert Storm.

Admiral Kelso, CNO, orders the design of an "affordable" submarine, as a follow on to the SSN-21 class. This is the beginning of the new SSN (NSSN), which will be named the Virginia-class SSN.

February 4, 1991

The Pentagon earmarks $2.8 billion for a Seawolf nuclear-powered attack submarine in the federal fiscal year 1992 budget.

1992

Secretary of Defense Richard Cheney terminates the SSN-21 program and asks Congress to rescind funds for two boats authorized in fiscal year 1991. Compromise is reached to cancel one unit and retain the other.

President Clinton supports construction of the third SSN-21-class submarine.

1993

USS *Kamehameha* (SSBN-642) and USS *James K. Polk* (SSBN-645) replace the SSN-609 and SSN-611 in swimmer delivery roles.

1994

USS *Mariano G. Vallejo* (SSBN-658), last of the original "41 for Freedom," is phased out of the strategic force.

1995

USS *Baton Rouge* (SSN-689) becomes the first SSN-688-class submarine to be decommissioned. Units of this class are still under construction. Dr. Robert Ballard explores shipwrecks in the Mediterranean Sea aboard *NR-1*. Admiral Boorda, CNO, proposes the "Arsenal Ship," a surface warship designed to carry a large volume of fire power. This concept will lead to ideas of converting some SSBN-726-class submarines into cruise missile submarines (SSGN).

1996

USS *Gato* (SSN-615), last of the SSN-593-class submarines, is decommissioned.

USS *Cheyenne* (SSN-773), the 62nd and last unit of the SSN-688-class submarines, is commissioned. Charleston Naval Shipyard and Mare Island Naval Shipyard are closed as a result of base realignment and closure decisions.

July 3, 1996

Sea trials for USS *Seawolf* (SSN-21) begin.

1997

U.S. Navy consists of 365 active ships, including 91 submarines (all nuclear-powered). Defense budget is $258.3 billion, representing 16.1 percent of federal spending.

April 7, 1997

Newport News Shipbuilding is awarded a $71.9 million contract to provide design and planning yard services for Seawolf-class submarines.

July 19, 1997

USS *Seawolf* (SSN-21) is commissioned in Groton, Connecticut. She is outfitted with the S6W reactor plant.

1998

USS *Connecticut* (SSN-22) is commissioned.

Tomahawk cruise missile strikes from submarines against targets inside Iraq emphasize a shift from "blue water" operations to the littorals.

General Dynamics and Newport News announce cooperative effort to build the SSN-774-class submarine. Each shipyard will build specific sub-assemblies for each boat.

September 10, 1998

Secretary of the Navy John H. Dalton names the lead ship of the new attack submarine class USS *Virginia* (SSN-774), designed to dominate the coastal region, while maintaining open-ocean supremacy. The class will include Tomahawk missile capability, advanced sonar systems for antisubmarine and mine warfare; reconfigurable torpedo room for special missions; advanced SEAL delivery system (ASDS) and nine-man lockout trunk, to launch unmanned underwater or aerial vehicles for mine reconnaissance, intelligence gathering, and other missions; enhanced stealth; and enhanced electronic support measures (ESM).

September 2, 1999

USS *Virginia* (SSN-774) keel laying ceremony at Quonset Point, Rhode Island. With construction begun at Electric Boat, Connecticut, and Newport News, Virginia, *Virginia* is expected to be complete in 2004.

APPENDIX II

LEADING INDIVIDUAL SUBMARINE SCORES

(TOP 25)

NUMBER OF SHIPS SUNK			
SUBMARINE	SHIPS	Snook	17
Tautog	26	Thresher	17
Tang	24	Bowfin	16
Silversides	23	Harder	16
Flasher	21	Pogy	16
Spadefish	21	Sunfish	16
Seahorse	20	Tinosa	16
Wahoo	20	Drum	15
Guardfish	19	Flyingfish	15
Rasher	18	Greenling	15
Seawolf	18	Jack	15
Trigger	18	Grayback	14
Barb	17	Kingfish	14

TONNAGE SUNK			
SUBMARINE	TONNAGE	Guardfish	72,424
Flasher	100,231	Seawolf	71,609
Rasher	99,901	Gudgeon	71,047
Barb	96,628	Sealion II	68,297
Tang	93,824	Bowfin	67,882
Silversides	90,080	Thresher	66,172
Spadefish	88,091	Tinosa	64,655
Trigger	86,552	Grayback	63,835
Drum	80,580	Pogy	62,633
Jack	76,687	Bonefish	61,345
Snook	75,473	Wahoo	60,038
Tautog	72,606	Sunfish	59,815
Seahorse	72,529	Archerfish	59,800

APPENDIX III

UNITED STATES NAVY SUBMARINES, 1900–2000

Naval Identification Symbols

SSN: Attack Submarine, Nuclear

SSBN: Ballistic Submarine, Nuclear

SSGN: Guided Missile Submarine, Nuclear

AGSS: Auxiliary Research Submarine

HULL NO. & NAME	COMMISSION DATE
SSK-1 *Barracuda*	
SSK-2 *Bass*	
SSK-3 *Bonita*	
SST-1 *Mackerel*	
SST-2 *T-2/Marlin*	
SF-4 *V-1*	
SF-5 *V-2*	
SF-6 *V-3*	
SF-7/SM-1 *V-4*	
SM-1 *Argonaut*	
SS-1 *Holland*	1900
SS-2 *Plunger/A-1*	1903
SS-3 *Adder/A-2*	1903
SS-4 *Grampus/A-3*	1903

SS-5 *Moccasin/A-4*	1903
SS-6 *Pike/A-5*	1903
SS-7 *Porpoise/A-6*	1903
SS-8 *Shark/A-7*	1903
SS-9 *Octopus/C-1*	1908
SS-10 *Viper/B-1*	1907
SS-11 *Cuttlefish/B-2*	1907
SS-12 *Tarantula/B-3*	1907
SS-13 *Stingray/C-2*	1909
SS-14 *Tarpon/C-3*	1909
SS-15 *Bonita/C-4*	1909
SS-16 *Snapper/C-5*	1910
SS-17 *Narwhal*	1909
SS-18 *Grayling*	1909
SS-19 *Salmon*	1910
SS-19 *G-1*	1912
SS-20 *F-1*	1912
SS-21 *F-2*	1912
SS-22 *F-3*	1912
SS-23 *F-4*	1913
SS-24 *E-1*	1912
SS-25 *E-2*	1912
SS-26 *G-4*	1914
SS-27 *G-2*	1915
SS-28 *H-1*	1914
SS-29 *H-2*	1914
SS-30 *H-3*	1914

SS-31 *G-3*	1914
SS-32 *K-1*	1914
SS-33 *K-2*	1914
SS-34 *K-3*	1914
SS-35 *K-4*	1914
SS-36 *K-5*	1914
SS-37 *K-6*	1914
SS-38 *K-7*	1914
SS-39 *K-8*	1914
SS-40 *L-1*	1916
SS-41 *L-2*	1916
SS-42 *L-3*	1916
SS-43 *L-4*	1916
SS-44 *L-5*	1918
SS-45 *L-6*	1917
SS-46 *L-7*	1917
SS-47 *M-1*	1917
SS-48 *L-8*	1917
SS-49 *L-9*	1916
SS-50 *L-10*	1916
SS-51 *L-11*	1916
SS-52 *AA-1*	1920
SS-53 *N-1*	1917
SS-54 *N-2*	1917
SS-55 *N-3*	1917
SS-56 *N-4*	1918
SS-57 *N-5*	1918

SS-58 *N-6*	1918
SS-59 *N-7*	1918
SS-60 *AA-2*	1922
SS-61 *AA-3*	1920
SS-62 *O-1*	1918
SS-63 *O-2*	1918
SS-64 *O-3*	1918
SS-65 *O-4*	1918
SS-66 *O-5*	1918
SS-67 *O-6*	1918
SS-68 *O-7*	1918
SS-69 *O-8*	1918
SS-70 *O-9*	1918
SS-71 *O-10*	1918
SS-72 *O-11*	1918
SS-73 *O-12*	1918
SS-74 *O-13*	1918
SS-75 *O-14*	1918
SS-76 *O-15*	1918
SS-77 *O-16*	1918
SS-78 *R-1*	1918
SS-79 *R-2*	1919
SS-80 *R-3*	1919
SS-81 *R-4*	1919
SS-82 *R-5*	1919
SS-83 *R-6*	1919
SS-84 *R-7*	1919

SS-85 R-8	1919	SS-129 S-24	1923	SS-172 Porpoise	1935	SS-215 Growler	1942
SS-86 R-9	1919	SS-130 S-25	1923	SS-173 Pike	1935	SS-216 Grunion	1942
SS-87 R-10	1919	SS-131 S-26	1923	SS-174 Shark	1936	SS-217 Guardfish	1942
SS-88 R-11	1919	SS-132 S-27	1924	SS-175 Tarpon	1936	SS-218 Albacore	1942
SS-89 R-12	1919	SS-133 S-28	1923	SS-176 Perch	1936	SS-219 Amberjack	1942
SS-90 R-13	1919	SS-134 S-29	1923	SS-177 Pickerel	1937	SS-220 Barb	1942
SS-91 R-14	1918	SS-135 S-30	1924	SS-178 Permit	1937	SS-221 Blackfish	1942
SS-92 R-15	1918	SS-136 S-31	1920	SS-179 Plunger	1936	SS-222 Bluefish	1943
SS-93 R-16	1918	SS-137 S-32	1923	SS-180 Pollack	1937	SS-223 Bonefish	1943
SS-94 R-17	1918	SS-138 S-33	1923	SS-181 Pompano	1937	SS-224 Cod	1943
SS-95 R-18	1918	SS-139 S-34	1922	SS-182 Salmon	1938	SS-225 Cero	1943
SS-96 R-19	1918	SS-140 S-35	1923	SS-183 Seal	1938	SS-226 Corvina	1943
SS-97 R-20	1918	SS-141 S-36	1923	SS-184 Skipjack	1938	SS-227 Darter	1943
SS-98 R-21	1919	SS-142 S-37	1923	SS-185 Snapper	1937	SS-228 Drum	1941
SS-99 R-22	1919	SS-143 S-38	1923	SS-186 Stingray	1938	SS-229 Flying Fish	1941
SS-100 R-23	1919	SS-144 S-39	1923	SS-187 Sturgeon	1938	SS-230 Finback	1942
SS-101 R-24	1919	SS-145 S-40	1923	SS-188 Sargo	1939	SS-231 Haddock	1942
SS-102 R-25	1919	SS-146 S-41	1924	SS-189 Saury	1939	SS-232 Halibut	1942
SS-103 R-26	1919	SS-147 H-4	1918	SS-190 Spearfish	1939	SS-233 Herring	1942
SS-104 R-27	1919	SS-148 H-5	1918	SS-191 Sculpin	1939	SS-234 Kingfish	1942
SS-105 S-1	1920	SS-149 H-6	1918	SS-192 Squalus/Sailfish	1940	SS-235 Shad	1942
SS-106 S-2	1920	SS-150 H-7	1918	SS-193 Swordfish	1939	SS-236 Silversides	1941
SS-107 S-3	1919	SS-151 H-8	1918	SS-194 Seadragon	1939	SS-237 Trigger	1942
SS-109 S-4	1919	SS-152 H-9	1918	SS-195 Sealion	1939	SS-238 Wahoo	1942
SS-110 S-5	1920	SS-153 S-42	1924	SS-196 Searaven	1939	SS-239 Whale	1942
SS-111 S-6	1920	SS-154 S-43	1924	SS-197 Seawolf	1939	SS-240 Angler	1943
SS-112 S-7	1920	SS-155 S-44	1925	SS-198 Tambor	1940	SS-241 Bashaw	1943
SS-113 S-8	1920	SS-156 S-45	1925	SS-199 Tautog	1940	SS-242 Bluegill	1943
SS-114 S-9	1921	SS-157 S-46	1925	SS-200 Thresher	1940	SS-243 Bream	1944
SS-115 S-10	1922	SS-158 S-47	1925	SS-201 Triton	1940	SS-244 Cavalla	1944
SS-116 S-11	1923	SS-159 S-48	1925	SS-202 Trout	1940	SS-245 Cobia	1944
SS-117 S-12	1923	SS-160 S-49	1925	SS-203 Tuna	1941	SS-246 Croaker	1944
SS-118 S-13	1923	SS-161 S-50	1925	SS-204 Mackerel	1941	SS-247 Dace	1943
SS-119 S-14	1921	SS-162 S-51	1925	SS-205 Marlin	1941	SS-248 Dorado	1943
SS-120 S-15	1921	SS-163 Barracuda	1924	SS-206 Gar	1941	SS-249 Flasher	1943
SS-121 S-16	1920	SS-164 Bass	1925	SS-207 Grampus	1941	SS-250 Flier	1943
SS-122 S-17	1921	SS-165 Bonita	1926	SS-208 Grayback	1941	SS-251 Flounder	1943
SS-123 S-18	1924	SS-166 Argonaut	1928	SS-209 Grayling	1941	SS-252 Gabilan	1943
SS-124 S-19	1923	SS-167 Narwhal	1930	SS-210 Grenadier	1941	SS-253 Gunnel	1942
SS-125 S-20	1922	SS-168 Nautilus	1930	SS-211 Gudgeon	1941	SS-254 Gurnard	1942
SS-126 S-21	1923	SS-169 Dolphin	1932	SS-212 Gato	1941	SS-255 Haddo	1942
SS-127 S-22	1924	SS-170 Cachalot	1933	SS-213 Greenling	1942	SS-256 Hake	1942
SS-128 S-23	1923	SS-171 Cuttlefish	1934	SS-214 Grouper	1942	SS-257 Harder	1942

SS-258 *Hoe*	1942	SS-301 *Roncador*	1945	SS-344 *Cobbler*	1945	SS-392 *Sterlet*	1944
SS-259 *Jack*	1943	SS-302 *Sabalo*	1945	SS-345 *Cochino*	1945	SS-393 *Queenfish*	1944
SS 260 *Lapon*	1943	SS-303 *Sablefish*	1945	SS-346 *Corporal*	1945	SS-394 *Razorback*	1944
SS-261 *Mingo*	1943	SS-304 *Seahorse*	1943	SS-347 *Cubera*	1945	SS-395 *Redfish*	1944
SS-262 *Muskallunge*	1943	SS-305 *Skate*	1943	SS-348 *Cusk*	1945	SS-396 *Ronquil*	1944
SS-263 *Paddle*	1943	SS-306 *Tang*	1943	SS-349 *Diodon*	1946	SS-397 *Scabbardfish*	1944
SS-264 *Pargo*	1943	SS-307 *Tilefish*	1943	SS-350 *Dogfish*	1946	SS-398 *Segundo*	1944
SS-265 *Peto*	1942	SS-308 *Apogon*	1943	SS-351 *Greenfish*	1946	SS-399 *Sea Cat*	1944
SS-266 *Pogy*	1943	SS-309 *Aspro*	1943	SS-352 *Halfback*	1946	SS-400 *Sea Devil*	1944
SS-267 *Pompon*	1943	SS-310 *Batfish*	1943	SS-353 *Dugong*	Cancelled	SS-401 *Sea Dog*	1944
SS-268 *Puffer*	1943	SS-311 *Archerfish*	1943	SS-354 *Eel*	Cancelled	SS-402 *Sea Fox*	1944
SS-269 *Rasher*	1943	SS-312 *Burrfish*	1943	SS-355 *Espada*	Cancelled	SS-403 *Atule*	1944
SS-270 *Raton*	1943	SS-313 *Perch*	1944	SS-358 *Garlopa*	Cancelled	SS-404 *Spikefish*	1944
SS-271 *Ray*	1943	SS-314 *Shark*	1944	SS-359 *Garrupa*	Cancelled	SS-405 *Sea Owl*	1944
SS-272 *Redfin*	1943	SS-315 *Sea Lion*	1944	SS-360 *Goldring*	Cancelled	SS-406 *Sea Poacher*	1944
SS-273 *Robalo*	1943	SS-316 *Barbel*	1944	SS-361 *Golet*	1943	SS-407 *Sea Robin*	1944
SS-274 *Rock*	1943	SS-317 *Barbero*	1944	SS-362 *Guavina*	1943	SS-408 *Sennet*	1944
SS-275 *Runner*	1942	SS-318 *Baya*	1944	SS-363 *Guitarro*	1944	SS-409 *Piper*	1944
SS-276 *Sawfish*	1942	SS-319 *Becuna*	1944	SS-364 *Hammerhead*	1944	SS-410 *Threadfin*	1944
SS-277 *Scamp*	1942	SS-320 *Bergall*	1944	SS-365 *Hardhead*	1944	SS-411 *Spadefish*	1944
SS-278 *Scorpion*	1942	SS-321 *Besugo*	1944	SS-366 *Hawkbill*	1944	SS-412 *Trepang*	1944
SS-279 *Snook*	1942	SS-322 *Blackfin*	1944	SS-367 *Icefish*	1944	SS-413 *Spot*	1944
SS-280 *Steelhead*	1942	SS-323 *Caiman*	1944	SS-368 *Jallao*	1944	SS-414 *Springer*	1944
SS-281 *Sunfish*	1942	SS-324 *Blenny*	1944	SS-369 *Kete*	1944	SS-415 *Stickleback*	1945
SS-282 *Tunny*	1942	SS-325 *Blower*	1944	SS-370 *Kraken*	1944	SS-416 *Tiru*	1943
SS-283 *Tinosa*	1943	SS-326 *Blueback*	1944	SS-371 *Largarto*	1944	SS-417 *Tench*	1944
SS-284 *Tullibee*	1943	SS-327 *Boarfish*	1944	SS-372 *Lamprey*	1944	SS-418 *Thornback*	1944
SS-285 *Balao*	1943	SS-328 *Charr*	1944	SS-373 *Lizardfish*	1944	SS-419 *Tigrone*	1944
SS-286 *Billfish*	1943	SS-329 *Chub*	1944	SS-374 *Loggerhead*	1945	SS-420 *Tirante*	1944
SS-287 *Bowfin*	1943	SS-330 *Brill*	1944	SS-375 *Macabi*	1945	SS-422 *Toro*	1944
SS-288 *Cabrilla*	1943	SS-331 *Bugara*	1944	SS-376 *Mapiro*	1945	SS-423 *Torsk*	1944
SS-289 *Capelin*	1943	SS-332 *Bullhead*	1944	SS-377 *Menhaden*	1945	SS-424 *Quillback*	1944
SS-290 *Cisco*	1943	SS-333 *Bumper*	1944	SS-378 *Mero*	1945	SS-425 *Trumpetfish*	1944
SS-291 *Crevalle*	1943	SS-334 *Cabezon*	1944	SS-381 *Sand Lance*	1943	SS-426 *Tusk*	1946
SS-292 *Devilfish*	1944	SS-335 *Dentuda*	1944	SS-382 *Picuda*	1943	SS-427 *Turbot*	1946
SS-293 *Dragonet*	1944	SS-336 *Capitaine*	1945	SS-383 *Pampanito*	1943	SS-428 *Ulna*	Cancelled
SS-294 *Escolar*	1944	SS-337 *Carbonero*	1945	SS-384 *Parche*	1943	SS-429 *Unicorn*	Cancelled
SS-295 *Hackleback*	1944	SS-338 *Carp*	1945	SS-385 *Bang*	1943	SS-432 *Whitefish*	Cancelled
SS-296 *Lancetfish*	1945	SS-339 *Catfish*	1945	SS-386 *Pilotfish*	1943	SS-435 *Corsair*	1946
SS-297 *Ling*	1945	SS-340 *Entemedor*	1945	SS-387 *Pintado*	1944	SS-436 *Unicorn*	1945
SS-298 *Lionfish*	1944	SS-341 *Chivo*	1945	SS-388 *Pipefish*	1944	SS-475 *Argonaut*	1945
SS-299 *Manta*	1944	SS-342 *Chopper*	1945	SS-389 *Piranha*	1944	SS-476 *Runner*	1945
SS-300 *Moray*	1945	SS-343 *Clamagore*	1945	SS-391 *Pomfret*	1944	SS-477 *Conger*	1945

SS-478 Cutlass	1945	SSRN-586 Triton	1958	SSBN-625 Henry Clay	1964	SSN-666 Hawkbill	1971
SS-479 Diablo	1945	SSGN-587 Halibut	1960	SSBN-626 Daniel Webster	1964	SSN-667 Bergall	1969
SS-480 Medregal	1945	SSN-588 Scamp	1961	SSBN-627 James Madison	1964	SSN-668 Spadefish	1969
SS-481 Requin	1945	SSN-589 Scorpion	1959	SSBN-628 Tecumseh	1964	SSN-669 Seahorse	1969
SS-482 Irex	1945	SSN-590 Sculpin	1961	SSBN-629 Daniel Boone	1964	SSN-670 Finback	1970
SS-483 Sea Leopard	1945	SSN-591 Shark	1960	SSBN-630 John C. Calhoun	1964	SSN-671 Narwhal	1969
SS-484 Odax	1945	SSN-592 Snook	1961	SSBN-631 Ulysses S. Grant	1964	SSN-672 Pintado	1971
SS-485 Sirago	1945	SSN-593 Thresher	1961	SSBN-632 Von Steuben	1964	SSN-673 Flying Fish	1970
SS-486 Pomodon	1945	SSN-594 Permit	1962	SSBN-633 Casimir Pulaski	1964	SSN-674 Trepang	1970
SS-487 Remora	1946	SSN-595 Plunger	1962	SSBN-634 Stonewall Jackson	1964	SSN-675 Bluefish	1971
SS-488 Sarda	1946	SSN-596 Barb	1963	SSBN-635 Sam Rayburn	1964	SSN-676 Billfish	1971
SS-489 Spinax	1946	SSN-597 Tullibee	1960	SSBN-636 Nathanael Greene	1964	SSN-677 Drum	1972
SS-490 Volador	1948	SSBN-598 George		SSN-637 Sturgeon	1967	SSN-678 Archerfish	1971
SS-522 Amberjack	1946	Washington	1959	SSN-638 Whale	1968	SSN-679 Silversides	1972
SS-523 Grampus	1949	SSBN-599 Patrick Henry	1960	SSN-639 Tautog	1968	SSN-680 William H. Bates	1973
SS-524 Pickerel	1949	SSBN-600 Theodore		SSBN-640 Benjamin Franklin	1965	SSN-681 Batfish	1972
SS-525 Grenadier	1951	Roosevelt	1961	SSBN-641 Simon Bolivar	1965	SSN-682 Tunny	1972
SS-526 Dorado	Cancelled	SSBN-601 Robert E. Lee	1960	SSBN-642 Kamehameha	1965	SSN-683 Parche	1974
SSK-1 Barracuda	1951	SSBN-602 Abraham		SSBN-643 George Bancroft	1966	SSN-684 Cavalla	1973
SSK-2 Bass	1952	Lincoln	1961	SSBN-644 Lewis and Clark	1965	SSN-685 Glenard P. Lipscomb	1974
SSK-3 Bonita	1952	SSN-603 Pollack	1964	SSBN-645 James K. Polk	1966	SSN-686 L. Mendel Rivers	1975
SS-563 Tang	1951	SSN-604 Haddo	1964	SSN-646 Grayling	1969	SSN-687 Richard B. Russell	1975
SS-564 Trigger	1952	SSN-605 Jack	1967	SSN-647 Pogy	1971	SSN-688 Los Angeles	1976
SS-565 Wahoo	1952	SSN-606 Tinosa	1964	SSN-648 Aspro	1969	SSN-689 Baton Rouge	1977
SS-566 Trout	1952	SSN-607 Dace	1964	SSN-649 Sunfish	1969	SSN-690 Philadelphia	1977
SS-567 Gudgeon	1952	SSBN-608 Ethan Allen	1961	SSN-650 Pargo	1968	SSN-691 Memphis	1977
SS-568 Harder	1952	SSBN-609 Sam Houston	1962	AGSS-555 Dolphin	1968	SSN-692 Omaha	1978
AGSS-569 Albacore	1953	SSBN-610 Thomas A. Edison	1962	SSN-651 Queenfish	1966	SSN-693 Cincinnati	1978
SSN-571 Nautilus	1954	SSBN-611 John Marshal	1962	SSN-652 Puffer	1969	SSN-694 Groton	1978
SSR-572 Sailfish	1956	SSN-612 Guardfish	1966	SSN-653 Ray	1967	SSN-695 Birmingham	1978
SSR-573 Salmon	1956	SSN-613 Flasher	1966	SSBN-654 George C. Marshall	1966	SSN-696 New York City	1979
SSG-574 Grayback	1958	SSN-614 Greenling	1967	SSBN-655 Henry L. Stimson	1966	SSN-697 Indianapolis	1980
SSN-575 Seawolf	1957	SSN-615 Gato	1968	SSBN-656 George		SSN-698 Bremerton	1981
SS-576 Darter	1956	SSBN-616 Lafayette	1963	Washington Carver	1966	SSN-699 Jacksonville	1981
SSG-577 Growler	1958	SSBN-617 Alexander		SSBN-657 Francis Scott Key	1966	SSN-700 Dallas	1981
SSN-578 Skate	1957	Hamilton	1963	SSBN-658 Mariano G. Vallejo	1966	SSN-701 La Jolla	1981
SSN-579 Swordfish	1958	SSBN-618 Thomas Jefferson	1963	SSBN-659 Will Rogers	1967	SSN-702 Phoenix	1981
SS-580 Barbel	1959	SSBN-619 Andrew Jackson	1963	SSN-660 Sand Lance	1971	SSN-703 Boston	1982
SS-581 Blueback	1959	SSBN-620 John Adams	1964	SSN-661 Lapon	1967	SSN-704 Baltimore	1982
SS-582 Bonefish	1959	SSN-621 Haddock	1967	SSN-662 Gurnard	1968	SSN-705 City of	
SSN-583 Sargo	1958	SSBN-622 James Monroe	1963	SSN-663 Hammerhead	1968	Corpus Christi	1983
SSN-584 Seadragon	1959	SSBN-623 Nathan Hale	1963	SSN-664 Sea Devil	1969	SSN-706 Albuquerque	1983
SSN-585 Skipjack	1959	SSBN-624 Woodrow Wilson	1963	SSN-665 Guitarro	1972	SSN-707 Portsmouth	1983

SSN-708 *Minneapolis/*			
St. Paul	1984		
SSN-709 *Ilyman G. Rickover*	1984		
SSN-710 *Augusta*	1985		
SSN-711 *San Francisco*	1981		
SSN-712 *Atlanta*	1982		

SSN-708 *Minneapolis/*
   St. Paul 1984
SSN-709 *Ilyman G. Rickover* 1984
SSN-710 *Augusta* 1985
SSN-711 *San Francisco* 1981
SSN-712 *Atlanta* 1982
SSN-713 *Houston* 1982
SSN-714 *Norfolk* 1983
SSN-715 *Buffalo* 1983
SSN-716 *Salt Lake City* 1984
SSN-717 *Olympia* 1983
SSN-718 *Honolulu* 1985
SSN-719 *Providence* 1985
SSN-720 *Pittsburgh* 1985
SSN-721 *Chicago* 1986
SSN-722 *Key West* 1987

SSN-723 *Oklahoma City* 1988
SSN-724 *Louisville* 1986
SSN-725 *Helena* 1987
SSBN-726 *Ohio* 1981
SSBN-727 *Michigan* 1982
SSBN-728 *Florida* 1983
SSBN-729 *Georgia* 1984
SSBN-730 *Henry M. Jackson* 1984
SSBN-731 *Alabama* 1985
SSBN-732 *Alaska* 1986
SSBN-733 *Nevada* 1986
SSBN-734 *Tennessee* 1988
SSBN-735 *Pennsylvania* 1989
SSBN-736 *West Virginia* 1990
SSBN-737 *Kentucky* 1991
SSBN-738 *Maryland* 1992

SSBN-739 *Nebraska* 1993
SSBN-740 *Rhode Island* 1994
SSBN-741 *Maine* 1995
SSBN-742 *Wyoming* 1996
SSBN-743 *Louisiana* 1997
SSN-750 *Newport News* 1989
SSN-751 *San Juan* 1988
SSN-752 *Pasadena* 1989
SSN-753 *Albany* 1990
SSN-754 *Topeka* 1989
SSN-755 *Miami* 1990
SSN-756 *Scranton* 1991
SSN-757 *Alexandria* 1991
SSN-758 *Asheville* 1991
SSN-759 *Jefferson City* 1992
SSN-760 *Annapolis* 1992

SSN-761 *Springfield* 1993
SSN-762 *Columbus* 1993
SSN-763 *Santa Fe* 1994
SSN-764 *Boise* 1992
SSN-765 *Montpelier* 1993
SSN-766 *Charlotte* 1994
SSN-767 *Hampton* 1993
SSN-768 *Hartford* 1994
SSN-769 *Toledo* 1995
SSN-770 *Tucson* 1995
SSN-771 *Columbia* 1995
SSN-772 *Greeneville* 1996
SSN-773 *Cheyenne* 1997
SSN-774 *Virginia* 1997
SSN-21 *Seawolf* 1997
SSN-22 *Connecticut* 1998

APPENDIX IV

SUBMARINE MUSEUMS

Submarines have so captured the interest of the public, not to mention those connected with the navy—and particularly some 300,000 living submariners and former members of this elite branch of the military—that there are more than 50 museums in the United States dedicated in whole or in part to the submarine. The text that follows lists them by name and provides information about how to contact them for details concerning their hours of availability to the public.

Drum (AGSS-228)
USS Alabama Battleship Commission
PO Box 65
Mobile, AL 36601
(205) 433–2703

Nautilus (SSN-5711)
Historical Ship Nautilus
Submarine Force Museum
NavSubBase New London
Groton, CT 06349
(800) 343–0079

Bowfin (SS-287)
Pacific Fleet Submarine
Memorial Assn., Inc.
11 Arizona Memorial Drive
Honolulu, HI 96818
(808) 423–1341

Torsk (AGSS-423)
Baltimore Maritime Museum
Pier Three
Pratt Street
Baltimore, MD 21202
(301) 396–3453

USS Marlin (SST-2)
Freedom Park
2497 Freedom Park Road
Omaha, NE 68110
(402) 345–1959

Ling (AGSS-297)
State of New Jersey Naval Museum
PO Box 395
Hackensack, NJ 07601
(973) 342–3268

Croaker (SS-246)
Naval and Servicemen's Park
1 Naval Park Cove
Buffalo, NY 14202
(716) 847–1773

Cod (SS-224)
Cleveland Coordinating Committee for USS Cod, Inc.
1089 East 9th Street
Cleveland, OH 44114
(216) 566–8770

Pampanito (SS-383)
National Maritime Museum Association
PO Box 470310
San Francisco, CA 94147
(415) 775–1943

St. Marys Submarine Museum
102 St. Marys Street West
St. Marys, GA 31558–4945
(912) 882–2782

Lionfish (SS-298)
SS Massachusetts Memorial
Battleship Cove
Fall River, MA 02721
(508) 678–1100

Silversides (SS-236)
USS Silversides and Maritime Museum
PO Box 1692
Muskegon, MI 49443
(231) 755–1230

Albacore (AGSS-569)
Port of Portsmouth Maritime Museum at Albacore Park
600 Market Street
Portsmouth, NH 03802
(603) 436–3680

HOLLAND BOAT #1
Paterson Museum
2 Market Street
Paterson, NJ 07501
(973) 881–3874

Growler (SSG-577)
Intrepid Sea Air Space Museum
Intrepid Square
New York City, NY 10036
(212) 245–2533, x7325

Batfish (AGSS-310)
Muskogee War Memorial Park
PO Box 735
Muskogee, OK 74402
(918) 682–6294

Blueback (SS-581)
Oregon Museum of Science and Industry
1945 Southeast Water Ave.
Portland, OR 97214–3354
(503) 797–4000

Requin (AGSS-4811)
Carnegie Science Center
1 Allegheny Avenue
Pittsburgh, PA 15212
(412) 237–3403

Cavalla (AGSS-244)
Seawolf Park
Pelican Island
2102 Seawall Blvd.
Galveston, TX 77550
(409) 744–5738

Cobia (AGSS-245)
Wisconsin Maritime Museum
75 Maritime Drive
Manitowoc, WI 54220
(920) 684–0218

Becuna (SS-319)
Independence Seaport Museum
211 South Columbus Blvd.
Philadelphia, PA 19106
(215) 922–1898

Clamagore (SS-343)
Patriots Point Naval and Maritime Museum
40 Patriots Point Road
Mount Pleasant, SC 29464
(803) 884–2727

The Naval Undersea Museum
PO Box 408
Keyport, WA 93845
(360) 697–1129

APPENDIX V

WEBSITES

The U.S. Navy maintains more than 700 official websites on the Internet and is constantly updating and adding additional entries that can be easily reached on most computers. These are listed on the U.S. Navy homepage both alphabetically and by category such as Aviation, Command and Control, Education and Training, Engineering, Logistics and Supply, Medical, Naval Bases, Research, Shipyards, and types of vessels. The following, most of which are listed alphabetically in this encyclopedia, are a sampling of those that apply to submarines and undersea warfare. One can also search the navy website for ships and submarines by name.

Atlantic Undersea Test and Evaluation Center
http://www.npt.nuwc.navy.mil/autec/

Commander Submarine Force U.S. Atlantic Fleet
http://www.atlanticfleet.navy.mil/index.htm

Commander Submarine Force U.S. Pacific Fleet
http://www.csp.navy.mil/

Commander Submarine Group 7
http://www.ctf74.navy.mil

Commander Submarine Group 9
http://www.csg9.navy.mil

Commander Undersea Surveillance
http://www.spawar.navy.mil/commands/comundersea-surv/home.htm

Fleet Anti-Submarine Warfare Training Center
http://www.fasw.navy.mil/

Helicopter Anti-Submarine Light Wing, Atlantic Fleet
http://www.navy.mil/homepages/comhslwinglant/

Helicopter Anti-Submarine Wing, U.S. Atlantic Fleet
http://www.globalsecurity.org/military/agency/navy/hswinglant.htm

Helicopter Anti-Submarine Squadron Four
http://www.hs4.navy.mil/

Helicopter Anti-Submarine Squadron Seven
http://www.navy.mil/homepages/hs7/

Helicopter Anti-Submarine Squadron Ten
http://www.hs10.navy.mil/

Mobile Diving and Salvage Unit One
http://www.mdsu1.navy.mil/

Naval Diving and Salvage Training Center
http://www.cnet.navy.mil/ndstc/

Naval Ocean Facilities Program
http://nofp.nfesc.navy.mil/

Naval Oceanographic Office
http://www.navo.navy.mil/

Naval Pacific Meteorology and Oceanographic Center
http://www.npmoc.navy.mil/

Naval Submarine Base, Bangor
http://www.bangor.navy.mil/

Naval Submarine Base, King's Bay
http://www.subasekb.navy.mil/

Naval Submarine Base, New London
http://www.subasenlon.navy.mil/

Naval Submarine Medical Research Laboratory
http://www.nhrc.navy.mil/nsmrl/

Naval Undersea Warfare Center
http://www.nuwc.navy.mil/

Pacific Fleet Submarine Force Naval Reserve Site
http://www.subpacnr.navy.mil/

Portsmouth Naval Shipyard
http://www.ports.navy.mil/

Submarine Group Two
http://www.csg2.navy.mil/

Submarine Logistics Support Center
http://slsc.navy.mil/

Submarine Maintenance, Engineering, Planning and Procurement
http://www.submepp.navy.mil/

Trident Training Facility
http://www.ttf.navy.mil/

The United States Navy
http://www.navy.mil/

U.S. Naval Observatory
http://www.usno.navy.mil/

APPENDIX VI

ACRONYMS

SUBMARINE TYPES

AGSS	auxiliary submarine
AOSS	oiler submarine
APSS/LPSS	transport submarine
SS	torpedo armed diesel-powered submarine
SSB	ballistic missile carrying submarine
SSBN	nuclear-powered ballistic missile submarine
SSG	guided missile carrying submarine
SSGN	nuclear-powered guided missile submarine
SSK	submarine designed for anti-submarine missions
SSN	nuclear-powered attack, or fleet, submarine
SSR	radar-picket submarine
SSRN	nuclear-powered radar-picket submarine
SST	target/training submarine

GENERAL

ABM	anti-ballistic missile
ACINT	acoustic intelligence
ADCAP	advanced capability torpedo
AEW	airborne early warning
AGI	auxiliary general intelligence (spy ship)
AIP	air independent propulsion
AIV	automatic inboard venting
AMP	assisted maintenance period
ASMD	anti-ship-missile defense
ATP	air turbine pump
BB	broad band
	bottom bounce
CEP	contact evaluation plot/circular error probability
COB	carried on board (spares)/chief of the boat
COMINT	communication intelligence
CZ	convergence zone
DEMON	demodulator equipment (sonar)
D/F	direction finding
DOT	distance off track
DR	dead reckoning
DSMAC	digital scene matching area correlator
DSRV	deep submergence rescue vessel
DWT	dead weight tonnage
ECE	external combustion engine
ECM	electronic counter-measures
EDC	error detection and correction
EHF	extremely high frequency
ELF	extremely low frequency
ELINT	electronic intelligence (recording radars)
EORSAT	electronic orbiting satellite
EP	estimated position
E/S	echo-sounder
ESM	electronic support measures
EW	electronic warfare
EZ	exclusion zone
FLTSATCOM	fleet satellite communications
FMOP	frequency modulation on pulse
FSH	full speed hours
GPS	global positioning system
HF	high frequency
HFDF	high frequency direction finding
IFM	instantaneous frequency measurement
JATO	jet-assisted takeoff
KW	kilowatt
LF	low frequency

LLQSA	limiting lines of quiet submerged approach
LLSA	limiting lines of submerged approach
LOP	local operations plot
MARV	maneuverable reentry vehicle
MBT	main ballast tanks
MCM	mine counter-measures
MF/DF	medium frequency direction finding
MIRV	multiple independent reentry vehicle
MPA	maritime patrol air
MSF	magnetic silencing facility
MW	megawatt
NB	narrow band
NDB	nuclear depth bomb
OPCON	operational control
OTC	officer in tactical command
PFV	programmable firing valve
PMOP	phase modulation on pulse
PWR	pressurized water reactor
RAM	radar absorbent material
RF	radio frequency
RORSAT	radar orbiting satellite
RPV	reactor pressure vessel
RV	reentry vehicle
SAM	surface to air missile
SATCOM	satellite communications
SATNAV	satellite navigation
SBD	submarine bubble decoy
SDI	Strategic Defense Initiative

SEC	submarine element coordinator
SG	steam generator
SHF	super high frequency
SINS	ships inertial navigation system
SLBM	submarine-launched ballistic cruise missile
SLCM	submarine (or ship) launched cruise missile
SOSUS	sonar ocean surveillance systems
SSE	submerged signal ejector
SUBOPAUTH	submarine operating authority
SUBROC	submarine-launched anti-submarine rocket
SVP	sound velocity profile
TAINS	TERCOM-aided inertial navigation system
TASS	towed-array surveillance system
TBP	time bearing plot
TDHS	tactical data handling system
TEDS	turbine electric drive submarines
TERCOM	terrain contour matching
TG	turbo-generator
TI/IR	thermal imaging infrared
TMA	target motion analysis
TSMA	temperature swing molecular adsorber
UHF	ultra high frequency
UQS	ultra quiet state
UWT	underwater telephone
VDS	variable depth sonar
VIMOS	vibration monitoring system
VLF	very low frequency

GLOSSARY

absorber Chemical atmosphere cleansing system whose contents temporarily or permanently combine with unwanted gases.

ADCAP ADvanced CAPability. Newest version of the Mark 48 torpedo on-board U.S. submarines.

adsorber Physical atmosphere cleansing system whose succession of sieves have molecular-sized holes to trap specific gases.

AFFF Aqueous Fire Fighting Foam.

AN/BPS-15A Navigation radar on many U.S. SSNs.

AN/BQQ-5 (A-E) Integrated sonar suite on most U.S. SSNs. The different variants include improvements in signal process and/or different sonar arrays.

AN/BSY-1 Integrated sonar/fire control system on improved Los Angeles-class SSNs.

anechoic coating Rubber coating applied to the exterior hull surfaces of a submarine to absorb active sonar pulses. Reduces the detectability by active sonars. Some coatings also reduce the amount of noise a submarine puts into the water; these are called decoupling coatings.

angles and dangles Test conducted by a submarine to ensure that everything is stowed properly before beginning its mission. The procedure calls for making large up-and-down movements with the submarine as well as using large rudder angles at moderate speeds.

AN/WLR-8(V)2 Radar warning receiver on 688-class SSNs.

AN/WLR-9 Acoustic intercept receiver found on navy submarines.

AN/WLR-10 Radar warning receiver with recording capability on 688-class SSNs.

Archimedes principle The physical law of buoyancy discovered by the Greek mathematician Archimedes. Basically, it states that any body completely or partially submerged and at rest is acted upon by an upward (buoyant) force, the magnitude of which is equal to the weight of the fluid displaced by the body. Buoyancy is caused by

the increase in fluid pressure at increasingly greater depths. The operation and navigation of a submarine is particularly governed by its buoyancy (or lack thereof) under a wide range of situations, functions, and operating maneuvers. Thus, for example, a submarine that has lost buoyancy—whether on purpose or because of an accident—might be able to counteract this lack of buoyancy by using its engines and bow and stern planes to move itself upward in the water.

AUTEC Atlantic Undersea Test and Evaluation Center. An acoustic test range located off Andros Island in the Bahamas.

bar Unit used in expressing pressure, where a millibar is a thousand dynes per square centimeter and 1 bar equals 1 atmosphere—or about 15 lbs./sq. inch.

bastions highly defended SSBN patrol areas. Established by the former Soviet Union, now used by Russia to protect its SSBNs from attack by Western SSNs.

blue/gold crew The policy of having two alternating crews assigned to strategic missile submarines.

BOL (Bearing Only Launch) Launch mode for Harpoon and Tomahawk antiship missiles that doesn't require range information. Essentially, the missile seeker is activated once cruising altitude is reached.

boomers U.S. Navy nickname for strategic missile submarines.

bottom bounce Term used to describe the route taken by sound waves as they bounce off the ocean bottom traveling from the noise source to the sonar receiver. For example, the noise source could be an active sonar pulse that bounces off the bottom and hits the target ship; then the echo bounces off the bottom again and is received by the sonar.

breech door Inner door of a torpedo tube.

bridge Small observation area on top of the fairwater. The officer of the deck (OOD) stands his watch here when the submarine is on the surface.

buttercup   U.S. Navy term for the "wet" or flooding trainer.

cathodic protection   Anti-corrosion protection of an underwater metal fitting achieved by making it the cathode in an electrolytic cell.

cavitation   Effect caused when a drop in pressure allows vapor bubbles to form in a liquid and then collapse again.

choke point   Geographical restriction that limits the maneuverability of a submarine.

Clyde   U.S. Navy nickname for the auxiliary diesel engine.

CO (Commanding Officer)   Title given to an officer in command of a ship. Often called "Captain" or "Skipper."

COB (Chief of the Boat)   Senior enlisted man in a submarine's crew. Usually a senior or master chief petty officer. Interfaces directly with the XO on issues that affect the enlisted personnel.

control room   Area on a U.S. Navy submarine where the ship control, fire control, and periscopes are located. Major submarine functions are controlled from this location. The OOD stands his watch here when the submarine is submerged. In communications the area is referred to as the "conn."

convergence zone (CZ)   Phenomenon whereby, if the water is deep enough, water pressure turns sound waves up toward the surface. This occurs at intervals of roughly 30 nautical miles. Multiple contacts are possible when the sound bounces off the surface and heads back down, eventually to be turned back upward again by the pressure.

COW (Chief of the Watch)   Leading enlisted man in control during a watch. Operates the ballast control panel to dive and surface the submarine and makes trim corrections when directed by the diving officer.

curfuffle, clunk and clong   Three of the many onomatopoeic words used to describe, and so help identify, transient noises heard by a passive sonar operator.

data shock   Paralysis of an electronic processing system—or the display operator—due to information overload.

direct drive   Main machinery system where a submarine diesel engine can be connected in a straight line to electrical generating armatures and —abaft them—a propeller shaft. Clutches are positioned between engine and armatures and between armatures and propeller shaft. With both clutches engaged, the diesel directly drives the propeller. With the tail clutch disconnected, the full power of the engine is used to generate current for the battery. With the engine clutch disconnected, but the tail clutch connected, the dual purpose armatures can be used as propulsion motors drawing electrical power back from the batteries.

direct path   Term used to describe the route that sound waves take from noise source to sonar system without interacting with the surface or the ocean floor. Roughly speaking, it is considered to be the straight-line distance between the two vessels.

discrete frequency peaks   Distinctive high spots on a noise frequency spectrum produced by rotating machinery and hull resonances.

dolphins   symbol of the submarine force in just about every nation. Also, the badge or pin that designates a sailor as qualified in submarines.

DSMAC (Digital Scene-Matching Area Correlation)   A second Tomahawk land attack missile navigation system used to improved the accuracy of the conventional variants. Uses a camera-like system to make detailed digital pictures of the terrain and compares them with stored images in the guidance computer.

DSRV (Deep-Submergence Rescue Vehicle)   A small rescue submersible designed to dock with a sunken submarine and retrieve the crew.

EAB (Emergency Air Breathing)   A low-pressure air system that crewmen can plug in to and obtain breathable—although dry—air. This system is to provide a source of air while a submarine ventilates to get rid of the smoke from a fire.

Electric Boat Company   The company started by John Holland to produce submarines for the U.S. Navy. Presently owned by General Dynamics Corporation.

emergency blow   Process by which high-pressure air is rapidly introduced directly into the submarine's main ballast tanks. An emergency blow makes the submarine positively buoyant, and it will rise to the surface quite quickly. This system was instituted as part of the Subsafe program following the loss of USS *Thresher*.

enabling   Process of sending instructions—down the umbilical wire—to the brain of a homing torpedo to tell it to arm its warhead and start searching.

EOOW (Engineering Officer of the Watch)   Officer in charge of the team that is monitoring and manipulating the submarine's reactor and propulsion system. Key responsibility is to maintain propulsion in a safe manner.

ESM (Electronic Support Measures)   A passive receiver system designed to detect radar emissions from aircraft and surface ships.

Ethan Allen   First U.S. Navy SSBN class designed to carry Polaris missiles. Larger than the George Washington class, the Ethan Allen class has more quieting measures to improve stealth.

fairwater   U.S. Navy term for the sail on a submarine. Sometimes erroneously called the conning tower.

Familygrams   Short (40 to 50 words) messages that U.S. Navy submariners receive from family members about once a week while on patrol.

first-line maintenance   Planned upkeep routines, which can be performed by the submarine ship's company at sea, if necessary using the on-board spares.

"Flaming datum" A ship that has been hit by a torpedo fired from a submarine. It is the place to begin searching for a submarine, because one is known to be in the area.

force multiplier Sensor or weapon system that not only provides capability itself but also enhances the value of other systems. Thus a "Home-on-jamming" capability in one missile of a salvo is a force multiplier for a radar homer head in another missile of the same salvo. Now, whether the enemy jams or not, one missile will hit.

George Washington First U.S. Navy SSBN class. Essentially Skipjack-class SSNs with a 130-foot hull insert containing 16 missile tubes for Polaris missiles.

Gertrude Old World War II phrase used to describe any equipment whose function is underwater communications. Underwater telephone.

girding An effect by which a towing vessel can be laid on its side, if the towed object starts to exert a lateral pull.

goat locker U.S. Navy term for the chief petty officer's quarters on a submarine.

GPS (Global Positioning System) A constellation of Navstar satellites that can very accurately determine the submarine's position.

Harpoon (UGM-84) U.S. Navy antiship missile, fired from an SSN's torpedo tube.

head U.S. Navy term for a washroom and toilet.

Holland (SS-1) First U.S. Navy submarine, designed and built by John Holland.

hot bunking Rotation system whereby two men share a single bunk. While one man is on watch the other is sleeping. When it is time for watch rotation, the man coming off watch climbs into a bunk that was recently vacated and is usually still warm.

hotel load Amount of electrical power needed to provide domestic services (heating, lighting, air-conditioning, cooking, etc.) and to run other auxiliary machinery—thus reducing power available for propulsion.

Hunley A Confederate Navy vessel that made history by being the first submarine to sink a surface ship in battle (USS Housatonic). Unfortunately, the Hunley herself also sank in the attack.

Lafayette Third generation of U.S. Navy SSBNs. Larger and quieter than the Ethan Allen class, the Lafayette class carries the Poseidon C-3 missile. However, 12 units of the Lafayette class were backfitted with the Trident 1 C-4 system during the 1980s.

legend range The range to which manufacturers guarantee that their weapons will run.

liquid metal coolant Metal with relatively low melting point, such as lead (327.5°C), circulated in reactor primary circuits to transfer heat energy to secondary plant at a higher temperature than is possible using water coolant.

LOFAR (LOw-Frequency Analyzing and Recording) Term used to describe the process by which narrowband "tonals" are displayed on a modern sonar system.

Los Angeles (SSN-688) Admiral Rickover's high-speed submarine design and once the most numerous submarine class in the world.

maneuvering room The reactor and propulsion control area located in the engine room. The engineering officer stands his watch here.

MGU (Midcourse Guidance Unit) The inertial navigation system used to guide Harpoon and Tomahawk anti-ship missiles to their targets.

MIDAS (Mine Detection and Avoidance Sonar) New mine-hunting sonar on improved Los Angeles-class SSNs.

Mk 48 (Mods 1–4) Designation of the active homing torpedo used by U.S. SSNs. The various modifications have improvements in wire-guidance capability and allow for deeper depths.

Mk 60 Captor A deep-water moored acoustic influence mine employing an encapsulated Mark 46 lightweight torpedo as the payload.

Narwhal (SSN-671) Basic Sturgeon-class hull with a natural circulation reactor. One-of-a-kind experimental submarine; fully combat capable.

Nautilus (SSN-571) First nuclear-powered submarine in the world. Commissioned September 30, 1954.

OBA (Oxygen Breathing Apparatus) A portable system that chemically generates oxygen for about 30 minutes. Used by damage control teams to fight fires.

octaves The frequency band that can be covered by a sensor antenna or array. In sonar systems, the octave top frequency is about double the bottom frequency. In ESM systems, the octave top frequency is about three times the bottom frequency.

Ohio (SSBN-726) Fourth generation of U.S. Navy SSBNs. Largest submarines in the fleet; each carries 24 Trident C-4 or Trident II D-5 missiles.

plank owners The original crew of a boat at the time of its commissioning.

platform correlation Making the connection between an intercepted transmission and the vehicle from which the transmission, radar or sonar, has been made.

Polaris (A1–A3) First generation of U.S. Navy submarine-launched ballistic missiles. The different variants each have improvements in range.

Poseidon (C-3) Second-generation U.S. Navy submarine-launched ballistic missile.

raft A large metal frame that supports various rotating parts of machinery, such as main engines or turbine generators. Through inertial damping it reduces machinery vibrations that could reach the hull. In other words, it's heavy, and the vibrations are absorbed as they try to move the raft.

RAM (Radar-Absorbing Material) A coating designed to absorb radar energy and reduce a target's ability to be detected.

RBL-L (Range Bearing Launch–Large)   A launch mode of Harpoon and Tomahawk antiship missiles that uses both bearing and range information. The "Large" refers to the size of the area where the missile is to conduct its search.

second-line maintenance   Planned upkeep routines carried out in harbor, usually at the base port with base staff assistance, during which the notice for being able to go to sea may be extended to 47 hours.

shutter door   Shutter doors are the external hull fairings covering the torpedo tubes' external hull penetrations. As such, they operate in conjunction with the torpedo tube outer doors, such that when the torpedo tube outer door is closed, the hull streamlining in that area is preserved. When the torpedo tube outer door is opened, the shutter door slides away to allow an unobstructed torpedo launch.

signal ejector   A small (usually three-inch) torpedo tube-like system for launching flares, noisemakers, and torpedo decoys.

SINS (Ship's Inertial Navigation System)   SINS is an electromechanical navigation instrument that employs a gyro-controlled stable platform. The platform is equipped with accelerometers that measure ship's movement in the X (north-south), Y (east-west), and Z (vertical) planes. Such movements are then computer-translated into a ship's positional updating from an external reference.

Skipjack (SSN-585)   First U.S. Navy SSN class to use the teardrop hull shape. Fastest SSN in the fleet until the Los Angeles class.

SOSUS (SOund SUrveillance System)   A series of fixed, bottom laid, passive sonar/hydrophone arrays used to provide early warning and tracking information of submarines in the open ocean areas.

SRA (Short-Range Attack)   A mode of firing the Mk 48 torpedo to accommodate a target that is very close to the attacking ship.

steerage   Any information given to a submarine to help it position itself for intelligence collection purposes.

Steinke hood   Combination breathing device and life preserver used during free ascents from a sunken U.S. submarine.

submove message   Sailing orders sent to the submarine in message form by the authority holding OPCON (operational control). It must contain: departure time, details of route to be followed, overall speed to be maintained along the route, dimensions of the moving exercise area (peace) or moving haven (war) established around the submarine, any CHOPS (changes in OPCON) to be made along the route, and the communications broadcast on which watch is to be maintained.

SUBROC (SUBmarine ROCket)   A submarine-launched ballistic rocket with a nuclear depth bomb payload.

Subsafe   Procedural and system changes instituted to increase the safety of U.S. submarines following the loss of the USS *Thresher* (SSN-593) in April 1963.

support personnel   Shore-based members of any submarine force indispensable if proper second- and third-line support is to be provided (e.g., periscope workshop artificers).

tail personnel   Shore-based members of any submarine force who provide important but not necessarily indispensable backup for support personnel (e.g., transport drivers, catering staff).

TB-16 (A–D)   Standard U.S. Navy SSN "fat line" towed array. The various modifications (mods) allow the submarine to search at higher speeds without degrading performance. The array is stored in a sheath that runs along the hull.

TDU (Trash Disposal Unit)   A tube that ejects weighted trash cylinders from the bottom of a U.S. submarine.

teeth personnel   Those fully trained and in a submarine.

TERCOM (TERrain-COntour Matching)   A navigation system on Tomahawk land attack missiles. The system uses the Tomahawk's radar altimeter to make terrain profiles at preselected points along the missile's route. These profiles are compared to a radar reference map to determine if flight corrections are needed.

third-line maintenance   Major planned upkeep routines carried out in a dockyard, during which the Notice for Sea may be considerably more than 48 hours.

TMA (Target Motion Analysis)   The process by which computers or men determine a target's course, speed, and range so that a torpedo or missile can be fired accurately.

TMPS (Theater Mission Planning System)   U.S. TMPS centers plan Tomahawk land attack mission routes to various targets around the globe, using maps and navigation information provided by the Defense Mapping Agency.

Tomahawk (UGM-109)   Family of cruise missiles that are launched from standard torpedo tubes or special vertical launch tubes on SSNs.

torpedo   The self-propelled torpedo was invented by Robert Whitehead, an Englishman, in 1866. Since then, the torpedo has undergone significant improvements in speed, range, and depth. Present-day torpedoes are all homing weapons using active/passive acoustics or wake sensors.

towed array   String of passive hydrophones towed at some distance behind the ship. By separating the hydrophones from the ship, the array was no longer limited by platform noise, thereby increasing detection range. The towed array can also be made as long as necessary to detect sounds with long wavelengths (very low frequency).

Trident I (C-4)   Third generation of U.S. Navy submarine-launched ballistic missiles.

Trident II (D-5)   Fourth generation of U.S. Navy submarine-launched ballistic missiles.

Triton (SSN-586)   Only U.S. Navy SSN built with two nuclear reactors. Originally designed as a radar-picket submarine, *Triton* made a submerged round-the-world cruise in 1960.

Tullibee (SSN-597)   First U.S. Navy SSN with torpedo tubes placed amidships to make room for the 15-foot spherical sonar array. This design is the basis for all later U.S. SSN designs. *Tullibee* was also fitted with a trouble-some turboelectric drive, which earned her the reputation of being a hangar queen, and she was often referred to as "Building 597."

Turtle   A semi-submersible craft designed and built by David Bushnell during the American Revolutionary War. It was the first submarine to conduct an attack, albeit unsuccessful, against a hostile surface ship (HMS *Eagle*).

Typhoon (SSBN)   A Soviet/Russian SSBN. The size of a small World War II battle cruiser, the *Typhoon* is the largest submarine ever built. Very quiet, and equipped with modern sensors.

VLS (Vertical Launch System)   A set of 12 external tubes located in the number two main ballast tank on SSN-719 and on the Los Angeles-class SSN.

SELECTED
BIBLIOGRAPHY*

Alden, John. *U.S. Submarine Attacks During World War I.* Annapolis: Naval Institute Press, 1991.

———. *The Fleet Submarine in the U.S. Navy.* Annapolis: Naval Institute Press, 1979.

Bak, Richard. *The CSS* Hunley. Dallas: Taylor Publishing, 1999.

Beach, Edward. *Run Silent, Run Deep.* Annapolis: Naval Institute Press, 1991.

———. *Salt and Steel: Reflections of a Submariner.* Annapolis: Naval Institute Press, 1999.

———. *Submerged: Voyage of the* Triton. Annapolis: Naval Institute Press, 2001.

Blair, Clay, Jr. *Silent Victory.* Philadelphia: Lippincott, 1975.

Bouslog, David. *Maru Killer.* Placentia, Calif.: R.A. Cline Publishing, 2001.

Calvert, James. *Silent Running.* New York: Wiley, 1997.

———. *Surface at the Pole. The Extraordinary Voyage of the USS* Skate. Annapolis, Md.: Naval Institute Press, 1996.

Clancy, Tom. *SSN.* New York: Simon & Schuster, 1996.

———. *Strategies of Submarine Warfare.* New York: Berkley Books, 1997.

———. *Submarine: A Guided Tour.* New York: Berkley Books, 1993.

Cline, Rick. *Final Dive: The Gallant and Tragic Career of the WWII Submarine USS* Snook. Placentia, Calif.: R.A. Cline Publishing, 2000.

———. *Submarine* Grayback: *The Life and Death of the World War II Sub.* Placentia, Calif.: R.A. Cline Publishing, 1999.

Conner, Claude. *Nothing Friendly in the Vicinity.* Conshohocken, Pa.: Combined Publishing, 1999.

Cross, Wilbur. *Challengers of the Deep.* New York: Morrow, 1959.

Duncan, Francis. *Rickover and the Nuclear Navy, The Discipline of Technology.* Annapolis: Naval Institute Press, 1990.

Enright, Joseph. *Shinano!* New York: St. Martin's Press, 1987.

Fluckey, Eugene. *Thunder Below: The Barb Revolutionizes Submarine Warfare in World War II.* Chicago: University of Illinois Press, 1994.

Friedman, Norman. *U.S. Submarines Through 1945.* Annapolis: Naval Institute Press, 1995.

———. *U.S. Submarines Since 1945.* Annapolis: Naval Institute Press, 1994.

Galantin, I. J. *Take Her Deep: A Submarine Against Japan in World War II.* Chapel Hill, N.C.: Algonquin Books, 1987.

Genat, Robert. *Modern U.S. Navy Submarines.* Osceola, Wis.: Motor Books International, 1997.

Grider, George. *War Fish.* Boston: Little, Brown, 1958.

Harris, Brayton. *Navy Times Book of Submarines.* New York: Berkley Books, 1997.

Holmes, Harry. *The Last Patrol.* Shrewsbury, England: Airlife Publishing, Ltd., 1944; also Naval Institute Press, 2001.

Hoyt, Edwin, and Christie, Ralph. Bowfin: *The True Story of a Fabled Fleet Submarine in World War II.* Short Hills, N.J.: Burford Books, 1998.

Keith, Milton. *Subs Against the Rising Sun.* Las Cruces, N.Mex.: Yucca Tree Press, 2000.

Kimble, David. *Chronology of U.S. Submarine Operations in the Pacific, 1939–1942.* Bennington, Vt.: Merriam Press, 1997.

Kimmett, Larry. *U.S. Submarines in World War II.* Kingston, Wash.: Navigator Publishing Company, 1996.

Langess, Robert. *U.S.S. Albacore,* Forerunner of the Future. Portsmouth, N.H.: Portsmouth Marine Society, 1999.

Lavo, Carl. *Back from the Deep: The Strange Story of the Sister Ships* Squalus *and* Sculpin. Annapolis: Naval Institute Press, 1998.

---

* Based on bibliographic lists published by various submarine sources and including books that focus on American submarines rather than those of two or more nations.

Leary, William. *Under Ice: Development of the Arctic Submarine.* College Station: Texas A & M University Press, 1999.

Lipscomb, F. W. *Historic Submarines.* New York: Praeger, 1969.

Lockwood, Charles. *Down to the Sea in Subs.* New York: Norton, 1967.

———. *Sink 'Em All.* New York: Dutton, 1951.

Maas, Peter. *The Terrible Hours: The Man Behind the Greatest Submarine Rescue in History.* New York: Harper Collins, 2000.

Martini, Ron. *Hot, Straight, and Normal: A Submarine Bibliography.* Sheridan, Wyo.: Ron Martini, 2001. The only current bibliography in print, with more than 6,000 references to books, as well as a comprehensive listing of articles from *Naval Proceedings* and *Naval Submarine League.*

Mendenhall, Corwin. *Submarine Diary: The Silent Stalking of Japan.* Chapel Hill, N.C.: Algonquin Press, 1995.

Michno, Gregory. *USS* Pampanito: *Killer-Angel.* Norman, Okla.: University of Oklahoma Press, 2000.

Milton, Keith. *Submarines Against the Rising Sun: U.S. Submarines in the Pacific.* Las Cruces, N.Mex.: Yucca Tree Press, 2000.

Morison, Samuel. *Coral Sea, Midway, and Submarine Actions.* Edison, N.J.: Book Sales, Inc., 1998.

O'Kane, Richard. *Clear the Bridge: The War Patrols of U.S.S.* Tang. Novato, Calif.: Presidio Press, 1989.

———. Wahoo. Novato, Calif.: Presidio Press, 1987.

Padfield, Peter. *War Beneath the Sea.* New York: Wiley, 1998.

Parsons, William. *Robert Fulton and the Submarine.* New York: Columbia University Press, 1922.

Perry, Milton. *Infernal Machines: The Story of Confederate Submarines.* 1965. Reprint, Baton Rouge: Louisiana State University Press, 1985.

Ragan, Mark. *The* Hunley. Charleston, S.C.: Narwhal Press, 1999.

Robinson, Patrick. *U.S.S.* Seawolf, New York: Harper, 2000.

Rockwell, Theodore. *The Rickover Effect. The Inside Story of How Admiral Rickover Built the Nuclear Navy.* Annapolis: Naval Institute Press, 1990.

Rodengen, Jeffrey. *The Legend of Electric Boat.* Ft. Lauderdale: Write Stuff Syndicate, 1995.

Roscoe, Theodore. *U.S. Submarine Operations in World War II.* Annapolis: Naval Institute Press, 1949.

Rupp, Albert. *Threshold of Hell.* Long Beach, Calif.: Almar Press, 1983.

Sasgen, Peter. *Red Scorpion: The War Patrols of USS* Rasher. Annapolis: Naval Institute Press, 1995.

Schratz, Paul. *Submarine Commander.* Lexington: University of Kentucky Press, 1988.

Sheridan, Martin. *Overdue and Presumed Lost: USS* Bullhead. Francestown, N.H.: Marshall Jones, 1959.

Sontag, Sherry. *Blind Man's Bluff.* New York: Public Affairs Press, 1998.

Spector, Ronald. *The War at Sea.* New York: Viking, 2001.

Spinardi, Graham. *From Polaris to Trident: The Development of the U.S. Fleet Ballistic Missiles.* Cambridge Studies in International Relations, 1994.

Sterling, Forest. *Wake of the* Wahoo: *The Heroic Story of America's Most Daring Submarine.* Placentia, Calif.: R.A. Cline Publishing, 1960.

Walkowiak, Tom. *Fleet Submarines of World War II.* Missoula, Mont.: Pictorial Histories Publishing Company, 1996.

Waller, Douglas. *Big Red, Three Months on Board a Trident Nuclear Submarine.* New York: Harper, 2001.

Williams, Marion. *Submarines Under Ice.* Annapolis, Md.: United States Naval Institute, 1998.

Winslow, Richard. *Portsmouth-built Submarines of the Portsmouth Naval Yard.* Portsmouth, N.H.: Marine Society, 1996.

Yokota, Yutaka. *Suicide Submarine.* New York: Ballantine, 1962.

INDEX

Boldface page numbers indicate major treatment of a subject. Page numbers in *italics* denote an illustration.